Mama's Boy

Lennox Lewis and the Heavyweight Crown

2006

To Grandad
Lots of love from

[signature] xxxx

Mama's Boy

Lennox Lewis and the Heavyweight Crown

GAVIN EVANS

Dedication

For Pat

Acknowledgements

Lennox Lewis has always been generous to me with his time, space and energy. I first interviewed him after the Frank Bruno fight in 1993, and the last time, specifically for this book, was in 2004, and in between he has never refused me access and has shown commendable patience, even when I phoned him at 3am, or went way beyond the allotted hour or criticised him in print. Without this co-operation over the past eleven years, *Mama's Boy* would not have been possible.

Aside from Lennox and the other boxers featured, there are several others I interviewed for this book who helped me with information and support, including Lawrence Lustig, Andy Powis, Bernita Drenth, Don McRae, Emmanuel Steward, Dennis Lewis, Violet Blake, Courtney Myers, Aisha Mike, Frank Maloney, Eugene Maloney, John Hornewer, Adrian Teodorescu, Judd Bernstein, Joe Dunbar, Harold Knight, Courtney Shand, Lou Duva, Panos Eliadis and Gene Heesaker.

I would like to thank in particular my agent Euan Thorneycroft of Curtis Brown and my editor Jonathan Taylor.

Published in 2004 by Highdown,
an imprint of Raceform Ltd
Compton, Newbury, Berkshire, RG20 6NL
Raceform Ltd is a wholly-owned subsidiary of Trinity Mirror plc

A CIP catalogue record for this book is available from the British Library.

ISBN 1-904317-76-6

Designed by Fiona Pike
Printed in Great Britain by William Clowes, Beccles, England

CONTENTS

CHAPTER ONE
SONS AND MOTHERS

L ennox Lewis vaults the fence, unlocks the gate and leads the way to the porch with its view of fields and mountains. He's tired but contented, his daily routine finally over. He excuses himself to enter the house where his mum, the former Violet Lewis and the current Violet Blake, is cooking the evening dinner of West Indian-style chicken and rice, plantain and yam, swaps snatches of quick banter with his Jamaican friend Scott DeMercado and his English friend Patrick Drayton, and re-emerges with the offer of a glass of orange juice and a request for an easy ride: 'No difficult questions today, I hope.'

The big man talks about his future – the way his life after boxing may unfold – and also about how his past and present will be remembered; he wonders what kind of 'legacy' he will leave. In contemporary boxing, this subject invariably brings comparison to the man whose legacy overshadows all the rest: Muhammad Ali. So Lennox detours to tell how, at the start of this boxing business, way back a couple of decades ago in Kitchener, Ontario, he imagined himself as the incarnation of the dancing, jabbing Ali before the picture of the future Lennox began to take shape, and how, ever since, he's taken Ali's image and example with him, reading the books, watching the movies and drawing constant inspiration from the man's courageous defiance in taking on his government and standing up for his principles and, most of all, his people. 'Definitely one of my idols,' he says.

After staying with Ali for a while longer he offers an alliteration-inspired list of the other heroes who've touched his life. He skips through Malcolm (X) and Martin (Luther King) and the sense of hope and identity they brought to black people, and the way they overcame adversity and persecution and fought for justice, pauses a while longer for Nelson Mandela – that combination of defiance against oppression and forgiveness of the oppressor – and settles on his mother.

With Violet just out of earshot he leans forward, changes tone and spells out her many virtues. 'My mother's my hero because I realise all the heartache she's been through during her life, and the kind of oppression she went through as well,' he begins. 'She went through a lot to bring me up in today's society, which was hard – not an easy task, raising sons in today's world – so it's important for me to grow up to be the best that I can to make her proud. You know, when she goes to the store and people say to her, "Ah, you've got a good son," those kinds of things make her feel good.' He pauses again to make sure these points are taken. 'So, yeah, I'm a self-professed mother's boy. I don't mind saying that: I'm a mother's boy. With me saying it, other athletes can say it too because there are a lot of mother's boys out there – people who really appreciate their mothers.'

Lennox is now in full flow, painting a picture of the woman cooking his supper in the kitchen – of her centrality in his life – his future as well as his past. 'If Mike Tyson had a mother like mine, he would definitely be a different person. That's what my mother says – that she wishes she could talk to him and be with him, because he needs someone who cares only for him, which is what I had.'

At this moment Violet reappears to say hello and have a quick, quiet word with her son. She also has her opinions on all this mama's boy talk. 'I think it's a compliment to call him that. Why shouldn't he be a momma's boy? Don't you want to be a momma's boy? And he's a good boy,' she says with a smile. 'He makes his bed, always cleans up, and takes care of people he loves. What's wrong with that? What's wrong with being a good boy?' She chuckles at this and then returns to the kitchen.

Lennox continues, talking quietly about the way she gets emotionally involved in his line of work. 'My mother used to watch karate movies when I was young. She loved those kind of action movies, which some people call violent but we just called action, and when she watches me fight she gets involved like she was watching one of those karate movies, except it's me who's the hero. There was once a camera filming her when I fought and in a way it was quite funny because her psyche got totally involved in the fight – in watching me fight. I can see that she enjoys it to a degree, but then she also realises her son is in there, so she's on edge too. I have the feeling that, in a sense, she feels she is there in the ring with me.'

He points with both hands. 'You want to know what kind of person my mother is? Very loving, very giving, very spiritual and very kind.'

The relationship between Lennox and his mother began through passion, followed by doubt and then acceptance and delight – all this before his first weigh-in, at 10lb 10oz, on 2 September 1965, born by Caesarean section in Queen Mary's Hospital in Stratford, London.

By then Violet Lewis was 27 hard years old. She'd grown up in the small town of Port Antonio on the Rio Grande in north-east Jamaica, a playground for rich men who liked to mess around in boats on the river before retiring to their hotels. Down below was a kind of shanty town for 11,000 locals. Her father was a casual labourer, her mother a big, strong washerwoman, and she had four sisters and seven brothers, all of them packed into a three-room wooden shack near the harbour. There was no room for Violet once she was out of nappies, so she was farmed out to live with her Aunt Gee, a vegetable hawker, and later, when Gee married, to another aunt, Lou. Farming out children to available relatives was more than just a custom; it was often a necessity, and it was a way of life Violet knew and accepted.

She seldom saw her parents and remembers this part of her Jamaican life as a struggle with no money and sometimes not enough food, a time when you had to do what was necessary to survive. Sometimes that meant selling sludgy ice drinks that would take the edge off the endless summer heat, and after classes she also helped provide for the extended family by selling vegetables. You made do any way you could. Lennox talks of the 'heartache' and 'oppression' of his mother's childhood and teen years – and difficult formative experiences that helped mould her view of herself and the world.

Still, Violet was by nature optimistic and usually managed to stay hopeful. She wasn't about to be battered into submission and grew into a short but big-boned and broad-faced young woman with a beaming, uninhibited, full-toothed smile and a rollicking laugh. She watched the comings and goings of the millionaires, such as the rowdy Errol Flynn, and heard stories about the glories of the Empire and the wonders of the 'mother country' where the streets were paved with gold and money flowered on trees. She dreamed of a different life, away from the hand-to-mouth Jamaican world, and the solution was to travel.

The early seeds were scattered in June 1948, soon after Violet's tenth birthday, when she heard about the departure of the first boatload of Jamaican ex-servicemen on the SS *Empire Windrush*. A few years later, when the British government decided it needed extra labour for the transport system, there was another wave that included Violet's aunt Gee and her husband Son, who settled in London's East End. Gee wrote regularly to tell Violet about the wonders of this new Old World, where there were pennies to save if you kept a tight-enough fist. The hopeful teenager wrote back to say she wanted to join her favourite aunt. She matriculated from Port Antonio High School in 1955, after which Aunt Gee posted her a one-way plane ticket to London Heathrow, and finally, in 1956, at the age of eighteen, Violet and her closest friend Hazel dressed up in their Sunday best, took their first trip to Kingston and boarded an aeroplane for their maiden flight.

London, with its pea-souper fogs, perpetual queuing and undercurrent of racial antagonism, wasn't quite what she'd imagined, but she wasn't about to let it get her down. She moved in with Aunt Gee and soon found a job at an electrical goods factory where her wages seemed like a small fortune compared to the pittance earned from hawking in Jamaica. Working hard was no problem and she was earning enough to have a good time – a happy, bubbly, silly girl, as she put it, having the time of her life. After a few months of living with her aunt, Violet decided she needed more independence. It was time to strike out on her own. She found herself the first of several flats near Upton Park, the ground of West Ham Football Club, and a while later began training as a nursing auxiliary, which led to a full-time post at East Ham General Hospital.

It certainly wasn't always easy being a black woman in the white London of the late 1950s and early 1960s. If you weren't being called 'nig-nog', you were frequently being patronised by people who smiled uneasily, spoke slowly and loudly and said 'Sorry, I didn't get that' because they struggled with the accent. But there were many compensations: the money, the camaraderie among the Jamaicans who settled in the East End like so many immigrant waves before them, and the sense of freedom from expectation and tradition, particularly for women, who were in a distinct minority within the West Indian community of the time and therefore in demand.

However, after five years the hard but essentially fulfilling life of London started to become more complicated. The 23-year-old Violet had a close friend and sometime lover in fellow Jamaican Rupert Daries, who worked as a swimming teacher (and, many years later, as a masseur whose clients included Frank Bruno). She liked Rupert but had never seen him as future life partner material. He felt more like a kissing cousin than a potential husband, so she had a dilemma when her pregnancy test proved positive in 1961: whether to settle down with a man she liked but didn't quite love or go it alone.

In the end, she tried both options, first by trying to make it work as a partnership until Daries's jealousy and possessiveness put her off, and in the end by deciding she'd be better off as a single mother after all, with the considerable compensation that Rupert was usually there to help when called upon and generally proved to be a dependable father by the standards of the time. It certainly wasn't easy being a single mother in a foreign country, but Violet felt fortunate that her first-born, Dennis Daries – named after Dennis the Menace, she later admitted – turned out to be an extremely 'easy' baby, toddler and child who slept endlessly, fed happily and adapted well to being looked after by Aunt Gee and a succession of childminders, and occasionally by Rupert.

Just when Violet was becoming comfortable with her single-mother routines and was about to start a new course to become a state-registered nurse, her life changed again, this time in a way that felt far more profound. She fell in love with another young man she met at a party. Carlton Brooks was a tall, good-looking motor worker from the Ford plant in Dagenham, and Violet was smitten at first sight. The two of them seemed to hit it off immediately and became extremely close, to the point that Violet allowed herself to make a place for him in her long-term dreams. When she found she was pregnant once again, she was more delighted than shocked. Carlton, she decided, was the love of her life. They would move in together, get married and raise a family. But there was one little detail he'd neglected to mention: he already had a wife and family back home in Jamaica. When he broke this news – 'Um, sorry, Vi, but I can't marry you. You see, I'm already married' – Violet was devastated and years later still spoke about the hurt caused by that discovery.

Instead of exploding into rage, she was overcome by a deep sense of sadness that lingered and was pricked every time she saw him. Once she had absorbed the shock she was hit by a sense of desperation as the practical implications of raising another child, without a partner, began to dawn on her. She could just about cope with three-year-old Dennis on her nurse's salary, but she had no idea how she would manage with two of her children at home. Her nursing friends gave her unambiguous advice: terminate the pregnancy without delay. Violet considered this option, carefully weighing up the pros and cons, but when one of the nursing sisters booked her in for an abortion she found she just couldn't go ahead with it. She was still in love with Carlton and the idea of aborting his baby was too much for her. As this huge child grew inside her she began to feel he was precious and special and chosen – that he was meant to be.

After the birth, when she was handed the baby for the first time, she took one look, saw how much he'd inherited from his father and knew she would love him for ever. Still, she decided to leave Carlton Brooks off the birth certificate and to give the boy her own surname. Lennox Claudius Lewis hasn't always been so keen on the name Violet chose for him, but he gradually grew fond of it. He likes to tell the story of its origins.

'Lennox is a very strong, noble name, but it wasn't my mother's idea – it came from the doctor when I was born. He came in, he had a look at me and he said, "Oh, yes, he's a real Lennox there – he's so bright and so strong."' Violet wasn't at all sure what the doctor was going on about, but she liked the sound of it and agreed it was strong and noble, especially after discovering that it meant 'chieftain'. After a few moments' thought she wrote it down and added the middle name, after the Roman emperor who conquered Britain in AD 43 – a fact she recalled from her Jamaican high-school days.

This new baby was very different in looks and character from his placid and pleasing brother, over three pounds heavier at the start and far livelier and harder to pacify from then on. He was full of boisterous charm, loud, busy and extremely energetic – a bit of a handful, in fact. As soon as he could walk he wanted to run, and he liked to wrestle with his big brother and take over his toys and games and make a noise. He seemed to take up the whole of their flat in Victoria Road, West Ham, and Violet had her hands full.

Although Carlton contributed now and then, Violet still needed to work several extra shifts a week at the hospital in order to survive. Rupert, Aunt Gee and, occasionally, Carlton also did their share of babysitting but these were occasional breaks; usually Violet had to pay other women to look after her boys when she went to work, with Lennox going to one childminder and Dennis to another, which meant the boys seldom saw much of each other. She would collect them on her way back from the hospital, do her shopping on the way home, feed them, put them to bed and then get down to the business of cleaning the flat before collapsing into bed. There never seemed to be time even to think about parties and love affairs and nights out. She was perpetually exhausted and under severe stress.

Violet had grown up in a culture where children were routinely raised by relatives – in her case aunts Gee and Lou – when parents were struggling. It was nothing unusual. She realised she wasn't coping, that her emotional resources were running dry, and decided that she would have to find another solution. In essence she had to make a choice between Lennox and her older son, Dennis: one of them had to go to live with his dad. Violet's complicated feelings for Carlton, combined with the fact that he had a family of his own, made for a tense relationship, but things were easier with Rupert since he'd married. So Dennis was sent to live with his father – a decision he accepted without complaint. 'I never saw it as a rejection,' he says. 'It made sense because I was nearly four years older than Lennox, and I was already in school, so I had more going for me in that way.'

Shortly after that, Violet decided it was time to say goodbye to this bleak life in England. The 1960s were drawing to a close but the spirit of peace and free love only went so far in the East End. For black immigrants like Violet there were also the bovver boots of neo-Nazis and reverberations of the apocalyptic, anti-immigrant, anti-black 'Rivers of Blood' ranting of Tory MP Enoch Powell (who, incidentally, had played a role in encouraging the arrival of Jamaican immigrants in the 1950s). She began to make plans to start a new life with her youngest son, far away from all this misery, in North America.

Chicago seemed a good place to start because some of her classmates from Port Antonio had settled there, so she scraped together enough money to buy a single ticket, left Lennox with the ever-reliable Aunt Gee and flew off with the idea that she would send for her four-and-a-half-year-old son as soon as she had found a regular job or a steady income. The trouble was, she didn't qualify for an American Green Card, which meant she was unable to work legally; her only option was to pick up the odd babysitting, childminding or house-cleaning job wherever she could find it. She stuck it out for a year, clinging to a desperate hope that something worthwhile would turn up, but in the end a message from Aunt Gee forced her to give up.

Lennox can remember snippets of early childhood, but says he retains no memory of that year he was apart from his mother. Violet, however, was always being reminded of the boy she left behind. She would receive reports from Aunt Gee that Lennox was acting up – regularly getting into fights with other children, whose mothers would complain. He punched this one, twisted that one's arm, pushed another one and so on. Gee simply couldn't handle him. Violet knew her youngest son was an extremely boisterous boy who seemed unnaturally large and strong, but she also knew that the complaints were clear signs of distress from a little boy in desperate need of parental love. As Violet remembers: 'Lennox was very upset when I left and we both cried a lot while I was gone.'

So, with her young son not coping with his mother's absence, she returned to east London and resumed her nursing life. Dennis continued to live with his father, but Lennox moved back in with his mother and over the next few months his behaviour seemed to improve. He started in Year One at the Green Street primary school near Upton Park and at first things went well there. Violet was working the night shift so she was able to spend more time with him during the day, taking him to school and collecting him in the afternoon.

He quickly settled into school life and made friends, particularly with the girls. Perhaps because he was so close to his mother and aunt, he seemed to find it easier to relate to girls than boys, regularly introducing Violet to his little girlfriends and asking them home for tea. With boys, however, things were sometimes more difficult. Lennox was used to pitting his strength against Dennis and the bigger boys at his aunt's house, but this caused problems at school. Because he was born on 2 September, two days after the cut-off date for Year Two, he was the oldest in his Year One class and half a head taller than most of the other boys in his year. The disruption and insecurity of his year of separation from Violet had also produced a more volatile temper: when things didn't go his way, he was inclined to hit out, and he hit hard. A nine-year-old like Dennis could just about absorb the punches and hit back with interest, but it was a different question for the five- and six-year-olds who got in Lennox's way.

It was Lennox's fists that prompted his first major clash with authority and, in his mind at least, set in motion a series of events that left their scars, both on his arm and, perhaps, on his personality too. 'I have some good memories of my early years in east London,' he recalled, 'and especially when I started primary school. I remember I liked to play outside a lot and I made friends and we used to hang out together and play lots of soccer. I was having a lot of fun, and I remember with my mother back things were going very well for me then. But then one day I was in the playground and some of the kids were playing with the soccer ball – kicking it around – and I wanted to join in because I loved playing with the ball, but for some reason they wouldn't let me. So I just took their ball away from them and started playing with it by myself. Then they tried to take it back, so I punched the boy in the face quite hard and I was taken down to the principal's office.

'I was still all angry and upset about the whole thing, and then while I was waiting outside his office they said I was really going to get it – like, the principal's really going to get me – and that made me more upset so I just reacted by punching the window out of frustration or whatever, but I hit it too hard and my hand went right through this window and it cut my hand up. If you look at my right arm you can still see the scars from where one jagged piece caught me and ripped it up. Well, that was the last straw for them and the last straw for me too, so they sent me home with a note that said something like, "Dear Mrs Lewis, sorry, but I'm afraid we have no option but to expel your son from school because he has proved to be a danger to the other children."'

When Lennox talks about this incident, and shows the scars on his arm, he invariably connects with what followed: Violet's decision to have a second try at emigrating, which was wonderful at first, and then terrible. Once again, reports from the Jamaican diaspora proved decisive. Some friends-of-friends had found good jobs in Kitchener, Ontario – a 150-year-old German-Canadian town with a population of 180,000 – so she decided it would be as good a place as any to start again, this time with an ecstatic Lennox in tow but, once again, no Dennis. They flew off together, full of hope for a bright new future in this huge, new, cold country Violet had read about.

Until then, Lennox's horizons had consisted of tower blocks, row upon row of terraced houses, punctuated by the school, the hospital, the high-street stores and the Upton Park stadium. The skies seemed low and the rare falls of snow soon turned into sludge. But arriving in mid winter in Kitchener, the skies seemed so high and blue, the fields of snow went on for ever and the houses stood alone; nobody locked their doors and the people spoke funny and yet most of them seemed so friendly. After the endless sprawl of London, Kitchener seemed manageably small.

Lennox's recall of those first few months in Canada revolve around vivid memories of snow – acres of whiteness, sledges and toboggans, snowball fights. His most specific memory, however, involves a fight. A red-haired boy came up to him while he was playing in the snow and said, 'I've heard you think you're tough and that you're English, so let's have a fight.' Lennox knocked him down a couple of times, but the redhead kept trying until the school bell rang, after which the boy suggested snowballs as an alternative to fists, and they made friends. 'I remember quite a lot of that time,' he said. 'I remember learning about the different kinds of snow and learning about winter sports and how to play them. I remember noticing when I arrived that people spoke differently than in London, and that they noticed the way I spoke, and I remember that red-haired boy, although I can't remember his name.'

With his new best friend, and all this snow and space to use up excess energy, Lennox was loving life, but Violet was sinking. 'For me that was a very happy time,' Lennox said, 'a time when I felt I didn't have a care in the world, but then my mother told me she was having problems looking after me so I had to go back to England.' Violet couldn't afford the exorbitant rent charged by the opportunistic friends-of-friends who weren't quite as reliable or as friendly as she'd hoped, and she had to pay full school fees because of her immigrant status in Canada, which meant that despite a decent factory job there was never enough money to afford basics. Violet is a woman who loves cooking and enjoys her food, but for Lennox to eat she sometimes had to go hungry.

Once again she drew from her own childhood experience of being sent off to live with aunts while her parents scratched out a living, and she decided this was the only option, even though she later described it as the most heart-breaking decision of her life. She appealed once more to Aunt Gee, who, as always, said yes. Lennox would go back to London while Violet established herself in her new country. She did her best to explain this decision to her son, and he did his seven-year-old best to understand, but it must have been hard for this big little boy not to see this as a kind of rejection. He vaguely remembered that things hadn't worked out with Aunt Gee a year earlier, during that horrible year when his mum was in America, and now he was going back, alone, while Mum remained behind in this lovely place.

Violet found some acquaintances who were flying to London and got them to agree to look after Lennox on the plane. They hugged, both burst into tears, and then, for five years without end, they went their separate ways.

CHAPTER TWO
MONTEGO BAY, JAMAICA, 2004

You have to remind yourself Lennox and Dennis are brothers when you look at the pair of them and then listen to them speaking. Approaching his mid-forties, the older sibling is starting to resemble his mum more – broad face, medium height and a physique inclined towards the chubby side – but his accent is neither Violet's Jamaican nor what Lennox calls his 'mid-Atlantic' but rather East End 'estuary English', reflecting the fact that for most of his life he grew up in a different part of the world from his brother and mother. You'd have to say that in most other respects there are few obvious sibling similarities: different dads; raised, mostly, in different households and then in different countries; they even had different surnames until Dennis changed his from Daries to Lewis after starting to work for the family firm.

But there's been a gradual, unsteady, merging of interests over the years, invariably from Dennis towards Lennox. One brother is tall and, even today after a quarter century of boxing, handsome, as well as being the intellectual of the family, an international celebrity and one of the world's two or three richest sportsmen. The other is, well, quite an ordinary Joe. So that's the way it tends to go, although Dennis will tell you he's had an influence too.

This merging of destinies is all about Jamaica these days. Lennox likes it here – the sun, the music, the sense of freedom, the relative anonymity, the absence of tabloid newspapers – and spends anything from a couple of months to half of each year with his Jamaican fiancée in his beachside house. Dennis likes it too. The weather, the space, the relaxed way people relate to you – it's all so different from the Upton Park side of the East End that he and Lennox shared all those years ago, or even the manicured lawns and high fences of Hadleywood a couple of decades later. Life in Montego Bay feels as if it comes in brighter colours, and for Dennis it has become home. He still pops back to London every so often to see how the barber shop and his properties and other interests are going, but most of his year is spent in the warmth of the West Indian coastline not far from Lennox's house, tending to his own Caribbean investments and staying close to his brother.

When it comes to his role in Lennox's professional career it's been a while since Dennis has done much more than carry the flag or the title belts into the ring and offer the odd friendly, tentative word of advice. But now that Lennox's retirement decision has finally been broached, concluded and announced and there's talk of marriage and starting a family, the big little brother has more time on his hands and fewer pressures, so it's an opportunity for the two of them to coincide again.

And coincidence remains important for Dennis. Back in 2000 there was a slight fissure in their relationship, or a major crack, depending on whose version you absorb, although Dennis portrays it in more hopeful terms: a serious conflict was actually avoided by his decision to withdraw from his role as Lennox's business manager. The catalyst was what Lennox describes as his own decision 'to change to a new team', former promoter Panos Eliades describes as an 'internal coup', and Dennis describes as a difference of opinion over sponsorship deals; but, insists the older brother, that stuff really is all in the distant past now. 'Rather than having a fall-out over this, as members of the same family, I thought it would be better for both of us if I just stepped down, so that's what I did, and since then my role was more of a personal one, as his brother, and we are still very close.'

Lennox shares this perspective. He continued to take his brother around the world as a member of the entourage for his big fights and made a point of thanking Dennis when he formally announced his retirement, which he didn't do for several others he left behind. He reiterates his point that all the talk that he dumped his own brother is grossly exaggerated. 'What you should realise is that Dennis was there to the end, talking to me and giving me advice, and we're still close.'

It wasn't always like that, though – the close bit, that is. The half-brothers spent most of their childhoods and early adult lives apart and never really got to know each other inside out the way most siblings do.

But their two decades of separation was eventually followed by a decade of proximity. For a while they shared houses and a big chunk of Dennis's working life was dedicated to furthering Lennox's. He accepted this role with a good deal of pride and certainly without complaint, because it's better to be employed as the sibling of the world heavyweight champion than to work hand to mouth as a ticket tout and DJ, even if that sometimes means submerging your identity a bit.

But while relaxing in the sun on a balmy Friday afternoon in Montego Bay after a day overseeing the businesses set up without brotherly intervention, sometimes it does no harm to remind yourself that it wasn't always like that, that there was a time when normal, chronological pecking order prevailed. Dennis was the pliable, easy-going older brother and Lennox the exuberant younger one, but most of the time the form went with seniority, at least in early childhood, when no one was minding them. In those days they would sometimes fight and the older brother would generally come out on top.

'He always used to want to play with us and often I didn't really want him to play with us because he was so much younger.' Dennis begins a touch reluctantly, but then starts to warm to the subject. 'Yeah, he was always wanting to play with the bigger boys, with my friends. Like when we were playing football his main concern was to try to get the football away from us. I remember one time when he must have been about ten he said he wanted to play football with us, and I said no because actually he wasn't very good at that stage, so he kept on asking until I just pinned him on the ground and then started flicking bits of grass in his face.'

Dennis laughs at these scraps of childhood memories, and you can see that despite his caution he enjoys imparting them. But then, quickly remembering himself, he throws out a few points in mitigation, just so you don't think he's over-reaching his natural limits with his fondness for the past. 'But of course I only got the better of him in those early days because I was nearly four years older,' he adds, giving a little chuckle. 'And actually we didn't really fight much as children and we got on great – most of the time.'

When Lennox talks about his first seven years – his earliest memory, at the age of three, of sitting on a rocking horse, bobbing back and forth as far as it would go; his formative experiences at his first primary school; those endless miles of bright, white snow in Kitchener – his tone is relaxed and his recall specific and vivid. They were not all good years, of course – after all, they encompassed his overworked mother's exhaustion and stress, the separation from Dennis, that hard year with Aunt Gee and his expulsion from school – but at least for most of the time there was enough love, structure and security to his life to make for a reasonably happy and well-adjusted child. Ask him about the next five years, however, and the chronology becomes more blurred, the details more vague, the gaps more telling. When pushed, what he's left with are a few regularly repeated snippets that substitute for a coherent narrative, and he seems relieved to move on.

He can't, for instance, quite remember the whereabouts of his first school after returning from his six months in Canada, or exactly why he was sent there. 'All I remember is that it was some kind of country boarding school run by this lord of the manor type and his wife, and that it was somewhere down south of London,' he says. 'They had a big mansion on about four acres of land and they had four dogs, three Alsatians and a Labrador I think it was. I'd say this boarding school was probably funded by the government but I can't even be sure about that, and I don't know too much more about it.'

After that the details become hazier, but it seems that Aunt Gee did her best to look after him but soon realised that she wasn't managing and that Lennox was turning into a disturbed child with a wild temper who was increasingly difficult to control. Somehow they managed to find a place for him outside London that passed as a boarding school for miscreants. He recalls that he was the youngest boy in the big house where they lived and learned. All the children had their school lessons together, taught by the man, who also led them in their outdoor activities, while his wife did the cooking and caring.

This period, however, was at least tolerable most of the time for this emotionally volatile young child although it certainly wasn't easy being a seven-year-old living far away from his aunt, brother and father and, particularly, 6,000 miles away from his mum in a place run by strangers. Violet phoned and wrote regularly, but she wasn't around when he badly needed her. It could get extremely lonely, but Lennox also remembers enjoying the space and opportunities provided by the countryside: riding a bicycle on country lanes, shooting at a target with a bow and arrow, playing table tennis with the man of the house, making things in woodwork and learning to read (so that he could absorb the letters he received every two or three days from Violet) and write (so that he could reply to her letters at least once a week).

This little boarding school had a strong emphasis on sport and outdoor activity and Lennox remembers experiencing there the first excitement of sporting competition, which has stayed with him ever since. 'Ever since then I've been a competitor by heart,' he said. 'If somebody says, "I can beat you up the stairs," I say, "Yeah? Let's go." It's a race, and the race is on, and that's what brings me excitement. And it's always important for me to come out on top.'

He got on particularly well with the man, whom he remembers as kind, patient and understanding. The man noticed the boy's energy, aggression and anger and looked for ways of channelling it, and this was how the boy had his first crude flirtation with boxing. 'That was actually the first time I ever put on boxing gloves,' Lennox recalled, 'there in that boarding school in the country. I think the headmaster must have wanted just to get all that hyperactiveness out of me, so he laced up the gloves. He would say, "Come on," and he would let me punch at him until I was absolutely exhausted. It wasn't really a boxing lesson and you couldn't even say it was my first introduction to boxing – that came a few years later. It was more like me just throwing wild punches at him, but I'm sure I wasn't throwing them correctly. I think it was probably his way of getting me tired.'

Lennox is not quite sure why he was whisked away from this countryside school after one year there, but he remembers that he returned to London and was sent to another boarding establishment in Forest Gate in the East End. This children's home had none of the compensatory virtues of country lanes, bicycles, boxing gloves and kindly-seeming parent-teachers. He talks of being cooped up in an institution near Romford Road, packed with large numbers of problem children, some much bigger and harder than him: boys abandoned by their parents; boys who were in trouble with the police; boys who were out of control or difficult to control. 'It was some kind of boarding school for all the bad kids and the hyperactive kids like me and it was much more controlled and a lot less fun than the school in the country,' he remembers. 'When I say bad kids, I don't want to overstate it. I mean, they weren't killers or anything and it wasn't even as if I had to fight all the time to survive or anything like that. I would say it was more that each kid there seemed to have a different kind of problem – basically problems like not being able to get on with their families or their families not being able to get on with them. During my time at that place I always felt I didn't really need to be there because I wasn't really one of the bad kids.'

Lennox did his best to keep out of trouble, but he had no alternative but to become one of them up to a point, although he never really made close friends during his three-plus years there. The other boys were simply acquaintances who might just steal your things if you turned your back, and you always had to be ready to stand your ground otherwise they'd walk all over you. He can't even remember any of their names, and the picture that emerges is one filled with loneliness and insecurity, punctuated by pockets of relief when he spent his holidays with his brother.

Despite its attempts to maintain control, Lennox has little memory of any lessons at the school. The boys were either kept inside watching television for hours or made to wash the dishes and clean the kitchen. Sometimes they were let out and they would run riot – nicking things, pelting shopkeepers with crackers, fighting and playing truant. Sometimes there were fights with boys from outside. 'I was fighting for football because I was a West Ham fan, fighting on the street with skinheads and mods,' Lennox said, although one presumes the skinheads and mods part may be the distortion of memory. He remembers running away several times, riding on the Underground with no clear destination in mind until, bored and hungry, he and his accomplices would turn up at a police station where they would be fed and sent back to the boarding house. They would then be punished and some of the punishments seem bizarre by contemporary standards, such as being forced to go barefoot and to wear shorts in the winter cold, but for the most part they seem to have had little impact on moderating the behaviour of the boys.

Lennox's father, Carlton, had previously made some kind of effort during these years to maintain links with his son. He sometimes sent money to Violet and, when asked, would occasionally spend time with his son. But Violet's absence weakened the link, and it was virtually broken by the time Lennox returned to the East End. Today Lennox has very little say on the subject: 'My memory of my father is that he was a mechanic from Jamaica and that in the early days he was around some of the time, but that he wasn't with my mother, and then later, after she left, I didn't see him too much at all.'

Instead, it was Dennis's father, Rupert Daries, who stepped in to help – partly because he felt sorry for the boy and liked him, but also because he wanted his own son, Dennis, to maintain contact with his younger brother. As a result, Lennox would stay with Rupert's family in Stratford during the school holidays and occasionally at weekends. 'I hardly saw Lennox's father at all in those days,' said Dennis. 'He never seemed to be around, but Lennox got on really well with my dad. They liked each other, and, in a way, I think he saw my dad as a substitute father.'

For Dennis, the experience of seeing his brother again after almost two years of separation was something of a revelation. The two brothers hadn't had much of a chance to be close, but when Lennox returned to east London they got to know each other better. Whenever Lennox arrived for the holidays between the ages of nine and twelve they would quickly become comfortable with each other again, and Dennis noticed the changes.

The vulnerable, cheerful boy had grown into a tall, tough little pre-pubescent tiger who was always up for a fight, even against Dennis's friends who were three or four years older, and he was prepared to have a go at his older brother too. 'Most of my earliest memories of Lennox, when we were kids, revolved around us having fights,' Dennis recalls. 'And, of course, given the age gap, I was always the winner.' But Lennox always refused to give up, even after the kind of ritual sibling humiliation that big brothers can impart to smaller ones. Once he was back on his feet he would have another go because he believed in the credo of never losing face. 'He was quite a rogue in those days,' Dennis continues. 'He was very mischievous, like any pre-teen I guess, and in a way he was a lot of fun. He'd jump on my friends and have a go. He fought a lot then, and while I wouldn't say he was a good fighter yet, he certainly was an extremely good trier. He never backed down. Never. Not even against much bigger and stronger kids. And, as he will tell you, he had quite a temper at that age.'

By the age of twelve, Lennox had experienced only sporadic contact with his father and had been separated from his mother for half his life, including six of the previous eight years. In that time he'd moved from a relatively secure existence with Violet and Dennis to a less secure existence living without Dennis at Aunt Gee's house, then back to live with his mother when she returned after a year away, from there to an idyllic half year in Canada, then back, alone, to live with Aunt Gee again, from there off to the countryside as the youngest boy in an institution for troublesome boys, back to his aunt's and then to a rougher institution that felt like some kind of reformatory and seemed devoid of love, structure and boundaries, albeit with the occasional respite at his half-brother's house.

It had been an extremely chaotic time, and it goes without saying that it had a profound impact on his identity and the way he related to people – not least his own mother, which he recognises today.

Years later, John Hornewer, his lawyer, friend and adviser for the first eight years of his professional boxing career, said he picked up hints of unease when he brought Lennox back to London in 1989. 'I got a strong sense that some of his experiences in those years must have been extremely difficult. I remember one time when we had returned to America and things weren't going well he said to me, "John, I'm starting to feel the way I used to feel in England when I was a kid." So I said, "Should I take that as a warning?" and he said, "Yes, I think you should."'

Lennox's first long-term girlfriend, Bernita Drenth, reached a similar conclusion. 'I got the feeling those years apart from his mother, when he was living in London, must have been pretty traumatic for him. He spoke about it in a few vignettes, but it was very hard for me to get a total picture. He was very cryptic, and he was reluctant to give me more than bits and pieces he chose. For example, he would say some really supportive things about his brother Dennis, but even then I felt he was going through the motions. I felt I was never allowed to be privy to the things that happened in that part of his life.'

Dennis believes his brother's life might well have gone further downhill had he remained in London during his teenage years. 'He could have ended up in prison or worse,' he said. His mother was reaching a similar conclusion from a different angle. By this stage Lennox's letters to his mother had become more sporadic and he wasn't always there when she phoned, and some of the things he reported worried her. He was running wild, the archetypal 'feral child', and she feared he might be in a situation where he was vulnerable to the worst kinds of predators. 'I knew I had to bring him back to Canada,' she said, 'because he had become very stubborn and hyperactive, and also because I thought someone would ill-treat him or abuse him.'

And so, after five never-ending years, Violet finally made the decision that was to shape both of their lives: Lennox would join her in Canada. By then her own life had reached a level of stability. She'd been working for five hard years as a packer at the Morval factory, which manufactured Styrofoam products, and despite spending a fortune on phone calls to her sons she'd managed to save enough to find a two-bedroom flat in Lancaster Street, on the down-at-heel side of Kitchener, and a plane ticket for Lennox.

When Dennis heard about this, he felt pleased for Lennox. He never considered for a moment that he might be asked to join him or that he was being left behind.

'Going to Canada wasn't something I really thought of for myself,' he said. 'It just seemed the right decision at the time that he should go, and later, when he was there, it was quite fun knowing that I had a brother on the other side of the world.'

For Lennox, the news provoked a feeling of momentous relief. He felt ecstatic. 'I felt really, really good when I heard I was going back to Canada to be with my mum,' he recalled, 'because I was a hyperactive young man with a very bad temper and I badly needed my mother's attention.'

CHAPTER THREE
KITCHENER, ONTARIO, 2003

A ndy Powis is sitting in his front room, half a mile from the down-at-heel area of Kitchener where he and Lennox Lewis spent their teenage years. He's drinking a glass of water after going a few rounds on the punchbag out back. Absolutely no alcohol these days, he insists, and he still does what he can to stay in shape. Mainly he practises the Japanese martial art *aikido*, but now and then he still goes down to the gym to spar – 'once you've boxed it's always in your blood' – although, at the age of 40, his main opponent is that trusty old heavy bag.

His one-time best friend has just arrived in town, staying at the family mansion in Bradford in the rich part of town. The former 'Junior' Lewis is visiting his old high school for the twentieth anniversary of their all-conquering senior basketball team, but so far he hasn't looked Andy up. Not this time. Not for a while in fact. It would be nice to sit down together and really catch up, Andy reckons, but then, things being as they are, it's Lennox's call, isn't it? 'We were very, very close friends for four years,' he says. 'I was Junior's closest friend, definitely – I knew him better than anybody – but then his lifestyle changed as he became successful, and when he became famous and entered the jet-set life we just kinda drifted apart.' Andy opens his hands in a you-know-how-it-is gesture and smiles bravely. 'These days he always forgets about me, but no hard feelings, none at all. I'm still one of his biggest supporters.'

And just in case there's any doubt on this point he emphasises the thrill he gets from following his old pal's career on television and in the papers, and once in a while there's the added bonus of running into his former friend when he's in town. 'If I see him in a bar or a restaurant we'll still have a little chat. The last time was at Popeye's gym. He came over and said hi and we started kind of goofing around like the old days. I said, "How you doing, Junior?" That's what we always used to call him; he didn't like being called Lennox until later. So he laughed and said, "Hey, don't call me Junior," and then he said, "I still owe you one," because we once had an amateur fight and I bloodied his nose.'

That's the best Andy can hope for these days – a hi, how's it going and a joke or two before they go their separate ways, Andy to his wife and children, his little house and his job in shipping reclining chairs at La-Z-Boy, and the erstwhile Junior to Miami, London, New York or Montego Bay and his job as the newly retired heavyweight champion of the world. What remains is mainly those sweet memories of their glory days together in the late 1970s and early 1980s when Andy, the awe-shucks youngest brother in a working-class family of fighting boys, befriended this tough but vulnerable newcomer from England and showed him the ropes in oh so many ways.

Andy picks out a couple of photographs of the two of them together – skinny Lennox in his tracksuit top with his modest Afro and his big grin and serious Andrew, a bit chunkier, with his brown disco shirt and big orange hair; and another, this time Andrew grinning with delight and Lennox pulling a face and displaying a peace sign. Andy points to the pictures with a wistful fondness. 'Junior was thirteen when that one was taken and I was fifteen, and by then we were already really good friends. We had just started boxing so we were spending plenty of time in the gym together. In fact, outside of school we spent just about all our time with each other.'

They met soon after Lennox moved into the neighbourhood to join Violet. Andrew, a friendly teenager who lived a block away, saw this kid who looked about his own age (but was in fact two years younger) kicking a ball in the park. 'That's Junior,' said another of his mates, so the friendly Andy went over to and said, 'Hi, I'm Andrew Powis, do you want to join in?' and the two lads hit it off immediately. 'I remember that first time I met him,' says Andy. 'We were playing football in the park. He'd been in Canada a few months already but he still had a slight English accent, which he soon lost. He was quite tall and lanky and, in fact, pretty skinny – not a big brute at that age because he only started filling out when he was about seventeen. And like me he was quite cocky, but never a bully in any way. Those were my first impressions.'

By the time Andrew Powis introduced himself, the boy from the East End was already starting the long process of calming down and adapting to this wonderful new life in Ontario. He was still suspicious of adults, reluctant to trust and introverted, but his temper was becoming easier to control, his inclination to hit out at the slightest provocation was dissipating, he was smiling far more often and he was becoming more open to friendship. The change in his mood, mindset and demeanour that followed his departure from a chaotic London life was underway, and, in a sense, the changes taking place in Lennox's life and those still to come offer a hopeful illustration for the idea that if there's a foundation of early love children can recover from the experience of childhood trauma, even if that damage leaves some scars in unexpected places.

Lennox flew into Toronto late in 1977 and remembers feeling slight embarrassment when Violet, who'd arrived early and had been waiting for several hours, rushed up with tears in her eyes and proceeded to give him a prolonged hug and kiss. She shouted out loud to no one in particular, 'Here's my son, look, my son!' But Lennox also remembers feeling wonderful relief and happiness. 'It was a really great experience seeing her again after all those years,' he said. 'A really wonderful experience. She's the kind of person who gets really excited, so she just kept on kissing me and even if it was embarrassing it was wonderful too.' He was back with his mum at last, and this time he would make sure they would never be separated again. He would try to be good. He would help her. He would make her proud. He would do good. He would achieve something big – maybe become a fireman or something like that.

By the standards of middle-class Kitchener, Violet's two-bedroom flat at the Sunrise Apartments in Lancaster Street wasn't much, but for a twelve-year-old who'd spent five years sharing rooms with boys he barely know, it was perfect. He had his own room, and across the road was Hawk Fields where he could charge about and kick a ball. He had a routine and security, he was safe from predators and he was back with his mother.

It wasn't all easy, of course. When he started at the Elizabeth Ziegler primary school he discovered that his fractured schooling left him several years behind his contemporaries. And it didn't help when they laughed at his East End accent, made fun of him, and tried to imitate him or correct his glottal stops. He said 'haitch' instead of 'aitch', "air" instead of 'hair', and spoke of 'fings' instead of 'things'. 'The Canadian boys made fun of my cockney accent,' he recalled. 'I think my accent really annoyed people, and I used all this slang, like when people told me to shut up I'd say, "It's not closing time yet," because that's what we used to say in London, and it led to a lot of fights. They would tease me a lot, so, you know, I had to defend myself.'

His routine response to such piss-taking was to climb in with fists and boots, but this wasn't tolerated in the Elizabeth Ziegler playground. A pattern developed: some classmate would tease Junior; Junior would thump him; an exasperated teacher would order him off to the school principal, who in those days was still permitted to 'paddle' his backside; and Junior would return to the classroom for another round of teasing. It happened once, then again, and then a third time until the headmaster told Junior he needed to 'channel his aggression' and that perhaps he should give boxing a try.

Most great boxers tell apocryphal stories about how they started. For Joe Louis it was those big hands and tin ears that couldn't handle the violin, prompting the secret resolution to spend his mum's money on learning how to box; for Muhammad Ali it was the stolen bicycle that sent him crying to the police gym, asking to learn how to fight; for Mike Tyson it was the kid who tore the head off his pet pigeon, turning the 'Fairy Boy' into a monster; for Lennox's countryman Naseem Hamed it was a schoolyard beating delivered to two bigger boys at once, witnessed from the top of a bus by an awed Irish trainer. For Lennox Lewis, appropriately perhaps, the story is more complex and layered, depending on the fortuitous combination of a new best friend, a proposed street fight that in the end never actually happened, the invitation of a kindly police sergeant and the arrival in his life of a father figure who doubled as one of the best amateur trainers in Canada.

The catalyst was Andrew Powis's arrival in his life. He became Lennox's first close friend in nearly six years – in fact his first real friend since he had said goodbye to another red-haired chum on his first visit to Canada. They were in different classes at school and later attended different secondary schools, but their common passion for sport, and boxing in particular, the proximity of their flats and the way their personalities meshed meant that, as Andy put it, 'we were inseparable in those days'.

Lennox enjoys being reminded of the good times he had with his older friend. 'He's one of the friends I remember really well from my first few years of living in Kitchener,' he said. 'Yeah, Andrew Powis, and also his three older brothers – I remember them very well. I would hang out at their house quite often and Andrew would come to my home quite a lot as well, and I have plenty of fond memories of the two of us doing stuff together. We started boxing together, we jumped off a big gorge into a pool of water together, we had a lot of fun. Yeah, I'd say we were pretty good friends.'

They have different angles on why this boxing thing happened. Andy suggests there was inevitability about that trip to the Waterloo Police Boxing Association gym. 'I was in grade school at the time and I got in a lot of fights with other kids, and a teacher of mine who'd boxed said I should go to the police station to box. Well, my brothers had also been into boxing, so that's what I decided, although in the end the way it happened was through a situation that me and Junior found ourselves in. You see, by then we were really good friends and we went together to this dance at the YMCA on Queen Street and had a bit of a quarrel with some guys. They wanted to fight, so we agreed to meet them outside the police gym, but they never showed up, so the fight never happened. And it was then that we met the head trainer, who was a police sergeant called Jerome "Hook" McComb, and we decided to join the gym together and start boxing, and we just stuck at it.'

For Lennox it felt like just one of those things that happen in an ordinary day, but later it took on the aura of a fortuitous, fateful event. 'By then I'd already got into a couple of street fights, and I won them too. I remember that these guys from the school dance were from another school, KCI I think it was called, and they were sort of a gang – well, not a proper gang, but they were tough guys. They wanted to fight us, but we realised that if we fought there at the school we'd get into trouble so Andy said to them, "Yeah, we'll fight you, but let's meet at the gym at the police station," and they said OK. Well, the KCI guys never showed up so we hung around for a bit, and you know how it is, you see all the bags and the gloves and you want to train with them. Well, Hook McComb watched us and then he called me over and said, "You! You want to box?" And that's how it all started.'

These two boys, up for a scrap and with the 'go box' advice of their teachers in the backs of their heads, were open to invitations. They wandered in, looked around and saw an indoor basketball court without a ring where the boys were sparring in circles, and they moved closer to the action, intrigued. They were joking around, pushing each other and laughing out loud until Hook came over and gave them his 'if you want to fight, you should learn to box' spiel, and they took his bait. But Hook had his way of doing things, of reeling them in, which involved teaching the basics before allowing the lads to have a go: give them a taste, build up the desire, but don't throw them in too deep too early. This middle-aged police officer might have been as hard as they come when the moment required, but he had a kind heart and he didn't want to see the boys' enthusiasm dampened by the taste of too many mouthfuls of their own blood.

He started them off with some warm-up exercises and then some instruction about stance, balance and correct punching. It was enough to tempt them back the next week, when they went through the same routine, until Junior decided he'd had enough and quietly announced, with his eyes on the floor, that he was ready to box, at which point Hook introduced the boy to a wiry man in his late forties with a full head of curly, greying hair, a droopy moustache and a big smile. Arnie Boehm noticed that this lanky new boy was shy and reluctant to look him in the eye, but he also observed that he was extremely keen to try his luck. He had a word with Hook, gloved Lennox up and called over a fifteen-year-old to square off with this nervously enthusiastic newcomer. 'I remember that Hook said to me, "You want to go a couple of rounds?" and I said, "Yeah," so they laced up my gloves and I sparred my first two rounds of proper boxing.'

By the end of the rounds Junior Lewis had a lump in his throat, his eyes were watering and his nose was hurting. He was close to tears, fighting the urge, and wasn't so sure any more that this boxing thing was such a good idea. 'At first – those first two rounds – I didn't really like boxing,' he said, 'because that kid punched me in the nose and my eyes started watering, so I wasn't sure this was for me.' Arnie sensed the doubt but also noticed the resolve to fight those tears and he geed him up: happens to everyone, this rite of passage; you'll see, it'll be easier next time. 'Most kids would say "That's enough for me" after getting hit like that, but Lennox just stayed in there and didn't give up, and I liked that in him,' said Arnie. Lennox took him at his word, and Arnie made sure he kept it by putting both boys in with lads who were also new to the game, and they started to enjoy themselves. 'This time I was with someone more or less my own level and it was much more fun,' Lennox recalled. 'I liked the feel of being in there – you know, just you by yourself, which makes it exciting in the sense that there's another guy who's trying to hit you and you're trying to hit him at the same time, and also to avoid getting hit, which means you have to learn new and different skills, and you're both looking at each other all the time. This one-on-one thing is what appealed to me most about boxing because it's so intensely competitive – ego against ego – and I'm an intensely competitive person.'

Lennox went home and told Violet where he'd been but she wasn't convinced. After five years apart her relationship with him was never going to be one of my-way-or-the-highway but she didn't want to see her son getting knocked around. 'What about basketball?,' she asked. 'You're so good at basketball. Why not concentrate on what you're best at – go with your strengths.' In this way she had a gentle bash at playing down the boxing thing, but it didn't work, and soon Junior and Andy were at it three times a week or more, running in the streets to keep fit, shadow boxing in the sitting room and talking about their next fights. Despite the occasional bloody nose, Violet gradually came round to the idea. 'At first, when he was twelve years old, I didn't want him to start boxing, but when he started doing it he had my full support. He never had black eyes but sometimes when he got home he had a bloody nose and I'd say, "Give it up, son, stop it," but he'd say, "No, I want this."' It took a while, but Violet became increasingly interested in the details of his progress and eventually came to accept the bruises and blood along with the trophies and medals. 'It's a contact sport, so you go in there and somebody has to get a little bruised. I didn't expect him to come out beautiful all of the time.'

The decision to take up boxing together sealed Lennox's friendship with his older friend and for a few years they were inseparable out of school. 'Junior and his mum were living in this two-bedroom apartment in a kind of low end of point of town, and it was nothing fancy, that's for sure,' Andy recalled. 'Later they moved to another apartment, but they didn't have a whole lot of money or things, you know. Like no car, which was unusual in Canada. Violet wasn't there during the day because she was a single working mum – a worker at that Styrofoam factory – but I used to see him after school every day. I was there at his place all the time and sometimes I'd have my dinner there. Violet would make us Jamaican food, especially dumplings, which were great. And one day, when Violet was out, Junior introduced me to Jamaican rum.'

Lennox's brother Dennis was occasionally present by proxy as someone the younger boy would refer to with pride and imagination. 'I never met Dennis,' said Andy, 'but Junior would talk about his brother and I got the impression he really admired him. He would say Dennis was a really good soccer player and great at this and that. He looked up to Dennis in a lot of ways and he liked to talk about him.'

In a sense, one of the roles Andy played was that of substitute older brother – but not so old as to be out of reach. When they first met, Junior was a streetwise twelve-year-old on the cusp of puberty and Andy was a young fourteen-year-old and their main idea was to have a laugh, compete against each other in every sport and see what they could get away with. 'We were typical boys when we were younger, me and Junior,' Andy said. 'We used to get up to a little bit of mischief, like nicky-nicky-nine-door [knock down Ginger]. You know how it is – you do what you have to do to get through your schoolwork and stuff but that's not your real interest. Junior certainly wasn't stupid but he certainly wasn't top of the class. His intellectual interest came a bit later on in high school, but at the time he wasn't much of a bookworm. He was more into playing lots of sport and having fun, and we sure had a lot of good times together.

'Like, we once jumped off Elora Gorge together. It was sixty feet in the air and we jumped off the top all the way down into that water, sixty feet below. Lennox did it with his arms extended, which wasn't such a good idea. He was scared all right, but I talked him into it, because my older brothers talked me into it, but he went first and of course he survived, but I can tell you his arms were really red and stinging, even with his dark skin, because when you hit the water from that height with your arms open it stings real bad. I know, because I did the same thing, and my white arms were red and stinging too.'

Though Carlton Brooks had popped in and out during Lennox's first few years, the link weakened over time. 'It was just him and his mother and they were real close,' said Andy. 'Junior never talked much about his father, although once he said his mom thought it best that they lived apart, but Arnie was like a second dad to him. Junior really treated him like a dad and he treated Junior like his son.'

Arnie Boehm, his wife Verna and their five children served as an alternative family. In his self-deprecating way, Arnie used to tell the boys he'd been a terrible amateur boxer but that he knew how to teach others the things he couldn't do himself. During the day he was an electrician, working on the power lines for a Kitchener-based hydroelectric company, but working with boys in the boxing club was his main passion, and when Hook McComb died it took over his life. 'Arnie Boehm wasn't just my amateur boxing coach,' Lennox says, 'he was more of a father figure to me than any other person in my life.'

Like so many amateur boxing trainers, Arnie saw his sport in terms of its potential for developing confidence and self-assurance in damaged boys. From their first meeting Junior struck him as a prime candidate. He could see from the start that this thirteen-year-old was reluctant to trust anyone, particularly adults. Difficult past experiences had made Junior an emotional 'basket case', Arnie guessed, and he noticed Lennox's 'terrible inferiority complex'. But this offered a challenge for a kind and caring man who prided himself on his ability to work with troubled boys and to help them develop confidence, direction and pride. By then his own children were leaving home and he had the energy and experience to spend time with Junior, who gradually grew to trust him.

Part of the attraction for Arnie was that the boy showed remarkable natural ability – the balance, rhythm, reflexes and power that rarely come so easily. The prowess he was already displaying on the basketball court was translated with effortless grace into the boxing ring. Moves that other boys took years to learn seemed innate in Junior Lewis, and on top of that he was a keen and dedicated student. 'I've never seen anyone work so hard in my life,' he said. 'He would run every day, often in snow and freezing rain.'

So Arnie was impressed with the physical raw material and with his attitude, but it was more than just a boxing thing. He was also impressed by his courage, determination and sense of principle. He would tell a story of a day in the gym when some local toughs arrived to cause trouble. Junior quickly surveyed the situation, walked over to the biggest one and flattened him with a right cross. 'He was really fearless,' Arnie recalled. 'And I couldn't help being drawn to a boy who had such a strong idea of what was right and wrong and was ready to work for what he wanted.'

He realised that the boy and his mother were poor, so he used his own money to buy Lennox his first boxing vest, trunks and handwraps, and later his first jockstrap, gumshield, baseball boots and boxing boots. He would also give handouts of pocket money, birthday presents and Christmas presents and invite him round for meals. 'Arnie played an instrumental role in every aspect of my life,' Lennox confirms. 'He bought me my first head gear and jock, he took me camping, he taught me how to drive, he taught me how to fish and he was instrumental in my social life too.' He offered the teenager advice about girls and sex and about why he needed to take his schoolwork seriously. He instructed him in all the little bits and pieces he felt fathers should teach their sons: about electrical currents and how to fix fuses; about the internal combustion engine; and about the properties of cement and how to mix and apply it. He even showed Junior how to cut his toenails. Occasionally Lennox would open up to him, usually tentatively, about his self-doubts and insecurities, and Arnie would reassure him.

'Everyone says I've got boats for feet,' Lennox once confided after they'd had to order special shoes.

'Ah, you see, a tall oak tree needs a good base,' Arnie responded. 'Soon the rest of you will catch up and you'll be a big man.'

There was a lot of growing to do and, as with his boxing career, Lennox took his time over it. On the physical side, his feet stopped at size 15½ and the rest of his body followed – mainly upwards at first. 'I kind of grew all of a sudden,' he recalled. 'I was really lanky as a kid. I remember one summer I just shot up and gained twenty pounds, so I rose a couple of weight divisions from 140lb to 160lb in four months.' He was closing in on sixteen before he started shaving, and it took a while longer before he began to fill out. By seventeen he was a broad-shouldered 6ft 3in but still thin-limbed and wasp-waisted; he only passed 200lb at the age of eighteen. He ceased his upward surge for a while at twenty, stalling at 6ft 4in, and then his body had a final spurt that ended in his mid-twenties, bringing him to his current height of a fraction over 6ft 5in.

Another boxer who started off lean and tall (and only stopped growing upwards at 23) was Muhammad Ali. In the autumn of 1978 Ali was about to win the world heavyweight title for the third time by outpointing his novice conqueror, Leon Spinks. Lennox and his mum watched the fight on television, with ABC's Howard Cosell eulogising the old champion as he danced to victory (with viewers offered a fifteenth round backbeat of Bob Dylan singing, 'May your hands always be busy/May your feet always be swift/May you have a firm foundation when the winds of change they shift'). Junior was a long-limbed kid with busy hand and swift feet, who like to pretend he was 'The Greatest' – 'I loved Ali and I would try to emulate him to a certain degree by moving around the ring and hitting without getting hit' – until the idea of becoming Junior Lewis and, eventually, at the age of seventeen and under Arnie's prompting, 'Lethal' Lennox Lewis.

Andy remembers Lennox's transition from interest to obsession in his chosen sport as a gradual process. 'When you're that young you don't know how big to make one sport or another so you do them all, as long as they're fun, and that's how it was at first,' said Andy. 'Junior was like all of us then and didn't take boxing so completely seriously at first, and of course, like all of us he had to learn the ropes. So he took some punches, as you do when you're learning the game. I mean, when we started we were sometimes fighting in the gym with guys who had five or six years' experience, although most of the time Hook and Arnie were very good about putting you in at more or less your own level so that you didn't get hurt too often. But whoever he was fighting, Junior could hold his own.'

By the time Junior Lewis had his first bout, against Junior Lindsay in 1979, he had sparred over a hundred rounds. He had no trouble blowing away Lindsay in two rounds and he was on his way. Soon after that, however, he experienced his first defeat in a tournament at the Police Recreation Club against his best friend Andrew Powis, who was almost sixteen. 'What happened was that the person I was supposed to fight didn't turn up,' Andy recalled. 'In fact we both had no one to fight, so we ended up being paired against each other, and even though we were close friends we both went all out and were trying our best. I managed to bloody his nose and I got the decision and the trophy, but that was really only because I was two years older and more physically mature and probably slightly heavier. It was his first loss, but they put the wrong result in the newspaper.'

When he reached junior high school at Margaret Avenue Public School Lennox had settled down and was no longer regarded as a disturbed or troublesome boy. However, he was still behind classmates who had grown up in the relative order of the Ontario school system, so it was decided he'd do best with a vocational education and he was sent to Laurel Vocational. Halfway through Year Nine he changed to a top state school, Cameron Heights, which had 1,800 students and a reputation for sporting achievement. As Andy recalled, 'Cameron poached him because of his sporting potential because he was already playing basketball really well.' He added American football, track and field and baseball to his repertoire and also tried ice hockey – 'I liked it because you could fight real free' – but his skating let him down. 'I also tried all kinds of martial arts, and I loved to wrestle with my friends and cousins. If the YMCA was doing some kind of judo programme, I would try to make time to go along. My school also had a karate class so I went along to learn the kicks, although I found it was most effective to kick no higher than the waist, so I wasn't too much into that side of it, and I also found that you can't compare the karate guys to boxers because their hands are no good.'

The other one-on-one activity Lennox discovered was chess. On a whim he joined the chess club at Cameron when he was fifteen-years-old, starting a life-long passion in which he sometimes displays the extremes of his competitive nature, occasionally accidentally-on-purpose knocking the board over when things aren't going his way or insisting on a return match even if it's the early hours of the morning. 'I got to be pretty good at chess quite quickly, although it takes time to get really good,' he said. 'In a way it felt a bit like boxing to me – the one-on-one thing. It's a strategy game because you always have to decide which is the better move, which you have to do in life generally: do I go down this road or is that road the better road? Chess helps you to recognise it. And that kind of thinking is especially useful when you're boxing. Do you throw a jab or a right?'

Arnie Boehm went out of his way to nurture Lennox's natural talent as a boxer. The other boys in the gym also began to take note, watching his smooth defensive moves and sharp combinations and trying to imitate him. 'You could see he had it from early on,' says Andy. 'I mean, you couldn't miss it because Junior was a really good all-round athlete – brilliant at basketball, great at football and really good at soccer too. The only thing he couldn't do well was skate. But in boxing it was obvious he was going to be really good. When he was going on for fifteen Arnie really saw that spark in him, and after that Junior became extremely dedicated and he really took off.'

When he arrived at Cameron Heights he had passed six feet in height, weighed just over 160lb and was already the Ontario Golden Gloves junior champion. Soon after that he had his first bout against a senior, Toronto's 22-year-old Kingsley Hataway, who was a former Canadian champion at 165lb. It was intended as a tough learning bout, but Lennox's natural ability carried him through as he jabbed and moved his way to a points win and what he thought was a lovely trophy for their living room. 'Aside from the intensely competitive aspect of it, the thing I liked most about boxing in those early days was the trophies I won,' he said. 'I wanted to build up my trophy and medal collection.'

In October 1980, a month after his fifteenth birthday, Lennox was thrown in with the soon-to-be seventeen-year-old Donovan Ruddock, who went on to become the heavyweight contender Razor Ruddock. The two of them had sparred together a few times, with Ruddock having an edge in the early days. But the gap was closing and Ruddock squeaked home on a 3–2 points decision. Lennox complained that they only gave it to Ruddock because they needed him to represent Canada in an international tournament. To which Arnie added: 'It was a pretty even fight, but what lost it for Lennox is that his stamina gave out in the third round.' Still he was pleased with his pupil's performance and told him: 'Junior, mark my words, one day you'll be the heavyweight champion of the world.'

It was an idea that had already occurred to Lewis, but it didn't hurt to have his mentor reinforcing it. 'From then on he really blossomed,' said Arnie. In fact, his only other loss over the next three years came in the Canadian national championships in 1982 but Lennox says he only lost then because he was slipping and falling all over the floor as the result of his first-ever pair of boxing boots (ordered from America by Arnie) having leather soles and the ring surface being made of a slippery vinyl.

Lennox soon overtook Andrew in terms of achievements in their chosen sport, but they continued to hang out together for a while longer, running together through the streets of Kitchener most mornings, going to the gym most evenings and picking up tips from their neighbour Donny LaLonde – a good-looking blonde-haired lad who was something of a hero in the gym. Donny, who went on to win the world light heavyweight title, used to train with them in the police gym and regularly offered them advice. 'He was a couple of years older than us and he sort of took us under our wing and used to teach us stuff,' Andy remembers. 'Lennox and I learned a lot from him and we all made the best of it – especially Lennox, of course.' Part of the attraction for these two working-class boys was the regular travel to compete in amateur tournaments. 'You know, that gym in Kitchener attracted a lot of Canada's top boxers, guys who later did well in the pros because Hook and Arnie were the best coaches in the whole of Ontario,' said Andy. 'So through them and through boxing we got to travel all over Ontario and it was one of the things that kept us excited about the sport.' To which Lennox responds: "Yeah, that was a big attraction. Through boxing I was getting to travel all over – first Ontario, then Canada, then America, and then the world.'

The teenagers would back each other up when fights broke out. 'We had a few fights, me and Junior,' Andy acknowledges. 'I remember one time a guy stole my bike. We were walking down King Street and Junior saw the thief with the bike, so he shouted, "Andy, there's your bike!" and we chased him. Junior was a pretty good runner so he caught the guy and gave him a couple of really good punches, and then the police came.' As they grew older and developed reputations as boxers and street fighters, the extra-curricular scrapping became almost an expectation when they went out. 'We'd often go to dances together – Junior was a pretty good dancer – and sometimes at these dances we'd get into the middle of a fight and we'd have to look after ourselves. But Junior would never start a fight – neither of us would. It was a situation of people picking on him, or me, because they knew we were boxers. You know, when people hear you know how to box they decide they want to have a go, and then you have to defend yourself, and as boxers we obviously knew how to do that, so we'd look after ourselves.'

Lennox stresses that he never picked on anyone. 'Boxing helped me control my temper. Once I got into it I stopped getting hyped up real fast like I did when I was a kid in London. I guess I developed a more constructive temper after I started. I've certainly never picked a fight in my life and I've never been one of the bully types, and I developed an easy-going manner that helped deflect antagonism. Also, I was always quite a big kid and people knew I could defend myself. If I'd come across intimidating or aggressive I think I would have been in more fights, but that's just not my nature. It no longer bothered me too much when people called me names. The only thing that bothered me was when they touched me, and then I would react – and that's how I got into a few altercations when I was at school, and I'll tell you this: I've never lost a street fight in my life. I'm very proud of that. You know how they say, in a room full of men I'm the last man standing, and I finish it quickly. I'm not into a long, drawn-out brawl unless I can't help it, but usually it was over with a couple of punches. One-two and they were out, and it was all over.'

CHAPTER FOUR
TORONTO, CANADA, 2004

Bernita Drenth has been through a lot of heartache recently. Her husband, Arthur Gelgoot, a Toronto accountant who was also a prominent supporter of the arts, died in February 2004, after a long battle with cancer. 'It's been an extremely difficult time,' she says. But Bernita is a kind and open person who finds time between the demands of wrapping up Arthur's business and seeing to her own, to speak about another relationship that ended two decades earlier. It doesn't take long to appreciate that she is about a million miles from what some might be tempted to expect of the first serious relationship of a world heavyweight boxing champion – not just well spoken and well-to-do, but strong-minded, independent, intellectual and, despite all the pain in her current life, witty too.

It's been a few years since she last saw Lennox but there are no lingering tensions. 'We see each other once in a while and we get on fine,' she says. Now and then she observes him being interviewed on television and tut-tuts when he sounds too belligerent, because he certainly wasn't like that at school; she also smiles when he goes on about his mum, because she remembers the conflicts as well as the love in that relationship.

Thinking back on the high-school years she spent as the girlfriend of Lennox still makes her smile. 'He may have been a goof to date but most kids at sixteen are, so we had lots of ups and downs and heartbreak and all the drama that any high-school relationship has, but he treated me very well and he was by no means your typical boxer.' Her idea of the typical boxer comes from the time she spent watching Arnie Boehm taking his lads through their paces, and from subsequent images of boxers on television, but to reiterate the point she adds that he wasn't the typical 'jock' either. 'I mean, if you knew me you'd know I've never been a groupie interested in dumb guys who can just play sport. Lennox was a jock, of course, but he had none of the characteristics of most jocks.'

She can't recall the first time she set eyes on this tall, lanky, good-looking basketball, football and track star, but she has a clear memory of his opening gambit. 'He used to really chase the girls, so one day he dropped down to the floor right in front of me and did some push-ups, to show off. He was a major cad in those days.' Bernita laughs at the memory of that overture, just as she did then, but soon they were talking and she discovered he had a lot more going for him than his looks and athleticism. 'What impressed me about him was that he was so totally focused on becoming the best. He had such huge self-confidence. He was doing a lot of sports at the time and doing extremely well in all of them, but even then, at the age of sixteen, he would say with absolute certainty he would be Olympic super heavyweight champion and heavyweight champion of the world. I would laugh and say, "Sure, sure," but he believed it. He knew it. He had no doubt. I had never come across such self-belief before and that's what attracted me to him.'

Lennox's sporting success gave him an enhanced status at high school. 'He became pretty popular with the guys soon after he arrived at Cameron Heights,' said Andy Powis. 'I think this was partly because he was becoming well known for boxing and other sports. Mostly he used to hang around with me and two or three other friends outside of school but he was one of those people that a lot of guys wanted to be with, and he certainly did all right with the girls. They really seemed to like him and he always had girls around him and he was a great dancer, which they liked.'

When he started dating Bernita in 1981, their friends were surprised. On the surface they seemed an unexpected couple – white, middle-class, brainy Bernita and black, working-class, jock-ish Junior – but they had a lot more in common than her admiration for his ambition. 'We met at high school when I was one of the guys who was kind of famous there, mainly through basketball, so everyone knew me, including Bernita,' Lennox recalled. 'I thought she was a very nice girl, and I liked her a lot and we got on really well, and she became one of my first girlfriends – well, my second actually – and I guess some people were surprised. I got the impression her mother, for one, didn't really understand me. It was, like, "Who's he?" Maybe I was wrong, but I guessed my colour never really helped with some of her family. But Bernita, she was really cool.'

He felt it necessary to stress that there was far more to him than just his prowess on the field and in the ring and showed none of the expected predatory machismo in the way he related to girls. 'Not at all,' says Bernita. 'Not even slightly. Actually he was very defensive about not being seen as a dumb jock. He was well read – even then – and very interested in ideas and in learning about the world, even though he did the least he could get away with to get by in his schoolwork. I remember once seeing him cooking away at the stove, so I asked him what he was doing and he said he'd decided to take Home Economics. But he was very literate and interested in ideas and he'd started playing chess, which he really enjoyed. We would have long discussions, just the two of us, about religion and politics and all sorts of issues. Once he went to meet Pierre Trudeau, the Canadian Prime Minister, in Toronto, and when he came back we spent hours talking about the politics of the Liberal Party. He was really waxing on about it. And he was quite philosophical. He used to say to me all the time, "You may be intelligent, but I'm smart."'

Lennox laughed at this description, but said it was spot-on. 'Yeah, Bernita and I would talk about the world and about politics and all sorts of things. You see, I was becoming very interested in what was going on around me at that time, like that time when I went to meet Trudeau. I wanted to find out more, so I asked him a lot of questions so that I could gain an understanding of his job.'

His boxing-induced absences and the constant demands of his sports coaches meant his schoolwork suffered. He was so sure he would become heavyweight champion of the world that he felt he could place his studies a poor second to this calling. 'I decided I should first take advantage of what boxing can offer me and then do what's necessary to get my grades at high school because education is always there but boxing isn't.'

He remembers one English teacher in particular showing enormous patience with him, which set the basis for his subsequent interest in reading. 'By then I was away a lot because of my boxing, and then I'd come back and I'd have to copy out a lot of stuff from other people's books on the things I missed in class, but then I started to realise that the teachers would help me when I returned from these trips and I had a couple of really excellent teachers. One of them was my English teacher at Cameron. Everybody hated her because she wouldn't give them any leeway, but I really liked her because she was the kind of person who said, "If you do the work, you get good grades." So if I did badly in a test, she would let me retake it after school. And then I would retake it, even though I had sports practice every day, and I would do better. So she really helped me. But in other classes – well, I sort of learned after a while how to stay ahead of the programme. There are certain ways you can stay ahead of the programme if you use your brains, and I did that.'

One of his ways was to call on Bernita in a crisis. 'Half the time I would do his homework assignments for him – well, not half the time, but definitely sometimes – and in the end he scraped through,' she said. 'What helped was that the teachers and the principal really liked him, so they supported him a lot. Part of it was that they just liked him as a person, but it was also because he was a VIP for sport. When they cottoned on to his success in boxing they supported him in that too, so they wanted him to succeed. I remember once the basketball coach phoned me and said Lennox just wasn't getting some essay done that he had to do so couldn't I help him out in some way, so, you know, I sat down and scribbled a few things for him. But he was actually really very intelligent.'

In addition to his four evenings a week of boxing training, he seldom had an afternoon free from training in football, basketball or athletics, depending on the season. He was top scorer in a high-school basketball team that went on to win the Ontario provincial championships. He became a running back in a high-school football team that won all its games, as well as the area championships, and he excelled in athletics: the best shot putter of his year, represented his school at area level in the long jump and set the school record in javelin. Despite his size he wasn't a bad runner either, capable of covering 100 metres in twelve seconds and he was particularly quick over short bursts of 30 metres.

Basketball was a game he took to effortlessly, and he continued to play it throughout high school and during his brief spell at college, and he still regularly plays pick-up games today. His spell in gridiron football was briefer, lasting two years. At first some of his football coaches resented seeing him missing games when he was travelling for boxing and it played into their doubts about his commitment. They observed an easy-going demeanour, which they interpreted as lackadaisical. Having never seen him fight, some of them wondered whether he had the energy, guts and heart to go for the kill, or the commitment to fulfil his potential. 'By then I was already excelling in boxing,' Lennox recalled. 'I was Ontario champion and national champion, so when I had to decide which sport to concentrate on a hundred per cent I chose boxing because I felt it would get me furthest in life. But at the same time, as a running back, I was one of the key players on the team, yet when I'd have championship football games I sometimes couldn't go because I'd be away for boxing, and the coaches didn't like that. One of them called me a prima donna.'

Despite his absences, the coaches began to change their perspective. They noticed the intense competitiveness beneath the laid-back demeanour and by the end of his first season he had become the darling of the team. 'It didn't take me very long to realise he was an absolutely fabulous athlete, very gifted with innate ability, and very coachable,' said Gene Heesaker, who coached Lennox in 1981 and 1982. 'He became our star offensive running back. I remember after one championship game I talked to a player from the other school, and he said, "It's unfair – it's like boys being made to tackle men." Junior was only sixteen then but I guess he was already nearly six three, and even though he wasn't bulky he was extraordinarily strong and really tough. His raw physical strength was unique for that level. Actually, our game plan was simple: give the ball to Junior and he will run with it and make us look good. He was quite quick, but the main thing is that he was extremely hard-nosed and so strong.' To which another of the Cameron coaches, Ron Bell, added, 'He was really a tremendous basketball player because he was tall and quick, and we thought it was a pity he gave up football after only two seasons because if he'd carried on he could have been an awesome professional.'

The coaches came to realise that with Junior boxing came first, so they'd best accommodate this diversion. 'As soon as I saw him, when he arrived at Cameron halfway through Year Nine, I knew he had a future as a professional athlete, in whatever field,' Heesaker continued. 'With track and field he did it without really training, but he set school records. He was really outstanding at basketball and football, but all those sports he played just for fun because he was already being groomed to become a world champion boxer, and we came to appreciate this. Some of us used to shadow spar with him before practice and we would raise money for Arnie and Junior to help with his boxing travels, because Junior and his mother and Arnie didn't have a lot of money. I guess I got to know him as well as I've known any athlete and I found him to be a really good kid, very respectful. Everyone liked him. Despite the fact that we had to accept that boxing was his first priority he was a good team player who got on well with his team-mates. He had a great sense of humour and was always lots of fun, and he liked to fool around but he wasn't a prima donna in any sense and he wasn't egotistical at all.'

It was the fooling around that worried Violet. As she later put it, 'He is a son you could always trust. Naughty, yes; untrustworthy, never.' But trust sometimes is not quite enough. She knew her son was intelligent and intellectually interested and harboured ambitions for him to go to university, perhaps to become an architect, but all he seemed to do was box and play sport and chess, and if there was time to spare it was spent with Bernita or hanging out with friends. He never seemed to focus on school work. With mother and son alone in the flat, things could get tense when there was a serious disagreement. 'They always relied on each other and were extremely close but it certainly wasn't always lovey-dovey between them,' said Bernita. 'She was at the centre of everything in his life and sometimes it could get quite intense. She would really scream at him, but he's a very stubborn guy and he had this remarkable self-belief and independence, so he would stand his ground, and they would fight like cats and dogs. When it got too rough between them, he would just go to Arnie's house for a while but he never talked about leaving home.' Lennox acknowledges that Arnie played a key role in keeping the peace. 'When I was a teenager, my mum and I had some difficult times when we were shouting at each other, and then Arnie would play the role of the conciliator between us.'

He remained close to Arnie in his late teens, always listening to his advice and regularly seeking it. 'At that stage of his life it was the relationship that seemed most important to him,' said Bernita. 'Arnie took him under his wing and completely made him part of his family. He would talk to him about everything in life and show him the practical things too. There was nothing Arnie wouldn't do for him. He would even phone me to apologise for Lennox when he'd behaved like a cad. He was so pivotal to Lennox's life and it was such a special relationship in a really deep and personal way. He gave Lennox emotional stability, he nurtured his self-confidence and helped him find his place in the world. I don't know where he would be today if it hadn't been for Arnie. I've thought about it a lot, and I really don't. He would dabble in different directions, but Arnie kept him focused. He was unbelievable.' Lennox paints a similar picture of an adult who eased his transition from childhood to adulthood. 'Everything good that's been said about Arnie Boehm is true. He was my father figure, my adviser in life and my trusted friend. He just did so much for me. I really was like another son to him, and he was like a father to me.'

When Bernita started dating Lennox, she found he often preferred to be alone, or with her, or with one or two rather than large groups or parties. 'Even though he could be very sociable he was never a big-crowd guy. He was very much his own person, very independent, and he had this strong sense of himself, which I liked.' However, she also found he could quickly adapt to fitting in with his fans when required. 'He was very popular with the in-crowd at Cameron, who were mainly white. He was very accepted by them and admired. And he also had a black group around him.'

It was partly through his black friends that he began to be exposed to new forms of music, including rap and reggae, and to new ideas about the world. 'I listened to hip-hop from the beginning,' he said. 'It all happened to me when I was in high school and went to a party and some guys started grabbing the microphone and talking over the music and rapping. I heard the Sugar Hill Gang's "Rapper's Delight" and I thought this is a new thing, this is great! And then later I began to train to rap music, and drive to rap music, and I started getting into gangsta rap and West Coast beats. I became a heavy [Dr] Dre fan.'

His love of reggae was even more profound, with its connections to his mother's past. Although he never visited Jamaica until his early 20s he already felt a strong affinity for the country. He was introduced to the music of Bob Marley and Peter

Tosh and became interested in their Jamaican world at the same time as he began hanging out with a group of students of Jamaican origin. 'I can remember him getting into Rastafarianism towards the end of our relationship,' Bernita recalled. 'I think it began with the reggae music and then they all started speaking in patois, but I couldn't understand what they were saying.' Lennox remembers being fascinated by their distinct looks and approach to life, as well as their music. 'When I was growing up in Canada there were some Rastafarians in my town and I was interested in their lifestyle and what they had to say. Rastafarians are always speaking about life and philosophy. They philosophise a lot, which is something I was drawn to, and of course I love reggae music, and I really love Bob [Marley].'

Lennox's devotion to boxing meant he usually kept clear of alcohol as a teenager. 'He was so focused on keeping fit that he didn't drink much,' said Bernita. 'If he ever got even a little drunk it was just once or twice to make an impression with his friends, but he wasn't really a partyer. It wasn't his thing.' Andrew Powis adds to this picture of abstinence. 'Arnie let it be known that we shouldn't waste our time with drugs and I never saw Junior smoke a cigarette or cannabis, let alone anything harder. He was too into his sport. I knew him better than anybody at that stage because we really were inseparable then, and even though I later heard rumours about cannabis smoking, I doubt it, because I never saw it and I think I would have heard.' Lennox is more reticent on the 'Have you ever?' question regarding cannabis, preferring to make a general point about its incompatibility with peak fighting fitness. 'I was first influenced by Rastafarianism when I was still living in Kitchener, but that doesn't mean ganja's necessarily part of the package. Of course a lot of people see me and think it must be, especially if you've got the locks like I have today, but that's not always the case. It really doesn't help you in boxing.'

Partly through his musical interests, Lennox began to develop a clearer sense of himself and his family origins, not just as a boy with dark skin who very occasionally faced racist taunts in a town of people with mainly white skins, but as a black person. 'When I was a little kid in London there was obviously racism,' he said. 'I mean, it was there. I noticed it, but not so much because it wasn't such a big thing for me then. But when I was starting to grow up I realised that it was a big thing to other people, so when it showed its face to me – let's say I noticed it. It came through things like being called nigger and, when I was younger, being chased by white boys shouting racist stuff at me. And then when I got older it was things like being ignored for some award, which makes you wonder. It was more like that, happening at an individual level, which is hard to fight against because you can't march or boycott a bus or any action like that. But it helped me to become very conscious of my blackness and proud of my culture and my history.'

Bernita says this was never raised as an issue between them. 'I'm white and he's black but we were both kind of blind to it, and we had a fairly lengthy relationship. I remember that when we were about eighteen he talked about how he felt the racism in London when he was growing up there, but my sense in Kitchener was that if white people were racist they didn't show it much, and I don't remember him complaining to me about racism here, although maybe that was because by then he was quite a local celebrity so he was easily accepted. In a way – and I used to say this to him – racial identity was more of an issue in the black community because they tended to be more possessive.'

Lennox's prime identity was as a boxer. It set him apart and offered hope for his future. By 1983 he had given up football to concentrate on the World Junior Championships in Santo Domingo in the Dominican Republic in November. He was determined to succeed, adding to his speed and mileage as he ran through the tree-lined streets of Kitchener on winter mornings, constantly thinking about his moves. 'I used to punch at raindrops as they fell off a branch of a tree,' he said, 'or, in the gym, if another boxer was skipping, I would punch towards him and try to get my hand out of there before the rope came back round again.' He increased his sparring load and threw in additional routines such as running up and down the steps of the main stand at the local athletics track, 25 times up and 25 times down without stopping, always trying to go a little faster in his bid to get his body into the kind of shape needed to take on the best and the biggest in his age group. Bernita found his confidence and enthusiasm infectious and couldn't help but get drawn in. She'd be there with Arnie, wearing her waterproofs against the winter rain, wrapped up against the cold, cheering her boyfriend on. 'I can still see it very clearly,' she said, 'Lennox running up and down those stairs at the Centennial Stadium with Arnie and me standing at the bottom. My little role was to hold the stopwatch and keep his times, but I also used to go with him to the police gym to watch him training.'

The change from the snow of Ontario to the heat of the Dominican Republic came as quite a shock, but Lennox's fitness paid off and after two impressive wins over an American and a Romanian he returned with the gold medal after his Cuban opponent pulled out with a broken hand. However, the medal came at a cost. Arnie insisted on accompanying Lennox, even though he had to pay his own way. His employers at the hydroelectric company were fed up with his regular absences and told him they'd had enough. He told them he was going regardless; they, too, dug in and told him that if he went he would be fired, which is what happened when he returned. After this Arnie became a self-employed electrician, which meant he no longer had a guaranteed income.

When Lennox returned from the Dominican Republic he was voted his country's junior male athlete of the year and felt he was ready to go after the big men. Arnie felt it was time to test his strength in senior tournaments and make a bid for selection for the 1984 Olympic Games, to be held in Los Angeles. Although Lennox had fought a couple of bouts against Canadian seniors from the age of fifteen, it was a far tougher proposition to be tangling with the top Americans, who tended to train with professionals, not to mention the Cubans and eastern Europeans, who were usually men in their twenties paid by their governments as full-time athletes. The gap could be closed only through better sparring. At least once a week, but often twice, Arnie would drive him to Toronto to spar with the twenty-year-old 'Razor' Ruddock, who had turned professional and was unbeaten after eight fights, but it was often frustrating. They would make the trip only to find Razor didn't feel like sparring because he was too tired after a workout or had a cold. Arnie therefore started getting the word around that the world junior champion was willing to travel across counties, states and countries to improve himself.

As it happened, an old man who lived in a huge white mansion in the Catskills in New York was looking for sparring for a teenager he hoped to make his second world heavyweight champion. Cus D'Amato phoned Arnie Boehm and made him an offer: bring your lad to the Catskills for eight days of training and sparring. Lennox was delighted. 'I badly needed good sparring, and except for Razor, who wasn't reliable, we couldn't find any, so Arnie told me about this young cat in New York called Mike Tyson and I jumped at the chance.' They flew together to Albany, New York, where Kevin Rooney, one of Cus's assistants, came with Tyson to collect them. Lennox was five inches taller so he took the front seat; Mike sat in the back. 'When we arrived in the Catskills they pointed out this little gym that looked like an old fire station, and it was there that we met Cus.'

At that stage he knew very little about Tyson, except that the great Cus D'Amato had saved him from a detention centre after a rough upbringing in Brooklyn and had big plans for him. But rough times come in different forms. Lennox had six chaotic, disjointed, years of separation from his mother, sandwiched between years of maternal love, and both left their mark. He had arrived in Canada angry, suspicious and fearful, but thanks to Violet, Arnie, Andy and Bernita his happiness was restored and he came across as a balanced, confident young man. 'I'm not saying I came from the ghetto,' he said, 'but I came through certain extremely hard times, and with the help of my mother, who went through a lot to bring me up in a difficult world, I overcame those trials and tribulations because I realised the sacrifices that were involved and I just persevered through.'

Mike, on the other hand, had had no respite from chaos and not much in the way of parental love to fall back on, with a no-show drunk of a dad who disappeared before he turned one and a drug-addict mum who took in deadbeat, violent men and eventually died of cancer. 'My mother might throw hot scalding water on her boyfriend,' he said, 'her boyfriend might beat her, break her eye socket or something, or her finger. The emotions were high.' Completing the picture was a huge bully of an older brother and a big sister who slapped him around. As he described it, 'My sister and brother used to beat the fuck out of me all the time but I just didn't want to fight.' Tyson lived in a gang-controlled, drug-rich neighbourhood where you were either victim or predator. In his early years, Mike, or 'Fairy Boy' as they called him, was pure victim, kicked around, battered and bullied in every way. In those early years he was knocked unconscious five times, regularly attacked with bricks and beaten by baseball bats. 'The world I come from, I been abused,' he said in 2003. 'I been used any way a person could be used. I got a lot of beatings. A lot of real murderous beatings. I was very afraid all the time.'

He developed into a frightened big kid who tried to get away from it all by nurturing pigeons on the roof of the apartment block across the street. He adored those birds and spent hours every day with them. But one day a bigger lad picked on him, choosing a pigeon to make a point. He taunted 'Fairy Boy' by holding the head of one of his beloved birds, and while the eleven-year-old Mike pleaded for mercy the bully smiled and twisted until they heard the neck snap. Something snapped in Mike that afternoon. He exploded and beat the bully senseless, punching and kicking until he was a bloody mess. 'After that I got off on the violence. I saw its power,' he later explained. It was his turn to become bully and predator, and soon, with the help of a gang called the Jolly Stompers, he was robbing other kids and old people with fists, knives and, by the age of twelve, guns too, a pattern of behaviour that led to numerous court appearances, juvenile jail sentences and, eventually, incarceration. 'I was a beast,' he said. 'I started breaking into houses in Brooklyn. I liked the armed robberies.'

In the Tryon detention centre Mike ran into boys who were older and, for a time, bigger, stronger and harder, and they knew how to get their way with him. He received more beatings from other inmates and also 'a lot of beatings from staff members'. He was forced to bend the knee until, quite quickly, he learned what it took to win respect and create fear, and when fear wasn't enough he learned the best ways to make use of his fists, boots, head and whatever else came to hand. He made other boys bend the knee until he became king of his pond. 'I was just a monster of a kid,' he said, 'the toughest alive, the meanest. You had to be willing to do what no one else would do. Being ferocious, bloodthirsty.'

His capacity for violence and his talent for using it was, of course, well known to his warders. One of these hard men, a former professional boxer called Bobby Steward, steered him in the direction of the prison's boxing gym where Mike made an enormous impression with his strength, power and speed in sparring sessions – so much so that Bobby contacted Cus D'Amato. As it happened, Cus was after one last shot at reflected glory. He had twice taken Floyd Patterson to the world heavyweight title in the 1950s, and Jose Torres to the world light heavyweight title in the 1960s, and he longed for another. When he saw Mike he knew he'd found his boy. 'There's the future heavyweight champion of the world,' he said to Steward. He rushed home and told his common-law wife Camille Ewald, 'This is the one I've been waiting for all my life – my third champion, the best one of all.'

After fourteen years of Brooklyn crackhouses and prison cells, Mike loved his wonderful new life in this 15-room mansion overlooking the Hudson River – a free place where he could run through forests and up hills, pick flowers in the spring, throw snowballs in winter, skip in the Catskills Boxing Club gym above the local police station and beat up the other boys in the ring. But there was more to it than just training, fighting and flower arranging. As a fascinated Lennox discovered during his eight days there, every meal was a seminar, led by the old guru. Cus would talk about astronomy, about the joys of fishing, about Thoreau's march to the beat of a different drummer and about destiny, but most lessons were drawn from boxing, from the lives of the great champions. Although he learned nothing about maths or science or grammar, Mike became an expert in the history of his game. He said of his early mentor, 'I was madly in love with Cus D'Amato. He broke me down and built me back up. I became totally loyal to him. I became his slave.'

Along with his natural strength, speed and power Mike also had a high intuitive intelligence. He was a quick learner and when he was with Cus he was as good as gold. But the learning didn't go far enough. He knew how to get his way with hard-core boys but didn't have much of a clue about how to relate to the girls. He was infatuated with half of them but most of the time his shy advances were too gauche or crude. He once confided in Cus that girls found him repulsive. Cus, the supposedly caring father figure, said nothing and walked out of the room, leaving Mike devastated by his own sad confession and his guru's cold reaction. Cus eventually returned wielding a baseball bat that he handed to the downcast boy. 'You'll need it when you're heavyweight champion of the world,' he said, 'to fight off all the women who'll be chasing after you.' Mike took the lesson to heart and acted like he was already there. When charm wouldn't work, he resorted to force. A condition of fostering Mike was that he attend a local school, but after one 'incident' too many he was expelled from school, which meant he had to look elsewhere.

One of D'Amato's young boxers was a doctor's son called Teddy Atlas who had gone wild as a teenager and had turned into a violent bully. Cus became his legal guardian to prevent him going to jail, and when Teddy's nascent boxing career ended with a damaged back he transformed the scar-faced young man into a trainer. Atlas worked closely with Tyson until Mike decided to make advances on his eleven-year-old sister-in-law. Today, Tyson says, 'I was a young boy and grabbed her butt,' but Atlas says Tyson was an abuser of girls and that what happened that day was intolerable. He 'kinda cornered her into a situation'. Teddy drew his gun, cocked it and held it to Mike's head. 'I pulled the trigger back. I told him he would never put his hands on anyone in my family or do anything like that to anyone in my family again, or he'd be dead. To make sure he understood, I stuck the gun in his ear, then pulled it out of his ear and shot it off. He crumpled away, but I told him, "Don't make the mistake again."'

As Teddy stalked off, a terrified Mike ran to tell Cus, who couldn't risk the prospect of explaining why he'd allowed an armed ex-criminal blow the head off a disturbed boy, especially since the State of New York had appointed him legal guardian. He told Teddy to pack his bags and never return. It was, quite obviously, the right thing to do. But Cus failed to do the other right thing: explain to Mike that one more incident like this and it would be goodbye breakfasts with Cus and the motherly Camille, goodbye to the Catskills, goodbye to the flowers, snow and forests, goodbye heavyweight title and hello again penitentiary. That was what Teddy proposed to the old man, in his final words before being banished. But the old man had only one thought in mind: 'my next and greatest champion'. And so he let it pass, giving Mike the message that whatever he did wrong, back-up was at hand – as long as he did the right thing in the ring. There were many more 'incidents', which Cus and his successors covered up, usually paying off the victims, all the way to the world heavyweight title and back to jail.

This, then, was the man-child Lennox encountered in April 1984 – aggressive and passive, bright and silly, swaggering yet shy; a strange and fascinating mixture. His first impression was of a friendly fellow with a manly swagger and a high, lispy, not very manly voice. 'Today I can't help but feel sorry for him,' Lennox said. 'This is definitely a puppy with some problems but in a way I found it surprising how he conducted himself as a professional because he was around a good atmosphere when we were together in the Catskills. I thought he was a rough kid, sure, but also a really sweet guy.'

Mike seemed taken with his tall, gentle visitor. 'Quite soon after we arrived they were laughing and joking and carrying on like old buddies,' Arnie Boehm recalled. Tyson instructed Lewis in boxing history and in the ways of the pigeons he kept in the loft. They shared a room, and sometimes Tyson would hang up a sheet to use as a movie screen and show Lennox films of old-time boxers: Jack Johnson, Jack Dempsey, Joe Louis, Sonny Liston and Muhammad Ali. 'He was really into those old-time fighters and he liked to talk about old-time fighting too,' said Lennox. 'Old-time fighting and life.'

On the subject of life, Mike's main interest was girls – Brooklyn girls, Catskills girls, Canadian girls. Lennox told him about Bernita and another girl he had his eye on, a beautiful cheerleader called Marcia Miller. Mike told Lennox about a girl from Montreal he lusted over and tried to phone daily. Lennox must know her – after all, they were both Canadian. These were often long chats, punctuated by even longer phone calls to this girl or that, including the one from Montreal. He seemed to take a scattergun approach, sending flowers to this one and chocolates to another before embarking on another round of phone calls in the slim hope that one of them would be willing to lay him or love him, or both.

The eighteen-year-old Lewis was almost 6ft 4in and weighed 207lb, a tall, graceful, boyish-looking athlete who was still growing and, despite his unusual strength, was a long way from reaching his adult power. The 5ft 11in Tyson was three months shy of his eighteenth birthday but had stopped growing upwards almost three years earlier and already weighed 200lb, a squat, muscular prototype of the monster D'Amato would unleash in the professional ranks eleven months later. 'I think he had matured, physically, faster than me, because he already looked like a young Joe Frazier then,' said Lennox.

By the time of their first sparring session, on their third day together, Lennox was down with a bad cold and Arnie suggested he wait a day or two before lacing on the gloves. Lennox wouldn't hear of it. He had been brought out to spar, and unlike Razor Ruddock, who had also arrived in the Catskills and then changed his mind without going a single round, he wasn't about to let a runny nose upset the plan. They had their sixteen-ounce gloves laced up, shared a couple of jokes, and then the bell sounded and Mike changed. 'I remember that first day we sparred he was very hyped up as soon as Cus rang the bell,' Lennox recalled. 'Mike just ran across the ring and wanted to knock me out. He did catch me by surprise and gave me a fat lip but he never knocked me down or anything, like some of his people later claimed. I gave him a bloody mouth. One time he smiled at me and there was pure blood in his mouth, so by the end of our first session you could say we were even in that exchange. Those sparring sessions were pretty explosive. To me it felt like he was Frazier, coming at me with his bob and weave style and throwing lots of hooks, and I was Ali dancing around him, boxing him from long range.'

Arnie was shocked by the speed and ferocity of Tyson's first attack. 'The bell rang and all of a sudden he turned into an animal. He came charging across the ring like a raging tiger, like a man possessed.' He felt that the first two rounds belonged to Tyson and remembered Lennox emerging with a bloody nose (not a fat lip), but after that it began to change, with Lennox learning to evade Mike's charges. By their third day of sparring Arnie felt his lad had the edge – hitting without getting hit. 'Lennox was taunting Mike and laughing at him, so Mike said, "Come on, chicken, come on, hit me, you son of a bitch."' Lennox obliged, but Cus jumped in and said, 'That's enough, Mike,' and, Arnie recalled, 'the funny stuff stopped right there'. By their final session he thought Lennox was clearly on top. 'My impression was that as each sparring session progressed, Lennox's dominance progressed. By the end of their fourth or fifth session Lennox was playing with him.'

Kevin Rooney, who took over as Tyson's head trainer after Cus's death in 1986, admitted to a vaguer memory, but said as far as he could recall Mike must have had the overall edge. 'What I remember is that we'd heard about Lewis and brought him up from Canada because we were having a hard time getting good sparring for Mike, and Mike did good with him. He more than held his own with Lennox, and Lewis didn't dominate.'

Lennox's memory is that they were evenly matched. 'I'm not the kind of guy to go out and say, "Yo! I beat him up," because it wasn't the case. I'm just jabbing and moving and using the sweet science and he's just coming at me, and that's the way it went: Tyson more aggressive, me winning on points. If you had scored us when we were sparring in the Catskills that week, you would have to say he won on aggression and I won on points. But you have to remember, I was an amateur boxer dealing with a young man who was basically a full-time professional already.'

Cus told the teenagers they were 'destined' to fight each other as professionals. So they said respectful but cautious goodbyes, assuming they would meet up in less friendly circumstances a few years down the line, after watching each other in the Olympics. But it didn't work that way. Tyson seemed set for the US team's heavyweight berth while Lewis was chosen to represent Canada at super heavyweight (over 201lb). Tyson, however, tripped at the final hurdle, losing a pair of disputed decisions to a jab-and-move, older man called Henry Tillman. Like Frazier twenty years earlier, he went to the Olympics as the alternate on an outstanding US team but unlike Frazier, who stepped in for the injured Buster Mathis and won the gold medal, Tyson would never get the lucky break.

The American and Canadian chances were boosted by a boycott that had been called by the Soviet Union, supported by Cuba and the Eastern Bloc countries, as a tit-for-tat response to the American-led boycott of the 1980 Moscow Games. In Lennox's division that meant the exclusion of the magnificent Cuban Teofilo Stevenson, who had won gold in 1972, 1976 and 1980. The competition in Los Angeles was therefore wide open, the favourites being the American Tyrell Biggs and the Italian Francesco Damiani.

Lennox was a few years younger and far less experienced but he was improving rapidly in the Canadian Olympic training camp in Klowna, British Columbia. He was running harder than ever, at six minutes a mile and at 215lb his power and strength had increased.By the time he arrived in the Olympic village Lennox fancied his chances but was still regarded as a kid in the Canadian team, overshadowed by older and more experienced hands like the sprinter Ben Johnson, who strutted around the village, staring down anyone who dared look him in the eye. Johnson, who was already a major-league steroid abuser, had developed a reputation as a man with an explosive temper. Lewis, in contrast, was developing a reputation as an easy-going, nice guy who went out of his way to help his Canadian team-mates, but on this occasion his helpfulness clashed with Johnson's rage.

'You couldn't go anywhere in the Olympic village without a dog tag, because that was your only form of identification,' Lennox recalled. 'One day, when we were playing pool, Ben Johnson took off his dog tag because it was getting in the way when he was trying to shoot, and he left his behind and went upstairs. So then I noticed he'd left it and I took it upstairs and went to his room to try to find him, but he wasn't there. In fact, he was on his way down – he took a different elevator – because he realised he'd mislaid it, so he waited around downstairs looking for it while I was upstairs trying to find him, and we missed each other. Well, I couldn't find him, so I went to the girls' dorm for a while because I was hanging out with the girls' four-by-four team. Then I remembered I had his dog tag so I gave it to one of his track team members and asked him to pass it on. I think Ben must have been late for something, and by then he'd heard I'd had his dog tag.

'I come downstairs and start playing pool again when all of a sudden he charges at me with a stick, cussing me in really fast Jamaican. He was basically saying, "Why did you take my tag? Do you know who you're dealing with?" So I said, "No, man, you left it behind and I was doing you a favour and bringing it up to you." But he was extremely hyper and he raised his stick to hit me, so I took it from him, threw it down and pushed him. At that point he just ran into my chest because he was mad-upset, so I got him into a cradle hold with his head bent down and every time he tried to move I squeezed tighter. He would struggle and I would squeeze until he said, "OK! OK!" But by that time I was the one who was mad because of the fact that he had attacked me in front of people, because – well, you can't mess with a boxer. So I pushed him down to the floor.

'I guess the only reason I didn't hit him was that he hadn't actually hit me, so really, in the end, it was just a little altercation that got blown out of proportion. It was just a weird pushing thing where I had to take his stick away and put him in a cradle hold. But I was still mad because of his disrespect, so I thought it best just to leave and go to my room. And then there were a whole lot of people banging on my door, but I didn't answer because I was really angry. Somebody said security were coming to get me. Somebody else said the whole track team was coming to get me, but I wasn't really worried because I was the super heavyweight boxer and they were just runners and jumpers. The funny thing is that the next day, when I saw Johnson after his race, he was rubbing his neck, and then I smiled and said to myself, "I'm the one who did that to his neck." He claimed it may have affected him in his race, but I doubt it because he won the bronze medal.'

After this, Lewis settled down to the business of winning in the ring. He'd always felt relaxed, calm and confident before fights but hadn't anticipated the scale of the Olympics, that sense of being at the centre of the action with the whole world watching, and for the first and last time he went in with a feeling of being out of his depth. He had a scare in his opening bout when the giant Pakistani Mohammad Yousof charged out and caught him cold with a huge right cross, and the referee gave him a standing eight count. After that he moved away from Yousof's hay-makers and stabbed his face with his jab. His confidence grew, and he began to step in and out with quick combinations. One minute into the third he feinted and sent his own right cross down the shoot to end the fight.

For his second fight Lennox drew the favourite, the 6ft 4in, 218lb Tyrell Biggs, a quick, skilful 24-year-old who had five years of senior international experience and came into the fight with a record of 104 wins and six losses. Biggs boxed with a cool confidence. Lewis, in contrast, was unusually tense and would later acknowledge that he was overawed by the occasion, and it certainly affected his performance. There was no flow to his work, he was over-tentative, and he struggled to get his punches off against the quick-stepping American. It was only in the third round that he settled down and began to score effectively, but by then Biggs had a clear lead and he won a unanimous decision.

Several opponents who would feature significantly in Lennox's professional future were present in Los Angeles. Biggs beat Damiani for the gold medal, but later fell to Tyson, Damiani and Lewis. Henry Tillman beat Canada's Doug De Witt to win the heavyweight gold medal, but would get stopped as a professional by De Witt, Evander Holyfield and Tyson before transferring to a prison cell after committing a murder. Holyfield went home with the light heavyweight bronze medal after being disqualified but went on to become one of the finest cruiserweights and heavy-weights of the modern era. And Tyson, who was regularly taunted by Biggs and consoled by Holyfield, beat them all to the punch, blasting his way through the pro-fessional ranks to become the youngest ever world heavyweight champion eighteen months after turning professional, and then going on to torture Biggs, flatten Tillman and fall to Holyfield and Lewis.

And Lennox? He took the long-term view, and outlasted them all. When he returned to Kitchener he had to make up his mind whether to turn professional or stick around in the hope of richer dividends in future. Most boxers wouldn't have hesitated to cash in immediately. He already had experience in this field, having turned down offers from basketball talent scouts to enter the college circuit as a prelude to a pro-fessional basketball career, and he'd been told by his football coaches that he had a certain future as a professional, but his first professional boxing offer was significantly more generous.

Mike Jones, an American who managed the top heavyweight Gerry Cooney, recognised the potential in this tall teenager and tried to entice him with half a mil-lion Canadian dollars. It was a sum unheard of at that level. Lennox, who was still living at home on his mother's factory wages, was tempted by the money and by the idea of making far more in quick time. As Jones stressed, over and over again, his contemporaries would leave him behind and there was no guarantee he would return home with gold on his second try. He might get injured or fall ill before the final; he might get cut or lose a dud decision, or get stopped courtesy of an over-cautious or biased referee. And if he hung around until Seoul he would be at least 23 by the time he had his first professional fight.

His coach and his mother both advised him to stay in Kitchener – Arnie because he felt Lennox wasn't ready for the rough world of professional boxing, and Violet, in part, because she wanted her son to remain in Kitchener and the offer implied a move to America. By then she had come to accept that Lennox would, inevitably, become a professional boxer, but she wanted him to complete his schooling, to have something to fall back on. 'He'd turned out to be one of the most beautiful kids possible,' she said. 'At first I didn't want this boxing life for him. I actually wanted him to be something like an architect because he likes planning out things, so I thought architecture might be a good option. But I came to accept boxing and to love it.'

Lennox felt he had let himself down in Los Angeles and needed vindication by winning the gold four years on. And there were also more personal reasons for stay-ing. During the build-up to the Olympics he'd become even more interested in the cheerleader Marcia Miller, regarded by his friends and classmates as the 'hottest' in the school. His relationship with Bernita drew to an end. 'It wasn't me who broke it up, it was him, and the Marcia thing was part of it,' said Bernita. 'But in a way, we'd grown bigger and moved on, and it had been a fairly lengthy relationship by high-school standards. We were both eighteen by then and I think we just went our separate ways. Part of it was that he was training for the Olympics and was very focused on that, part of it was the fact that Marcia came on the scene, and part of it was that there may have been pressure from his clique about having relationships with white girls because at that stage there was a lot of focus on returning to his peo-ple. So it was all these things. It wasn't a clean break, though. It was on-off, on-off, so it was really messy, but eventually it came to an end.'

Now that he finally had the space to focus on his new lover, Lennox was reluc-tant to leave for America. He didn't feel ready to walk out on Violet or Arnie either, and the idea of abandoning his studies without a high-school diploma didn't appeal. He weighed it all up carefully and made a decision: he would stay an amateur for another four years. Jones and many others in the boxing world were shocked. Poor boys from single-mom homes don't turn down half a million bucks for honour. It was more than unusual – it was unprecedented. But then, Lennox Lewis was far more than just an unusual boxer.

CHAPTER FIVE
HUNGARIAN COMMUNITY
CENTRE, TORONTO, 2004

Adrian Teodorescu has just arrived for his evening session with his latest batch of promising Canadian professional boxers. He has a busy evening schedule today but he always has time for a chat, particularly if it has anything to do with his greatest success, Lennox Lewis. They've had their ups and downs over the years, mainly ups, but there was a spell when Adrian seemed in reach of a fortune as Lennox's manager-trainer until the deal collapsed and it all soured. Harsh words were avoided, but so were meetings, phone chats and back slaps. But now they're back on friendly terms and have been ever since Lennox invited him back into the fold for a couple of fights five years ago.

Broad, bald Adrian offers a big, crinkle-eyed, accepting, winning, diplomatic smile so that his moustache spreads to his cheekbones when asked about the mutual parting of ways all those years ago. 'Actually, whatever happened then, there's never been any hard feelings between me and Lennox, and whenever we meet it's just like it was back in those early days,' he says. 'He's the same character he was then and we still joke around whenever we see each other. He teases me, like he would blow my hair because I have so little of it, and he always listens to my advice.'

Listens, but not always follows, he might add. Lennox recently picked Adrian's agile brain and years of experience on the fraught subject of whether or not to plough on with his professional career in his thirty-ninth year; Adrian hedged his bets just enough to keep onside, whichever way he fell. He's always been good at playing people the right way – as he had to, learning to survive and while growing up under Nicolai Ceausescu's brutal Romanian regime. When he chose the life of the exile 21 years ago, Adrian's contacts, charm and competence allowed him to walk straight into the coaching job for Canadian boxing, from there to head coach of Canada's boxing teams for the Seoul and Barcelona Olympics, and onwards to become one of the country's top professional trainers. Five of those years, and then in the late 1990s once more, were spent working with Lennox.

From the first day Adrian and Lennox met, in April 1983, they took to each other: Lennox was impressed by Adrian's professionalism and attracted by his warmth and joking camaraderie as well as by his prowess at chess while Adrian was impressed with the potential of this tall, slim, likeable teenager. 'I first saw him when he was a six-foot-three seventeen-year-old who must have weighed just over 190lb, and after watching him in action I immediately told the guys in Ontario that Lennox had the calibre to be Olympic super heavyweight champion, but they laughed at me.' Adrian wears the grin of a man who likes to remind you of predictions that have come true.

He also reminds you of how he helped his prediction come true, but prefers not to prompt too hard, so talks instead of innate athleticism, strength and dedication before offering an illustration of their relationship: 'He treated me very well – always. I had two rules in the gym. It was kind of a joke but also a point I wanted them to recognise. One, the coach is always right. Two, if the coach is wrong, go to rule number one. So Lennox would tell the other boxers, "Hey, don't argue with Adrian." He was a really good team player who didn't bother anybody, and he never had anybody to bother him.'

Lennox Lewis regularly had cause to wonder whether he'd made the right choice in staying an amateur after the Los Angeles Olympics. He watched Tyson winning the WBC heavyweight title in his twenty-eighth fight after twenty months; Holyfield winning the WBA cruiserweight title in his twelfth bout after twenty months; both Ruddock and Biggs breaking into the world ratings. And yet he seemed to be getting nowhere; everything was going wrong. He seriously considered further professional offers during his final four years of fighting for fun, but in the end turned them down because he was convinced that despite all the setbacks and obstacles he would emerge as Olympic champion in 1988.

One of the advantages of remaining an amateur was that he could remain in Kitchener with his mother, mentor and girlfriend, and continue with his education. 'I completed grade twelve and then I took a little business course at Conasoga College, where I was also involved in playing basketball,' Lennox explained, 'but I never really considered going to university because from early on I realised my priority was boxing.'

What he did not anticipate was that boxing would soon take him away from home. Six months after Lennox returned from the Olympics the city council pulled the financial plug on Arnie's gym and he was forced to close it. He'd already lost his job but the loss of his life's vocation through the club was an even greater blow and he began to drink – binge drinking. In his early fifties, after a lifetime of preaching against cigarettes, drink and drugs, he fell to alcoholism. This was also devastating for Arnie's children, and particularly for his wife Verna, who had to cope with the dire personality changes. Feeling guilty, Arnie would try to hide it. It saddened Lennox, who could always tell when Arnie was off the wagon. He would plead with him to stop, and sometimes it seemed to work: Arnie would dry out for a while, but when he took his next knock he would find it hard to resist the urge. Eventually, several years later, he tamed his demon and never had another drink again until his death in 2002, telling everyone who asked that, yes, he was still an alcoholic but one who no longer touched alcohol. At the time, however, it was a serious problem, even if it was usually kept under control during daylight hours.

With a reduced income as a self-employed electrician, Arnie reluctantly accepted a job as assistant coach with Boxing Canada, which meant driving 120 miles a day to and from Toronto. Lennox and two other Kitchener amateurs would go with him every day to train with Arnie and spar with the Toronto-based boxers, and once they'd finished they had to wait for Arnie, who had a wide range of coaching duties.

One compensation was that he was now working under Adrian Teodorescu on a regular basis. But Adrian's expertise did not prevent the nineteen-year-old Lennox's first and only amateur stoppage defeat after a body punch from a highly experienced Russian super heavyweight. 'He was up against their top guy and he was caught with this huge left uppercut to the body. It was a really violent punch that took his wind away, and I think Lennox's knee touched down and the referee stopped it immediately without a count. It was the only time in his amateur career he was stopped.'

Teodorescu, however, did not change his perception of Lennox's potential. But while he was getting good tuition and better sparring than before, his daily travel routine put an end to any prospect of further studies and also ruled out continuing with the part-time work he'd been picking up in Kitchener. He was eating takeaways on the hop and was always short of money, despite getting C$450 a month from Sports Canada. He felt unsettled and unfulfilled, and eventually he decided he'd had enough. After seven years of living with his mother, he transferred his belongings to a friend's flat in Toronto. He hoped he could justify his decision when he travelled to Reno, Nevada, for the 1986 World Amateur Championships, but his preparations had been far from ideal and not for the last time he found himself a victim of the politics of world amateur boxing.

Professional boxing is scored by three judges who assess each round on the number of clean punches landed, the quality of those blows, as well as aggression, with the winner receiving ten points and the loser nine points, or less if there are knockdowns (although in Britain the archaic system of a single scoring referee still prevails). The amateur system has always been different. In Lennox's day five judges scored each round subjectively (although unlike professional boxing, aggression and weight of punch weren't taken into account and there were no additional points for knockdowns). The judges had considerable leeway, and it was common to find countries forming alliances to ensure that a boxer from a favoured country received the most votes. This is what happened when Bulgaria's Peter Stoinomov was given a 3–2 decision over Lewis, meaning he was once again out of the medals – which would have earned him an extra C$200 a month from Sports Canada. 'No question, we won that fight,' said Teodorescu. 'It wasn't fair.'

It took a while longer before Lennox finally picked up his first senior gold medal – at the Commonwealth Games in Edinburgh in July 1986. This also allowed him to visit London for only the second time since he'd left nine years earlier (he visited briefly in 1985 to take part in a London versus Ontario tournament).

This time he took a week off and used it to spend time with his brother. 'I was DJing in London at the time,' Dennis recalled, 'working in various clubs playing soul and R&B, so he came with me to some of our sessions and saw what I was doing. He seemed impressed with the work I was doing as a DJ and of course I was really impressed with what he'd achieved – you know, having a brother who was Commonwealth super heavyweight boxing champion – so we both admired each other. We went around everywhere together and hung out for a week, and it was at this time that we really started getting to know each other as brothers again, after nearly nine years apart. I think it was then that he started to see himself as English again because he started to remember some of the places where he'd grown up. I introduced him to some of the old East End guys I knew, and I took him to Upton Park to watch West Ham United because that's the area we came from, and when you grow up in that part of the East End West Ham is the club you support, although I've since seen sense and I'm an Arsenal man now.'

Beating the best of the Commonwealth was fine, but the Eastern Block and Cuba presented far stiffer competition, and Lennox suffered several more disputed split decision setbacks – most of them reversed in return fights. Lennox dropped a controversial 4–1 decision to Cuba's top super heavyweight, the 6ft 7in Jorge Gonzalez, at the Pan American Games in Indianapolis in August 1987, when four Latin American judges banded together to outvote the American judge. 'It was never going to be easy against Gonzalez because he was far better as an amateur than as a professional, but no question, Lennox definitely won that fight,' said Teodorescu. 'It was one of several bad decisions that went against Lewis. He could be a slow starter so I think he didn't do enough in the first round against Gonzalez, but he clearly won the second and third rounds, and yet somehow they gave the split decision against him.' A fortnight on they fought again at the North American Championships in Toronto, and this time Lewis won easily. Many years later Gonzalez, after abandoning Cuba to turn professional in Florida, told American writers he'd outclassed Lewis and few bothered to check the details. 'That was untrue,' said Lennox. 'He whipped Riddick Bowe – knocked him down twice – but he never genuinely beat me. It's true he got the first decision against me but he was extremely lucky because everyone who watched felt I deserved it, and when we fought the return I beat him very easily.'

Much of Lennox's time during this period was spent criss-crossing the world fighting in international amateur tournaments, and it helped him develop self-discipline and stoicism about adverse conditions. It also helped develop his prowess as a chess player, with Adrian as his usual sparring partner. 'Whenever we were travelling to boxing tournaments we'd play game after game to pass the time, and Adrian was quite a good player so my game really improved during those years.'

Lewis dropped two more close verdicts to East European boxers in the run-up to the Olympics, raising the fear in Canadian boxing circles that he was an inconsistent performer destined to fail on the big occasions. National coach Taylor Gordon, criticised him for being too laid back, easy-going and lazy. He felt Lennox's work rate was too low and said he lacked stamina. This brought an incredulous response from Adrian, who insisted that with every fight Lewis was improving and that he would peak at Seoul. 'I had to spell it out to them: "Look, guys, he's a heavyweight with long limbs so he can't jump around like a buzzsaw flyweight, but he's a quick heavyweight and a great natural athlete and he always works extremely hard for me and never seems to get really tired." I know he might sometimes look tired, but it's deceptive because then he comes back really hard. He has great stamina, and I knew he had the heart as well as the talent. One day we did some hard running at our camp in Lake Placid and Lennox had this blister that took off the skin on his sole. The next day he didn't say a word, he just ran like nothing had happened, and when he took off his shoe it was full of blood. That showed me that when he wanted to do something he'd do it, even if it meant fighting through a serious pain barrier.'

Cuba boycotted its second Olympics in a row – in solidarity with the North Koreans (who refused to participate because their request to co-host the Games was denied). This did not substantially affect Lewis' chances as he had already proved he had the measure of Gonzalez. It was, however, a relief to the Americans and their 21-year-old Riddick Bowe. 'We knew Bowe very well,' Teodorescu said, 'even though Lennox had never fought him. I had seen him box many times. I watched him getting dropped twice by Gonzalez – although he also dropped Gonzalez once – and he was well beaten. I knew Lennox was all-round better than Bowe – stronger and faster – and that if he used his jab he'd have no problem.'

The Americans, whose press adored Riddick, heralded him as a sure thing. Here was the good boy from the same neighbourhood that bred bad Mike Tyson – and they believed Riddick when he said, 'I do think I'm a decent guy'. Son number seven and child number twelve out of thirteen, he was raised in a fatherless family by his headstrong mother, Dorothy. Uzi-wielding crack dealers controlled their apartment block at 250 Lott Avenue, Brownsville. People were regularly shot dead, sometimes in their building, and every night they could hear shots and screams, but he doggedly side-stepped the drug merchants on his way to the gym. Shortly after the Olympics the *New York Daily News* ran a story quoting Dorothy on her son's achievement in becoming such a fine fellow amid such scum. One of her daughters sent a bouquet of flowers to congratulate her for speaking out. It duly arrived on her doorstep in a garbage can that also contained the murdered deliveryman, prompting Riddick's decision to move his family to Maryland. But in 1988 they were still in Brownsville – Dorothy, Riddick, his wife Judy, their two children, a brother and a sister – seven in a two-bedroom apartment, all waiting for deliverance. Three weeks before the Olympic team was chosen, Riddick's sister Brenda was stabbed to death by crack dealers. A month later he heard one of his brothers was dying of Aids.

In addition to the Cinderella plot, journalists liked him because he came with an attractive, boyish charm and easy smile, and despite an official IQ of 79 (three more than the young Muhammad Ali, incidentally, and as good an indication as any that intelligence and IQ are different animals completely) he was clearly a smart guy with a sharp wit and an engaging sense of fun. This he demonstrated particularly with his on-the-ball mimicry, which served as his favourite party trick (and included passable impressions of Ronald Reagan, Bill Cosby and Stevie Wonder). He liked to joke and tease and fool around.

To add to the tale, in the six months prior to the Games Riddick ran into a few physical problems on top of his family problems, picking up a hairline fracture on his right ankle and also having to have surgery on his right hand. By the time he arrived in Seoul, however, both these injuries were fully healed and he felt he was in the best shape of his life. At 6ft 5in and 225lb he certainly looked the part, and he was impressive in the run-up to the Games – a polished boxer who could work at all ranges and a big puncher with both hands. He was seen as destined for triumph, and this confidence rubbed off on him. He came to see himself as the anointed one and spoke of the gold medal as an inevitability – to be followed, after a respectable apprenticeship, by the professional demolition of Mike Tyson.

Lennox also experienced injury troubles. In his final pre-Olympic fight he knocked out an American in the first round, but his penultimate punch landed at the wrong angle, leaving him with a broken right thumb. Teodorescu instructed him to spare his right until his first fight, which saw him bowl over a bulky Kenyan in quick time. His next test was more serious – the East German Ulli Kaden who had out-pointed him at the World Cup in Belgrade eleven months before. 'Another one of those 3–2 political decisions,' said Teodorescu, 'but we couldn't be sure it wouldn't happen again so I told Lennox to just go out there and knock him out because there was no way we were going to allow the judges to rob us there, so Lennox was really up for the fight, really confident. He wasn't at all nervous. He was just very cool as he always was, but not lackadaisical, never, and he went out there and bombed Kaden out in thirty-four seconds.' In his third bout, the semi-finals, he was drawn against a Pole he'd bashed up at a training camp in Warsaw in 1987, prompting him to pull out of the tournament that followed. He did it again in the Olympics, claim-ing a broken hand, which set Lennox up for the final against Bowe.

After watching Bowe Lennox was convinced he had the beating of him; so much so that when he had his first chat with the American a week before their fight he offered him some friendly advice on how to beat an opponent he'd previously encountered. He came away with the impression that Riddick wasn't listening. A few days later, when both men reached the final, he watched a television interview where Bowe dismissed him, predicting he would 'take this Canadian to school' and spoke of the gold medal as a certainty. This stirred Lennox's intensely competitive juices and made him determined to do a job on the American. His sense of mission was further excited when one of Bowe's American team-mates, the heavyweight gold medallist Ray Mercer, approached him saying that Riddick was a 'loud-mouthed piece of shit' and he hoped Lennox flattened him.

Meanwhile, the Games was about to be engulfed in scandal. Everyone knew ana-bolic steroids were fuelling the astonishing records set by East German athletes, particularly women whose performances were boosted by the drugs' testosterone-mimicking properties. Suspicions that it went beyond the Eastern Bloc were raised when America's Florence Griffiths-Joyner shattered the world 100 metre record in 10.49 seconds – a time no one has since come close to matching. These doubts were reinforced by the claim made by a US sprinter that Flo-Jo paid him to buy her a consignment of the banned but undetectable performance-enhancing drug Human Growth Hormone. It is widely believed that her massive drugs intake contributed to her death from a heart attack a decade later. But this was just a niggle compared with the controversy surrounding the men's 100 metre final, won by Lennox's team-mate, Ben Johnson, in the remarkable time of 9.79 seconds. Second was America's Carl Lewis, who should not have been allowed to compete having already failed a drugs test that American track and field officials chose to cover up. Third was Britain's Linford Christie who tested positive for a banned stimulant but escaped a ban after claiming he absorbed it through ginseng tea (although a decade later he tested positive for steroid abuse). Johnson was less fortunate, and was banned for two years, largely because he didn't do enough to flush the evidence out of his system (and later admitted to an investigating committee that in addition to steroids he paid $10,000 for ten bottles of HGH). The great Canadian triumph turned into the great Canadian disgrace, after which the Canadians decided he was really a Jamaican.

This was followed by a ringside disgrace when America's Roy Jones Jr was robbed of the 156lb gold medal. While Bowe was the face of the US boxing team, it was Jones who delivered in the ring with his scintillating combination of speed, skill and power. In the final he boxed rings around Korea's Park Si-hun. It was not one of those close fights where you could mount an argument either way: Jones won every minute of each of every round. Before the bout, however, there were rumours of money passing hands and of the desperation of the South Koreans to do whatever it took to secure a gold medal. While the Soviet and Hungarian judges made Jones the winner, the men from Uganda, Morocco and Uruguay over-ruled them. Olympic president and former Spanish fascist Juan Antonio Samaranch, himself not a man exactly untainted by controversy, was outraged and repeated a prior threat to have boxing scrapped from the Olympics. An embarrassed International Amateur Boxing Association decided their judges could not be trusted and introduced the new 'computer' scoring system, which relied on the inclination of the same men to punch the right buttons for the right punches. They also awarded the Val Barker Cup, for the most skilful Olympic boxer, to Jones – an admission that the decision was a travesty. Jones went on to become one of the finest professionals of all time, although he too was not immune from scandal – later getting away with a positive steroids test because the International Boxing Federation decided the result belonged under its own giant rug – a move illustrating how random the drugs control lottery could be in professional boxing.

The super heavyweight final came immediately after the Jones fight. As soon as Lennox and Teodorescu heard the boos in their changing room they knew there was the potential for trouble, fearing the officials might decide the Americans needed a favour after suffering such a blatant robbery. 'You could beat this guy with a jab alone,' Adrian advised, 'but we can't give the judges any excuses to rob us, so I want you to go out there and take him. Our first strategy is to knock him out.'

But Lewis is seldom a quick starter, and when the first bell rang he decided to wait and see for the first minute, which allowed Bowe to take the early initiative in a scrappy round. He landed a hard jab that bloodied Lennox's nose, several body blows and a stiff uppercut on the inside, but Lennox fought back with his own jab, and even though he missed with most of his big punches he looked like the stronger man and the more powerful puncher. Late in the round Bowe received an official warning, requiring a one-point deduction, for continual dangerous use of his head. Teodorescu felt that with the point's deduction Lewis shaded it but that he wasn't doing enough so he yelled, 'What the hell do you think you're doing? Just get out there and fight! Knock him out! But don't allow him close and don't brawl. Just keep your distance, use your jab and bang him with your right cross. I want you to really hurt him. OK? Now go out there and kill him!'

Lennox didn't hesitate. He advanced, landed two jolting jabs and then a three-punch combination: right cross, power jab, right cross. Bowe wobbled and fell on the ropes, breathing heavily from the shock of being hit so hard. 'I could see from the corner that he had no chance after that,' said Teodorescu. 'That first combination hurt him so badly that he never recovered.' The East German referee, Gustav Baumgardt, issued a standing eight count – the usual practice in amateur boxing when a man is hurt. Lewis cracked in another good right that rocked Bowe's head back, and then a reflex left hook. Teodorescu was sure it was over. 'That second time Lennox caught him with the right, it was actually not quite so damaging as that first combination, but he was still dazed. I could see by the way he was looking to his corner that he was still dazed.'

Baumgardt issued a second standing eight count, and then, 43 seconds into round two, waved Bowe to his corner, indicating that despite the American's raised-arm plea the fight was over. The devastated American protested that the stoppage was premature, that he could have fought on. Lennox dismissed this as nonsense and said that from his vantage position a few feet from Bowe's eye level he could see the American was wobbly and that his eyes were glazed. He felt that with one more punch he would have knocked him cold. 'I hit him with some really good shots and he was gone, so the referee had to stop the fight.' Hardly surprisingly, Teodorescu agreed. 'He had no cause to complain because the referee asked him if he was ready to fight on and he said nothing, so he had no option but to stop it. If I'd been in his position I would have done the same thing.'

A fascinated observer was the professional trainer Emmanuel Steward, who came away extremely impressed with this tall underdog – and determined to sign him up. 'My impression in that first round was that this Canadian might not have the skills of an American kid raised in New York, with top American trainers and sparring part-ners. At first I thought Bowe was outboxing him but then the Canadian came back. I was watching carefully and I saw that it was just becoming too physical for Bowe. Lennox knew he was losing the fight and got so excited that he came out in the next round and just physically overwhelmed Bowe. He said, "I can't beat him being tech-nical so I'm going to do what I have to do to win," and he came out and crushed him. He overpowered Bowe because he had too much physical strength and power for him, and also too much mental strength. He broke Bowe. He basically knocked him out and I was just so impressed.'

Back in Kitchener, Violet watched the final round on a small television set with three friends and a television crew who were filming her reaction. Her leg was in plaster following an accident at the Styrofoam factory – a fork-lift truck ran over her foot, shattering the bones, which never completely healed – and this prevented her from going ahead with her planned holiday to Seoul. But when the referee waved it off and she realised her boy was the Olympic super heavyweight gold medallist she leapt up from her couch, whooped with delight and began to dance around the room.

She watched Lennox's face as he realised that all the waiting had been worth it, and then saw Adrian clambering through the ropes, grabbing Lennox and lifting him up for a few seconds until the weight proved too much, at which point Lennox raised his hands, beaming ecstatically and running around the ring until a pair of anxious-looking Canadian officials stepped in his way. Their faces speaking of borderline panic, they instructed Lennox to leave the ring, saying, 'You have to do your drugs test now so don't drink anything and don't touch anything or anyone. Nothing. Hear?' Clearly worried about a repeat of the Ben Johnson fiasco, and concerned that all eyes were on Canada for this reason, they stayed with him and let no one near until he had successfully peed in the bottle and they had witnessed its sealing and signing.

At last, Lennox could return to the ring and mount the fourth step of the podium with Riddick Bowe's Afro below him and a bit of his own blood over his heart on his vest. Feeling shattered about the loss, and placing the full blame on the referee, Bowe made the bizarre request to join Lennox on the top step, which the gold medallist refused with a smile, a shake of the head and a handshake. The shattered silver medallist responded with bitter resentment. 'See you in the pros,' he spat.

When Lennox heard the first bars of 'O Canada, Our Home and Native Land' he stood ramrod erect, his eyes on the back of the hall. He was holding a little Canadian flag in one hand and a large bouquet of flowers in the other, and when he bent down for the gold medal to be placed around his neck, his mother's moment of calm came to an end. She burst into tears and praised the Lord.

CHAPTER SIX
CHICAGO, ILLINOIS, 2004

Sitting in his attorney's office, with one finger near the pulse of boxing and another on more mundane legal matters, John Hornewer will admit that, yeah, OK, regrets, he has a few, but then again … hey, you can't keep on looking back, can you?

He reels off the names of champions he's represented since the big break-up: Roy Jones, Antonio Tarver, Chris Byrd … Trouble is, when you've had eight formative years as friend, lawyer and adviser to a man like Lennox Lewis it's hard not to compare. You can't really help glancing back once in a while with a mixture of nostalgia, regret and, if you don't catch yourself in time, a bit of hurt and bitterness too. Ask John how he feels about Lennox today and what you get is a little wave of criticism followed by a stronger undertow of affection. It's a mixed message, but in the end it tends towards the positive.

They fell out in 1996, ostensibly over money, but also over things closer to the heart, like hurt feelings, lost influence and advice ignored. It's been a while since they chatted. 'We were close – he was one of the groomsmen at my wedding – very close, but people came between us who resented my influence and I think that was the cause of all the problems.' But now, with these manipulators exposed, falling one by one, he says, 'I feel vindicated, because everything I said to him about them has proved to be correct.'

His way of resolving this ambiguity is to draw a distinction between the friend, Lennox, the young man he first got to know in Kitchener, and the celebrity called Lennox Lewis surrounded by a growing entourage and remote from some of his former friends. 'Ah, you see, money and power change everything,' the now 43-year-old John says with a shake of the head. 'I liked Lennox a lot, and I still like Lennox, but I don't like Lennox Lewis very much. Lennox is a very sensitive person, raised by his mom and then by Arnie Boehm, who told him not to trust a lot of people, yet his biggest flaw turned out to be his willingness to trust the wrong people – people who are always complimenting him. So I didn't have a problem with Lennox so much as with the people around him. I used to tell him things he didn't want to hear, and that's an unpopular position to take with him because he likes to have peace and hates confrontation in his life. But I did it because I always looked at him as Lennox, my friend, and I respected him. Trouble was, I wasn't as rich as some of the fraudsters so in the end my opinion didn't count as much because he'd be wondering if I was so smart how come I wasn't raking it in like some of them. But, you see, I wasn't stealing his money. And if you're the one person who's telling the truth and nobody wants to hear it, well, you're the bad guy. But now I feel sad for Lennox. He's so bitter about it because he trusted those people.'

So what was that Lennox like? John throws out a mixed bag of adjectives – confident, playful, sensitive, cautious, gullible before settling on another one: curious. 'He's so full of ideas and so interested in the world. He's not well educated in the formal sense because of all his athletic travelling when he was at school, but he's a really bright, intelligent guy who always wants to learn. One time he phoned me and said he wanted to learn more about the Nation of Islam, and seeing as I was from Chicago couldn't I go to their offices and get some reading material? So I did it and he read it all. Another time we'd been talking about rap, so he asked me to bring him some records and information about Public Enemy because he wanted to learn more about where they were coming from. And when Kurt Cobain killed himself he phoned, waking me up at three a.m., and said, "John, isn't it terrible?" I said, "Uh, what?" and he said, "I've just heard, Kurt Cobain killed himself. That's just terrible." So I said, "Yeah, that is terrible, but it's also three a.m., Lennox. So goodnight.'

After seven years apart, with only memories like these to fall back on, Hornewer's sole remaining connection with Lennox comes through occasional conversations with his former friend's mother, Violet – conversations he values highly. 'She loves her son and so did I, and I had a great relationship with her – very good. When we see each other nowadays she'll say things to me like, "You were right about this fraudster and that fraudster." He loves her very much and keeps her included. She's the one constant in his life, extremely loyal to him, to a faith. She's a stand-up person who really appreciates what I did for him, and she's changed less than he has. This is not a nice business and unfortunately he hasn't learned to extract himself from it, but I think now that he's retiring Lennox Lewis will become Lennox again. I hope so.'

Lewis' victory over Riddick Bowe in Seoul was seen throughout the world. His brother watched it on the BBC in Britain, his mother on CBC in Canada, and most of America's leading boxing managers, trainers and promoters watched on NBC. Everyone watched except the Cubans, North Koreans and South Africans. With those big rights that landed on Bowe's face and chin, Lennox transformed his fortunes. His size and physique, his good looks and sharp brain, that long left jab and vicious cross, and most of all that gold medal made him the most desirable amateur commodity in the world. But Lennox is a cautious man. When he returned to Kitchener's favourite-son welcome he decided to take his time about making any deals. He didn't want to jump too quickly.

As far as Canadian businessman David Hurst was concerned, Lennox and his friend Egerton Marcus (who won the silver medal for Canada at middleweight) had already jumped. That was also the perspective of Teodorescu, who told would-be suitors, 'Sorry, but Lennox is spoken for. He's signed up with the Mallet group already.' Eight months earlier Adrian introduced Lennox to Hurst, whose exposure to the sport came through his boxer nephew, Nick Ruppa. He proposed a promotional deal for Lennox and Egerton, paying them both C$200 a week, providing them with the finance for their first cars (Lennox chose a Thunderbird), with the money lent at an annual rate of 15 per cent. On these terms it was hardly a costly risk for Hurst, especially considering the potential payload if they delivered in Seoul. This sweetener was intended as a prelude to a future deal that would net them 65 per cent of the profits from a company called Mallet Sports Inc., based on the initials of the protagonists: Marcus, Adrian, Lennox Lewis, Egerton and Teodorescu. The debt would be waived once they signed the promotional agreement after the Olympics, when they would be paid 'substantial' signing bonuses. However, in their relief at being handed some pocket money and the keys to their first cars they did not quite absorb this little rider: if they failed to sign up after the Olympics and had not paid back the loan by a date set five months *before* the Olympics, they would owe Hurst C$100,000. Adrian, who was offered an annual salary of C$100,000 for his role as trainer, as well as his fee as a director of Mallet Sports Inc. and a small percentage of the boxer's earnings, emphasised the upside of the deal without getting into the penalties. Lennox and Marcus trusted Adrian, and on his advice they went along to Hurst's office and signed the contract.

The Mallet group got moving as soon as the boxers returned home. The way Hurst saw it was that he'd made an investment by advancing some money prior to the Olympics, and now he was due to cash in. Teodorescu, who assured Hurst there would be no problem delivering the medal winners, was given the task of wrapping it up. Lewis understood Adrian's role as future trainer but never realised it went further – four days after he beat Bowe, Adrian was installed as Mallet president, which meant he would effectively become their manager and promoter as well, with Hurst pulling the strings in the background. Lennox later acknowledged that if he'd known this from the start he would have been far more wary about signing the pre-Olympic agreement, but all he'd been concerned about at the time was getting his body in shape for Seoul.

He went along with the deal at first, assuming he was about to be paid a whopping signing bonus – more than the C$500,000 offered in 1984 – but instead, when he asked for the figure, he was shocked to discover it would be only C$25,000. Teodorescu says he too was surprised and insists he had nothing to do with this side of the deal. 'I really don't know why the whole thing went wrong. I thought David Hurst was looking after us, but then something strange happened, which I still don't understand. Lennox and Egerton were asking for their bonuses but then this gentleman and his company didn't put real money up front. They wouldn't come up with a proper bonus, so, in the end, it didn't work out.'

Lennox declared there was no way he was prepared to consider such an insulting offer and that if necessary he would look elsewhere. The downside, he was told, was that he would then owe Mallet a fortune. When they continued with their refusal, Lennox was billed almost C$170,000, and Egerton C$115,000 (the penalty plus expenses). The pressure increased, but Lennox listened to Arnie's advice. 'Listen, Lennox, the people who want you to stay in Canada are doing nothing for you, only for themselves,' he said.

At this stage another key player entered the scene. Desperately keen to rescue the deal, Adrian introduced them to a young Chicago lawyer he'd met, John Hornewer. 'You see, one of my journalist friends introduced me to John,' he recalled. 'Without me Hornewer would never have met Lennox, but then he really didn't do a nice thing. He just bypassed me and took Lennox to other trainers and promoters.' John says that in addition to Adrian's introduction he was independently recommended to Lennox by Canadian media people because of the work he'd done for another promising Canadian boxer, Matthew Hilton, in negotiating several favourable fight contracts.

Hornewer was a small, youthful-looking but extremely self-confident 27-year-old attorney who had completed a spell at the accounting firm Arthur Andersen before taking a year off to complete a business studies degree. He followed boxing and liked to photograph the big fights, and through this hobby he came to meet several of the leading players in the American game. His success with Hilton prompted the invitation to Toronto to help Mallet by ironing out some of Lennox's problems with the promotional deal, with the potential sweetener of a future role in the company. But John prided himself on his probity and felt he had a duty to give Lennox direct and honest advice, and it helped that he took an instant liking to this young man. 'The first time I met him I got an impression of a big, playful young guy who had a lot of confidence, but he wasn't like some of the streetwise boxers I'd come across by then. Maybe I was wrong, but when I first met him I thought he was as much like a white guy as you get – the way he lived his life in Kitchener, although I later discovered that some of his earlier experiences growing up in England weren't so wonderful. But he wasn't from the ghetto and it was also pretty clear that he was an intelligent guy who was eager to learn. I soon realised that he'd been very close to Adrian Teodorescu, but I also soon realised that Adrian had put him in a bad situation, and he felt let down. So when we met I could see he had a lot of justified caution about being abused and he was therefore quite cautious towards me.'

The Chicago lawyer felt that if he played it straight and made it clear he was not there to take advantage he could do well out of the relationship, so what he offered the boxer was the business equivalent of the no-win-no-fee lawyer's deal (and he explained he had an additional interest in making this contract-seeking mission the case study for his business degree). 'Right from the start, when I first came in to advise him, I said we can take it entirely on results,' he recalled. 'I said, "If I get results then you pay me; if not, you don't." I was the first person who helped him without demanding a contract, and he liked that. What I did for him at that stage was to encourage him to look at everyone who was available and to make sure he made the right decision.'

Lennox was impressed with the way this aggressive little lawyer shouted the odds to bigger, older, more experienced hands, and soon John became his friend as well as his lawyer and business adviser. Within a month he had positioned himself as the most important person in the first stage of his boxing career. He was not impressed by the Mallet group, feeling that Hurst had no experience in boxing, and he wasn't convinced of their approach in exploiting Lennox's professional potential. He also felt Adrian had been too vague about the details of the business deal and that his success with amateurs did not necessarily make him the best man to train Lewis as a professional. So, even though he had been brought in by Teodorescu, he advised

Lennox to refuse their offer, even if it meant paying back some of the money they claimed. Instead he should shop around for the best possible contractual deal. 'By the time I arrived on the scene there wasn't a great deal of interest in Lennox Lewis from other promoters because everyone had been told unequivocally that he had been promised to the Mallet group and was therefore completely spoken for. So I encouraged him to look around at everyone who was potentially available as a promoter, manager and trainer to make sure he got the decision right.'

Hornewer made it known that his man was available for offers and he was immediately approached by two more Canadian business consortiums, neither of which could deliver the terms required. With the Canadians out of the way, he opened the process internationally. Virtually all the major players in world boxing came courting but none would pull it off. An early probe came from Don King, but Lennox had been warned by Arnie to keep the charming jailbird at a distance. As Hornewer recalled, 'Arnie drilled it into him not to trust a lot of people, and to stay away from King in particular, and it was one lesson he never forgot.' Or, as Lennox recalled, 'My attitude to Don King then was like, how can you trust a guy who never stops talking and you can't understand a word he says? But actually, even though King wanted me I don't think he was too concerned at that stage because he was too caught up with Tyson at the time.'

The powerful Main Events group, headed by the promoter Dan Duva, had the finest boxing stable in the world, including Holyfield, who was breaking through the heavyweight division after an unbeaten reign at cruiserweight; Biggs, who was coming back after a loss to Tyson; and some outstanding little men. Lou Duva, Dan's father, who played a managerial role as well as training the boxers with former middleweight contender George Benton, auditioned Bowe soon after the Olympics. 'He's a piece of shit,' he concluded. 'He's got no heart at all and no balls at all. I had him here three times and three times I threw him out, until finally Tyrell Biggs knocked him out in sparring by hitting him in the belly, and then we threw him out for good.' And as the dust settled behind Bowe, he commented, 'When the going gets tough, he's not going to be there.'

They then issued an invitation to Bowe's conqueror. Hornewer was interested but concerned that Lennox should control the process. 'I advised him not to throw a punch while there, in case he broke his hand or got injured in some other way. I said, "just watch and see if you like it". Lennox did as instructed, refusing to spar. After all, he'd already won Olympic gold, so why the need to audition? Lou Duva, who was used to being the boss, was incensed. 'What I remember is that Dan called me up and said, "Look, we've got this kid who won the Olympic super heavyweight gold medal and they want to come down here and train and see what you think." So, OK, he comes down to Virginia Beach and the next day we go down to the gym and he's not there. So I go up to his room and I say, "What's happening?" And he says, "Oh, on the advice of my attorney I'm not going to train, but I am going to spend a few days with you, looking you and George Benton over to see if you know how to train my talents." So I said, "Look, you're a nice kid, but I thought you came here to get into the gym so that we could see you spar so that both of us can see if the chemistry is there so we can work together." So he says, "Well, my lawyer said I should go along just to see if I like what I see." So I said, "We're giving you forty years of experience and if you didn't think so you wouldn't be here. We know what boxing is all about here, and if you don't have confidence in us then don't come here. So get your bag, get on the train and get out of here because we should be looking you over."'

Early in 1989, with Bowe and Mercer both in training for their maiden professional fights, Lennox, John and Violet Lewis's solicitor Jim Tait arrived in Las Vegas to spend a few weeks considering further offers while preparing to watch several major fights, including Tyson's world title defence against Frank Bruno. By this stage the fight reporters had forgotten Lewis and few even recognised him, but the promoters were still out for his contract and they all knew why the boxer and his lawyers were in town.

Soon after his Olympic victory Lennox had sent his brother Dennis an air ticket, inviting him to stay in his Toronto flat and join in the celebrations. Dennis jumped at the chance and had a fine time in Canada, but he left with the impression that Lennox was being undersold and suggested an alternative plan: why not base yourself in London? 'It was me who first suggested to Lennox that he box out of the UK,' said Dennis. 'You see, with me coming from Britain, it was all around me every day so I could see the potential. I realised that Britain only had Bruno in heavyweight boxing and that there was room for a rival. I felt that with Lennox being Olympic champion and British-born he would really make a name for himself quickly here, because everyone knew that most great boxers came out of the Olympics. How much better to have the whole country behind you, which he'd have in Britain, than struggling to make a name in America? So he sat down and he listened to all of this, and when I'd finished he said, "Yeah, sounds like a good idea."' While not yet entirely convinced he certainly felt it was worth considering. 'I saw Britain as a good place to start, and it wasn't just an economic thing,' he said. 'It was also because it was my birthplace.'

Lennox raised the idea with John, who conceded it made good marketing sense, even if he didn't relish the prospect of regular trips to London. 'I advised him that Britain might be a good idea, partly because I felt that in the United States Lennox would be competing with Americans like Bowe, Mercer, Tyson and Holyfield, and would not be as readily accepted as them because he was Canadian, but in the UK there was just Frank Bruno and Gary Mason at the time, which created interesting possibilities, so I felt it would be a better fight environment for him and that he would be able to go for titles early – British, European and Commonwealth – which would be good for public exposure and for his progress. So we talked about it and once again he expressed strong interest in the idea of going back. Part of the pull was that his brother lived there. One of the drawbacks, though, was that Violet was opposed to this at first, partly because her earlier experiences in the UK weren't great, and neither were Lennox's for that matter.'

It was left to lie for a while until the British promotional partnership of Mickey Duff and Jarvis Astaire arrived in Las Vegas, ready to catch a big fish.

At first there was a stand-off – the visiting Englishmen pleaded with John to name his figure but were reluctant to come up with an offer of their own.

Meanwhile, a concerted campaign was led by Emmanuel Steward, who felt Lennox was the kind of boxer he'd love to train – a tall ectomorph with a big right cross. Steward would take on the role of manager and trainer with the leading American promoter, Bob Arum, playing the promotional role. Steward's presentation impressed Violet enough for her to advise her son to take it up: she liked the man and the package he was selling. Teodorescu, having accepted that the Mallet deal was dead, was keen to stay on board and made it known that he also liked what he heard. 'Emmanuel was the only one to come up with a serious bonus. His people came to talk to me and to offer a half-a-million-dollar signing fee, but someone put it in Lennox's mind to sign for a million so he turned it down.'

Steward always believed his failure to sign Lewis first time around was a case of bad luck and unfortunate timing. 'I always wanted to work with him because I thought he was one of the most naturally talented athletes I'd ever seen,' he said. 'When he crushed Riddick Bowe to win the Olympic gold medal I was so impressed with him, and he always wanted to be with me too. I was one of the first people he approached. He later came to Detroit to sign a managerial contract with me but unfortunately I had to take off a few days to take care of some other business and I left him in Detroit by himself for a few days and he was sitting there restless and ended up going back to Canada, but he always wanted to be with me and I always wanted to have him.'

Hornewer acknowledges they were tempted by Steward's offer. 'It was a serious option but in the end we said no for two reasons: they didn't come up with enough money and we were worried that Emmanuel might not have the time to give Lennox the kind of exclusive attention he needed, because he was also managing and training other top boxers like Tommy Hearns, Michael Moorer and Gerald McClellan then.' Years later, however, Lennox admitted to moments of regret about not having taken his mother's advice. 'Yes, I regretted it,' he said. 'Well, yes but also no, because you live and learn and I don't live in regret about these kinds of things. There's always a reason for everything. Maybe if I'd taken Manny on then, right at the beginning, I wouldn't have ended up coming this far.'

By the end of their Las Vegas sortie they were tending towards a rival offer from an American fight manager Lewis liked called Stan Hoffman and his multi-millionaire oil heiress business partner Josephine Abercrombie of the Houston Boxing Association, but instead his future was decided by a chance event that sent him in an unexpected direction – one of those fortuitous circumstances that fall into categories like luck.

It depended on Lennox sitting in a hotel foyer, reading a newspaper, waiting for the press conference to announce the return fight between Sugar Ray Leonard and Tommy Hearns; on the simultaneous presence of a British photographer, Lawrence Lustig, who recognised the big man as the Canadian he'd seen beating Bowe on the BBC, and on his memory that this particular Canadian was actually a Londoner. It further depended on Lustig's friendship with a little cockney boxing manager called

Frank Maloney, who, by his own admission, had just 'moved from the sport's Conference League into its Third Division' by working for an ex-con called Ambrose Mendy, who fancied himself as a future Don King. It also drew on Lennox's irritation that most Americans had no idea of who the hell he was. Finally, it required the instant liking Lennox took to the little photographer who offered him help while asking for nothing in return. All these pieces had to be in place for the scheme to work. Without them Lennox would have been based in the United States, the British connection would have remained dormant, and his career would have taken a different path.

CHAPTER SEVEN
WEMBLEY, LONDON, 2004

It's mid-morning, and Lawrence Lustig is on his way to photograph a London-born Olympic super heavyweight champion who dreams of professional glory. This time the man's name is Audley Harrison, and, just like last time, Lawrence believes he has the potential to go all the way, but, inevitably, the conversation turns towards the promoter of his fight, who just happens to be the last London-born Olympic super heavyweight champion Lawrence helped to introduce to Britain and the world.

The 47-year-old photographer is about to meet up with his old friend again, which always pleases him. The pair of them still get on just fine, although Lawrence regrets that he does not see as much of Lennox Lewis as he once did. In a way, he feels that the business of boxing intruded on the rest of his friend's life or at least the small part of it he once shared. This is partly a consequence of the fact that these days the world champion spends far more time in Jamaica and America than in England, but also because, 'it's a circumstance of his change of management: he has a lot of people around him – new people'. And, more specifically, because one of those people, Lennox's business manager Adrian Ogun, 'doesn't particularly take to me for some reason I don't understand', and as Lawrence sees it, 'you can earn trust but you can't make someone like you'.

On the subject of trust, the unusual thing about Lawrence Lustig is that he did a great deal for Lennox's career yet never expected anything in return (and would never have accepted anything had anyone got around to offering it), and there aren't many people like that in boxing. 'People say I'm crazy, but my attitude is that I'm a photographer and I get paid for taking photographs, so I've never received a penny for anything else I've done for Lennox or his managers or promoters and I've never asked for a penny. My only motivation was that I wanted to see the world heavyweight title in Britain. I'm a patriot.'

Lawrence's lack of pecuniary ambition meant Lennox felt safe in his company and enjoyed spending time with him. He liked and trusted him – still does – and this was important in his formative professional days when he was short of friends in his new old town.

Hornewer recalled, 'In his early days in London Lennox had one person in the press he regarded as a real friend, and that was Lawrence.' Or, as Lennox put it, 'Lawrence was one of the people in the press I knew I could really trust, right from the start, and that was very important to me. He was always around me, always taking pictures – fantastic pictures of me in Western outfits and all sorts of things. He's one of those camera guys who gives you something for his picture and says, "Take hold of this – hold it up," and you do it and he gets an interesting picture. But most of all, he was a really good friend to me.'

So the two of them would hang out together, the tall bachelor boxer and the little family-man photographer, and sometimes the big man would express a kind of resigned envy at the little man's life. 'Lennox always said he wouldn't marry while he was still in boxing because he realised everything that went with being heavyweight champion of the world and didn't think it was a good life for a family man. He really loves children, and I've seen from the way he played with my daughter Laura that he's fantastic with them, and he said that when he has children he didn't want to be an absent father. He really wants to spend time with them. Now I've got four children, and I remember once he said to me, "You know, Lawrence, when I finish boxing I want to be like you." I laughed and said, "What do you mean, short and curly?" and then he laughed and said, "No, I want to be able to walk around with my children in the park with no one staring at me." I shook my head and said to him, "You know, Lennox, that's never going to happen to you – the no one staring bit, I mean," and he smiled and said, "Yeah, I know." But that's still his wish and I think it's one of the reasons he spends so much time in Jamaica: to be himself without all eyes on him all the time. Even as heavyweight champion he wanted to be famous just for doing his sport well but not for being an outrageous personality, and he would tell me he seriously hoped that when it's all over he and his family could lead a normal life.'

When Lawrence first met Lennox, in the foyer of the Caesar's Palace Hotel in Las Vegas on 6 February 1989, the young boxer had the opposite problem: it was just over four months after the Olympics and no one seemed to recognise him any more. The hotel was full of journalists and photographers, in town for Lloyd Honeyghan's world welterweight title defence against Marlon Starling, for the announcement of the Leonard–Hearns return and for the build-up to the Tyson–Bruno fight later that month, and they all passed this tall, handsome young man without a nod or a blink. All except Lawrence.

'Before I saw him that day, I already knew that Lennox was from London,' he said. 'I remembered seeing him box in a London versus Ontario match at the old international press centre at the back of the *Daily Express* building, and then again at the Commonwealth Games. I tried to track him down then and found out he had family in London, and I followed him through the Olympics, so when I saw him at Caesar's, sitting there in the foyer reading his newspaper, I recognised him straight away and went up and said, "Excuse me, are you Lennox Lewis?" and he seemed really surprised that someone knew him. So we got chatting and hit it off straight away, and then the two lawyers, John and Jim, came down and I found John had a great knowledge of boxing, so we all chatted until the press conference where no one introduced Lennox or recognised him, and then we chatted some more, and that's when Lennox and John told me precisely why they were there – that they were meeting various people about Lennox turning professional.'

Lawrence then made his pitch on behalf of British boxing. It went like this:

'So tell me, Lennox, why are you turning professional in the United States? You're from Britain. Why not the UK?'

'We've met with Duff and Astaire,' John cut in, 'and we're going to dinner with them again tonight, but so far we aren't impressed, and we don't think Frank Warren can offer us anything.'

'But, you know, there are other promoters in Britain.'

'Are there?' they both said together.

'Yeah,' said Lawrence. 'There's this up-and-coming group called World Sports Promotions owned by Ambrose Mendy and Frank Maloney, and they have Nigel Benn and some other good boxers.'

'Ah, Benn, yeah, heard of him,' said Lennox. 'I think he might be a friend of my brother's. Do you think you could maybe set it up so we could speak to these guys?'

'Sure,' said Lawrence. 'I'll try to set it up for midnight.'

Lennox and John, who were young enough to appreciate a good free meal but wise enough not to let that sway them, were treated to a sumptuous dinner by Duff and Astaire that evening. The English pair did their utmost to woo them, convinced that they could impress these youngsters with their good taste and their boxing suss. They argued that a fortune awaited Lennox if he placed his fate in their own safe hands. It was all going fine until their pitch fell on the tricky issue of a signing bonus. Duff and Astaire did their best to convince them that this signing bonus was a red herring and that they wouldn't have to wait long before earning huge sums from purse money and endorsements. Thanks but no thanks, said John, and while he went off to bed, Lennox walked over to the Hilton to find Lawrence, just to make sure he'd set things up for his telephone chat with these other promoters.

One of the reasons Lawrence recommended Frank and Ambrose was, simply, that he liked them. 'It was nothing against any other promoter,' he explained, 'but I knew they'd rejected the idea of Warren and I could see they were about to reject Mickey Duff, and I knew Frank Maloney very well on a friendship basis and I also knew Ambrose Mendy and liked him. I mean, he may be a bit close to the edge in some areas, but that's not my business. To me he's a very nice person – a lovely, friendly, charming character. And I'd watched their rapid rise from small-hall shows to promoting Benn at the Royal Albert Hall, and you have to remember that everyone in British boxing was against them, including the journalists, but I admired what they were trying to do' He knew them well enough to have their home numbers and when that drew a blank he tried their office in Tower Bridge Road, asking for Ambrose. But it was only eight a.m. in England and he hadn't arrived yet. It was Frank who answered, so Lustig gave him his excited spiel.

'Frank, Lawrence here. Listen: how would you like to manage the next heavyweight champion of the world?'

'Are you pissed?'

'Hey, you know me, Frank.' Maloney then recalled that Lawrence seldom touched a drop, and never when he was working. 'I'm serious. There's never been a world heavyweight champion from the UK, not unless you count Bob

Fitzsimmons who never boxed in Britain and he was a hundred years ago.'

'Yeah, yeah, but what's that got to do with me?'

'Listen, Frank, there's a kid here called Lennox Lewis who won the gold medal at super heavyweight in the last Olympics and he wants to go pro. He's talking to Mickey Duff, and he really wants to come to England because he's English, and he's not happy with Duff's offer, so why don't you make him an offer yourselves?'

'Lawrence, Lawrence, hold it there, hold it. I'm not stupid. We've never won a gold medal at the Olympic Games at super heavyweight.'

'No, Frank, but Canada did.'

'Yeah, well, then he's not English, is he?'

'Yes, he is, because he was born in east London and he went to Canada when he was twelve. Check it out, Frank.'

Maloney quickly checked and phoned Lustig back a few minutes later. 'Hey, Lawrence, you're right,' he said. 'I'd really like to speak to this kid. How do I get to do it?'

Lustig instructed him to be in his office same time the next morning and he'd receive a call from Lennox and John, and it was up to him to make an impression. A few minutes later Lennox knocked on Lawrence's door to check that he'd set it all up. So Maloney had 24 hours to put together enough to keep them interested. 'I had absolutely no idea how I was going to fund this thing,' he recalled, 'so I got hold of Ambrose and we sat down and tried to work out a plan.'

Ambrose Mendy always had a plan of one kind or another. Sharp as they come, extremely confident, highly ambitious and always impeccably groomed, he bought his first Rolls Royce at nineteen and began to make a mark in football in his twenties before homing in on boxing in his early thirties, viewing it as his route to a quick fortune. He seemed to model himself on Don King, though in every way he was in a different league. Take their dealings with the law. King, the former numbers runner, first went to jail for manslaughter – kicking to death a man whose last words were, 'I'll get you the money, Don!' He had previously killed another man but got off on a self-defence plea. Once he arrived as a player on the boxing scene he liked to make light of his heavy reputation. When his light heavyweight Ray Anderson moaned about not getting fights, King responded, 'Ray, we're from the same gutter. Let's not jive each other. You could pick up that phone and have me dead in a half-hour; I could pick up that phone and have you dead in five minutes.' Later, he was tried and acquitted on 23 counts of tax evasion and then again for insurance fraud, and the Feds were forever on his tail, trying to bust him for one thing or another.

Ambrose was less audacious in his crimes and less successful in persuading juries that he deserved to be free. When this debonair father of four was sentenced to six months' imprisonment for burglary in 2003 it emerged he had 42 previous convictions for theft, burglary and fraud, going back thirty years. Unlike in America, where such inconveniences are hardly impediments to promoting, the British Boxing Board of Control wasn't keen on proven crooks. So Mendy brought in two front men: Frank Maloney and Terry Marsh, a former IBF world light welterweight champion, who managed to go through his entire career unbeaten and had once been trained by Frank. Together they made a success of things, with Benn as their main drawcard.

When Maloney mentioned the Lewis idea Mendy realised his criminal record would be an impediment, so he'd better let Frank do the public running. He looked at his junior partner and said, 'No one in the boxing establishment likes Ambrose Mendy. You want to do this, Frank, but I can help you set it up. You've got to think big, Frank – think big. Now listen, I know these people who want to break big into the sports business – you've heard of the Olympic Gold group?' Maloney shook his head. 'Well, they're a new sports subsidiary of the Levitt Group, who specialise in financial advice on insurance, pensions and things, and they're owned by this multi-multi-millionaire called Roger Levitt, and he has huge ambitions for Olympic Gold, so let me help you prepare a project and take it to them and see if they'll buy it, and then maybe you can get me in there. OK?'

Lewis and Hornewer phoned the next morning, and Frank was ready. He'd always been a good talker, and during a fifteen-minute conversation he offered enough to keep the two men interested, although John made it clear it all depended on quick proof of capacity to deliver. Lennox hung out with Lawrence for a while longer and then returned to Kitchener to spend time with Marcia and his mum while John did some more fielding of offers and then returned home to Chicago.

What followed was a delicate juggling act: Maloney needed to keep the two men interested long enough for him to get a sponsor on board. He made an attempt to get television sponsorship but drew a blank, after which he decided to go all out to attract the Levitt Group. The first pitch came from Ambrose, but while the suits at Olympic Gold liked the idea of getting into boxing they were reluctant to commit themselves to an ex-con. He picked up on their hesitation and suggested Maloney try again. So off he went, all 5ft 3in of him, with his east London accent and his best suit, in a bid to persuade the privately educated executives of a company ostensibly worth £150 million that he, a 36-year-old pub owner and Third Division promoter, was the man to deliver them a world heavyweight boxing champion.

'This was a star-struck place,' Maloney recalled. 'Sebastian Coe was there and all sorts of people who'd been to top public schools. I'd never been to such plush offices. You sank into the carpets, and being so small I had to climb. Everything was luxurious and everyone talked posh, but there was a nice guy called Charles Meaden who had boxed for Harrow school but was now a chain smoker, and he was still very keen on adding boxing to their profile. He gave me a quick seminar in business etiquette and in how to present myself at meetings because he could see I was still very much a kid from the streets.'

When they sat down, Maloney stood up. 'Look, I got this great proposal for you,' he announced. 'I've heard you want to get into the sports business and the only way you can be number one is if you can have the world heavyweight boxing champion – look at Muhammad Ali.' He told them all about Lennox Lewis, that he was British and brilliant and certain to bring them the crown. When they asked 'How can we get him?' Maloney closed the show. 'I can get him for you as long as you give me the go-ahead.' They instantly agreed. 'This is what it's going to take,' Maloney continued. 'Fly him to England first class, put him in a top hotel, talk to him, show him your references, tell him I've got the clout to move him, and offer him a contract that is better than the Americans can offer.' The executives looked at one another, they all nodded, and Measden said, 'Fine, you do it.'

Maloney had never phoned America before and didn't quite understand the time difference, but after twenty calls, including one to John's mother at three a.m., he finally reached the lawyer, who, in the meantime, had continued to listen to promotional offers in Las Vegas. Maloney pleaded: 'John, I hear you're still talking to everyone. Well, please, can I also have an opportunity to meet with you and Lennox and represent my case? I feel I might be able to give you something that might interest you and revolutionise boxing.'

Hornewer and Lewis agreed to fly in to discuss a potential deal. By then, Maloney was looking the part. The Levitt Group gave him a £25,000 annual consultancy fee, a percentage fee for all the boxers he signed, a new white Mercedes 190, his own office with its walnut furniture, a secretary and his first ever mobile phone. 'I felt I'd made it,' he said. 'I mean, what else could you want in life?' He drove to Heathrow's Terminal 3 with his daughter, Emma, and waited for the arrival of the early-morning flight from Canada. His eyes fastened on a tall, handsome young man striding into the terminal, and he thought, 'There's my man and I've got to sign him because this guy is clearly going to go all the way.' He talked up the whole deal while waiting for Hornewer to arrive on the Chicago flight, then drove the pair to the Churchill Hotel in Portman Square in Bloomsbury.

Lennox and Frank took to each other immediately. They went out for a meal at an Indian restaurant and then to Maloney's pub in Crayford, and along the way the boxer discovered more about their common past in the East End and a common interest in football. In Maloney's case this verged on the fanatical and focused on Millwall, a club known not only for its diehard approach on and off the pitch. In Lennox's case it was more curiosity than fanaticism: he'd once supported West Ham United and had periodically played 'soccer' while living in Canada. But it was something in common, and they took it from there. 'We clicked from that first meeting,' said Maloney. 'It was quite clear to me that he was going to be someone special. He seemed so self-assured and confident in a quiet way, and he was such a gentleman.' Lewis was impressed with Maloney's bubbling confidence and his straightforward approach. 'He was really enthusiastic about my career, which was good, and I got the impression he was honest and direct, the sort of guy who says what he means with no nonsense, which was important for me.'

Hornewer, however, was wary. He did not feel confident that these British suitors were serious, or that they had the financial muscle to back up their boasts. As Lustig recalled, 'When John and Lennox came over for the first time, John told me, "I've decided to ask for the most outrageous contract I can think up and if they agree to all of it then we won't sign, because then we'll know that this Levitt Group are either suspicious or idiots." So he put in some ridiculous things no one serious would agree to, just to test them.'

The next day they began negotiating, with Hornewer making demands and the Levitt Group agreeing to most of them but balking at the wilder ones, which impressed him. Still, by the end of their stay they had yet to receive a firm offer and the executives seemed to be prevaricating. Lewis returned to America empty-handed, which irritated Hornewer and exasperated Maloney. His standing with the visitors was hardly helped by rival British promoters who made a point of contacting John to say that Frank was a nobody and suggesting, falsely, that he had mob connections, while emphasising that he was a front man for the crook, Mendy. But Maloney felt the main problem was the arrogance of the Olympic Gold executives. 'Negotiations broke down through their stupidity,' he said. 'Some of the directors were just pompous people, and when Lennox flew back I felt utterly dejected. I didn't realise that people with so much education could be so stupid on basic things like how to treat people. So I said to myself, "I mustn't become like them. I must take parts of what I watched and keep my own personality."'

He was sitting morosely at his desk, fearing his car and secretary were about to be taken away from him and wondering what else he could pull to re-ignite the deal, when he noticed a sudden change of mood in the building. 'All of a sudden I hear a lot of noise and I say, "What's going on?" And they say, "God's coming on to the floor." "God?" "Roger Levitt." So everyone's polishing their desk, cleaning up, making themselves look nice; the girls are putting on lipstick and they're saying to me, "You'd better tidy your desk," but I did nothing. I always work in a mess.' Then a thin man with a big moustache appeared in the doorway wearing a long coat with a big fur collar and a red scarf, puffing on a cigar. He coughed – 'Ghuh, ghuh, ghuh!' – and everyone snapped to attention. All except one.

'Can I help you?' said Maloney.

'Don't you know who I am?' said the man.

'No.'

'I am Roger Levitt.'

'Hello, Mr Levitt, I'm Frank Maloney.'

'Aha! You're my boxing man.'

'No. I run what used to be your boxing department but I don't think it's going to exist any more.'

'What?'

'Well, we just lost Lennox Lewis, thanks to some of your stupid directors, full of egotism and high opinions of themselves.'

Levitt's face went red and he banged the table, screaming, 'What do you mean?'

'He's gone back to America without a contract.'

'Hmm. My enquiries suggest you're very good at your job and you're very ambitious. Let me see how good and ambitious you really are. Get yourself on a plane and don't come back without Lennox Lewis's signature, and I don't care what it takes.'

Maloney flew off to New York – his first ever business-class fare – and they met with them again, apologising and assuring them that it could all be sorted out. 'Please, please, will you come back and negotiate? Just tell me what you want – the main points – and I'll get them all for you.' Frank didn't take to John as a person, but felt he was a straight man who saw sense when it came to negotiation. 'Yeah, in fairness to John he saw us as a revolutionary idea in boxing, and so, together, we worked out what we could do.'

They finally talked themselves into a deal, and the package was sealed: a signing fee of over £150,000 (less than some other offers but counterbalanced by many other advantages), a rent-free house for Lennox in Crayford, the use of a Mercedes, a gold watch, £2,200 a month in pocket money, £750,000 in health and life insurance policies, provision for Lennox's tertiary education when he retired and a sum to cover his outstanding debts in Canada. Most important was the way profits would be split: 70 per cent for Lennox and 30 per cent for the company when it came to purse monies for his fights, with the added proviso that Lennox's training expenses plus the salaries of his training team would be covered by the company's share. And when it came to additional earnings such as commercial endorsements and advertising fees, the split was 75–25 in Lennox's favour. Hornewer had also added a term to the contract that allowed Lennox to deal with rival promoters if, in his opinion, the group failed to provide him with the right fights. And crucial to Lennox and Hornewer, the boxer would have the final say on all important decisions, including the choice of trainer and opponents.

A head trainer had to be found before the contract was signed and Maloney decided that with the deal still precarious it was wise to step back. Violet strongly advocated an American trainer and was still pushing for Emmanuel Steward, but the decision to base Lennox in Britain meant that this was no longer a viable option, because of Steward's commitments to the professionals based at his Kronk gym in Detroit. Another was Teddy Atlas, but Lennox remembered the story of how Cus D'Amato had fired him for pointing a gun at Tyson's head and decided that this wasn't the kind of man he wanted in his corner. At Maloney's prompting they also met with Angelo Dundee, former trainer of Muhammad Ali and Sugar Ray Leonard, but they felt he wanted too much money and were concerned about his reluctance to travel to Britain for long periods.

They preferred to follow an idea proposed by Stan Hoffman, who, despite losing the contract race, was drawn in to advise on the American boxing scene. He advocated the cause of a tough, unsmiling, 48-year-old ex-Marine drill sergeant from New York, John Davenport. Lennox knew of Davenport's reputation from his Canadian amateur days and felt this might be what he needed – a taskmaster who would give him a crash course in the fresh range of skills required for the professional game. Maloney felt Davenport lacked the experience for the job but held back from being too critical, at least until the contract was signed. 'It was primarily my decision,' Hornewer conceded, 'and I still think it was the right decision. He was the right person to choose for that stage of Lennox's career and I think he did a great job teaching Lennox, and developed him correctly – at that stage.'

Finally, they agreed on other key staff appointments. Maloney would be Lennox's boxing manager, with a salary and a 3 per cent stake in the purse money, while Hornewer was formally installed as his lawyer, with an annual retainer in addition to his fees for legal work and business advice. The families were well catered for: a job for Violet and a job for Dennis while Maloney's mum was employed as a secretary, and his brother, the former professional boxer and ex-con Eugene, was appointed head of security.

Lennox was happy, particularly with the control he would retain over his future. 'I knew I was going to get used and abused in boxing,' he said, 'I just didn't want to get used and abused too much. I wanted to control my own destiny. I wanted a say in when I would fight, and where, and who I would fight. I didn't want to get thrown in against someone before I was ready. And what I liked about the deal with Frank was that it allowed me more freedom, more say, than any of the others.'

Hornewer might have had a personal preference for operating closer to his Chicago home, but he was clear that this should be subservient to Lennox's professional interests, which he felt lay with the Levitt deal in London. 'When all the elements were put together it was definitely the best offer we'd received. None of the others could match it. Lennox and I discussed the details and we decided together it was the right option to take, and I still think it was the right move. Right from the start it meant he had a great say in his own career back then. He was the boss, and no one else was offering that. In fact, that contract was unique in boxing history because it meant he was in charge and they were working for him.' Or, as Maloney recognised, 'I had no illusions of power. I was working for Lennox and he made the final decisions, not the other way around.'

At six a.m. on 23 April 1989 Lennox Lewis flew to Heathrow from Canada and John Hornewer from Chicago for a press conference to announce the deal. The delighted Lawrence Lustig quietly shot the event in the background, eleven weeks after his first meeting with Lennox. Later that morning they signed the contracts, and Maloney, who claimed to have lost sixteen pounds through nervous tension since receiving Lustig's call, could finally relax for a moment. He was now known in the boxing world as Frank Maloney, manager of Lennox Lewis. As he saw it, 'We had put together a deal that shocked the world and it made me a major player in boxing.'

CHAPTER EIGHT
THE EAST END, LONDON, 2004

Frank Maloney is having trouble with his lines. He knows the point he wants to make – all about being English and British and definitely not European – and he knows he's supposed to thump the heavy bag at the climax of his spiel. But Frank's essentially an ad-lib man, and this scripted anti-European Union soundbite requires precision. So Frank, the mayoral candidate for the right-wing UK Independence Party, does it over and over again, and then one more time, until finally the director says that's a wrap more out of exasperation than satisfaction.

It's quite a way from the Maloney of six years earlier who campaigned for the pro-European Liberal Democrat Party and offered to run for parliament for them. It's even further from his east London working-class childhood, when his Irish immigrant parents were diehard Labour voters. And a million miles from the increasingly cosmopolitan world of Lennox Lewis, who says German racism is more bearable than the British variant and criticises the British colonial past and military present in Iraq, would prefer to get beaten by a black opponent than a white one, and who spends more time in Jamaica, America and Canada, than in Britain.

The truth is that towards the end of their twelve years of co-existence Lewis and Maloney were pulling in different directions. Cockney Frank, with his Union flag suit, no longer fitted the bill, so when he shacked up with Lennox's most devoted critic, Frank Warren, and then criticised Lewis to the press and showed reluctance about signing a confidentiality agreement, it was time to break the long relationship. For a while there was hurt on both sides, with Frank's more public. He made snide remarks and harsh criticisms and predicted Lennox's demise. Lennox sucked it up and held the high ground, expressing disappointment about being let down. But for both of them that's all over now.

The pain of separation didn't run too deep and each is clear-headed enough to remember better times. Thick-skinned Frank, who doesn't hold grudges for long, released a bowdlerised autobiography with more kind things to say about Lennox than harsh ones. 'When I first started writing my book,' he says, 'I was going to bury a lot of people, but then I thought, no, I won't bother. It's really not my nature to do that. And you don't want to get sued, do you? You don't want a lawsuit over nothing because boxing books don't have massive sales, and anyway, I've got no hard feelings and I'm not the sort to go and spill the beans on the private lives of people I worked for. That way no one will trust you.'

He may still carp on about Lennox's lifestyle between fights, his occasional fondness for brandy and champagne, and will go a bit further on his belief that Lennox was over-enamoured with people he, Frank, didn't care for. 'You see, Lennox is overly impressed by money and power and importance,' he says. 'He'd look at the house they have, look at the car they drive, look at the bank accounts they've got. Lennox was impressed by that sort of thing. Lennox was one of those people who wanted to keep up with the Joneses all the time. That's not derogatory towards him. That's just his nature. Lennox judged people by what they had and what they were worth at the time.'

But then, just when you think he's on a roll of negativity, he'll stress his respect for the fighting man by telling you how hard he trained, how he always abstained from alcohol or sex to get himself in peak shape. He'll tell you that Lennox was the best of his era and would have beaten Riddick Bowe if they'd met in their primes, and why 'a hundred per cent fit Lennox will still beat anyone out there at the moment'. If pushed, he'll tell you how gentle, playful and caring Lennox was with his two daughters, how kind and considerate he could be, and finally about what a wonderful person Violet is, and how she still phones for a chat. But Frank has a tougher hide than, say, John Hornewer, so he won't go too far down the fond memory lane. Brushing off the crumb-covered front seat of his cluttered Mercedes and then driving from one gym to another, he makes the point that he has his own life to follow, his own boxers to worry about and his professional relationship with Warren to protect. What's happening in Lennox's life is his own business. 'I don't know any more and I don't really care either,' he says with a shrug. 'I know it's a flippant thing to say, but I have no interest in Lennox's career any more.'

Fifteen years ago, however, it was, by a long way, the prime interest in his life. It was the relationship that made him wealthy and gave him prestige; the business relationship that drove him to the edge of suicide when it looked set to collapse; the relationship that made Maloney the public figure he is today. It brought a good deal to Lennox, and a good deal more to Frank. As he put it, prior to their split, 'Once you've got a real winner like Lennox, it lifts everyone else up. He's done a lot for British boxing and he's certainly done a lot for Frank Maloney. Without him I wouldn't be in the position I am now. Lennox Lewis has made Frank Maloney.'

Frank was a dyslexic East End lad who left school without any qualifications but made up for it with his energy, his capacity to invent and innovate, his memory for detail, his self-deprecating wit and personable charm, and his ambition. He was torn to pieces by his parents' divorce and, perhaps as a consequence, never tired of chasing new wives of his own, new lovers and fresh flings – as long as they were pretty and preferably blonde. But between all the women and the booze he found time to hustle ceaselessly and to box as an amateur – 44 wins in 66 fights. He considered turning professional until he realised there was no money for second string flyweights. 'I saw how all the other younger fighters were looked after, which was really bad. They never had no money and they still had to pay some out of their £75 purses, and then I saw the world light heavyweight champion John Conteh and the way he was looked after and paid, and I said to myself, "If I can't be like Conteh there's no way I'm going professional."'

So, he continued hustling. He'll admit to occasional breaches of the law in his early days – small-scale nicking, selling stolen goods and, just once, breaking and entering and burglary – but, unlike his street-fighting younger brother Eugene, who was in and out of jail, Frank strove mainly within the law – trainee jockey, chef and caterer, greengrocer, publican. And on the side was professional boxing, starting as a trainer for Frank Warren.

Today, working for Warren's Sports Network organisation, he says they originally split up after Warren told him it would be better if someone else took over. He once gave it a different spin: 'I didn't like some of the things he was doing and then he wanted me to work in the corner of my brother's opponent, who was one of his biggest prospects, and I refused. "No way is this fight gonna happen because I'm not gonna see my brother getting the hell kicked out of him just to save the show" I said, and after that our relationship went downhill, and there was also a personal reason. So I stayed out of boxing for three years.'

He tried small-hall promoting while working as a matchmaker for Mickey Duff, until they too split. 'One of his young stars was fighting a boxer I promoted. Duff's boxer came in overweight so I insisted he take the weight off and my boxer stopped him, and then Duff started screaming, telling me I'd never work again because of what I'd done, and a little while later he called me into his office and told me he no longer required my services.' After that he promoted on his own, without financial backing or television or any stars, until Ambrose Mendy recruited him, which is when he moved into the 'Third Division'. 'Together, we moved to the top of the Second Division, until I signed up Lennox Lewis and leapt into the Premiership.'

Immediately after the contracts were signed in London, Maloney flew to New York to join Lennox and John in announcing the deal to the sceptical American media, who laughed at the prospect of this unknown little cockney managing the Olympic super heavyweight gold medallist. He then flew to Canada for the first time, for another press conference in Toronto, where it was gently broken to the Canadians that their man wasn't quite theirs any longer. He visited Kitchener for the first time, where he started getting to know Violet, met several of Lennox's friends, as well as his girlfriend, Marcia – 'I suppose she was OK too' – and got to see Lennox on his home pitch, observing the little details of his life, like the meticulous way in which he ironed, folded and packed away his own clothes, which Lennox explained was a product of his years on the road wearing the Canadian vest.

The reaction to his defection tended towards the cynical. The Canadian press suggested this British thing was a marriage of convenience and for some this resentment went further, although, over time, there was a reluctant acceptance that he hadn't totally abandoned his adopted country. As Andy Powis put it, 'It took a while for people here to accept the move to Britain, but now I think there's a lot of admiration for what he's done for people here, particularly the way he helped Arnie Boehm, and also for the way he keeps on coming back here, going back to his high school – things like that. Even though he was born British, to us he's Canadian, and most people around here would say he's Canadian, and whenever he's here he starts sounding Canadian again after a few days.'

When Maloney returned to London, he was surprised by the level of hostility he found, particularly from rival promoters who regarded him as a minnow who had snatched the big prize from more deserving hands through brazen bullshit. The

Levitt Group had a firm contract with Lewis, so the idea of getting the boxer to change his mind passed. Instead the whispers were directed towards the ears of the boss, Roger Levitt, and they invariably concerned Maloney's shortcomings. 'Everyone was phoning or talking to Roger telling him they had problems with the boxing programme I was running,' he said. 'And in fairness to Roger, he kept coming over and telling me everything.'

Maloney also faced understandable resentment from Mendy, who felt let down by his exclusion from the Lewis deal. Frank's perspective was that he had no alternative but to leave Mendy behind: the Levitt Group made it clear they didn't want Ambrose. It came down to a choice between Lewis and the Premier League and Mendy and the Second Division – so no choice, really. But Ambrose felt abused. As he saw it, he had drawn Frank into his promotional team; he was the man Lustig phoned first when he thought of finding a British promoter; he suggested the idea of the Levitt Group; he introduced Frank to the Levitt executives and voluntarily eased back when he realised his overt presence might cause a problem. Without Ambrose, Frank might have remained a 'Southern Conference' player; certainly he would never be in the position to take on the Lewis project. Frank might have scored the goal but it was Ambrose who made the play and he wanted acknowledgement of his playmaking role, a share of the glory and a share of the money too. Yet he was getting none of this. He'd been dumped.

Mendy's resentment flared up in May 1989 at the Michael Watson–Nigel Benn fight. He took a swing at one of the Levitt Group accountants, had a screaming row and a fists-clenched stand-off with Maloney, whom he accused of betraying him, and then had to endure the sight of his best boxer and prime earner, Benn, getting stopped. Maloney went home to continue preparations for the launch of Lewis's career; Mendy went home to try to resurrect the fortunes of his shattered career. He returned to the habit of fraud, and went from there to jail, out, and back again. 'Funny thing, but just about everybody I was involved with in those days was busted for fraud at some time, including Ambrose,' said Frank, 'but not while he was with me because the Watson fight was the last thing I ever did with him. From then on everything I did was funded by the Levitt Group, who bought my whole stable of fighters and told me to go and sign some more.' For the time being, Maloney's tensions with Mendy were resolved by divorce (although four years later, after a contractual dispute over an undercard fighter, Ambrose punched Frank in the mouth, cutting his lip and loosening a tooth).

Divorce was not an option with Hornewer. Lennox liked both men, but they were less impressed with each other. Right from the start Maloney decided Lewis would do better without this small baby-faced American who was too cocky by far and ten years his junior. 'I didn't exactly warm to him,' he acknowledged, 'and maybe I was wrong, but I certainly got the impression he didn't like me.' It went well beyond questions of warmth. Maloney saw Hornewer as an undeclared conniving enemy, out to undermine him. Whenever John presented Frank with a problem raised by Lennox, Frank assumed that it was John speaking on his own behalf rather than him representing his client.

Hornewer says he had 'no particular problem with Frank', although he admits he could have handled the relationship better. 'Listen, I wasn't there to make friends. I was there to represent Lennox as his lawyer, and also I was twenty-eight years old at the time, so, yes, I was an arrogant arsehole. I certainly wasn't as diplomatic as I could be.' When pushed, he acknowledges he initially had his doubts about this small baby-faced Englishman. 'It wasn't personal, it's just that I thought he shouldn't be Lennox's manager. I mean, it was clear to me he was the white guy with the licence, rather than Ambrose, who was black and had no licence, and that's the only reason why he came into the picture.'

Later, he came to shift his view, maintaining some reservations while recognising that Maloney brought unique qualities to the Lewis team. 'What I'll say for Frank is that it was fantastic to have such a strong British connection, and he provided that, which was important early in his career when Lennox was being undermined for not being English enough. And also he's a lot fun. He's a lovely guy to be with and he's a real survivor, a classic ducker and diver, and I give him credit for that. And Frank would have lived and died for Lennox, and you've got to give him a hundred per cent credit for that too, and he was also great in terms of building Lennox's British image abroad.'

What kept this pair from open warfare was their shared sense that they had a huge amount to prove. 'The Brits didn't like Lennox because they said he was Canadian, the Canadians didn't like him because he went to the UK, and the Americans just thought he was a foreigner,' John recalled. 'Sometimes it felt like he was floating in the ocean looking for a port to dock, but in a way it didn't matter because it soon became clear the guy was a winner. Except if we'd lost at that time he would have been a dog in all three places.'

It was John Davenport's job to ensure that never happened and again Hornewer and Maloney had a different perspective on his suitability. Frank was worried about the impact of Davenport's antagonism to all things British. This former military man couldn't seem to understand British ways and sometimes he couldn't understand what these Brits were saying; he felt sure they knew nothing about boxing. He started out with this attitude, and it grew worse when a series of cock-ups over work permits, documentation and the contents of his luggage meant that he was turned back three times at Heathrow and Gatwick. Finally, they gave up and decided that Lennox would be trained for his first fight at Stan Hoffman's gym in the Catskills, not far from where he'd sparred with Tyson five years earlier. This sticky start seemed to seal Davenport's attitude to Englishmen, both within the team and beyond. At the best of times he tended to be surly and monosyllabic with anyone outside the inner circle, but with the British press his attitude was one of open contempt. His job was to train Lennox, not to talk to assholes with silly little tape recorders.

Maloney was trying his best to get Lennox accepted as British, highlighting his east London childhood, having him pictured by Lawrence Lustig at West Ham United games, bringing Dennis, with his estuary accent, into the foreground and encouraging Lennox to express his ambitions in British terms: his London home, his aim to win the British, Commonwealth and European titles and his desire to become the first Englishman in a century to win the supreme prize in boxing. Davenport tended to undermine this goal, which was not helpful at a time when the Lewis project was being attacked from all sides. 'It was clear to me that right from the start we had a lot of antagonism from the British Boxing Board, from other promoters and from the press,' said Hornewer. 'There's no doubt there was a lot of resentment from the boxing establishment because Lennox was taking on the status quo by doing it his own way and the fact that he didn't have an English accent hurt because it meant they could say we were trying to force-feed him to the English public, and this attitude spread to some of the journalists. In fact, other than Lawrence Lustig, Lennox regarded just about everyone else in the press as an enemy at first.'

Davenport was unimpressed when he first met Lewis. 'I was approached to see if I was interested in the job but Lennox turned up twenty minutes late to our meeting so I looked at my watch and said, "I expect people to be on time when they arrange an appointment.' He felt he'd blown it and was surprised when invited to the Catskills to start work. By then Lewis had been out of the ring for seven months, and his fitness, timing and reflexes were nowhere near Olympic level. Davenport also complained about Lewis's upright 'European style' and was worried he would never adapt to the professional ranks. He later admitted he considered resigning after their first days together but once Lennox recovered his rhythm, he changed his mind and came to the conclusion that Lewis had more innate ability than any other boxer he'd trained: fast, flexible, athletic, strong and fit, with sharp reflexes and an ability to learn new tricks quickly, which was unusual for a heavyweight (with most big, athletic lads pursuing basketball or American football where there was a better prospect of making a financial killing, with considerably less danger). He realised after watching Lennox sprint, move around the ring and play with a basketball that this was an athlete who could excel on the court, field or track and that he could go all the way in the boxing ring.

Lennox was ready for his transition to the professional ranks after six weeks preparation. His first fight was set for London on 27 June 1989, two months before his twenty-fourth birthday and nine months after the Olympics. By this stage Bowe was training for his fifth fight and Mercer his sixth. He returned to London a week before his debut against the 215lb Midland-area heavyweight champion Al Malcolm, a six-round fight that was the main focus on a bill at the Royal Albert Hall dubbed 'The Birth of a Champion'. Maloney succeeded in drumming up publicity in all the major British newspapers and the event was covered by ITV, giving Lennox national terrestrial publicity to complement the fading memory of his Olympic triumph.

He was keen to make a decisive impression and it was immediately clear he had far too much strength, talent and size for Malcolm. He was a bit wild at first, overanxious to excel, but managed to drop him with a heavy right cross followed by a left hook, and then continued to batter him until the bell. Early in round two Malcolm missed with a wild right and Lennox caught him with a power jab that sent him sprawling headfirst to the canvas for the full count. The crowd roared its approval and the press verdict was that he had shown impressive power but had been a bit over-eager, even clumsy. Lennox's verdict was that he won in style. It was his first taste of professional boxing in Britain and he loved it.

He might have felt less comfortable had he returned to Britain in an earlier era. Eight decades before, when the first black world heavyweight champion, Jack Johnson, won a couple of fights in Britain, the grandees of the National Sporting Club were so outraged by his lack of deference to their pompous white skins that they banned black men from fighting for the British title. It took 40 years to overturn the ban, but overt racism continued to be a feature of the British game. The most notorious example came in September 1980 when the Englishman Alan Minter was about to defend his world middleweight title against Marvin Hagler. Minter declared that 'no nigger is going to take my title' and the Wembley crowd took this sentiment to heart. As the BBC's Harry Carpenter put it, 'the Arena reeked not so much of patriotism; it had a decidedly rancid smell'. When Hagler shredded Minter, the crowd pelted him with bottles and full beer cans. Within a few years, however, this brand of thuggery disappeared from British boxing or was absorbed into football, which grew and grew, pushing all other sports, including boxing, to the fringes. Many British clubs, not least Lennox's West Ham, had problems with racist fans, but such sentiments were submerged in boxing. Crowds happily displayed their jingoism and would occasionally riot out of regional or sectarian lunacy, but black boxers received the same treatment as whites: cheered if British; booed, if foreign. A recent exception illustrates the change. When Scarborough's Paul Ingle, a white boxer managed by Frank Maloney, challenged Sheffield's Naseem Hamed, an Arab Englishman, for the world featherweight title in 1999, an Ingle family member began chanting, 'Fucking Paki, Naz, you fucking Paki bastard!' The pro-Ingle Manchester crowd ignored him. When Hamed knocked Ingle out, a yob tossed a chair and yelled at the black footballer John Fashanu, 'Fucking nigger, fucking nigger!' Again the crowd ignored him, but an embarrassed friend put him in a headlock, slapped his face and dragged him away.

When Lennox decided to return to London he thought of the East End, but Maloney, who knew the terrain, was worried about the kind of abuse he might face and instead chose a house in Bexley Heath, Kent, not far from his own house and pub in Crayford. Lennox was a bit taken aback to discover it was a terraced town house with neighbours on either side who would complain politely if his reggae and hip-hop was played too loud, but he soon settled in, joined by his brother, his mother and her white poodle, Ty (after Tyson, although Lennox disapproved, insisting its name was Thai). They were the only black family in the neighbourhood, which seemed a bit odd, but soon the white kids learned that the Olympic champion was among them and began knocking on his door for his autograph. Lennox, who relates extremely well to children, always obliged.

Every now and then, however, he saw hints of the racism of his early childhood. Soon after the Malcolm fight he drove home from Maloney's pub in his white Mercedes with a black friend in the passenger seat when he noticed two white men in a car following them. A minute later several police cars materialised with sirens blaring and ordered him to pull over. Lennox demanded to know why he was being stopped, but the officer in charge glared at him, refused to answer, demanded he place his hands on the hot bonnet and, with his truncheon at the loose, barked, 'One move and we'll beat you.' Lennox glared down at him and said, 'You're crazy, man,' while thinking he had no intention of getting clubbed by a bunch of racist cops and that he would flatten a few of them if they tried. The other cops were handcuffing his friend, who was yelling, 'D'you know who that is? That's Lennox Lewis.' They didn't recognise the name. The situation deteriorated until a gentler policeman explained that there was a problem with the car's registration, and asked him to accompany them to the police station. He was body searched and told to make a statement about the car before he was allowed to phone John Hornewer. He was then locked in a cell where he curled up on a blanket and went to sleep. Hornewer arrived, and after a few calls of his own discovered the Mercedes had been reported stolen when it had been legitimately repossessed and resold. Lennox and his friend were released without apology, but Hornewer complained, and for the next fortnight Lennox had several visits from policemen asking him to sign papers stating he hadn't been assaulted or abused in any way.

He decided the lesson was that black men driving smart cars were automatically assumed to be up to no good in suburban England. He felt sure that had two white men been driving a Mercedes the incident would never have arisen because there would have been no suspicion and no registration check. 'That's one of the many ways I've experienced racism in Britain,' he said. 'It comes out in the way the police treat you by stopping you and harassing you or something. It comes out when they look at your colour, not your heart. It comes out when people change their bag into the other hand when they see a black man. These are things you get used to because you learn to expect them in a certain way. You look at TV and see it's happening on the screen, and then you find it's also happening in real life, and you think, really, what can I do about it? So you learn to accept it to a certain degree but at the same time you can't just ignore it. I mean, if I was to see people getting beaten up on the street, I would make a point of publicly condemning it by saying, "No, that definitely shouldn't happen." I would take a stand. But racism expresses itself in all sorts of ways. Here in England, and in America, they hide it and whisper behind your back and that's the worst kind of racism there is. It's things like this that have made me very conscious of my blackness and therefore more aware of my culture and history.'

A decade later, however, Lennox appeared in a police recruiting advertisement praising their determination and restraint when dealing with one of the categories of criminal he most despises, wife beaters, reflecting his belief that it is a worthwhile project to recruit more good people, including black people, into the police force.

He returned to the Catskills after his night in the cells to train for his American debut on a Don King-promoted show headed by Tyson's world heavyweight title defence against Carl Williams, in Atlantic City, New Jersey on 21 July. His 192lb opponent was an Ohio cruiserweight, Bruce Johnson, who was giving away 33lb, and once again he picked up an easy second-round stoppage. He then returned to Britain for a few more fights, touring the country and becoming familiar with British ways. Frank was particularly impressed with the way he mucked in. When in Cardiff to attend a tournament he was happy to sleep on the couch in the front room of one of Frank's friends after discovering the hotel was overbooked, and when back in London his manager would smile while watching him enjoying himself eating fish and chips in East End markets, and he was surprised to see that Lennox was happy to babysit his daughter and prepared to do tasks such as cleaning up and washing the dishes. He never felt like a bosom buddy of Lennox's and soon realised there were aspects of his life he kept to himself, but the two of them got on well, laughed a lot together, sometimes ate and drank together and took the piss out of each other. After a few months of this Maloney felt his project of making his young heavyweight suitably British was working out, despite the accent, which the Canadians claimed was becoming suspiciously English and the English felt was sort-of American.

For fight number six he returned to Kitchener with the idea of spending a few weeks over the festive season with his on-off-on-again girlfriend Marcia. So it was back to running in the snow, with Davenport leading the entire team, prompting his second brief run-in with police in a month. The group was stopped while jogging in what resembled military formation during one of their training expeditions, but this time it ended with smiles, light apologies and best wishes. Once again Lennox had a cruiserweight opponent, the 198lb Greg Gorrel, who was dropped early in the first round but managed to survive until the fifth when he was rescued from further punishment.

When Frank Maloney returned from Canada, Roger Levitt called him over for a chat. 'I'm getting a lot of calls from your enemies,' Levitt said, 'but I want you to know that I'm going to stick with you, Frank. All I need to know is, do you feel you need any help with the promoting?' Maloney hesitated. 'Well, not at the moment, but to be honest, we may do in time.' Soon after, Barry Hearn, the suave, fast-talking Essex man who promoted Chris Eubank, phoned Maloney offering to assist him with television exposure. 'Instead of going through the back door he always came direct to me and he didn't attend that meeting with Levitt, when the other promoters were speaking against me, and I've always respected Barry for that. He phoned me direct and said, "Frank, I want to talk to you about working with Lennox. I can deliver the TV." So we had a chat, and then I went to Roger and said, "You know what you were talking about the other day, well, I feel there's an opportunity to work with another promoter and get TV backing for Lennox."'

All but one of Lennox's early fights were shown on ITV, but the new deal with the Sky channel Eurosport, brokered by Hearn, meant his fights would also be screened throughout Europe. The opening event was a show at Crystal Palace on 26 February 1990 with Lewis facing the 6ft 6in African champion whose fight name was Proud Kilimanjaro. At that stage there was no routine Aids testing for boxers in African countries (although a little later South Africa made it compulsory and 33 professionals immediately lost their licences after testing HIV positive). Visiting African boxers were therefore required to take an Aids test in the UK, and shortly before the fight Kilimanjaro tested HIV positive and was banned from boxing in Britain. At the last minute a Welsh substitute stepped in, but bad weather meant that flights were cancelled, leaving Maloney with an angry crowd and a bunch of agitated television bosses. 'It would have been wild if Lennox hadn't climbed in the ring to say that if anyone wanted to try their luck they were welcome to replace Kilimanjaro, which helped calm things down,' he said

A week before this cancellation of Lewis' eighth fight, Mike Tyson went ahead with his thirty-eighth, in Tokyo – a routine assignment after seven months' inactivity, against James 'Buster' Douglas. The 24-year-old Tyson, who showed signs of decline against Frank Bruno a year earlier, barely bothered to train. With the expensive collapse of his violent marriage, his intake of alcohol, anti-depressants and recreational drugs, and his string of extramural assaults and other distracting 'incidents', he was in no mental or physical shape for war. On top of this, having fired D'Amato's disciple Kevin Rooney as his trainer, he had had an incompetent team in his corner. Still, he was considered unbeatable. Douglas, in contrast, had been beaten by a couple of Tyson's victims and even with his advantages in height and weight was considered a no-hoper. Yet despite the death of his father shortly before the fight, he displayed a focus and intensity previously alien to his phlegmatic nature and pulled off the biggest upset in heavyweight history. He put pressure on Tyson with aggressive jabbing, evaded his swings, survived a bad knockdown and knocked Tyson out in the tenth round. Lennox watched on television, at first with amazement and then with understanding. 'Buster Douglas gave me the blueprint on how to beat Tyson,' he said. 'You just look at that fight and you say, "OK, this is when Tyson was supposed to be at his most ferocious, and this guy's father's dying, he's out in Japan by himself and everybody's against him, yet he came out on top."' Don King, with the help of the tame WBA and WBC, tried to push Buster down again, demanding the result be reversed because of a long count when Douglas was dropped, until public opinion forced a climbdown. But Douglas, ate himself out of contention, losing his title in his first defence to Holyfield – which meant that for over four years King was frozen out of the heavyweight picture.

While all this was happening at the top of the pile, Lewis was struggling to move beyond the foothills. There was further confusion before his next fight with constant changes of date and opponent, and for the first time Lennox let rip at Maloney, castigating him for his organisational failures. He was backed up by Hornewer, who suggested that Maloney was out of his depth. 'From my perspective, Frank wasn't always on the ball and he made mistakes,' he said. 'Like he wanted Lennox to fight one of Britain's top heavyweight contenders, Hughroy Currie, in his second fight, so I said to him, "Sure, Frank, and he can fight for the European title in his third and the world title in his fourth." Another time he brought out a southpaw sparring partner when we wanted an orthodox one. Maybe that's how it was done at his level in British boxing, but from what I could see there wasn't a great deal of sophistication and professionalism there, and it worried me.'

Maloney made sure things went more smoothly as Lennox picked up five wins in four months under the tutelage of Davenport and his assistant Harold Knight, a former top-rated super featherweight. Opponents were picked to test moves practiced in the gym and bowled over quickly. This is the way it goes with most top professionals – a line of tomato cans to knock over while the boxer adjusts to the discipline of fighting for pay. 'I fought a lot of stiffs in my first year,' he admitted, 'but then so did Tyson and just about everyone else. They all fight stiffs to start with. Our attitude was that we had a major commodity – me – and we didn't want to take any chances, so we went at a comfortable pace for the first few months.' Once Lennox's professional record reached double figures they began to set more demanding assignments. 'We didn't want to push him too hard at first, but at the same time we never gave him a completely easy ride,' said Hornewer. 'We would never get away with the kind of opponents Audley Harrison chose twelve years later. Even if we'd wanted to the British Board wouldn't have allowed us, because they were against us.'

Fight number eleven saw Lennox driving to Sheffield to take on the 6ft 3in, 210½lb Nebraskan heavyweight Dan Murphy, who came with a decent record of 24 wins (fifteen on stoppages), three losses and a draw. The original opponent was the world-ranked former WBA champion James 'Bonecrusher' Smith, but Davenport felt he was too risky for so early in Lennox's career and instead chose Murphy, who came with a reputation as a slippery mover with a sound chin, but without great power. The challenge was to cut off the ring and stop him. Murphy ran and Lennox pursued without much sense of urgency. He chipped away at Murphy's body to drain his resistance, but became frustrated, missing frequently and seeming to lose concentration. At last, in round six he slammed a heavy hook to the body and then landed several head-jolting uppercuts before pounding Murphy in the corner, ending his flurry with a pair of right crosses that forced the referee to stop the fight. 'He showed all the fiery aggression of Mother Teresa with a hangover and fumbled and swiped like a raw beginner,' wrote *Boxing News* editor Harry Mullan.

Number twelve, after one year as a professional, was a further step up when he took on Puerto Rico's former world heavyweight title challenger and former WBA cruiserweight champion, Ossie Ocasio. The 224lb Lewis was outweighed by five pounds by an extremely cagey spoiler with vast experience in riding punches, tying up opponents in the clinches and landing sneak punches. Ossie was a little past his best, but he was still capable of pulling off upsets and making good boxers look bad. Early in the first round he caught Lennox coming in with a quick, hard right cross to the chin, which he later admitted shook him for the first time in his professional career – a 'wake-up shot' that made him realise he was in with a far higher calibre of opponent. Lennox kept trying for the knockout, but his efforts were frustrated, and he had to be content with a wide-margin eight-round points win. Davenport was delighted, feeling his boxer had shown fortitude in pacing himself without tiring and had therefore gained invaluable experience.

A week later Lennox returned to Canada to prepare for another fight, a second-round battering of a 235lb American, Mike Acey, in the Ontario town of Mississauga – and for a more prolonged stay with his long-distance girlfriend Marcia. Trying to maintain this relationship through phone calls and occasional visits proved even more difficult than expected. When they started dating as eighteen-year-olds their friends assumed they were destined to be together forever, but Marcia's lack of enthusiasm for her lover's profession and the months spent apart meant they struggled to keep it going. 'I thought Marcia was a very nice girl,' said his Canadian childhood friend Andy Powis. 'And the way they looked when they were together, a lot of us thought they'd get married. They started going out when we were still friends and they were still seeing each other when he was boxing professionally, but I know she didn't really like boxing and I also just think long-distance relationships are hard. They don't often work out because, you know how it is, you're apart so you see other people and things get in the way, and in the end you struggle to hold it together.'

The Acey fight was his last in Canada. Until then, Hornewer felt that Lewis should stress his dual British and Canadian heritage and challenge for both the Canadian and British titles. When he entered the ring they would fly the Union and the Canadian flags, and would do his best to play it both ways: 'I love Canada and I love England too,' he'd say when interrogated. 'My roots are here, but I learned to box in Canada.' But sometimes he would forget himself and go further. 'It seemed like an advantage to go back to England and hide out there for a while,' he once said in an American interview. This honesty compounded his problems with the British press, who suspected he was using London as a base of convenience. 'It's true we were try-ing to go back and forth between Britain, Canada and America in his first year as a professional,' said Hornewer, 'but then the Levitt Group said it was time to base himself here more firmly and to get rid of the Canadian flag, and we went along with that, and I must say that Frank Maloney really helped there. I mean, what a story! To have a London publican as your manager. We played it up, and that really helped to establish Lennox's reputation as a British fighter.' Maloney, naturally, heartily agreed with this compliment: 'John is right there: Lennox's image in Britain was down to me. In fact, if anything, I made him – not the fighter, obviously, but I made Lennox the person in Britain. I made him English with the English people.'

They set out to win the British, Commonwealth and European heavyweight titles. The easiest leg was the most prestigious of these, the European title, held by a French gypsy, Jean Chanet, who did well as an amateur before deciding, at the age of 30, that it could be used to supplement his income from selling candyfloss at a fairground. He established a reputation as a globetrotting heavyweight who could be relied on for a good show, but in his mid-thirties he managed to step it up and earned a shot at the European title. His opponent was Derrick Williams, a big Londoner seen as a potential Lewis rival. Chanet won on points, an outcome Williams blamed on food poisoning. They fought again, and Chanet repeated the feat, setting him up for the Lewis gig at the National Sports Centre in Crystal Palace on Halloween. He demanded and received £70,000, a purse that allowed him to buy a fairground ride (and meant that the Levitt Group made a loss).

Back home in Saint-Dizier, Jean Chanet had a twelve-year-old son, Jackson, who went on to win the Olympic heavyweight bronze medal before dropping down to super middleweight to excel as a professional. But his balding, moustachioed father, who arrived in England with a record of 22 wins and ten losses, had neither the size nor the skill to cope with the thirteen-fight novice in front of him. He gave away five inches and 18½lb to the 224½lb Lewis, and although he kept trying he never got near his challenger. A jab cut him between the eyes in the opening minute and from then on he was picked apart; when he tried to close the gap he was battered with heavy uppercuts. Lennox then started to hammer away at his body. A huge left to the solar plexus doubled Chanet up, and the fight became horribly one-sided. Early in round six Lennox landed eight unanswered punches leaving the Frenchman's face in a bloody mess, and the Swiss referee, Franz Marti, finally decided it was time for the ringside doctor to have a look at the damage, and it was over. His British critics retained their doubts about whether he had the power or passion to go all the way but after just fourteen professional fights Lennox Lewis was the European champion – his first professional title – and he had entered the world ratings.

CHAPTER NINE
BLOOMSBURY SQUARE,
LONDON, 1994

A first impression of Panos Eliades is of a man who seems mighty pleased with himself and his achievements, particularly his achievement in promoting the man who may be the world's best heavyweight. Walk to his office and you pass a Bentley turbo with a customised PANIX numberplate. When his secretary ushers you inside, your eyes are drawn to a picture of the 6ft 5in Lennox and the 5ft 6in Panos, beaming on the wall behind him, along with his degrees, professional qualifications and various other mementoes suggesting brains, wealth and success. And in case you miss the point, the loquacious Panos is delighted to fill you in the moment you enter the room.

He's finally made it, a rampant 42-year-old success as Britain's self-styled leading liquidator of the assets of companies that spend more than they earn and a leading figure in the strangely fulfilling world of professional boxing, a man who can look Don King in the eye, metaphorically at least, or slap his back, whatever the need. With Lennox Lewis in his corporate portfolio Panos believes he is, indeed, a made man. 'We could be seeing a legend,' he says, and then, just so you don't think he's talking only about himself, he adds, 'and I'll be in the back room.' Well, not really the back – a bit closer to the front actually. He has a story about an American television commentator seeing him standing beside King in the ring and remarking, 'Will you look at that! The murderer and the liquidator.' It tickles him whenever he tells it. Me and Don, equals.

The point he stresses, over and over, is that like Don, all this success is based on his own sweat, brains and ingenuity. He offers his bootstraps credentials in back-to-back clichés. 'I'm a self-made multi-millionaire,' he says, smiling. 'I didn't inherit any money. I was a poor boy. I made my own fortunes through hard work. I've done the groundwork on the ladder that goes through life. I wasn't born with a silver spoon in my mouth. I had to work hard, and I know good times and bad. I'm proud of the fact that I've worked hard and made money, so my grounding is perfect and I haven't forgotten where I come from.'

Where he came from – or rather his parents – is the Greek side of Cyprus, but where he grew up is London, and not the Bloomsbury part. He had to hustle to become an accountant and liquidator, but he reckons he has retained his common touch. 'For success in life,' he instructs, 'you've got to be able to relate to people on their level. So I can talk to a busman and he will be comfortable, but it's no use talking to a busman the same way as you'd talk to Prince Charles. Understand? It makes them feel uneasy. The prime example is you and me now. I hope you don't feel anything other than very comfortable, and that you're looking at me as your equal.'

His killer point, implied rather than stated, and offered with a wide grin, is that this charming illusion builds the trust and confidence to make him rich. 'I may have twenty-five million pounds more than you, but you don't feel it. Know what I mean? I relate to people at their level. I adapt. Other promoters, they don't. They got their level and other people got to move to their level. But in one day I can talk to different societies and I adapt, and that's why I'm successful, because they give more than if I treat them any other way.' This approach works particularly well with Lennox, he insists. In fact, it works even better than with, say, Prince Charles or the busman because there really is a deep and genuine bond there, a mutual admiration.

What, then, are the things that Panos admires about Lennox? 'Special man, special man,' he begins. 'Terrific qualities. To be able to do what he does you have to have special qualities. To be able to bear the pressure twenty-four hours before a fight without cracking up and to isolate yourself for six weeks you need total commitment. Not a lot of people can give that commitment. A lot of people would back off under the pressure of that last twenty-four hours before a fight. The pressure must be enormous, and it's not a team game where there's eleven of you and if you have a bad game you can be carried by the other ten. The stakes are very high – enormous stakes. So he's a man of special qualities.'

Anything special beyond the courage to fight other men? 'For a boxer he's highly intelligent. He's actually unaffected by his success, which is also a fine quality. Feet on the ground, very mild and a real gentleman. Terrific with children. When he went down on the Wembley pitch when England was playing he was the only one signing autographs for the children. He never says no and he's always there. He's a fabulous role model for sport, with very, very fine qualities.'

And what makes it all so perfect is that as far as Panos is concerned Lennox feels exactly the same way about him. He knows for sure that Lennox identifies intimately with the details of the extraordinary Eliades success story. 'Yes, Lenny really relates to that,' he says. 'He may be a couple of feet taller and a different colour, but we're the same animal. There's a mutual respect between us and I've developed a personal relationship with Lenny.' How personal? 'I talk to him when he needs some consultation, when he needs some help. I'm his adviser. I advise him where to invest his money.' Yes, but the personal bit? 'We go out for dinner once in a while, but we don't live in each other's houses. We keep our distances. He leads his own social life and I lead mine. It's a fatherly relationship, although I prefer to call it brotherly.'

And the funny thing is that this mutually beneficial, balanced, fatherly-brotherly relationship started by pure coincidence. 'You see, I live in the same road as Roger Levitt,' Panos explains with a you-won't-believe-this shake of the head. 'The only boxing matches I'd ever seen were when Roger took me to two of Lennox's fights because he was a neighbour and we were actually friends, and it was Roger who asked me to buy the contract of Lennox Lewis, who, as far as I was concerned, was still an unknown quantity. But, you know? Who dares wins.'

It goes without saying that the Lennox view of the father–brother–son dimension of their relationship was never quite the same as the Panos view, and that their perspectives on each other would eventually change decisively and irrevocably, but back in the early 1990s Panos Eliadis was viewed as a saviour. Lennox saw him in this light and, even more so, did Frank Maloney, who remembers his arrival as a second shot at heaven after a month of hell. Without Panos, the British phase of Lewis's career would have ended. Without Panos, all that security they had built into the contract would have been in doubt. Without Panos, Frank would have been back to the Conference or worse. With a saviour like that, it's best to suppress any lingering doubts you might harbour.

After sixteen months of fighting for pay, Lennox Lewis's professional apprenticeship was over. The European title delivered a world ranking with the largest of the international control bodies, the World Boxing Council (eleventh contender for Holyfield's world heavyweight title), and his team decided he was ready for the big boys. But the step required was far larger than anyone in British boxing expected and a little more than his management might have planned if they had a prior inkling of all the trouble to come.

British champion Gary Mason was the top contender for the European title and Lewis the top contender for the British title, so the British Boxing Board of Control called for purse bids after the persistent prompting of Mason's manager, Mickey Duff, who felt the European title would be useful in Mason's world title campaign and that it was best to get Lennox when he was still in the nursery stages of his career. He won the bidding war with a record purse of £276,000, evenly split between the two champions.

The 28-year-old Mason was rated fourth in the world by the WBC, with a record of 35 wins, no losses and 32 knockouts. He was a powerful, 6ft 1in tree stump of a man who usually weighed over 240lb, with a solid chin and heavy hands. His biggest win was a seventh-round stoppage over Tyrell Biggs, the man who beat Lewis on his way to the 1984 Olympic super heavyweight gold medal. The prevailing view within British boxing circles was that this was a premature and extremely risky assignment for a novice professional who had not always impressed. As a result, Mason remained a 4–6 betting favourite throughout the long build-up. 'I remember people saying, "Ooh, it's too early to put Lewis in with Mason,"' Lewis recalled, 'and it's true, I could have lost to him, but I had great confidence in my ability.' Duff, who was openly contemptuous of Maloney's management, accusing him of 'doing a Cecil B. De Mille in reverse – they're taking a star and turning him into an unknown', was astounded when Frank said yes. Frank was equally astounded at Duff's folly. He'd studied Mason's fights carefully and felt sure of victory.

With this thought, Maloney drove to his office on a Friday morning two and a half weeks before Christmas and was astonished by what he found. 'The minute I arrive I can see something's different. Then, when I to try to go in I find the police are there. And then I find that everywhere is locked up and I can't get in and the staff, who are outside, tell me the Levitt Group has just gone bust.' After several frantic calls he discovered his own company, Frank Maloney Promotions and Management, was still permitted to trade, and he was allowed into his office while the others waited outside. He learned over the next few days that the Levitt Group, valued at £150 million, hit the rocks when four major investors pulled the plug after discovering its companies were trading on air – a fact brought to their attention when Levitt begged for an emergency £20 million rights issue. On 7 December 1990 the group went into administration as a prelude to liquidation and, later, to the sequestration of Levitt, who would face 60 charges of fraud before absconding to America.

Lennox and John were inside the group headquarters when they heard the first hint, via a memo sent by Levitt to his staff, saying there might be some adverse publicity in the Sunday papers but that they should ignore it. John promptly instructed: 'Listen, something bad is coming down so go now and get all your valuables out of your house and store them somewhere else, and park your car somewhere else too.' Two days later the *Mail on Sunday* came out with the headline DEATH OF A SALESMAN, its story heralding the demise of the 41-year-old Roger. When John and Lennox returned to the group headquarters the next morning, Levitt told them he needed their support and that this was just a minor mishap that would be sorted out, after which business would resume as normal.

With that bit of encouragement Lennox joined Violet in flying off to Kitchener for Christmas. Later that day Levitt was arrested, but after being released on bail he raced off to a meeting with the liquidators, doing his utmost to sell them the idea that the Lewis investment was worth a mint. He told them the contract itself was worth £2 to £3 million and that the European title belt alone was valued at £100,000. The gullible liquidators seized the belt – until Maloney informed them its actual value was £200. They then informed him they would sell Lewis' contract. Maloney politely replied it wasn't theirs to sell. 'I told them that the contract was worth nothing unless Lewis and I signed it.' The liquidators looked at each other, searching for a riposte, and Maloney gave them a way out. 'I said the only thing you can do is keep trading until we trade out of trouble because this guy's gonna be world heavyweight champion.' The liquidators were forced to accept all this but did their best to seek out potential buyers, all of them having to go through Maloney, including some of those who'd previously bypassed him. 'Everyone phoned me then: the First Artist agency, Jarvis Astaire, Frank Warren, Barry Hearn …'

There was nothing Maloney could do on the boxing side other than sit around hoping for an offer to entice Lennox and John to sign for a second time. He was no longer receiving a penny, his cars – by then he had a Jaguar as well as the white Mercedes – had been seized and he was worried his house might be next. He sunk into a severe depression. 'The good life stopped and I couldn't pull myself out it,' he recalled. 'I felt I'd nearly got there, but I'd lost it.' Levitt, however, was still doing his utmost to keep his troops onside. 'He phoned me out of the blue one morning and asked me how I was surviving. And I said, "Well, Roger, actually I'm not surviving. I'm Lennox's manager but I can't do anything. I'm not even coming out of my house." I was in a state of terrible shock.'

And he wasn't the only one. None of the team was getting paid, and with Christmas looming and presents and plane tickets to purchase they were becoming agitated. One morning a car drove into Maloney's driveway and out stepped Hornewer, Harold Knight and John Davenport, who was in a foul mood. He slammed the car door, glared at Maloney and threw out a few choice insults about the British. When they went inside, Davenport could no longer contain himself and launched himself at Frank, knocking him to the floor and gouging his face with his high-school graduation ring. Maloney managed to get a hand free and jabbed his fingers into Davenport's eyes while Knight pulled him off. Maloney's face was badly bruised; Davenport required hospital treatment.

The trainer was convinced he would be fired for this assault, rather than merely retained without pay, but said nothing about the incident in the faint hope of survival. Maloney also said nothing because, as he saw it, he wasn't a rat, and this earned him a little respect from the American, who a week later shook Maloney's hand and told him, 'Frank, you're a man. You never said a damn word about the fight.' It's a position Davenport continued to hold long after he'd parted ways with the camp. 'I was in a bad mood that day,' he recalled. 'I was fed up with many different things going on. I was waiting for somebody to detonate me, and Frank happened to be that person. He said something and I jumped up and hit him. It was completely wrong of me. He hadn't done anything. I apologised, and Frank was a total man about it, and when he said "Forget it, mate" I felt really bad, even more like a fool.'

Desperate to salvage the situation Maloney met with a UK-based American millionaire, David Smith, about buying the contract, and when Smith showed enthusiastic interest Frank set up a meeting with Hornewer. But when Maloney and Smith spelled out the details, John turned to Frank and told him that whatever deal was reached his role would be reduced, along with his percentage. For the tear-choked Maloney, who had never liked Hornewer, this was a clear case of betrayal. 'He was basically trying to get me out of the organisation,' he said. For Hornewer, who had never respected Maloney's managerial skills, it was perfectly reasonable. After all, Frank sold them the idea of the Levitt Group and assured them they were in the safest of blue-chip hands, which had turned out to be a long way from the truth, and therefore Frank should expect to take a knock when the whole thing fell to pieces. In fact, he could reasonably expect a lot worse. Lennox and John owed him nothing, and the gesture of keeping him on in any form was one of kindness. 'The way I saw it was that Frank was always there as a manager but at the same time he was fairly marginal when it came to strategic decisions, and he made mistakes,' said Hornewer.

Smith dropped his offer after observing this little spat, and Maloney sank further into despair. He became temporarily impotent and began to consider suicide as his only way out, at one point accelerating his car towards some trees before swerving to avoid them at the last second. 'It just seemed like everything was going wrong with me and I just couldn't pull myself out of it. I was separated from my wife and going through a messy divorce, and at the time I really didn't need it. But my daughter, Emma, who was fourteen, was still living with me and my father used to come to visit, and that made the difference.' One day, when he was unable to move, his father came round in a bid to motivate him. He told his son, 'Frank, I've never taught you to quit in life or just give up, and there's one thing worse than being broke and that's looking like you're broken, so pull yourself together. I'm sure you'll survive. You're a survivor.'

A few minutes later, Levitt phoned and asked Frank to come round. Heeding his father's advice he dragged himself off the sofa and headed off. 'Once again he asked me how I was and I told him straight. Then he pulled out this big wad of money, and I thought, "This guy's supposed to be broke, how does he do this?" He peeled off five hundred quid and said, "Take this for Christmas and buy yourself and your daughter a present."' Frank, who'd been funding Lewis' California training camp from his own credit card (with some help from Hornewer), brightened up. Levitt smiled and told him not to worry, and before Maloney could reply he added, 'By the way, I may have some people who are interested in buying the Lennox Lewis contract. Could you come to a meeting?'

So off he went to a meeting at those plush Bloomsbury Square offices, where he found himself face to face with a friendly, smiling, talkative, moustachioed 38-year-old who, like Levitt, was smoking a Churchillian cigar. 'Mexican bandit from a spaghetti western,' Frank said to himself as he sat back, but soon he found himself smiling and chuckling and relaxing because Panos Eliades had a way of putting bus-men and princes at their ease. When they got down to business, however, Maloney made no attempt to soft-soap him. 'I knew Hornewer wanted the same deal as Lennox had with the Levitt Group – word for word – so I told Panos it would cost him between a million and a million and a half to take Lennox to the heavyweight title.' He also explained that Lewis would need to beat Gary Mason if he was to have any chance of fighting for the world title. 'I told him exactly what it would take and how much it would cost, and he smiled and said, "Well, it's worth a little try – it's only money after all" – and I nearly died.'

Levitt reiterated that the only way Lewis would agree was if the original contract survived intact. He wanted Maloney as an ally, so he insisted that this include Frank's role as manager, along with his original percentage and fee. And despite the fact that he was in public disgrace, Levitt also demanded he remain a minority shareholder (through a family trust) and, more significantly, in an executive role with the title of commercial manager and a job description that involved finding sponsorship deals. Eliades (who also stood bail for Levitt) and his silent partner Conrad Morris agreed to all these terms, including paying the liquidators £18,000 and Lennox the £70,000 still owed on the signing-on fee.

At this stage Lewis was in training camp, working like never before to prepare for Mason, so he didn't have time to devote himself to the details but when he met Panos he liked him. As for Levitt, well, despite all his troubles he was one of those people who made you want to believe in him. He spoke of grand plans with an infectious enthusiasm and took you with him in a way that made you want to forget the dark side. Lennox remained intrigued by him, but was wary too, although today he'll recall those early feelings of caution better than the susceptibility to Levitt's charm. 'It didn't really surprise me when I first discovered Roger Levitt was going under because there were whispers on the street that something like this was about to happen,' he said. 'You see, Roger was a great talker. He could talk the coffee out of the cream, but I wasn't completely taken in. I got my first inkling that he wasn't quite straight when he was trying to get me to fight Bonecrusher Smith. The way he was trying to sell this idea to me didn't feel quite right and it was then that I started to realise he wasn't quite as straight as I'd thought.'

Maloney, who admits he was also taken in by Levitt's panache, wealth and charm, said that he never noticed much scepticism from his boxer. 'He put too much trust in Roger because he was so impressed by the money, power and importance.' Hornewer, the one person in the team who voiced his suspicions about Levitt from the start, agrees. 'Lennox is a really bright and sensitive guy but his biggest flaw is his willingness to trust people who are always complimenting him. But eventually, through experiences with people like Levitt who took advantage, he learned not to trust people so easily.' Hornewer himself, however, went along with all the terms of the deal, including Levitt's part in it. His only objection was to Maloney retaining his previous status, but in the end he allowed Levitt to get his way. It seemed too small a detail to get in the way of a hugely advantageous settlement, and no one could foresee it might have serious implications in the future.

Eliades and Morris set up a company called Products of the Far East (based in the tax haven of Jersey), decided on the promotional brand name of Champion Enterprises (later, Panix Promotions), drew up the contracts and raised the finance. 'I saw it as a financial deal for me where I invested money in Lennox to bring him up to a certain level in world boxing,' Eliades said. 'But it was a big risk because he was an unknown quantity about to fight a top contender with thirty-five straight wins. And we had to finance everything, including all the management team, the trainers, conditioners, bodyguards, and pay all Lennox's bills, the travel arrangements, with a very small return at first.'

While all this going on Lennox was staying in a ranch house owned by a fundamentalist Christian who, in return for board, lodging and the use of his on-site gym, insisted the entire team close their eyes and put their hands together for grace before every meal. Lennox, while not conventionally religious himself, was at least used to this because his mother had converted to Pentecostal Christianity, but for his trainer all the accusatory talk of evil spirits and the power of prayer was too much, and they relocated to Bristol, once again on Maloney and Hornewer's overstretched credit cards.

On 28 February 1991, with one week to go before fight time, Lennox and his training team arrived in London, tossed around a few insults and boasts at the head-to-head press conference and headed off to Panos's office to sign the contract. The tension between Hornewer and Maloney was temporarily eased, and for once John complimented Frank on his good work. Maloney, who remained at his post as manager on the same consultancy fee and percentage, was ecstatic. 'I don't know about Lennox because he never seems to show any emotional reaction, but I was in a state of – well, something like winning the lottery all over again. The first time was winning the pools, and now it seemed like I'd won the lottery. For the first time in nearly three months I felt safe.'

The remaining obstacle was Gary Mason at the Wembley Arena on 6 March. Maloney felt certain that Lennox could not be beaten by this world-rated British champion, despite his hugely impressive record, his vast advantage in experience, his edge in weight, his power, strength and chin, and despite the fact that they'd heard that Mason was working harder than ever before in his training camps in Florida and New York. He reasoned that Mason had never achieved much as an amateur and that his professional record was inflated with blown-up cruiserweights who could not cope with his strength. He also knew that a year earlier Mason had had to undergo surgery for a detached retina in his right eye. Davenport took advantage by placing tape on the headguards of Lennox's Mason-sized sparring partners, just above their right eyes and he would jab at the tape (although he later said it made no difference and he merely aimed at Mason's large head). Lewis also did more strength work than ever before, with weight programmes designed by his close friend Courtney Shand, who had joined the team.

Maloney was so sure Lennox would prevail in style that he placed a big bet on a sixth-round stoppage. 'I still don't know why Duff took that fight when Mason was number four in the world and Lennox had only had fourteen fights,' he said. 'It taught me that the master of boxing – and I always had the greatest respect for Mickey – had finally lost it and was on his way down. I was just so sure that Lennox would win this fight that I was willing to use my American Express card to pay for his training camp in Los Angeles and his flights, because I knew he'd win and I'd get everything back, even if I didn't find a backer in time for the fight. I was completely confident he would win.'

The Wandsworth-raised British champion was usually jocular and relaxed, but now his whole career was at stake. Unlike Lewis, he had no alternative to boxing for his salvation. His first line of employment was as a bouncer, then as a West End security manager. He then tried the jewellery business, buying shares in two shops that went under. Finally he turned to professional boxing and excelled, winning the British title in 1989. But his hope for the big money lay in a world title shot. He saw victory over the European and Olympic champion as the way to secure that goal, and with his eye troubles he knew it had to come quickly. So even though he went through the pre-fight motions with his usual smile and quips – 'Lewis always says Gary Mason has got something I want. Well let me tell you, Lennox Lewis, I've got something to give you' – he did his best to needle the cool 25-year-old novice. But Lewis seemed unfazed. 'As soon as Mason feels me hitting his eye, he's going to think about it and it will affect him mentally,' he predicted.

There was mild shock when their weights were announced: Lewis at 227lb was about average at that stage of his career, but a more slimline Mason, at 235lb, was ten pounds lighter than expected. He had trained with commendable focus and had cut down on fatty foods because he felt he would need speed to assert himself early and be prepared to fight at an intense pace for longer than usual. The Lewis camp, however, were pleased with Mason's weight, believing it would take away some of his power without offering him anything useful in return.

Lennox was driven from Crayford in Barry Hearn's stretch limousine, had his usual sleep in the changing room and then started faster than usual. He easily evaded Mason's swings while landing sharp jabs and stiff crosses. Mason began to find his range late in the round and planted some hefty digs to the body and a hard right to the chin in the second, but most of the point-scoring punches came from Lennox, who was using his jab as an aggressive weapon that made it costly for Gary to bore inside. 'He was trying to come in all the time, but he found that it's not that easy,' said Lennox. 'He could see things when he watched my fights and he believed he could take advantage and do things to weaken me, but when he found himself in the ring with me, it didn't work.'

Early in round three Lewis hurt Mason with a well-timed right cross and then continued to rake him with his stiff, accurate jab until his right eye began to swell. But Gary kept on coming, banging heavy hooks to the body and now and then to the head. This invariably produced a rally from Lennox, although his work was becoming ragged. Mason head butted him at the bell, prompting Lewis to push him and referee Larry O'Connell to jump between them. It had become a hard, tense, hurtful fight.

Mason's cut man, Denny Mancini, tried to reduce the swelling by pressing it with an endswell – a cold metal tool – while his trainer, George Francis, urged him into an all-out attack. He came out with a new determination, putting everything into his body attack and Lewis just invited him in, taunting him. Even though Gary won the round and Lennox returned to his corner, tired, with a swollen lower lip, he felt he'd taken the best the British champion could offer. 'He thought he was hurting me with his body punches but I was just soaking them up and I think he was surprised that I could stay with him,' he said. 'He tried to get me out of there as soon as possible because I'm sure he felt worried his eye would go, but unlike some of his recent opponents I'm a real heavyweight, so I could soak it up.'

Early in round five Mason landed his biggest punches of the night: a crunching left hook to the chin and several hard uppercuts. Lennox had never been hit like this before, but he took them well, and kept on firing back until Mason was squinting out of the remaining slit of light afforded by his right eye. Davenport tried to induce more urgency: 'Why you carrying this man? He's ready to go. He's drunk as a skunk. Now get him out of here.'

Within a minute of round six the slit was closed and Mason was a one-eyed man. Lennox raked him with long punches. Almost everything he threw landed flush and he seemed to have found fresh motivation while Mason was tiring and his punches no longer had the same venom. His troubles were exacerbated when a jab opened a cut above his left eye. When the bell rang for round seven Lewis moved in to finish it. He threw an overhand right and a left hook and the champion wobbled. Just when it looked like he was going, Gary piled in with a final effort but his punches had lost their sting while Lewis' three-punch reply was hard and accurate. O'Connell looked at Mason's grotesquely swollen and bleeding face and waved it off, and Lennox Lewis was British champion.

Some writers, surprised at Lewis' strength and dominance, over-compensated for their prior scepticism by describing it as a clinical and one-sided victory, but it had really been an intense battle with Lennox finding his resilience, stamina, heart, chin and pain threshold seriously tested for the first time in his short professional career – an excellent learning fight. 'I'm never pleased with myself,' he said when the cheers died down. 'I've got a long way to go and I still have lots to work on but I was just taking my time, boxing him, soaking up his punches and putting a lot of pressure on him.' Three years later he admitted, 'You may be surprised but of all my opponents, Mason hit me the hardest.'

For Mason the defeat began a long downward spiral so sadly typical of this brutal profession. The damage to his confidence and his eye, which required further surgery, prompted retirement. 'After losing to Lennox, I just didn't want to play any more,' he said. Later he picked up a couple of wins in America, but after being refused a UK licence he lost the will to continue, retiring for a second time with a magnificent 37–1 (34) record but very little to show for it. 'I'm a bit of a wheeler-dealer so I tried my hand at a lot of things,' he explained, but most of these things soaked up money without earning it. He made a pilot programme called *Who's Gary Mason?* and hawked it around the television studios, 'but nobody seemed to want it'. He signed up for the London Crusaders rugby league side but gave up after three games. He invested in a small clothing line called 'Punch and Style', 'but that didn't work out either'. He then worked for a while as a commentator on Sky Sports but was dropped when he said on air, 'Clarence, where's my fucking tie?' He headed for Tenerife where, among other things, he tried promoting arm-wrestling shows, 'but no one would invest in it'. Finally he returned to boxing. 'In time I will be as devastating as a promoter as I was as a boxer,' he said, but instead he flopped.

Victory changed Lewis's British image. He went in as an underdog taking on an unbeaten, world-rated danger man, all for the honour of winning the British title, and showed guts as well as skill in pulling it off. Frank Bruno, in the early throes of a rebuilding campaign following his defeat at the hands of Tyson, had never bothered to challenge for the British title, but Lennox bothered and it went down well. Most of Lennox's previous fights, including his European title victory, had been shown on ITV, but the Mason fight, shown live on the BBC, gave Lennox far greater exposure.

His arrival coincided with the takeover of major league boxing in America by cable television networks and its withdrawal from the terrestrial channels, which, in turn, prompted a loss of newspaper interest. The most direct reason was simply that cable could pay more, which made it desirable for the top boxers who were trying to earn as much as possible in a short space of time. Cable could dangle top dollar because of their subscription fee on top of their advertising revenues, particularly for the 'super fights', which could be shown on pay-per-view to a dedicated audience prepared to pay up to $60 a pop.

Another reason for the disappearance of boxing from terrestrial television and newspaper back pages was that its popularity declined among American sports fans (with the notable exception of Hispanic Americans), which made bidding for big fights less enticing for corporate sponsors. Stinker decisions and the behaviour of many of the boxers also had an impact, as did the over-abundance of titles and alphabet soup control bodies. It wasn't like the old days when there were eight champions in eight divisions. There was also more competition, along with a wider choice of channels, so boxing became a niche sport, invisible to the casual fan but amply available to the devotee through cable, Internet sites and specialist magazines. The exceptions were a handful of stars who had previously made their names with a mass terrestrial audience, mostly through the Olympics. For the next decade the best of these fighters formed boxing's A-list – men whose names were known to the general public; the rest had to make their mark via the more limited feeder markets, and, if they cut it, through HBO and its smaller competitor Showtime.

This was the world Lennox Lewis entered after beating Mason. Both Seth Abraham, a Woody Allen sound-alike who headed HBO, and Jay Larkin, the anglophile who headed Showtime, came calling, proposing deals involving exposure in the United States. Panos played them off before settling for HBO. Abraham suggested a partnership with a major American promoter and they chose Main Events, the New Jersey-based group headed by Dan Duva (the son of Lou Duva, who had booted Lennox out of his gym a couple of years earlier). One reason was that they promoted the undisputed world champion, Holyfield. Another was that Lewis, Maloney and Eliades felt an instant rapport with the understated Dan. 'I liked him,' said Panos, 'and I thought he was a very professional solicitor, a very educated man, and you don't find a lot of educated people in boxing. And when I say educated, I mean with morals. I find Dan a man of great integrity and high morals.' Their programme involved conquering America on HBO and consolidating in Britain, mainly through the Rupert Murdoch-controlled satellite network BSkyB, which was following the US example by edging boxing off terrestrial television.

His first fight on HBO, four months after the Mason match, was held in an outdoor arena by Lake Tahoe, 6,300 feet up in the Sierra Nevada mountains. This was a short drive from Carson City, where 104 years earlier the Cornish-born Bob Fitzsimmons whacked Gentleman Jim Corbett in the solar plexus to become the first British-born boxer to win the title. Bob, who never returned to Britain after emigrating to New Zealand at the age of nine, weighed in fully clothed at a career-heaviest 167lb. Lewis, who weighed in wearing his underpants, came in at 225lb – 10 more than his opponent, the former WBA world heavyweight champion Mike Weaver, who was having his fifty-second fight.

Weaver held his title for three years in the early 1980s before losing it controversially to a coke-head called Michael Dokes, after which his record became erratic: routine wins and surprise blowouts of contenders punctuated with decisive defeats. He'd won seven of his last nine, and despite his age – 39 – was still superbly conditioned and dangerous. Davenport warned Lennox that Weaver's favourite trick was to lure his opponent to the ropes and then catch him with his big left hook, instructing him to back off when Weaver tried this. Lennox boxed a disciplined defensive fight and showed no signs of panic when he picked up his first cut after a clash of heads (later requiring eight stitches) and no sign of frustration when the crowd booed his caution. In round six Weaver threw a lazy jab and Lennox knocked him cold with a fast, heavy right cross counter. Watching from ringside was Emmanuel Steward, who pronounced himself 'very, very impressed with Lewis', adding that while he may still be six or seven fights from beating Holyfield, he felt Lewis had the style to beat the former world champion Mike Tyson immediately.

Lennox returned home for his first British and European title defence, against the former IBF cruiserweight champion Glenn McCrory at the Royal Albert Hall. A severely weight-drained and dehydrated McCrory lost his world title in his previous bout and decided to return to heavyweight for a final payday. Having sparred a hundred rounds with Tyson, this popular Geordie was not too fazed by the prospect of a beating from Lewis, provided he received sufficient compensation. He was desperately in debt and his fees as a part-time Sky commentator couldn't get him out of the red.

His aim was to rile Lennox enough to secure the fight. He went to the Boxing Writers Awards dinner, got drunk, sat near Lewis and began to insult him. 'I started saying, "I'd beat ya, ya Canadian, ya can't fight – you're no good."' Actually, it was a good deal tastier. 'Yeah, well, I really, really wound him up. I gave him all sorts of abuse.' Lennox glared at him until he could take it no more and stood up with the idea of ripping Glenn's head from his shoulders. They were held apart, and McCrory was satisfied. 'I knew what I was up to. All the press was there and we were standing up shouting at each other. Within a week I was named top contender for Lewis's European title. That was the only time I ever had a pop at an opponent, and fortunately Lennox, a class guy, is all right about it now and we get on fine, but I had to clear that debt and that's why when they first offered me the fight I asked for more money until, eventually, they paid me enough to wipe out the debts.' He was helped by the fact that the man negotiating on the other side of the table was Levitt rather than Maloney. Glenn demanded £100,000 – an astounding sum for a recently beaten challenger – Levitt agreed, and the fight was on.

The 6ft 4in McCrory looked like a real heavyweight at 221lb, but when they squared off in the ring it was clear the gap in strength and power would be huge. They were fighting in the shadow of the Michael Watson tragedy nine days earlier, when the delayed effect of a massive twelfth-round Chris Eubank uppercut sent Watson into a coma and left him with severe injuries. Both men had to switch off the unavoidable sense of physical risk their calling demanded. Lennox wanted to get it over as quickly as possible and McCrory knew he was in for a hiding. As the moment drew closer he began to wonder. 'I knew I couldn't beat him,' he said. 'I knew he was too big. It was one of the hardest things I've ever had to go through with, getting the crap kicked out of me. I didn't wanna be there.'

Lennox landed with virtually every punch he threw, starting with the body and then hammering the head. By the end of round one McCrory was seriously hurt. Lennox dropped him with a short right cross early in the second. He rose at nine, feeling he had to earn his fortune, and was battered some more before being dropped on all fours by another right and counted out – a quick and decisive end rather than the long, drawn-out competitive variety that causes brain damage. 'The strength he had to push you around was incredible,' recalled McCrory, long after the bruises had healed and he'd made friends with his batterer. 'When he hits you it feels like someone whacking you over the head with a bag of wet cement, and he's so fast too. Tyson never manhandled me like that. No one has done that to me. I've been in with a lot of heavyweights, and from my personal experience Lewis is the most powerful heavyweight I've ever known. He's very, very physically strong – unbelievably strong. He looks very athletic but he's an extremely strong man.'

Seven weeks later in Atlanta, Georgia, hometown hero Holyfield was dropped and almost beaten by the cruiserweight Bert Cooper, a late substitute for Francesco Damiani who in turn was a substitute for the injured Tyson. Evander survived his crisis, recovered from a short-circuit in energy levels and rallied to stop the under-trained Cooper in round seven, but that night, on his home patch, he looked like an extremely vulnerable champion.

On the same bill Lewis was up against Tyrell Biggs, the man who beat him in the 1984 Olympics. Soon after winning the gold medal, Biggs found himself having to rally from his own crisis. Like so many American heavyweights he developed a drug problem – cocaine in its various forms – and had to kick it in a recovery programme. Lou Duva steered him towards the top through a tough-love programme of hard tests and harder knocks, and Tyrell felt compelled to prove he had the heart to overcome. He dislocated a shoulder in his sixth fight, but boxed one-handed to prevail. He suffered a horrific facial gash in his fourteenth, requiring 32 stitches, but held on for victory. Two fights on he challenged Tyson, who hated him and delighted in the chance to make him pay. Biggs was tall, quick and skilful but lacked power and strength, and Tyson walked through him, punishing him with brutal severity before knocking him out in round seven. Mike then explained, with a benign smile, that he knew he had Biggs where he wanted him by round three because 'every time I hit him to the body he screamed like a woman'. After this Biggs was damaged goods and lost to Damiani and Mason before claiming redemption with a run of wins that had ended nine month before in an eighth-round defeat at the hands of Riddick Bowe.

The challenge for Lewis was to see if he could do better than Bowe. He started fast, zeroing in his long jab, mixing up his combinations, weakening the 231lb Biggs with his uppercuts and cutting off the ring to prevent him running. In round three he dropped his former conqueror with a right cross. Biggs pulled himself up at eight but another right cross put him down again and this time he made it by nine. After a third knockdown it was over. 'I'd been waiting seven years to pay him back,' Lennox said. To keep his delighted American backers sweet at a time when the heavyweight title seemed up for grabs, Lennox agreed to forgo his winter holiday to train for a February 1992 fight on an HBO-televised bill from Caesar's Palace, Las Vegas, entitled 'The Night of the Young Heavyweights', which also featured Emmanuel Steward's unbeaten heavyweight prospect Michael Moorer. This time his late replacement opponent, the 31-year-old Levi Billups, was a squat 228lb former wrestler with an unthreatening record of sixteen wins and five losses. In his last fight he'd beaten the former WBA heavyweight champion 'Bonecrusher' Smith, but in the one before that he'd been stopped by Moorer. He was five inches shorter than Lennox but three pounds heavier, and he wasn't carrying any flab. He managed to find his way inside and stung Lennox with uppercuts in rounds three and ten, but for the rest of the fight Lennox dominated without figuring out how to stop this awkward dump truck. Even though he won all ten rounds on one judge's card and eight and nine on the other two, it was a poor performance in front of an international television audience of 25 million. Lou Duva shook his head afterwards in an I-told-you-so gesture. 'Lewis isn't sensational,' he announced. 'He's not ready for a title fight because he just can't fight that well. Not like Michael Moorer – now, he fits right in.'

Even before the inevitable internal post-mortem, trainer John Davenport showed his most defensive side when interrogated by the British press, telling them they couldn't tell a left hook from a fish hook, and that when God made dumb people he placed the whole lot in England. Part of his problem with Britain, his problem more generally and his problem with living in Upper Belvedere, Kent more specifically, was loneliness. His marriage had broken up and he was away from his two children, the boy just nine years old. Another part of his problem was his acerbic manner. Lennox did not like being treated like an army private or an errant child. At the age of 26 he was smarting at taking orders and could see that his trainer's negativity was affecting other team members. The mood in the Lewis camp had become too gloomy. After talking to other trainers while in America, Lennox began to feel that he wasn't being given the room to innovate. He felt he was becoming too robotic and programmed, and that his athletic gifts were not being utilised. The Billups fight brought this home to him.

The fiercely patriotic Maloney, who was regularly riled by Davenport's anti-English remarks, agreed it was time for Davenport to go. Hornewer, who picked him at the outset, wasn't so sure. 'Lennox developed correctly under Davenport,' he said, 'and I think he did a great job of teaching him. I still think he was the right person at that stage of his career.' As always, the final decision rested with Lewis, who decided this ex-Marine's role in his life had reached its logical conclusion. Lennox sat him down, spelled out the problems and gave him the verdict. The trainer pleaded with him to think again. Lennox explained that it was a hard decision to take, but his decision was final.

Davenport was gutted. Although he was paid enough to keep him going for another two years his longer term financial security was gone, as was his dream of training the world heavyweight champion. He accused Lewis of disloyalty and of making the wrong decision; of wanting a yes-man; of wanting to be the boss in the gym rather than the pupil. He felt he was in the process of transforming Lennox into a complete fighter – a long-range jabber, equally adept at in-fighting. He said he should not be judged on one mediocre performance by his pupil after so many outstanding ones – nineteen fights, nineteen wins, sixteen knockouts; European title after thirteen; British title after fourteen. He'd transformed Lewis into a world-rated professional. 'The trainer usually gets the blame after a loss, but we didn't have any losses, so I couldn't understand it,' he said. 'So where did I go wrong? A combination of people and things conspired against me. It was probably because I was too demanding and spoke my mind and I wasn't afraid of Lennox, and it didn't help having that fight with Frank Maloney.'

While this was happening, Mike Tyson was fighting to save his career – or at least to stay out of jail for anything up to 63 years after being charged with rape, confinement and two counts of deviant sexual conduct. On 18 July 1991, six days after Lewis beat Weaver, Tyson had done some public praying with the Rev. Jesse Jackson in Indianapolis, and then, a few hours later, popped downtown to the Miss Black America beauty pageant where he got down to fondling the buttocks of the 23 contestants. Patrolling the line like a sheikh with his harem, he resorted to his favourite wooing tactics: 'I want to fuck you, and you, and you,' he said, 'and bring your room-mate too because I'm a celebrity and you know we do that kind of thing.' When he asked them what they liked, one of them replied that Southern ladies like to cook. 'That's good,' said Mike in his high-pitched lisp, 'because I like to eat, and I'm not talking about food.' He felt up a few more bums, apologised profusely, and felt some more before telling one of them, 'If you don't want to go out with me, I could move on, because I could have any one of these bitches here.'

He eventually settled on an eighteen-year-old college student with a little girl's voice called Desiree Washington. He thought she was up for it. 'I explained to her that I wanted to fuck her,' and she said, 'Sure, just give me a call,' Mike claimed, adding that this led to some heavy petting in his limousine and then some heavy-duty consensual sex in his hotel bedroom. The 108lb former convent girl had a different version – that she refused his invitations to join him in the limousine, but, intrigued by his celebrity and the fact that her dad was a boxing nut and a Tyson fan, agreed to join him in his room for a few minutes, but only after he assured her he 'just wanted to talk' and promised he would take her to a few parties to see some other celebrities. She collected her camera, to take a picture of her date, and knocked on his door. She said the then-240lb Tyson picked her up, tossed her across the room, pinned her down on the bed, stuck his fingers and then his tongue into her vagina and, with considerable force and despite her screams, raped her. He then ordered her to leave, which she did. 'I was in pain and I just beared it,' she said before resuming her beauty pageant duties and then telling all to her parents the next day. A few weeks later, when her mother observed how reticent she had become, she replied, 'Mom, I'm not Desiree any more. Desiree is gone, and she's not going to come back.'

Tyson turned down the offer of pleading guilty in exchange for a six-month sentence, saying he would rather go to jail for a hundred years than admit to a rape he didn't commit. But the jury unanimously agreed beyond reasonable doubt that Desiree was telling the truth and Mike was lying, even though one of them later acknowledged she might have got it wrong (and 13 years later the prominent American defence attorney Alan Dershowitz wrote a book arguing that Tyson did not receive a fair trial). Tyson was sentenced to three years in jail, Don King lost $100 million, and Lennox Lewis became one of the major players in the heavy-weight division.

CHAPTER TEN
EAST LONDON, 1994

Pepe Correa has a nonchalant air as he struts into the Peacock. He wants to let you know that this gym is his domain, that everybody takes his cue from him – everybody except Lennox Lewis, of course. He's the boss and he's paying Pepe well – $100,000 a year plus 2.5 per cent of every world title purse, and that after a $25,000 start-up package – so the 'big guy' can do whatever he pleases.

The Puerto Rican-born, New York-raised, Washington-based Pepe has a droopy moustache and black spectacles, and the lines on his 54-year-old face speak of experience, but when he opens his mouth and tilts his head up you get a different impression – something closer to casually cocky if you're being benign. For instance, his approach to the opposition is to show open contempt with child-like glee; childish you could also say. His speciality is visual metaphor – a pillow for one (he'll need it when Lennox puts him to sleep, see), a suspender belt for another (that's the only belt he'll be taking home, see) – and he has a knack for inventive obscenity.

His approach to his employer is to let it all flow, to see what fits on the day, see what the big man wants and offer him constant praise and encouragement because a boxer needs to feel good about himself to be at his best. Lots of rest and recreation too: that's essential to get those innovative juices flowing. 'Once he's done his road work and taken his shower and had his breakfast and his sleep, he'll come to the gym and then the question of how much he works all depends on what I put together, and after that Lennox has no problem relaxing, believe me. He's always doing things to stay relaxed, like chess and snooker, lots of things.' Most of the other regular boxing business – boring stuff like running, gym exercises, watching videos of the opponents – is down to his underlings, like assistant trainer Harold Knight, conditioner Courtney Shand and camp coordinator Ollie Dunlop. 'Actually those guys are with him more than me,' Pepe happily admits. 'Harold's constantly with Lennox, doing things like deciphering those tapes.'

Lennox, a bit late today, enters the gym and undresses to reveal a T-shirt saying 'It starts with the right attitude' on the back. Pepe wanders over for a chat, then turns back to the champion and suggests just two rounds of sparring today, two or three – 'See how you feel, big guy.' He bandages Lennox's hands and tapes them, and then, after Lennox has climbed into the ring, watches him shadow boxing, telling him to 'visualise' his opponent. He then acts as referee while Lennox puts in the full three with a fat, slow sparring partner.

Courtney Shand comes over, talking quietly because he doesn't want to disturb Lennox's concentration or Pepe's equilibrium. He tells how strong his friend is and how serious he is about their strength work together. 'We use weights for building strength and endurance,' Courtney says. 'We start with the heavy weights in the training camp and he can easily lift over 300lb, but he'll regularly do seven reps of 225lb and then we'll do more reps with lighter weights later in the camp.' Pepe then returns to offer extra details about Lennox's regime. 'You know, the one thing he don't do is mess with weights. Not at all. He won't touch them. These heavyweights using weights are cruiserweights trying to be heavyweights, and he's a genuine heavyweight, so he don't need them weights.'

While this is digested, Pepe stresses the need for flexibility and instinct – his own, primarily – when it comes to designing the day's gym programme. 'You take every day seriously because you can't get those days back if you blow them, but I go by what I see on him. It depends on what I see when Lennox walks through the door because I don't have anything in mind about what I'm going to do until you walk through the door. I may ask him to go six rounds, he may do ten, and I could call off the sparring sessions or ask him to spar until the day before the fight. It all depends. But I don't ever plan a workout.'

When Lennox fired John Davenport in February 1992 he already had his favoured replacement in mind. About a month earlier, when Lennox was visiting a girlfriend in Washington, D.C., he went to try on a pair of shoes in a shop. Pepe Correa spotted him, said a garrulous hello and they got talking, or rather Pepe got talking and Lennox listening. They talked some more when they met up at a local boxing show, and Lennox liked what he heard. He discovered Pepe was the man who 'made' Sugar Ray Leonard – trained him as an amateur and later as a professional. And Pepe had other top boxers too, like Andrew Maynard, the American who won the Olympic light heavyweight gold medal in Seoul. All this was true, but it wasn't quite the whole truth. For instance, there was quite a gap between the fourteen-year-old Leonard he trained as an amateur and the 34-year-old Leonard he coaxed to a cautious win, a lucky draw and a bad loss, while Maynard was on his way to becoming one of the great failures of amateur-to-professional transition.

But there was no doubt that Pepe was a world-class salesman. He knew how to sell himself and to say the words Lennox wanted to hear. Pepe told Lewis how well he could move and jab, and about his brilliant boxing brain and his innate athleticism and he warned that Davenport was sapping his greatest asset by reducing his mobility, making him box by numbers, stifling his creativity. His pitch was that he, Pepe, understood how to work with quick, mobile, innovative boxers – men like Sugar Ray; men like you. It went down well. 'I always liked Sugar Ray,' Lennox said. 'More my natural style.' So the decision was made and Maloney was informed he should expect a call from the man to take him to the world heavyweight title. When Davenport heard the news he reacted incredulity. 'To be replaced by Pepe!' he said with a perplexed shake of his baseball-capped head. 'People couldn't believe it. "Leaving you to go to him – he's just a cheerleader," they'd say. And that's all he was – in my view too.' The rest of the team, including Harold Knight and Courtney Shand, remained in place.

Lennox's next fight, in April 1992, was for the Commonwealth title held by Derek

Williams, a large Londoner whose record showed 21 wins and three losses. He'd picked up three knockouts and his Commonwealth title since losing his European title two years earlier and had Angelo Dundee in his corner, but bearing in mind that two of his losses were against Jean Chanet, Lennox had nothing to worry about. They were fighting for all three titles – British, European and Commonwealth.

Lennox's desire to add Derek's Commonwealth crown to his collection meant negotiating for the first time with Frank Warren, who was attempting to come back after a series of disasters. Warren had hustled his way to becoming Britain's top promoter but then was blown apart in November 1989 when a balaclava-clad man stepped out of the shadows, pumped four bullets into the promoter's chest and departed. Warren lost half a lung but survived. The man charged with his murder was his first world champion, Terry 'The Fighting Fireman' Marsh (once trained by Maloney and later one of Maloney's promotional partners). Marsh was acquitted but Warren was less fortunate. By 1991 his empire was going under. Nine of the companies on which he served as a director went into liquidation and he was in debt to the tune of £30 million, mainly through the collapse of the London Docklands Arena development, where he invested heavily. Already down, he was confronted with a series of stories in the *Sun* focusing on an extra-marital affair, the first instalment a blow-by-blow account of a doorstep encounter between his wife and his former mistress. But he held on. 'I'd lost a helluva lot of money, my businesses, my personal life,' he said, 'but I worked hard to get myself back in the game and I worked hard at keeping the family together, which I managed to do.'

The Lewis fight came in the middle of all this, and Warren, with survival a powerful incentive, did his utmost to secure the best deal. What made it easier was that it was Levitt on the other side of the table, which meant no haggling. 'It was like taking sweets from a baby,' Warren later told Maloney. Five years later, when there were no more sweets to be taken, they met again in Don King's office in Nashville and failed to agree on a boxer's ownership, and this time Warren's response was to punch the consumptive-looking Levitt, and then happily confirm this fact to Sky, the *Sun* and the world.

Lewis took six minutes longer than necessary to get his message across to the 233lb 'Sweet D', prompting a chant from the Royal Albert Hall crowd: 'Bruuu-no! Bruuu-no!' After two rounds of fiddling, Pepe instructed him to forget everything practised in the gym. 'Just go and knock him out,' – not the last time he'd take this approach. Lennox marched in and landed a right cross chin, followed by a left hook and a right uppercut, and Williams collapsed. He dragged himself up at the count of nine but his eyes were vacant, his arms flopping loosely, and referee Larry O'Connell waved it off, giving Lewis his third title and the Lonsdale Belt for keeps – an honour awarded to boxers who win three British title fights. Again, the contrast with Bruno was stressed, but the crowd shouted for Frank again, prompting Lewis to shout: 'I hear you calling for Bruno. Bring him on – any time.'

However, his prime focus was to secure a shot at the world title. Also in the running were two other feasible challengers and one not so feasible. The not-so man was a South African bleeder called Pierre Coetzer, who was in the picture for only one reason: Cedric Kushner, his US-based South African promoter, 'bribed' the International Boxing Federation boss Bobby Lee to secure rankings for his boxers. The two more legitimate contenders were Bowe and Razor Ruddock, with the huge-hitting and more experienced Ruddock widely rated as the most serious threat to Holyfield's crown.

Dan Duva favoured giving Lennox first shot at the crown. The fact that he was already Lewis's American promoter offered security and he liked dealing with Maloney. But when serious negotiations started Dan was surprised to find himself faced with Roger Levitt. He didn't trust Levitt and was worried about the 60 fraud charges Roger was facing, so instead he opted for Bowe. As Maloney recalled, 'I later had a meeting with Dan, who was one of the best, most honest and knowl-edgeable boxing people I ever worked with, and he assured me that the problem wasn't anything to do with Lennox or with me. He said if Levitt hadn't been involved he would have made Lewis–Holyfield immediately, but he felt Levitt could cause lots of problems. He was worried Roger would try to keep the title in England and he felt that by getting Holyfield and Bowe to fight in America they could have some control over Rock Newman (Bowe's manager), and that's one of the main rea-sons why we never got the fight with Holyfield then.'

The fact that Bowe was American also influenced Duva's calculations. This galled Lennox who felt he had prior claim – not just because he'd stopped Riddick in the Olympics but also because he'd beaten a top-rated contender in Mason. Bowe's best opponent had been the fat, substance-abusing, one-time WBA champion Tony Tubbs, and most ringsiders felt Tubbs deserved the decision. Yet the American press adored him while ignoring Lennox. This exasperated both boxer and manag-er. 'Jingoistic people, the Americans,' Maloney complained. 'They can't look any further than America. They call their baseball series the World Series when the only people playing are Americans, but they can't compete in real world sports, like soc-cer – sports they don't govern.'

There was some truth in this perception of myopic bias, but the reason related as much to marketing as patriotism. Despite his failure at the Olympics, Bowe was beginning to prick up public ears because he arrived with a good tale and, in a sense, it kept on developing intriguing new twists. With his wife, Judy, and two chil-dren to support, he considered dropping his sport and joining the Marines after the bitter disappointment of Seoul, until approached by the 37-year-old Eugene Roderick 'Rock' Newman, a chubby, belligerent, chip-on-the-shoulder radio talk-show host and former used-car salesman who was doing some publicity work for the promoter Butch Lewis. When Butch turned Bowe down, Newman sold his BMW and used his credit card to finance the operation. Like so many of his calling, he identified himself as a loving father figure for the Brooklynite, although Bowe would later dispute this image. In any event, they were extremely close at the time. Perhaps more to the point, Riddick represented Rock's only hope for fame and for-tune and he fought tenaciously for his man, sometimes physically – like the time when one of Bowe's opponents fouled Riddick, and Rock leapt onto the ring apron, leaned over the ropes and tried to throttle the fellow.

He hawked Bowe around, but the top trainers concluded he was just too lazy. Finally, he offered him to Eddie Futch, a semi-retired 77-year-old who was one of the most knowledgeable veterans of the game. Futch had been Joe Louis' sparring partner in the 1930s before a heart murmur put an end to his own brilliant amateur lightweight career. He went on to train seventeen world professional champions and still had enough vigour for activities like satisfying the pretty young Swede who married him in his seventies and flattening a racist punk in a Las Vegas parking lot. Papa Smurf, as he was known, agreed to give the 21-year-old a trial. He told the lad he had to fly home but that he wanted him to run in the hills of Las Vegas at five a.m. the following day. Would he do it? Bowe said yes. The next morning Eddie drove to the hills at 4.45 and waited. Fifteen minutes later he spotted Riddick labouring his way uphill. He had passed his trial. 'This boy has been misunderstood,' Futch declared and began teaching him the tricks he'd learned in 50 years in the game. Despite periodic displays of indiscipline – particularly when it came to eating because junk food was Riddick's prime passion – he developed into a well-schooled boxer, equally adept on the inside and outside, and an outstanding body puncher with a good jab and a heavy right cross, and he had the size and power to beat most of the world's best big men. Aside from his lucky escape against Tubbs, he usually looked impressive, and this talent, when combined with his usually sunny personality, his penchant for mimicry and his compelling life story, meant he was becoming a highly marketable commodity to American sports writers and editors looking for an antidote to Mike Tyson.

Lennox watched several of Riddick's early fights and was convinced he would stop him, just as he had done in the amateurs. Lennox reasoned he was faster on his feet than Bowe, had far more innate athletic ability, sharper reflexes and quicker hands. He felt he had a sharper jab, a harder right cross and a better uppercut. Although Bowe, at that stage, was a little heavier, Lennox was naturally the bigger man and he was sure he was significantly stronger, in mind as well as body, and far more disciplined. He felt the favouritism shown to Bowe proved the bias of the American press and promoters. 'I don't think the American media will ever accept me,' he said with a sigh. 'There's a certain arrogance and ignorance that makes them really patriotic when it comes to Bowe. I've watched him when he looked terrible, yet they never really say anything too bad about him and I just sit there thinking, "Jeez, if that was me they'd be cutting me up left and right."'

Lennox and Riddick took an instant dislike to each other from the day they met as amateurs. Bowe felt Lennox stole his birthright and was a beneficiary of a dubious refereeing decision at a time when there were too many distractions for him to focus; Lennox felt Bowe was a poor loser who lacked the grace to acknowledge a legitimate defeat. John Hornewer recalled Lennox's reaction on seeing Bowe at a world welterweight title fight in Las Vegas in February 1989. 'He was sitting right in front of us at ringside, and he turned around and instead of saying hi, all he said to Lennox was, "They stopped our fight too soon," and Lennox bristled. I can tell you, he really didn't appreciate that.'

Duva's decision to give Bowe first shot at Holyfield exacerbated this dislike, although Lennox was not completely out of the picture – not yet anyway. Duva set up a meeting with Maloney, Newman and Murad Muhammad (Ruddock's promoter) and put together what he called a 'box-off, elimination package'. 'We reached a deal so that everyone would have a box-off,' said Maloney. 'Holyfield against Bowe; Lewis against Ruddock.' At first glance that seemed equitable, but in reality it wasn't. It meant Bowe had an easy ride to a shot at the erratic Holyfield, while Ruddock and Lewis, whose credentials were more solid, would have to fight each other before one of them got his chance.

Bowe's only remaining obstacle was a fight billed as an IBF final eliminator against Coetzer, who had never learned to move his head out of the way of a punch. Yet he made a meal out of it, both before and during the fight. Coming in over-weight, he laboured his way through the rounds, losing a couple along the way, taking too many punches, and resorting to blatant fouling to weaken the South African. The referee was a showman of a minor judge called Mills Lane who liked to be the centre of attention in the ring but sometimes made major mistakes. He warned Bowe a couple of times for low blows but, not for the last time, failed to be appropriately positioned when his attention was required. Late in round seven Bowe buried his fist low in Coetzer's groin with all the force he could muster. As Coetzer bent over in agony Riddick belted his unguarded head with five huge punches. Lane pulled him off, but instead of disqualifying him or giving Coetzer time to recover, he declared Bowe a technical knockout winner, with one second to go in the round. Later, when asked why he kept on pounding the 6ft 3in Coetzer's groin, the 6ft 5in Bowe explained, 'I hit him low because I'd never fought anyone as tall as him.'

Lennox was offered the consolation of an easy warm-up as a last supper before facing the formidable Ruddock. He was put in with the small (205lb) trial horse Mike Dixon in Atlantic City, where he was watched from ringside by Ruddock and his trainer, the former world heavyweight champion Floyd Patterson, as well as by Bowe and Newman. Lennox went through the gears, boxing behind his jab for a couple of rounds, before dropping Dixon with body punches in the third and then stopping him early in the fourth. When asked to predict the result of the forth-coming Lewis–Ruddock fight, Bowe said, 'I'm willing to bet my house on Ruddock. This fight isn't going to go long.'

After this Lennox finally decided to give Roger Levitt the boot. He felt he could manage better without him, particularly since he was making little progress with his job of attracting commercial endorsements. He summoned Roger (and the rest of his staff) to his hotel suite in Atlantic City and informed him his time on the mana-gerial team was up, although he allowed Levitt to save face by claiming he'd resigned because of his court case and family pressures and to claim he would always be around to offer advice. Needless to say, such advice was never sought, but, a bit like Ricky Gervais's fired manager in *The Office*, he kept popping in unin-vited. Eventually Frank Maloney threatened to punch him, and the other team members had to step between them. Later, Eugene Maloney, Lennox's head of security, attacked Levitt after he tried to block a bonus payment. It was only after impassioned pleas from Dennis Lewis that Panos began to ease his former neighbour out of the company, although he hung on, a little further in the background, for another year. 'It's true, Roger certainly tried to stay on as long as he could,' said Lennox. 'But I think part of that desire was that he was having what I might call personal problems at the time.'

Eliadis agreed to pay Ruddock over $2 million to fight at the London Arena in Earl's Court on 31 October 1992 and refused Duva's offer to underwrite the losses in return for the exclusive right to promote Lewis' next three shows, preferring the potential rewards from the existing fifty-fifty deal. These rewards were dependent on victory. 'Our investment in Lennox was gradually going up until we reached a maximum of £1.6 million before the Ruddock fight, and that's when we peaked,' he explained. Having previously played a background role in the boxing side of the business he felt it was time to make his presence felt, starting at a press conference when he reserved seats for his housekeeper and his housekeeper's daughter, both operating as his personal spell-binders. He asked them to cast a bad spell on Ruddock and a good spell on Lennox's gloves. Violet Lewis disapproved and made sure they were banned from her son's changing room.

Shortly before the fight another obscure figure emerged into the sunlight: Lennox's father, Carlton Brooks. After an absence of fifteen years, he popped up again to request ringside tickets to see his son in action. He told Lennox about how much he'd thought of him during their years apart and how he wanted to be part of his life again, but Lennox remembered his mother being hurt by Carlton and wondered why his father took so long to contact him, and whether it had anything to do with his increasing fame and fortune, so there were no warm hugs, home visits or handouts. They went their separate ways.

Ruddock was viewed by the rest of the boxing world as the short straw; the man to avoid at all costs. Throughout the build-up Lewis remained the underdog, for the second time in his short career. As Maloney put it, 'Lennox had only been a professional for three years and had just twenty-one fights, and he was up against the most feared heavyweight in the world who no one else wanted to fight and who had been a professional for ten years.'

When the Jamaican-born, Ontario-raised Ruddock turned professional in 1982 he was a lean, quick-moving, 183lb jab-and-move eighteen-year-old. He gradually grew into the heavyweight division and went unbeaten in ten fights until a mid-bout asthma attack caused his first loss. He returned a year later, significantly bigger and a far more powerful puncher, and worked his way through the ranks with wins over three former champions. The decisive manner of his fourth-round knockout over Michael Dokes, with a hook-uppercut hybrid christened 'Razor's left smash' made the entire division take notice.

Tyson pulled out of a scheduled Ruddock fight, claiming 'pneumonia', but finally relented after losing his title. Razor demanded they both take drug tests but Tyson refused, and after accepting $25,000 from the Tyson camp to waive this demand he went ahead and duked it out, hurting Mike and taking hurt. When Ruddock stormed back after a flash knockdown, Tyson resorted to low blows and head butts before shaking the Canadian in round seven, prompting referee Richard Steele to step in and declare Mike the winner. A clear-eyed Razor uttered a loud and indignant 'What?' and the crowd erupted into a chorus of boos, remembering that Steele had done a similar favour for another King fighter, Julio Cesar Chavez – stopping his world light welterweight title unification fight against an upright Meldrick Taylor with two seconds to go, with Taylor too far ahead on points to lose in any other way and Chavez too far away to land another punch. Perhaps Steele was just an over-cautious referee, but a return was demanded and secured.

This time, when they met at a pre-fight event, Mike gave him his best jailhouse shot: 'I can't wait to kiss those great big lips of yours. I'm gonna make you my girlfriend. Don't you know that you're really a transvestite?' He looked around at his audience and added, for their benefit, 'It doesn't count if he isn't dead. It doesn't count if he isn't dead.' And then back to Ruddock: 'You're dead, you pretty thing, you.' But if Razor was intimidated he didn't show it. He came in too heavy – an enormous 238lb – and lost some of his speed, but none of his determination. Tyson dropped him twice in the early rounds, breaking his jaw, but Razor astonished him by battling back. He wore Mike down, met him punch for punch and became the first man in four years to take him the distance, even though he lost the nod. Tyson described his left smash as 'like the kick of a mule', adding 'no-one else hit me that hard'.

Razor returned to stop another former WBA champion, Greg Page, and followed that by knocking out the unbeaten American contender Phil Jackson. He was already in shape when he arrived at his Puerto Rican training camp and by the time he made it to London he was in the finest condition of his career. He arrived with a twenty-person entourage (all paid for by Lennox's promoters, who spent £40,000 in air fares alone) and with the exaggeration that comes with the passing of twelve years, he reminded Lewis he'd 'whipped' him as an amateur and 'splattered' his blood on the canvas in sparring. At the opening press conference Murad Muhammad came to the microphone and smirked: 'Welcome to the world of big-time boxing, Mr Maloney. Enjoy it. It's going to be a very short time for you.' Then at the pre-fight press conference Ruddock made the same demand he'd made of Tyson – a pre-fight steroids and Aids test. In fact Lennox had already given his blood sample (mandatory under WBC rules), but he was riled by the implication. Ruddock told him to shut up. Lennox responded, 'Come on, why don't you shut me up then?' and Razor leapt to his feet before the minders stepped in. 'I was just trying to intimidate him,' he later explained, 'but I guess it didn't work.'

Lennox also worked longer and harder at his Mount Poconos training camp in Pennsylvania than for any of his previous fights. With Harold Knight beside him he studied videos of Ruddock's fights and noticed some faults. They decided he was one-dimensional, relying too much on his left hook or 'smash'. They also noticed he liked to jab to the body but made the mistake of keeping his right too low, meaning he was open to a right-cross counter. They worked hard on tactics and even harder on strength and fitness. 'He was so sharp that it got to a point where we worried about his weight,' said his conditioner, Courtney Shand. 'In fact he got right down to about 220lb, which was too light at that stage of his career, so we had to ease off the training to get him back up.' He finally weighed in at 227½lb, five lighter than the massive-shouldered Ruddock, but he was two inches taller and, at 84 inches, had a two-inch reach advantage.

Frank Maloney was a nervous wreck, gobbling ice creams and talking non-stop at high speed as he popped in and out of the changing room, while Lennox calmly played chess and draughts and watched television with his camp aides. He paused to reassure Maloney there was no cause to worry, finished his game and then had his usual sleep on the rub-down table. He didn't even wake up when Ruddock's brother stopped by and turned his ghetto blaster to full volume. Maloney then headed off to Ruddock's changing room and found him all gloved up, pounding Floyd Patterson's hands and ready to go. 'No, no,' Frank insisted. 'The rules state that a representative from each camp is permitted to witness the other fighter getting gloved up. I'm Lennox Lewis's representative and I demand you glove him up again so I can be sure it's all within the rules.' Ruddock yelled, protested and swore at Maloney, but in the end Patterson had to glove him up again.

At one a.m. – a time chosen for the comfort of the American HBO television viewers – they were told to go. Pepe got them into a prayer circle, finished with 'in Jesus' name, Amen' and off they went – to party, as Courtney put it. Lennox, wearing his shades, began his slow walk, hearing the satisfying roar of a capacity crowd yelling at full voice 'Lew-wis! Lew-wis! Lew-wis!' As he approached the ring he passed a cheering, smiling group of striking mineworkers, beneficiaries of a Lewis ticket donation, and his extremely anxious mother, who attended all his fights, and his old mentor Arnie Boehm. A minute later Ruddock arrived, trying to look menacing. He stalked past and, like Moriarty, muttered, 'Finally we meet again.' Lewis met his eyes and stared.

Lennox evaded the opening foray, circled clockwise and landed a long, quick jab and a hook. Razor responded by charging but Lewis held his head and they fell on to the bottom rope. He was the first to find his range, landing three jabs in succession while Ruddock missed by a fraction with a monstrous hook. 'I clearly remember feeling the wind from that punch,' Lennox said. He landed his first right cross and Ruddock responded with a long left jab to the body, his head exposed, just as they'd watched in the videos. 'Razor did something he shouldn't have,' he said. 'He didn't realise what he had in front of him because when he jabbed to my body he kept his left hand out there and I just seized the opportunity straight away.' He countered with a long, overhand right, which landed flush on Ruddock's temple. He'd certainly thrown harder punches before, but its accuracy, combined with the momentum of Razor's 232½lb body coming forward, had a decisive effect. His legs did a little involuntary jerk, he wobbled back and then pitched forward, crashing heavily to the canvas. Lennox backpedalled quickly to reach the neutral corner and referee Joe Cortez counted. Razor rose at the count of nine, his legs still wobbly, but by then the bell had ended the round. Sitting on his stool with water being poured on his head, Razor's eyes were glassy. Correa instructed, 'Go out there and knock him out.'

But Lennox knew he shouldn't be rash – that even a hurt Razor was a dangerous man – and he had to avoid a couple more big swings before landing with his own left hook. Ruddock's knees dipped again and he tried to smother the attack but Lewis was punch perfect and another cross dropped him for a second time. He hauled himself up and tried two more desperation hooks but was met by two jabs, a right uppercut and then six short, extremely fast punches to the head and one to the body, ending with a cross that drove Razor face-first to the canvas for the final time. Cortez took a look and waved it off.

This one-sided outcome was unexpected and made a huge impression on the boxing world. Even former cynics like Lou Duva and Mickey Duff pronounced themselves converts. George Foreman, who was covering the event for HBO and who was in the middle of his strange and wonderful comeback, gave a verdict that he would repeat often in the future. Asked whether he would contemplate a fight with Lewis, he replied, 'Are you crazy? That man's dangerous. That man could rip your head off.'

Frank Maloney was beaming for England with tears in his eyes and a lump in his throat. Later that morning he went to find Lennox at an after-fight party held at a West End night club, but left because he wasn't comfortable with what he called 'the heavy smoke and pungent smell'; years later he stated that 'some of the people there and the things they got up to didn't really appeal to me'. Instead he detoured for some heavy drinking at another party at the White House Hotel where hundreds of Lewis supporters congregated. When it was all over he recalled he'd never had a moment's doubt about the outcome. 'Lennox is a unique individual and a unique boxer,' he said. 'I saw it from day one and that's why I was so confident. He has a brain that is probably four or five steps ahead of anyone else's, he has a great survival instinct in him and the most important thing is that he wants to win. You don't go and knock out Razor Ruddock after twenty-one fights unless you're well on your way to becoming one of the greats.'

Panos Eliades had a look of great relief on his face. 'Thank God Lennox actually came through,' he said. 'Had he lost I would have actually lost £1.6 million, but then he who dares win. Now we can start recovering all the money we invested.'

But no one could match Violet for a display of ecstasy. Throughout the fight she seemed to feel every punch, wincing whenever Ruddock missed and clenching her fists whenever Lennox landed. She gave a shout of joy and began bouncing up and down once she'd absorbed the result; then fought her way through the minders, television crew members and officials to climb through the ropes, rush up to her smiling son, grab him around the waist, hug him over and over again and then kiss him, with tears pouring down her cheeks. 'I always believed Lennox would beat Razor,' she said. 'He told me, and I believed him, as I have always believed him. A lot of people thought there would be a problem with this fight, but they didn't have enough trust in him.'

CHAPTER ELEVEN
JOHANNESBURG,
SOUTH AFRICA, 1993

Riddick Bowe certainly looks like a heavyweight champion as he strolls into the concourse of Johannesburg Airport, followed by his tall, lean wife Judy and his short, plump manager Rock Newman. Two weeks earlier 'Big Daddy' weighed in at a thick-waisted 243lb for the maiden defence of his two-thirds of the world title, but now he looks like he's pushing 270lb. There's a fresh roll of fat settling comfortably above his ample hips and a hint of an extra chin, but that's all OK because his current priority is not so much fighting as eating, handshaking, receiving blessings and eating some more.

Their last stop was the Vatican, where they popped in for a quick blessing from the Pope, and now they're off for dinner with Nelson Mandela and a credibility-enhancing tour of Soweto. They requested the trip but officially they're guests of a politics-in-sport outfit called the National Sports Congress, which is linked to Mandela's African National Congress and enjoys tight links with the World Boxing Council. The two organisations are in the midst of a public love-in because the WBC took a firm anti-apartheid stance while its rivals, the IBF and WBA, broke the sporting boycott of South Africa. So, for the time being, in Mandela's emerging 'new' South Africa the WBC is in and the IBF and WBA are under suspicion. Which is all a bit awkward because it was the WBC's championship belt that Riddick dumped in a rubbish bin after the organisation demanded he fight their top contender, Lennox Lewis – an undertaking he'd previously promised to fulfil. Lewis then became WBC champion by default.

Still, now that he's made it all the way from Maryland to London to Rome to Johannesburg, Riddick's hosts are doing their bit to make him feel wanted. It's what they do. Not anything like the show planned for Muhammad Ali in six weeks' time, but politely ingratiating nevertheless. He is, after all, the American who beat that Boer policeman Pierre Coetzer, albeit with low blows. Riddick and Rock, however, do not quite grasp the politics when they arrive on this hot February morning. So when the first questioner demands their reasons for disrespecting this esteemed WBC belt, Riddick launches into a tirade about the iniquities of this disreputable organisation, ending with the promise that he will 'never again wear their belt because the WBC stands for everything we're against'. His hosts respond as they might to an awkward but honoured guest who breaks wind at a dinner party, giving each other sideways glances behind raised hands.

Sensing their embarrassment, Rock cuts Riddick off in mid-flow, throwing in a mention of how much they admired the WBC 'in their efforts to stand up against apartheid'. Bowe, however, fails to appreciate the sensitivities. His second question, on when he intends to fulfil his promise to fight Lewis, produces another sneer: 'If Lewis denounces his WBC title, then we can fight or we can fight for my two titles and he can leave his at home.' He is then asked if he's perhaps a bit scared of the man who stopped him in Seoul. 'I can beat Lennox Lewis as easily as I can beat anyone in my career,' he shouts. 'I don't see that fight going on too long because I can beat him in any department.'

Newman, who had anticipated an effusive welcome, not just a stream of questions about Lewis and the goddamn WBC, is also getting a testy. 'The Lewis camp ain't interested,' he snaps, cutting off Riddick for a second time and prompting a sotto voce question from a Sowetan reporter to a colleague: 'Who's this whitey who tries to talk like a brother and keeps on answering for Bowe?' The colleague replies, 'He's Bowe's manager, and I think he's black.' Newman steams on: 'Last week we made several offers – legitimate offers – to Lennox Lewis, and not chump change either. One was for about ten million dollars and another a winner-take-all deal, but these were refused.' He indicates to his hosts that enough is enough, while Riddick indicates he's hungry again.

'Excuse me, but, Mrs Bowe, um, how will you be preparing the diet of this great man?' she is asked as they stride away.

She looks down and smiles. 'I'm taking him straight to McDonald's.'

Leaving aside for the moment the issue of those offers supposedly turned down by Lennox (whose account was rather different from Newman's – quite the opposite, in fact), the question arises, why did the world heavyweight title get fractured again? The short answer is that Riddick and Rock refused to honour their prior agreement to fight the mandatory contender, preferring to do as they pleased for as long as they pleased. The longer answer is basically the same but involves subsidiary issues of protecting cable television investments, the implications of medium-term risk assessment, negotiating-table brinkmanship and, perhaps, simple, uncomplicated fear.

Lennox was the hottest commodity in world boxing for thirteen days in November 1992. His premier heavyweight rival, Holyfield, had not impressed in his title defences. He outboxed the 43-year-old George Foreman but failed to stop him, pulled off a wobbly win over Bert Cooper, struggled with the 43-year-old Larry Holmes and was considered fortunate to have avoided Mike Tyson. For all his skill and guts he seemed to lack the size and power to compete with big, young men like Lewis, although at least he'd proved his metal against cruiserweights and fat, aged heavyweights. Bowe, on the other hand, had yet to prove anything. He was still the lad who lost to Lewis. These perceptions would change when he met Evander in Las Vegas on 13 November.

Lennox and Frank flew in with the idea of seeing the next opponent in action. Though the bookies' odds narrowly favoured the champion, most pundits were tending towards the challenger's view: 'I'm going to knock out that little man you call the heavyweight champion of the world.' The weigh-in strengthened this perception. The 6ft 5in Riddick came in at an unusually sleek 235lb; the 6ft 2in Evander looked frail in comparison, coming in at 205lb, his lightest-ever weight since moving up from cruiserweight. Unlike most other heavyweights, the harder Holyfield trained the heavier he got, and his weight suggested that either he hadn't worked hard enough or had miscalculated.

Still, when Lennox put on his headphones as an HBO analyst, he predicted Evander would prevail. He went this way for several reasons, some analytical, others merely hopeful. For a start, he doubted Bowe's heart and chin while he had no doubts about Holyfield's. He also despised Riddick as a man while admiring Evander. More to the point, he trusted Holyfield's promises, but not Bowe's. Evander made a written agreement that he would fight Lewis if he won, and Lennox was sure he would keep to it, not least because the champion was determined to hold on to all three title belts. Rock Newman, on the other hand, had already hinted that a victorious Riddick might make a first defence against Foreman in China. And, finally, he knew a Holyfield bout would be easier to put together because the pro- moter Dan Duva had a stake in both of their careers. Either way, however, he felt certain he would soon become undisputed world champion.

What happened in the ring over the ensuing 47 minutes changed all that. It turned out to be one of the finest fights in heavyweight history, twelve extraordi- narily intense rounds that strengthened Holyfield's reputation for bravery and reinvented Bowe as a big man with the commitment and energy to go with his size and talent. This new view would be reassessed in time, but the old image of funny, lazy, gutless Riddick passed that night.

For nine rounds they fought with fervour and skill, Bowe's heavier arsenal giving him a slight edge, and then in the tenth it exploded. Holyfield, who'd been shaken at the end of the round nine, was horribly battered for two minutes. He reeled, he wobbled, he staggered as Bowe slammed back his head with jabs and belted him with crosses and hooks. The referee, Joe Cortez, looked like he might step in but then it was Evander's turn to come on, banging home his own hooks and driving Bowe across the ring. It was a remarkable comeback, later explained in understated but suitably heroic terms: 'He was laying a lot of leather on me,' Holyfield said. 'He hurt me, and he had me going from pillar to post. Yet I felt, "This is the round I have the chance to knock him out." Even though he had me hurt he was expending a lot of energy. I knew he was going to miss one and I was going to have a chance to catch him. I did catch him, but he proved he was a champion by staying in there.' Early in round eleven Holyfield moved into a clinch and Bowe slipped under his arms and landed a right hook behind the head, dropping him. Once again he fought back, but the knockdown sealed the result and Bowe won a unanimous decision.

What followed the announcement of this verdict exacerbated Lennox's dislike of his rival. As the new champion was leaving the ring he spotted Lewis at ringside, pointed at him and said, 'You're next.' Lennox responded with a smile. 'Yeah, bring it on,' he said. But Bowe didn't leave it there. He stepped through the ropes, pushed his face to within an inch of Lewis's and threw out some choice insults. Lennox glared at him and said, 'Why don't you fight me?' Bowe nodded and said, 'I'll fight you,' and Lennox cut back with the threat, 'I'll knock you out.' They were talking about the present, there and then, rather than some time in the future, with gloves on. Maloney, sitting nearby doing commentary for Sky, thought they were about to have a go at each other, and Lennox later admitted that he was serious about his threat and that he was on the verge of flattening Riddick with his ungloved fist because he felt the American had gone too far, but then he spotted Holyfield and realised that the man goading him had just gone twelve of the hardest rounds in recent boxing history and that it wouldn't look good to whack him under the circumstances. Instead he kept Bowe's gaze until the new champion was led away by his minders.

By the time of the post-fight press conference Lewis had been praised by Maloney and the HBO team for keeping control, and decided it was time to go further, by showing magnanimity. He accepted Newman's offer to join them at the top table where he congratulated the new champion. Bowe, however, was a long way from forgetting their spat, or, for that matter, his defeat of four years earlier. 'You're so kind, you big ugly bum,' he sneered back and then he glared at Lewis and said: 'I've got sisters who could whup you.' Lennox decided he could take no more and rose to leave, followed by Frank. As they departed, Bowe yelled, 'Get your great feet south!' And then, as he continued walking, trying to hold a smile, 'I like your pony-tail, Lennox, you big faggot.'

He spat out the word faggot, giving it extra emphasis. For a moment Lennox froze, contemplating his options. 'I came quite close then to just turning around, rushing back to that table and punching him in the face because I knew I could beat him up inside or outside the ring, but then I thought, no, I'll punish him when we meet for the title, and I walked away with dignity.' His friend, Lawrence Lustig, was sitting next to Violet at that press conference and later left with them in the same car. 'I thought Lennox's behaviour was impeccable that night considering what was going through his head,' he said. 'Afterwards, when we were driving back to the hotel, he was still livid. He said, "Can you believe the nerve of that guy, calling me a faggot in front of my mother? Where did he get off calling me that in front of my mother?" He was fuming.'

The incident, incendiary in itself, had an additional spin-off. Within days of Riddick's 'faggot' remark, rumours began to circulate in boxing and press circles that Bowe must have been on to something – in short, that Lennox was gay, or, when they learned of his female lovers, bisexual. The stories spread rapidly through the worldwide web, and included speculation about who might be the special one, ranging from football stars to members of his own entourage. The 'evidence' invariably started with something like this: look, he's a big, handsome world champion, so where's the wife, where are all the babes on the side, where are all the babies? He has women as friends, for God's sake. He still lives with his mum. And why's he always so private about his private life? And what's with that white poodle? 'You know where I think it comes from?' said Lustig. 'He's very gentlemanly, especially the respectful way he treats women. He always gets up when a woman comes in and he always opens the door for his mum. He truly respects her and she's everything to him, and people who are used to other boxers think it's feminine or something, which, if you think about it, is ridiculous.'

Soon tabloid newspapers went trawling, building up files full of gossip in the hope of linking it to something more substantial. On one occasion a Sunday newspaper started digging around after hearing a false rumour that Frank was supplying rent boys to Lennox. When Maloney discovered the paper was taking it seriously he secretly taped the reporter trying to pay his driver to set up a 'sting' along these lines. 'And I've still got that tape as proof of how far they went,' he said. In the end the paper gave up, and beyond asking Lennox things like, 'How did you feel about being called a faggot?' no one dared to take it further, until finally, in 1999, it all came out in the open – the rumours and Lennox's denial. This should have been the end of it, but was in fact a new beginning, because from then on every newspaper, tabloid and broadsheet seemed to feel it was open season on Lennox's sexuality. And the more he denied the allegations, the more they were repeated.

All this had a significant impact on the way Lennox dealt with the press and the public. He became more suspicious of the motives of journalists, more reticent about his private life and more insistent on retaining control over every aspect of his image, which, of course, fuelled the rumours and fresh attempts by Lennox to safeguard his privacy. 'It's important that my life isn't an open book like Mike Tyson's,' he said long after the gay tittle-tattle became public. 'I would hate for people to know everything about my life because I think some of it should be private. Once they start to know you they always try to think of some way to try to get into your life and try to wreck it. My life is mine.' Needless to say, that was not the way the tabloid press viewed it.

Some of his friends, such as Lustig, were happy to fill in the gaps by addressing the question openly. 'When people ask me about his sexuality, I just say, look, I've met his girlfriends. Lennox and I have talked to each other about his relationships, but he always said he wouldn't get married until after he retired from boxing.' Others, however, were more reluctant. Frank Maloney, who frequently had to field questions from journalists too scared to ask Lennox directly, would routinely deflect the question. 'Look, whatever Lennox gets up to outside the ring is his own business,' he'd say. 'I have no interest in what he does in his private life – only what he does in the ring, and it's the same with all my boxers.' When asked where the rumours stemmed from, he replied, 'I honestly don't know how or why, but the first time I heard it was when Bowe called him a faggot.'

This exacerbated Lewis's antipathy towards the boxer who started all this trouble – and for a man from his background, earning his keep with his fists, it made for a lot of trouble. His attitude shifted from contempt towards hate. 'If there was one boxer he really wanted to hurt it was Bowe,' said Hornewer. 'He just didn't like the guy – didn't like him then and even less so later, and he would have hurt Bowe if given the chance.'

Lennox acknowledged his feelings went beyond the competitive urge he felt against other opponents. 'I would say it was a personal vendetta for me at first, and even though I later came to see it mainly in business terms, I would still have taken that fight personally. I basically just wanted to get him in the ring, so my door was always open to him, because I wanted him to make that one mistake of saying yes.

It's the fight I've always wanted, that chance to get at Bowe, because I believe he deserves to be treated for what he did. I mean, I never really insulted him, or only after he'd insulted me, and the way he did it – what he said in front of the cameras – gave me an added edge when it came to the prospect of fighting him. I realised he had a big mouth and I felt, OK, if you've got so much mouth, let's sort it out. I didn't feel the need to speak to him with my mouth. I wanted to speak to him with action. I said to him once, "You have a problem with me, let's get in the ring," but of course he wouldn't because he was all mouth. I don't hate my opponents, and even with Bowe it wasn't a situation where I wished him dead, but I basically had it marked in my mind: "Yeah, you called me a faggot. All right. You'll see." In my mind I was always saying, "Don't worry, redemption will come one day. I'll give you a beating and send you home to your mother."'

The day after the fight Newman gave further cause for resentment by beginning a concerted wriggle to get out of their prior agreement. His only way of escaping was to relinquish the WBC title, and Newman duly began to hint that this was what he had in mind. The way he played it was to launch a justified yet expedient attack on the integrity of the organisation. He said the acronym stood for Will Be Corrupt, spoke of the WBC president, Jose Sulaiman, as a Mexican dictator and drew attention to some of his most nefarious practices, such as routinely favouring Don King and his boxers. All this was fair comment, but it would have been more convincing had he also mentioned a few of the atrocities committed by the WBA and IBF, which were even less credible than the WBC. In reality it was a thin excuse for getting out of a dangerous pickle: the showdown with Bowe's amateur conqueror. Lennox saw it as cowardice dressed up as morality. 'I look into Riddick's eyes and I see fear,' he said. 'I think he will side step me.'

As Newman became more vocal with this convenient line, Maloney hit back through show-and-tell, handing out business cards to the American press with Riddick on one side and a boxer with a chicken's head and the words 'Chicken Bowe' on the other. When Bowe visited London a month after winning the world title Frank hired two actors to dress up in chicken outfits to meet him and hand out the chicken cards. At a subsequent press conference he released a live chicken into the room. Bowe and Newman responded in kind, pre-empting the WBC's decision to strip Riddick of their title by relinquishing it. 'As long as I remain champion I will not be involved with any part of the WBC and today I am withdrawing recognition from them,' said Riddick, who then dumped a replica of the WBC title belt in a rubbish bin (but collected it again, once the photographers departed). 'If Lennox wants that, we can call Lennox the garbage picker,' Newman said. As they left the St James's Court Hotel, he was met by ten clucking men, dressed as chickens.

The WBC accused Bowe of running scared and of dishonouring the belt worn with pride by Ali, Holmes and Tyson by reneging on his prior agreement to fight Lewis. They duly appointed Lewis as their world heavyweight champion. For Lennox, who was on holiday with his mother's family in Port Antonio at the time, it was the worst possible way to become champion. Only once before had this happened, and with embarrassing results. Fifteen years earlier the WBC appointed Ken Norton their heavyweight champion after Leon Spinks decided on a return with Muhammad Ali rather than face certain defeat at Norton's hands. Norton, however, lost his first defence against Holmes, which meant he served four months as champion without ever winning a world title fight. Bowe was still widely recognised as the world heavyweight champion: he was the man who beat the man. Lewis was now in Norton's position. Never mind that he flattened Ruddock and was avoided by Bowe; he was just an appointed champion, awarded the title belt at a function at London's Marriott Hotel, dressed in a penguin suit. Through no fault of his own, Lennox was derided as no more than a title-grasping appointee. He was the boy left without a dance partner, and it was all a bit embarrassing – and infuriating too.

In another, perhaps more important sense, he also found himself without a partner for the first time in over eight years. Lennox and Marcia Miller had been lovers, on and off, since 1984. They had started dating at the end of their final year at high school when the tall, handsome Lennox, the star of the basketball and track teams, a former god of the football field, was bound for the LA Olympics and Marcia, rated by many of the lads as the prettiest girl in the school, was a cheerleader. For most of their first five years together, when Lennox was living in Ontario, they saw each other regularly, but his boxing career, his life in London and his regular training stints in America meant they were more often apart once he turned professional. This caused strains, particularly since Marcia was never very keen on boxing to start with. They broke up, got together again, and he proposed marriage. She accepted, but eventually they ended the engagement.

'Marcia was a very nice person and she was gorgeous looking,' said Lawrence Lustig, 'but they had a very fiery relationship. Part of the problem was all the time apart, but also they came from very different backgrounds. Lennox is very gentlemanly towards women and he treats them extremely well. He reads books, plays chess and so-on but he's not from the same background as her. He's not from the middle class. He's still very working class in terms of where he came from. His mum brought him up in a situation where many kids from his background could have gotten into a lot of trouble, yet he had none of that because of her and because of boxing. But Marcia came from a middle-class, professional background, and it's true that she didn't much like boxing. So they had lots of breaking up and making up. They went out, they broke up, they got together again after splitting up and got engaged, and split up again for good.' Characteristically, Lennox is more reticent than some of his associates when it comes to discussing Marcia, although he still speaks highly of her. 'It was a very serious relationship and it lasted eight years,' he said. 'Unfortunately we split up, but I'm glad to say we remained friends.'

After this he placed all his hopes on the career-defining task of securing a unification bout, but Newman made it clear he would have to wait. Rock picked the drug-ravaged Michael Dokes as Riddick's first challenger. Champions routinely make easy first defences but the choice of Dokes was particularly cynical. Twelve years earlier Dokes had been a quick and dangerous fighter who briefly held the WBA title at a time when Holmes was the real world champion. He got there through a dubious refereeing decision in his fight against Mike Weaver and was fortunate to be awarded a draw in the return before getting blown away by the combination of Gerrie Coetzee's fists and his habit of sniffing thousands of dollars of white powder up his nose every week. He descended into uncontrollable addiction. In the late 1980s, however, he cleaned up and returned to the ring, but an intense give-and-take beating at the hands of Holyfield and a wipe-out defeat against Ruddock sent him back to the coke. His habit cost money, so he fought on with diminishing returns and was thrown in with Bowe, although by then he was old, fat, drug-dependent and inept. He lasted two minutes and nineteen seconds, went home to snort up his purse money and beat his woman into a bloody pulp, after which he headed to jail.

Meanwhile the WBC insisted that Lewis fight their new number one contender, Tony Tucker, who, as usual, just happened to be a Don King fighter. Tucker's story had a similar theme to Dokes's, with a different conclusion. In the late 1980s he was the most naturally talented heavyweight on the horizon. He was 6ft 5in tall yet moved like a smaller man – a quick, skilled boxer with fast hands, a big punch and a great chin, but he smoked, partied and took drugs. For a while he got away with it and stopped Buster Douglas to win the vacant IBF world title before taking on Tyson in a unification bout. He shook Mike early, held on late and was never off his feet, but lost on points. He then discovered his own father had been absorbing his purse money, after which his little drugs habit became a big one. But then, like so many American heavyweights, he found salvation in God, and, unlike Dokes, cleaned up and became completely dedicated for the first time in his career. He began to knock off decent contenders along with bums, and with King behind him moved through the rankings. By the time he secured the Lewis gig he'd won fourteen at a trot and his record showed just one defeat – to the peak-form Tyson – in 50 fights. At the age of 34 he'd reached his peak – not as quick as in his youth, but more experienced, wilier, harder, bigger, stronger and cleaner. He had never been dropped or cut and had a 76 per cent knockout ratio, his right cross the main culprit. Lennox, in contrast, had major problems for this fight: his own right hand and the insatiable attentions of Mr King.

Tyson's imprisonment meant King was at a loose end within boxing's premier division. He had some good big men, including Tucker, but he really wanted a youthful star with huge pay-per-view potential and the ability to reunify the title and he chose Lewis. He remembered Lennox kept clear of him back in 1988, but that was never enough to discourage King. These boxers always said no-no-no, but in the end he persuaded them they really meant yes please Mr King. It worked with Ali, Holmes, Tyson, so what made Lennox Lewis so different? Talk the street talk to them, show them bags of crisp notes, offer them girls and cars, paint a big, glorious picture, tell them they are being undervalued and underpaid by whitey and that they could only trust a brother like him, inform them that no one cometh to the title but via Don. Whatever it takes.

His first strategy was to get to Lewis through Maloney, so he decided to recruit Frank to his cause. He thought it would be easy enough – he'd just wave a few dollar bills at the little Irish-cockney barrow boy and he was sure to bite. Don phoned him, calling him 'my little man'. He informed Frank that they both came from the same repressed minority background – 'I'm black; you're Irish' – spoke about the nineteenth-century potato famine and offered to make him 'the biggest name in boxing Britain has ever seen', ending with the question: 'How does a million dollars sound to you?' Maloney politely told him that he was spoken for, and informed Lennox and Dan Duva of the call.

Don's next play was to separate Lennox from Frank. To do this he felt he needed time to woo the boxer and he also needed to make a grand impression. He therefore refused to cut a deal with Main Events and made sure the Lewis–Tucker fight went to purse bids. When the envelopes were opened everyone was shocked: King's bid was for $12 million, meaning that Lennox would be paid $9 million for his first title defence, to be held in Las Vegas on 8 May 1993. One reason for the size of this bid was that Don needed to make sure he won, so that he could get access to Lennox; another was to illustrate that he could pay more than Eliades or Duva. Despite being beaten in the bidding war, Maloney and Hornewer were delighted, although, knowing King's past record, they insisted the money be guaranteed by a letter of credit and paid in a single lump sum. Lewis was less sanguine because he wanted to make his first title defence in London.

King went all out to seduce his quarry, flying him out on Concorde to do an advertising spot and trying to sweet-talk him while launching a tirade against Maloney at their first pre-fight press conference. The response of the Lewis camp was to do the contractual minimum when it came to selling the fight, which infuriated King, who eventually lost almost $4 million on the promotion. Once they arrived in Las Vegas he really got to work, taking every opportunity to compliment Lennox while doing his utmost to undermine Maloney, describing him as an underqualified little man doing a big man's job. 'Maloney's a mental midget, a little weasel, a treacherous snake in the grass,' he said. 'When I am near him I feel like a porcupine because of all the arrows in my back.' Frank smiled and thanked him for making his name. He later took to carrying around a Don King doll, in gratitude for the American promoter's role in making his name.

Don became desperate. He even approached Frank's mother and asked, 'How can such a beautiful woman have such a horrible son?' In a final move, he copied a four-page letter addressed to 'Lennox, Family and Genuine Friends' entitled 'The Indiscretions of Frank Maloney. Vicious, Stupid or Both', which was pushed under the doors of the media and the Lewis camp. Its tone was to praise Lewis and defame Maloney. 'Lennox, you are a potentially awesome heavyweight boxer,' it said. 'But you are being held back by this mental midget, this pugilistic pygmy, named Frank Maloney. You can't fly a multi-million-dollar airplane properly when you are being guided by a ten-cent control tower.'

But when it came to King, Lennox was never easily impressed. He remembered Arnie Boehm's warnings, and he also knew from Hornewer and Maloney that Don's word was not always his bond. Several past King-promoted boxers complained of being exploited. One of them, the former WBA heavyweight champion Tim

Witherspoon, successfully sued Don for a million dollars. Lennox was certainly intrigued by King, fascinated even, and he sometimes enjoyed his verbal rambles and found his malapropisms funny, but he also felt he knew the score. He insisted he never meet King without a third person present and moved out of his hotel. He even made sure he never drank anything other than his own, British-bottled water. 'In the world of boxing there's people that are despicable and people that you never want to deal with, but, sometimes, you have no option but to deal with them,' he said. 'I realised that in this game you're going to be used and abused all the time, but my thing was to keep it to a low level and that means not signing no blank contracts that Don King puts in front of my face.'

But his problems went beyond being the object of an aggressive seduction campaign. First there was a minor setback at their training camp at Hilton Head Island in South Carolina when Tony Tubbs, the former WBA champion chosen as Lennox's chief sparring partner, failed to turn up one day and was found in a part of town where the drug dealers did business, after which he was fired. Then, a week into his six-week camp, Lennox injured his hand during sparring. When the pain grew more intense they had to break camp to fly to New York, where a specialist X-rayed the hand and informed him he'd split the extender tendon in the top knuckle of his little finger and it would require an operation to repair. Lennox knew he stood to lose $9 million if he asked for a postponement and would also have to endure a longer spell as a champion who'd never had a title fight. The specialist conceded he could go ahead with the fight provided he didn't use his injured hand in training. He was banned from hitting the heavy bag, had to cut down on sparring and was under strict instructions never to throw a right, and at night he had to keep his hand in a bucket of iced water, affecting his sleep. He also had to walk around town with his severely swollen right hand in his pocket in a vain attempt to prevent the press and his rival's camp from discovering his injury. He was not in impeccable condition, he knew he hadn't put in enough sparring rounds and he wasn't sure whether he would even be able to use his right, but he felt he could beat Tucker one-handed.

A week before the fight King gave up, for the time being, on his plan to poach Lewis and instead turned his resentful attentions to Tucker, showing him a shiny black Mercedes 500 SL car and telling him: 'You knock this motherfucker out and the Benz is yours.' He turned the fight into America versus Britain, and encouraged Tucker to undermine the novice champion's confidence, with rehearsed quips like 'Lennox, you will fall down like London Bridge'. Lewis, who'd been out of the ring for six months, weighed 235lb – seven and a half more than against Ruddock. Tucker also weighed 235 – twenty lighter than he'd been three years earlier, which wasn't surprising considering he'd put in over five months of continuous high-intensity training.

Lewis' performance was an uneven mix of boxing brilliance and power, vulnerability and inexperience. In the early rounds he showed easy flowing movement as he danced around Tucker, spearing him with long jabs. Now and then he would throw testy rights, but nothing serious. Tucker's corner knew about the hand injury and saw that Lennox was being tentative. 'He's got no right hand, he's got no right hand,' said Tony's notorious trainer Panama Lewis (who'd once been jailed for removing the stuffing from his boxer's gloves, causing serious damage to an opponent). Lennox stepped it up in round three, increasing the power of his jab and then whipping over his first heavy right cross to drop the American for the first time in his professional career. 'If that was Bowe, he would have been out,' Lennox said. 'But Tucker has a great chin.' To Lennox's surprise, Tony rose at the count of two and stood for the eight count. Lewis battered him for the final half minute, finishing the round with another big right cross to the point of the jaw.

Over the next two rounds the benefits of Correa's free-flowing methods were apparent. Lennox was using his sharp reflexes to slip and ride punches and he was working the body as well as the head, but his previous success meant that he had overcompensated for his prior caution by going right-hand crazy and he was starting to tire, fighting with his mouth open. 'Actually, I got a cramp in the fifth round,' Lennox said, 'and I had to work it out before I could go back to throwing combinations.'

Tucker was learning how to read the rights and counter them. Cheered on by an ebullient King, he was slowly working his way into the fight, but late in round eight Lennox struck again, shaking him with an uppercut and then wobbling him with a right cross. The bell curtailed this assault, but twenty seconds into round nine Lennox caught Tucker with another cross and down he went again – and once again he was up at the count of two. Lennox had time to finish him and threw everything into his onslaught, loading up on his hooks, winging away for 45 seconds until he became arm weary. 'I thought I had him going, but he just comes back,' he recalled. 'I realised I'd hurt him and thought if I just catch him with one more hard punch he'll go, but they kept on bouncing off him and it was harder than I thought. He showed a lot of guts and was in pretty good shape.'

With Lewis tiring, Tucker slipped the jab, stepped inside and landed his honey punch, a short, heavy right cross that landed flush on the chin. Lennox absorbed it without going down but his world seemed to stop for a couple of seconds, long enough for Tony to land three more hard rights to his jaw and face and several hooks and jabs. But just when it seemed Lennox was in peril, he fought back. 'He might have been shocked by getting hit like that,' said Maloney. 'Most people don't like getting hit. Some people criticise him by saying he can't take a punch, and then when he gets hit hard and shows he can take a punch they criticise him for taking it. And after that his boxing was masterful.'

Correa told him to stay outside and jab his way to victory, which is what he did for the final three rounds, enduring a few boos along the way but emerging to yells of praise from his army of travelling fans with a wide unanimous decision (118–111, 117–111 and 116–112). Tucker praised Lewis as 'a good fighter and a better man'. Lennox admitted, 'I wasn't satisfied. I can always do better,' before announcing, 'I did it for Mother's Day,' and then turning to Violet and saying, 'Happy birthday, mother.'

Two weeks later Bowe made his second defence in Newman's hometown of Washington, D.C. His original opponent was the 1988 Olympic heavyweight gold medallist Ray Mercer, but he blew it in a warm-up fight against a plodder called Jesse Ferguson, who had lost eight of his previous twelve. When Ray realised he was losing he whispered in a clinch that he'd pay Jesse if he took a dive. He was later tried for offering a bribe but acquitted after his plea was accepted that this was no more than fight tactics. The 36-year-old Jesse stepped in and was knocked out seventeen seconds into the second round. No one had treated the title with such contempt for more than twenty years, not since Joe Frazier avoided giving Muhammad Ali a return shot at the crown and instead defended it against a pair of no-hopers outside the world's top 50. And, as with Joe, the effect on Riddick of this kind of complacency was seen in the spread of his waistline.

Lewis's people had done their utmost to secure a fight against Bowe since the day after Riddick's title-winning triumph. Lennox made it clear this was the fight he wanted and was prepared to make financial compromises to secure it. Despite the fact that he beat Bowe in the Olympics his managers said they would agree to Riddick receiving three-quarters of the purse money. HBO made it known that there was potentially $32 million in the pot, and the Lewis camp was willing to accept $8 million (25 per cent). However, it soon became apparent that Newman was reluctant to enter serious horse-trading. 'The way they were negotiating made it clear to me that they felt they had to take as much security as possible,' said Maloney, 'and that was why they wanted to take all the money at once. At one point they wanted ninety per cent, and ten per cent for us. I got the feeling that Rock never really wanted the fight when Bowe was champion.'

Despite Newman's claim that his offers were realistic, the details support a different conclusion. His first proposal was less than 10 per cent ($3 million) for Lennox, although he later raised that to a package that amounted to $5 million. Lennox was willing to accept it (and said he was even prepared to take $3 million), but Maloney was strongly opposed. The $5 million offer was, after all, $4 million less than he was to receive for the lower risk Tucker fight. Another proposal was that Lewis relinquish his WBC title and take $2 million to fight on a Bowe under-card, with the offer of giving Lennox a shot at the title for $9 million on an unspecified date. But Maloney was not prepared to take him at his word about a vague future date and felt uncomfortable about abandoning the WBC. 'It's a matter of principle,' he said. 'We made a commitment to the WBC, they backed us, and we have to honour that agreement.' Newman then offered a winner-take-most fight with both boxers receiving $5 million each and the winner getting the rest of the kitty. Lewis liked this idea and Maloney sent Rock Newman a fax agreeing without any qualifications. However, no more was heard from Rock, and the Lewis camp came to the conclusion that Bowe's people were playing games. They felt they were wasting their time and needed to look at alternatives.

So why was the Bowe camp so reluctant to entertain Lennox Lewis? Shortly before his death, Eddie Futch said he'd wanted the fight but Newman blocked it. 'I thought it was an ideal match for Riddick. That match should have been made in Riddick's time.' However, Emmanuel Stewart cast doubt on the old man's retrospective confidence: 'I once spoke to Eddie about this and he told me he didn't want Bowe to fight Lennox because he knew Bowe could never beat him – that Lennox had too much mental strength and physical strength for Riddick. I'm convinced that is why the fight never happened.'

When still managing Lewis, Maloney insisted fear was the prime deterrent. 'No matter what excuse you want to use, Bowe was frightened to box Lewis,' he said then. Now that they have parted he is less certain. 'I don't know if they were scared. I just got a sense they didn't want to play because they wanted all the money.' Hornewer explained it in terms of cold risk assessment: 'I don't think they were scared but it made sense for them to avoid the fight at that stage. If you were them, would you have risked it against Lewis when your boxer was world champion?' This view is supported by the fact that in August 1993 the unpredictable Newman phoned Eliades with his first realistic purse offer ($11 million for Lewis; $22 million for Bowe) for a unification bout in November. However, by then the Lewis camp had formally agreed to fight Frank Bruno on 2 October and the details had already been announced. Dan Duva, Lennox's American promoter, refused to consider backing out of the Bruno deal to accommodate a loose verbal offer from Newman.

Hornewer and Maloney believe the Bowe camp's early display of caution went beyond Newman's recalcitrance and involved the hidden hand of HBO. 'The fight could realistically have been made after Lennox beat Ruddock,' said Hornewer, 'but Bowe chose the right course for him, and avoided it, and HBO protected him. He was their guy. They were from New York and so was Riddick, and he was with Eddie Futch, which made for a great story. Lewis just wasn't their guy and they wanted Bowe to have some easy options first.' Maloney said this attitude from HBO's boss Seth Abraham was seldom overt but was part of an undercurrent that became clear over time. 'I always got the sense that HBO wanted Lewis beaten. We had to negotiate twice as hard as anyone else when we were negotiating with HBO, and when they felt that it was one of their favourites – and they did have a love affair with Bowe for a while – they would try and protect him and I think that's what they tried then. If they felt a hundred per cent sure Riddick would have beaten Lennox they would have made negotiations a bit easier. Lennox didn't give himself to the press and cooperate in the way they wanted and there was always this thing that he wasn't an American, and the Americans hated not having the world championship. They thought they had a divine right to have the world heavyweight champion and they couldn't understand how an Englishman could own the world title.'

For HBO the choice between the rivals was less about simple patriotism than three essential marketing ingredients: narrative, image and potential. Boxing is sold on story lines, and Bowe's was a simpler tale to tell. For all his chiselled features, natural athleticism and smarts, Lennox's story seemed too complex and cerebral for the casual punter to embrace – incomplete, ambiguous, with an over-abundance of tricky subplots; more satisfying in the longer term, perhaps, but as yet devoid of easy soundbites. There were flags and anthems, but too many of them, and they seemed to exist only out of convenience; riches but no real rags, and his roots didn't show. Not only was Lennox a non-American – a substantial drawback, especially as he was the kind of foreigner who showed a maddening reluctance to do

America's bidding – he was also devoid of any clear national identity. An Englishman, yes, but also a Canadian and a Jamaican too, and yet, really, none of those. The tale of the London lad left to fend for himself before reuniting with his West Indian mum in Ontario and proving his worth on the playing field and ultimately in the ring, over and over again, for Canada, for England and for Mum but mainly for himself, might have been a good one for Freudian analysts but it was hardly the stuff of ring legend. That would come much later, when new bits were added that were easier to grasp: justice, vindication, vengeance.

Bowe lacked Lennox's looks and intellect but came with a tale that was easier to digest; a satisfying story with a beginning, a middle and, if played right, a scripted end. Tyson's story was cautionary and depressingly unAmerican. Bowe's, in stark relief, was pure Horatio Alger. The narrative invariably started with the observation that both men come from the same part of the Brownsville ghetto and both had ended up as champions. But there the similarity ended, because with every fresh account of assault, wife beating and rape, the Tyson story fitted the cliché 'you can take the lad out of the ghetto but …'. It was devoid of redemption, saying that bleak conditions breed bleak boys whereas Bowe's was the antidote: goodness comes from good hearts and good mums and no matter how horrible your start – single mother with huge family in slumsville, surrounded by guns, drugs and violence, with brothers and sisters falling – you can pull yourself up by your Nike laces if you can find the character inside you. Riddick, the smiley ghetto kid with a gift for impersonation, refused to let the extremes of adversity get to him. To keep out of harm's way he took to the ring and fought his way to the Olympics. This being Horatio Alger, it required obstacles to test the hero and entice the reader, and they were piled on, one after the other: his sister's murder, his brother's Aids revelation, his loss to Lennox and his rejection by the professional establishment. It was a time of doubt, when guidance was needed. Enter Rock, the fervently loyal big brother who fights Riddick's corner with impassioned intensity, and Papa Smurf, the wise, calm grandfather who gently corrects the mistakes, showing the lad the wisdom of the past to allow him to become the force of the future. And so Riddick arrived, still smiling, but now, finally, a man fit to rule his world.

The reality was quite different, which meant there would be no salutary ending. For all his charm and talent, Bowe would emerge as a failure, and often a nasty one at that. Inside the ring he was a dirty fighter who avoided his best rival. Instead he and his rapacious manager were in the process of discrediting the title, taking on some of the worst challengers in recent history. Outside the ring it was worse: at first just minor sins such as gluttony, bullying, indiscipline and poor judgement, but in time, assault, wife beating, kidnapping and jail would be added to his ledger. In Tyson's case the fall was scripted; there were no surprises. In Bowe's case there was real disappointment. In 1993, however, you could still close off the doubt – like the foul fighting in the ring and the overeating outside it – and stick to the easy line, rather than the more difficult one lived by Lewis. The difficult one had the potential to ruin the easy one, and for HBO that made no sense at all.

When Lennox realised his American television backer was favouring the enemy he began to resent their role. 'He really hated that HBO chose Bowe and that this worked to his own detriment,' Hornewer confirmed. It also strengthened his sense that America and Americans were against him, and his resolve to stick their words, their judgements and their hopes down their throats. 'It's difficult for me because my mission has been sideswiped by the politics of the sport, which has devalued the sport,' he said in 1993. 'I think the only thing for me to do is keep winning and show them everything they think is wrong. I'm making the Americans take me seriously with every heavyweight I beat from America. That's part of my motivation: socking it to Bowe, socking it to Rock Newman, socking it to the Americans by proving that I'm the best out there. They have to wake up.'

So what would have happened had HBO put the squeeze on by getting the rivals to meet when they were both champions? Bowe's supporters argue he was a more complete boxer at that stage. He'd had 34 fights by the time he beat Ferguson to Lennox's 23. He was tutored by one of the best men in the business whereas Lennox's teaching came from the less experienced Davenport and the self-promoting Correa. And while Lennox was a slow burner who matured late, Bowe was a meteor who peaked at 25 in his first fight with Holyfield. In that fight he was outstanding, beating Evander on the inside as well as at range and showing the fortitude to suck it up when hurt and tired. Shortly before his death, Futch gave his final testament on this question. 'They were both about the same height and both were good boxers,' he said, 'but Riddick could fight on the inside whereas Lewis didn't do anything inside. He would tie you up. I think Riddick could have beaten him.'

Lennox and his camp were adamant in 1993 that Lennox could do a job on Bowe. Over a decade later they haven't changed their view, arguing that even at that early stage Lennox was quicker than Bowe, with more athletic ability and better reflexes, and was far stronger. He also had the psychological advantage of knowing that he could beat Bowe. In 1993, Emmanuel Steward, who was training some of Lewis' rivals, felt certain that Lennox would stop his rival if they fought. He still feels he was correct, even though Lennox has since shown huge improvement under his tutelage. 'Bowe would not have coped with that intensity,' he said. 'I don't care what they say about Bowe's ability back then. Lennox would have broken him whenever they fought, just like he did in the amateurs. Riddick was afraid of Lennox because of what happened in the Olympics. I watched the way Lennox stopped Bowe then and I know that Bowe never forgot that strength.'

In 1993 Frank Maloney felt Bowe would have had no chance against Lewis. 'I have no doubt that Lennox would knock out Bowe easier than he would knock out Holyfield,' he said then. 'You would have heard the word "Timber!" and Bowe would have fallen on that big fat backside of his.' Eleven years later, and no longer a fan, he still feels he got it right. 'Do I think he would have beaten Bowe? I'm not going to change my mind now. I can't turn around and say no after all these years I've said he would beat Bowe. It would have been a war, but I think Lewis may have had just that mental edge over Bowe because of beating him in the Olympics. So, yeah, Lennox would have beaten Bowe back then.'

CHAPTER TWELVE
OLD KENT ROAD, LONDON, 2004

Eugene Maloney sits back in the soft chair in his little office at the back of his famous old gym, now and then turning to watch through the window as his boxers go through their paces. He's a player now, Eugene. Not a major player, but then again not just Frank's bigger, tougher, younger brother either. He promotes his own shows, manages his own boxers and trains the lads. At the moment his brightest hope is a former Thai boxer called Matt Skelton who is now the British heavyweight champion.

It's quite a good life actually. Better than doing the bidding for other players when half the time you'd prefer to kick their heads in. And a lot better than alternating between prison cells and the professional boxing ring. He's in his late forties now and feels he can sit back and enjoy himself. Of course, if the need arises he can still kick arse with the best of them, but his waist has spread a bit because after so long staying fit he no longer feels compelled to get in his morning run. He leaves that to the lads.

Back in the old days, Eugene did a lot of running, one way or another. He had barely reached his teens when he started nicking cars and driving them down the high street, inviting the local girls to jump in for a ride. He was always in trouble, always going down and getting up again, always fighting. He boxed at bantamweight as a professional, a hard and dirty crowd-pleaser who won more than he lost, but he was never going to be champion and his career was interrupted by his problems with the law. He was more formidable on the streets, where he learned early how to make the best use of his head, knees, elbows and the rest. If there was a spot of bother, you could count on Eugene to sort it out. On the other hand, sometimes he'd make spots of bother – just the kind of fellow you wanted if, say, a celebrity needed minding because usually one look at Eugene with his broken boxer's nose, scar-tissue eyes and the attitude packed into his walk and his talk and you were liable to forget he was under 5ft 6in tall. His other key attribute in the minding business was that his older brother, Frank, was always looking out for him. So when Lennox needed a bodyguard/driver/minder/fixer, Eugene got the job, which was soon formalised into the post of head of security – a position he held for five years.

Today, a decade after his up-yours departure from Lennox's life, sitting back in his own 'Fight Factory' gym with this manager and that one (and his older brother too) popping in with offers and proposals, he looks back on those days with a mixture of fondness and distaste. Fondness for most of the time he spent with Lennox; distaste for the personal disagreement that prompted his sudden resignation. But more of that later. Between 1989 and 1994 Eugene Maloney relished his position as Lennox Lewis's shadow.

The two of them made an odd couple – tall, gentlemanly, black, cosmopolitan Lennox and, a foot below, white, East End Eugene whose usual banter and opinions were even further from what might be considered politically correct than Frank's – but despite these differences, or perhaps because of them, they liked each other. Frank used to drink with Lennox occasionally and tease him, and get teased, but because of his managerial role he never got quite as close to his boxer as Eugene. 'I got on very, very well with Lennox until late August 1994,' Eugene says. 'Up until then it was perfect. We used to hang out together all the time, especially after fights when I used to take him to nightclubs, to the pictures, take him to pick up his girlfriends, take him everywhere. I used to spend time in his house in Hadleywood when he didn't want to go out, and instead we'd play pool or chess or whatever. He used to phone me at two o'clock in the morning sometimes to ask me to come round to his house and play pool, and I'd always go.'

After one of these pool games, with the competitive Lennox up by £300, he told Eugene to take a break by going off to buy them some fish and chips. While waiting for his order, Eugene bumped into his sometime connection the former world snooker champion Alex Higgins and invited him to the house. Lennox, who did not follow British snooker, failed to recognise Higgins and allowed him into the game, and within minutes Alex had won back Eugene's money for him. He was about to make Eugene a profit when Dennis entered and inadvertently gave the game away, which prompted the heavyweight to chase the former bantamweight around the table until they all collapsed with laughter.

Once they entered training camp his job changed. The boxer became more focused and the bodyguard had to respond accordingly. 'I used to spend six weeks in camp with him, getting up early every morning to go with him and Harold Knight for his roadwork, because I used to love running. I was a long-distance and cross-country runner from when I was a small kid, and Lennox was a good runner too. No matter what he was doing, running, playing chess, ping-pong, he always wanted to win, but if you asked him honestly, face to face, he'll tell you I'm the only person he couldn't out-run. And then I'd go to the gym with him twice a day, drive him everywhere he wanted to go and make sure everything was done for him, and then he was OK.' Doing everything for him also involved protecting Lennox from over-exuberant fans and keeping the groupies away – often young women who would pull everything they could think of to find their way into his hotel room. It also meant looking after Violet when the need arose. And occasionally these jobs required more than just hard words and looks.

One of his more vivid memories goes back to their final months together in 1994 when Donna Summer was playing at the hotel where they were staying. Violet, who was part of their camp, wanted to see the show so Eugene arranged to meet her at reception, together with Harold. 'When she got out the car she was really upset and crying. I asked Harold what was the matter and he said that when they came through the barrier at the security gates and showed the security guards Violet's hotel ID, a big white guy – an ex-cop with a big moustache – was extremely rude to her. What this guard said was very, very personal and extremely insulting, and Mrs Lewis was very upset. I actually thought Harold should have got out of the car and bashed him up there and then, and not let Mrs Lewis get upset and crying about it. I mean, sure Harold's a laid-back guy, but how laid back are you, you know? When do you get stirred? Everybody's got a stirring moment, don't they?'

Eugene's stirring moments arrive quickly, and having seen Violet's state he was close to reaching his, so he got Harold to take him to security and show him the culprit. 'I called this guard over and said, "Listen, you made a terrible mistake," and when he didn't remember I repeated word for word what he'd said to Violet. He just said, "Oh, yeah," so I asked if he knew who Lennox Lewis was. "Yeah, he's the champ staying here." I said, "Yeah, and that woman is his mother and if you don't come down and apologise Lennox will come down and break every bone in your body. But it's my job not to tell him, so you got two options: you come down with me and apologise or I'm going to break your bones rather than worry Lennox." Now, I'm not a big guy, so he started laughing. I then took my jacket off and proceeded to bash him up, and then took him down to the hotel with Harold and met Mrs Lewis there. By then the owners had come down because they had heard there was fighting going on at the gates, so I explained the situation and they were going to sack the guy, but I said no, if he apologises that will be good enough, so he apologised.' He laughs about it now and remembers it as just one of those things you occasionally have to do when you're head of security for a celebrity. 'Except that time was heavy duty because that guy I bashed up had a gun on him and a cosh, so it could have been the end of me.'

The relationship between Lennox and his security chief began to deteriorate soon after that and came to an abrupt end after an acrimonious personal dispute in September 1994, a few hours before Lennox defended his title against Oliver McCall. Two days later Eugene went to Panos Eliades's office to collect the £30,000 he claimed was still owed to him. Panos spoke to him using the generic pet name used for all his employees: 'Bobsy, the champ doesn't want to pay you because you jumped ship an hour before take-off.'

'Bobsy, I was in camp for months,' Eugene countered, 'and I only left an hour before the fight when I had no more work to do, and let me tell you nobody would have stood for what was going on.'

'Well, I can't pay you,' said Eliades.

'OK, keep it, stick it up your arse,' said Eugene.

Today, he shrugs his shoulders over that loss. 'I just walked out of his office and I haven't seen Lennox or Panos since. I don't feel nothing, to be honest. He's done what he's done. I was very loyal to him and I never let him down once.'

Eugene lives a different life now, less on the edge and more his own boss. He hasn't seen his old employer for ten years and feigns indifference about his fate, but when he gets chatting about 'those days' he can't help smiling. 'Yeah, I liked working with him. He was like a big kid, and I have to say, I really enjoyed the job, especially in the early days. In fact right up to about a month before the end it was perfect. He was nice, but unfortunately, like most things, as time went on the bigger he got the more he changed.'

Lennox went to New York for an operation to repair the tendon damage to the knuckle on his right hand, and then returned to spend some time in the Hadleywood mansion he shared with Dennis and Violet. By then his team had decided on two tasty title defences. The first was the showdown with Frank Bruno in Cardiff on 2 October 1993; the second was a big-money defence against the popular American Tommy Morrison. They decided to get Bruno out of the way first because Lewis saw the fight as essential in consolidating his British image. It was vital to him that he was universally recognised as the top big man at home as well as abroad, and this meant months of turbulent negotiations with Bruno's promoter, Mickey Duff, who pressed hard for the bout to be switched from Cardiff to Frank's home turf at Wembley, until Lennox took the phone from Panos and gave Mickey a rendition of the American freedom song 'We shall not be moved'.

His desire to see off Bruno was not so much about the money. Lennox accepted £3 million ($4.5 million) – half what he received against Tucker – while Frank's purse was £1 million. It related to identity – not just of British heavyweight boxing but of black Britain more generally. He saw Bruno as a figure of the past, a figure of fun, a minstrel whose image lacked gravitas, a man who sent himself up by playing the fool. Whenever he imitated his rival's stock-in-trade soundbites he made no attempt to hide his disdain.

Frank was targeted by the neo-Nazi group Combat 18 because of his marriage to a white woman, but his public support extended to home counties housewives, old-age pensioners and public schoolboys who loved his buffoonish 'know what I mean, 'Arry' persona. He played stupider than he was; or, put differently, the man who talked sagely about boxing as 'showbiz with blood' was more astute than the image he cultivated, which did not impress Lewis, for whom the idea of black pride meant, among other things, behaving with dignity. He viewed Bruno as a black celebrity who had 'sold out'. He was, Lennox felt, an archetype of the lickspittle Uncle Tom that his heroes like Malcolm X and Muhammad Ali used to ridicule. He felt Bruno abrogated his potential as a black role model and allowed himself to be used to the detriment of black Britons. He would wince while watching Frank hamming it up with Harry Carpenter, saying it reminded him of black American actors from the 1950s, forever playing cringing servants.

Bruno's politics strengthened this feeling. His decision to break the anti-apartheid sporting boycott, his declaration of adoration for Margaret Thatcher, his offer to stand for the Conservative Party and his 'threat' to leave Britain if the Labour Party ever came to power did not endear him to Lennox. 'This stand is kind of unusual for a man who really stayed out of politics,' he said. 'I mean, the Tory party hasn't had the best history on issues of race, has it? Just look at their history. And each one of their leaders seems to have indiscretions that the public becomes aware of, which is why they're losing support. So that's unusual for him to get involved with politics, very unusual, because if you ask him about any political incident – say, people getting beaten up in a street protest – his only comment will be [and here he imitates Bruno to perfection], "Oh, no, no, I don't want to get involved." He doesn't have a stand on anything. To draw the correlation between me and Frank Bruno, I stand up for what I believe in and I don't give in to something that I'm not. Or rather, that's the difference between me and him. He will come up and shake my hand and behind my back it's "I hate that guy" and this and that. He might as well say he hates me in front of my face because I'm into that kind of realism.'

On top of this there was the boxing. Lennox felt Bruno reinforced the American view that the only British heavyweights were those of the horizontal persuasion. He found it demeaning to the essence of his profession that, as he put it, 'Bruno's a national hero for being a loser'. Every time Frank was thrown in with a top American he fought his big heart out before being battered to brave and noble defeat, after which he would dust himself off and try again, beating up lesser men until he next tangled with a champion.

Looking at the contrast between Bruno and Lewis, you might think they emerged from very different environments. In fact they came from pretty much the same place. Both grew up in working-class areas of London and had parents who emigrated from Jamaica. Both had caring mums who worked as nurses. Both had dads who, for different reasons, did not or could not play a major role (Frank's belt-wielding father, who died when he turned fourteen, was bedridden with diabetes and later suffered a stroke). Both were expelled from school (Frank in secondary school, for punching a teacher). And, like Lennox, Frank was sent to a boarding school for miscreants, where he continued to fight. But their histories parted after that. Bruno, a self-acknowledged 'bully and bad boy', left school without qualification at sixteen and worked at a succession of menial jobs. Like so many young men with a penchant for violence he turned to boxing. Unlike Lennox, whose life had several sporting, cultural and intellectual hinterlands, Frank's options were limited, and it is tempting to see parallels between his life inside and outside the ring: great determination, strength and resilience along with hidden vulnerability and a propensity to short-circuit. His one outlet was family life with his harder, emotionally stronger wife Laura, whose opening move was to pinch his bum at an ice-skating rink.

After proving himself Britain's top amateur heavyweight, Frank came to believe he was on his way to winning the world heavyweight title as a professional, pinning a note to the wall in 1981: 'Frank Bruno, Heavyweight Champion of the World 1986.' Managed by Terry Lawless, trained by Terry Francis and promoted by Mickey Duff and Jarvis Astaire, he turned professional in 1982 and began knocking them over.

If his movement was a bit robotic, he made up for it in strength and power. But in fight number nineteen his primary weakness was revealed. He took on a heavy-handed American, Jumbo Cummings, and got whacked. For several seconds he hovered but instead of going down his legs and arms stiffened. On that occasion he was saved by the bell and went on to win, but three fights later against the slow but huge-hitting future WBA champion James 'Bonecrusher' Smith he was caught by a left hook in the final round when way ahead and once again his body froze. This time there was no bell. Smith teed off until Bruno collapsed.

Despite his vulnerabilities, Frank presented a picture of a gentle and lovable goof having a fantastic time. For instance, in 1986, a few wins after the Smith defeat, he took on the out-of-shape former WBA heavyweight champion Gerrie Coetzee and bowled him over in one round, leaving Gerrie dramatically splayed on the canvas, his head halfway out the ropes. 'He'd have to be a baboon to stand up to that right,' he said, and then jogged over and kissed Coetzee. Carpenter said, 'They love you, Frank,' and Bruno replied, 'I'm not that way inclined, but I 'ope they love me in a different way. There'd 'ave to be six baboons in there to beat me tonight. I'm sorry, Arry, I'm sounding a bit aggressive. I think I'll go for a run. I need to sweat a bit.' He went to speak to Coetzee. 'I'm sorry to have disgraced you in front of your wife and children, but that's cricket, old sport.' Actually, not quite cricket, it emerged. Coetzee later confided in his heavyweight protégé Frans Botha, among others, that he threw the fight. 'He was very proud of it,' said Botha. 'He told me he hurt his hand so he decided to take a dive. He got a brother to bet on him losing in the first round – a huge amount, he said – and he told me he was laughing in the changing room afterwards. He thought it was a big joke.'

Bruno was serious about his calling but he also liked a big joke. He was gauche and funny and, in his odd way, charming. A lot of it, however, was an act – playing to the image his public adored. Behind all the chirpy banter and cockney rhyming slang about his 'Black and Decker' and the like was a fragile ego; a sense of self needing constant reinforcement. There were bouts of depression and hints about a paranoia that others were out to get him – in love with the adoration of strangers yet suspicious of their motives. Interviewed before facing Pierre Coetzer in 1992, he looked down at the notebook facing him and said, 'I don't want to tell you my tactics because you might have a tape recorder hidden there and pass them on, know what I mean?' He wasn't joking either.

Anyway, the Coetzee victory put Bruno back in contention and Duff secured a fight against Tim Witherspoon for the WBA title. His odds were improved by the fact that Terrible Tim had what his countrymen might call substance abuse issues, and was also overweight, but it was ripped, muscle man who started tiring as a result of his inability to relax while the fat man came on strong. Tim caught him in round eleven, and once again Frank froze until he was bludgeoned to defeat. Laura and Terry picked him up while Duff worked on his promotional rehabilitation, all the way to his second title bash against a declining Mike Tyson in 1988. But he lacked the speed to take advantage of his moment when he hurt Mike in the first round. Tyson was pulled off him in round five and everyone thought that was it for Bruno: time to retire – an option he refused to consider.

There's an old adage in boxing that you can't build muscles on chins, and like most old boxing adages it is at best half-true. Boxers can be trained to take a better punch and building muscle is part it. A flyweight may knock out a bantamweight but his punches will have little effect on even the softest heavyweight. The boyish Cassius Clay was twice dropped by men who would be considered small cruiserweights today, but the manly Muhammad Ali took the hardest shots thrown by George Foreman and Ernie Shavers without falling. Did his 'chin' improve? In a way, yes. A stronger neck and stronger legs are particularly helpful, but a blow to the jaw is absorbed by the whole body. Added to this, improved stamina helps you recover quicker. Foreman, who had one of the best chins around, was knocked out by the arm-punching Ali and dropped by the feather-fisted Jimmy Young because exhaustion sapped his resistance. On top of this, an ability to 'read' punches prevents boxers getting caught cold, and it helps to know how and when to clinch, when to go down after being hurt and when to get up again.

While Laura patched up her husband's shattered ego, Terry built Bruno physically, adding more muscle to his 6ft 3in frame. He also worked on refining Frank's technique – a heavier jab, more variety in his infighting skills – and along the way, a fresh array of fouls. Frank's favourite was to pull an opponent in close and belt him behind the neck to shake him up – the 'rabbit' punch – but he was also no slouch at holding-and-hitting, kidney punches and the odd elbow strike and low blow. They also worked on his stamina, flexibility and speed and tried to teach him to relax in the ring and it seemed to work, up to a point. He looked a more complete boxer – enough to get him past a couple of lower level contenders. With his popularity and Duff's persistence, these victories secured him a top five ranking with all three control bodies and his third bash at a version of the world title.

The Brunos regarded the Lewis fight as their final shot at glory, which meant that Frank followed Laura's shrill example by getting nasty, particularly in the way he treated the 'hostile' press. Laura periodically gave vent to her emotions with tirades in the direction of Frank Maloney or anyone else who got in the way. Lawrence Lustig, for example, was seen as part of the enemy camp and treated accordingly. 'I had a great relationship with Frank until Laura turned on me when she found out that I was close to Lennox,' he recalled. 'She couldn't understand how I could be friends with two people at the same time and she gave me a lot of venom, even though I was still doing personal photos for Frank. She abused me a couple of times because of my relation to Lennox, real heavy abuse, including on the night of the fight, and this spread to Frank himself. Once, outside the Marriott Hotel in Cardiff, Frank hurled a volley of abuse at me down the road, and it was all because I was close to Lennox. I took some pictures and he stuck his middle finger at me and said, "Swivel on this, you cunt." That's exactly what he said.'

Relations between Lennox and Frank were cordial until they arrived in Cardiff. Part of the change was Pepe Correa, who had his own line in insults, such as, 'You will eat your feet. I'm going to take a pillow to ringside for you,' and throwing underwear around. Bruno annoyed Lewis by using the fight's 'Battle of Britain' marketing theme to hit at his ambiguous national identity. 'He's not British,' Frank said. 'Nobody cares about Lennox Lewis in Britain. I'm the one who's famous.' Later, at a pre-fight press conference, he claimed, 'I'm a true Brit, you're not.' He then turned to the press. 'You don't need to be Ironside to know that the man doesn't live in this country. He's taking the mickey out of the country.' He maintained this tone all the way to the fight itself, stressing his homeboy credentials by entering the ring wearing a Union flag tracksuit behind a big Union flag to the sound of 'Land of Hope and Glory'. Lennox felt he'd gone a long way in showing respect for the land of his birth – returning to the city of his childhood, turning professional there with a British manager, winning the British title, defending it twice to secure the Lonsdale Belt, buying a home in the shires and living there with his English brother and his Jamaican mum for much of the year. His response was to give vent to his true feelings. 'You're an Uncle Tom,' he said. Frank bristled. Unlike Lennox, he couldn't and threatened legal action for slander. Lennox made a joke out of the threat and refused to withdraw the insult, while Maloney publicly tore up the legal letter.

Lewis worked hard for this fight at his camp near Washington, D.C., sparring with a strong former Olympic bronze medallist from Poland called Andrej Golota and a future British and Commonwealth champion, Julius Francis, among others, and pushing marathon man Eugene Maloney all the way on their early-morning runs. 'For a big man, Lennox was a good runner – a great runner, in fact – and he always liked to win,' Eugene said. And he made it through the training camp without any of the medical problems or interruptions that had plagued his preparations for the Tucker fight. But once he arrived in Cardiff he went down with a severe cold and a slight temperature. Eugene, who was with him throughout the long build-up, called a doctor to examine him, and although he was cleared to fight he had not fully recovered by fight time. He came in at 229lb, six fewer than against Tucker, while the 31-year-old Bruno weighed 238lb.

On a cold, wet night, the drizzle occasionally giving way to hard rain, 30,000 people poured into Cardiff Arms Park. Pepe was his usual bumptious self in the changing room, but Lennox appeared unusually on edge. Meanwhile, the normally agitated Bruno was relishing the happy mood of his changing room – full of flags, with music blaring and plenty of laughter – and he entered the ring to a stirring reception. Lennox was still in the early stages of his warm-up routine when the television batmen hurried him into the ring, afraid that another downpour might scuttle the fight. He later acknowledged, 'I hadn't warmed up enough, so I felt too cold at the start.' As usual he entered the ring to Bob Marley singing Rita Marley's anti-racist classic 'We're gonna chase those crazy baldheads out of town', to a reception noticeably more restrained than Frank's.

The WBC's curious choice of referee was Mickey Vann, a cigarette-puffing little man from Leeds who, three weeks earlier, made his name in the boxing world for all the wrong reasons. He was appointed to judge a 'superfight' in San Antonio between Mexico's King-promoted darling of the WBC, Julio Cesar Chavez, and the brilliant American Pernell Whitaker. Most ringsiders had the quicker, more imaginative and versatile Whitaker four rounds ahead, but to the astonishment of the non-Mexicans in the 63,000 crowd two judges made it a draw, outvoting the third who went for Whitaker. It was bad enough that one of the culprits was Vann; what made it worse was that he scored round six to Chavez – a round Whitaker dominated. He explained this in terms of Pernell's low blows, despite the fact that the referee made no point deduction and Chavez also put in his share of fouls. Vann achieved instant notoriety in US boxing circles, falsely accused of taking a $20,000 bribe to secure this result (in fact he was underpaid for his duties). The WBC's Mexican boss Jose Sulaiman phoned to commend him on a job well done while appointing him to referee the Lewis–Bruno fight. When Mickey was introduced to the crowd, he was booed, although he would later describe it as the best night of his whole life.

Before hostilities started Vann yelled into the microphone, and to a television audience of several million, 'I don't want no shit off any of you! Don't give me no shit!'

Lennox looked like he didn't give a shit. He circled to his right, poking out his jab and receiving the same in return. Bruno, the 3–1 underdog, returned to his corner with his left eye slightly swollen but his confidence boosted, while Lewis returned still feeling cold and lethargic. Harold Knight wrapped him in a thick blanket but he seemed even less energetic in round two. He kept throwing his right cross, but Frank, who boxed behind a high guard, blocked them. 'Frank really did his homework,' Lennox said. 'He never stopped watching out for my right.' Bruno landed a decent right of his own and was also edging the battle of the jabs, and consolidated by whacking Lennox behind the back of the neck, over and over again. Lewis replied in kind and, slightly too late, Vann stepped in for a lecture that would earn him a disciplinary hearing and an official reprimand from the British Boxing Board of Control. 'Come here!' he yelled. 'Now don't fuck with me! Don't act like a couple of tarts. Don't piss me about no more. I don't want no shit!'

Bruno connected with a heavy overhand right flush on the temple early in round three and Lennox's legs dipped slightly. In his hurry to retreat he fell back on the ropes and Bruno steamed in for more, but Lennox ducked the next right and clinched. Bruno had further success late in the round, landing another cross and two beefy hooks to the body, while Lewis's work was ragged. His footwork seemed unusually clumsy, his timing was off and he was lunging and struggling to find his range. He returned to his corner with a swollen left cheekbone. 'It was tough in there,' he said, 'a lot tougher than I expected. He was pretty warm while it took me a while to get started. Maybe it was because it was so late at night and my body wasn't used to waking up then, but I can't make too many excuses about that. You know, some nights you're on, some nights you're off.' With Pepe imploring him to use his jab more, he willed himself to work harder in round four, and gradually warmed up, doubling up on his jab and using his reflexes to slip the incoming flak. He upped the pace in the fifth with three-punch combinations, exacerbating Frank's eye damage. Bruno, however, got in one more hard right, a few more stiff jabs, several more hard rabbit punches, and opened a small cut on Lennox's left eyebrow.

In round six, Lewis took over. He had finally boxed his way into a comfortable rhythm, winning the jabbing battle, pushing Bruno back, landing hard to the body. 'Those right hooks to the belly seemed to slow him down,' he said. 'I realised as the fight went on that Frank would slow down because a lot of his punches were missing me, so I just kept my composure and in round six my speed came into play.' Once more Bruno resorted to rabbit punches – again without receiving a warning. The two American judges had the fight even, three rounds apiece, while the Welsh judge had Bruno up by a ridiculous four points. Pepe decided Frank was ready to be taken. Terry Francis, who was worried about Frank's eye, told Bruno to throw everything into the seventh. As always, Frank obeyed, charging out, bundling Lewis into the ropes and thumping away, but his cavalier attack lacked precision and caution. Lewis covered up and saw Bruno dropping his right as he prepared to fire, and that fraction of a second was all he needed. It took one huge, wide left hook flush on Bruno's exposed chin to end his challenge.

The punch had a crippling effect on Bruno's central nervous system, rendering him incapable of resistance. Lewis drove him to the ropes and landed sixteen bombs, ending with a sickening uppercut that lifted Frank's head way back. Finally, Vann jumped in to rescue the stricken challenger – or so it seemed. But instead he led Lennox to the neutral corner for a long lecture on the crime of steadying Bruno's head with his left while throwing his right. 'I don't know why Vann did that,' said Lennox. 'He said I was holding but I wasn't. I was just throwing my right. I was upset and I just wanted him to hurry up so that I could go and take Bruno out because I realised he was still groggy-eyed and not even putting his hands up, and that the ropes were holding him up. I just wanted to take his head off and I thought all it would take was one more right.' Ten seconds elapsed before he was permitted to resume, but on this cold Cardiff night ten minutes would have been too quick. Bruno was incapable of moving off the ropes. His eyes were glazed, his torso slumped and his body unable to react. Lewis landed seven more monstrous punches, ending with a terrible overhand right to the jaw, and Frank collapsed, the ropes breaking his fall. At last, several punches too late, after one minute and ten seconds of the round, Vann rescued him.

Laura jumped into the ring to comfort her husband and Violet followed, embracing her son with delight. Lennox admitted he'd under-performed. His assessment of his night's work was no better than 'pretty average' – a bad start but a great finish. 'There are a lot of things I have to work on,' he said, before paying tribute to Bruno's performance. 'I don't keep no grudges and I don't hate Bruno. Nuff respect to him.'

The Brunos felt less respectful. When Maloney went to commiserate with Laura, she spat in his face. Later that morning her husband acknowledged he had been whipped 'fair and square' but said they would continue the fight in court over the Uncle Tom remark, which he was not prepared to forgive or forget. Banging his fist on the press conference table, he said, 'I'm a proud, proud, proud, hombre.' Lennox refused to withdraw the slur and continued to deride Frank in these terms for the next few years but there was no legal action, and the spat eventually burned out. After Bruno retired he gave vocal support to Lewis in several fights, while Lennox was one of the first to declare his admiration for Frank when in 2003 he was sectioned under the Mental Health Act.

Two interested observers were Lou Duva and Eddie Futch, both liking what they saw. Futch said that despite Lennox's natural ability he had not learned all the basics of defence, and would require hours of repetition in the gym to get it right. Lennox had gone 'power crazy' at the expense of his skills and was not preparing for the day when 'he faces someone who won't go down, or who he can't catch squarely'. He pointed to the way Bruno kept Lennox on the back foot. 'He was pushing Lewis back for six rounds. Then, in the seventh, Bruno pushed him back to a corner and decided to go for a knockout. Bruno stepped back with his right foot, which gave Lewis the range to throw. It gives you a pretty good idea what pressure does to Lewis, but that was one of the faults of Bruno. When he got hurt, the fight left him.' Duva was more ambiguous. 'He didn't use his jab properly until the fifth round, he did lots of amateurish things and made lots of mistakes. He looked hurt in the third but Bruno was too slow to follow up. But on the other hand he proved he was capable of being a far better fighter than he showed tonight. He can box, he can punch, and he showed heart in coming from behind to take it. I think he could become a great boxer but he needs to look very carefully at the mistakes he made. At this point I'd say he'd have a lot of trouble with Evander and I'd also say that if they'd fought tonight Bowe would have knocked him out, but in six months the situation may be different.'

Maloney's initial reaction was one of relief. 'I was amazed to see Bruno outjabbing Lewis in those early rounds,' he admitted. 'I think Lennox may have been taken aback by the crowd response, and in fairness, Frank boxed like I've never seen him box before. He would have beaten anyone else who came out of the other corner, but unlucky for him it was Lennox who came out, and you got to remember that a bad Lewis beat a two hundred per cent Bruno, so what would Lennox have done on form?' But why was he so bad? Not warmed up, after-effects of a cold – feasible but not enough. There were also problems with technique: defensive sloppiness, too many telegraphed rights, too much lunging, clumsy footwork. The inevitable question was raised: is Pepe up to the job? Lennox raised this issue with Frank for the first time, worried he wasn't receiving the coaching he needed and concerned that Harold Knight was being sidelined. Maloney spoke to Pepe and told him he was worried, in particular, about Lennox's tendency to telegraph his right and to throw too many of them, and his failure to use combinations. He hoped the message sunk in and left it at that. 'I've sat and talked to Pepe, and let's say the team are happy,' he said.

Frank considered seeking additional help. One possibility was a former champion whose skills he admired, Larry Holmes, who was starting to play the Jack Johnson role to Lennox's Joe Louis. Johnson, the first black world heavyweight champion, made a point of deriding Louis when Joe was on his way up in the mid-1930s, calling him slow-footed, 'not a very bright boy' and a sucker for the right with 'poor craftsmanship' and 'marked mechanical flaws'. He kept predicting Louis's defeat (and eventually got it right when Joe was stopped by Max Schmelling in 1936) and kept on offering his knowledge and experience to his young successor, but the offer was never accepted.

Holmes, too, made a point of pouring scorn on Lennox's technique, forever predicting his demise and getting it wrong. Even at the end of Lewis's career he continued to snipe. 'Lennox didn't want to fight anyone who could fight, and never has,' he said in 2004 after Lewis had beaten every heavyweight of his era. 'They will remember he didn't have any heart. He was always scared he would get his butt kicked. Lennox is an OK fighter but I don't think you can call him one of the greats. I'd have beat his butt.' But despite the persistent criticism, Maloney was intrigued. 'Larry approached me and said, "Let me come to the camp and help you with Lewis. I can made him as good as I was."' For Maloney, 'as good as Larry' meant superlative. 'I think Holmes would have beaten every heavyweight who ever existed. Of course, if Lennox had fought him in 1993 he would have destroyed him, but then Larry was way past his best, but in his prime he would have beaten every heavyweight out there.' But he let the offer pass. 'I often wondered whether I made the right decision. Should I have recommended Larry to Lennox? I always liked Larry and got on with him, but you see, at the time Holmes was still fighting and I thought there was an ulterior motive for him offering to come to our camp, so I said no.'

Lennox's next fight was supposed to be a high-profile, big-money ($7 million), low-risk meeting with the exciting, big-hitting, soft-chinned, American heavyweight Tommy Morrison, who held the inconsequential WBO title. Morrison, however, decided on a warm-up three weeks after the Bruno show. He chose an unranked, British-born heavyweight, Michael Bentt, and was knocked out in the first round, a result that made Lennox despair. 'Can you believe it? Tommy missed out on a five-million-dollar fight with me just because he wanted to make an extra million dollars. Just for a million dollars.'

A week later Bowe made the third defence of his title against Holyfield. 'Big Daddy', who'd been champion for a week less than a year, expected an easy anniversary. After all, he'd already beaten the little man and now he was a year more experienced, while Evander, at 31, was merely a year older. He trained hard but ate even harder and came in at 246lb – eleven more than in their first fight. Evander, at 217lb, had added twelve pounds to his frame, but in his case it was all muscle. With Emmanuel Steward hired for the job he came in significantly stronger, and from the start it was apparent that he was hitting harder than ever before. He met Bowe punch for punch and amazed the Las Vegas crowd with his intensity. By the halfway mark he was driving Bowe back, and by round seven a stoppage victory began to look like a possibility. But the fight will be remembered for something else. Two minutes into the round 30-year-old James Miller, strapped to a parachute and a huge fan, flew in through the hole in the Caesar's Palace roof. As he descended the cords of his parachute became entangled with the lights and he landed with one leg over the ring ropes, at which point Bowe's goons pounded him into unconsciousness, one of them hitting him twenty times, with Newman later claiming they feared an attack on the Nation of Islam leader Louis Farakan, who was at ringside. Miller, who committed suicide a few years after pulling similar stunts at the Arsenal football ground, and Buckingham Palace (in the nude), was taken to hospital and from there to jail, later explaining his action as a protest against violence in spectator sport. This odd incident gave Bowe 21 vital minutes to catch his breath. He fought back and dominated the final round, but not even Rock Newman had the nerve to complain about the decision.

As Maloney put it, 'He lost fair and square and hasn't screamed about it. He's accepted the decision. Amazing. It's the only sporting thing the pair of them have done.'

The boxing world had seen enough of Riddick and his obnoxious manager and there was much rejoicing. Maloney was assured by Duva he needn't worry about the prospect of Holyfield–Bowe 3. 'They were not interested in letting Rock back in with any chance of getting his hands on the heavyweight title because of the way he's been treating everybody,' he said. 'I mean, sometimes you have to be a bit respectful even if you are the world heavyweight champion's manager. Now, Evander's different. He wants to honour the agreement he made in 1992 by fighting Lennox. That's his number one priority in his mind.' Lennox began to get his mind focused on an April 1994 engagement with Holyfield. 'This will give me a lot of motivation because I really want to become undisputed champion,' he said. 'I'm going to box him and use that great jab I have.' Soon afterwards, however, the honourable Mr Holyfield changed his mind, deciding instead that he would first accommodate the more manageable 214lb contender Michael Moorer.

So, once again, Lennox was without a dance partner. To fill the time his team decided on a national publicity tour. As always Lawrence Lustig stepped in to help and refused to take a penny for his troubles. 'They decided they needed sponsorship for this tour but couldn't find anyone,' he recalled. 'The trouble at that stage was that the public had started to forget about Lennox, so I went to the *Daily Star* and asked them to sponsor it and they agreed, and I think it did a lot for his profile in the UK.' Lennox had a grand time answering questions and swapping jokes with the students at the Oxford Union and talked about one day studying philosophy there himself. He then toured Britain and Ireland, promoting his autobiography while putting in appearances on several popular television programmes and taking the odd break from all the fun to drink his team members under the table before emerging fresh and unscathed in the morning.

Six months after beating Bruno, Lennox returned to Las Vegas to watch another hope subside. Holyfield, who economised on training expenses for his defence against Moorer by refusing to re-employ Steward at the demanded rate, managed to drop his weak-chinned challenger in the second round but grew more lethargic as the fight progressed. The cautious Moorer wasn't much better. His trainer, Teddy Atlas, was becoming so exasperated that he sat on the stool between rounds and asked if he would rather he himself did the fighting. It was enough to carry Michael through on a majority decision. Holyfield yelled robbery before heading off to hospital, emerging later with his left arm in a sling, claiming a shoulder injury. He also claimed to have sustained a heart problem in the ring, explaining that it was an oxygen shortfall as a result of a hole in the heart, and later that this malady was divinely healed. Finally, after another set of doctors said there'd been no hole to start with, he said his troubles were caused by water retention. The general consensus was that Evander had been through too many brutal fights, and most felt it time for him to retire. Lennox shared this view. 'I think it's sad. I ask myself, how can a man be in such great physical shape and eat so well and have a heart condition? Boxing would definitely be better served if he didn't fight again. I mean, what is the reason he wants to fight? He doesn't need a faith healer. He needs a psychologist.'

Moorer, meanwhile, hinted that a title unification date with Lewis was not on his agenda and his management stated that if they were ever to contemplate such a fight it would be on the basis of tying Lewis up with a long-term share of his contract.

By then Lewis, who was training at the Caesar's Brookdale hotel resort in the Pocono Mountains, was two weeks away from his third defence, against the fifth-ranked contender Phil Jackson – a filler gig for £2.5 million ($3.8 million), but he wasn't satisfied. 'It frustrates me so much because my goal is to become undisputed champion, and once again it just seems like everybody's ducking me. They don't really want to get in with Lennox Lewis,' he said, in an early rendition of an emerging habit of referring to himself in the third person – a Caesarean reflex, perhaps, or maybe a suggestion that Lennox Lewis the boxing champion was an entirely different human being from Lennox the private man.

The 29-year-old Jackson was a big-banging Miami contender who had grown up surrounded by crack dens and criminals. He had six brothers, one of them paralysed by a bullet, and six children of his own, and had not been immune from the temptations of his environment: he twice did time in youth offender institutions for bag snatching and developed a reputation as a fearsome street fighter. But behind bars he found God, and then boxing. Standing just over six feet tall and weighing around 220lb, he was a heavy hooker who raked up 25 wins (24 on knockouts) before running into Ruddock, who stopped him in four, after which Jackson said, 'He didn't hurt me at all. When he hit me with that hook, I went down on one knee. I felt, "Why get up?" My heart wasn't in it. There was no need to prove anything.' A wise attitude for a normal mortal but not particularly desirable in a fighter. But sometimes a display of what is viewed as cowardice can later spur a boxer to extremes of courage. Over the next two years Jackson strung together five wins to take his record to a 30 wins, one loss, 28 knockouts. He promised, 'Everything will be completely different with Lewis. I am ready for him.'

As he would later admit, his first look at Lennox in the Atlantic City ring, stripped to the waist and looking down at him gave him a shock. He had not realised quite how huge he was and given his memory of the Ruddock experience the temptation to fold must have been overwhelming, especially when, half a minute into the first round, he was dropped with a right hook. But he kept winging hopeful left hooks and late in the round landed a stiff right hook that had no effect. Over the next three rounds he tasted that long, heavy jab over and over while still pressing and throwing hooks. Teddy Atlas commented, 'He wasn't jabbing at all, and to me that was a guy frozen by the moment. Jackson's what I call a game quitter – hanging in there, showing gameness but not trying to win any more.' That was a little uncharitable. It was more that Jackson lacked the equipment to prevail.

He launched a serious attack in round five, backing Lewis on to the ropes, but even there he failed to register as the big man displayed his blocking, parrying and slipping prowess. 'He came at me with hard punches but I showed some skill and kept my composure in there,' Lennox recalled. Later, Jackson landed his best left hook of the night and Lewis stumbled back, off balance rather than hurt, but came back with one of his quick, heavy, perfectly timed right crosses, and this time Phil pitched down on his face and struggled to make it upright by the count of nine. Another barrage, continuing for a second after the bell and earning Lennox a point deduction, put the Miami man down again. 'I thought he showed real bravery,' said Lewis, 'because I hit him with some good, solid shots and I thought he would stay down, but he got up and kept on trying.'

Lennox was putting his punches together beautifully but breathing heavily through his mouth, and his hands were coming down. Pepe encouraged him: 'Come on, Lennox, he's tired too. You can take him out, but remember, keep your right hand up to protect yourself against his hook.' Lennox didn't listen and Jackson caught him again, but he soon started raking the American with jabs and rights. By round eight Phil's right eye was closing and he was taking a fearful beating. Lewis then began to work inside, banging to the body and snapping his head back. A five-punch combination of hooks and uppercuts prompted veteran referee Arthur Mercante to step in as Jackson collapsed. Violet was quickly into the ring, kissing her son, smiling and raising his hand.

He was happy with his performance. 'I did what I wanted,' he said, 'and showed speed, skill, movement and composure, and I also showed what an effective jab I have. I think I'm one of the best boxers in the world today.' But the neutral verdict was equivocal. Atlas didn't think it was the kind of performance to send a message to America. 'What if the other guy had done more persistent work? In the period when Lennox hadn't woken up, he got away with it. Maybe he was hampered by the mind-set he took into the first round – the idea that he would set the guy up, hypnotise him with the jab, then knock him over with the right and go home. But by the end he was putting his punches together well. He knows what to do when he gets you hurt, he's got a good chin and he has confidence about himself. He believes he's going to win.' George Foreman also offered a mixed review. 'Lennox is a genuine puncher. No doubt about it, he's the hardest-punching heavyweight in the game today, the best puncher out there, but he needs to go back to his original trainer to get his footwork back, and he drops his hands too much. Put him in the ring with the right fighter and he can get knocked out easily. He should stop moving around with his hands down. He doesn't need that in his repertoire. He should get a better trainer.'

Lennox, however, felt he was sharp enough to allow Pepe one more low-risk chance. After all, his next fight was a mandatory against King's recovering drug addict Oliver McCall, who hardly presented a risk. After that, a deal had been sealed for his first 'superfight', against Riddick Bowe, who, without a title of his own, had finally come begging. Sure, that may require another trainer, but, as yet, he was reluctant to admit his mistake. He had a stock answer to the trainer question, whether put by Maloney, the media or anyone else: 'If it ain't broke, why fix it?'

CHAPTER THIRTEEN
HILTON NATIONAL HOTEL, LONDON, 1994

It's two hours after the fight but Oliver is still bouncing. He can't stop himself. Up and down, bouncing and whooping, 'Hooh! Hooh!' and 'Whooh! Whooh!' The enormity of his triumph is just beginning to register – and, now, at three a.m. on 25 September, with his shower and the press conference out of the way, he can finally end those long days of abstinence and celebrate non-stop. 'Hooh!' he says again. 'Man! I'm gonna have me a beer – the first in six weeks. Hey, Don! I hit him right in the mouth. Bang! Whooh!' He downs the beer in six big gulps and grabs another.

Don King is no less delighted, but not so much for Oliver, who is really no more than a useful pawn who made it to the other side of the board, allowing for his main player to return to him, as for himself, because after four-and-a-half years in the heavyweight wilderness he's back with a piece of the world title, and that may soon be enough for total control. His chosen instrument is another man, sitting in a cell and waiting for release.

'We gotta talk to Mike Tyson,' Don tells Oliver, and the new WBC champion offers an accepting smile because he too knows the score, and then turns to explain. 'I talked to Mike this afternoon and he said I should keep the pressure on him, and I did. My ultimate goal is to fight Mike Tyson when he comes out.' As they're walking to the phone, Don's batman, Mike Marley, says quietly, 'Yeah, this victory is all about Mike. Oliver's done good, but Mike'll be the governor.'

Don passes the phone to Mike's former sparring partner. 'Mike! I did a number on the punk, Mike!' Oliver yells. 'I did a number on the punk!' He takes Tyson through the final moments – the big right when the punk was coming in, smack in the punk's mouth. 'Yeah! You! Champion! I planned it all, Mike. Thanks, Mike.'

There aren't supposed to be any journalists present. This is a private party to celebrate the return of the King. It's strictly family: Don and Oliver, obviously, Don's beaming British sidekick Frank Warren, Frank's scowling, harder looking younger brother, and all the trainers and promotional assistants and sparring partners. And, of course, the WBC boss Jose Sulaiman. But Jose has two problems. First, he's not so sure he should be seen at Don's table on a night like this, because you never know who might slip through. More immediately, he's been left behind in the elated scramble. He was standing outside the arena, looking lost, when a friendly Englishman approached, offering help, summoning the hotel minibus and accompanying Jose to the Hilton.

'I can't stay here in case I'm seen,' Jose said as they approached.

'Why?' asked the Englishman, feigning ignorance.

'You don't know who I am, but I'm telling you there's going to be controversy for me, so I can't be seen there.'

Still, he popped in to say hi and bye, and, feeling grateful to his helper who was just dying to have a look at the new champion, escorted him past the doormen saying, 'Don't worry, he's with me,' and into the party, before making his own excuses.

An hour of backslapping and phone calls later, Don spots the little tape recorder. He feigns alarm but, what the hell, he can't resist. 'Oh, you jolly old Englishman, how did you get in here?' he says, roaring with laughter and extending a welcoming arm. 'Never mind. What can I tell you?' But he doesn't wait for an answer. 'From now on there's gonna be quality control in the heavyweight division because we only put on the best against the best, so while we wait for Mike to return we gotta look for the rest of the best for Oliver McCall.' And who might they be? 'Someone like Frans Botha or Pete McNeely,' he says, referring to a mediocre white South African he promotes and an incompetent white American. 'You see, you gotta give the white man a chance,' Don King says with a delighted smile and a hearty laugh.

Meanwhile, speaking quietly in the corner, drinking first a glass of water then a glass of white wine is the architect of this coup, the trainer-supreme, Emmanuel Steward. He's smiling in satisfaction with a job perfectly planned and executed. 'Lennox is a magnificent athlete,' he says. 'He has immense natural talent – more than anyone I've seen – and there's no doubt he could be champion again but everything came too easy for him and he didn't have the right trainer, so there were mistakes creeping into his work that we could take advantage of. He would telegraph his right before he threw it and we worked on how to step inside and counter with a right. Oliver worked extremely hard, he always listened and I had no problems with him at all and I developed a lot of respect for him. He was a perfect gentleman to me. A sweet man.' But was the referee right to stop the fight? 'Oh, yes, there was no way Lennox could have survived. But if he corrects his mistakes and gets the right trainer, he'll be back. No question. He has immense potential and, yes, I have no doubt he will be world heavyweight champion again.'

Oliver downs another beer, bounces over to his mentor of the last few months and, thinking aloud, has an even better idea. 'No, no, no, I must give a call to my dad now. I said I would after I won.' He jogs to the phone, dials his dad, says hi, and listens. 'I love you too, Daddy. I done it, Daddy. I done it. I'm the champion of the world.' Then comes his father-in-law and then another bounce, with that big, hard body going up, six inches above the carpet, and down, up and down. 'Oh, shit, what am I thinking of? I gotta phone my kids.' He dials again. 'What am I, Elijah? I tell you what I am. I AM THE HEAVYWEIGHT CHAMPION OF THE WORLD. What am I, son?' Oliver gives a bellow of a laugh, shakes his head and turns around to his one-man audience. 'He sure knows his stuff, my son does. You know what Elijah said? He said, "Daddy, you're the WBC heavyweight champion of the world."'

Lennox Lewis was thrilled with the prospect of fighting Riddick Bowe. After one more easy fight he would finally get his chance to flatten the rude boy who called him a faggot – humiliate him; hurt him; destroy him. It was hard to think of anything else. The whole thing just felt so magnificent.

Dan Duva, who also promoted Michael Moorer, would have nothing to do with Riddick any more, not after the way they'd been treated in his brief reign, so there was only one avenue left for the former champion and his manager, the one they'd previously tried so hard to avoid. The two men who'd vowed never to dirty their hands with the WBC and refused to accommodate Lewis had no option but to come begging. Lennox was enjoying this humiliation and was happy to show magnanimity, provided it came with a whopping payday. It gave him the chance to retire Riddick by giving him the beating of his life. 'Bowe and Newman deserve to be frozen out because of the way they behaved when he was champion,' he said, 'but the fact remains that it's the fight I'd still really like – that one chance to get at Bowe. I want to stuff all his insults down Bowe's throat, although it's funny, but he doesn't really insult me any more now that he's no longer a champion. He's basically humbled himself a great deal.'

Panos Eliades sealed the deal, bypassing an infuriated Duva. With Newman hovering in the background, he negotiated a contract through Bowe's attorney, Milt Chwasky, securing a deal for Lennox to receive a career-highest purse of £12 million ($18 million) and Bowe £8 million for a 'superfight' in Las Vegas in March 1995.

Since losing to Holyfield, Bowe had been extremely fortunate to get a 'no contest' result rather than a disqualification loss for pounding the unprepossessing Buster Mathis on the canvas after dropping him. He fouled his next victim, Larry Donald, before the fight, slugging him in the face with his bare fist at a press conference.

Lennox was getting used to the idea that once a year he had to face the WBC's mandatory contender, which inevitably meant that once a year he had to face a Don King protégé. It was just one of those irksome tasks to get out of the way before you could move on. Last time it was Tony 'TNT' Tucker; this time, Oliver 'The Atomic Bull' McCall. If anything, standards were slipping, and Don was reaching the bottom of his rapidly emptying slime bucket. Tony, after all, had outpointed Oliver two years earlier. 'It gives me great pleasure beating Don King's men,' he said, 'but McCall is not like Tucker. Don believed in Tucker and that's why he put up twelve million dollars up front. He didn't do that for McCall because he's not up to Tucker's skill level. So I look at it as a warm-up. He's a stepping stone to help me prepare for my next fight against Bowe.' An easy stepping stone at that. 'He's a recovering this and a recovering that. Look, McCall's been around a long time but if he was any good he would have been at the top long before me because I came yesterday and look where I am. And all of a sudden he starts saying things about what he's going to do to me. Well, I guess that's provocation enough, but I can't hate him. Hate's too strong. Disdain would be a better word.'

And what of McCall's two-and-a-half-year stint as Mike Tyson's sparring partner, when he managed to drop Mike but was never dropped himself? 'Actually it's a weakness that he's been a sparring partner for so long because being in the gym is different from being in the ring. I definitely feel I can put him down, and not just once. He seems to think he can just march inside and catch me, but to do anything he has to get through my arms which are longer than his and through a barrage of punches, and I'm a heavyweight who moves, so it's not going to be easy for McCall, who's a man who comes straight at you. I hope he'll be in my face all the time because I'll be boxing him, giving it to him.' This, then, was the attitude he took to his training camp in the Catskills.

By then he was close to reaching a decision that this little tune-up would be his last with Pepe. One of his problems was that the rest of his camp aides were struggling to contain their contempt for the trainer. Courtney Shand, for instance, complained, 'Pepe worked against you. He wouldn't listen and he wasn't interested in what you were doing. So I may work Lennox hard in the morning and then Pepe would overwork him in the afternoon, and when I tried to tell him he would say, "I'm the trainer – you just do your job." He wouldn't listen to anything, and sometimes he seemed mad. Like it would be raining outside and he'd say it's a sunny day. That actually happened once.'

Lennox was also becoming irritated. He found Pepe's behaviour increasingly exasperating and began admitting this to his aides. At one point Maloney, who was shocked by the lack of unity in the training camp, suggested they fire Correa there and then and ask Harold Knight to take over as acting head trainer. Lennox considered this option but in the end reverted to his 'if it ain't broke, why fix it?' line. It seemed unfair to fire a man with a winning formula, and there were contractual difficulties too. As Eliades put it, 'We decided prior to the fight that Pepe would be replaced but it's very difficult to disrupt a winning formula – you only start changing a losing formula – so people were still reticent, and maybe they were wrong.' The compromise was that the Puerto Rican would be given one final chance, even though Lewis struggled to contain his unease about the man he'd chosen. 'I was disappointed in Pepe,' he later admitted. 'He was basically a cheerleader. He was self-hyped. He was a muppet. He was obnoxious.'

Partly because of all the tension in camp, Lennox began to miss training sessions, disappearing without warning – something he'd never done before – and the work he put in lacked his usual focus. One problem was that his sparring was not up to scratch. His chief sparring partners were a skittish Puerto Rican called John Ruiz and a fat, short American, Garing Lane, who had lost as many as he'd won. Neither could match McCall's big-hitting aggression and Lennox began to feel there was little point in going through the motions. This situation deteriorated when he pulled a muscle in his back, three weeks before the fight. He refused Maloney's suggestion of postponing the fight and instead worked with a physiotherapist, but he had to cut down his sparring and found he lacked his usual flexibility. The rest of his programme went ahead without his usual competitive intensity. 'For the McCall fight he hardly ran at all,' Eugene Maloney recalled. 'I remember he came and said to me on a few mornings, "Go on, you go ahead and I'll run with the team," when it used to be me and him running away from the rest of the team. He just had no real interest. He kept slipping in and out of camp, slipping away for two days and then coming back, so I knew he wasn't right. I actually phoned up my brother at that camp and told him that Lennox ain't doing his roadwork and things ain't going right, and all that was going on with the trainer and everything, and fights all around.'

His personal life was less stable than when he was engaged to Marcia Miller, with a succession of short-term flings but no real stability. 'He's kind of between relationships at the moment,' his brother, Dennis, said at the time. 'No I'm not,' Lennox cut in. 'You can't even say that – that I'm between girlfriends. No, I'm not. I don't have one. What I have is a lot of women who knock on my door, but just to, uh, find one with harmony – always difficult.' He had a new group of friends but there was concern among the professionals in his camp that these newcomers were getting in the way of his preparations, particularly when he returned to London for his final fortnight of training. Correa brought out only one sparring partner, the incompetent Lane, and Lennox barely seemed to be going through the motions, arriving late, curtailing workouts and putting minimal effort into his sparring.

Still, most of his aides praised him to the hilt, refusing to acknowledge the truth. 'I've taken my training very seriously for McCall,' Lennox stated twelve days before the fight. 'We've been working on specific things – secret moves – and I'm still sparring hard. I'd say I'm up to ninety-eight per cent. This training camp is a very special one. Everybody in my team works hard together and everything is going really smooth.' Correa nodded enthusiastically and pointed at his employer. 'He'll soon be undisputed champion of the world. Just a matter of time. He's advanced a lot since his last fight – you guys bear me out.' Knight, camp coordinator Ollie Dunlop and Garing Lane nodded, smiled and grunted. 'Lennox Lewis is all about work,' said Knight. 'He's like a fine-tuned car now, and our job is to keep him oiled and keep him great. He's the world champion, but he's always willing to learn.' To which Lane added, 'Oh yes, he's among the best. He's quick, and there's nothing wrong with his punching power. In fact he's quicker than he was against Jackson, and putting his punches together better, so I'd say he's at a higher level than before.' And, finally, Dunlop: 'Yes, so professional, and such a nice personality.'

Eugene Maloney, who was on call 24 hours a day, felt there was a false complacency in camp and that Lennox's attention was being diverted by people who had little understanding of boxing. 'My impression was that he had the wrong people about him, people who weren't actually doing anything financially or physically. I call those people hangers-on, ponces, and Lennox started to get these kinds of characters socialising in his company. I think he underestimated Oliver McCall because of what these people were telling him. Basically he had a lot of yes-men around him. All they used to say was, "Yes, Lennox, how high do you want me to jump? Three bags full," and all that. I'm convinced that if it was a hundred degrees baking out there and Lennox said to these guys, "It's raining," they'd put umbrellas up because they were that sort of yes-men. Well, I don't think those yes-people are good to any sports people. They don't do no good.'

If Lewis had followed McCall's progress more carefully he might have taken a different approach. Three negatives blighted Oliver's early career. First, he came without an amateur pedigree and had to learn the professional game on the hop, picking up five points losses in his first 24 fights. Second, his early progress was marked by his draining role as Tyson's chief sparring partner. He developed a sparring partner's mentality – conserving effort so that he'd have enough for the next day. Third, he periodically took drugs and abused alcohol. But his attitude changed in the two years before Lewis. He cut out cocaine, cut down on drinking and worked hard. He came to King's attention by mauling the future WBA champion Bruce Seldon and then another genuine contender, Francesco Damiani, and he'd won five in a row, all on knockouts since dropping a decision to the more experienced Tucker. McCall still had marked weaknesses, including the novice habit of closing his eyes when taking a punch, but he was fighting with fresh intensity, landing more punches with greater venom and learning to place them correctly – one of the biggest hitters in the division. His jab had improved, along with his hook, footwork and defence. He also had the best chin around, perhaps the best in heavyweight history. Tyson never dropped him in over 300 rounds of sparring and he would never be knocked down in 48 professional fights, despite taking flush blows from several of the division's biggest hitters.

At a minimum, this meant Lewis could expect a long night and would need to remain alert because of McCall's power. None of this was enough to test even the worst version of the reigning champion, or at least not without a fat dose of luck, but the gap was narrowed by King's foresight in hiring Emmanuel Steward as head trainer. Manny would have preferred the job of helping the heavyweight he really admired, Lennox Lewis, but no such offer arrived. He saw himself as a hired gun, so when Don came calling he accepted the gig, with the added incentive that it would allow him to prove a point to Lewis.

McCall knew this was his only hope of making money for his six children and proved to be a model student when working with Steward for three months – mostly spent at a high-altitude camp in Mexico. 'I heard all those stories about his indiscipline and wild ways but he listened to everything I told him and I can honestly say I never had a moment's trouble with him,' said Manny. They would study Lewis fight videos, making ample use of the slow-motion button. Steward's respect was undiminished, but he felt that Lennox had regressed under Correa. He saw flaws – problems with his footwork and balance, an over-reliance on the right cross, a tendency to flick out the jab rather than pump it and a habit of flinching slightly and dropping the left guard before throwing the right – and began to work on ways to counter them. Using Tucker as chief sparring partner, they practised slipping the right, stepping in and countering with a cross or hook, until it became a reflex response. 'I think Oliver will knock out Lewis,' Steward commented. 'McCall is not the kind of guy I would like Lewis to fight if I was training him.'

The gap between the approaches of the two trainers was exposed at their first head-to-head press conference ten days before the fight. While Steward remained calm, respectful and measured in his comments, Correa was merely hysterical. He threw a red suspender belt at McCall and yelled, 'This is the only belt you'll be taking from here!' McCall stormed out, but his training team just shook their heads and later expressed their disdain for Pepe's qualifications. Lennox, however, was determined to retain the image of solidarity by standing by his trainer. 'Well, if it ain't broke, why fix it?' he said once more. 'The reason why Oliver McCall's people have to say these things about Pepe is that they fear the fact that he's in my corner, so it doesn't really matter to me. Doesn't affect me.'

The difference in the attitudes of the two fighting men was clear at the pre-fight press conference at London's Britannia International Hotel two days before the fight. Fired up by King's long, praise-singing speech, complete with a Yankee Doodle variation and a homily to Oliver's hunger – 'this is a man who is so hungry for the title, he has an insatiable appetite; he's aching and paining with anguish because he can hardly wait; he's almost becoming uncontrollable' – McCall became belligerent. He talked of breaking Dan Duva's neck before glaring at Lewis. 'You stand out and I will knock you out right now,' he said. There'll not be no fight. I'll beat your ass right now. Right now! We don't have to put on the gloves. Right now! Right now!' He diverted to say he was a 'man of class' and had always respected Lennox's mother before reiterating his right-now offer. 'And it won't go no further because I'm gonna walk over two seats and knock the shit out of you.' Lennox gave a tired smile, barely bothering to go through the motions. 'Tell you what, sounds like Oliver McCall has got his knickers in a twist,' he said. 'I'm not really into too much hype.' He talked of what a wonderful, disciplined training camp he'd had and smiled again. 'Don't leave on the night for any hotdogs or anything. See you guys on the night.'

At the weigh-in 30 hours before the fight the 6ft 2in McCall stripped off to display a body rippling with high-tension muscularity. When his weight, 231½lb, was announced he glared at the press and stalked out, looking like he was on the verge of exploding. A softer-looking Lennox lingered, waving victory signs over King's head, after weighing in at 238lb, the heaviest of his career. Mike Katz of the *New York Daily News*, expressed the prevailing American wisdom. 'He don't look in great shape. There are rumours of back troubles and he's talking of retiring. I'm telling ya, he's ready to be taken.'

On the day of the fight the Lewis camp was hit by yet another mini-crisis when Eugene Maloney, who had been a constant presence in his life for five years and was one of his few close confidants, walked out. When Lennox didn't arrive in time at Wembley, Frank Maloney put in two frantic calls to his brother to find out why they were delayed. 'When I reached Eugene I asked him where the hell Lennox was, and he said, "I've no idea. I'm sitting here at home. I've just resigned."'

Lennox's lackadaisical attitude to training had frustrated Eugene, and he didn't like Correa and several of Lennox's other aides, but on the surface at least they were getting on fine until a few days before the fight. Eugene was on duty in Lennox's quarters at the Britannia Hotel when he was phoned by the police and told that an intruder had been spotted in his own garden. He asked Lennox if he could take time off to see if his girlfriend was OK, but Lennox insisted he remain at his post. He suggested Eugene send one of his mates instead but his security chief slipped off when his boss was asleep, which annoyed Lennox when he found out. Their final fall-out happened shortly before they were due to leave the hotel. 'There was an incident in the hotel an hour before we were supposed to leave that you can describe as a personal disagreement,' said Eugene. 'Something happened which I didn't agree with and I basically told him to stick his job up his arse and walked out, got my car and went home. I didn't have to walk out, you know, but I walked as a matter of principle an hour before the fight.'

Some of Lennox's friends were under the impression that the catalyst related to his harsh response to what he regarded as a planning error prior to the fight. 'Whatever the reason Eugene felt he'd been slighted,' said Lawrence Lustig. 'He's one of those old-style East End men for whom everything is either black and white, and he felt it was a matter of principle, which isn't the way everyone would see it.' Eugene, however, said it was 'utter bollocks' that any minor spat would have prompted him to walk out. 'To me, it would be grassing if I was to say exactly why I walked after what I saw in that hotel, and I'm not a grass, you know. I was still owed thirty grand and I was offered a hundred grand by the newspapers to say what happened but I'm not going to say because I was not brought up like that. I'm from the street. But I know what happened and Lennox knows what happened and anyone with any type of principle would have done the same thing.'

Lennox was clearly not as focused as Eugene on the details – hardly surprising as he had other things to worry about, like Oliver McCall. But he is still bemused by the memory of Eugene's sudden resignation. He has no hard feelings, but he does feel that the act of resigning so soon before the big event was an over-the-top reaction to what seemed to him no more than a minor dispute. 'I expect when people walk out, for them it must feel like a big reason, because obviously it's big enough for them to leave, and that seems to be how Eugene felt about it, but from what I remember of it I will say that I didn't agree with his perspective on the dispute and I still don't think it was a good reason for resigning.'

On fight night some of this tension seemed to have spread to Lennox's family and friends. They shuffled in at ten p.m., headed by Violet, who was fidgeting nervously and refusing to talk. She was followed by his guest for the evening, a young woman friend called Sandra, who kept on saying, 'Ooh, I wish it was over, I wish it was over and he wins,' a thirteen-year-old boy, who said he'd made friends with Lennox in Wales, Panos Eliades grinning away in his fur coat, Dennis Lewis, who settled his mum in before heading off to Lennox's changing room, and several other minders and friends. While this was happening Lennox, as usual, was fast asleep in his changing room, apparently unfazed. McCall was pacing up and down, talking to himself.

When McCall entered the ring at one a.m. on 25 September 1994 to the disco sound of 'Take it to the top' the crowd gave him their usual big British boo, while he gave them his usual pre-fight sobbing. The tears were pouring as he climbed through the ropes, but then he began punching at the ring posts and his face took on a look of explosive intensity. Lennox was irritated to discover someone had put on the wrong song for his ring entrance, but by then he had reached the point where he was beyond making a scene. He just wanted to get into the ring and finish the job as quickly as possible. He walked in behind the Union flag, trying to retain his cool as 7,000 people chanted his name.

McCall came out aggressively, missing his opening jab. Lewis responded with a couple of sharp jabs and a right, and then, when Oliver rushed in, tied him up. McCall broke and landed a hook to the body but missed with several more. Late in the round, however, he caught Lennox with a short, hard left uppercut that prompted him to hold again. 'I tried to catch him with my right in the first round, but I missed,' said Oliver, 'but then I nicked him on the jaw with the left uppercut and he held on for dear life.' Lennox came back with a sharp long right and a stiff left to shade the round.

The gap in the proficiency of the two trainers was vividly displayed between rounds. Steward started with the encouragement his emotional fighter needed and moved towards detailed advice. 'You're fighting good, baby, looking good. You're fighting a very intelligent fight and you're taking his big punch away from him, his right hand. He got in twice and every time you rolled and countered. You caught him once and every time you make him quit throwing the right. And that little kind of hook you're doing is working. It's glancing but it's working. He's blocking it, but keep doing it because even though it's not landing it's keeping him off balance every time you're throwing that shot.' Correa's advice was vacuous in comparison. Lennox, Maloney and Panos claimed his final words were, 'Forget the game plan. Just go and knock the bum out.' In fact, a variation of this theme with an emphasis on the right cross came earlier. His final words were, 'Stay with the jab. That's the key. Nice and easy now. Stay on him. See? Keep on him and try to catch him with the uppercut coming in.' The overall message was that it was time to close the show.

Lennox came out for round two with his head up and guard down. He landed a quick left hook and then a long, hard jab flush in McCall's face, and then another. He was more aggressive than before, determined to finish the job. Oliver respond-ed with his own left hook, just as Steward had instructed, and Lennox lunged forward, pulling back his right in what looked like a bid to blast McCall out of the ring. Oliver stepped in, closed his eyes, and fired with every ounce of his weight and strength – the biggest right of his career. It's hard to tell whether McCall's blinkered reaction fell into the category of luck, as Lewis insists, or preparation, as McCall and Steward insisted. 'We both threw rights and unfortunately his went in first and my momentum was taking me forward at the same time, when he was coming off the ropes,' said Lennox. Or, as McCall remembered it, 'He loaded up with his right and I caught him straight on. I'd watched all those videos of Lewis's fights and I saw that every time he throws a right he shows that he will throw it, and just as we planned, I slipped inside and, bang! That was it, baby.'

The punch landed on the zone between Lewis' mouth and chin, cutting his upper lip and jerking his head back as he fell. The loud, cracking thud of this huge blow reverberated shockingly at ringside; the combined momentum of two huge men moving towards each other doubled its force. It was one of those dramatic blows that made you think the victim has no chance of getting up in time. Lennox fell heavily and pushed himself up, looking bewildered. By the count of six he was erect with his gloves up. The Mexican referee, Lupe Garcia, continued counting while motioning Lewis forward, asking if he was OK. Lennox nodded and raised his guard to signal he was ready to defend himself. However, as he stepped towards

Garcia, who was one pace in front of him, his legs shuddered slightly and simultaneously his upper body bent forward, his gloves touching the referee. Garcia immediately waved his arms. The fight was over. McCall was the new WBC world heavyweight champion.

A decade later the debate over whether Garcia was right to stop the fight when the champion was on his feet at the count of six, with his hands up, his eyes clear but his legs unsteady, has yet to be settled. Three questions remain. First, was there a fast count? Second, could Lennox have survived? Third, was Garcia biased in favour of Don King and King's Mexican friend Jose Sulaiman, and therefore McCall? From the moment Lewis hit the canvas to the moment Garcia finished his count of nine, 8.9 seconds passed. Technically, that barely qualifies as a fast count. However, by normal standards, the count was quick. In fights involving a knockdown the count is invariably slower than actual time. The referee often picks it up only after the puncher approaches the neutral corner and each number he calls usually takes slightly longer than a real second. On average around twelve seconds will pass before a referee reaches the count of nine. After that he will wipe the fallen boxer's gloves, and if he has any doubt about his condition he may look into his eyes and ask him if he is OK. It is not uncommon for seventeen or eighteen seconds to elapse from the time of the fall to the time when the puncher is able to land his next blow. In this sense, yes, Lennox had a quick count, but it was also not one that was unacceptably fast by the laws of the game.

The second question is impossible to answer with certainty. Lennox remains adamant his head was clear and he had the strength to hold when McCall moved in. Though he later blamed himself for being cavalier in his tactics and for being in less than pristine shape, he felt he was the victim of a bum decision. 'I just can't believe it,' he said immediately afterwards. 'It was a lucky shot and an awfully fast count. I was up at six and the referee asked me if I was OK, and I said yes. I was trying to get my feet in position, and they got caught up, but I really was OK to fight on.' Later he gave a more considered verdict: 'I was hurt, but not so badly that I couldn't continue. I feel cheated because I thought the count was fast and it was unfair of the referee not to give me the chance to fight on. It was early in the fight and I was still fresh and I could have gone on to win.' His US promoter Dan Duva, taking over the adversarial role from Maloney, who was too shattered to say anything comprehensible, picked up on this theme and led the charge for an immediate rematch. 'It was a very lucky punch and an outrageous refereeing decision. I've seen fighters much more hurt than this. That referee should have let him fight on.'

McCall, naturally, presented a different view. 'He was hurt bad. Another punch and I might have killed him, and there was two and a half minutes left in the round. There was no way he could have survived.' At the time Steward agreed with his boxer, but today, after training Lennox for eight years, he holds a different opinion, believing that with Lennox's sharp boxing brain and his recuperative powers he had a good chance of doing what was necessary to survive the round. 'The fight was prematurely stopped. I say that even though I was in the other corner. It should never have been stopped the way it was.'

Frank Maloney, on the other hand, has changed his position in McCall's direction. At the time he was adamant Lewis was the victim of an outrageous injustice and could have fought on to win. Now that he has parted with Lewis he offers a different view: 'I've seen Lennox knocked out twice and both times it was no different. He's totally gone for about two minutes and then all of a sudden he comes back again, so that referee may well have saved his career. We can never be sure, but when you analyse it you see that when he was on his feet he was wobbling and wasn't exactly steady and you say to yourself, "Maybe that referee and the controversy it caused did save his career." We'll never know. Maybe Lennox would have recovered, but what would have happened if he hadn't and got hit again on the chin, and out? Then he would never have gotten the rematch.'

So was Garcia biased in favour of Don King's fighter? Referees may show unconscious bias for esoteric reasons such as a stylistic preference or for reasons of national or ethnic pride. Or a promoter may wine and dine a referee, give him presents and offer him a route to regular high-profile work, making the official feel obliged to give his patron's boxer a helping hand. And at times it goes further. The British promoter Barry Hearn, for example, lost a legal suit against his former boxer Steve Collins after a referee gave evidence that officials from Hearn's Matchroom group tried to persuade him to swing a fight in favour of Collins's opponent, Chris Eubank.

A biased referee can disrupt the rhythm of the opponent by giving him gratuitous warnings. If the opponent likes to fight on the inside, he can keep them apart; if he prefers long range the referee can allow the favoured son to clinch. He can give warnings for legitimate body blows, calling them low, or, when the favoured boxer goes low, he can ignore it. When the promoter's lad is cut by a punch he can rule it was caused by a head butt; when a butt cuts the opponent, he can rule it a legitimate punch. When the favourite son is dropped or hurt, he can give him a long count and spend several seconds wiping his gloves, looking into his eyes and asking him if he's OK; when the opponent is dropped or hurt, he can wave the fight off and declare he is protecting his health.

Lennox felt this is what happened. 'I was totally robbed,' he said. 'I'm not crying over spilt milk but I do believe there was malice against me.' A few seconds after Garcia waved his hands, Lennox turned to Dennis and said, 'Why did he stop the fight? Why did he do that?'

While this was happening his shocked manager clambered into the ring and jabbed his finger at Sulaiman's face. With a look of rage on his face he began his tirade with these words: 'You cheated us out of our title. You gave us a Mexican referee.' Although he later felt it politic to apologise, he still feels he did the right thing. 'My job is to make a big fuss and to jump up and down and scream and holler because I managed Lennox Lewis, and I believe what I done and the fuss I kicked up got Lennox the rematch. So I done my job.' Three months after the fight, however, when Maloney went to plead Lennox's cause at the WBC's convention in Seville, he felt his early perception was confirmed when he saw a smiling Garcia, together with his family, sitting at Don King's table – although today he concedes that might have been coincidence.

Garcia, who'd been refereeing his first-ever heavyweight title fight, insisted his decision was taken entirely on the grounds of safety. 'I'm absolutely sure of what I did. Lennox was knocked out. If I'd allowed more punches it could have had fatal consequences. I stopped it to protect the health of the boxer.' Sulaiman backed him in this view: 'I thought Lennox was very hurt. Lupe said Lewis fell against his body with his gloves because he was unable to stand up.' Also at ringside was Stan Christodoulou, one of the world's most experienced and respected referees with over a hundred world title fights behind him, and he expressed astonishment at what he'd just seen. 'I don't like to criticise another referee's decision, but I will say if I'd been in that ring I wouldn't have stopped the fight. This wasn't a novice fight. It was a world heavyweight title fight, and when the champion is dropped and gets up at six you give him the chance to fight on.'

While this debate was raging, Lennox was trying to come to terms with the fact that he'd been beaten for the first time and was now an ex-champion who would no longer get his chance to beat up Bowe. He spoke of his outrage at the referee's decision and his view that he was a victim of a plot. He said he wouldn't rule out the possibility of retirement before changing his mind. In the same breath, he felt the need to reiterate his British credentials, which the press had been questioning. 'I will come back in England,' he said. 'I am not moving to the USA. I never said I was leaving Britain. Only Don King said that. I said I was going to fight in the USA in order to beat the best, but I live in England.'

With that he left the floor to King. 'What you seen happening tonight is history,' said the beaming Don. 'It was what I prognosticated and predicted. In the words of Winston Churchill, "We owe so many, so much, for so few." As I said, "We will fight them in the beaches and we'll fight them in the battlefield."'

After his lip was stitched, Lennox finally made it to the Britannia Hotel at 5.45 a.m., with Violet, Dennis and his English middle-distance running friend Patrick Drayton in tow, although it was the fallen champion who seemed to be the one doing most of the consoling. He found a wake in his honour with some of his friends getting drunk; he told them there was no need for sadness and he would be back. He then went up to his room.

Meanwhile, Frank Maloney walked two miles to the hotel in a state of exhausted devastation. 'I have this cloudy impression,' he said. 'I just remember it being a blank for the next few weeks after he lost. I thought of resigning, leaving it, calling it a day, but I didn't want to be known as a one-hit wonder. That was motivating me more than anything else.' What he recalled of the hours immediately after the fight are a few fleeting memories such as the gloating of his critics. He felt particularly incensed with Frank Warren, who had been the most animated of all his rivals in his celebration of the American's victory. 'When a British boxer fights for a world title I always support him, no matter who he fights for,' he said. 'So I can't understand how anyone from here could celebrate Lennox losing his world title because it was a terrible blow for British boxing.'

He went to his room, worried that his run had come to an end and that even if he survived, with King on top again, it would take several years before they got another chance. After failing to fall asleep he got up and went to Lennox's room.

'We sat there on his bed and all I could do was put my arm around him and comfort him. I don't know who was in the worst state, him or me, but I remember looking at him and his lip was bust and he was sitting there and he was sucking on ice and he looked into my eyes and said, "It ain't over yet, Frank." Them sort of words picks you back up.'

Lennox slept two hours that night before being evacuated from the hotel after a fire broke out on the fifth floor. He posed with the firemen, signed autographs and spoke of his determination to climb back to the top and to fight again, in Britain, before Christmas. His emphasis was on the theme that nothing major had changed, right down to the question of the future of his trainer. 'Pepe's done a great job and I say, if it ain't broke, why fix it?' He went out of his way to convince everyone that this result, unjust as it was, did not fall into the category of a personally shocking event. 'When I started boxing I realised something like this could happen,' he said. 'I had to prepare myself for a moment like this, when things don't go your way. It's a setback, but a minor one. I'm definitely fighting on because I don't want to end on a bad note.'

Later that day his family heard yet another piece of bad news. For the past month they had all been secretly interviewed for the television programme *This is Your Life*, but when Lennox lost his title the show was dumped, which upset Lennox when he heard about it. The next morning, however, the Channel 4 show *The Big Breakfast* filmed a spoof version outside the Lewis house in Hadleywood. One of those who went was his friend Lawrence Lustig, who took along his eight-year-old daughter Laura. 'I thought Lennox would be really depressed, but a few minutes after I got there I found him rolling around on the carpet with Laura, play-wrestling with her, and they were laughing together and really enjoying themselves like neither of them had a care in the world. I mean, obviously he was quite devastated by what had happened and what he'd lost, but he's always had this ability to separate his boxing life from the rest of his life.'

CHAPTER FOURTEEN
HADLEYWOOD,
HERTFORDSHIRE, 1994

L ennox Lewis has just returned from his Jamaican retreat having critically examined his recent past while walking the hills above his mother's house in Port Antonio – the mistakes analysed, the implications absorbed and his purpose in life restored. But back home, he finds himself all dressed down with no one to fight. For five years his life has moved coherently in a single direction, but now it has stalled and he's not sure how to deal with it. In a strange way he quite likes the feeling – at least, it's tolerable – but it's not a state of being he wants to last for too long.

For the first time in several months he's based himself for a sustained period at his English home, together with Dennis and Violet and Ty the poodle and he likes the experience of spending time with family. Now that they're all together, they're becoming house-proud. While Lennox takes calls upstairs and Violet chats to the Jamaican domestic worker in the kitchen, Dennis asks the guests to circumvent the white carpets or at least to take off their shoes, as he begins to show off the mansion's delights: black leather couches, huge flat-screen television, office, pool room, an acre of manicured lawns, tennis court, the garden's arboreal splendours and, out front, a new Range Rover, bought shortly before the McCall fight, with the number plate L2 TKO (Dennis laughs at this one), and a new, top-of-the-range Mercedes with the more hopeful plate A1 TKO.

'It's funny,' says Lennox after his mum calls him to come downstairs, 'I'm a person that's always busy and yet I don't have anything do. You know, there's the business side to attend to, and television interviews, and fighting with this London traffic, and my phone never stops ringing. I've even got a little part in this sci-fi movie – more grunts than lines though.' Good guy or bad? 'Um, I'm playing an FBI agent, so that would be bad, I guess. But you see my point? I say I don't have anything to do, but I'm still busy.' What he means is that while his life may be full of little tasks, without the title it lacks direction and purpose. And yet, now that he's accepted his lot, he seems surprisingly contented. 'This loss just gives me time to sleep,' he says. 'So right now you could say the lion is sleeping.'

Lennox's sleeping is punctuated by runs in Trent Park and endless games of pool and chess. He takes time out to read and at the moment is perusing Thomas Hauser's biography of Muhammad Ali, rediscovering how his hero came back from defeats to Joe Frazier and Ken Norton to beat them both and then regain his title by knocking out George Foreman. That was 20 years ago and now this same George, at nearly 46, is getting his first shot at Michael Moorer's titles, while Oliver McCall is planning his first defence against 45-year-old Larry Holmes. Two dodgy champions fighting two old men. 'After something like this you start to appreciate how integral those twins, politics and business, are to boxing,' he says. 'It's the politics that will keep Lennox Lewis out for a while, but, you know, I still have great confidence in my ability. I'd been going strong for four years straight – steady, steady. People said it's too early to put me in with Mason and I could have lost to him. They said I'd get destroyed by Ruddock but I destroyed him. And then the guy to take it away was McCall, but I'm not depressed about it because when I first came into boxing I realised there would be a point where I could lose and it happened, and you live and learn.'

The living bit means he's doing his best to find the positive side in all this – like the way the British public, with its fondness for losers, has responded to him. 'It's funny and kinda weird but great too, because people who are not into boxing are suddenly taking note of me now.' And the learning bit means everything is up for grabs again. He makes it clear that he will take time out to ponder his options while recognising the need for humility, patience and outside advice. This enforced time-out offers him an opportunity to decide how his career should advance and whether he should cut deals with other promoters to get back to the top – even the dreaded Don King, because for the moment nothing is ruled out, and nothing's in either. 'In the boxing world there's people that are despicable and people that you never want to deal with, but, uh, sometimes you have to deal with them.'

The most significant opportunity is the chance to choose a new trainer. Within 24 hours of his loss he'd come to realise that the 'if it ain't broke, why fix it?' cliché only served the status quo when nothing was broken, and going down to an inferior fighter was a neon sign that some fixing was required. So, having fired Pepe, he's determined to avoid being rash in choosing a successor. He won't easily be wooed by fast talk and smooth compliments. He'll take it nice and slow, audition the candidates and then decide – just as he did with the promoters five years earlier when he turned professional. Every boxing person who passes his door gets interrogated about the qualities of each man. What do you think of this one? Would he work well with my style? What do you think of that one?

The decision to dump Pepe was made the day after the McCall fight, but they decided to hold off for a month before announcing it (after which Pepe tried to sue – without success). 'We didn't replace him immediately because we didn't want to rush out in public and sack him,' said Panos. 'The public was demanding his head but we had our own agenda, and I didn't want people to think Pepe was responsible for the loss because he wasn't. Pepe certainly didn't help with all his hype talk but it's like telling you to go jump off a cliff. Do you jump? It didn't help. It didn't help. It didn't help. But you can only blame one man and that's the man with the gloves on. You can't blame anyone else.'

An early favourite among the five candidates was George Benton, a master of defensive technique. He came to London, played pool with Lewis, downed a couple of bottles of red wine over dinner and they got on well, but not quite well enough for Lennox to take him on board. His strong preference was for the architect of his defeat. His mother had long advocated Emmanuel Steward's abilities, and this time she was backed by John Hornewer. Lennox had always liked Steward, who possessed considerable charm and an ability to dish out compliments without being gushing or obsequious, and also to criticise without sounding too negative. In Lewis's case this sunny perspective came easy, because ever since the Olympics six years earlier Manny had spoken of the Lewis as the most naturally talented heavyweight he'd ever seen.

Lennox, in turn, could not help being impressed with Steward's role in planning his own downfall and was mature enough not to take it personally. The man from Detroit had trained a string of world champions from scratch and had built on the talents of several others. He particularly relished working with tall boxers with quick hands, long jabs and big crosses, and Lewis fitted the mould – so much so that Steward was willing to step away from the man who beat him, to test his faith in the victim's potential. His 'audition' went particularly well, with Lewis appreciating the respect Steward showed, the intricate boxing knowledge he revealed and the ease he displayed in advising, correcting and encouraging. When it was over, 'Manny' told him, 'If you're interested in being just a good fighter, rather forget it.' Lennox assured him his interests went far further: he wanted greatness.

Steward, however, came with baggage. He was on good terms with Don King; he was the most expensive of the lot; and when he worked with a boxer on a long-term basis, he liked a role in management, not just in training (because aside from the financial benefits he felt it essential to play a major part in choosing opponents). Lewis reluctantly agreed to let the idea pass and moved onto another outstanding American, Thell Torrance, who refused to be auditioned and stood on his reputation. This was almost enough for Lewis, who pronounced himself highly impressed. Maloney took his lead, made Thell an offer and sent him tickets to fly to London to take up the job, but Lennox changed his mind and Frank had to tell Thell that, sorry, he was no longer wanted. Instead of suing Torrance accepted his fate with a polite shrug.

Lennox dug in and insisted Steward was the only man for the job. 'Everybody in his camp was against Emmanuel, except me,' said Hornewer. 'So you can ask today, would he have been trained by Steward without me? No.' Lennox agreed to all Steward's conditions, including a role in his management team. In return Steward agreed to remain loyal to Lennox on a long-term basis, and he was as good as his word, even when King offered him more money to work with Tyson on his release from prison. In fact, to accept the Lewis job Steward had to make a break from King, which meant giving up McCall, an option to train Tyson and a deal to train the Mexican hero Julio Cesar Chavez.

'With the first McCall fight, King called me in as a hitman, a hired specialist,' he said. 'But I had no desire for a long-term contract with him. I did my job, I was paid very well, but I always, always thought the best fighter was Lennox Lewis. I thought he was just ill-prepared, so after that fight I gave up the WBC heavyweight champion to pick up the man he beat. I have that much faith in his talent. This is the only heavyweight around with the ability to be a superstar, to be great, to put himself into boxing history along with Johnson, Louis, Marciano and Ali. If I didn't believe that, why would I leave McCall when he was a winner to go with a loser? Why would I pass up a chance to work with Tyson when he came out of jail, turning my back on a million dollars that I could have earned in the next few months? My credibility is on the line here.'

Steward's role in the decision making, which increased as boxer and trainer grew more comfortable with each other, irked Maloney, who felt wary of the charming, articulate, white-wine-drinking former amateur boxing star. 'I'm sure he'll be pissed off with me when he hears this, but I have no love for Emmanuel Steward,' he says today. 'My nature is to be very honest, and I don't rate Steward as a top trainer.' Everyone else disagreed. You don't take a feather-fisted lightweight like Tommy Hearns and turn him into one of the biggest-punching, sharpest-boxing welterweights, middleweights and light heavyweights in the sport's history unless you know what you're doing, and he performed miracles with several other champions. After two months of working together, Lennox felt he'd already made significant improvement under his new head coach.

'Emmanuel Steward is what you call a real trainer,' he pronounced. 'His past speaks for itself. He's a trainer of champions, he has so much to offer, and he's got such a history in the sport. I'm just one of his eager students who wants to learn what he has to give, and the great thing about him is that he's not a praise singer like Pepe. He'll tell you the absolute truth. If you look like shit, he'll tell you straight, or he'll tell you he's unhappy with the way you're performing in the gym, which is great. And he'll also speak the truth when he praises you, which is also great. People will say, "Ah, it's all talk from Manny – he's trying to hype the guy up," but it's what he really believes. It's the truth. He's giving me the confidence to do things that my two other trainers held me back from, by helping me to realise that I'm a big heavyweight with a great right hand and a great jab, and then to utilise these assets, and I can also see he's already adding to my technique, improving it a lot. He's got me shortening my punches, not winding up, he's correcting my tendency to tilt over to my left and lose balance when I jab, and getting me to use the left hook more, and he's helping me to deal very specifically with the tactics of the opponent I'm facing.'

While Steward was choosing the long march in preference to shorter term success with one of King's protégés, the picture in the rest of the division was changing rapidly, mainly for the worst, and each change affected Lennox's prospects.

The porcelain-chinned and extremely temperamental Moorer, who held the major share of the title, had no intention of tangling with anyone as big, young and dangerous as Lewis. His early career, when Steward trained him, cast him as an explosive southpaw light heavyweight. But at a broad-shouldered 6ft 2in he was too big for the 175lb limit and his lack of discipline regarding eating and training and his inclination to get drunk (as well as rowdy and violent) meant that he outgrew both that division and the next, settling in as a smallish heavyweight. At first he continued with his bash-'em-up ways, but an atavistic brawl with the cruiserweight Bert Cooper, which saw Moorer dropped twice before prevailing, changed his approach. He defected from Steward to George Benton and became a boring but effective defensive boxer, and then from Benton to Teddy Atlas, who in his idiosyncratic 'Do you want me to do the fighting?' way prodded him towards the title.

He chose as his first challenger the highly marketable and beatable George Foreman, who seemed more of a novelty act than a genuine threat. Once, George had been a different kind of monster, the prototype of a new generation of menace. For anyone around in 1973 it was hard to forget the five minutes when he brutalised Joe Frazier in Kingston, Jamaica, after which he became the embodiment of the title he held: silent and violent, with his Afro and his Alsatian and his aura of menace. He seemed enormous (though at 217½lb he was small by today's standards) and invincible. And then it evaporated. The world watched, disbelieving, as the inexplicable happened in a jungle setting under Mobuto's brutal US-backed dictatorship in Kinshasa, Zaire. Muhammad Ali discovered George's weak link – a lack of stamina, and an obsession with finishing the job quickly – and exploited it to a thoroughly illogical end by knocking him out in the eighth round. From then on George was stamped with the mark of Muhammad. Forget what he did to Frazier and Ken Norton before, or Frazier and Ron Lyle after; he was forever the giant who fell in the jungle. Ali would not risk his life by giving him a shot at redemption, and so, in 1977, after a religious epiphany and a second secular defeat, George retreated.

There must still have been something mean about him – how else do you explain his decision to name all his sons George? But in his calculating way he realised that only a complete makeover would sell. During his decade in the pasture, this former street thug pickled his body in fat, acquired the appearance of wit and wisdom, played at being a preacher man and waited. In the lengthy interim, Larry Holmes's pear-shaped body and abrasive greed seemed apposite in the jaded late-disco world of the time; except that he just happened to be a sublime talent and there was no way George would have lived with him. But by the mid-1980s Larry was burnt out and the man of the moment was a terror in the mould of the old Foreman – Mike Tyson. There seemed no place for the aged anymore.

When Foreman returned in 1987, at first it seemed like a classic case for Marx's dictum on two Napoleons and historical repetition: first as tragedy; then as farce. Except perhaps they should have allowed for a third option, because once the farce was done George had another hand to play. In millennia to come he'll be remembered not just as the seventies hard man who fell so far to Ali, but also as the nineties joker who reinvented himself with such magnificent American chutzpah, rose high again and wreaked soft vengeance on the sneering lot of them. By then he had attracted a slew of aged clones, including the masterful Larry, but in the world of comebacks there was room for only one gigantic geriatric prototype and the original was not for stepping aside.

He achieved this by recasting himself as the humane, self-deprecating, tubby fellow with the joke on himself, and, ultimately, on all of those who laughed. To be sure, he had some good lines. It was all to raise money for the Church (like hell), and was fuelled by those triple cheeseburgers (yeah, yeah), but his best crack was about his Ali thing. What a laugh, the way he couldn't handle it in those days, and America chuckled along with him, delighted he'd found a way of overcoming such a life-defining setback. If they'd looked closer they would have noticed that those laugh-at-myself guffaws were in themselves a clear pointer to George's steely missionary zeal, because privately he was still seething and this anger was detectable in the way he displayed his cold intelligence. Even on his sunniest days it was only partly disguised by the avuncular smile. There was method, method, method behind the mirror of madness. Boxing promoters and just about anyone else who had to deal with him outside the ring described him as the hardest son-of-a-bitch around. Larry Holmes, admittedly never one to pass a compliment when an insult will do, called him a 'total fraud who is the opposite of the nice guy he pretends to be'. And he added, 'The guy is a con artist and it's time people stopped being fooled by his nonsense.'

In a way, it was the same in the ring. While pretending to be training on burgers he was, in reality, slaving away in his Houston gym, building the biggest and strongest set of arms the division had ever known, creating a new style designed for preserving energy, and perfecting it by beating up the hired help with cold-eyed cruelty while handpicking opponents for maximum effect. The best of these come-forward white men, like the eager bleeder Pierre Coetzer, discovered too late just how serious he was. 'You think he's just old and slow and fat,' said Coetzer, 'but every time he hits you, even with a jab, your whole body shudders. It takes everything out of you, and he's so damn accurate.'

Sure there were failures – first a sound beating by Holyfield, then a closer one against Tommy Morrison – but even then George was out-earning the lot of them while waiting for the next opening. It came when the out-of-sorts Evander lost his title to Moorer, who wanted some safe money. The big man had his final chance. For nine rounds he absorbed a severe pasting as Moorer peppered him with right jabs and hooks and bopped him with left crosses before moving out of range. But the smaller man grew weary of shifting all this weight and hung around for a second too long, and with one slow but impeccably timed and accurately placed right cross on Moorer's extremely fragile chin it was all over. Twenty years after Zaire, Foreman was, again, king of the whole wide world.

He reigned as he pleased, placing the title on ice, returning to his diet of white boys, which was how he came to be stripped of his titles. He admitted that Lennox would have beaten him even at his youthful peak. 'Lewis was the greatest heavyweight of all,' he said when Lennox announced his retirement. 'He was good enough to compete with anyone.' So there was no way he would ever contemplate fighting him. In fact, there was no way he would consider fighting anyone within the world's top ten. His first defence was against a moderately accomplished German called Axel Schulz, who received his rating and his chance when the IBF boss Bobby Lee was bribed with $100,000 to place him in the top ten. He proved far too young and quick for George and soundly outboxed him, but the IBF judges looked the other way and gave George the decision. After that the old man decided he'd keep clear of anyone within the world's top 30, but eventually lost his 'linear' title on a dubious decision to his first black challenger, Shannon Briggs.

Foreman's cynical expedience meant the world title was fractured beyond recognition, which aided just one man, Don King. In the 1980s he had sent Mike Tyson on a mission to clean up the reigning pretenders, and now, nearly a decade later, he was ready to do it again, as soon as Mike was released.

Tyson would never agree with this, but jail might have been the best place for him in the early 1990s. If the jury's verdict was correct (and there is still some doubt), he certainly deserved to be there, but aside from this, his life had been veering out of control. After the death of Cus D'Amato and the discovery that his other managers were ripping him off, he took solace in the arms of the television starlet Robin Givens, who still claims to love him and who, together with her gold-digging mum, managed to divert a huge chunk of Mike's millions and convince him that he needed to take anti-depressants to control his moods. Mike regularly beat up Robin, backhanding her across the room two weeks before their marriage, knocking her out; bashing her in the face with a phone; 'choking me, kicking me and things like that,' she said. 'But he felt bad, really bad. He'd cry like a baby. I used to hold him. I'd console him. I held him a lot. He'd cry a lot. There was really something about him. I was ga-ga over him.' And still he'd run around propositioning other women. 'Once there were lipstick stains on his crotch,' she said in a joint television interview with him. To which he responded, laughing, 'I'm a pig. A dirty dog.'

Eventually they parted, Robin painfully richer and Mike painfully more suspicious of people generally and women specifically, and more inclined to lash out when the darkness descended. He told his biographer, the former Cus D'Amato champion Jose Torres, how much he liked to hurt women when he had sex with them, and it emerged that he did a lot of hurting. He spun increasingly out of control, totalling his car by driving it into a tree, beating up strangers and former opponents, harassing women, drinking too much and taking drugs. His psychiatrists decided he had attention-deficit disorder, hyperactivity and a learning disability; Tyson himself decided he was hopeless and sad and expected to be betrayed by the people he loved. 'I have no self-esteem but the biggest ego in the world,' he once said, adding that he was aware these two were related. For a while he seemed to reform after the shock of losing his world title, but his behaviour soon returned to form, ending with his arrest for raping Desiree Washington.

In prison (or the Indiana Youth Center, as it was called) he was cleaned of his substance abuse problems and put in an environment where there was an incentive to learn. Early release depended on passing his school leaver's exam, but in the end he fell one percentage point short, his maths letting him down. He wasn't much good at writing either, but when it came to reading he showed promise, making nonsense of the claims that he was a thick oaf. Don King famously tried the same thing when he was behind bars for manslaughter, although from the evidence of his renditions of Shakespeare, Churchill and 'St Thomas Aquinine' it often seemed he had gone no further than the index. Tyson delved deeper, absorbing bits and pieces from an eclectic range, and from the evidence of his interviews he certainly understood a fair amount of it. His choice of writers was said to range from Jack London (implicitly racist in everything he wrote, said Mike) to Maya Angelou, Frederick Douglas and W.E.B. Dubois. He liked the hard-headed logic of Nietzsche, Genghis Khan and

Machiavelli as well as the revolutionary zeal of Marx and Engel's *Communist Manifesto*, Mao's *Little Red Book* and Che Guevara, and he also claimed to have dipped into Tolstoy, Voltaire, Plato, Socrates, Dumas and Hemingway. He acquired new tattoos – Mao and Arthur Ashe – and a new religion – Islam – which meant further reading (of the Koran) and plenty of prayer. This being prison, he had to look after himself in the usual way. Once, when he was dishing out Christmas gifts to fellow inmates, an enormous prison gang leader objected to his own role being usurped, and threatened Mike. It took one punch, with the gangster finding himself on his back several metres away, for the message to sink home that Mike Tyson was a different category of inmate.

His release was the most eagerly anticipated event in sport and there was a race to his heart and signature. Inevitably, despite claims about Tyson money being channelled in the direction of King family members, it was Don who took the prize. He quickly set him up to knock over the three heavyweight skittles balancing on the increasingly ridiculous podiums of the rival alphabet bodies. Needless to say, King had no intention of allowing Lewis anywhere near Tyson, or anywhere near the WBC title. Oliver McCall said, 'I'll give Lennox Lewis a rematch if the money is right,' but Don King, who made the decisions, said: 'His chances of a rematch are slim, and none, and slim has just left town.'

The opponent Lewis most desired was Riddick Bowe. 'Even after my loss, I'm still talking about a Bowe fight,' he admitted three weeks after his defeat to McCall. Bowe, however, had stopped talking about Lewis. This might have made sense if he had better options but he'd lost his last chance of fighting for any of the recognised versions of the world heavyweight title. Foreman was not remotely interested in anyone as big and black as Bowe, and neither was McCall, for different reasons. 'I'll never give him a fight because of what he done with that WBC belt,' he said. 'We don't want Riddick Bowe.'

Bowe therefore fought for the meaningless WBO title, a belt generally used for temporary convenience and then disposed of when something more respectable arose. His opponent was yet another small, quick, china-chinned, out-of-control young heavyweight, although this time it was a Nigerian-born Englishman rather than a ghetto-born American. Herbie Hide outboxed Bowe for a couple of rounds, hit him hard and hurt him before succumbing to the combination of Riddick's superior size, strength and experience and also to Bowe's inclination to shake up opponents by landing well-placed punches behind the neck. But Bowe quickly and appropriately grew tired of this bauble and instead hung around, growing fat, waiting for something juicier. As it turned out he had only one more outstanding performance left in him. In 1995 he re-yoked himself to Papa Smurf's discipline and worked his way to impeccable shape to take on his one-time Cuban sparring partner, Jorge Gonzalez, exposing the gulf between the amateur and professional games by stopping him in six rounds – before incensing Lennox (who was commentating for HBO) by dishing out some choice insults, this time aimed at his mother. 'Lennox was very angry and upset about the extremely personal things Riddick said about Violet at the press conference after the fight,' Steward remembered, 'He never forgot or forgave him.'

Without Bowe, Tyson or Foreman, Lennox's best option was to secure a mandatory title shot. Once again he chose the WBC, partly because the dispute over the McCall stoppage gave him an edge and also because the WBC, for all its sins, was larger then its rivals and retained the appearance of some form of democratic accountability, which none of the others bothered with. Maloney and Eliades attended the organisation's annual conference in Seville, where Frank went out of his way to grovel before Sulaiman, apologising profusely for insulting him in a moment of madness. King responded with a booklet featuring the picture of an enraged Maloney poking his finger into Jose's face while calling the Lewis camp enemies of the WBC. But in the end the combination of Maloney's lobbying skills and a fine speech by Eliades swung things their way, a majority of delegates voting to offer Lewis a final eliminator against the highest challenger.

This, however, was not what King had in mind. His plan was to clear the decks for Tyson, so Sulaiman tossed in a caveat that Mike would become mandatory challenger as soon as he secured a win after coming out of jail, despite the fact that he hadn't fought in four years and that there was no stipulation about the quality of his first comeback opponent. His straight-faced rationale involved comparing Tyson's situation to Muhammad Ali's in 1967, when Ali was unjustly stripped of his world title and threatened with jail after refusing to serve in an American military involved in what he considered an unjust war. In the world according to Jose, Tyson, like Ali, was an innocent man, unjustly jailed. The rule of law – that he was charged, prosecuted and convicted of rape by a jury of his peers – was of no interest to a man who felt he was better able to decide the rights and wrongs of Tyson's case than, say, twelve jurors, or, say, the delegates of his own organisation. In effect, it meant the WBC had made two contradictory decisions: one by the delegates for Lewis to be the top contender if he beat the top challenger, and the other, from Sulaiman, that Tyson would be top contender if he beat anyone.

Tyson emerged from prison, rolled over the inept Pete McNeely in one round on 19 August 1995 and was inserted at the top of the WBC's ratings. Meanwhile, his former sparring partner struggled to handle his celebrity status and returned to his old druggie ways. McCall's first defence was against the ancient Holmes and he squeaked through on points. Lennox, in contrast, was given what seemed like a rather more demanding assignment. The top contender was, once again, Tony Tucker, but King decided Tony couldn't cut it. He therefore picked someone he felt was dangerous enough to present a threat to Lewis's ostensibly fragile confidence. Lionel Butler, who once put in a brief, wild spell as a Lewis sparring partner (Butler walked out midway through his stint), was even less reliable than McCall, and he had even more of a problem with over-eating than Bowe. But when he had his mind on the job this squat, 5ft 11in American could be a potent fighter: unbeaten in the previous four years with fifteen of these sixteen wins coming inside the distance, including stoppages over two former 'world' champions. Even when his mind was on the fridge, the bottle and the white powder, he could take you out with one punch and was rated the heaviest puncher in the division. As King viewed it, 'Lewis has shown he ain't got no chin. Butler will destroy him, just like McCall did.'

Lennox trained for a month in Steward's famous Kronk gym in Detroit and then for six weeks at 7,200 feet altitude in Big Bear, California, before arriving in Sacramento to settle in for his 13 May 1995 return. He was delighted with his new trainer's approach and was enjoying his training for the first time in ages – driving himself in running and cycling, sparring with more focus and intensity than in the past and building up his strength by doing a fresh range of resistance exercises. Steward won the respect of the rest of the team, including Harold Knight and Courtney Shand. After the first few days they were smiling, immensely relieved they were finally working under a grown-up who knew his job and let them do theirs. 'There's no comparison between Manny and Pepe,' said Shand. 'The biggest difference is that Manny works with you instead of against you, which is what Pepe was doing. I could see from day one after Manny came on board that Lennox was developing. Every day he works on new things and on correcting old things, so it's a very different type of regime. He doesn't believe in being the kind of boss who never listens, so when we tell him things that he doesn't see, he listens. And he always asks what we're doing. Pepe would never do that.'

By the time they completed their preparation Lennox looked a different man. For one thing he was growing his 'locks' as a sign of his increasing affinity with Jamaican reggae culture. For another he was bigger, coming in at 248lb, ten more than against McCall. This time, however, the extra bulk was all muscle – a tribute to the heavier weights and strength exercises devised by Shand. By the end of the camp he could benchpress 385lb and would regularly do sets of eight lifts with 225lb, in addition to four sets of twenty chin-ups in the morning and five sets of fifteen in the afternoon, and the same with dips, neck weight exercises, back-raises and a range of other strengthening exercises. Some days he would total 300 push-ups.

When Steward arrived he observed Lennox's chess-playing approach and tried to transform him into a more instinctual boxer. 'We're talking about a guy who is six foot five and the best-built heavyweight I ever saw, with big, long muscles that give him tremendous power while leaving his body flexible and athletic. He has a good chin, strong legs and excellent stamina and he's an amazingly accurate puncher. Properly prepared and going out as a confident, kick-ass Lennox, he whips every heavyweight in sight and Tyson would be one of the easiest. With his talent it's a disgrace he hasn't achieved more and that he has had so many drag-out wins against men he should've annihilated, but he's still a big baby in many ways. He's surrounded by so much love, people happy to devote their lives to him. It helps that his mother Violet is with us to cook his food and look after him, and Courtney, who's been his friend since they were kids in Canada and has done a marvellous job on his conditioning, is always there for him to rely on. But some of those working with Lennox gave him an easy ride, ducked the responsibility of making him confront the realities of this tough and violent business. For me there's an advantage in this because the fact that he's never been taught much means he's not set in too many bad habits.'

The 27-year-old Butler took a different approach to training: abstinence. King hired Pepe Correa for the job, hoping this would give his man an inside edge, but even a more mature trainer would have struggled with this version of Butler, who returned to his old ways of drugs and gluttony and came in at 261lb – 30 more than his best. A few days before the fight his breath smelled boozy. Still, Pepe could always talk a good fight. 'Lewis is just a punk with no heart and no chin who blamed me and everyone else except himself when he was knocked out by McCall,' he said.

Steward was worried about Butler's unpredictability. 'You don't know what to expect from a guy like that, he told Lewis. 'Butler won't be passive and you'd better take some ferocity of your own in there. You should say to yourself, "I'm a big man, and dammit, I'm going to make you respect me. Bring your little ass in here – you're just something for me to look good with."'

Butler's plan was to take it early because he was in no shape for protracted war. He certainly looked threatening in the first round, catching Lennox flush with a heavy overhand right and a meaty left hook, but Lewis took them well, even if the shock prompted him into more caution than planned. He'd been out of the ring for eight months and despite all the sparring it took him a while to relax when faced with such heavy-handed aggression, but midway through the second round he began moving fluidly, landing sharp jabs, quick crosses and the occasional uppercut, and by round three Butler's left eye was closing. Correa screamed before the fourth, 'You gotta get inside!' but he had nothing left. Lionel groaned after being caught with a heavy right and Lennox dropped him with a left-right combination early in the fifth and then asserted his dominance by pushing him down again. Late in the round he landed another flurry ending with a big right cross, and Butler slid down the ropes until his ample posterior reached the bottom strand, a bit like a slob collapsing on the sofa after too much dinner, prompting referee Marty Dinkin to stop the fight. It took over twenty seconds before Butler could get to his feet again.

Steward felt reasonably satisfied with his pupil's performance. He had boxed more or less to instructions but took a round longer than anticipated to complete the job. 'When I got Lewis he was boxing at only forty per cent of his potential,' he said. 'Now he's up to sixty per cent.' He wanted to see Lewis in another fight against a short, strong heavyweight of Tyson-like proportions, albeit one far less risky than Butler or Mike and the man chosen for this routine assignment in Dublin, seven weeks later, was Justin Fortune, a muscular, 29-year-old, 5ft 9in, 216½lb former power lifter whose record of two losses in fourteen fights suggested his limitations. But he was strong and aggressive, with a decent left hook that he managed to land in round one, although it had no visible effect on the 246lb Lewis. The idea was to try out all the moves practised in the gym – getting his guard up quickly whenever Fortune came in, working on the inside, using his uppercut more. By round four the Australian was badly cut under the left eye and Lennox went out to close the show, throwing a trio of massive uppercuts at close range, jerking Fortune's head back at an alarming angle. Referee Roy Francis leapt in to save the Australian as he fell to the canvas. Lennox was relieved. 'I didn't want to hurt him too badly,' he said.

Meanwhile, Frank Bruno was training as fanatically as ever for his fourth bid at a version of the world title, this time against an increasingly wobbly Oliver McCall.

His chance arose through two overlapping decisions: Don King's to pick Frank Warren as his British partner; and Bruno's to drop Mickey Duff and sign with Warren and King.

In the early 1990s Warren was struggling to survive financially, so much so that the British High Court later banned him from taking up a position as a company director for seven years following a four-year Department of Trade and Industry investigation that found he'd been trading while insolvent. Then along came King, who needed a British partner and who had already been turned down by Maloney. King provided Warren with the prestige, backing and connections to take him back to the top of British boxing promotion. He later claimed to have helped Warren 'when he was on his deathbed' and said he 'brought Frank back from destitution and ill repute to high esteem and stature in the world of boxing' – a view Warren described as 'absolute bullshit', taking particular exception to King's suggestion that 'my arse was hanging out of my trousers when we met'. In return, Warren negotiated British television deals for King, supplied him with British boxers and sang his praises to the heavens, claiming that criticism of Don often amounted to racism. 'When doing a deal with Don King, the negotiations are very tough, and whatever the deal is, that's the deal you got,' he said then. 'If you make money from it, great. If you don't make money from it, that's your problem.' He would later see other dimensions to his honest Don partner. At the time, however, with King's backing, he signed up several of the biggest earners in British boxing. Some, like the retreaded Bruno, he shared with King from the start; others, like the mercurial, bombastic and wonderfully marketable featherweight 'Prince' Naseem Hamed, he managed to keep for himself. By 1995 the King–Warren alliance, funded locally by a lucrative Sky television deal, had pushed Warren's Sports Network Europe organisation into the premier position in British boxing promotion.

Bruno was just the sort of heavyweight King needed – massively popular at home, which meant he would pull the punters, and easily beatable, especially by Tyson. King offered him the Oliver McCall gig with the promise, or threat, that if he won he would make his first defence against Mike. It is unlikely Bruno would have survived twelve rounds with the version of McCall who defeated Lewis, but a year later, without Manny Steward as trainer and once again full of doubt and drugs, Oliver managed no more than the minimum motions of training. He seemed uninterested in proceedings, even when the packed Wembley stadium booed him to the rafters. He later admitted he should have been in drug rehabilitation, not in the ring, at that time. Bruno fought a disciplined fight, with his guard high and his heavy jab pumping. McCall blinked, closed his eyes and fell asleep for eleven rounds. Nothing Bruno landed seemed to have much effect on him but he was throwing little in return. Finally, with one round to go, his corner persuaded him he was heading for oblivion unless he flattened Frank and this roused him out of his stupor. He walked through Bruno's jab and bashed him on the chin. As usual, Bruno's body went stiff and lifeless, only this time he fell against McCall and found the flicker of consciousness to cling on. In his wild desperation McCall lacked the composure to give himself room to plant his biggest bombs. He landed several more clubbing blows but none with the precision to close the show. Bruno rolled around like a drunk but retained enough awareness to grab, and he survived. When the decision was announced and Bruno became the new WBC champion, he wept, repeating over and over again in memory of Lennox's slur, 'I'm not an Uncle Tom, I'm not, I'm not. I'm not an Uncle Tom.'

The Fortune fight saw Lewis returning to Sky television. He fell out with them a year earlier when the Sky Sports boss Kelvin McKenzie decided to fork out £10 million to Barry Hearn and Chris Eubank for the privilege of showing Chris getting awarded a series of dubious decisions in defence of his nonsense WBO belt, usually against boxers outside the world's top thirty, in what was billed as his 'world tour' but with one exception was really his tour of Britain and Ireland. McKenzie grudgingly offered Lewis a reduced deal but Lennox told him where to stick it and defected to a short-lived rival, Wire TV. With McKenzie out of Sky and a more generous offer on the table, he agreed to return.

At the same time HBO offered a lucrative contract to fight in a 'tournament' to determine the best heavyweight in the world not promoted by King. Others they had in mind included Tommy Morrison, Ray Mercer, Holyfield, Bowe, Moorer and the unbeaten Pole Andrej Golota. HBO boss Seth Abraham maintained that King would never allow Lewis to fight for the WBC title and that the other 'alphabet organisation' titles were becoming worthless bits of garnish, passed from one nonentity to another. It was better to go against heavyweights who meant something in America, even if no title belts changed hands. Lennox was not convinced. After all, the WBC delegates had voted to secure him the next mandatory shot at McCall and the WBC supervisor at the Butler fight had publicly reiterated this position. While he waited, however, he went ahead with Abraham's HBO plan, starting with a fight against Tommy Morrison in Atlantic City on 2 October 1995.

Morrison was an extremely popular heavyweight for several reasons. First, he was a fighter who loved a good tear-up, possessed quick hands and a cracking left hook, was vulnerable around the whiskers and yet had the guts to fight through the pain of multiple knockdowns – and, on one occasion, a broken jaw – to win. Second, with his peroxide-blond hair he was regarded as white (although in fact he said his mum was a 'full-blooded' Native American) and was therefore branded with the clichéd epithet 'Great White Hope' – a product both of a racist yearning for a return to the days of Jack Dempsey (and of the fact that there've been no white American world heavyweight champions since Rocky Marciano in the 1950s). Third, he achieved fame outside the confines of the ring by co-starring with Sylvester Stallone in the movie *Rocky IV*, playing Rocky's protégé Tommy Gunn. Fourth, he came with a great story line: a trailer-park kicker from Oklahoma who claimed to be related to John Wayne (very distantly, it turned out) and lived his life in a suitably idiosyncratic way – cougars, leopards and monkeys at home, a love of guns, more women than Magic Johnson, and, in his early professional days, a habit of drinking nine pints of beer a night. Most of all, he relished a good brawl.

Between the ages of seven and thirteen Tommy claimed a 229–13 amateur record, after which he felt hard enough to leave home. He worked on construction sites in the Oklahoma panhandle during holidays, supplementing the income by fighting on the Toughman circuit. The minimum age was 21, but with his fake ID the thirteen-year-old was accepted and had no trouble taming the half-drunk hicks gloved up to face him, winning 59 out of 60 fights. 'I was never a bully,' he said, 'but if somebody wanted to fight it didn't take a lot to get me interested. My brother and I had a reputation, but I think it was a good one. When we walked into a bar-room everybody's attitude kind of calmed down a little bit.' He turned down a football scholarship and returned to amateur boxing with the idea of making the US Olympic team, but lost to the eventual gold medallist Ray Mercer, after which, at the age of nineteen, he turned professional, winning 28 in a row, 24 on knockouts. Then in fight number 29 he fought Mercer again, outboxing him for four rounds, until Ray battered him into unconsciousness in the fifth. Too over-confident, too inexperienced, not yet learnt to relax, said Tommy. Too soft-chinned, said the media. He bounced back and learned a few new tricks to outbox Foreman in 1993 but two fights on he was knocked out in one round by Michael Bentt, which scotched the original plan for a Lewis–Morrison fight. But Tommy's problems were less in the ring than out. As his trainer Dr Tommy Virgets explained, Morrison worked hard for the big ones, but once it was over he would go wild for a month or two, partying non-stop. 'He drinks too much and can't handle alcohol, he hangs out with an entourage of assholes and he's the world's greatest bimbo-magnet.' He also struggled to separate work and play, and had to pay $40,000 in an out-of-court settlement after blurring this distinction in an incident in an Iowa restaurant.

Still, after the Bentt disaster he bounced back, and in his last fight prior to facing Lennox he climbed off the floor to stop Razor Ruddock in six rounds. He was unbeaten in his previous eight fights and saw victory over Lewis as his final opportunity. Having fathered two children with different women, he tried to settle down with a third and had a serious bash at becoming a Seventh Day Adventist – his childhood faith. He also cut out alcohol for two months and trained harder than ever before, Virgets constantly emphasising the necessity of keeping his hips low, fighting from a crouch and attacking the body. By fight time he was sure he would break Lewis. 'I'd never been more confident,' he recalled. 'I thought I'd take him out in two or three rounds.' The key, he felt, was not only his preparedness but his opponent's vulnerabilities. 'I question Lewis's balls,' he said before the fight. 'I don't think he's mentally a tough person.' Asked about his own vulnerabilities, such as his reputation for a glassy chin, he joked, 'If I got a dollar every time anyone asked me that, I'd be a rich man. Come to think of it, I am a rich man, so I may have a glass jaw.'

The 6ft 2in Tommy, who entered the ring with his cropped hair back to its natural mouse and a thin line of beard, looked in superb nick at a ripped 227lb, but he was fourteen pounds lighter than Lennox and this gap in size told from the start. After a cautious opening round – 'I came out really relaxed,' said Lennox – he dropped Morrison with a short left hook to the top of the head; then used his jab to cut him on the side of his right eye. By the third Lennox was starting to hook off his jab, something he seldom tried in his pre-Steward days. 'Everything flowed from the left,' said Steward, 'and the left hook was the key.' Morrison's left eye began to swell and there was an air of desperation about his work. He was struggling to reach the taller man, his efforts hampered by clouded vision. 'My eye started closing and it got hard to fight with one eye,' he said later.

Lewis knew he could pick him off without getting hit. 'I realised as long as I kept patient, used my jab and threw some combinations, it would be too much for him,' he said. Morrison finally got his chance to test his own theories when he landed a big right to the side of the head and then a solid uppercut, but the punches had no effect and Lennox continued outboxing him, opening up with quick combinations and slicing open a second cut under the left eye. Late in round five he dug in a hurtful right hook to the body and then a right uppercut under the chin, and Tommy was down again. Virgets implored, 'Tommy! You got to take him into a war this round. We're not going to win on points.' Tommy tried but lacked the tools. Lennox raked him with jabs and then dropped him with a right cross a minute into round six. Thirty seconds later he put him down for a fourth time with a left hook to the temple – 'he was watching out for my right so I figured I would throw the hook' – and referee Mills Lane stopped what had become a one-sided battering.

Steward would have preferred overwhelming force rather than a systematic sapping of resistance, but he was pleased with his pupil's mindset. 'He came out with a cocky, arrogant attitude like a gang leader, which was the opposite of what he had in the past.'

Lennox left for his holiday in Jamaica with his friend Courtney Shand feeling frustrated with the way his life was going. He talked of being 'in the wilderness' – 30 years old with no children, no steady girlfriend and nothing to show for his career. He was out walking one afternoon, thinking about his life, when a family friend came over to say he'd just heard on the radio that Morrison was diagnosed HIV positive. Lennox remembered those cuts he'd opened around Tommy's eyes and the way his blood had splashed around, and he thought of the times he worked up close and the times Tommy grabbed him. He worried that maybe a drop reached his own eyes and began to wonder how much longer he had to live. Maybe he wouldn't die in one of the ways he'd imagined – peaceful and old in his bed, or from a bullet fired by a jealous husband or lover, or even from the wrong punch at the wrong time in the ring – but instead from some horrible Aids-related disease.

Then he began to consider how Morrison must be feeling and tried to phone him in America, but Tommy had left home in a daze after the shock diagnosis and Lennox never managed to reach him. After a few more days of panic he abandoned his holiday plans and flew to Toronto where a doctor he knew well gave him a blood test. Before he received the results the doctor told him that while the chances of contracting Aids from unprotected sexual contact, blood transfusions and sharing needles were extremely high, the odds of the disease passing through skin contact with a cut eye were negligible. As long as he took care in these other areas he would probably be fine. To Lennox's immense relief the result came back negative and was subsequently confirmed. His second chance would come.

CHAPTER FIFTEEN
PHOENIX, ARIZONA, 1996

L ying back on his bed in the luxury suite at the Camelback Inn, four days before Christmas, the best Lennox can say about his 1996 is that at last it's coming to an end. He's managed just one fight this year and soon it will be just one in sixteen months – and his biggest victory was in the courtroom. He's seen his third major opportunity for a fight with Bowe evaporate. He's seen Bruno falling to Tyson and then Tyson falling to Holyfield, but nothing much for Lewis, except a close shave. Even his coming fight, his return with the mad McCall, keeps on being postponed.

But now he's allowing himself hope. Oliver McCall may be in a state of drug rehabilitation after several arrests, but Lennox feels sure he'll turn up for their return fight on 7 February 1997. 'McCall's personal situation – with him getting arrested and all – that doesn't really worry me,' he says, 'because I definitely don't think there's any possibility he'll pull out. I absolutely guarantee you he'll be there. Don King will not only look bad if he isn't, but he'll lose a lot of money, so McCall will be there.'

Lennox feels he is finally set to return to where he left off two and a half years before. He's repeating this particular litany over and over again, to convince himself as much as anyone else because he still has seven more weeks to go, and the prospect of further disappointment is just too sickening to contemplate. 'Yeah, he'll be there all right,' he insists, 'and then you can look at it as, basically, payback time for me. Don King kept Oliver McCall away from me because he realised he beat me with a lucky punch, and he realised what I am able to do, and the fact that all his boxers will lose if they come up against me. That's why he didn't want McCall or Bruno or Tyson to fight me, but my perseverance and the public's knowledge and the courts forced his hand.'

Not that his forthcoming engagement is ideal. He'd prefer Riddick Bowe. 'I think Bowe can still take a lot more punishment. I hope so,' he says. 'And I would also love to take the H out of Holyfield,' he adds, with a smile at his attempt at a joke. 'And if I get in there with Tyson, I will box him aggressively and beat him up.' The idea of getting back with the only man to beat him holds less of a thrill. More like relief after waiting so long. Relief combined with impatience because he's anxious to move on to beat these other, more deserving men. But at least he's focused on the present this time. The long period of contemplating what went wrong – lucky punch, fast count, bad referee, and, yes, the lapse in commitment under the wrong trainer and the lack of concentration in the ring – all that is in the distant past. 'I'm just getting myself prepared for the fight – ready for the night. Nothing else matters, not even all the chopping and changing, and the fact that this is my second leg of training for this fight. And I don't really ponder on what happened back in 1994. I just realise what took place and I know it will never take place again. This time, second time around, I will definitely beat McCall. I will do a job on the guy.'

He talks with animated enthusiasm about his daily routine, starting with the task of lugging his heavier-than-normal body around for those early-morning runs in the desert cold and then the details of his gym work and the qualities of each of his sparring partners, the new techniques he's learning under Steward's supervision – how to catch the jab better, for instance – and finally how Courtney Shand is helping him build additional muscle to allow him to manhandle McCall. These are the subjects that consume him in training camp and it's a relief to be discussing them as present reality because it's what he does. It's what makes him Lennox Lewis. It's his current purpose in life.

But this discussion soon reminds him of the lack of purpose of the rest of his year, the perpetual frustration of the long gestation period since he beat up Tommy Morrison. There were brief moments when the temptation to pack it all in occurred as a quickly passing fancy. 'Yeah, somewhat,' he acknowledges, before offering the reassurance that it was never one he pondered for long. 'There's just that void there that's unfulfilled. Basically I needed to feel comfortable with myself before I really allowed myself to think about that.' And when will that comfort zone be reached? 'Oh, I'd say I've got about four more fights before I retire. Yeah, and then I'll probably become a great basketball star.' He laughs softly at this one. Four more fights. A life after boxing. Bit of a joke really.

Soon after the Morrison fight the talk turned to that elusive showdown with Bowe who was training for his 'rubber' match with Holyfield. It was, for once, serious talk, backed by genuine negotiations, prompting the assumption that if Bowe prevailed the Lewis fight was a done deal. Once again this pair delivered an exciting, vicious scrap. Evander managed to drop Bowe heavily but was too exhausted to finish him, and was knocked down and then bludgeoned to defeat in round eight (after which he claimed to have been seriously ill before the fight and therefore lacking his usual energy levels). Lewis was invited to the post-fight press conference, where his fight with Bowe was set to be announced. But with Rock and Riddick you could never be sure. As Bowe turned his lumpy face towards the tall man with the suit and dreadlocks, he let out a growl from his bruised lips. 'Lennox, you look like a pussy,' he said. 'I think I'm gonna come down there and cut off your dreads and then make you my bitch.' Lennox glared at him and smiled slowly, with a look of utter contempt on his face. Soon after he got up to leave, and Bowe yelled, 'Don't go away because I'm gonna knock you out in 1996.'

But Bowe prevaricated, turning his gaze towards Tyson while dismissing Lewis as a fall-back option. An alarmed Seth Abraham, who was keen on making a Bowe–Lewis fight as part of his bid to build an alternative to the King axis, then put forward an offer for Lennox to receive $8 million and Bowe over $11 million. While their managers and lawyers chewed this over, Lewis's US promoter, Dan Duva, died of a brain tumour and was succeeded as head of Main Events by his less able and honest brother Dino, who had another idea. His father, the family patriarch Lou Duva, managed and trained the exciting, unbeaten US-based Polish heavyweight Andrej 'Andrew' Golota. Lou and Dino favoured Golota over Lewis and persuaded Riddick that his interests lay in fighting the Pole first and so, once again, Lennox was bypassed. 'That was the third time Lennox realistically could have fought Bowe,' said John Hornewer. 'HBO made a serious offer but Main Events had Golota and decided to give him the Bowe fight. That's the reason it didn't happen then. Basically, Main Events wanted Golota in there and not Lennox.'

The first unexpected observation about this strange encounter was how much stronger the Pole was than the American. Golota pushed Bowe around, bashed him from one side of the ring to another, walked through his punches and hammered him, winning five of the first six rounds. Bowe, invariably a dirty fighter, put in his share of the rough stuff – rabbit punches, low blows and fighting after the bell – but for once he was outdone. Despite Golota's success in battering his opponent with legitimate blows he could not resist the temptation of teeing off on the crotch. Finally, late in round seven, the severely battered Bowe sank to the canvas after being whacked once again in the testicles and was declared the winner on a disqualification. Black American anger at Golota's tactics and Polish-American anger at the manner of Bowe's victory prompted a wild Madison Square Garden riot, with chairs and fists flying inside and outside the ring, leading to sixteen arrests and numerous injuries. One of Bowe's cornermen rushed over to the confused Golota and bashed him on the head with a mobile phone, opening a cut, which was more than Riddick managed. As more ringsiders leapt into the ring to join in the brawl, Lou Duva looked like he was having a heart attack, although he later recovered in hospital.

Bowe's excuse was that he took Golota too lightly, so instead of Lewis he agreed to a return five months on, and this time arrived looking in fine nick, back to his title-winning weight of 235lb. But his beating was even more severe. Golota was so much more powerful than this streamlined version, and Riddick was once again knocked around. He managed to drop the Pole once but was twice dropped himself and absorbed a severe pounding. Once again, Golota was unable to resist the groin as his target of choice, despite reaching a position of dominance through his bona fide punches. In round nine he fixed his hungry eyes on Riddick's balls and sank three of his finest about six inches below the belt line, and once again Bowe collapsed in agony, escaping with another disqualification win. What was even more alarming, however, was the way Riddick spoke after the fight, fluffing his consonants and prolonging his vowels. He sounded punch-drunk.

Lennox watched with great disappointment, aware that his wish was getting snatched away from him again. 'I just hope that Golota never knocked all the stuffing out of Bowe,' he said a week later. 'I think that maybe there's a little bit of stuffing left in there for me. I hope so.' Instead, Bowe decided to fulfil his teenage ambition to join the Marines, but gave up after a week. He then announced his retirement, and with that lost his purpose in life, grew obese and began beating up his wife. Lennox hoped his enemy would try to find meaning in the ring again. 'In my mind, I'm still saying, "I think redemption will come one day,"' Lewis said. 'I definitely still want Bowe and my doors are open. They've always been open, and I feel he may just make that one mistake. Bowe went to join the army and didn't want to face me, but there's talk going around that he's back in training. He's started punching at his wife first, and then his sister punched him out, but I think there's a little bit left in there for me to beat.' Whenever he heard rumours of a comeback his hopes would rise, but he was always disappointed. It was one of the great regrets that he never received the opportunity to prove his professional superiority over the man he whipped in the Olympics, never had the chance to beat up the man who had called him a faggot, a pussy and a bitch and who insulted his mother. As Maloney put it, 'I think Lennox was cheated out of becoming one of the greatest heavyweight champions because he had no major fight in his prime. His major fight would have been Riddick Bowe.'

In the end, he could take consolation in the fact that not only did he beat Bowe in the Olympic final, but that his record as a professional way surpassed his rival's, and there was no comparison when it came to their conduct as men. For all his talent, Bowe was one of the great under-achievers in heavyweight history. He retired with only two outstanding performances: the first against an underweight Holyfield when he won the title in 1992, and the second his stoppage victory over the amateurish Cuban Jorge Gonzalez in 1995. He'll be remembered as much for his title loss to Holyfield and the two beatings he received from Golota, as well as his cynical reign as champion, his gluttony, his mental decline and his descent into domestic violence, kidnapping and prison.

Once Bowe made himself unavailable the Lewis team put all their energy into securing their guaranteed shot at the WBC title Bruno lifted from McCall. Eliades offered Bruno $7 million but Warren scornfully turned it down, saying it was 'nowhere near' the figure his man deserved. The British Boxing Board, wary of being caught between the conflicting interests of two British boxers, proposed that Warren and Maloney meet to reach an agreement, but instead they yelled at each other and, said Maloney, would have gone further had it not been for the intervention of mediators. But even if Warren had wanted to accept this option he was not in a position to deliver because his man was already spoken for. King decided Bruno would be fighting Tyson next, and there wasn't much anyone else could do about it, a fact illustrated by Bruno's purse for the Tyson fight – $6 million ($1 million less than Eliades offered).

The WBC immediately sanctioned this fight, contradicting its prior promises that Lewis was next in line. He could have used the American courts to interdict them from continuing with this course but his lawyers made the mistake of launching their writ in the Britain and it was thrown out, the judges making the point that the United States (where the Bruno–Tyson fight was scheduled and where the WBC had a major base) was the appropriate site. They therefore had to launch a fresh American action, choosing Paterson, New Jersey, where Judge Amos Saunders accepted his lawyers' argument, based on the principles of administrative law, that organisations are required to abide by their constitutions and rulings, and the WBC was not immune from this obligation. He ruled that the WBC could not allow anyone else to fight for their title until Lewis had his shot. Referring to the forthcoming

Tyson–Bruno fight in Las Vegas, Saunders accused the WBC of 'making up your own rules' and even warned Sulaiman and King that they were close to being thrown into jail for their behaviour. 'This fight against Mr Bruno should have been Lennox Lewis's, not Mike Tyson's,' he said. 'There are some things money can't buy. Money is no compensation. There is no question he has suffered irreparable damage. I am in no doubt that the WBC have treated Mr Lewis unfairly. He was promised this fight and should have had this fight.' After further pleadings he agreed to allow the Tyson–Bruno fight to proceed, but issued an interdict preventing the winner from defending against anyone other than Lewis. This judgement was confirmed on appeal.

Bruno was therefore permitted the dubious privilege of making his first title defence against Tyson, with the proviso that the winner fight Lewis next. Seven years had passed since his first encounter with Mike and in that time he'd built up 20lb. of additional muscle and had the confidence from winning the WBC title, while Tyson, having his third fight in five years, could hardly have improved. Yet Frank, a fighter previously renowned for quixotic courage, entered the ring in a state of terror, crossing himself over and over again like a Catholic dissident on his way to the Inquisition, and seemed ready to succumb before the first bell. Mike walked through him and whacked him out in three rounds. Bruno had no more chances for reinvention. His doctors told him that if he fought on he could lose his eyesight as a result of a detached retina.

Despite allowing for the first stage of Tyson's ascendancy, the New Jersey judgement was devastating to King. His plan had been to set up three weak champions and allow Tyson to knock them over to become, once again, the unified champion. To achieve this King ensured his own minnows won the title belts – a task made easier by what could euphemistically be called his cosy relationship with the bosses of the alphabet bodies. Aside from Bruno, there was the South African Frans Botha, who won a disputed decision over the mediocre German Axel Schulz for the IBF title, and the weak-willed Bruce Seldon, who won the WBA version by beating the aged Tony Tucker. But Botha's post-fight drugs test revealed he'd been taking anabolic steroids, and after a court case by rival promoters the IBF was reluctantly forced to strip him of his title. King therefore had to buy up the man who succeeded him, Michael Moorer (for the second time). King then planned to unify the WBC and WBA titles by putting Tyson in with Seldon, but the New Jersey judgement prevented this, so he was reluctantly forced to negotiate with Lewis.

It seemed, at first, King might just be serious. Because this was a mandatory challenge it was open to purse bids unless the parties agreed to a deal beforehand. King could not afford the risk of being outbid, because he didn't want any other promoter getting his hands on his prize asset, so he began making offers, starting with $6 million and ending with twelve. Eliades, who was convinced he would win a purse bid, said no and countered by offering Tyson an unprecedented $50 million. King turned him down and it soon became clear that there was no way he would allow Tyson–Lewis to go ahead unless it met three conditions: he was the promoter, it was screened on Showtime and he retained promotional control over both men.

Inevitably King made another bid to entice Lewis towards his stable, but when this failed Don realised he was in a quandary and changed his position, concluding that the risk of letting his man take on such a dangerous opponent was too high. He started bombarding Lewis with step-aside offers to allow the WBC–WBA unification bout to go ahead unhindered, or, for an extra million dollars, allow Tyson to make a voluntary defence against Holyfield and then take on Lewis some time in 1997.

Steward assured Eliades there was no way Tyson could beat his man, but, as always, the final decision rested with the boxer. After analysing Tyson's three comeback fights, Lennox agreed he had Tyson's number. He was therefore reluctant to accept a step-aside deal, arguing that Tyson had proved to be an unreliable character outside the ring and an inconsistent performer inside the ropes. It was possible that he'd slip up against Seldon or Holyfield or find himself in jail again or die a violent death. It was therefore too risky to allow him another year. In addition, Lewis doubted King's inclination to stick to a long-term deal. It was better to dig in for their right to an immediate shot at Tyson.

King tried a different tactic. To get around the spirit of the judgement he announced Tyson would fight Seldon for the WBA title alone (his WBC title would not be defended). The Lewis camp was about to sue when King offered to pay Lewis in lieu of damages. At this point Eliades received bad news from his lawyers, who said their case was weaker than previously thought. It would take two months to be heard, and King could take it on appeal all the way to the US Supreme Court where he might win on the grounds that preventing Tyson fighting anyone other than Lewis was restraint of trade. Panos accepted their advice to negotiate but played hard, turning down $2 million, then three and finally settling for four. In return, Tyson agreed either to defend against Lewis by 30 September 1996 or relinquish his WBC title. This was portrayed as proof that Lewis accepted 'step-aside' money. The reality was different. His choice was between accepting $4 million for doing nothing or accepting nothing. Either way he wasn't going to fight Tyson.

Tyson went ahead with his challenge for Seldon's WBA title and proceeded to win in the first round; Seldon so terrified that he collapsed without actually being hit. After this, to no one's surprise, Tyson relinquished his WBC title rather than go ahead with his obligation to fight Lewis. 'In a way it's a compliment that King kept Tyson away from me,' Lennox commented. 'Mike and Don gave up the WBC belt because they knew he would lose if he came up against me. That's why they wouldn't fight Lennox Lewis.' His trainer agreed. 'Was Tyson scared of Lennox? Yes, he was. Well, not so much him, but people in his camp. Guys don't just give up the WBC title, but that's what Tyson did.'

More than seven months after beating up Tommy Morrison, Lennox had his next fight at New York's Madison Square Garden. It was expected to be a routine assignment against a strong, durable, world-rated opponent who was unlikely to provide too many puzzles. Ray Mercer's early career met with the expectations of an Olympic gold medalist. He was strong, heavy handed and soon proved to have one of the best chins around. After stopping Francesco Damiani for the WBO title and flattening Morrison he was seen as a future star. He then took on 42-year-old Larry

Holmes for a filler fight. The WBO, in a first and last fit of conscience, decided it was such a mismatch that they would strip Mercer of his title if he went ahead. He ignored them and was stripped, after which Larry exposed their ignorance by out-classing the still-raw Ray, who then developed the usual substance abuse and discipline problems. This attracted Bowe but Mercer blew his chance by coming in such appalling shape that he lost his warm-up to the unrated Jesse Ferguson – a les-son that returned him the path to righteousness. He found the Lord, avenged the Ferguson defeat and added a fresh range of skills to his renowned brawling abili-ties; in particular, a well-timed and extremely solid jab. In his last fight before Lewis he came in as the underdog against a peak-form Holyfield and pushed him all the way before losing a close decision. In his first after Lewis he outworked the rejuve-nated former champion Tim Witherspoon to begin a five-year unbeaten run. Lewis fought him at his peak.

Although he took time off to attend the court case and to keep abreast of the negotiations with King, he toiled for five weeks at his favourite camp in Pennsylvania, never missed his eight-mile pre-breakfast runs and worked over his sparring partners. It was not quite the load he would have put in for a fight against the likes of Tyson or Bowe, and at 247lb he came in six pounds more than against Morrison, but he felt ready to face a man who viewed victory as part of his destiny. 'I'm not desperate,' said Mercer, 'I'm just hungry. It's a very important fight for me. God let it happen, and it's time for Ray Mercer to get his due. I've sacrificed, I've made a lot of mistakes, and I've paid a lot of dues.'

The crowd of 17,000 booed Lewis as he entered the surprisingly small ring, after which he received an even lustier reception from his 6ft 1in, 236lb opponent. He was taken aback by the jabs that thudded into his face and it was soon clear he was in for a rough night. Lewis moved more and mixed up his punches in round two, but Mercer kept coming, landing hard every time Lennox eased off. The American started round three with a thumping jab and a right uppercut and ended strongly. It was Mercer's first clear round, and to Lennox's continued amazement the jab was the key. Although he was landing plenty of his own – more than Mercer – he was caught more than usual. 'I was definitely getting hit with the jab more than in any other fight,' he said. 'It was weird because I didn't expect it, but then Mercer had a really good jab. I saw it against Witherspoon in his next fight and it's not an easy jab to protect yourself against. Any boxer would have problems with it but I learned a huge amount from that, and if we ever fought again he would never hit me with that jab because Manny taught me to place my right hand in a different position – across my chin rather than on the side, so his jab wouldn't get through.'

Lewis powered back, snapping Mercer's head back with an uppercut and landing several draining hooks to the body. He then slammed home several extremely heavy unanswered punches, visibly wobbling Mercer with a particularly spiteful combina-tion. It looked like he might be close to a stoppage, but a clash of heads left him with a deep cut on his left eyebrow and Ray regrouped. Early in round five Mercer's face started to swell and his mouth was bleeding, but he kept landing that jab to stay in the fight. 'Move your head and let your hands go!' Steward yelled. Lennox ripped

A youthful Lennox Lewis poses with childhood friend Andrew Powis.

Another blistering attack on Francois Botha.

Lewis listens intently to Frank Maloney at a press conference following his victory over Michael Grant.

Mama's boy

A face-off with David Tua before their fight at the Mandalay Bay Casino in Las Vegas.

A blistering left-hand jab rocks Mike Tyson back onto his toes.

Tyson is dumped on the canvas.

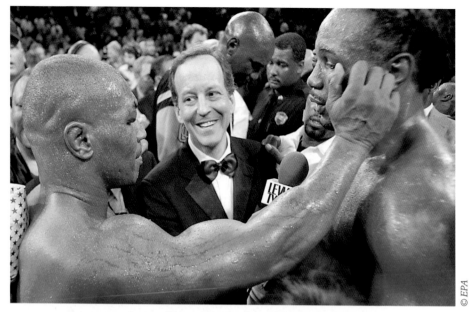

Tyson congratulates Lewis

Numero uno!

Lewis lands a left hook on Vitali Klitschko, then celebrates his victory after the doctor stopped the fight for a cut over the Ukranian's eye.

Lennox at a Press Conference after the Klitschko fight.

Lennox Lewis and Nelson Mandela.

home another uppercut at the start of round six but Ray came again, firing a succession of hooks to drive Lewis against the ropes. This time it looked like he might be in trouble but he too powered his way back. It had become an intense, draining battle, fought mainly at close quarters, with both men fighting through pain and exhaustion in their bid for dominance. Mercer started strongly with his jabs and hooks in round seven but Lewis closed with a barrage of six heavy punches. 'A lot of people had questions about my chin,' he said, 'but after that they realised that not only do I have a good chin but I have the will to win.'

Lennox felt he'd won almost all the rounds and was on his way to a wide points victory, but Steward knew better. He was sure his man deserved to be leading but he also knew that in New York, with American judges and the crowd solidly behind the local man, there was room for doubt. 'You can't afford to lose any more rounds,' he shouted at Lennox. 'You gotta be first.' Shocked by the tone of Manny's assessment, Lennox staggered Mercer with a vicious right cross. Yet the American fought back again. With the crowd shouting 'Go Ray!' Mercer hit Lennox on the break, and after being warned for the infringement he landed another right, but Lennox responded with a far harder cross of his own. It landed flush on the top of Mercer's jaw, knocking his head sideways, but again he remained standing. 'I'm telling you, Ray Mercer has got some tough chin,' he said. 'I hit him with some shots that I felt in my hand, yet he kept coming.'

Still, Mercer looked like he was punched out. He collapsed in exhaustion at the end of the round, panting heavily. Steward glanced up and instructed, 'Make him use his legs because he's tiring badly.' So Lewis changed tactics and began to move and jab, although this was more difficult than usual because the 18 foot ring (in contrast to the usual 22 feet) made it harder for a 6ft 5in heavyweight to maintain mobility without running out of space. 'The effect of that small ring on a heavyweight as big as me is that you take two steps back and you hit the ropes,' he complained. He caught Ray with yet another cracking cross but instead of falling Mercer responded with three big jabs and the pattern was the same in the tenth, Lennox moving more, landing single jabs and rights, but still getting caught. By the final bell Lewis' right eye was closing and his left was swollen, but Mercer was in a worse state, his mouth dripping blood and his face badly bruised and swollen.

The crowd favoured Mercer's better-than-expected performance, but in reality he was caught more than he landed – even with the jab. Ray threw an average of 38 punches per round – 22 jabs and16 power punches; Lennox averaged 53 per round – 32 jabs and 21 power punches. Lewis was caught 223 times – more than ever before – but landed 320 punches, an average of an extra ten per round.

The scoring, however, was surprisingly close. One judge gave it to Lewis by two points, another by one and the third scored it even. Lennox gave a so-so verdict on his showing. 'I took the Mercer fight because he's a pressure fighter and so is Tyson and he gave me a lot of pressure and caught me with some good shots, and he showed he has a really good jab and a great chin, but I thought I did enough to win.' Steward was less ambiguous. He felt the technical problems could easily be remedied, and more importantly, his pupil had shown him that 'his chin was sound and he had the balls for a hard fight, and that he could really dig deep when he had to'. Later, Steward added, 'Lennox will perform a lot better than that but he won't often be required to produce so much character in the ring. It's the kind of performance I can live with. He showed me he had guts, that he wasn't going to run away when the going got tough.'

This fight was Lewis's last with John Hornewer. One catalyst for their break-up was Bowe's decision to sign to fight Golota in preference to Lewis. 'That turned out to be the end of Bowe and that was also a nail in my coffin too,' he recalled. However, he feels the underlying reason was the persistent antagonism from Eliades, who was taking over his role in contractual negotiations and undermining his position. Hornewer, never been one of nature's diplomats, was candid in his opinions about Panos. In essence, he warned Lewis not to take Panos at his word and also to keep clear of Milt Chwasky, the attorney who went from representing Bowe to becoming the lawyer for Eliades and later for Lewis as well. Lennox ignored this advice, suspecting that John was concerned about his power base, and he made it clear he felt Panos was doing a fine job. 'The thing about John,' said their mutual friend Lawrence Lustig, 'is that he's very shrewd and a very good judge of character and there is nothing crooked about him. But he couldn't accept it when Lennox took Levitt's advice and Panos's rather than his. When I gave Lennox advice, I wouldn't take it badly if he didn't agree but John would take it personally, which perhaps he shouldn't have. I'd say that of all the people Lennox dropped, I felt most sorry for John because he's as straight as a dye and he always had Lennox's best interests at heart.'

Lewis decided his American lawyer, adviser and chum was surplus to requirements because he was no longer playing a major role within the organisation and was being paid for next-to nothing. It was a simple cost-cutting business decision. John saw it differently. He felt let down. Today he says an underlying reason for their differences was that money, style and charm too easily impressed Lennox. 'His biggest flaw is his willingness to go along with people who are always complimenting him, like Levitt, Eliades and others,' said Hornewer. 'You see, I used to tell him things he didn't want to hear and that's an unpopular position to take. I always looked at him as a friend and I respected him but I wasn't as rich as Panos so my opinion didn't count.'

Finally, after eight years working together the relationship came to an end in December 1996. As John recalled: 'I received a call from Lennox and Dennis, who said it was time we parted ways but I think the decision was pretty much triggered by Panos. We were very close, but Panos came between us. Lennox left some of the negotiations of contracts to Panos and I didn't appreciate it. Basically I felt Panos wouldn't let me do my job. I didn't want to have the title of Lennox's lawyer and not be able to do my function, and I didn't think he was being told the truth. Panos resented my influence and I think he was the cause of all the problems but now I feel vindicated because everything I said to Lennox about him proved to be correct. But at the same time I also feel sad for Lennox. He's so bitter about it because he trusted Panos.' Eliades was surprised by this attitude and insisted he was not central to his dismissal. 'Really, I had no problem with John, and as far as I knew we were getting on OK,' he said. 'It was Lennox's decision to dump him, not mine and I never completely understood it. I think it was because Lennox felt John was overpricing himself and that he no longer needed him. But I felt for John at the time.'

One of the remaining issues dividing them was that Hornewer said Lewis owed him money for his role in negotiating the Mercer fight. 'I billed them for my contributions to that fight and they disputed this and said they weren't the right figures,' he explained. To which Lewis responded: 'That was Panos's department, definitely, and I really didn't know anything about it.' Eventually, seven years on, Hornewer negotiated a settlement with Judd Burstein (who, by then, had become Lewis's lawyer and business adviser). 'Am I satisfied with the deal?' John asked. 'Well, that depends on whether you're talking legally or morally. But as Judd put it to me, "Neither Lennox nor you are happy with the settlement, which probably makes it a good deal." And I guess I have to go along with that.'

Maloney was relieved, feeling that Hornewer had been plotting to oust him. Today he recognises that whatever their differences, John was an honest man and that it would have been better if they'd worked together rather than against each other. 'I certainly got the impression he didn't like me but maybe I was wrong,' he admitted. 'My main problem was that he tried to get me out of the organisation, but maybe I was mistaken. You see, people like me and John were truthful to Lennox, but he'd be told something else by someone else and he'd think, "Look at the house they have, look at the car they drive, look at the bank accounts they've got." When I think about it now, if John and I had worked together we could have kept the rascals out, but we didn't – we worked against each other.'

Meanwhile King and his allies were working to ensure their courtroom defeat was no more than a temporary setback. He decided that Tyson had to vacate his WBC title rather than face Lewis and that he would have to find an alternative opponent for Lennox. The man who came to mind was, once again, Oliver McCall (who scored two quick knockout victories following his title loss, the second of these against the top Russian Oleg Maskaev, which gave the WBC an excuse for offering the shot at their vacant title).

King felt sure McCall would beat Lewis again and decided to give his charge every possible advantage, employing one of the finest trainers in the world, George Benton, and bidding $9 million to promote the fight It was scheduled for November but then King requested a 30-day extension from the WBC, who, always obliging, went one better, giving him permission to stage the fight in January 1997. This meant Lennox had to break training camp, which annoyed his team so much that they returned to Judge Saunders, who ruled that the terms of the delay were contrary to WBC regulations. King therefore lost the right to promote the fight, which was transferred to Lennox's US promoters Main Events, despite the fact they bid $3 million less than King. They eventually settled on the 7 February slot in Las Vegas.

While this was happening, King suffered a more drastic setback. Earlier that year, he saw an underweight, out-of-form Holyfield labour his way to an unimpressive stoppage over the cruiserweight Bobby Czyz on the Lewis–Mercer bill. This convinced him Tyson would have an easy time with Evander – an opinion shared throughout the boxing world, so much so that he was derided for his cynicism in staging the event. Many feared Holyfield would lose his health or his life.

They forgot two things: First, Holyfield was an erratic boxer. He always trained hard, but could not always fight well. He looked magnificent when first winning the heavyweight title against Buster Douglas but struggled in his three defences before failing against Bowe. He was inspired in the Bowe return but looked finished in his first defence against Moorer; sharp against Mercer but flat in his third fight with Bowe. You could never rely on his decline any more than you could rely on his brilliance. And second, Evander was a man of faith – in his God, in himself, and especially the combination of the two. He was the most competitive man in the game, with a mania about being the best, at all costs, in everything he tried, and an inability to admit weakness to the world or himself. This gelled with his fundamentalist Christian faith, which led him to believe that God would use him as his vehicle to prevail against the odds. This time the odds favoured a convicted rapist who had espoused a variant of the Islamic faith. Evander believed Tyson was the man God picked out for him to conquer; Tyson saw the fight as a routine assignment. A few big digs and this little old man would fold – die perhaps. Who cares?

Mike strolled into the ring in his black shorts and boots, completely disdainful of the opposition. Evander entered in his purple shorts and a gown, smiling and praying and chanting, in the finest shape of his life. Tyson began to belt Holyfield with his big guns, but Evander held firm, clinched and fought back and Tyson discovered he was in with a man who could match him for strength and surpass him in boxing ability. Evander clinched, he butted and he threw quick, hard punches. As Tyson tired, Holyfield took take over. Mike went down, but fought on, until in round ten, utterly exhausted, he went down again, and after taking a pounding in the eleventh the fight was stopped. Evander was the new champion. King had, of course, taken the precaution of signing him up before the fight and compelling him to agree to an immediate return and a long-term contract, but it was not the same. Holyfield was admired as the comeback hero who defeated the monster, but he lacked the visceral magnetism and money-making potential of Iron Mike.

Lennox felt intense frustration that Evander got there first. 'Really, this is yet another situation where King has not helped his boxers. He put Tyson in with bum, bum, worse bum, and then he puts him in with somebody who could rise to great heights – heights he wasn't prepared for. All the time King's telling him, "You're the greatest thing since sliced bread", and then all of a sudden he's in there thinking, "Why is this guy hitting me and hurting me, and why can't I hit this guy?" Holyfield is supposed to be washed up but he basically made Tyson a boy. He pushed him back, outmuscled him, outboxed him and it affected him mentally. If I boxed Tyson it would have been in the same way as he boxed, only better. I'm definitely not running away or backing up from Mike and I think I'd knock him out quicker than Holyfield.'

While King absorbed this latest blow, his next hope, McCall, was falling to pieces. A combination of drugs and alcohol fuelled outbursts of violent and unpredictable behaviour that led to three arrests. Before he could start training he had to negotiate with prosecutors wanting to charge him for possession of crack cocaine in Virginia, and with prosecutors in Chicago wanting him for parole violation, but the most publicised incident happened in Nashville, Tennessee, where he took to wrecking his hotel, throwing around its Christmas tree and spitting at a police car after a tequila binge; it took eight burly cops to restrain him. He was sentenced to eighteen months' probation and ordered to attend a drug rehabilitation clinic, after which three female drug counsellors remained at his side until he stepped through the ropes. Emerging from the clinic he called himself a 'changed man', declaring he was 'clean and sober' and that God had transformed him. He read the Bible every night, watched Christian videos and listened to Christian cassette tapes as part of his ambition to become a 'Minister in my own church'. The Nevada State Athletic Commission demanded a drug and alcohol test before the fight and he came out clear, but there was concern that all was not well. A week before the fight he woke up his wife, Aletha for some Bible reading. After exchanging verses, they agreed boxing wasn't 'godly' enough for born-again Christians – too much humiliation and pain.

Still, he seemed in fine nick, coming in at a solid-looking 237lb, five and three quarters more than in the first Lewis fight, but without a hint of excess flesh – testament to six weeks' work under Benton. Although he sometimes looked distracted, he put on a passable display of belligerence, dismissing the possibility that his former trainer could help Lewis. 'They can tell him how to fight but they can't put the fight into him,' he said, promising he'd knock Lennox out again. Steward responded by pointing out that in the first fight 'Lewis was the better fighter but McCall was better prepared', but this time Lennox had the advantage on both scores. He elaborated: 'The people working with Oliver have allowed him to forget most of what I taught him and whereas I respected Lennox when I was in the other corner, they are filling Oliver's head with the belief that Lennox lacks the mental toughness to hold up in a brawl. They say he will be terrified when he remembers what happened last time and will quit or fold as soon as Oliver gets to him.'

He smiled at this perception but acknowledged the truth would be revealed only when they started fighting. 'Regardless of what I say or Lennox says, you can never tell what will occur inside a man's head. Who knows what memories will come flooding back when he sees McCall rise off the other stool? The first minute or two could be dangerous. There is not just the risk of a bad reaction if big punches are thrown at Lennox but the possibility that he will be hesitant about letting his own stuff fly, because last time he was hit while in the process of throwing a punch.' Lewis dismissed this possibility, insisting that unlike Bruno against Tyson, he felt no McCall-sized demons haunting him. 'Why should I? Look at the way the last fight ended, with me on my feet. I wasn't beaten up. Basically I beat myself. I'm longing to get in there and prove this man doesn't have anything over me.'

The Lewis camp spent $250,000 on training expenses for this on–off fight. When they resumed camp they chose the warmth of Scottsdale, a few miles outside Phoenix in Arizona. Lennox worked hard in the Fifth Street Gym in Phoenix but complained of being slow and sluggish on his morning runs, which might have been a result of the fact that he was heavier than before. According to Maloney, this was a product of the great food at the luxurious Camelback Inn Resort and his inclination to make use of room service. The rest of his team maintained that the additional weight was a conscious tactic. 'People were concerned about his weight against McCall, but we chose that weight,' said Shand. 'It was a calculated decision. You have to remember McCall wasn't the same weight as two years earlier either and we figured he'd have two rounds or so to try to back Lennox up and therefore we needed the extra weight because we didn't want him to be bullied. We thought McCall would come in heavier, so we trained Lennox to carry the extra weight.'

Lewis weighed in at a career-highest 251lb, but, like McCall, he looked solid and muscular, and in sparring he was extremely sharp. Four days before the fight he went ten fast rounds with Al Williams, a decent heavyweight with only one loss in eighteen, and showed no sign of tiredness, moving and punching constantly and ending the final round with a quick and sustained combination. He was ready.

Steward outlined Oliver's tactical options. 'All of them are designed to get him in close, which is his obvious hope of doing damage against a giant. One method would be to come in swinging haymakers, brawling from the start. Or he could cover up and try to walk in without getting hurt. He could also bob and weave, slipping punches, moving his body side to side, staying low, attempting to penetrate but whatever he does, we'll be ready. McCall has never been stopped but I can't see him lasting the distance this time. Oliver won't be the same man I sent out, and Lennox won't be the same fellow we beat that night. I've cured him of that nonsense about the right hand being the answer to everything. I'm working on making him the complete fighter, improving his jab and his body movement, getting him to throw left hooks and, above all, to concentrate on maintaining his balance at all times, avoiding those awful habits of crossing his feet and sprawling.'

McCall ran towards the ring and then raised his arms triumphantly, and this time there was no sobbing, but nothing else unusual to report. As expected, he came out quickly but Lennox met him with a heavy right that landed flush. McCall looked alarmed and took a couple of steps back before attacking again. Lennox drove him back with his jab, moving well and confusing him. 'I went out there and just asserted myself,' said Lennox of that first round. 'I think he found it difficult to get through my jab. I was just playing with him, with my jab – just popping it out and making it difficult for him to make a move.'

Encouraged by Benton to keep attacking and throwing the right, McCall charged at the start of round two and landed two good hooks, and later two hard right crosses along and several jabs, but this time Lewis soaked them up. His response was to bring up his right uppercut, catching McCall under the chin, and then move out of range, pumping in jabs while using his footwork to evade further rushes. Towards the end of the round he delivered two overhand rights and another hurtful uppercut, but Steward warned that his work was becoming sloppy and he had to keep his right hand up to protect his chin.

He became totally dominant, landing heavy jabs followed by power punches. McCall fought hard but was being outboxed, outpunched and outmuscled and his punches were bouncing off Lewis, who was so much stronger, better prepared and more defensively adept than the man he faced in 1994. A minute into round three, Lewis landed a quick hook to the chin and followed it with a big right cross that caused McCall's legs to shudder for the first time in his career. He'd taken heavy punches from the likes of Buster Douglas, Tony Tucker, Bruce Seldon and Frank Bruno, but nothing like this and it seemed to dent his confidence. When Lewis followed it with a succession of jabs he looked dispirited. 'He couldn't counter it or control my jab, so he sort of gave up,' Lewis said. The first stages of his breakdown, towards the close of round three, were ambiguous. He clowned aimlessly for a few seconds; then backed off, while still punching but when the bell sounded, he refused to go to his corner. Benton called to him to sit down, but McCall kept walking.

He continued to walk away from Lennox in round four, and occasionally he'd grab, but he was no longer punching. Lewis, like everyone else, seemed confused – still wary of what Oliver might try. 'When he started walking away I thought it was a joke,' he said, 'and he was trying to lull me into something and catch me like in our first fight'. Lewis kept his distance for a while and then began to set him up with the jab and step in with quick and heavy rights, but he seemed reluctant to really bash up his weeping adversary. 'When you see a man crying in the ring like that you know it's not related to anything going on in the ring and that makes it very difficult to attack him physically,' said Steward. 'I don't care what people say. Everyone has emotions and feelings. It was all very frustrating for Lennox until, finally, at the end of the round, I told him, "Just go out and do something quickly before they call it a disqualification."'

Mills Lane ordered the sobbing McCall to sit and yelled, 'Do you want to fight?' McCall replied, 'I gotta fight, I gotta fight,' and this was good enough. After watching for a while, Lennox decided to end the fight and walked in to land fifteen unanswered punches to the head and body. At last, 55 seconds into round five, Lane stopped it, declaring Lewis the champion on a technical knockout 'because Oliver McCall refuses to defend himself'.

Lennox experienced an initial sense of relief at Lane's intervention, feeling he might have seriously injured his defenceless opponent if he'd been required to land any more punches – a position shared by the rest of his team. 'He's the greatest finisher in boxing,' said a relieved Maloney, who had entered the ring in a state of palpable nervousness wearing a double-breasted Union flag suit designed by an East End tailor, a practice he would continue throughout his portion of Lewis's career. 'When he gets a fighter in trouble he ain't getting out of trouble, and McCall was in trouble. He would have killed him if the referee didn't step in and stop the fight. He would have killed McCall.'

So, at last, Lennox was back where he'd been in 1994, as WBC champion. He not only stopped the only man to beat him, he'd also upset King's plans and defied Sulaiman's will. He was pleased to be 'out of the wilderness', but the victory felt tainted. 'McCall ran away from me and Don King helped the situation, which meant I had to take him to several courts to get that fight, and finally, when I get there, the guy's not mentally present. He just gave up. But, anyway, I've undone that one loss on my record, so, in a way, my career is back to zero.' That was the best you could say because no one talked about the three rounds when he beat up McCall, or the way he shook that previously unshakeable chin. Few made the obvious point that whatever else was going on in Oliver's odd head it was Lewis' punches that had prompted his disintegration. All they remembered was that McCall broke down mid-fight, and they concluded, appropriately, that a man in recovery from drug addiction should never have been in the ring in the first place. As Maloney conceded, 'It was a disgrace to the human race for his people to allow him to fight.'

McCall, however, was able to claw back a semblance of self-respect. He continued to have periodic drug problems and did time in jail, but continued to box and win. In fact over the rest of his career he went undefeated, and though most of his thirteen victims were patsies, one of them, Henry Akinwande, was a top contender and Oliver knocked him out. Lennox, however, was so disgusted by what happened that he never contemplated a re-run. 'I always say I never lost, in a sense, because I came back against the guy I lost to and made him cry,' he said. 'And when I've looked at McCall since then, I've always felt there's no need for a rubber match because when we fought in 1997 it was all one way and it could never be any different. It would make no sense. Lightning can only strike once.'

CHAPTER SIXTEEN
BIG BEAR, CALIFORNIA, 1997

L ennox slips in silently, sits on a bench and starts wrapping his enormous hands. He seems wary and uncommunicative, not wanting to be disturbed. He peers up and gives a quizzical 'yes, what do you want?' look, then softens a bit. 'I was just watching you, checking you out,' he says with a little half smile, but that's it. He goes back to his hands, the flicker of conversation over, and then hauls up his huge body, pulls on a woolly hat, climbs into the ring and begins shadow boxing, moving fluidly as he imagines what he will do to his next opponent, Andrew Golota, the hefty Pole who ended Riddick Bowe's career.

Emmanuel Steward enters, and the converted garage turns silent. 'Change the music, please,' he commands in a voice polite but firm, and one kind of soul goes off and another comes on. Manny climbs through the ropes and Lennox's shadow boxing becomes more focused, his coach calling out moves and offering bites of advice, particularly about balance. After three rounds it's Courtney Shand's turn. He has Lennox on his back doing complicated stretching exercises, his long legs and arms getting bent and twisted into quite surprising angles for fifteen minutes.

His working day started at 5.30 a.m. with a five-mile hill run led by Patrick Drayton; he's also been through a gruelling uphill cycle with Scott DeMercado, starting at 6,800 feet, ending at 10,000. Next came skipping, shadow boxing and strength exercises. And now his afternoon gym routine starts with four rounds on the 100kg heavy bag, throwing fast punches in combinations of eight, ten and twelve with Harold Knight keeping count. He then puts on a scrum cap with weights dangling from it and completes four sets of neck exercises to improve his ability to absorb punches, but takes care to issue the instruction, 'No pictures of this'. Pull-ups follow – hauling his body up and down without touching the floor – five sets of fifteen, followed by sets of dips, back-raises, press-ups, sit-ups. 'We're going for muscle endurance as well as strength,' Courtney explains. 'It's just like doing rounds in the ring, except we don't allow him a full minute's rest.'

Manny watches from a distance and then moves in for a chat, outlining his vision of what will happen against Golota. What it comes down to is this: as long as the kick-ass version of his man turns up in Atlantic City on 4 October, it'll be over quickly because Lewis has too much of everything, including the intangible of fortitude. 'The general public here believes Lennox doesn't have the heart, chin or desire to be a great prize fighter and I cannot fault them because he hasn't demonstrated them yet,' he admits. 'So it's a justifiable misconception. But I know what I've seen and I feel different, and time will tell.' Age isn't a worry either. 'I've had boxers who are finished at twenty-six, but everyone ages different. Lennox hasn't been in lots of gruelling fights, he lives very good, he's a natural, gifted athlete and he's very young mentally and spiritually – a young man of thirty-two, learning things for the first time, and that keeps him enthusiastic.'

Manny's only real worry is all this damn chess he plays, every goddamn night, and what it reveals about Lennox's mindset: too analytical, too much the thinker. Manny hates chess. He would like to see less intellect and more wild animal but he knows it's not always there. 'That's the one thing we need to judge him on because he does not have that staying-in-trouble street mentality.' He pauses – a point worth acknowledging, and then he remembers another. 'But he has a real competitive attitude. When I went to Canada and started talking to the guys he grew up with I discovered he was a sports-type rough guy and we have to bring that out. There's a little too much of the diplomacy, a little too much of the British conservatism within him and that's his biggest problem: too much chess.'

Steward started boxing at the age of eight and became a rangy and brilliant bantamweight who won the US national championships. But he decided there was more money to be made training and managing boxers than fighting them and founded the Kronk gym in Detroit, where he nurtured a string of world champions. Lennox, he says, is the most naturally talented of the lot. True this analytical chess thing is a caveat, but it does not detract from his undiscovered brilliance and Manny wants you to know that these opinions are not hyperbole. After all, he was speaking of this untapped potential way back, years before he was appointed head trainer. He seldom rolls with laughter, but this is worth a chuckle. 'They say I'm a very respected man in boxing except for this Lewis thing,' he says, enjoying some self-mockery. 'It's the only time I've been knocked but I have to say what I believe: Lennox Lewis is the best heavyweight I ever saw in my life.' Better than Muhammad Ali? 'The Lennox I'm training now would have knocked out Ali and all the heavyweights I saw before him. I have no doubt. Ali wasn't a strong heavyweight and would not have been able to outbox Lennox, who is tall and has a fine jab himself. The only guy Ali fought who was that tall was Ernie Terrell but he bent down and crouched up and was over thirty pounds lighter than Lennox and he was intimidated, but Lennox, with his strong jab and his physical strength, would have been a big problem for Ali. I know people don't believe that but I look at the problems Ali had with Kenny Norton, physically strong guys who were not intimidated by him, and I think Lennox would have beaten Ali.'

Like most boxing people, it does not take much to draw Manny into the mythical terrain of time travel fights and so he continues. 'Now, Larry Holmes would have been a much more difficult fight than Ali because he had a very good fast jab and was fairly strong, but, no, I think Lennox would have beaten all of them.' Tyson, Holmes, Foreman, Frazier, Ali, Liston, Marciano, Charles, Louis, Tunney, Dempsey, Johnson, Jeffries, Corbett – all the great ones? 'Yes, I think he's the best heavyweight that has ever been in professional boxing. His physical size, his all-round natural athletic talents ... but it has to be proved.' He smiles knowingly again. 'And everyone keeps laughing at me about this.'

The monologue is broken by a cheer on the other side of the gym as Lennox steps off the scales. He bet them he'd be under 250lb today, and he's 249, with exactly one month to go: right on schedule – slightly ahead perhaps – and feeling wonderful. He marches triumphantly to the showers, and when he emerges ten minutes later his mood is changed. Usually he has a final weights session after supper, but today his work has ended early. The rest of his evening is all pleasure: a chat, a meal, some videos, a game of chess, perhaps a game of pool and then eight hours of sound sleep. He's already relaxed and at ease, teasing Scott and Patrick and getting teased in return, but he's ever so gracious to the outsiders. A ride to his bungalow? A glass of juice? Is it OK for you outside on the porch?

Is this the British conservatism that Manny derides? Lennox smiles. Conservatism? He remembers the British general election just over three months earlier and talks for a bit about the 'indiscretions' of various Conservative Party MPs that contributed to their defeat. Not that he voted, mind – out of the country, training – but anyway, British electoral politics isn't his thing. 'I don't really support any political party. Well, I support the Love Party,' he says, and laughs again, happy to talk about something other than fighting for a change. And the British thing? Well, you know, that might be Manny's American perception, but who cares? Frank Maloney can wear his Union flag suit, but really, the necessity to stress national credentials is fading. 'It's weird, you know, because when I'm in England I speak a lot of English slang, but people aren't used to me and they listen to this and they say I sound American. Then I go over to Canada and they say I sound English, so I just say I'm mid-Atlantic. I live on planet earth. And actually, I haven't even decided where I'll end up when I retire. Probably just enjoy the planet earth.'

He raises his hands in a nonchalant gesture, settles down to watch the sun descend over the San Bernardino mountains, then returns to the subject of the election he missed and the changes he'd like to see from the new government: stronger laws to protect children, punish polluters and prevent traffic congestion. For a while he sounds like the soft-hearted Englishman his trainer tries to keep at bay, but then out pops the survivalist.

'You know, I don't like the gun law they just came out with – taking the guns away from the people because of the Dunblane massacre in Scotland. They ask, "Do you think they should allow guns?" Well, after that everybody is obviously going to say no, but they don't realise what they're doing to themselves, because when you take guns away from the people that makes the government able to control you a lot easier and that's just going to make the guns go underground, and anyway, it's not guns that kill people it's the people who control the guns who kill people. Yeah, well, that's my pet peeve at the moment.'

He laughs at himself before returning to his theme of government control. 'I like reality books, books that teach you something. I'm reading one at the moment about the American government.' He shakes his head when asked to elaborate. 'I can't really tell you about it because the guy that wrote it got assassinated and they took all his books out the library and if you want his book you have to kind of order it and put your name down on a big list. I'm into those kind of books right now.'

Once again, a little laugh, just so you don't think he's losing it or getting too con-spiratorial, or taking himself too seriously.

He sweeps back his untied locks and shifts to a more comfortable subject – his heroes Nelson Mandela, Malcolm X and Martin Luther King. 'Look at their life sto-ries and what they've been through, all their trials and tribulations and what they've overcome, and the impact they had on so many people and the way they changed people's lives, and what they achieved for their race,' he says. And while he doesn't pretend to emulate them, he feels he sets an example by not compromising his beliefs. 'I stand up for what I believe in and I don't give in to something I'm not. I would rather be real and deal with reality than deal with fallacy, like other people would. I'm a real person.' That is why he prefers the more direct attitude of the Germans to the under-the-covers racism he experiences in Britain and American. 'If you go to Germany you can tell who doesn't like you. They don't hide it, and that's one of the reasons I like Germany. Because if I don't like you I say, "Look, I don't like you." I won't play with you. I'm into that kind of realism.'

And finally, because he's into realism, it's back to his sport and its reluctance to honour him. 'I'm better than all of them, yet I'm not getting the glory, so I'm show-ing that I don't duck anybody because I want to prove that I'm good. I just want to prove I'm the best boxer on the planet. Muhammad Ali made his footsteps. Lennox Lewis is going to make his footsteps in a big way.' But at the age of 32, how much longer to reach the mark Ali achieved at the age of 22 – undisputed world heavy-weight champion? 'Two more years and five more fights and then I'll retire, and after that I think I'll become an entrepreneur and get involved in all kinds of busi-ness ventures, and I'll get married and have children – as soon as I find the right girl, but I haven't found her yet.'

Nice to think ahead, to dream, to put the world right and to allow the realism to slip a little at the end of a hard day. But tomorrow he'll be up at five and off for another hill run because it's what you have to do to stay at the top in this strange, compulsive profession.

As soon as Oliver McCall was led out howling, those incorrigible doppelgangers, Don and Jose, were plotting their next move. Every time Lennox had to fight a mandatory contender or 'final' eliminator Don would dredge up one of his lads and Jose would nod. Non-Don heavyweights need not apply. Tucker, McCall, Butler, McCall again and now Henry Akinwande: what they all had in common was that Don King promoted them.

When Lennox learned of the first mandatory challenge he tried to remain hopeful. 'You know, I'm the kind of guy who looks at the good side,' he reasoned. 'All these things happen for a reason. Did you ever see that film *Nikita*? Yeah? Well, I'm can-celling out all King's pretenders and it gives me a lot of pleasure to beat his guys, because each time he puts one up against me I realise, boy, I'm just beating Don King.'

That was his always-look-on-the-bright-side spiel. But then he sighed in recogni-tion of what he was up against. 'Look, Don's a very smart man. He's basically using these idiot guys as pawns to keep me away from his best one, Tyson, and I have to admit he's done a great job – for himself. The problem in his plan is me because I won't be in his corner and the reason I made that choice and stick to it is that I realise so many guys involved with King went down in some way, whether drugs, getting fat, getting into trouble with the law, women problems. He's a very clever man and a fascinating man, but I won't let him too close. I keep the abuse down to a small, manageable level without ever giving him control over my career, so you won't see me getting sucked into the game of, oh, here's a suitcase of money. I ain't sucked in like that, because nothing good has come out of Don King.'

Henry Akinwande seemed like he might just be that rare exception: a King-backed heavy without problems with drugs, violence or madness. He was the last opponent a champion would choose if offered a free choice. At 6ft 7in and almost 240lb he was taller than Lennox and nearly as heavy, and he had a fast and accurate right cross, the sharpest of jabs and a highly effective defensive system, combining quick reflexes with a sound blocking and parrying technique, along with fine balance and footwork. His drawback was his reluctance to engage. He could look sublime dominating from a distance but whenever anyone came too close he would tie them up with his long arms. If there was a choice between taking a risk and winning ugly, he would go ugly every time. This made him an extremely frustrating boxer to watch or fight – boring, awkward, yet highly effective, having gone unbeaten in 33 fights with several decent scalps on his record.

Henry spent his early years in Dulwich before his family returned home to Lagos, Nigeria, but at sixteen he decided to break free of his domineering dad and return to London. Living in a squat and cleaning the streets of Westminster, he spent his spare time in the gym, honing his skills. After beating Herbie Hide to win the British amateur heavyweight title, he turned professional. He soundly outboxed Axel Schulz in Germany for the European title, but you don't beat Germans at home by just outboxing them, so they made it a draw. He won the Commonwealth title and then took on Schulz again, and this time outclassed him so overwhelmingly that even the Germans had to give him the win. After six years of being avoided by the likes of Bruno and Hide and being denied the chance to fight for the British title, he cut his losses, moved to Miami and fell into Don King's outstretched arms. He secured the minor bridgehead of the WBO title, which he defended twice, earning a respectable reputation but no real following. King then cut a deal with Sulaiman that Henry would get the WBC's number one slot if he vacated his WBO belt.

Maloney and Steward groaned when they learnt Akinwande would be the next opponent, although for different reasons. Steward complained that the Nigerian-Briton was not marketable and did nothing to enhance Lennox's reputation. 'He might have knocked out a couple of contenders but he's still not that accepted in America. As a general fan I would not be interested in Akinwande–Lewis because neither one has beaten a big-name fighter.'

Maloney, however, feared Akinwande was the kind of boxer who could spoil his way to an upset. 'Let me be truthful: if it was a fight we could avoid, it's a fight we would have avoided,' he admitted. 'No matter what people think, this isn't an easy fight. It could be Lennox's hardest, but unfortunately it's been forced upon us because he's a King fighter and the politics of boxing means that every year we have to fight a King fighter.'

Two weeks before the Akinwande fight, at the end of June 1997, Tyson fought his return with Holyfield in Las Vegas. He was better prepared this time and after two rounds seemed to be gaining a slight edge. Holyfield, however, tried to even it up by ducking down low and smashing his head into Tyson's face. He did this several times and it didn't look accidental. Referee Mills Lane did nothing, not even when one of these butts opened a nasty cut under Mike's right eyebrow. In round three, Tyson gave a streetfighter's response to Evander's foul tactics by taking a mouthful of Holyfield's right ear lobe. Evander shrieked, jumping into the air. Lane issued a warning, deducted a point and waved them on. Holyfield attacked furiously but Tyson tied him up and bit again, and this time the world watched nine-tenths of an ear spurting blood and one tenth lying on the canvas – enough for a disqualification. King tried desperate damage control, but the Nevada State Athletic Commission did the right thing and banned Tyson from boxing for a year.

Lennox said he felt disappointed with both boxers – Holyfield for the head butts that contributed to Tyson's crazy reaction, and Tyson for losing control. 'Mike let himself down in my eyes,' he said. 'And it's clear to me he could lose his mind like that again but I still hope he gets his licence back and I certainly wouldn't object to fighting him, even though I realise he's capable of anything. I don't think he would try to bite me because I'm a clean fighter, but if he did I certainly wouldn't jump up and down like Holyfield. It's always important for me to maintain my composure.'

King needed back-up, so Akinwande became Don's second stringer. He talked of the London-born, Lagos-raised, Miami-based Nigerian as 'my Zulu warrior' (the logical equivalent would be to call King 'my Masai shyster') and tried to sell the idea of Henry as the logical successor to Holyfield. The obvious venue would have been London, given both boxers' roots, but the Duvas, who staged the fight, decided on a converted lounge in the Caesar's Palace Hotel in Lake Tahoe, which barely held a thousand people. The event didn't really wash in America, but in Britain it was taken seriously. Mickey Duff, for one, bet on an Akinwande victory, and several boxing writers went the same way. As the fight approached this message began to reach the serious punters, and by fight time the odds were closing.

In a way, the outcome was decided at the weigh-in. Akinwande came in at 237½lb, only 3½ less than Lewis, but looked puny in comparison. He'd been told that Lennox was unfit and would weigh over 250lb, but the 241lb body before him looked not only huge but hard too. After seven weeks of training in Big Bear Lewis was in fine shape, his resting pulse rate down to 42. 'This was a fight we were really well prepared for and by the end of camp we were really looking forward to it,' said Steward. When this sleek, fired-up giant stared imperiously at him, Henry licked his lips nervously and you could see the self-doubt flooding in. He was further unnerved on discovering that they were to fight in a small ring that would restrict his movement. He looked terrified walking towards it.

Lewis's instructions were to force his weaker challenger into a brawl. 'We decided Lennox should let him know who's boss right from the beginning,' said Shand.

'He had to stay with him and never give him room to breathe.' Lewis charged, landed a jab, and Akinwande clung. 'I wanted to maul him from the start,' said Lennox, 'because I realised he wasn't mentally or physically tough enough for me. He couldn't even handle that first jab I put in his face.' Lewis threw six hooks to the ribs and slotted in a big right cross, while slipping a couple of jabs, and Henry clung again. 'The first punch Lennox missed, not landed, just totally freaked Akinwande out,' recalled Steward. 'He was really scared. It was the left hook that didn't even land, and then a couple of uppercuts that almost landed that really frightened him, and that was it. From then on he was just trying to clinch. When he went back to his corner at the end of the round we were listening to them and I clearly heard him say, "He's too strong." I'll never forget it. Very few people realise that Lennox is the most intimidating heavyweight of our time.'

Lewis walked through Akinwande's skittish jab-cross offence and landed a right cross and an uppercut at the start of round two. All the Nigerian could do in response was grab until Mills Lane forced them apart. After several more clinches Lane deducted a point from Henry's score. When he grabbed again, a frustrated Lewis whacked him behind the head a few times. 'I was trying to fight, but all he wanted to do was throw a left–right and hold, and what can you do with a guy who doesn't want to fight?'

Akinwande had his only moment of the fight in round three. After Lane separated them, Lewis landed another right cross-uppercut combination, and for once Henry punched back, landing a hard right that caught Lennox on the top of the head, but he seemed terrified by his success and rushed to grab at the same as Lewis was bending to punch again. This meant Lewis went so low that his right glove dusted the canvas as he came up to punch. Both boxer and trainer refuted the idea that this was an unofficial knockdown. 'No, I dipped to slip his punch, but really, he never hurt me,' said Lewis. Steward was even more emphatic. 'No, no, no! I saw it myself from ringside. Lennox was going low when Henry was throwing the right so that he could get set to come up with a hook. Henry threw that right and when Lennox tried to go underneath Henry pushed him downwards, but Lennox kept right on fighting. He wasn't shaken and that was no knockdown.'

Steward said, 'throw the left hook to the body' and Lewis came out aggressively, digging in to the short ribs. Akinwande, visibly suffering, held but Lewis jerked him around violently to free himself and then hurt him again with a right to the body and a hard left hook to the chin that sent him flying into the ropes. Henry was wobbly but managed to clutch again, earning another warning. He was exhausted from the effort of trying to hold a far stronger man and from the effect of the body blows and was gulping in air as he wrapped his arms around his torturer's back with a look of terrified desperation. 'With the small size of that ring, and the way Akinwande chose to fight, it would have been very hard to keep away,' said Shand. 'He could never have outboxed Lennox so he chose to hang on. I think part of his problem was that he made the mistake of training at sea level, so he got tired quickly, and Lennox never let him into the fight. He jumped on him and stayed on him, and after the fight Akinwande couldn't breathe.'

Henry looked unsteady coming out for the fifth and clutched as soon as Lennox hit him. Lane deducted another point while his trainer, Don Turner, yelled, 'Get out there and fight! You gotta fight!' But his only idea was to prevent himself from being hit, his only tactic to cling for life. Lane walked Henry to his corner and gave him his final warning, asking Turner to reiterate the point. 'All you have to do is fight him,' Turner pleaded, but that was like telling him 'All you have to do is jump in the fire.' Henry just wasn't going there. Lennox hit again, Henry grabbed again, and Lane issued his disqualification notice.

Once again Lennox felt disgusted and disappointed, and blamed it all on Don King. 'He's always throwing these idiot guys in with me,' he complained. 'Look at Akinwande. Thirty-three fights without defeat, nineteen knockouts, by far the most important fight of his whole career and he elects to hold. I felt disappointed because I wanted to show off more of my talent, but every second he got he just held on to me. He obviously just didn't want to fight.' Steward felt his pupil was beyond criticism. 'I was very satisfied,' he said. 'Lennox did everything he could. He crowded Akinwande and took his fight away. He took his physical strength away, and took his mental strength away.'

Akinwande's disgrace left King unmoved. In the absence of better candidates he recycled his 'Zulu warrior' and a year on, after a few decent wins, persuaded the WBA to make Henry their mandatory contender. But the day before his challenge for Holyfield's title he was diagnosed with hepatitis B and the fight was cancelled. Neither deterred nor embarrassed, King did it again eighteen months later, trying to force Lennox into a return with Akinwande, which never came off, but he kept him in the picture until 2002.

Lennox had four weeks to rest and play before returning to Big Bear to train for the biggest fight of his professional career, against Golota in Atlantic City on 4 October. Everyone agreed there was a strong chance of this one going wrong because Golota was a wild, volatile and violent character, but it was also the kind of fight to define Lewis's career. Andrew was exciting, unpredictable and dirty, and his notoriety, following two disqualification defeats against Bowe, meant he was wonderful box-office material. He went into the first Bowe fight as an Olympic bronze medallist with a record of 28 straight wins, 25 on knockouts, and came out of the second one claiming to be the best heavyweight in the world – and a man so mean that he was not content just to beat up Bowe; he had to break his balls too. That's the kind of thing that sells pay-per-view hits.

Maloney and Eliadis didn't want him. Aside from their concerns that he was a dangerous boxer with an excellent jab and a heavy right, not to mention their worry that Lewis was destined for another disqualification mess, they were convinced that their US partners, Main Events, wanted Golota to win because Lou Duva trained him and because Andrew's notoriety made him more marketable. 'Main Events was Golota's sole promoter and we weren't getting on well with them at the time, and I had no doubt from the way they were acting that they wanted Golota to win,' said Panos. But Steward was eager. 'Man, let's do it!' he told Lennox. 'You need to fight Tyson, Holyfield, Golota, someone the American public accepts as a good fighter, because it gives you a chance to exhibit a few skills.' Once the fight was made he was delighted with Lewis' response. 'He's more motivated and enthusiastic about his training than in all the fights I've been with him because he realises this is the fight to give him the credibility he thrives and hungers for.'

Golota fled to the United States in 1990 to avoid assault charges arising from an incident when he beat up a man in a bar fight in Warsaw (although he eventually returned, was convicted and fined), and a few years later he again faced charges for beating up a stranger in another Polish brawl. This behaviour was carried over into the ring. On his way up he sank his fangs into the neck of the Samoan Samson Po'uha before stopping him, and one fight before Bowe he smashed his head into the face of the American Dannell Nicholson before stopping him. There were also questions about that pimply back and observations about how he managed to get so big so quickly. When he fought in the 1988 Olympics he weighed 200lb; when he turned professional in 1992 he had grown to 217lb but when he fought Lewis he was a solid 244lb (the same as Lennox, who was only thirteen pounds heavier than his debut weight eight years earlier).

While the public viewed Golota's foul-fighting tactics as commendable nasti-ness, Steward had another explanation. 'I don't think he has the biggest heart. Any time he gets in distress or discomfort, whether it's fatigue or a fighter challenging him, he snaps and starts doing dirty things. It's something you have to deal with. You can't say you don't worry about it because he doesn't even know why he does it himself. Therefore it's damn sure a possibility because it's nothing he plans. He just does it and doesn't really have any control, but I believe if Lennox comes out and attacks him he's not going to have much opportunity to get into that, which is why I want him to come out with a very aggressive style. How the fight goes depends not so much on Golota but on Lennox. If he comes out with that, "I want to get it on and get you out of here quick" attitude the fight's over within three rounds because Lennox is too strong, too sharp a puncher, too accurate and too seasoned. He's spent a lot of time becoming a complete fighter and he has such an assortment of weapons he will have too much of everything, including the intimi-dation factor. When Lennox attacks him he's not going to have much opportunity to get into the dirty stuff. This fight will be over quick because I don't think this guy has a good chin.'

For Lennox, the idea of losing to a white boxer felt worse than losing to a black one. 'It's not that it means more to me to beat a white boxer,' he explained. 'That doesn't mean anything, really. But it would be worse getting beaten by a white boxer because black boxers have it so hard in the first place, just to get by. It's always easier for the white boxer.' As he watched videos of Golota's fights he felt certain there was no danger of this happening if he struck hard and early from a dis-tance. 'I'm going to see where his balls are at,' Lewis said, 'but I'm going to do it with reason. I mean, I'm not going to fight inside, and even if he hits me low I won't do it back because I'm not into that kind of fighting.'

What no one could have predicted was that the disintegration happened before the first bell. Again, the weigh-in seemed decisive. As with so many opponents it was the sudden realisation of Lennox's size that unsettled Golota. Although he weighed the same as Lewis and was only an inch shorter he looked softer and smaller. And, again, that impassive stare made him doubt what he'd been sure of. When Golota arrived in his changing room this feeling of dread overwhelmed him and even affect-ed his cardio-vascular system. He began to hyperventilate and had to receive attention from medics. His people tried, without success, to delay the start of the fight by twenty minutes to allow him a bit more time to get his head straight. He seemed anxious when he got into the ring, too, trying to focus but struggling to ban-ish the doubts. 'I was too nervous,' he said later. 'There was too much pressure.' Lennox had a look of burning intensity in his eyes. Everything else was shut out. 'I wanted to go out and hit him before he could commit any fouls,' he said. 'I wanted to go out there and get rid of him, take him out.'

He probed with a jab, and then, after Golota missed with a couple of out-of-reach punches, he shot a quick right cross to the face. 'I realised he was a bit tentative with his punches. He was waiting to see what I would do and he's never seen anything like me with my speed, accuracy and punching power. Once he got hit, he recoiled in a negative way and I knew he was gone.' Golota barrelled for-ward, but Lennox turned him on the ropes and then crashed in an overhand right followed by eight brutal and accurate punches – four lefts, four rights – all landing on Golota's head, face and jaw, driving him to the canvas where he stared up with a wide-eyed look of shock, fear and astonishment on his face.

He rose unsteadily at the count of six. The referee, Joe Cortez, watched him stumbling but decided to give him time to recover by checking and re-checking that he could defend himself. Twenty seconds elapsed between the moment Golota hit the floor and the time Lennox was permitted to resume his bombardment. 'The ref-eree took a long time with that count, but I knew it was the end and I felt very intense.' He started with a power jab and followed it with nine huge rights to the head, a mixture of crosses, uppercuts and hooks, and Golota went down and out. One minute and 35 seconds had passed.

With his manager Frank beaming for Britain in his Union flag suit, his cycling friend Scott grasping him from behind, his trainer Manny beside him, smiling at a job well done – 'he's gone back to the old days when he really was an aggressive per-son in the street' – and his travelling army of fans yelling in delight as thousands of Poles held their heads in their hands, Lennox felt ecstatic glee for the first time in a long while. He called it his 'statement to the world', said that he had proved he was the 'best heavyweight on the planet', and warned that Golota had 'woken the sleep-ing lion'. As for the beaten Pole, he looked relieved it was over, but ashamed too. 'I love to fight,' he said, 'but people thought I was an accident waiting to happen. What can I do? Sorry.'

CHAPTER SEVENTEEN
BIG BEAR, CALIFORNIA, 1998

Harold Knight never misses a beat as Lennox pounds the hand pads. He can't afford to, because one slip could mean a heavyweight punch in the face. Harold might be 30lb heavier than in his fighting prime but he's still a little guy. He's also one of the best pad men around, so when Manny's out of town he takes over this once-a-week task with aplomb. The small man calls the moves and the big man fires – jab, jab, jab, left hook, right cross, the pads going up and down, this way and that, mimicking the movement of head and body. 'Pedal on the metal, come on baby, pressure, pressure, pedal on the metal, go into another gear.' Both men are sweating heavily, Harold feeling the force of his boss's punches all the way through his arms and shoulders. 'Lennox is a massive guy,' Harold points out during the inter-round break, 'but you can see, he's just so quick and nimble.'

He's a friendly and talkative man, Harold, as is Manny, but whereas the head trainer exudes authority and ego his deputy is deferential. Everyone quite likes him because he's unobtrusive, easy-going and cooperative and does his job with under-stated efficiency, without complaint. They're all mighty pleased he's around.

Not an alpha male by nature, Knight has been content to play the back-up role ever since joining the Lewis camp in January 1990, making him the longest-serving member of the training team. He arrived before Lennox's third fight as assistant to his mentor and former trainer John Davenport. He stayed on as Pepe Correa's assistant – an extremely difficult time because Harold didn't have the force of character to stop the rot or the experience and temperament to be head trainer of a world heavyweight champion. When Lennox chose Manny Steward, Harold survived the cut, and once again adapted to the new man's needs. 'Harold is the left hand to Manny's right,' says Lennox. 'He provides a different perspective that has proved invaluable in my improvement.' Or, as Harold puts it, in his modest way, 'I see things because four eyes are better than two, so I might see little details someone else missed. I work on his punching, particularly on the bags and sometimes the pads, and on filming his sparring and helping to give advice in his corner.'

If you want to know about Lennox's preparation, Harold is the man to ask. So a question like 'What did Lennox do today?' brings a detailed response. 'He started with fifteen minutes of stretching at five forty-five, and then we went for a five-mile run, and after breakfast he did strength exercises in the gym – five sets of twenty chin-ups and fifty sets of sit-ups, and light weights – and then he rested and played pool, and at four p.m. he went to the gym for two and a half hours and did more stretching and callisthenics, and then four rounds on the heavy bags, ten minutes on the speed bag, eight minutes of rope jumping and also, as you saw, we worked on the pads, so he takes a break from sparring but tomorrow he'll do eight rounds, and Violet's cooking a West Indian dish of fish and rice for dinner, and then he'll watch tapes and play chess, and it's lights out at nine p.m.'

This is not a role he envisaged when he started boxing as a nine-year-old and went on to win 103 of 116 unpaid fights and a clutch of titles, boxing for his country. He won't labour the fact, but he's the only person in the training team with any experience of boxing professionally. Davenport christened him 'The Shadow' because, as Harold puts it, 'I was always on people in fights, just like a shadow'. He won his first nineteen fights for pay, fifteen on knockouts, and lifted the American junior lightweight (130lb) title. But in his last fight, a premature challenge for the WBA title, he lost on points over fifteen rounds to the reigning champion Rocky Lockridge, and was forced to retire on medical grounds.

That was in April 1988 when he was 25 years old. It was a desperate blow and he wondered what would become of his life. 'Even now I hate to think about it but without a doubt I would have won the world title and possibly two,' he says. With no other options he decided if he couldn't box himself at least he could teach others. He was delighted when his former trainer, Davenport, invited him to join the Lewis team and had no problems with the idea of following them to Britain and all over the world. Gradually, as his expertise developed and Lewis's fight schedule became sparser, he started to train other boxers – men and boys who appreciated his knowledge and skills and didn't need to be bossed around. He also puts in some voluntary youth work back home in Plainfield, New Jersey. But when the call comes, he drops everything for a boss he adores.

'Right from the start, when we first met, I really liked him because of his nature as a person and I grew to respect him tremendously,' he says. 'What I appreciated most was the way he treated other people and this honestly hasn't changed.' Asked to elaborate, he can't stop. 'I've been around sport since I was a little kid and I've seen that some people get a lot of money and status and they change. Well, today Lennox has all these things but I haven't seen major changes in his attitudes to people. He still loves playing practical jokes and having a bit of fun in the camp, and this makes it easier for me being in camp for so long because having to be away from my family, sometimes for more than eight weeks, is the hardest part of this job, but he's such a personable guy that it makes it easier. Really, from that first time we met, I found him one of the most down-to-earth guys I've come across in boxing, and he's still like that. He really is a good guy. This man will still stop to talk to anyone, and when they talk to him he's all ears, and it's the same in his approach as a fighter. He's a world champion but he's still all ears and all eyes, always willing to learn something new. And also, when he arrives in camp he's not like some other fighters I've worked with who want to take it slow for a week or so. When he arrives he's all work.'

Lennox's hopes of an immediate unification bout were quashed. There were several obstacles in the way: Don King's reluctance to conclude an agreement unless on his terms; Evander's insistence on a $20 million purse; and the fact that the boxers were contracted to rival cable companies. King's inclination to extract as much as he could out of Evander's reign before risking him against Lewis proved the biggest hurdle. He played a long game, starting with a Holyfield–Moorer return, to unify the WBA and IBF titles. This time the much-improved Evander overcame early difficulties to overwhelm Michael in eight rounds. King was still reluctant to deal, driving Lennox demented. 'This will affect not just my marketability but boxing's marketability,' he complained. 'In a sense we're entertainers. We put our lives on the line to entertain, and this is the fight the public want to be entertained by. They want to see who's best, and if we boxers are denied the chance to prove this, we all suffer because the public is what keeps us alive. Without them, we're nothing.'

While Lennox was resting, two other major heavyweight events unfolded: First, Tyson, having completed his year's suspension, returned to action against Frans Botha. While being handily outboxed for four rounds he tried to break Botha's arm in a clinch and hit him after the bell, before finally connecting with his payload right to end the fight late in the fifth. But he was soon in more serious trouble: after assaulting two motorists in a road-rage incident he found himself back in jail. Shortly after his release he fell out with King, physically booting him out of a limousine and accusing him of stealing his money. He also sued King for $100 million. 'Greed reaches at the deepest core of people,' Tyson later explained. 'Just reaches deep at them, and they, the promoters, are fighting for me and stuff, and then that made it easy for Don King to sneak in. Oh man, he got me good. He's a very interesting individual.' After this Tyson became a free agent as far as promoters were concerned, although he was tied for life to Showtime Television. He fought on; almost every subsequent bout involving some kind of stink inside or outside the ring. Without Tyson, King's heavyweight ambitions were focused on Evander.

Second, Foreman's reign as the 'linear' world champion finally came to a questionable end. He won this honour legitimately, by beating the chinny Michael Moorer (who in turn had beaten Holyfield, who beat Bowe, the last unified champion), but George was soon champion in name only because each of his three white challengers seemed worse than the last. But eventually he lost concentration. HBO offered him serious money to take on a popular, intelligent and loquacious New Yorker, Shannon Briggs, who was different from Foreman's other opponents in several respects – he was big, talented and black – but he came with the kind of limitations the old man figured he could exploit.

In an early outing he was stopped by a fringe contender, later claiming he suffered from an asthma attack as a result of a dust mite allergy. Foreman reckoned the problem lay in an allergy to hard work and big punches, a view reinforced when Shannon's demanding trainer, Teddy Atlas, abandoned him. So, George took the Briggs fight and at the age of 48 gave one of the finest performances of his comeback. Most ringsiders felt he deserved the nod, but in a reversal of fortune he lost and retired.

The new 'linear' world champion was Shannon Briggs, although very few in the boxing world bothered to emphasise this honour. Still, this title and Briggs' popularity in New York made him an attractive filler opponent for Lennox and the fight was set for Atlanta, New Jersey on 28 March 1998.

Steward cautioned that Briggs might not be the pushover everyone assumed. He was reasonably large, at 6ft 4in and around 230lb with an 81-inch reach, quick on his feet, with fast hands, sharp reflexes and sound counter-punching skills, and he was also a banger, with serious knockout power in the left hook and right cross. His only loss in 31 fights (24 stoppages) might have had an asthmatic explanation, but he had clearly improved in the two years since. 'I saw him fight Foreman and I watched the way he dug in over the last three rounds,' said Steward. 'It made a man out of Shannon and he came through that fight a much more dangerous heavyweight than most people think.' Certainly he gave an impression of the kind of cockiness suggesting he'd successfully banished his residues of self-doubt. Lennox trained hard, but with a week to go he came down with a bad cold.

Lewis, at 243lb, fifteen more than Briggs, went straight into the attack and walked into a hard right-cross counter. Briggs darted in and out, using his jab well. He moved into range and threw an extremely well-timed left hook that landed flush on Lennox's temple, driving him back. He was shaken but covered up as Briggs followed through with three rights to the back of the head, prompting a retreat in an undignified backwards run to avoid taking more. When his back touched the ropes, he turned his pursuer and held; the crisis over. 'He tripped me up and I was kind of off balance when he hit me at the back of the head, but my defence was too good for him when he jumped on me and after that I realised he would try everything in his power to get a good shot in,' he said. 'I think all his New York fans got quite a kick out of seeing their man hitting me on the back of the head.' As the bell rang Lewis landed a right that put Briggs on his bottom, but Steward was worried. 'You gotta watch your balance,' he said. 'You're getting off balance. Keep your balance! And if you get hit again, tie him up and take your time. That's the power.'

Soon everything was flowing from the jab. Lewis landed a stiff right cross, but the New Yorker bounded back with a hard hook and a sharp cross of his own. When Lennox shook his head, Briggs tried again, but this time was met with a string of jabs and a three-punch combination. Lewis took over in round three, starting with a heavy cross to the jaw, two quick jabs and some meaty hooks to the ribs. But Briggs was disproving the slur that he lacked spunk. He shook his head disdainfully and kept firing back, but again it was Lennox who had the last word, ending the round with a spiteful hook. He was starting to load on the hurt, wobbling Briggs with a hook and nailing him with three rights. Shannon grabbed the top rope to stay up and was battered with short punches until he went down. Although up at seven, sixteen seconds elapsed between the knockdown and referee Frank Cappuccino's order to resume hostilities. Late in the round, Lewis became arm weary and Briggs caught him flush on the chin with another cracking hook, but he came straight back to drop Shannon with a right. This time Briggs dragged himself up at eight, and when Cappuccino asked 'Are you all right?' he nodded.

Lewis landed his right and several hurtful hooks and he was also using his jab as an offensive weapon before firing a massive cross that left the New Yorker lying out on his back with his legs spread. Amazingly, Briggs was up before the count of eight but Cappuccino was worried. He looked carefully before asking again, 'You all right?' His question was met with another nod. Cappuccino allowed nineteen seconds, but it wasn't enough. Lennox was hurting him with every punch, and it was clear that Shannon's legs and lungs were gone. Wobbling alarmingly, he missed with a desperate swing and fell flat on his face. Cappuccino shook his head and waved his hands and Briggs did not protest. Lewis was now the linear world heavyweight champion as well as the WBC champion.

'Sometimes you're not a hundred per cent for a fight,' he said. 'Sometimes you go down to eighty per cent, and that's where I was for Briggs. I wouldn't say I was really tiring, but being off for a week when I was training did affect me. Anyway, I was glad he came to fight because that made it interesting, and I'm in the entertainment business.'

While he continued to wait for Holyfield, he was able to focus more directly on some of his concerns outside boxing. He set up his own model agency, helped to sponsor the black British professional golfer Robert Forde, put in many hours on the golf course and tennis court, had several short-term romantic relationships, sponsored a team of motor racers he called the Lennox Lewis Motor Racing Team, and bought the first of two moderately successful race horses, this one also called Lennox Lewis.

But his major passion was Lennox Lewis College, the school he founded in east London. The idea was hatched in 1994 when he decided that he wanted to give something to the kind of community he roamed in as a child. He talked of his bleak experiences with British schooling and his positive experiences in Kitchener, where his sporting talent was nurtured and his intellectual interest stimulated. Panos Eliadis suggested they could find a comparable formula with the added benefit of boosting his image. Having purchased the freehold to a disused factory in Hackney, he proposed they turn this into a school for troubled teenagers and in 1994 they set it up with Lewis as patron. It was announced that both men would donate £1 million (although today Eliades says this figure was 'just for the press' and that in reality he put in £1.2 million and Lennox £300,000).

Its aim was to transform the lives of a selected group of fourteen- to nineteen-year-olds by offering education, skills training and a sense of purpose. 'Nowadays a lot of young people are getting into trouble with the law and they're sending them to prison, and they're not educating them properly, so Lennox wants the children on probation to come to the institute and he is going to be the role model,' Panos said, adding, rather oddly: 'Lennox is black and Hackney is ninety per cent black, or should I say coloured [sic]? They'll look at Lennox and think, "Ah, I like that, I'll do boxing." Or it could be gymnastics, snooker, car repair or bricklaying, so they'll be educating themselves so that one day they can earn some money rather than be mugging people on the street.'

They put plenty of effort into ensuring the building was painted, carpeted and stocked, with a gym, a woodwork room, a hairdressing salon, a plumbing classroom, a sound recording room, a decorating classroom, a mechanics shop, a computer room, an electronics room. By 1995 they were ready to start and the first 40 students were enrolled, two thirds of whom had been excluded from school; 40 per cent had been arrested at least once, 19 per cent had served custodial sentences, 41 per cent were in care and 56 per cent were from single-parent households. In addition to sport and vocational courses, literacy and numeracy were stressed. They had one teacher for every six pupils.

The head teacher, Liz Jones, dismissed the fashion for 'zero tolerance' and 'tough love' when dealing with teenage tearaways. Like her school's patron, she believed in second, third and fourth chances. 'You have zero tolerance and put them away, and at the end of that, when they've served their sentence, you just end up with career criminals,' she reasoned. 'Sure you get dramatic results with crime figures, but you're creating a problem for these kids for life. Most of the young people you see locked up have missed out on huge chunks of education. All they can rely on is the street and stealing. If you're serious about rehabilitation and keeping the crime rate down, you have to give them a future, and that has to mean giving them a chance to read and write and have a bash at a skill.'

The school won rave reviews and whenever Lennox visited he came away feeling it was making a significant difference to the lives of these teenagers. But it was not immune to the problems of its environment. Average attendance was only 70 per cent, although the teachers were quick to stress that most students had had a zero per cent attendance record at their previous schools. The staff were not all ideal and yet were protected by law. In 1997 a teacher won an industrial tribunal case against the college for not receiving the correct severance pay. But the main problem was funding: it cost £12,000 per pupil per year, compared to £2,500 a year in state education. Together with all the equipment and salaries the bill was £750,000 a year. They raised money from the Prince's Trust, sponsorship from a computer company and dribs and drabs from other businesses, but some of it came from their pockets, with Panos starting to balk at this loss, bemoaning the difficulties in raising grants from government or the National Lottery. When the school was established he boasted, tastelessly, that it would be so hot that kids would be 'doing muggings to get in'; when he discovered it was starting to drain his personal finances he complained, tastelessly, that it was easier for 'one-legged homosexuals' to get state funding.

Today he says he did everything possible to secure its future. 'We were taking kids off the streets and teaching them computers and electrical skills and all sorts of things, but the government said they were not prepared to invest in it, which was a great shame. We ended up putting a fortune into it, and especially me, and we couldn't keep going.' Lennox, however, has a slightly different take. 'I was out of the country most of the time, training and fighting, but I started hearing of the problems about the lack of funding from Panos. We wanted government involvement and we didn't get it, but part of the problem was that Panos was supposed to be managing it and in my opinion he didn't do a very good job.'

Lennox addressed Hackney Council about helping with funding and came away with a commitment to raise bridging funds. 'Lennox made a big impression when he came to speak to us,' the council's executive director Sarah Ebanja gushed, and she went on to praise the college's contribution to improving the lives of Hackney's teenagers and to claim the financial package would help 'secure its future permanently.' They raised £100,000 of public funding – enough only for it to limp on before grinding to a halt in August 1998. The younger pupils were transferred to other schools in the area, the older ones to Hackney colleges. Lennox protested that the school was 'too important to close' and talked about 'when, not if' in terms of it reopening but by 1999 he had to accept it was over.

The experience left a bitter taste with teachers who lost their jobs, and because the school bore Lennox's name they directed their anger in his direction. As Ann Malech of the National Union of Teachers put it, 'We didn't have a very good experience with Lennox Lewis College, and we weren't very happy with the way our members were treated.' In the end, Lennox felt that there was nothing more he could do to revive it. He was spending most of his time away from London, he had fights to focus on, and he felt he had exhausted his options. 'I found the whole thing very upsetting,' he said. 'I had been so positive about it at the beginning but then it ran into problems that we couldn't solve without government help. I was really gutted when it finally closed.'

In the meantime, negotiations dragged on about the goal of unifying the title and Lewis began to doubt his rival's nerve. 'Sometimes I think Evander is joking when he says he wants to fight me,' he complained. 'I mean, I crave that fight and will do anything to get it, but I hear a lot of people saying that Holyfield is ducking me by playing games with money, which makes me think that he's both greedy and afraid. I always respected Holyfield, but I'm starting to lose my respect. Basically I think the Americans are afraid to lose their piece of the world title, because I don't see them pushing hard enough for this fight, and this is embarrassing for the sport of boxing.'

As they waited, both men fulfilled mandatory defences. On 19 September 1998 Holyfield outpointed the inconsequential Vaughn Bean, while a week later Lewis faced the unbeaten European champion Zeljko Mavrovic. The 29-year-old Croat had won all 27 professional fights, 22 on knockouts. Despite his number one ranking he had never fought any American contenders but dominated in Europe. Usually weighing 220lb, he was not a huge heavyweight, but he was tall (6ft 4in), with an 82-inch reach. He was a strong, attacking boxer and a sharp puncher who preferred leading to countering, but he moved his head, parried effectively and had one of the best chins in the division

The Croatian football team reached the semi-finals of the World Cup, their tennis star, Goran Ivanicevic, won Wimbledon, and there were hopes that Zeljko was next, although unlike Goran and so many of their football fans, he did not descend into the deeper realms of ethno-nationalism for a nation whose symbols harked back to its Nazi-supporting days. Always accompanied by his British gypsy trainer Darky Smith, Zeljko, with his Mohawk hairstyle, his commitment to organic food and his disarming politeness, came across as a likeable character who genuinely believed he was destined to win. He would say, for instance, that his astrologer girlfriend had told him victory was 'written in the stars', but he certainly didn't leave this to chance, training unremittingly in hot, humid conditions, which brought his weight to a career-lightest of 214½lb, 28½lb less than Lewis.

Lennox trained in the dry, high-altitude atmosphere of Big Bear, despite the fact that the fight was to be held in a humid dome at sea level in Connecticut. When Frank Maloney arrived he observed that Lennox was in a bad mood and that there were tensions between the boxer and his head trainer. Soon afterwards, Lennox told Courtney Shand to bar Maloney from his training sessions, after deciding that Frank was too inclined to interfere and offer unwanted advice. The furious Maloney bit his tongue and respected the boss's wishes for a few days before sitting down with Lennox and sorting out their differences, but it was an early sign of a gradual parting of ways between boxer and manager.

Lennox invited two of his old Canadian connections to join him: fellow Olympic medal winner Egerton Marcus (employed as a sparring partner and all-round helper) and his old Olympic coach Adrian Teodorescu, who was there partly for old times' sake, partly to help with the training, but also because he'd studied Mavrovic during his days as an international amateur trainer. Both were delighted by the invitations and in Adrian's case neither he nor Lennox alluded to the tensions of ten years earlier. Once he arrived the atmosphere in the camp lightened. 'It was like we'd said goodbye yesterday,' said Adrian. 'I was pleased to see he was the same character as he was then. He would still listen to my advice and we could still joke around and tease each other.'

Lewis's men were worried about his stamina. That spell of arm weariness against Briggs wasn't his first and they felt it needed addressing before he faced Holyfield. They hoped more intensive cardio-vascular work at 7,200 feet might be the answer, but Adrian warned against the common assumption that you gain simply by training up and performing down. 'I kept telling his guys that you need to adjust to the change of altitude, even if you're going down. Either you arrive one day before, or at least two weeks before, but if you arrive a week before your blood doesn't carry the oxygen properly.'

Halfway through camp they were joined by another outsider – sports physiologist Joe Dunbar. 'I was in Big Bear working with two other heavyweights and got chatting to Courtney about what I was doing for them and various other athletes,' he recalled. 'I then talked to Adrian and he implied it would be a good idea if I joined the team, so Courtney and Frank brought me in.' Joe, who was about the same age as Lennox and Courtney and came from the same town (Purley) as Patrick Drayton, fitted into the bantering family atmosphere of camp and took an instant liking to Lennox, even if he was never drawn into his inner circle at a personal level. 'My first impression was that he's a very private person, but I have no problem with that, and also that he's a perfect gentleman,' he recalled. 'In fact, right from the start I kept thinking, "He's almost too nice to be a boxer." I quickly discovered he had a great sense of humour, a really fantastic sense of humour – you know, always playing practical jokes and little tricks – and he's quite light-hearted, and this keeps him very relaxed. In fact, he's the most relaxed athlete I've ever seen.'

Unlike some of the others in the camp, whose job description included things like keeping the champion company, Joe's job was technical: to conduct physical tests, take blood and heart measurements and make recommendations on diet, hydration and dietary supplements. He arrived with a master's degree in physiology and a reputation for working with Olympic rowers, athletes and tri-athletes, and he was told to measure everything measurable. 'As soon as I arrived they told me Lennox had an endurance problem, and they were worried about getting that right for Holyfield. So my main emphasis was on endurance.' He began his battery of physiological tests while offering the same advice as Teodorescu. 'With altitude training there can be a serious problem in going down to sea level at the wrong time,' he warned. 'You have to get the timing right. I've seen it working in rowing and athletics, and the worst time to come down from altitude is seven days before the event. My other worry is that you're training in a dry atmosphere but fighting in an extremely humid atmosphere, and that can also cause tiredness problems.'

But the team insisted their hands were tied by press obligations, which meant they needed to arrive seven days before fight time. Anyway, few believed that Mavrovic could last long, despite Teodorescu's warning that Lewis should expect a long fight. 'Zeljko's a really tough guy,' he told Lennox. 'I watched him fighting in two Olympics and even the great Cuban puncher Felix Savon couldn't drop him. He has a helluva chin.'

Mavrovic made a confident start, showing fast hands and quick reflexes to the delight of a vociferous contingent of Croatians crammed into the hot, humid, tented arena. Lennox, who looked so much more powerful, was content to box from long range, raking him with long jabs, and Zeljko's right eye began to mark up. Early in round three Mavrovic struck with the kind of right that flattened European title challengers, but Lennox did not seem fazed and kept pumping out his jab. 'He weighed under 215lb, so he didn't really hurt me,' he said. 'Those overhand rights of his just bounced off me.' A round later it was Lewis's turn to land a clean cross and Mavrovic was shaken and forced to hold before absorbing some body blows and a few hearty whacks behind the neck.

Lewis began breathing heavily with his mouth open, but, as Knight explained, 'Lennox always seems to fight with his mouth open in rounds four and five,' and he was still whacking his challenger in a way that would have finished off most heavyweights. Steward implored him to pile it on. 'Look, this guy can't counterpunch, so attack him.' He pounded the body, picked him off with heavy head blows and began to improvise – for instance, using an uppercut to counter a slipped right cross. Bleeding from both nose and eye, Zeljko finally registered in round seven, starting with a strong right cross and later, a sharp left hook, right uppercut combination and then a solid cross. Lennox looked exhausted – 'that's because they wouldn't listen to me when I said that the worst time to arrive was a week before the fight,' Teodorescu muttered – and the Croat took this as his cue to go all out, cornering him and throwing his all. Lewis blocked and slipped most of them, and those that connected seemed to bounce off him. After his short rest he came back with some rather heavier hooks and crosses of his own. 'I thought I would be able to breathe out there but he put good pressure on me,' he admitted.

The veil of exhaustion lifted and he began bouncing on his toes, firing off long, well-placed punches, including several huge rights. At times he looked like a young Ali, gliding with speed and grace as he jabbed, moved and countered with hands low, slipping the incoming flak with ease. 'I prepared wrong and in the end I had to use my experience and pull out some tricks,' he said. Zeljko had intermittent success with single punches, including a hard right that raised a swelling around the right eye, but was being soundly outboxed. In round 11 Lennox worked his way out of another spell of treacle walking, got back on his toes and stiffened his challenger's legs with a heavy-handed combination. He boxed beautifully in the final round, sharp-shooting from long range, leaving Mavrovic's face in a mess. 'That was his best round, despite all the tiredness,' said Teodorescu.

One judge gave Lewis eleven rounds, another nine and the third, eight – a wide decision, but still his hardest fight in two years. As Lewis left the ring he held onto his manager's shoulder as his legs weakened, and when he reached his changing room he plonked himself down, exhausted. 'Now we understand: altitude can be a problem when you're coming down, as well as the other way around,' said Harold. 'We came too early, or too late, and didn't realise how hot and humid it would be with that air conditioning in the tent. Also, we expected him to run, so our tactics were based on that, but he didn't.' Lewis nodded in appreciation of a valiant challenge 'You got a guy who dedicated his whole career for me, who had his entire country behind him and trained for ten months, and he really came prepared and I had to pull it out, all the way to the last round. I thought I'd knock him out but he's got a great chin,' he said.' They all grunted in agreement when it was suggested Mavrovic had the stuff to become world champion. Instead, it turned out to be his last fight. He contracted a wasting disease, lost 30lb and couldn't box again.

By then, King had reached the point where he needed money badly enough to become serious about concluding a deal without tying Lennox up in perpetuity, but it took a while to get all the parties to agree. On one side there was Lewis, who wanted $10 million (although he settled for half a million less), and his British promoter, who wasn't getting on with his American promoter; on the other side there was Holyfield, who demanded $20 million, and King who had a series of demands, including that he promoted the fight with the option of a return if Lewis won or the first mandatory defence. He agreed HBO rather than Showtime could televise the event, on condition that he made a massive profit. And then there was HBO itself, which had to agree to the numbers demanded by King (which meant putting up $30 million) but balked at paying all of Lewis's purse. In the end, Eliades nudged Duva out of the final phase of the talks and cut a deal with King, who made a minor compromise by guaranteeing to pay $2 million of Lennox's purse, while still walking off with a deal that would make him a mint if he filled Madison Square Garden and sold a million HBO pay-per-view hits (and he achieved both goals – a packed Garden and 1.2 million HBO buys – and made a $14 million profit, while HBO barely broke even).

At last, 13 March 1999 was set, and Lennox finally approached the prime goal of his boxing life: the chance to fight for the undisputed world title. 'I really see victory in this fight as part of my destiny,' he said. 'There's always gold at the end of the rainbow.'

CHAPTER EIGHTEEN
SCOTSRUN, PENNSYLVANIA, 1999

Courtney Shand is not an easy man to get past. If his broad, weight-boosted physique is not enough of a deterrent, he'll stare you down with disdainful, long-lidded eyes, and soon you'll find yourself talking a little too quickly, perhaps even in a slightly higher pitch than normal. That's if you haven't got your credentials sorted, or you want something beyond what was agreed, or you're taking advantage. When Manny's not around, it's usually Courtney who is in charge. Lennox is the boss, but his old high school buddy is the man you have to go through to reach the boss. And while Manny is genial and gentle in his undisputed authority, Courtney can be hard and immovable when he feels the need, and the need relates entirely to his reading of the interests of his friend and employer.

Ever since they met as fifteen-year-olds and started playing together as running backs on their high-school football team in Kitchener, Ontario, Courtney has been minding Lennox and singing his praises. 'Courtney was one of the toughest guys we ever had playing football here,' their high school football coach Gene Heesaker recalls. 'He blocked for Junior in games, and in a sense he's been doing that ever since. My impression, watching them together, was that he was sort of like Lennox's compass. He kept him on the straight and narrow, in a way, and he always looked out for him and protected him.' They had time apart in the latter days of Lewis's amateur career and early days of his professional career, a time when Courtney was completing a course in physical training studies at a college in Ontario, and then gaining practical experience, before joining Lennox as his conditioner at the end of 1990. While Steward and Knight concentrate on technique, sparring, tactics, bags and pads, the job of Shand and his assistants is to get Lennox into peak physical shape by supervising his fitness regime: stretching, weights, exercises, running, cycling and diet.

Everyone in camp respects him because there is never any doubt about his reliability and absolute loyalty, even if it goes against his own immediate interests. He made no complaint about the hiring of Adrian Teodorescu for a couple of fights, even though this cut into his own role, and he pushed for Joe Dunbar because he realised this outsider had more expertise with diet and supplements. Other employees fell out with Lewis, or with each other but none had a bad word to say about Shand because they knew he was straight and wouldn't speak behind their backs. As Lennox puts it, 'His total honesty and attention to the smallest details have been invaluable to me.'

His job gradually expanded to include handling visitors, so here at the Caesar's Brookdale, with Manny out of town for the day, he's the boss, the flak catcher, the minder, as well as the conditioner, and with Holyfield looming he's taking no prisoners. 'You want to go running with him tomorrow? Nope. Lennox says no outsiders for his runs. Next request?' And that unblinking stare again that makes you inclined to reduce your demands. That's the way it is with Courtney – until you're in, that is, on the boss's say-so, after which he rediscovers his previous friendly, talkative, relaxed, informative self, giving more than requested because he's eager to place his friend in the best possible light.

Courtney is most loquacious when recalling their high school time. 'Lennox was good at everything at school, a really great all-round sportsman,' he begins. 'I mean truly outstanding at everything – football, basketball, athletics, chess, table tennis and obviously boxing, and since then golf and tennis too. He was fast and unbelievably strong, which made him an incredible running back and he was absolutely brilliant at basketball. By sixteen he was probably six three and nearly two hundred pounds and he was really powerful and this amazing athlete. I've never seen more of a natural athlete in my life, so he was always doing sport, on top of his boxing, and yet managed to be a diligent student compared to the rest of us. He was just really good at everything he applied himself to, including fighting of course, although by the time I got to know him well he wasn't getting into many fights outside the ring because he was so involved in sport. But, you know, you always get guys who think they're tougher than you, until they find out differently.'

Pointing to three sparring partners on the other side of the gym, he says, 'See those guys? He's far, far, stronger than any of them. All the sparring partners who work with us are shocked how strong he is. He's just a naturally strong man – much, much stronger than he looks. We work with lots of repetitions of lighter weights and with own body weight resistance, so we're not concentrating on heavy weights, but he can benchpress almost four hundred pounds. He's definitely one of the strongest guys I've ever seen in my life.'

He doesn't take kindly to negative suggestions about stamina or flexibility. 'We stretch in the morning before we go running, and then we do extensive stretching in the gym, and I can tell you he's extremely flexible for such a big guy. And he has great muscle endurance and cardio-vascular conditioning. Lennox can do sets totalling five hundred push-ups some days, and he doesn't take a full minute's rest, and you should see him running or cycling uphill – hard climbs, increasing three thousand feet in altitude. Sometimes we all go with him and some of us are also in great shape too, but it's very hard to keep up, and he seems to reach a higher level in that last week or so, towards the end of the training camp, when his resting pulse rate comes down to forty-two or forty-three.'

So, basically, the perfect boxer, perfect athlete, perfect man. And for his forthcoming fight his condition is better than ever before because they all agree that this is Mr Perfect's biggest moment and that Holyfield is his finest opponent, which means that Courtney and everyone else has to work harder than ever before – harder on getting Lennox into impeccable shape and harder on keeping the rest of the world at bay.

When Evander Holyfield was searching for Bible verses to spirit him towards his first encounter with Mike Tyson, it was to the New Testament he turned. Evander is an Old Testament kind of guy at heart, but he's also a selective reader and learner, which means he's able to skip the bits about turning the other cheek, loving your neighbour, that kind of stuff – and settle for a statement of absolute faith from St Paul's letter to the Philippians: 'I can do all things through Christ who strengthens me.' That was what he had them embroider on to his purple trunks, and never a verse better chosen. Because Evander is a man of childlike faith in his Lord and himself. It's a combination that time and again has provided the will and heart to overcome bigger, younger men; more than anything else, it was what sorted Tyson. 'All things' meant what it said – moving mountains, healing his heart, beating the unbeatable. 'I'm a Christian,' he explained. 'I don't have the spirit of fear. I'm a conqueror, and such people don't lose from fear. Winners make things happen, while others let things happen. I fear no man, and that enables me to fight at my best.'

Lou Duva, who guided Evander to his first two world titles, never doubted his man would prevail against Tyson. 'One thing you've got to realise with Evander: there are better boxers and bigger punchers, sure, but no fighter, ever, has invested so much in winning; no fighter has his drive and will power; no fighter is as competitive. No fighter has his heart.' No fighter has his heart – that word always with Evander, one that defined his career. But its literal and metaphorical senses parted ways at one point. There was a fear that Holyfield, who was all heart, had a heart problem. It started when Tyson cracked a rib in sparring and exchanged his date with Evander for his date with the prison cell. Instead, Holyfield defended against Tyson lookey-likey Bert Cooper whom he bashed up until suddenly his energy source short-circuited and he went down and almost out. The problem re-emerged when he lost to Michael Moorer. His hands turned to lead and he fought on metaphorical heart alone, talking, for a while, about a heart problem.

Evander, a born-again Christian of the wilder Pentecostal brand, went to a healing service and after being 'slayed by the Spirit' (down three times – more than any mortal managed), he was healed, or so he said. Later, the original diagnosis was overturned and Evander was pronounced to be of sound heart. He experienced a similar problem energy shortfall in his 'rubber' match with Bowe, and once again blamed illness. He looked out of sorts again in beating the cruiserweight Bobby Czyz, when, aside from his loss of form, there was also a loss of size. Ever since conquering the sport's premier division, Evander's weight declined out of training. He was always small for a 1990s heavy (though bigger than most past greats – Johnson, Dempsey, Louis, Marciano, even Liston), but managed to pump himself up to impressive proportions through weight training, diet and who knows what else. But for Czyz he looked skinny – spindly legs, 29-inch waist, and an absence of those mighty biceps. His body appeared to be rebelling by returning to its natural state. Where had it all gone? Was the source of his past musculature and his heart problem a common one? Had he taken too many punches? These were the questions before his first Tyson fight, compounded by reports that he'd been taking a pasting from one of his sparring partners, David Tua. His own people were desperately concerned, and when Rory Holloway, one of Tyson's nastier batmen, speculated that Mike might just kill Evander, the sense of outrage was strengthened by the perception that this might just happen.

He really didn't need all this trouble. Here was a man with the biggest mansion in Atlanta, $100 million in assets, nine children and a wife who was a doctor – a psychiatrist, for heaven's sake – yet he was still longing to step up to the most feared unarmed man on the planet. Why? Manny Steward, who trained him for two fights, thought he knew. 'Everyone who doesn't know Evander thinks of him as this humble, nice guy, but I've never met anyone with an ego like his. That's why he's doing it.' His egotism – self-obsession really – came out most comically and most tragically in his single-mindedness about being the best. Best fighter, richest man, biggest house, best in bed, best body, best in the eyes of God. Lennox too has a bit of this in him but at least he can laugh about it. Evander's competitiveness is on a higher plane. When visiting his Atlanta mansion, he would show you around but not in the way of the usual southern host. See my pool table? I can beat you. My pool's Olympic size. I can whip you in a race. See my courts? I'll wipe you off them. Somewhere in what he described as his 'respectable working-class childhood' in Atlanta, via Atmore, Alabama, where he was raised by a single mother (who died in 1996), he acquired a mania about proving himself, insatiably, which was later combined with a belief that God could do it with him: Jesus and Evander together. Not an easy man to live with, then, as his succession of women attest, but then again not an easy man to fight.

His narcissistic personality made it difficult for him to reach an appropriate perspective on his own motives and actions. In anyone else you might be tempted to describe his moral inconsistency as hypocrisy (as Lennox did), his inability to admit defeat as self-delusion (as Lennox did) and the gulf between what he said and did as dishonesty (Lennox again), but in Holyfield's extreme case this would feel unfair because there's a real sense that he can't help himself. Still, some of these inconsistencies were breathtaking. Take, for example, his Christianity. He believes that the Word of the Lord is to be taken literally, chapter and verse, with no detours for contemporary interpretation, and strictly obeyed. He talks freely of the Gifts of the Spirit – divine epiphanies, healings, visions, tongues and the interpretation of tongues, casting out demons. He speaks about talking to Jesus, in an everyday way, much as anyone else might refer to little chats over the garden fence with a next-door neighbour. Between rounds, when training for Lewis, he played gospel tapes, quietly repeating the words – 'In Your presence that's when I'm strong, Oh Lord, My God, that's where I belong, touching your grace' – followed, at the end of each bit, by a loud 'Amen! – an exclamation his team felt obliged to echo.

Yet on the seventh Commandment he falls consistently short, and not just once or twice, because the Devil tempts the faithful more than the faithless, but all the time. Five of his nine children were born out of wedlock and two were fathered while his wives were pregnant. Evander responds to this with the observation that 'every man has to take his trousers off from time to time', but it gets worse, because his failure on the seventh runs into his forgetfulness when it comes to another verse: 'The love of money is the root of all evil.' Evander is a miser who particularly resents alimony payments. So he demanded that one of his wives take a DNA test in a failed bid to wriggle out of paying, and after fighting Lewis he contested and lost another massive claim, this one from his third ex-wife.

Within the ring, Evander takes his lead from a faux-Christian saying not found in the Bible: 'God helps those who help themselves' (and in his case, by any means necessary). His magnificent heroics obscures the fact that he's one of the dirtiest heavyweight champions ever – right up there with Dempsey, Marciano, Tyson and Bowe. Even in his amateur days there were worrying signs. When he was seventeen he fastened his teeth on to an opponent's shoulder – teenage exuberance, he later claimed. And in his final unpaid fight he was disqualified for felling his opponent on the break. But he really took to the rough stuff as a professional. Lou Duva tells a story of Holyfield getting punched low in his fight with Michael Dokes. 'When Evander comes back to the corner, I say, "Look at me. You go out there, get your right hand and put it right into his cup. You got that? Hit him low. You heard what I said?" So he says, "OK." And he goes right out there and, boom! Dokes is falling over and calling foul and he has to have a rest and everything, so I hollered out to Dokes, "You damn dog you, next time I'm gonna rip your balls. You keep hitting my boy low." And he did it no more. With Evander, if I told him "Walk through that wall over there rather than walk around it," he just said "OK" and he did it.' Soon he didn't need telling, and his speciality became the head butt. He would go in low, then straighten up, his head slamming into his opponent's face or bore forward with his head down so that the top of his head connected with a nose or eyebrow. He was also adept at nodding his head into opposing brows. And these were not occasional aberrations: by the second half of his career they had become an integral part of his tactics.

So, Evander fought dirty inside the ring and out but you could forgive him just about everything because he always fought his heart out, one way or another. After beating Tyson he was hailed as the comeback king, the returning warrior, the white-hat hero who gave the bully a bashing, and a man you could never write off. When he lost a piece of his ear in the return there seemed no end to the public's love and support. If you bear in mind that the American heavyweight competition included a rapist, a kidnapper, a menagerie of substance abusers and a bevy of extramural thugs, the adulation for Holyfield and the tolerance for his peccadilloes made sense. His formal claim to being world heavyweight champion was no stronger than Lennox's, but Americans regarded him as the man.

Despite his age (36), there was no reason to believe he'd gone on the slide in the sixteen months since his excellent performance in gaining revenge against Michael Moorer. This assumption had been made too often in the past, only for Evander to surpass his best. The available evidence suggested that he was a better all-round fighter, certainly a stronger man and a heavier puncher, than during his first and second reigns as champion. He was extraordinarily strong for his weight. He could absorb frightening punishment through a combination of his superb conditioning, his nineteen-inch neck and his sturdy central nervous system. He'd also developed into a big hitter, particularly with the left hook – the first man to drop Bowe and Mercer and the first to drop Tyson twice. He could also be a superb tactician and an outstanding defensive boxer, with a tight, high guard and quick reflexes, and his speed of hand and foot was impressive. And although he preferred to attack, he was an accomplished counter-puncher. Put it all together and add in his persistent aggression and that will to win at all costs, and despite his inconsistency he had to rate as one of the finest heavyweights of the modern era.

Holyfield had become a 'legend' and this meant he could count on a fair quota of grace and favour if the precedent of heavyweight history was anything to go by. Jack Dempsey, for example, was heaved back into the ring by journalists to allow him to go on to victory in his fight against Luis Firpo; Joe Louis was dropped twice and soundly whipped by Jersey Joe Walcott, but walked away with a split decision; Rocky Marciano was allowed to get away with blatant and consistent fouling; Muhammad Ali escaped with a couple of dubious decisions, and one outrageous one against Ken Norton. And with Holyfield there was the added bonus that the promoter was Don King, and King fighters tended to get the nod if it was close, sometimes even if it was not so close.

Evander trained to the backbeat of his gospel music with the same focus shown for Tyson and Moorer, and this time no doubts emanated from his sparring sessions; there were no whispers about his physical preparedness from his training team. They decided that the key to victory was to use his size to his advantage by concentrating on speed, and they had him moving in and out quickly, using the lead right cross to counter the jab. But in retrospect, his mental state was far from ideal. The combination of his religiosity and egotism and the length of time he had to focus on Lewis took him to an exalted level of passion. This zeal was raised even higher by the way Lewis goaded him. Evander could handle the talk of death from the Tyson camp because God would protect him. He could handle Bowe's jibes about being too small because his superhuman strength came from God. But he found it far harder when Lewis questioned his courage and moral integrity.

For Lennox, this was and remains a real issue, not least because he is serious about his own beliefs. 'I am religious in the sense of being a spiritual person,' he said. 'I do believe in a higher being – in God and in only one God – and I believe in love.' But he was wary of Evander-style proselytising, particularly in the face of such glaring inconsistencies between the preaching and the practising. In one joint public appearance he honed in on this weak point by drawing a distinction between Holyfield's ability to resist big men in the ring and his inability to resist small temptations outside the ring, making particular reference to his habit of fathering children outside marriage. 'I called you a hypocrite, not a hypoquit,' he said, clarifying the point. No one ever called Holyfield a hypocrite before and this drove him a few steps over the top. He started to see visions of victory. More specifically, he had a vision that he was destined to knock Lennox out in the third round, and he duly announced this to the world, which had never been one of his habits. He repeated over and over again that he would knock Lewis out in round three. Four days before the fight, after a final sparring session in his grotto gym in Manhattan, he turned to the cameras, put his hands on the ropes and announced, 'It's going to be a short night. Lennox Lewis is going down in three rounds. I keep saying it, but I'm not putting Lewis down. I give him respect. I'm just letting you know what's going to happen.'

While Holyfield was getting stewed up about the hypocrisy jibe and putting pressure on himself by predicting the round of his ascendancy, the Lewis camp was facing its own range of irritants. In the background there were tensions within his managerial team that were beginning to emerge. Maloney was becoming unsettled by what he saw as an attempt to squeeze him out. He had an increasingly tense relationship with Eliades, a man he felt knew nothing about boxing, and was also suspicious of Adrian Ogun, a former television weatherman who previously helped Dennis Lewis with marketing but was becoming more centrally involved in press work and business decision making. He felt the ambitious Ogun was edging him out by moving into a managerial position.

Even with Dennis, a man he'd previously regarded as a mate, tensions were emerging. After boarding a plane for the pre-fight press tour, Dennis attacked Maloney physically, grabbing him by the neck. Maloney took it as an indication of the problems within the organisation. 'I had no strong feelings against Dennis because he never did anything bad to me except that one altercation in the plane,' he said. 'In fact, the only problem I saw with him was that he let it go to his head when Lennox became famous – the fact that he was the brother of the world heavyweight champion. Unlike me, Dennis forgot his old friends and thought he was important, but, still, I always got on well with him. But it is true that I was losing respect for Panos and I was also wary of Adrian.'

Dennis apologised and returned to his default state of friendly bonhomie, but he complained strongly about a sponsorship deal with the clothing firm French Connection UK that Panos concluded without his approval, accusing Panos of disrespecting him and not following agreed procedures. His caution proved apposite because the nudge-nudge, wink-wink fcuk logo did Lennox no favours in America, where this kind of prurience was not admired. The problem first emerged in the hotel shortly before the fight when Maloney was asked to see the manager who said he'd received complaints that the Lewis team were wearing labels saying 'fuck'. Any pretence that, honest guv, this was not the intention evaporated when fcuk became a verb rather than an acronym and was placed on the back of Lewis' trunks. He entered the ring bearing the slogan 'fcuk fear', prompting titters from the British section of the crowd and tut-tuts from the Americans.

With these tensions bubbling away, Maloney was considering an offer to join Don King, who needed a British representative after his partnership with Frank Warren ended acrimoniously. By then both Maloney and Eliades were working closely with King, arranging several UK–USA fights, so the antagonism of the past was broken. King hoped to secure Lewis's signature for at least two fights and Maloney's for a longer term contract, and he went out of his way to court the man he had once called a 'mental midget'. He offered to double his salary, but Maloney hesitated because it would mean an end to his association with Lewis. Instead he informed the Lewis family he was considering the offer and also told Panos, who seemed happy for Frank to play along because he believed this would improve the chances of securing a Holyfield deal, but later came to a different conclusion. He conducted an interview for London Weekend Television (broadcast on the morning of the fight but recorded three weeks earlier) where he stated that Maloney would be fired. 'Don't even start about Frank Maloney,' he said. 'He's out. He's out. If this is showing on March the twelfth, Frank better not be watching, because he'll be out on March the thirteenth.'

It was a bad week for Panos. An English tabloid exposed the fact that his wife, Angela, was staying in one hotel while he was staying in another with his girlfriend and things were about to get worse. Maloney, who only heard of the LWT interview on the day of the fight, stormed into Panos' room where he found his boss in his underpants, clearly unnerved by his employee's rage. He pleaded ignorance, even when Maloney showed him a Press Association fax quoting the interview. He later announced to the press that he had no idea where it came from and that Maloney was not about to be fired.

In addition, Lennox had to parry the old rumours about his sexuality, this time in public. It began with an American reporter asking, during a telephone conference call, whether Lennox had a 'significant other' in a tone laden with innuendo. Lewis replied, 'Pardon me? What does this have to do with boxing?' But the American reminded him he was a public figure and continued, 'Well, are you … ?' Lennox cut him off and said, 'No.' This was picked up by the press, the *Observer* going furthest with the headline CRUISING FOR BRUISING garnished with the strap, 'What's the best way to stir up interest in "our boy" before his fight with Evander Holyfield? Ask him if he's gay. By phone …'

The *Sun* then went for a scoop, sending its highly respected boxing writer Colin Hart to put the question directly, which no one had dared before. Hart asked Lennox, 'Do you know the rumours that have circulated about you for years?' According to his report, Lennox smiled and said, 'You mean the ones about me being gay? I must say I find it comical. But let us put the silly rumours to rest once and for all. I'm certainly not gay. I love and adore women. I date girls and do not date boys … At the moment I date several girls, though no one serious.' The rest of the story mentioned that he was a 'mummy's boy', a bachelor, and was 'rarely seen with a girl on his arm', but none of this presented a problem. If anything, he was relieved to have finally put it to rest, or so he assumed.

But the *Sun* had no intention of leaving it there. It went for the tabloid equivalent of James Carville's famous remark, 'drag $100 through a trailer park and there's no telling what you'll find' and ran a panel alongside Hart's story saying that if any readers had dated Lewis or had had an affair with him they should let the *Sun* know. While Lewis tried to laugh it off, the rest of his team, and particularly Shand, were enraged (and later blocked Hart from receiving press accreditation for a Lewis fight). Maloney immediately contacted the *Sun*'s sports editor to complain and received a fax in response, saying, 'If we trapped a nerve with you and Lennox then

I apologise. Colin assures me Lennox was comfortable with the piece and happy to put the rumours to the sword. The invitation to former girlfriends may have been a bit OTT. I can assure you we will not pursue it.'

These distractions made his team determined to show absolute unity. Lewis trained harder at his eight-week Mount Poconos camp than for any other fight. Joe Dunbar, who worked with Lennox for his final ten fights and measured the details of his performance, diet and physiology, said that he peaked for the first Holyfield fight in terms of total workload. 'There's no doubt he was in the best shape of his career for that fight. You can see that from his training data, and the reason was that it was his biggest challenge.'

Together with Steward and Knight, Lewis studied scores of previous Holyfield fights to find an additional edge. With a month to go he felt he needed an additional sparring partner who approximated Evander's style and size more closely, and was prepared to fork out $10,000 for three and a half week's work from Jeremy Williams, a 26-year-old former US amateur international with a record of 34 wins in 36 bouts. He was quick, a sharp boxer and a good puncher, and at 6ft 1in and 220lb had similar proportions to Holyfield. He also shared Evander's competitive instincts and became exasperated with his inability to make an impression on Lennox. After taking a licking during one session he grabbed the big man and tried to pull him down. Lennox smiled and jokingly stuck out his leg to trip him. Williams, a judo black belt, responded by throwing Lennox, which proved a costly mistake. Lewis jumped up with a cold look in his eyes, proceeded to dish out a painful lesson about taking liberties and continued to batter Williams for the rest of their time together until finally, after one particularly brutal four-round thumping, the American spat out his gumshield from between his swollen lips and announced that there was no way he was coming out for round five. 'He's hit me enough for one day,' he said.

Lennox always felt he would beat Holyfield, but this conviction became more specific as he studied him. He watched the way Evander was almost taken out by Bert Cooper after being hit on the side of the head, and worked on landing hooks to the temple rather than the jaw. They tried various tactics to nullify head butts, but their prime strategy was based on dominance with the jab. Steward wanted Lewis to fight aggressively, but to do this behind a heavy jab to break Holyfield's rhythm, and then use his strength and power to drive him back. Lennox was convinced he could do this without too much trouble. 'You watch Evander's fights against Foreman and Bowe – the way he steps into range to throw his punches – well, I think he's definitely going to get hurt that way against me. He just won't have enough strength to push me back. I fought at the Olympics at super heavyweight, and he was a light heavyweight, so I'm a natural heavyweight and he's not. I'm not saying I'm the perfect boxer, by any means. Certainly, if you look at my history you can see there was a time when I neglected my jab and had a tendency to over-rely on my right, but that was in the past. I honestly think I can knock out Evander Holyfield.'

For the third time in his career, Lennox was not the favourite by the time of the fighting. When the books closed it was an even money encounter, and the majority of fight pundits, promoters and fellow boxers tended to go with the American. Larry Holmes chose Evander, on grounds of 'heart' and 'know-how', but Ray Mercer, who had fought both men, favoured Lennox. Angelo Dundee went for Holyfield on heart; Teddy Atlas for Lewis on legs and age. Frank Warren confidently declared that Evander would win inside the distance, but Mickey Duff bet £10,000 on a Lewis victory. Wayne McCullough went for Evander, Glenn McCrory for Lewis, while the doyen of British sports writers, Hugh McIlvanney, favoured Evander, as did a majority of the American writers. Wally Matthews of the *New York Post*, for instance, went along with the Holyfield third round prediction.

The announcement of the judges presented no particular concerns. The WBA choice was Stan Christodoulou, who, despite playing a questionable role in his days as chief executive of the apartheid-era South African Boxing Board, was a highly respected referee whose probity was not in doubt. The WBC nominee, the Englishman Larry O'Connell, was another fine referee, and although some of his past performances as a judge seemed idiosyncratic, his honesty wasn't questioned. The odd one was the IBF judge Eugenia Williams, who had no experience at this level and whose main qualification seemed to be her association with IBF boss Bobby Lee. A few months earlier the FBI launched an investigation that later led to Lee's indictment on charges of receiving bribes. The evidence shocked the boxing world, or at least those with no previous IBF dealings.

The IBF was once seen as an antidote to the nepotism of the Venezuelan-based WBA. To take an example, the American promoter Bob 'I was lying then but I'm telling the truth now' Arum admitted paying bribes to a Puerto Rican fixer, Pepe Cordero, whom he called 'the WBA's bagman'. Cordero's boss, Gilberto Mendoza, needed allies to maintain power and chose the white South Africans, ensuring that one Mr Justice H.W.O. Kloppers, a member of a secretive Afrikaner apartheid society, the Broederbond, became president. The Americans, led by Lee, mounted a takeover bid in 1983, but Kloppers used his casting vote (ruling in a way 'you'd expect from a South African judge', said *Ring* magazine) to ensure that Mendoza survived. Lee complained that an organisation headed by Latin Americans and South Africans could never be trusted and set up the IBF. The last thing professional boxing needed was another international control body (soon after, Cordero formed the WBO, which never cut it in the US, partly because it was more openly corrupt than the others but also because it wasn't American), but the promoters wanted an alternative to the Mexican WBC and Venezuelan WBA so the IBF became one of the big three. In no time Lee was doing business with the white South Africans and anyone else who would slip him something under the table.

The way it worked was that this former cop would send his own bagman, one C. Douglas Beavers, to pick up between $10,000 (to get a boxer rated) and $100,000 (for a heavyweight title shot). It emerged that all four major US-based promoters – King, Arum, Kushner and Dino Duva – acquired this habit. Beavers became the FBI's snitch in exchange for immunity, which led to the production of undercover tapes of hundred-dollar bills being stuffed into duffel bags and handed from the promoters, via Beavers, to Lee. This persuaded Kushner, Arum and Duva to admit their role and testify against Lee. Duva, for example, testified that he gave Lee $25,000, disguised in a bag of candy, to get one of his fighters a higher rating. 'Look, I made a mistake, but I did it and it's something I have to live with,' he said, while also admitting to cocaine addiction and cannabis abuse and taking medication for clinical depression. However, it was King who emerged as the biggest payer and therefore the leading beneficiary. Kushner complained, 'I always knew I was second fiddle or fourth. No matter what happened, Fuzzy Wuzzy came first.'

Lee was later convicted of racketeering charges, money laundering and tax fraud, sentenced to 22 months in jail and fined $40,000, but he was acquitted of receiving bribes because the jury accepted that the IBF was a business peddling ratings and titles, rather than a world sporting control body. All this was beginning to unfold during the countdown to the Holyfield fight, when it was already clear that the future of the IBF was in jeopardy. King was emerging as Lee's biggest briber and Holyfield was King's man. Any bias shown by a Lee-appointed judge towards Evander might be taken as an illustration of guilt. So Williams's appointment was seen as idiosyncratic rather than corrupt.

When the team arrived at the Madison Square Gardens changing room two hours before the fight the calmest man was Lennox, who promptly lay down and had his usual sleep, to the amazement of Joe Dunbar, who had never witnessed this before. 'I couldn't believe my eyes,' he said. 'I was really astonished. He just lay down and fell asleep. I don't think it was a deep sleep, but it was very relaxing and it seemed to be right for him, although for anyone else it would make them lethargic.' Everyone else bustled around, rechecking equipment, filling the water bottles, cutting strips of tape to cover the hand bandages and finding ice for the cutman's bucket. When all this was done Lennox was woken up and taken through his final routine: toilet, groin protector, trunks, boots, and finally, with Holyfield's representative present, the bandages, tape and gloves. Maloney, who was constantly popping in and out, chatting quickly and nervously, put on his Union flag suit, after which Manny Steward took Lennox, Courtney, Harold and Frank to the bathroom, gave them a little pep talk about destiny, and then said a prayer. With his team chanting words of encouragement, it was time to go.

With Dennis leading the way, carrying the WBC title belt, Lennox started his long walk to the ring, cutting out everything around him, including a huge approving roar from the Britons who made up one-third of the capacity crowd of 21,284. There was a complaint about carrying the flag into the ring – Madison Square Gardens banned displays of nationalism – and another about the number of people in his entourage, but eventually the team made it through the ropes, followed by Lennox. After a quick observation that the ring was smaller than expected, he returned to his state of focused intensity. A minute later it was Evander's turn, and he arrived in his usual state of religious fervour, heartily singing one of his gospel songs while smiling and then mumbling away to himself, looking almost as bonkers, in his way, as Oliver McCall. As they stripped off their gowns and towels both men looked in magnificent shape, their bodies glistening with taut muscle. Lennox, at 246lb, was in the finest shape of his career; Holyfield, at 215lb, was a couple of pounds lighter than usual. The difference in size seemed formidable.

Lennox opened with a quick left hook, then followed Manny's instructions of establishing his dominance with his jab while also landing several tasty rights. In round two he started with a stiff cross and then a two-fisted combination, and kept the jab in Holyfield's face, ending with a hard right hook to the body. Two in the bag, but now he knew he was going to have to show resilience because Holyfield believed he was destined to carry out the Lord's third round will. 'I'm going to get him this round, right here,' Evander said. 'He's outa here.' Don Turner, his trainer, responded, 'Don't get careless.'

Holyfield threw himself into a violent attack, catching Lewis on the chin with a hard jab and a solid hook. Lennox responded by bringing up his right uppercut but Evander continued to pour it on, driving him back with a right cross and then an even better one, followed by a jab and several more rights and hooks to head and body. Although Lewis was retreating he was firing back and by the bell was taking over again. The round belonged to Holyfield, but the victory to Lewis. Evander's plan had failed, and he later admitted feeling desolate. 'Right then I could have walked to my corner and through the ropes and right out of the arena. I knew I'd done wrong picking the round. It gave him an advantage, no question, when I failed to knock him out at that point. I could easily have quit, but I didn't because that's not my thing. Quitting is for other guys.'

Both trainers were eager to get in their advice, Lennox's to instruct him to take up where he had left off at the end of round two, Holyfield's to assure him that all was not lost. Turner said, 'I know you can get him. All you have to do is do it. Feint with the hook and then hit him with the right first.' Steward's last words were, 'Get back to your jab again. The jab is the key.' Which is just what Lennox succeeded in doing. His dominance with the jab became absolute in round four. Holyfield could not get past it without getting caught over and over again, throughout the rest of the fight, without respite. He managed to land a few hooks and rights, but they were single punches that failed to move Lewis and were offset by the more accurate and effective punches he had to absorb. Still, Manny wanted more. 'You haven't hit him to the body at all tonight,' he complained. There was a higher note of urgency, in Turner's voice. 'You gotta back him up,' he implored.

Holyfield was caught up in a stream of jabs in round five and responded as so often before, by boring in with his head. This time, however, it was ineffective, as Lennox landed behind the left ear and Evander's legs dipped. Lewis whacked hard to the body, the hands came down and he threw his right uppercut with massive force, staggering the smaller man, and then digging into his ribs again. Evander was already wounded when Lennox caught him on the side of his head with a full-force right cross that knocked him into the ropes. He was out on his feet, head in a fog, legs unsteady. It was a moment for an all-out offensive, but Lennox wasn't convinced – the memory of the first McCall fight still lingering. He feared Holyfield might spring off the ropes with one of his scything hooks and he also recalled Ali's tactics against Foreman when he covered up, waiting for George to punch himself out. 'When I'm hitting the guy three times to one and it's still the middle rounds, I'm saying to myself, "Well, is this guy using his experience?" And when he was covering up on the ropes I ask myself, "Is this his version of the rope-a-dope, trying to get me to punch myself out so he can come on in the later rounds?" You have to be strategising all the time, because he's thinking too, and you have to make sure his strategy doesn't beat yours. But, yeah, maybe I should have taken a few more chances then.'

Lewis was slotting in heavy, accurate head and body punches but there was a hint of caution in his attack. Instead of blasting his opponent, as Steward was yelling for him to do, Lennox picked him off with something less than the overwhelming force displayed when putting away Ruddock, Bruno and Golota. Holyfield remained backed up against the ropes, covering up desperately, taking hard and unanswered punches, but was permitted to survive. After 52 seconds on the ropes his head cleared enough for him to fight his way out, although it was Lewis who closed with another heavy combination. Remarkably, almost comically, Eugenia Williams gave the round to her fellow American.

Holyfield charged in at the start of round six, landing a leaping left hook, but Lennox covered up and then started to drive him back, once again landing a huge uppercut and closing the session with some sharp combination punching. He really cranked up the punishment in the seventh. A big lead right cross knocked Holyfield's head back, and Lennox then banged him around the body, after which he jerked his head back with yet another uppercut and hammered him on the ropes. For the second time in the fight Evander's legs wobbled and he returned to his corner with a nasty 'mouse' over his left eye. Amazingly, Larry O'Connell, scored the seventh round even. When Evander reached his corner, Turner tried to press away the swelling while coaxing him into more concerted aggression. Steward encouraged Lennox to start loading up on his punches. 'A little more power on your shots now,' he instructed, 'and get back to your jab.'

Lennox was outboxing Evander by constantly landing that long, accurate jab, but in the ninth he eased off, taking very few punches because his defence was excellent but not landing much either. Steward was sure his boxer was well in front but thumped the air with his hand and implored Lennox to show more urgency. Holyfield, however, was beginning to recover his sense of purpose, which was enough for Turner to offer some words of hope. 'All he wants to do is survive,' he said. 'Don't let him survive.' Evander's hands were busier in the tenth and he was also effective with his head, butting Lennox blatantly. He threw everything into another effort, catching Lennox with one of his best hooks of the night and, later, a decent cross, yet another butt and a low blow. Lewis seemed untroubled, but his own work rate declined. Steward was yelling again to step it up, which prompted Maloney to shout at the trainer, 'Manny, what's the problem? The television has Lennox winning easy.' This drew the irritated retort 'It doesn't matter what the television judges say. Television judges don't matter. It's what these guys at ringside say that counts.'

Lennox outjabbed Holyfield in round eleven, also landing several hard rights, and at the end of the round raised his hands, certain he was on his way to victory. Steward, like just about everyone else, had no doubt that his man was comfortably ahead. His estimate gave Lewis eight rounds to three, but he wanted a big finish and ordered his man to throw more harder punches. 'You ain't doing nothing,' he said again. Lewis got on his toes and trebled his jab so that Holyfield's head was bobbing back on his shoulders. Evander, his face distorted, lumpy and swollen, could offer nothing in return, and when Lennox closed with a final right-hand lead that shook him once again, the exhausted older man fell into a desperate clinch. He was rudely pushed away, before being rescued by the final bell.

Lewis raised his hand, knowing that not only had he outboxed Holyfield, he'd outclassed him too, and that he'd closed the show with a one-sided beating. He was beaming with delight as his team rushed up to congratulate him on a job well done, and he then went off to offer condolences to his crestfallen victim. 'That's the way it goes,' Evander replied. Lewis could have ended it in the fifth and he'd eased off in the ninth and tenth, but what the hell, he'd put on a master class and won by a mile. He'd beaten Holyfield, beaten the system, beaten Don King. Even Don's stepson, Carl, gave it to Lennox by three points, and that was about as conservative as it got. Just about everybody else had it wider. The average press verdict, including the Americans who'd tipped Holyfield, was a five-point win for Lewis – eight rounds to three with one even – and several prominent ringsiders went wider. For instance, both the fight's referee, Arthur Mercante Jr and Lou Duva, gave it to Lewis by nine to three while Tyson's former trainer Richie Giachetti and the New York Post columnist Jack Newfield made it ten to two.

Analysing the fight punch by punch, it seemed that the only rounds Holyfield won clearly were the third and tenth, while Lennox won nine. The official punch-count showed Lewis threw 613 punches and landed 348 while Evander threw 385 and landed 130; when it came to 'power-punches' (rights, hooks and uppercuts), the margin was 161 to 78; and the jab count 187 to 52. In other words, for every two punches Holyfield landed, Lennox landed five, and no one disputed that Lennox was the harder hitter.

All that remained was the formality of the decision. First came Eugenia Williams, the IBF judge from America: '115–113, Holyfield.' Lennox looked utterly perplexed. Next, Stan Christodoulou, the WBA judge from South Africa: '116–113, Lewis.' That too sounded a few points too close, but at least it was on the defensible side of strange. And finally, from Britain, the WBC judge, Larry O'Connell: '115–115.' The fight was a draw.

Lennox opened his mouth in astonishment, then looked around at his people for an explanation, asking, 'What's happening? What's going on? Somebody tell me what's happening?' Maloney replied, 'Fuck this, we've just been robbed,' and Lewis' eyes filled with tears. As the crowd booed, long and loud, Violet climbed into the ring to console her son, and then, with Holyfield already beginning his pretence that the judges know best, she turned to him and said, 'You know you were beaten. Why don't you say so?' A few seconds later Lennox began the long walk back to his changing room, still asking, 'What happened?' Maloney explained, 'You won the fight but they didn't give it to you.' Lennox plonked himself down on a bench, a bereft look on his face, and with some of his team asking, 'didn't you finish him off in round five?' he murmured, 'I feel so empty.'

Three weeks later, Lennox's friend, the former England football star Ian Wright, threw him a loose ball on his live, prime-time ITV Saturday-night show. 'We hear you're a bit of a rapper in your spare time. Show us your stuff.' It was a barely rehearsed moment and for a few seconds he hesitated, but then, what the hell, he went for it, treating the ecstatic studio audience to a not particularly memorable ragga-style rap in Jamaican patois, full of obscure references to the history of the heavyweight division. When it was over the audience was on its feet, roaring with unrestrained delight, and Lennox was beaming. So was Frank Maloney, who made his final decision to refuse Don King's offer and stay with his man immediately after the draw was announced, and then made the wonderfully daft call for Tony Blair to 'cut off all diplomatic relations with America'. He had worked so hard to get Lennox accepted as an Englishman, and now, finally, it was happening because of a fight in New York. 'Suddenly it's Lennox mania over here,' he gushed. 'The boxing fans have always known him but now it's the non-boxing public too. The British response has changed, with everybody recognising him now, and they all want to know him.'

Until the Holyfield fight the British public and Lennox Lewis had never quite got it together. The relationship lacked the vital elements of spontaneity and passion. Respect, certainly; love, not quite. But the draw changed all this. It had taken ten years, but his new status as a victim of injustice transformed his image. This went way beyond the adoration of his army of travelling fans, transcended the previous recognition of his talent, his cool and his success, and overcame the reserve about his curious accent. He was an Englishman wronged by the Americans, and this perception bridged the gap between respect and adoration. While this change stemmed primarily from the outrage against an injustice committed against a homeboy, there was also a belated recognition that, as Maloney put it, 'we have the best heavyweight boxer in the world'.

There was a different combination of emotions in America. Anger and, for the first time, respect were certainly part of the mix, but there was also shame. It started seconds after the result was announced when HBO's Jim Lampley announced, 'What we have here is a fraud. Boxing's cesspool has opened up to give an unconscionable odour. You have seen the fight. Lennox Lewis won the fight and two judges converted it into a draw. Lennox won it in every way imaginable. The draw means there is no undisputed heavyweight champion of the world – but there should be.' He was followed by HBO's inter-round analyst Larry Merchant, who added a touch of collective remorse to his Shakespearean bit: 'It is almost beyond a stench. Lennox Lewis suffered so many slings and arrows in America. He has a really wonderful career and despite being the best fighter in the heavyweight division he has been shamelessly avoided by everyone this decade. He came to fight the best of the best right now, decisively controlled the fight throughout, beat Holyfield up and didn't get a decision. The slings and arrows ought to be aimed at those who denied him respect. I am ashamed as a boxing fan and an American who has seen this foreigner take so much stuff simply because he is not American. His moment of glory was taken away from him.' And from there to world light heavyweight champion Roy Jones, who added to the mood of mea culpa by saying, 'Tonight I feel ashamed to be American.' This set the tone for the remarkable outpouring of anguish that followed. It is true that Americans had bypassed and disrespected Lewis, but now they were making public penance. Only in America, and perhaps only in New York, could a foreign boxer robbed of a decision become the recipient of so much favourable fury and mass apologia.

The next wave came from the unanimous US press verdict that dominated both the front and back pages. IT STINKS yelled the front page of the *New York Post*; IT'S ROBBERY screamed the front page of the *New York Daily News*. And inside, every sports columnist ranted against the audacity of the crime. 'It was the worst decision I have ever known in any championship,' the *Post's* Jack Newfield wrote, adding for good measure that 'it's like the Vatican has been burgled'. On a similar, religious terrain, his colleague, the previously anti-Lewis Wally Matthews, noted that 'the scorecards bore the mark of the Devil'. An editorial in the *New York Times* stated, 'The decision resembled a Brinks Trust heist.' The *Washington Post's* Tony Kornheiser wrote, 'It was like Three Blind Mice were scoring. Two Blind Mice anyway.' And so it went, up and down the country, the message reinforced as Lennox did the rounds of the major terrestrial television shows. Holyfield, his battered face a reminder of what happened, doggedly stuck to his line that 'the fight was in the judges' hands, and once the fight is in the judges' hands that's where it stays'. Lennox, his face free of lumps (but showing two small cuts, one on the top of the nose and the other over the left eye, both courtesy of Evander's head), said the judges' integrity was open to doubt. 'I feel I was robbed,' he said to Holyfield on *Good Morning America*. And then, turning away, he added, 'He should be a man and admit it. I felt I won the fight hands down. I felt I was a much more superior boxer than Evander.'

A few days later, this verdict moved to a new level when the Governor of New York State, George Pataki, and the Mayor of New York City, Rudi Giuliani, took up the cause. Pataki demanded the New York Athletic Commission investigate the judging, and soon the FBI was involved. Within days a special committee of the New York Senate was grilling the prime suspects, Eugenia Williams and Don King. Their hypothesis went like this. King 'bought' the verdict for two simple reasons: first, he did not want to lose control of the title; second, a draw guaranteed him a bigger-bucks return, and this is why the odds shifted so dramatically in Holyfield's favour two days before the fight. Pataki asked the Commission to place particular focus on Eugenia Williams's financial situation. King claimed she was paid no more than normal expenses plus the usual $5,000 fee but the investigation also revealed this ledger clerk had debts of $72,000 and had filed for voluntary bankruptcy in New Jersey seven weeks before the fight, yet had an undisclosed bank account containing over $20,000. The FBI and the Commission sifted through all this but found no hard evidence of 'uttering' (receiving bribes).

Immediately after the fight Williams claimed she had made her decision because she saw Holyfield landing more punches than Lewis. 'I scored the blows that connected,' she reiterated. When presented with the official CompuBox statistics showing that Lennox had connected with two and a half times more punches than Holyfield, she replied, 'I don't have the privilege of boxing stats.' The New York Senate committee showed her a film of Lewis battering Holyfield in round five and then asked her to comment. 'From what I've now seen on television it looked like Lewis was the winner of that round,' she admitted. 'But what I saw on TV was not what I saw on the night. I viewed the bout from a different angle.' When asked to explain, she added weight to the blind-mice jibe by claiming that her view had been blocked by photographers, which turned out to be nonsense.

Yet the incompetence of her scoring remains her strongest card. A bribed judge would have an interest in disguising corruption and would not be so idiotic to score a one-sided round for the wrong man. That does not absolve her from bias, however. Far more likely than receiving bribes is that she was influenced by being a friend of Lee's, a countryman of Holyfield's, and by the knowledge that Lee was a friend of King's and that King wanted Evander to win. To go along with his wishes meant the certainty of more work (which, in fact, happened); to go against them could mean no more $5,000 cheques. On top of this, King's customary pre-fight wooing might have reinforced the idea that Evander was the man, his man. So when she took her place at ringside she had eyes for only one boxer. She saw what she expected and had neither the competence nor experience to appreciate this bore no relation to the reality. So, no proof of bribery in the legal sense, but bias, probably, incompetence, indisputably, and, in a looser sense, corruption too.

What, then, of the British engraver Larry O'Connell, who was also questioned by the FBI? He took his first battering in America, where boxing writers still shuddered at the memory of Mickey Vann's bizarre decision in the Whitaker–Chavez fight. His first response was one of mea culpa: he claimed to be astonished when his score was announced. 'I felt very surprised I had given it a draw,' he said. 'I felt it could have marginally gone to Lewis … I thought Lewis had won it.' Later, after returning to his village of Hartley, Kent, he added to this contrition. 'If I did make a mistake, then it was an honest mistake,' he said. But by then the wave of outrage was threatening to drown him. British Boxing Board boss John Morris contradicted O'Connell by disagreeing with his verdict; Tony Banks, the British sports minister, called it a 'disgrace'; reporters demanded to know why he'd let Britain down and when he planned to apologise. He received abusive calls, was spat at, sworn at in the streets and called corrupt. He felt besieged in his own home for several weeks. 'Overnight, I went from being an ordinary guy to Public Enemy Number One,' he said. The truth is that O'Connell is, indeed, an honest man and one of Britain's fairest referees, with a career spanning 28 years. However, he was not always competent when scoring fights, and it is possible that one burst of incompetence led to overcompensation the next time, all the way to the Lewis débâcle.

Two years earlier he was the scoring referee in a Commonwealth light welterweight title fight between an Englishman, Bernard Paul, and a Zambian, Felix Bwalya. Everyone at ringside agreed it was one-sided with Bwalya winning about ten of the twelve rounds, but O'Connell gave it to Paul, who then lost his title to another Englishman, Paul Burke, who was obliged to defend against Bwalya. The Zambian Boxing Board, fearing another British robbery, emptied its account to bid for the bout and won. By then Bwalya was seriously ill (suffering from malaria) and entered the ring seven pounds under the limit. He faded in the midday Lusaka heat, getting dropped four times and knocked out in the last round. But the local referee decided that the final bell had sounded before he reached the count of ten, despite only 66 seconds having elapsed, and awarded the fight to the prone Zambian. There was no medical equipment available and doctors did not treat him. He later fell into a coma and died. While O'Connell was in no way to blame for this leg of the tragedy, his bad judgement set in motion a train of events that ended in death.

A month before the Holyfield fight, he was appointed by the WBC as a judge for the welterweight title unification bout between America's Oscar de la Hoya and Ghana's Ike Quartey in Las Vegas. The American view was that de la Hoya secured victory by dropping Quartey in the last round and battering him. Two judges gave it to Oscar by wide margins but O'Connell gave it to Quartey. Had he bent over backwards for an African against an American? Whatever the truth, he was widely criticised and feared he'd never be offered a major gig again. So when Sulaiman appointed him to judge Holyfield–Lewis he was enormously grateful, but once again reached the wrong decision – so wrong that his scoring of the seventh round was almost as bizarre as Williams's in the fifth. The most likely explanation is that he bent over backwards not to show bias against an American favourite again, particularly when his opponent was an Englishman. In other words, in his bid to be seen as fair to Holyfield, he turned out to be blatantly unfair to Lewis. So, no malice, corruption or conscious bias; just a lack of appropriate neutrality.

And yet, it all turned out for the best. If O'Connell had agreed with the other two judges on round seven, Lewis would have won a split decision, taking the title without controversy. The American reaction would have been along the lines of, 'Yeah, well, that's only because Evander's on the slide.' No anger, no debate, no inquests, no Leno, no *Good Morning America*, no story. Instead, Lennox became an American celebrity and a British hero. He began to take shape as a personality. He told Leno, for example, about his habit of refraining from sex before a big fight, making the unlikely claim that he abstained for three months – 'like being in prison'. Leno responded by asking his weight, before shaking his head with this happy conclusion: 'It's just great that there's someone out there who is 245lb and isn't dating the president of the United States.' Lennox laughed along with the audience, happy in the knowledge that he was on his way to becoming bigger than the title he held.

For the first time he was one of 'ours' at home and a star abroad, and he relished the feeling for the moment. 'In a funny way this despicable draw has made people recognise me,' he said. 'I've never had this kind of public reaction before, and it feels great because I have the sense that now the whole country and the whole world knows I'm the heavyweight champion of the world.'

CHAPTER NINETEEN
MOUNT POCONOS,
PENNSYLVANIA, 1999

Lennox Lewis counts as a regular at the Caesar's Brookdale. It's been his favourite training resort for a decade, a place where he feels comfortable and relatively undisturbed, set deep in Amish country in the foothills of the Pocono Mountains. It's at its best now, surrounded by forests of beech, oak and willow in their shocking autumn colours, with miles of mountain bike paths and a fair-sized lake for honeymooning couples and heavyweight champions to wander around. He comes once or twice a year with his ever-growing entourage of helpers, friends and sparring partners (sixteen this time). They stay in log cabins, doing their big jobs or little jobs, all for the cause. 'This is the kind of environment I love to train in,' he says. 'I play pool, go for long nature walks, go fishing. I like to relax here, to meditate and to concentrate on the fight.'

Their arrival seems to delight the staff – not just for the business they bring, but also because these visitors are unlike most other celebrity parties they attract. They keep to themselves and behave impeccably, taking their lead from the boss.

Vincent Manning, the 62-year-old handyman who doubles as a bag carrier and ring clearer, counts himself as a serious boxing aficionado. 'I used to hang out with Joe Frazier's brother, Tommy, in the seventies,' he says, 'and then got to know Joe through his band the Knockouts and I guess he was a nice guy, although Muhammad Ali was always my favourite. Ali was great to me the couple of times we met but I'd still have to say that of all the sports stars I've met Lennox is the nicest. He's a real prince, a class A gentleman. Like, he always shows me respect and comes to speak to me, he's never rude and when you want your picture taken with him, no problem, and you never hear a bad word from him. You won't find other stars like that. His mother too. I love having her here. My children are grown up now so to me it's like they're family. Beautiful people.'

Lennox's five sparring partners are also made to feel at home: invited to family meals, required to report for the morning runs, offered advice by the benign, dreadlocked paterfamilias, after taking their lumps. The lumps cannot be avoided. Harold Knight says that though Lennox never sets out to hurt sparring partners, because he doesn't have a bullying bone in his body, he can't afford to hold back either. The head guards and twenty-ounce gloves soften the blows, but still, sometimes they go down and out. 'He doesn't go to knock these guys out but he doesn't lighten up either because he ain't gonna come off the pedal in a real fight – he's got to put the pedal down to the metal every time.'

First up is 28-year-old Luan Krasniqi, a 6ft 3in, 220lb Albanian-German who won the Olympic heavyweight bronze medal and is undefeated as a professional.

He's on his fourth camp, and each time Lennox puts more pressure on him. 'I was very nervous the first time I sparred with him two years ago,' he says. 'Actually I was afraid but he was good to me because he didn't try to kill me. Now, he goes all out, I think, and I try the things he does, but obviously I'm still learning. He's just so quick and relaxed in the ring and it's hard to describe how strong he is. Also it feels to me he's still getting better, so it's not easy in there because I'm just not as good as him. But as soon as it's over he's very nice. He's always showing me new moves and things to watch out for. Honestly, I've never met a boxer so smart, normal and caring.'

The next two rounds are reserved for Derrick Banks, a 6ft 1in, 224lb, 28-year-old who has won all but three of his 22 fights. He previously worked as a sparring partner for Bowe and Moorer and first sparred with Lennox in 1996. He's in camp again because he resembles Holyfield in size and certain characteristics of style: he moves quickly, trying to dart in and out and land the occasional punch, although unlike Evander he won't stand and trade. 'I give him lots of movement and speed,' he says after his session is over. 'That's my job, but I have to be real careful and focused in there. I mean, he's so much sharper and more focused than Bowe or Moorer and he feels far bigger and stronger than both of them. I think he uses his reach and size better, which makes him bigger still, and this time he's also a lot quicker than he was for McCall. If he wants to let loose, he's gotta let loose, and the closer the fight comes the harder the work gets. But I don't take it personal. It's just a job, and when it's over he's real courteous, real polite with all of us.'

Lennox's current favourite is a skilful, 6ft 4½in, 220lb, 23-year-old fringe contender called Maurice Harris, who is also in his fourth camp. Harold Knight says Maurice is always the first man they call. 'Lennox obviously has more power and the edge in speed too, but Maurice takes him to another level,' he says as they go three intense rounds together. 'You watch, they're both really firing, and firing quick.'

Harris, however, admits it wasn't always like that. 'My first time was when he fought Golota and I left after he knocked me down. I just wasn't ready for that kind of power, but he gave me a second chance and invited me back and he's played a big role in my improvement. You might be surprised to hear this, but I think he's improved. He's definitely punching faster and he's getting his punches off better. It's strange, but at thirty-four he's a better boxer than at thirty-two. Some days sparring is real tough; other days, like today, it's a chess match, but we both know we have to pay for our mistakes. I can tell you, it's not easy in there because he's so big with those long arms and he hits so hard and he also has a pretty good defence, particularly when it comes to parrying.' When Maurice leaves, Lennox talks. 'I kind of feel like it's the Muhammad Ali–Larry Holmes syndrome where Larry was an excellent sparring partner for Ali because he kept him sharp,' he says. 'That's what Maurice does for me. He keeps me sharp, because I can't really lower my guard against him. He's a contender so he doesn't really act like he's a sparring partner.'

After showering Lennox picks a spot in the sun on the gym's veranda and offers cold water and peppermints while chatting away about a charity football game that he played in shortly before returning to America. He seems even more relaxed than normal, especially for a fighter just two weeks away from a career-defining engagement. The harmonious camaraderie of his friends and sparring partners, the absence of pre-fight complications, tensions and interruptions, the beauty of his surroundings and the sense that the task before him is not particularly daunting all help to make this a less pressured camp than normal.

Already he feels close to peak fitness, and he's sure that in a fortnight he'll have no trouble knocking Holyfield out. 'I think styles make fights and moments make fights, and this is the right moment for me to take Holyfield out and put him into retirement. In the first fight, maybe I was a bit cautious, but in this fight I won't be. I'm planning on trying to knock him out.' Not that he's taking anything for granted. In fact, there are some things he's doing better this time – 110 rounds of better quality sparring, for one – and they're working on a range of new tactics. 'Last time the only advantage Holyfield had over me was his head butts, which caused those two little cuts, so Manny has shown me how to deal with that, mainly by controlling his head when he uses it to bore in, or with the uppercut.'

At this point Manny comes over to add his bit. 'Yes, that was his biggest problem in the last fight, Holyfield's head butting, so we're working on countering that and we're also spending more time on shadow boxing to get him to maintain a perfect balance and to increase his speed around the ring and perfect those combinations. I want him to be faster on his feet so that if Holyfield charges he can move quickly into position, and I can tell you he's already there. I feel he's in his prime. Last time he only used seventy per cent and totally dominated. This time he'll use the other thirty per cent he keeps in reserve, and that makes me feel very good. I'm confident Lennox will stop him.'

Lennox smiles and nods – definitely a happy customer. He's feeling particularly satisfied with his physical shape at the moment. 'I really feel I've improved, that I've become a more consummate professional, that everything in the ring is becoming easier for me and that I'm better at the things I'm working on.' He just wishes it was all over and he could go back to the world of parties, sex and the odd drink, and staying up as late as he likes and having fun – as the undisputed heavyweight champion of the world. 'But now that the boredom is setting in, you realise you have only a couple of weeks left so you can tell yourself to put your nose to the grindstone, and then time goes pretty fast.'

In fact, they're already nearing the stage when they have to start winding down because, as Manny puts it, 'He's peaking now, so we have to slow him down a bit to ensure he doesn't lose it because we want him to be at his best in two weeks.' And this means more time for watching movies and videos of Holyfield's fights, more time for walking or cycling in the forest, more time for fishing in the lake and definitely more games of chess with Scott and Ron.

Manny offers a few choice insults about Lennox's favourite game. When he leaves Lennox smiles, clearly not taking it seriously. 'The funny thing is that Emmanuel always talks about my chess, but he doesn't know the game. He says it will slow me down, but how can it? He's never played in his life. And it's not just Manny. People like Don King are always jumping on my chess.' At this point he offers a passable imitation of King's tone and accent. 'He should be boxin', but instead he just plays chess!' Lennox rolls his eyes. 'These guys don't know about chess. They don't realise that it's just a relaxation thing. They find it unusual for a boxer to play chess every day, so they jump on it. If I played pool every day, they'd say, "Oh, he's a pool player." But, you know, it's good, because all this nonsense makes chess more popular and I'd recommend it to any kid.'

The next day Manny raises the subject again. 'People think I'm joking about this chess business, but I'm serious,' he says. 'It's the one thing we disagree on because I think it makes him too analytical in the ring when I want him to be more spontaneous and aggressive. I want him to go out there and just knock Holyfield out.'

Lennox held a high opinion of his rival before their first fight, with the small caveat of the gap between Evander's public religiosity and his private adultery. After the fight this respect dissipated, with Lennox noticing similar inconsistencies in the way he dealt with failure. His distaste spilled over into full-blown contempt.

It started a minute after the decision was announced, when the battered Holyfield offered the judges-know-best defence that so starkly contradicted his complaints about the scoring after his defeat against Moorer. Watching this, and also King's defence of the judges (inevitably followed by his 'let's get them back in the ring' call), Violet quivered with anger at the injustice dished out to her son, giving voice to his own feelings. 'I think it was disgusting,' she said. 'Everyone knows Lennox won the fight. But this is America. The result is a disgrace. I think it was all politics and I don't want to get involved in that. All I know is that my son won the fight. I don't know what fight the British judge was watching. It is for others to explain their decision. If they can live with it, that is for them.'

But Holyfield persisted. Forcing a slow growl through swollen lips, he muttered, 'I don't judge, I fight,' before offering a kind of double-edged praise for Lewis, saying, sure he shone, 'but that's not my best'. He later added to this defence, claiming he was hampered by leg cramps. For a while he could manage no more than variations on these themes. 'When you have two good fighters, that's a matter of opinion,' and, 'It's real simple: people around the ring are not the judges.' But he gradually became more resolute, blaming 'biased TV commentators and the media' for 'false impressions' while insisting that 'one thing I know is that I didn't lose'. Then he tried a new angle: Lewis deserved no more than a draw because you have to rip the title from the champion. 'If he wants to be champion he has to move out of his comfort zone. He's got to risk getting knocked out.'

This new line was particularly galling. There are no scoring rules placing added onus on challengers. Both boxers start with blank slates. And anyway, this was a unification bout – they were both champions. On top of this he felt he had ripped it from Evander. It was not one of his great performances but he came close to stopping him, rocked him three times after that, consistently landed the heavier punches, outworked him throughout and dominated the closing rounds. He felt Holyfield deserved maybe two of the twelve rounds.

As the negotiations dragged on he began to suspect that despite all the sympathy and adulation he was receiving he would never reach the desired pinnacle of his career, and that the return would never happen. 'There is still an emptiness there,' he admitted.

Holyfield had different emotions. As soon as the pain subsided, the hurt to his pride grew unbearable. This was already clouding his memory of what occurred in that New York ring. He could not bear to see Lennox paraded around as the real world champion, while he himself was derided as a sad old beneficiary of a tainted system. When Eliades demanded purse parity for the return fight, Evander bit hard and agreed. More than anything – more, even, than an edge in riches – he wanted vindication.

Once again there were several obstacles, mostly derived from the stink of the first result. Though no one was charged with any crime and no criminality was proved, there was a strong public perception that the result was corrupt and that the man behind the stench was Don King. For him to be profiting from this by promoting the same fight again seemed unconscionable. Added to this problem was the speculation that King might be indicted to face charges in the IBF trial. HBO was wary of a tainted fight and offered Don $10 million to step aside. Eliades argued King should be excluded because of the possibility of his arrest and that the inscrutable businessman who should take his place was none other than himself. Soon after, however, Scotland Yard arrested Panos on charges of defrauding the British government, which rather undermined his cause (even though the charges were later dropped). Then both King and Dino Duva were cited as 'unindicted co-conspirators' in the IBF trial, but unlike Dino, Don maintained his silence and in the end was never arrested. He chuckled over Panos's predicament and made a point of publicly defending him because, of course, he was an innocent until proven guilty. HBO duly dropped its objections, held its corporate nose, and went along with King, provided he agreed to pay Holyfield's half of the $30 million purse money.

Eliades was therefore forced to accept subservience to King one last time, and Lewis had no option but to go along with another fight promoted by a man he distrusted. He made a little stand by declining to have his picture taken with King at a pre-fight event. 'I refused because I was saying to myself, "What am I doing being photographed with a man who's basically promoting Holyfield to beat me?"' he explained. 'Because anything Don is involved in, you can rest assured I'm worried. There's always that thing in the back of your mind saying anything can happen in a funny way when he is involved.'

This time the funny thing happened under Eliades's nose, well before the fight. In his eagerness to conclude the deal he ended up making a concession that later had negative implications. King insisted a clause from the first contract be carried over to the return, granting him the right to promote Lewis's next defence if he beat Holyfield. It was a sly move from Don, who knew that even if Lennox conceded, HBO would never bankroll it because the man he had in mind was Henry Akinwande, who had already disgraced himself. The penalty clause for refusing was that Lennox would be obliged to vacate the WBA version of his title. In this way

King was ensuring a continued stake in the title if his man lost. Pat English, the lawyer for Main Events, argued vociferously against this clause, and the likelihood is that if they'd maintained a united front in refusing to consider it King would have buckled because he needed the millions Lewis–Holyfield II was sure to generate. Instead, Panos blinked first and the clause was included in the final contract.

After over four months of bargaining, the fight was set for the Thomas and Mack Center in Las Vegas on 13 November 1999, and Lennox returned to the Poconos. By the end of camp both Lewis and Steward insisted he'd reached a new level of preparedness for this fight, but this view wasn't shared by everyone. 'No, he didn't do quite as much work for the second Holyfield fight as for the first fight,' said Joe Dunbar, who logged in all his physical details. 'Lennox's total workload for the return was definitely a tad lower. Without a doubt, he didn't do as much as for the first fight.' Still, no one questioned that he'd worked hard and there were worries his weight was getting too low, threatening to fall below 240lb, but Steward cut his training schedule over the last two weeks. A few days before the fight his bad mood arrived – sullen, tetchy, irritable – just as they wanted it.

Lewis weighed in at 242lb, four lighter than in the first fight (perfect, said Shand; too light, said Steward). Holyfield came in at his ideal weight of 217lb, two more than last time. He'd worked relentlessly for ten weeks, training in the evenings as well, to get his body attuned to the eight p.m. fight time, with the emphasis on increasing speed and aggression, slipping the jab and landing his own double jab, followed by the left hook and his hard, shiny head. Keep it up close and personal, and when in doubt always use the head. 'I know what I have to do now,' he said. 'I didn't understand that properly before the first fight and so I was disappointed in my performance. I kind of felt old for real because I wasn't able to do what I wanted. I'd always thought it was a question of mind over matter, but I couldn't overcome my actions with my mind. But this will be a performance that may make everybody forget everything that's happened in the last year. I guarantee victory.'

Lennox, the 2–1 favourite, entered to the roar of 6,500 British fans (out of 18,000) and stood impassively in the ring centre for five minutes, hardly moving and ignoring everything else around him. He wasn't quite sure what he'd do – break him down with the jab like last time, or just go out there, take a gamble and roll him over, like he did to Ruddock and Golota, which is what Manny wanted. In the end he thought he'd probably start with the jab and then see how it went with an all-out attack. Holyfield, booed heartily and hatefully by the Brits, did his singing, chanting, praying thing, but this time without the vision of an early knockout blocking out a more sensible plan. He needed no reminding of tactics: bore forward, get close, hook, head, hook, head, over and over again.

Lewis made a perky start, pumping out his left and banging in the uppercut. Holyfield's contribution was an early head butt for which the 32-year-old referee, Mitch Halpern, issued a prompt 'watch the head' warning. Evander responded by doing it again. After the bell Lennox told his trainer he was concerned about the butts. As he later explained, 'When I was jabbing he was coming in with his head, and trying to use it up close, so the whole time I was concerned about that head at the same time as trying to score points.' Steward gave him sound instructions along with some encouragement. 'Touch him up top and then rip him underneath, and you're tying him up right.' Turner also offered specific advice. 'I want two jabs and then throw the overhand right. He's leaning back, so don't go straight in. Always give him a little feint first.'

But instead it was the Lewis jab and uppercut that made it home, and once again Holyfield's main response was to use his head. In training Lennox practised a move where his sparring partners bored in with their heads. He would push them down on the neck as soon as they came in, and this is what he tried, leaning on Holyfield and pushing him down and also hitting with the uppercut, which turned out to be his most effective punch of the fight. Evander would throw a hook and follow through with the head, and as often as not Lennox would evade and then time a right uppercut that would jerk his head back. Turner was becoming worried that the pattern of the first fight was being repeated. 'Don't get flat-footed,' he warned. 'I want two jabs and a right. Jab to his chest or shoulder – and he's trying to hit you with the right uppercut.' As if Evander hadn't noticed.

In round three Lewis made a fast start with his jab and then began to throw combinations. Again Evander came in with his head, and again Lennox pushed it down, moved away, jabbed and threw a stiff right cross. He was picking him off with ease, dominating with his left and displaying a tight defence, but he drifted off over the final half minute and Holyfield took advantage, landing an overhand right flush on the temple before moving in again, holding with his left and hitting with his right. It still seemed a clear Lewis round (although one judge, Jerry Roth, disagreed), but Steward was worried. 'You have got to get back to the jab,' he warned, 'and then come with the uppercut underneath.' Afterwards, Steward said that this punch was the key to Lennox's performance. 'I told him to throw his right uppercut when Evander was coming in, and it was one of his greatest strengths. It didn't always land, but it kept Holyfield apprehensive. He wasn't taking chances because Lennox was stopping his onslaughts with perfectly timed uppercuts.'

Holyfield picked up where he left off, countering the jab with a hard cross to the jaw, before coming in with his head again. Lewis came back at him by turning his long jabs into hooks, landing on the side of the head several times. Evander rallied over the final 30 seconds but this time Lennox responded with a four-punch combination, and closed by countering Holyfield's left with his own right cross. He was now well ahead, winning four out of four rounds on two cards and three out of four on Roth's card, but Steward wasn't satisfied 'He's putting in something big at the end of each round,' he warned. 'You gotta take some aggressive stuff at him without coming over the top. You gotta come underneath on the shot first. Even the simple jab, jab, left uppercut, right cross, but come from underneath. You're throwing the right too high. Get right down and throw it straight.'

This time it was Holyfield who landed by coming in from underneath – first with a heavy hook to the jaw and then with a head butt that opened a cut by the side of the right eye. Halpern warned him but an infuriated Lewis bulled Evander into the ropes, bending his body over backwards so that he almost fell out of the ring. This time Halpern warned them both before leading Lennox to his corner to get the blood wiped from his eye. Holyfield had finally succeeded in angering him and breaking his rhythm. It was the edge he needed. Lewis forgot his jab and decided to duke it out, which was precisely what Evander had in mind. At a distance he was lost but up close his hooks and his head could do serious damage. Rather surprisingly, Roth gave the round to Lewis, while the other two judges, Chuck Giampa and the 83-year-old Bill Graham, went the other way.

Turner was delighted. 'All you gotta do is get a little bit closer, a little bit closer.' But Steward did not yet seem perturbed. He wanted meanness and now he had it. 'Shoot that short right, just the way you're doing, straight and low,' he said. 'The uppercut is fine, but keep shooting that right real short. The right is the key now.' He later defended himself against criticism that he should have implored Lewis to get back to the jab. 'Lennox's mindset drifted into a less-jab mode and he began lowering his hands and coming forward,' he said. 'When Lennox does this his confidence is running high and he's very dangerous. Rather than try to convince him to change back to the jabbing style, which could have led to round after round of me trying, I decided to convert to his way of thinking and help him get the most out of the style he was fighting with.'

It was clear the changing pattern was not a temporary aberration. Lennox's jab was little more than a range finder, which meant Evander was fighting at his most comfortable range, and while Lewis was throwing hard, single punches, he was being outworked. 'You just cut off completely,' Steward yelled. 'You're going to sleep. You're not fighting, and he's doing better than you.' Lennox later claimed he eased off deliberately. 'I was concerned he was trying to conserve energy because he wasn't doing much work at the beginning of the round but was coming on strong later to try to steal it, so I slowed my own pace early in the round.'

Still, Lewis started fast in round seven, with a short right, an elbow and a push that prompted a furious attack from Holyfield, who ripped in a hard left hook to the chin. Lennox smiled, keen to advertise his contempt. Evander's response was to come in low and whack him in the groin; then follow through with a hook and cross to the head, and soon after, another right and then his best left hook of the night, which landed with a cracking noise on the side of Lennox's chin. The bigger man was suddenly looking tired, perhaps wounded, fighting with his mouth open but he later claimed it was all an act. 'I know it looked like I was hurt, but I wasn't. I was just playing. I wanted him to sap his energy a bit and get him to come out blasting with combinations and to throw lots of punches and get tired and it worked because he started breathing heavily after that. I was just egging him on.' Steward agreed. 'I know my fighter and I knew he wasn't hurt,' he said. 'Lennox was letting Evander exert a lot of energy.' Lewis came back in the last minute, meeting him in the ring centre as they went toe to toe and then hurting him with a huge right. His old rival Frank Bruno was yelling from ringside, 'Don't fight his fight, Lennox! Don't fight his fight!' and he was right. It was certainly the most thrilling round of the fight, but it was also the third in a row taken by Evander. 'You gotta pick it up!' Manny said. 'The fight is close. The fight is definitely close. You gotta land stiff jabs. Use the jab hard and then shoot that right hand to his jaw.'

Round eight seemed at first to be following a similar plot: Holyfield aggressive, Lewis, tired and panting heavily. Yet he was landing more clean punches while Evander's were losing steam. Midway through the round Lewis switched to the body and then landed some uppercuts. He was still neglecting his jab but seemed to have drawn Holyfield's sting and was now beating him at his own game by finishing stronger, and the pattern was maintained in the ninth when Evander started with a double jab and a right cross to which Lennox replied with a pair of uppercuts and some big hooks to the body. Back came Evander with the double jab, left hook, and then a low blow. Lennox was still looking tired but he was ripping hurtful body blows and several uppercuts, including a huge one that snapped Evander's head back on his shoulders. At the end of the round Lennox ducked under a left hook and then landed two more punches after the bell.

'You gotta get that jab working more,' Steward implored, and, finally, Lennox listened. With Evander tiring, he started stabbing out his jab with conviction for the first time since round three, and soon everything was flowing again – crisp, quick combinations and solid single hooks. Lennox feinted with a left, and as Holyfield ducked it he smashed in his right uppercut to end the round. Now it was the opposition corner's turn to talk in desperate terms. They reminded Evander of his faith in God, that he was a 'work horse' and also that he should do some more combination punching on the inside. But the exhausted veteran looked bereft of ideas, except the one he'd been trying all night long: the trusty old head butt. 'When I was exchanging with him,' said Lewis, 'he was keeping his head low and then coming straight in with it and it was hard to engage him up close without getting butted, so I tried to move to the side and throw combinations or to catch him with the jab when he was coming in, but it was difficult because he kept using his head.' Now and then Lennox would step in, hook powerfully to the body and bounce off again. The tiredness of the middle rounds lifted and he ended the eleventh with a six-punch combination that cut Evander below his left eye. Steward, fearing a repeat of New York, wasn't complacent. 'Don't hold back,' he said. 'Let it go. You gotta win this last round.'

But it was Holyfield who fought with greater urgency, starting with a trio of hooks and then yet another butt. Halpern, who soon after would descend into depression and take his own life, should have deducted at least one point from Holyfield's tally by then but instead issued another mild warning and waved them in again. Lennox caught Evander with a right cross, and once again Evander butted, but when he came in with his head for the third time Lewis brought up his right uppercut, catching Evander under the chin and knocking his head back, after which they went at each other all the way to the bell.

A hard, intriguing but seldom explosive fight was over. To most ringsiders, Lewis prevailed but by a closer margin than in New York, and this was also the view of the commentators who took the message to the world. HBO analyst Harold Lederman gave it to Lennox by four rounds, but the press average was two points and a few dissenters called it a draw or went with Holyfield. To Steward, this minority view displayed either bias or ignorance. One of the distortions was that 'people expected so little from Evander' and anticipated more from Lewis. 'I believe Lennox didn't push as hard as he should have and I am a little disappointed because I know what he is capable of,' he admitted. This made people assume Holyfield was doing better than he really was – a perception encouraged by his tactics. 'He would throw punches at the end of each round, which created a lot of excitement because he had been so inactive for the rest of the round. Winning the last fifteen to thirty seconds can have an effect on the judges but even when Evander applied pressure in these final moments he wasn't landing as many clean punches as people think. Even in close quarters Evander couldn't really hit him. Lennox was getting the better of the action on the inside, particularly with his right uppercut. He could have done more, and he didn't live up to his full potential, but he definitely won the fight.'

Professional boxing is scored on a round-by-round basis, not on overall punch totals, which means it's a bit like US presidential elections: the man who lands the most blows is not always the winner. But the statistics offer an indication of dominance. According to the CompuBox punch analysis, Lewis landed 195 punches to Holyfield's 137 (therefore connecting with 58 more than Evander compared with 214 more in the first fight). He outjabbed Holyfield (landing 76 to 52) and connected with 119 power punches compared with 85 for Holyfield, but perhaps more significant was the impression that his big hits, particularly the uppercut, were bigger than Evander's.

Lennox looked edgy during the long wait and Maloney told him to raise his hands in a display of victory but he was too nervous to look convincing. 'You never know what the judges are looking for,' he said afterwards, 'especially after the last time.' Eventually, the ring announcer, Jimmy Lennon Jr, read the scores: Roth made it 115–113 (seven rounds to five), Giampa 116–112 (eight to four) and Graham 117–111 (nine to three). 'All three in favour of the winner and the undisputed heavyweight champion of the world, Lennox Lewis!' A huge grin of relief and then of joy spread across his face as he raised his tired arms. He knew he'd come in over-confident, put on one of his worst performances in recent years against an improved Holyfield, yet he'd won a wide, unanimous decision. After a decade as a professional he'd finally beaten the last Don King man standing. 'With perseverance, and through trials and tribulations, I was vindicated,' he said a few minutes later. 'It was hard work to go through it but I finally achieved my goal. This is my dream.'

Immediately after hugging Violet and Frank he felt magnanimous enough to praise his rival's effort – up to a point. 'He fought a good fight,' he said. 'In our first fight he didn't know what to do but this time he had time to study me and work out a plan. This time he came in more with his head. He butted me and it's difficult to fight someone with his style, and styles make fights. I expected a different fight.'

Later, after watching it on video, both Steward and Lewis decided his relatively poor showing was all about complacency. 'Lennox won the first fight so clearly that he felt Holyfield couldn't present any kind of a problem for him,' Steward explained, 'so he went in not expecting much of a challenge. His body was well pre-pared but in his mind he was expecting an easier time, whereas Holyfield was fired up. Lennox always fights best when he sees a real challenge against an opponent he regards as dangerous but he didn't think Evander offered that kind of challenge.' Lennox agreed, saying he'd been convinced he would knock Holyfield out. 'In the first fight I trained hard and in my mind I won easily. So in the return I went in knowing I'd beaten him once, so it was like, "What can he possibly do now?" My premise was, "This is just another fight where I'm going to beat you, so are you pre-pared for that again?" But he knew what I was going to come out with so he changed his game and got a chance to better himself.'

At first, Holyfield offered only a hint of dissatisfaction. 'Of course I was sur-prised, but we are all surprised by the decisions that man makes,' he said. 'The only thing I can do is fight, and the judges make their decision. Of course everyone is disappointed when things don't go their way, but life is life.' The truth was that he gave his finest performance in at least two years and would never again fight close to this level, yet he fell short against Lewis at his worst. As the months passed, how-ever, he began to complain, about the judges not knowing best. He claimed he was robbed because of the controversy surrounding the first fight and used this as his initial justification not only for fighting on, but for campaigning as a court witness to get the heavyweight title dismembered again.

Lennox observed Holyfield's decline, listened to him talking with thick-tongued consonants about why he needed to fight on, and felt enough pity to decide that he should never contemplate another re-run. He believed he'd won about 18 of the 24 rounds they'd been through together and that there was nothing left to prove. He also feared he could leave his rival with serious brain damage and wondered whether Evander's decline was, in part, a product of the 543 Lewis-sized punches he'd absorbed. 'If we ever had a third fight I would certainly knock him out, but there won't be a third fight,' he said. 'Holyfield's age is definitely showing on him to the point where he has started to look pathetic in there.'

But beyond the pity he felt contempt for Evander's subsequent return to the status of WBA champion, particularly when this was justified by claims that he wasn't really beaten. 'Holyfield always has excuses. He always wants to say the other guy lost. He never wants to give the other guy credit. He's a bad sportsman. When he lost against me he didn't want to admit it. He would rather go in with a different premise. [Imitating Evander's slurred drawl] "Oh, the judges went Lewis's way, but that's just the way the judges went." Now, if it was me in his position I would have said, "You know what? I didn't look my best this time. I thought he won. Next time I'll get him." Be a man about it. He's not a man.'

Lennox Lewis had finally reached the status of The Man. In Steward's view he'd given only 70 per cent first time and 50 per cent in the return, but his 50 per cent was enough to make him the best in the world. He felt he'd arrived and that he deserved a spell of prolonged celebration, yet he knew he couldn't turn it in just yet. In his twenties he talked of getting out by 30. At 32, he gave himself two more years. Now, at 34, he felt that until he'd knocked out Mike Tyson any talk of hanging up his gloves was premature. 'I don't know when I'll retire,' he said. 'I can't really break it down in years any more. I'll continue until I'm satisfied, and I'm not satisfied yet.'

CHAPTER TWENTY
MANHATTAN, NEW YORK, 2004

Aisha Mike calls herself an 'artist and aesthete', and it's to this cultural world she has returned, composing and singing her own soul and R&B songs, promoting a Nigerian painter and working on a range of design projects while earning money to pay for having what she calls her 'very active and creative mind'. The earning comes mainly from her artistic 'promo company', and from modelling. 'It makes sense because, well, I'm six feet tall and I still have my looks,' she says with extreme matter-of-fact understatement. 'I do it to make money because I'm producing my own music, so I have to pay for band rehearsals, and the modelling helps to support my artistic side.'

When she first met Lennox Lewis in 1999, she had just returned from two years working and studying in Nigeria and was hoping to break into the New York musical and artistic scene that had been integral to her upbringing. Aisha grew up with her Chinese-Jamaican mother but was supported by her black Brooklynite father, a prominent theatre director and playwright. She went to a private school, trained as a classical soprano soloist and studied for a BA in film studies before moving to Lagos to complete a master's dissertation on Yoruba art. To fill the time after arriving back in New York, and to pay the bills, she took a job as a receptionist in a fashion photography studio.

One day Adrian Ogun came in to arrange a shoot for Lennox. 'I was explaining what was needed and Adrian said I should tell the champ.' At that stage she had no idea who Adrian was talking about. She'd never heard of Lennox. But she's a friendly person and it was her job to be polite, so she offered to pick out some music for the shoot. After that, Lennox and Aisha chatted and then, rather to her surprise, he invited her to dinner.

'Before I met Lennox I said I would never date a professional athlete,' she recalls. 'I mean, I don't know how it is in Britain but in America professional athletes have a terrible reputation with women. But when we met in the studio I didn't know who he was because I knew absolutely nothing about boxing, and anyway, I didn't think he would pursue me. We talked and got on well but I just didn't think he would call.'

Still, she accepted the invitation out of curiosity, discovered that he was about to enter his Pennsylvania training camp for the second Holyfield fight, and was intrigued by his continued interest. 'I was quite surprised when he ended up spending a huge amount of time with me,' she says. 'When he went to training camp he used to phone me from his bedroom for three hours a night, and then after the fight he invited me to stay with him and his mom in Florida over

Christmas and New Year, and I ended up being there for a couple of months and that's when our relationship really got started.'

Lennox took a keen interest in her artistic projects and worked with her as executive producer on one of her records, and by early 2000 they were seldom apart. She was astounded by how different he was from her perception of boxers, showing an intellectual curiosity that constantly surprised her and lacking any of the macho arrogance she associated with professional sportsmen. 'He really gives of himself a lot, sometimes to the detriment of personal relations,' she says. 'Like when we were out together the fans would always interrupt and bust in and he was always courteous to those people and give them what they wanted. But what surprised me most was how he was so intelligent and such an analytical thinker, and also that he was so well read – and not just for a sports star, but for anyone. He did a lot more reading than most people, even when he was in training camp, so we talked a lot about books and all sorts of things. Like, say, he loved sci-fi and was shocked to find that I did too, so that was one of the things we had in common. He introduced me to Dune and I introduced him to some of the sci-fi books I've read.'

Their relationship was punctuated by the constant call for Lennox to go to training camp – at the end of 1999, three times in 2000 and again early in 2001 – a place where girlfriends were not welcome and where abstention from sex was one of the self-disciplines Lennox imposed on himself. As he explains it, 'There are aspects of training where I admire the approach of the old-time boxers. For example, some modern trainers prefer their boxers to run on the treadmill, but I still like to put in the miles on the road, and it's the same with this thing about abstaining from sex. I've read of old-time boxers refraining for months because they believed it used to get them pent up and ready to fight, and, in a way, that's how I look at it. It's nothing to do with this nonsense of it tiring you out. I mean, if you think about it, having an orgasm takes up no more of your energy than running up the stairs. I think of it more as a good sacrifice to make. It's something you can basically look forward to having afterwards, like a reward, and also it clears your mind.'

These periodic withdrawals of contact, along with the constant demands for travel, would put a strain on any relationship. Lennox and Aisha's finally came to an end in mid-2001 with what she calls a 'mutual decision'. Still, she says she found it traumatic. 'By that time it was becoming so intense and then it ended dramatically,' she says. 'I got to know him very intimately and my time as his girlfriend was a very impactful period for me, and, you know, when you've had a close relationship, break-ups like that are very hard to go through. If I think about it now, I would say that after about eighteen months it had reached its end, but, still, it was a really intense experience and it took me about a year to finish grieving over it, and I had to find myself again. I wrote songs about Lennox and thought about him a lot. But both of us went back to our own lives.'

She hasn't seen him since because she wanted a clean break, but the one bad aftertaste was the ongoing pressure from British tabloids who bombarded her website with interview requests in the hope that they could entice something salacious out of her, without success. 'Both of us got on with our own lives, but even though I have put all my memories of that period to rest I must say that I still feel positive about Lennox. I thought he had a really great character and a very warm heart, and I still do.'

Lennox slept with his title belts under his bed for a week after beating Holyfield, and for a while he was content to be paraded around, talking of his triumph, receiving awards and plaudits to commemorate it, and, of course, celebrating. The celebrations, with and without his new girlfriend, started late on 13 November 1999 and continued through his spell in Florida over the New Year and for a good deal longer than his usual post-fight fare. On this terrain Frank Maloney invariably outdid him, but on one occasion it was Frank who had to cover for Lennox. He was invited as guest of honour to a lunch hosted by the British Boxing Writers Association, with most of Britain's leading boxing reporters on hand for a quote, a meal and several drinks.

But much to their irritation Lennox didn't turn up, and Maloney made a half-hearted attempt to say he had the flu, before giving up this line and admitting that, OK, fair cop, he was the victim of a force-ten hangover – a managerial admission Lennox was never allowed to forget.

'He was no teetotaller,' Maloney says today. 'He likes to have a drop of champagne, a drop of brandy and sometimes a drop of both together. Many a time I've been with Lennox and he's got me absolutely legless, so he's not exactly the greatest clean liver between fights, although I must say, you can't begin to compare him to the likes of Tyson and so many other boxers and sportsmen. I mean, he wasn't on depression drugs, and uppers and downers or cocaine or whatever. None of that. Never. And once he's in training camp it's a completely different story. Particularly if he feared a fighter he'd go to the gym and he would really prepare properly, mentally and physically, and he would never touch alcohol or anything else not approved by his conditioners. Whatever you say about Lennox, he almost always trained right for his fights.'

Lennox has never pretended to be a teetotaller, but after experiencing Arnie Boehm's alcoholism during his transition to adulthood he knows the dangers and has been careful to avoid them. He believes it's all a question of time, place and variety. 'There's always different periods when you can do that. Champagne is OK, but when it comes to the harder alcohol like rum, that's where you may have a problem.'

Maloney, who has never had restrictions like world title fights to train for, came down from the celebrations to find his relationship with Panos Eliades reaching the limits of his endurance, and once the post-fight hugging, backslapping and champagne toasting had lost its allure he also found he'd lost ground with Lennox.

Frank had never respected Panos as a boxing man, feeling he'd made mistakes through getting too directly involved, but he also lost trust for him as a person. Their relationship became increasingly tense, particularly when Eliades dissed Maloney's mother in 2000. He was reaching the point where he couldn't stand the sight of Panos and cautioned Lennox to be careful about the way his promoter was handling his finances. 'I always thought it wrong that Lennox put all his eggs in one basket,' he said. 'I constantly told him that he should have independent financial advice, independent accountancy, independent legal advice – people who could go through the books and report back to him – but Lennox wanted to do it his way. He told me he knew what he was doing, and that his other business advisers knew what was going on, and that they were happy with Panos, so I just took it at that, feeling, well, I done my job, so every night I knew I could put my head on the pillow and go to sleep and get up in the morning and look at myself in the mirror.'

The next dispute was of his own making. Tyson's manager, Shelly Finkel, decided Mike needed a break from America or America needed a break from Mike, and chose Britain. He also decided the appropriate opponent would be British and Commonwealth champion Julius Francis, a former Lewis sparring partner who was managed by Maloney. He put in a bid to promote the fight on behalf of Panix, but Finkel settled for Frank Warren, mainly because of Warren's tight relationship with Showtime, the network bankrolling Tyson and screening his fights. Panos then resolved that Francis should be withdrawn but Maloney refused, arguing that as the boxer's manager he had a duty to secure the best deal and that the offer of a $500,000 purse was too good to refuse. To add to Francis's earnings, he signed a contract with the *Daily Mirror* to sell advertising space on the soles of his boxing boots, which everyone assumed would be facing upwards before long. Eliades was furious with Maloney's insubordination and he had the support of Lennox, who agreed that Frank's obduracy was a sign of disloyalty. But despite their objections Maloney went ahead with his role in the fight, which meant working with Warren once again. As Eliades put it, 'It's true that Frank and I didn't have a great relationship by then. I let him do what he wanted for the first eight years and then reeled him in and he rebelled because he believed his own hype. I really didn't like what he did with Francis because I should have been the promoter of that fight, and also I suspected that he was starting to get too close to Warren, which proved to be correct.'

The Home Office could have refused Tyson's entry to Britain because of his criminal record, but eventually gave the go-ahead, and for once he behaved impeccably (aside from an enlivening threat to 'kill Francis'). The public response he received was sometimes alarming in its implications. For instance, this convicted rapist was mobbed by fans in Brixton, where he seemed to be viewed as a symbol of defiant machismo, a real man, a people's hero and one of us. When he went walkabout the traffic stopped for a mile around as thousands rushed to reach the high street to see him. Tyson took refuge in a police station where he was overcome with emotion, babbling on about the 'love' shown by the British people. When he appeared waving from the third-floor window of a police station, shouting his thanks through a loud hailer, the crowd below, which included a fair sprinkling of women of Desiree Washington's age, roared their approval. Over the next week he roamed around, spending over a million dollars on presents and delighting the crowds that turned up wherever he appeared before making it on cue, without complications, at a packed MEN Arena in Manchester. He flattened Francis in two rounds, dropping him four times along the way, and the *Mirror's* investment paid off handsomely.

After this, Maloney was effectively demoted. Their fights had previously been promoted under the banner of 'Frank Maloney of Panix Promotions'; now the Frank Maloney bit was cut. He was also cut from Lennox's camps, under the guise of spending more time on local boxing bills. It was clear his role was being reduced although Lennox denied he was due to be fired, returning to the ominous 'if it ain't broke, don't fix it' line.

By then Lennox and Panos were insisting all their staff sign a confidentiality form. Maloney was upset by this demand, viewing it as an indication that Lennox didn't trust him. 'I used to think it was Panos demanding I sign that thing and then I didn't know who it was,' he said. 'Panos was saying it was Lennox, Lennox was blaming Panos. But whoever it came from, if I went ahead and signed it would mean I would have to clear everything before I spoke to the press, and I wouldn't be able to speak off the record, and that would make my job untenable, so I didn't agree.' Lennox says he is still mystified by this response and feels there is nothing unreasonable about asking employees who are privy to details of his life to agree to keep it private. 'You can see it with other celebrities – they all get their employees to sign confidentiality agreements and I was no different. I thought, "I'm getting my business in hand, so now let me protect myself," because you know what can happen. Even with the Queen, her maid tries to tell all. So I got together a confidentiality agreement and I got everyone on the team to sign – not just Frank – and none of the others had a problem. I don't understand why he refused this demand.'

Maloney was still batting for Lennox on another terrain – a court case to protect his status as WBA champion. The background was the clause King inserted into the Holyfield contracts compelling Lewis to make his first defence for him against the WBA's top contender. By this stage King had ensured that John Ruiz replaced Akinwande in this slot. Ruiz, a former Lewis sparring partner, was best known for getting knocked out in nineteen seconds by another contender, David Tua. Despite offering no challenge, Lewis agreed to fight him and Panos offered Ruiz $2.5 million. But it turned out that the Puerto Rican-Bostonian was unavailable until July 2000 and they decided they couldn't wait and instead went ahead with a more lucrative and interesting defence against America's Michael Grant, while challenging the contractual provision in court. But, having signed the contract, they had no chance and the court compelled Lennox to relinquish his WBA title, after which he decided he would never again let the alphabet bodies get in his way.

Holyfield outpointed Ruiz, then Ruiz outpointed Holyfield, then they fought a draw, then Roy Jones beat Ruiz and relinquished the WBA title, after which Ruiz won it back again. But no one paid much heed to the fate of this belt because everyone in the game recognised that there was only one world title, and that belonged to Lennox Lewis. After four months of partying, taking it easy and doing very little serious exercise, Lennox got down to the business of defending for the first time against the huge, unbeaten and highly fancied Grant. He usually kept in reasonable shape between fights – playing basketball, golf and tennis, and sometimes going for runs – but this time he'd let it slip, and as some of his team admitted they had to take short-cuts to get him into shape.

The Grant fight was one HBO had long been proposing. The Lewis camp suspected they wanted the challenger to win when they fought at Madison Square Garden on 29 April 2000. 'There was always this thing that Lennox wasn't an American,' said Maloney, 'and I had the strong sense that HBO wanted Grant to beat him. They really liked Grant.'

If you ignore questions of loyalty you can see why an American network selling fights primarily to American buyers might want a big, popular, good-looking, clean-living, unbeaten young American as champion in preference to an older, more enigmatic Englishman. The 27-year-old Grant fitted the profile of your perfect imaginary heavyweight champion in every superficial category. He really looked the part: 6ft 7in, perfectly built, usually weighing around 255lb with an 86-inch wingspan, and he was handsome to boot. He was also a former college boy who could throw a 90mph fastball and was offered the chance of a professional career in American football. He was also intelligent, articulate and, naturally, a born-again Christian; he played the piano, sang in the church choir and wore spectacles outside the ring. There was a good deal of Clark Kent about his image: gentle and urbane-looking in his suit; huge, ripped and imposing when stripped down. HBO executives, salivating over his potential, called him 'the anti-Tyson'.

The only remaining question was, could he fight? On the optimistic side, after six years as a professional he boasted an unblemished record of 31 fights, 31 wins, 22 knockouts. He earned his top ranking by beating several men in the top twenty, including a gutsy win over Golota. Grant was powerful and athletic, he hit hard and had the courage to fight back when badly hurt. He was also superbly conditioned, working relentlessly for three months at his North Carolina camp under Don Turner, who enraged Lewis by saying he had no heart while adding that his man would be too young, strong, determined and athletic for him. Grant picked up on this theme by predicting that Lewis would be 'intimidated' by him and would be unable to cope with his workrate.

Having taken to boxing at the age of twenty he had nothing approaching Lennox's amateur pedigree, which meant there was a question of whether he'd learned enough. His technique was sound and his punches heavy, but his movement looked ponderous when compared to Lewis's, and there were questions over his punch resistance. The Golota fight offered a key to his assessment. His detractors said it revealed his vulnerabilities. The more experienced Pole dropped him twice and dominated for nine rounds until Grant finally caught him, battered him and knocked him down heavily in the tenth, after which Golota's notoriously fragile self-confidence collapsed and he gave up. Grant's supporters looked at the same fight and said it proved his patience, his resilience, his courage and his power.

With the 247lb. Lewis in slightly less than perfect shape it seemed a dangerous assignment, but he wasn't worried. He watched Grant's fight against Golota from ringside, and after observing how he dropped his left, leaving him open to the right, he was convinced there was minimal risk. Yet the strongly pro-Grant crowd, the extensive publicity, particularly in New York, the narrowing odds and his irritation over Turner's remarks, gave Lennox enough of an edge to get excited. After his trio of distance fights against Mavrovic and Holyfield he was determined to do a job on this giant – his first-ever opponent who was both taller and heavier than him. He wanted to bash Grant up in a way that would re-establish his reputation as a serious banger.

Grant, at 250lb – lighter than usual – came in looking drained and nervous. He prayed earnestly in his dressing room, licked his lips compulsively on his way to the ring, hugged Turner during the announcements, and when he touched gloves with Lewis he said, as always, 'God bless you.' But he came out quickly, landing a jab and a right, and a few seconds later another jab, a right and a left hook. Lewis slotted in his own right, but Grant came back with hard jabs to the head and midriff. 'He came out pretty gutsy,' said Lennox. 'I was shocked he came at me like that, really surprised, but I always said if he did that it would be a short fight because he's been fighting B-class opponents and I'm an A-class opponent. I realised I had superior speed and I could see him winding up his punches.'

Certainly nothing in Grant's fighting experience or 120 rounds of sparring had prepared him for the speed and accuracy of Lennox's response. A quick left hook was followed by a heavy right uppercut under the chin and then a clubbing, overhand right to the side of the head, and Grant was on his back. He was up at seven, but by the time Lennox was permitted to resume his assault seventeen seconds had passed. Lennox moved in and Grant tried to grab, but found himself steadied with a glove behind his head and absorbed four more clubbing rights that sent him collapsing into the ropes for a second eight count. He was out on his feet when Lennox probed with a jab before detonating a massive right cross on the jaw that swept Grant's feet off the canvas and deposited him heavily. He lay flat on his back with his legs spread, but woke up just in time and scrambled to his feet at the official count of eight, as the bell rang.

Turner yelled, 'You gotta use your legs, you gotta move your legs! Hear what I'm saying? You gotta move your legs!' But it seemed a hopeless exercise. As Lennox came out for round two, Grant tried to hold and push him down but found himself getting whacked behind the head in response. He rallied after they were parted, catching Lewis with a good left hook and the response this time was unusually wild, although dangerous enough for the wobbly Grant to grab again. Lewis planted some more uppercuts, driving his challenger back, and although his work was ragged every punch had a visible effect.

But the American hadn't given up and was still throwing with as much fire as he could find. As Lennox came in again, Grant met him with the best of his 22 scoring punches of the night: a full-weight right cross. It landed flush, but Lennox seemed unmoved; a few seconds later he stepped inside again and hurt Michael with a right of his own. As Grant grabbed, the world champion extended an arm loosely behind his head and then slammed home a massive right uppercut that jerked Grant's head back. 'He kept his head down,' Lennox explained, 'so I kept his head in one position and hit him.' Once again the effect was devastating: Grant dropped instantly and fell on to his back, his legs and arms apart. He took the full count at the two-minute-53-second mark.

As Grant sat on his stool, the ringside doctor looked into his eyes and asked him what happened. 'I just got knocked out in the second round,' he replied. Then, a few seconds later, 'I'm a strong man, I'm strong.' Lennox stooped down and held him gently for a few seconds, while offering words of compassion and commiseration. A minute later he commended Grant's courage in going on the attack, but said he was fortunate to have been stopped early. 'Styles make fights, and Grant was the perfect style for me to showcase some of my talents,' he said. 'If it had moved into the later rounds I would have shown some more but I don't get paid for overtime. I just come to conquer, and I improve with each fight.' At times it had been crude, but it was the kind of overwhelming display of power and aggression that wins respect and admiration in the United States, and the fact that it came against a bigger, younger, unbeaten American added to its appeal.

There was also plenty of admiration for Lennox's ringside guest, with cameras clicking on the beautiful young woman who was quickly identified as Aisha Mike. Until then Lennox had fiercely protected his private life. He would decline comment on lovers with the polite put-downs like, 'I kind of like to keep the personal, personal because it has nothing to do with my boxing career', but this did not stop speculation. There were regular stories associating him with celebrities – film and television stars, models, singers and sports stars.

Among those who received media attention for their public flirtation with Lewis were the ill-fated celebrity groupie Paula Yates and the Spice Girl Mel B, while the actress Halle Berry was vocal in her admiration. 'I'm a real fan,' she told one newspaper. 'He's a class act. I'm sure the British accent helps because every time he opens his mouth I like what I hear.' Usually Lennox ignored this kind of attention; occasionally he would make a joke about it. When the actress Julia Roberts kissed him after they'd filmed a scene in the Steven Soderbergh movie *Ocean's Eleven* he sighed dramatically and said, 'Oh, those luscious lips.' Sometimes he would issue an outright denial. For instance, he used an unrelated court case to scotch one of the more persistent of these stories. 'I heard rumours,' he said, with reference to the dealings of his promoter, 'just like there were rumours I was going out with Naomi Campbell – all whispers and rumours.'

In reality, while most of the whispers and rumours had no substance, Lennox had affairs and friendships with several women, including celebrities, while managing to keep the details within his inner circle. As Steward put it, 'He's one of the most desirable and sought-after men I've been involved with in my career. Not only is he a handsome guy but he's a perfect gentleman and women are attracted to that but he doesn't appear an excessive womaniser. When he has a girlfriend, even a long-term girlfriend, he'll never flaunt her. He thinks it would be very embarrassing for both of them to do that. He watches himself carefully, and when he goes out with a girlfriend and it looks like a bad place or a bad situation he'll say "Let's go" because he doesn't want negative publicity. I think part of that is that he's very ethical in the way he treats people. He's not deeply religious like me, or like his mother, but he's very ethical and believes in setting a good public example, so it's important to him to be respectful of women and not to be in any scandals.'

But his relationship with Aisha was serious enough for Lennox to take what for him was the unusual step of giving it a cautious airing in public. In a way he had no option because they were spending so much time together between fights. He began to take her as a guest to his fights, as well as to restaurants, clubs and premieres, prompting the tabloids to describe them as lovers, although when Maloney suggested setting up a picture session of them for a newspaper, Lennox was irritated. For Aisha, the constant media attention was tiresome. 'I wouldn't say they were cornering me all the time, but it used to happen now and then, particularly when we were in Britain together,' she said. 'Like once, when Lennox and I went to Stonehenge, a photographer was hiding in the bushes and popped out to take pictures. I became very careful who I would talk to about him because of journalists contacting me so much through my e-mail address.' On the one occasion she agreed to a short interview with a British tabloid, she maintained that 'they twisted my comments to sound like I was implying that we were getting married, when I had made it very clear this wasn't true, so naturally I have never trusted the press in any capacity after that'.

Lennox's desire for privacy and for separating his public and private lives also extended to some details of his family past. For instance, it was not widely known outside his inner circle that his mother had a third son, got married and had a granddaughter. At one point this son arrived in London and met with members of Lennox's managerial team. 'Lennox once introduced me to this other brother,' said Eliades. 'He'd just come out from the West Indies and Lennox asked me to give him ten thousand dollars of his own money, which I did.' But when a newspaper wanted to write this story, his management persuaded the journalist to drop it, as they did with several other stories relating to his private life.

Later, however, when the screenwriter Melissa Mathison wrote the text for a book of Lewis photographs taken by his friend Blaise Hart, he didn't object to the mention of Violet's granddaughter Marissa, who had come to live with her in Kitchener, and went out of his way to recommend the book. While Dennis remained coy on the subject, saying Marissa was 'a child my mother adopted', Lennox confirmed he had another sibling and a niece while Violet added that Marissa was the daughter of a son born after Lennox and that 'it is a joy to have her in my life'. The important point was that they maintained as much control as possible over the details that emerged about their family life.

He was also trying to assert more direct control over his boxing life, with the idea of clearing the way for a final 'showdown' with Mike Tyson. At this point Tyson was about to return for his second fight in Britain, against the 6ft 5in, 240lb American Lou Savarese, whose record of 39 wins and three losses suggested he was a more formidable opponent than Francis.

Mike arrived in London in a less amicable mood than before, which some explained as his response to the murder of a close friend, others to his decision to stop taking his mood-altering prescription drug Zoloft. This time the spark was a

£500,000 writ for a jewellery bill – a result of his spending spree during his previous trip, when he left without paying. Tyson decided it was Warren's duty to cough
up. Warren knew otherwise, and the conflict that followed was the most comical
aspect of Tyson's odd visit.

When Warren disappeared for a few days, several newspapers reported variously that Tyson had broken his jaw, cracked his ribs, smashed his cheekbone and tried
to throw him out of the window – all untrue. Warren, a man of prickly pride,
seemed to have no problem with reports of him slugging Roger Levitt but did not
enjoy hearing about anyone getting the better of him. Soon after this, for example,
a British broadsheet published an interview with the former British and European
heavyweight champion Joe Bugner in which he referred to 'grabbing Frank around
the neck and choking the life out of him, until I saw sense and put him down'.
Warren felt this merited a lengthy response, in which he huffed, 'He certainly never
put his hands around my neck. If he had, he would have come second.' He definitely did not appreciate hearing that anyone, even Tyson, had actually managed to
land a punch on him and threatened that if anyone repeated the allegation he would
sue. He turned up at the fight with nothing worse than a pink eye.

Still, the dispute over the jewellery bill and Tyson's bad mood put the fight in
jeopardy. His British debut attracted a capacity crowd of 21,000 hours after tickets
went on sale; for his return against Savarese there were hopes of 50,000 fans pack-
ing Glasgow's Hampden Park football stadium, but in the end the combination of
the Scottish rain and cold and Tyson's behaviour meant only 20,000 punters
stumped up for what turned out to be 38 seconds of action. Tyson charged in,
slipped a jab and whacked Savarese with a left hook on the chin. Lou went down,
got up again, and Mike drove him back to the ropes where he drilled him with three
more hooks and a right and then a further massive hook that snapped Savarese's
head sideways. The British referee, John Coyle, promptly called a halt, but Tyson
wasn't quite done and continued with his efforts to separate body and head. Coyle
jumped in and Tyson punched over him, his forearm knocking the bald referee to
the deck, at which point Tyson's trainer, Tommy Brooks, leapt through the ropes
and the victorious Tyson finally got the message.

He declared, 'I am the most ruthless, brutal champion ever. I am Sonny Liston
and Jack Dempsey. There is no one who can match me.' With this off his chest he
directed his rage at Lewis. 'I want to eat your heart out,' he said. 'I want to eat your
children [sic].' Then, admitting that he wasn't quite ready for this meal, he said, 'I
need more training. I am rusty.' And finally, 'He is no match for me when I am right.
I have only fought twelve times in ten years. I want to rip his heart out and feed it to
him.' An hour later, after showering, he walked into the post-fight press conference
by mistake. 'Oh fuck,' he sneered as he stalked out. 'Fucking press.' The British
Boxing Board fined Tyson £125,000 for misconduct and using 'bad language' while
Warren and Tyson announced they would never work together again.

Lennox would have his turn to feel Mike Tyson's teeth, but for the moment his
heart and unborn children remained safe because he was 5,000 miles away, completing his training in Pennsylvania for his homecoming title defence at the London

Arena on 15 July against Frans Botha. This was not an easy sell for Maloney and Eliades: the fight took place three weeks after the ill-fated Tyson show, coincided with the Euro 2000 football tournament and the Wimbledon tennis tournament, and Botha was not considered a threat.

Warren was also involved in this show through his position as manager of the Americanised South African. Over the previous eighteen months he'd been through one of the tougher spells of his promotional career. In January 1999 he agreed to pay £7.2 million to Don King in a legal settlement a month after losing an appeal against a High Court judgement that froze his assets. He had also come through a lengthy criminal trial, having been accused of £1.2 million worth of VAT evasion. Two months before the Botha fight he was acquitted, but his partner, Chris Morris, was convicted of tax evasion. These trials cost him a fortune and by then he'd also paid the £1.2 million he owed the government. On top of this he parted ways with his biggest earner, Naseem Hamed, and lacked a comparably marketable champion to succeed him. Botha provided a chance to recoup some of these losses and he was not prepared to sign him away cheaply. The fight also offered the hope of achieving his ambition of taking one of his heavyweights to the undisputed world title. He confidently predicted victory for his man. 'This is a big mistake for Lewis,' he said after the fight was arranged. 'Frans Botha has a big heart, he gives his all, and I believe he is so inspired that he will pull off a big upset.'

Botha was a heavyweight who went a long way and made a huge amount of money on relatively little. He was a decent but not brilliant boxer, a solid but far from ferocious banger, his chin was sound but not undentable and he was a big man but certainly no giant. What he possessed was just enough ability to make it into the rankings, and for the rest his talent for self-promotion and for finding men who would bankroll him carried him through.

Growing up in an Afrikaner family in the Northern Transvaal, the first fight he watched, when he was eight years old, was a film of Ali beating Foreman. 'That's where my dreams started,' he said. 'I said to my dad, "One day I'm going to win the heavyweight championship of the world."' Despite losing his first five fights, he stuck it out. 'Of course I was extremely discouraged,' he said, 'but in my heart I never thought of giving up.' Working as a fireman he picked up 353 wins and 25 losses, but it is the losses that are remembered – particularly four against his more talented local rival Corrie Sanders. Still, he won the national heavyweight title before turning professional in 1990.

He looked sluggish at first and only maintained his unbeaten record courtesy of a clutch of white South African judges who granted him dubious decisions against black opponents. One of his problems was an injury to his right arm sustained while fighting fires. 'I had no power in the right because it was very painful and my hand was numb,' he said. But none of this held him back. He teamed up with the former WBA heavyweight champion Gerrie Coetzee and they relocated to the United States, where Frans took fights wherever he could find them. Eventually he moved to Newport Beach, California, where he was enticed by Don King. An incensed Coetzee demanded money from Botha and went for him. 'We had a helluva fight and I gave him a helluva beating,' said Botha. 'By the end he was lying there, covered in his own blood.'

King ensured that Botha received a world rating with the IBF and tried to talk him up, branding him the 'White Buffalo'. Botha took to this new image, never forgetting to emphasise his skin colour. 'It's time to declare war on the heavyweight division,' he announced. 'I'm white, but I can fight. Anyone who wants the title will have to come through the White Buffalo.' To cover all bases he draped himself in the flag of the new South Africa and declared that he would 'win the world title for Nelson Mandela'. But while King was happy to mouth whatever mixed metaphors he thought his audience might stomach, Botha believed them. On the 'Great White Hope' issue, for example, he commented, 'People are crying for a white heavyweight champion, including blacks.'

It dawned on Don that this fellow had the knack of talking the talk, and his ostensibly unbeaten 35-fight record offered the illusion he could also walk the walk. So instead of using him as a morsel for Oliver McCall – his original plan – he had another idea. The IBF matched him with Germany's Axel Schulz in perhaps the worst-ever pairing for a vacant title. Neither belonged in the top ten and it was an awful fight, Botha scraping through on a split decision before testing positive for anabolic steroids. He should have been summarily stripped of his title, but Bobby Lee ignored the test until rival contenders issued legal summons, forcing the IBF to declare the result a 'no-contest' and their title vacant. 'I have never knowingly taken steroids,' Frans protested. 'The positive test was a result of medication for my right arm injury. I could name steroid users in boxing but look at my body. Do I look like a man who has been working out on steroids?' Well, no. He remained his podgy self, but his high steroid count and his association with a proven cheat, Panama Lewis (his trainer), meant he was damned by both science and association. Still, the IBF gave him first shot at their new champion, Michael Moorer, who dropped him three times and stopped him in round twelve. 'Technically speaking it was a win for me,' Botha said. 'Moorer went to hospital and I was ready for a big steak.'

He left King, signed with Warren, applied for US citizenship and denounced his homeland, claiming he was disillusioned that Mandela's government had never been on his side. He also went for a makeover, dispensing with the moustachioed mullet style and replacing it with an eclectic Ali-G variant, without the irony: skullcap, wrap-around shades, chunky rings, a bleached goatee and blond hair while the road-warrior existence was replaced by Californian urbanity, with shares in a restaurant, a wine-importing concern and a champagne glass retailing business.

His debut under Warren came against Tyson, who was having his first outing in nineteen months. Botha was not intimidated – not even when Tyson tried to break his arm in a clinch and hit him after the bell – and his boxing seemed more accomplished than before. His confident combination of jab, move and clinch enabled him to win four rounds out of four, but he got too close and was blasted out by a solitary right in round five. 'I just lost concentration for a second,' he explained, reiterating that he was still better than anyone else in the division.

His next fight shored up his opinion. Shannon Briggs was attempting to re-establish himself chose Botha as his victim. But Frans picked himself off the canvas and bashed Briggs around the ring to emerge with a draw. He was back in the rankings, and after another quick knockout felt sure he was ready for Lewis. At the age of 31, with a record of 40 wins (24 knockouts), two losses, one draw and one no-contest, he had reached his prime. The rehabilitation of his right arm had clearly added to his power, his once-soft torso had acquired definition, and he seemed fitter, stronger, faster and more accomplished defensively. Certainly, his self-belief was impressive. 'I think of Lewis trying to prevent my family from eating or of him hitting my children,' he said. 'That gives me the aggression I need. What gives me the confidence is the shape I'm in and the fact that I know I can fight against any kind of style, since I spar against a variety of styles.' He went on to declare that he was the 'number one heavyweight in the world' and that he was 'using this fight as a stepping stone to get back at the real man, and that man's Tyson'. But there was a less savoury reason for his sense of mission. 'I hope I can persuade more white heavyweights into coming out,' he said. 'I would like to have more friends out there – white friends – and I hope I can be a role model for the white heavyweights.'

Lennox, who was reading Zadie Smith's anti-racist novel *White Teeth* at the time, considered himself a role model for all heavyweights and had plenty of white friends as well as black. But he quite liked Frans because despite his boasts he showed respect, and so he made a point of returning the compliment, praising Botha's achievements and, more importantly, turning up in prime condition. He looked taught and glossy by fight time, after six weeks of training in Pennsylvania. 'He was in quite good shape for Botha because he had just fought Michael Grant, so didn't have long between fights,' said Joe Dunbar. 'I always preferred it when he was fighting more often, and the Botha fight showed the difference that made.' He weighed in at 250½lb, the second heaviest of his career, but there was speculation that the calibration of the scales was a couple of pounds out. The 6ft 2in Botha was also slightly heavier than expected, at 236½lb.

The packed London Arena booed the foreigner as he walked in to the Rocky theme, wearing a knowing smile and a white sheepskin rug (for a White Buffalo). Once he'd stepped through the ropes Botha began to waltz around the ring with Warren as Lennox was escorted by female Beefeaters in mini-skirts to the sound of a tinky-tonky version of Verdi's *Rigoletto* that turned into Bob Marley singing about chasing those crazy baldheads out of town, which was perhaps more appropriate than usual given Botha's pre-fight comments on white hopes. The normally impassive Lennox went over to the ropes and raised his hands to milk his delighted 12,000 fans. When Larry O'Connell was introduced to the crowd as the referee for the night, they gave him an even heartier boo than Botha (although Lennox's own sentiment was 'Good referee, lousy judge').

Lennox dwarfed Botha and found it easy to keep him on the end of his long punches. He opened with a quick right cross that landed. Botha tried his own right, but it fell short. The South African's strategy was to keep out of range and use his quick rights to counter, but he was unable to get past the Lewis jab. After two minutes Lewis landed a hard right cross to the chin and Botha's legs folded into a crouch, although he managed to straighten up and survived to the bell. Lewis took his time in round two, controlling the fight and setting the pace; Botha's contribution was to fire hopeful rights while backing off. Late in the round Lennox landed another right cross flush on the jaw and Botha's legs dipped again. This time there was no escape. Lewis steadied him with a left hook and then fired an extremely fast and heavy right cross that lifted Botha off his feet. He fell head-first over the bottom strand of the rope and nearly out of the ring. He hauled himself up at the count of eight, and O'Connell asked him to walk forward. He observed that Botha was still dazed and uncoordinated and waved it off. 'It was a good stoppage,' said Lennox, 'because when he had to step forward he was actually wobbling.'

Lewis climbed on the ropes, held his hands above his head and clapped the crowd, delighted that his first British fight in six years had gone so well. 'I wanted to prove I was a pugilist specialist,' he said for the first time – a phrase he would use regularly over the next couple of years. 'I don't take punches, I give them, and I want to show the public the sweet science.' After this speech he had a friendly chat with Botha and invited him to his post-fight party. The defeated challenger didn't turn up because he was too busy holding court after the post-fight press conference, where he told everyone who would listen that he was still the best heavyweight in the world.

CHAPTER TWENTY ONE
NEW LONDON, CONNECTICUT, CHRISTMAS 1996

David Tua is impossible to miss if you happen to share a Holiday Inn with him for a week. With his skin-headed scowl, melon-balled swagger and a physique with the dimensions of a tank, it's also hard to avoid an initial response along the lines of 'thug'. So you anticipate sullen, aggressive machismo and approach with caution, particularly since it's five days before Christmas and he's about to tangle again with the Nigerian David Izon, who handed him his last defeat, over four years ago at the Olympics.

What comes back is an infectious, awe-shucks grin, a high heavyweight voice, an eager friendliness and loads of laughter. He plonks himself on the bed and without much prompting begins to chat away with his flat, slow New Zealand vowels, mixing his own life story with talk of the Polynesian poetry he writes and about why his people back in Samoa are part-human, part-spirit. Along the way he lets slip that, yes, he was a bit of a thug in his rugby-playing, council-estate days in Auckland and definitely not a fellow for a safe 'Yo! David!' or even a meeting of eyes. But these days the thuggery is confined to the ring, a place he was groomed for from childhood, and earlier, all the way back to his martial ancestors. He believes he's descended from a warrior king called Talimatasi and talks of the days when 'giants' walked the islands and how his ancestors accompany him. Giants, it turns out, are a big part of his consciousness, as is the business of fighting them. 'We're a family of fighters,' he says. 'My grandfather used to do it and passed it on to my father, and again, it passed through the genes to me.' That's a romantic explanation, but, as with most fighting men, much of the truth is more mundane and brutal.

He was raised on the tiny Western Samoan island of Faleatiu, as a member of a community of 300. His father, Tuavale Mafaufau, ran a convenience store and smallholding, which earned enough to keep his nine children in good health. But he always harboured ambitions of making it in the ring, and when this failed he imposed the burden on his five sons. Tuavale taught David to box from the age of eight, and three years later began to select men off the street to spar with the lad. 'If they won he'd give them a loaf of bread and I would get the strap, so I tried to avoid those sparring sessions, but if my father saw me sneaking off I'd get more straps.' When he was twelve his parents and four siblings moved to Auckland in the hope of earning more money, with the rest of the children remaining behind. He joined them a few months later, in the winter of 1984, and discovered that his island life had been exchanged for a small, cold, government flat shared with another family. His father found a factory job as a machine operator, and to subsidise the family income David helped his mother to clean the local school during the week while working on a farm in the holidays. 'I know what it's like to be poor,' he says. His once happy life turned bleak, with regular fights and plenty of 'straps' for truancy and other misdemeanours. After a year, Tuavale ordered his son to join a local boxing club. 'I was hanging out with the wrong crowds and doing a lot of wrong things,' David recalls, 'but the boxing separated me from the trouble, together with the loving and caring from my parents.' Loving and caring – and regular, often gratuitous, beatings from a bitter man.

With his sharp eye, quick reflexes and surprising speed he excelled at sport, playing in the trials for the New Zealand secondary schools national rugby team, rugby league out of season and also representing his school at hockey and cricket. 'You can refer to me as a sports fanatic,' he says with an eager nod. 'I love sports, particularly rugby. I'm not bragging, but I used to be devastating on the field. I played second five eight [centre] and when the team was in trouble, say on our own twenty-two-metre line, when the only choice for the guy with the ball was to kick, I'd say, "Don't kick the ball!" and because the guys were scared of me they would throw the ball out and I'd run it. I had the mentality that I was an individual, playing for myself, and I hated losing.'

This individualistic streak was directed mainly through boxing. He won the national junior heavyweight title at fifteen, even though he was only a middleweight, and became the youngest boxer ever to win the senior heavyweight title a year later. Then in 1992, aged nineteen, he was selected to represent his country in the heavyweight division at the Barcelona Olympics, and despite his sparse international experience he scored two knockouts over favoured Europeans before being outpointed by the older and far more experienced Izon. Still, with the bronze medal hanging proudly from his neck he became an instant celebrity in Western Samoa – the first Polynesian ever to win Olympic honours.

While he's recounting this history, there's another knock on the Holiday Inn bedroom door, and in steps another friendly New Zealander, his manager Kevin Barry, who is best known for winning the 1984 Olympic light heavyweight silver medal by beating Evander Holyfield on a disqualification. After that fortuitous triumph Kevin made friends with Evander and used his help to open doors for David in America. 'When we arrived in America Evander took us to lunch, and then to church,' Barry recalls, 'which was a great motivational thing for David because it meant that even before turning professional he got to know the heavyweight champion of the world.'

From then on David was an émigré, living in New Jersey and longing for home. 'When I was starting out it was so difficult being away from home,' he says. 'I lived in a room with four other guys and the meal money I had wasn't enough. I used to go to McDonald's to eat because it was cheaper and I could eat more, and I finally made friends with the manager and he fed me.' What got him through those early years was the dream of one day returning to the islands as a hero. He still talks of retiring to pursue a political career there, or in New Zealand – perhaps standing for parliament. 'The last few years have been a really hard struggle for my people – in New Zealand, in Samoa and on the other islands,' he says. 'I want to use my fame to campaign for them and for their rights and do the best I can for the Polynesian communities.'

A minute on there is yet another knock and in shuffles Lou Duva, who takes over the conversation, telling of his part in the Tua story. Holyfield introduced Kevin and David to the old man who, as always, ordered a trial and after a few rounds pronounced himself impressed. He became David's co-trainer (with George Benton) when Tua started his professional career in December 1992. 'What I liked about him was that raw courage, the way he just went out there swinging,' Lou says. 'You know, I was very close to Rocky Marciano as a young man and I've always thought one day I would get a heavyweight who would be another Rocky, but for a long time no one came. I have a big, six-foot-four guy in Golota, and I also have Holyfield who I had to build up to heavyweight, but when I saw David, I thought, he's the one – another Marciano. He's rough, strong and he hits real hard. He walks in, takes a great shot, he wants to fight and it was just a matter of teaching him how, so I got him to move his head, move his body, put him at different angles so that he can ride the punch, which takes away its impact, and he did it all very well.'

David, beaming like a little boy being praised by granddad, cuts in to tell of his 'very interesting and competitive' sparring sessions with Golota. Naturally the Pole took the opportunity to hit him in the groin, 'but only once, only once' David says and bursts out laughing, knowing he has no need to add a rider about making him pay. But the real test was to see how David would handle three weeks of daily sparring with Holyfield, as he prepared for Tyson. 'They wanted someone with a Tyson-like style,' Lou explains. 'David said, "No problem – it's a good challenge for me," and he went terrific. They gave each other hell down there and he did real well. I mean, they had some pretty good wars and he sure held his own and helped Evander tremendously. Evander loved him and David came away thinking he's ready for anybody.' David excuses himself and cuts in again. 'Yeah, I was just buzzing through it,' he says. 'I mean, not like we were trying to knock each other out all the time, but the sparring with Evander was very, very interesting.'

It's a word he uses often when referring to fighting: interesting. He bashed his way through 22 vaguely interesting victories before being given his first truly interesting test against the Puerto Rican prospect John Ruiz. It took one left hook to separate Ruiz from his senses and his next two opponents also went in round one, which took David into the world's top ten. 'He's convinced me he will become world heavyweight champion,' says old Lou as he leaves for bed. 'I mean, if Tyson could do it and Marciano could do it and Frazier could do it – all guys under six feet – then David Tua can do it for sure, because he's one of the outstanding fighters I've had.'

A few minutes later it's David's turn to leave, because it's ten p.m. and he has a date with Izon. As he follows his manager, he turns at the doorway and drops the friendly smile. His dark eyes take on a deep-freeze frown as he starts pounding his meat-mallet left fist into his palm. 'Listen, my time will come, and soon,' he says. 'I have to prepare myself for that time because I want to be ready to face the outcome.'

The following night he hangs his Polynesian beads around his 21-inch neck, pulls on his sarong and heads out for what he expects will be another early night. But instead Izon gives him hell, jabbing and moving and bouncing right crosses off his hard head. Tua bobs, weaves and unleashes his hooks but can't quite nail the tough and talented Nigerian clean. It's a close, absorbing battle, going down to the wire until, with one minute left, David unleashes a head-severing uppercut and then obliterates Izon with a trio of wrecker-ball swings. It's five minutes before the legs of the Olympic silver medallist can support his 224lb body again. Everyone agrees that they've just witnessed an astonishingly chilling display of extreme power, but neither the 223lb David nor his trainer is quite satisfied.

In the morning, as they prepare to return to New Jersey, they mention another heavyweight, Lennox Lewis, who is in Las Vegas completing his training for the second McCall fight, and then talk about the need to grow big enough to compete with someone that size. 'I put David in with guys weighing 280, 300lb and they try to push him around but he pushes right back,' says Lou. 'He's too strong for them. But I still believe in building his body, like all my boxers. A lot of people don't take advantage of that, but I got a good bunch of physical guys on my staff and I believe in building their bodies.'

As David says goodbye he returns to his talk about giants, a subject that obsesses him. 'There will come a time when I have to fight bigger heavyweights than Izon – I mean a really big heavyweight, someone like Lennox Lewis,' he says. 'If I can't take a giant like that out with one punch it's going to go into the later rounds, and with his weight leaning on me throughout the fight I will get tired, so that means I have to have more muscle to handle that situation. I need more weight.'

Six months later, and a mere three pounds heavier, Tua fought his first near-giant – a Nigerian called Ike Ibeabuchi, who was bigger, stronger, harder-hitting and more talented than Izon. They were both unbeaten and determined to stay that way, and over twelve wonderfully savage rounds they threw over 1,700 punches between them. Tua, as always the heavier hitter, hurt Ibeabuchi and was never hurt in return, but in the end the 6ft 2in, 235lb Ike outworked the 5ft 9in, 226lb David and squeaked home on a disputed decision. It would be Tua's only blemish in 38 fights before fighting Lennox, but there would be no return. Ike, who was as mad as McCall, rammed his car into a wall after kidnapping his estranged girlfriend's son, severely injuring the boy. When he got out of jail he beat up a sparring partner outside the ring and whacked his own trainer. He then flattened a future champion, Chris Byrd (with the gloves on), but soon after that was arrested for raping a hotel maid, among other offences, and eventually, after being declared mentally fit to stand trial (just), he was jailed for fifteen years, still unbeaten in the ring.

After his sole setback against big Ike, Tua grew bigger and more ruthless. When unbeaten Hasim Rahman outboxed him he wounded the powerful American with a huge hook after the bell ending the ninth round, then finished him off in the tenth, and he continued to knock over everyone he faced. By the age of 27, having won ten in a row, he felt ready for Lewis. He was the top contender with a record of 37 wins (32 knockouts) and that one loss. His fighting weight went all the way up to 253lb by the beginning of 2000, although he brought it down to a solid 245lb by the time of his 11 November 2000 Las Vegas date with Lennox Lewis – big enough to face a giant, he thought.

By this stage Tua had dropped the Duvas, taking on another outstanding trainer in Ronnie Shields and had signed with a new promotional group called America Presents. For Lennox, 2000 was also a time of change in terms of the management of his career and control of his finances. He was beginning a year-long process that would see him taking over his own promotion with a new team of employees, which meant dispensing with the old team. The major surprise was that the first to go was his brother, Dennis Lewis.

Dennis had served as an employee both of Eliades and, more directly, of Lennox, looking after his brother's money. As he described it, 'When he was promoted by Roger Levitt I didn't have a formal title but I helped out with the promotional company, mainly through putting on small-hall fights, but it changed after Panos took over and particularly after John Hornewer left. At that point I got more centrally and directly involved in Lennox's career. Things were getting much bigger then, and we were promoting our own fights with major fighters, so I was involved in that, as well as being Lennox's business manager, and one of my many roles was to get sponsorship deals for him.'

In late 2000, however, Dennis was replaced by his former assistant, Adrian Ogun, who first came on the scene during the 1993 Lewis–Bruno fight after meeting Maloney and getting to know Dennis. 'How it happened was that I was looking into sponsorship deals for Lennox,' Dennis recalled, 'but they were difficult to secure because boxing didn't have a very strong image at the time, and unlike other sports stars, boxers are only as good as their last fight and blue-chip companies are not interested if you have a bad fight. So I felt I needed help, and I knew Adrian and introduced him to Lennox, and after that he worked with me on trying to arrange sponsorship deals.'

This newcomer cut an impressive figure: tall, well spoken and well educated (with a degree from the London School of Economics), Ogun once worked as a television weather presenter and knew how to project his personality. He had experience with major corporations and in representing the interests of musicians so he was comfortable with the rich and powerful and used his charm to work his way up. 'The way it worked,' said Eliades, 'is that Dennis wasn't very well educated so he used Adrian to compose letters and things like that, and when Dennis told him to jump Adrian would ask how high. But gradually it changed. Dennis was looking after Lennox's affairs in the UK, but because Lennox didn't feel like flying here all the time, Dennis would get Adrian to meet him abroad, so he got to spend lots of time with Lennox and his influence increased.'

Eliades clearly underestimated Ogun, referring to him contemptuously as 'Dennis's tea boy'. Frank Maloney took him more seriously, saying he was 'wary of Adrian from day one', viewing the newcomer as 'ambitious and obviously desperate to get involved with the team'. Eugene Maloney, who was head of security when Ogun arrived, offered a string of curses when asked about what he remembered of him. John Hornewer, who first met him at the Bruno fight, made it clear he had no time for Adrian, to put it mildly, and neither did Judd Burstein, who later became Lewis's lawyer and business adviser. But none of these reservations made much difference to Lennox, who was impressed, viewing Adrian as highly capable and easy to work with. He was getting positive comments about Ogun from businessmen he dealt with from outside their circle. For instance, Rodney Berman, the South African promoter, described Ogun as 'extremely charming and amicable and a pleasure to deal with'. Lennox therefore began to increase Ogun's responsibilities, and by the time of the first Holyfield fight he was a key member of the management team.

After unifying the title, Lennox began to consider the option of taking complete control over his career, with the idea of cutting out the middlemen and promoting himself. He viewed Ogun as someone who could play a central role in managing this transition, which meant reducing Maloney's role and easing Eliades out. He decided that Ogun should manage the financial side of his business and also drew in other outsiders, most notably his close Ghanaian friend Prince Osei-Poku. This meant a reduced role for his brother. Dennis, however, maintains he made the final decision to leave and that his departure was precipitated by a disagreement over sponsorship. 'Lennox wanted to go with one of the big agencies, William Morris, and I didn't think that was a good idea,' he said.

Eliades takes a more jaundiced view on the subject, suggesting that Dennis is protecting his brother. 'The way it happened is that first they went for Dennis and then they went for me,' he complained. 'I mean, you'd have to say something bad about Dennis to get Lennox to drop his own brother. I think some of Lennox's friends got to him by saying Dennis was living on his brother's name, because he used to get tickets through being Dennis Lewis and that kind of thing, but really, that's no crime. It wasn't like he had his fingers in the till or anything like that. Dennis was earning well because he was on a bonus per fight, but he was doing a fine job. He knew what was good for Lennox and he protected him, and he did a very good job of looking after Lennox's finances.'

Lennox does not dispute that his brother was serving his interests and insists it was his own decision to remove Dennis from his post as business manager, but also argues that this did not amount to 'firing' him. 'The situation with Dennis was that I was starting to take hold of my own business and I decided I definitely needed to employ people who could be part of a new team where everybody's job needed to become more specific,' he said, 'but even though my brother's position changed he remained involved in the sense of being my brother, so I still talked to Dennis regularly and he continued advising me, so in that sense he never really quit, and our relationship is good.'

Ogun replaced Dennis as business manager, taking on a key role in contractual dealings and promotion. Eliades was formally separated from his managerial role in Lewis's business affairs in August 2000, while his promotional role was pared down. In fact, the Lewis–Tua fight was the last to be formally promoted by Panos and the first where Ogun called the shots. As Eliades put it, 'After the Botha fight Lennox decided that Ogun would take over Dennis's position as his business manager while I stayed on as his token promoter for one last fight, but by then Adrian had complete control to the point where I had to ask him for my tickets for the Tua fight, which didn't go down well with me because I'm a dignified man and I won't let people push me around.'

Just over a year earlier, in what Frank Maloney described as a 'boozy lunch on the beach', Frank Warren proposed that he join his Sports Network Europe group. Maloney, whose previous antagonism to Warren went beyond mere rivalry, finally made his move after the Botha fight. He saw that Panos was about to be dumped by Lewis and had reached the point where he felt he could no longer work with a man he regarded as patronising and arrogant. When he explained his decision to Lennox and Adrian he made it clear he wanted to continue in his managerial role, and came away with the impression that they had no objection to his move. 'I told them what was on offer and what I planned and they said they had no problems with it so I took them on their word.'

In one sense their nod and wink was unsurprising because they were in the process of setting up Lion Promotions as an alternative to Panix and had shown no indication of wanting Maloney to join them. But in another sense it was strange because Warren, more than any other promoter, had made a point of slagging Lennox off over the years, regularly predicting his demise. Maloney, however, said this should not have been an issue because there was nothing personal in Warren's attacks. 'I would always say Lennox would beat so-and-so. That's the nature of the business. You always talk up your fighter and not your opponent. Manchester United don't talk up Arsenal. I've never heard Alex Ferguson say anything good about Arsène Wenger. What's the difference?' Lennox can accept this point, but said he was still surprised by Maloney's choice because of the negative things Frank had previously said to him about his namesake. 'My feeling was one of, "Why are you working with a man, Warren, who you broke off ties with all those years ago? How can you go back to that man?" It seemed to me like one step forward, two steps back.'

Maloney, however, is not a man to harbour grudges or let past feelings get in the way of a good deal. 'Frank Warren was my competitor and competition is good for the sport because it causes excitement but I think underneath all we used to say about each other we always had respect for what we'd each achieved in our different ways,' he began in a euphemistic appraisal of their historical antipathy, before getting to the point. 'End of the day, you have to look at what's out there, what's the best way to go, the best way forward for your career. I looked at everything when I was falling out with Panos. I looked at Sports Network's set-up, I liked the meetings I had with Frank and by then we were getting on well and it was good to work with people who had boxing knowledge because in Panix I was the only one and I was shouldering the burden which was quite a responsibility. Within eight months of me leaving, Panix Promotions crumbled.'

The deal from Warren's side was that Maloney would be paid to work for him as a 'consultant', which guaranteed a substantial income. He, in turn, delivered most of the boxers he managed to Warren's stable. This meant regular, well-paid work for them, regular managerial fees for Maloney and better boxers for Warren. The advantages for both men were obvious, yet the arrangement had one caveat: by far the most important boxer Maloney managed was headed elsewhere. This meant that while he was remaining Lewis's manager, he was working for a promoter who showed no respect for Lennox and was acting contrary to his emerging promotional interests. It was an arrangement that was bound to fail.

Still, rather to Maloney's surprise he was invited to join Lennox in the Mount Poconos training camp – the first time he'd been permitted to spend time there since he'd made a couple of fleeting visits during the second Holyfield fight. They discussed the Tua fight and Maloney's position with Warren, and despite the gradual estrangement of the previous two years they seemed to be getting on well. Then, during a meeting in his bedroom, Lewis popped the surprise question: 'How much am I paying you, Frank?' Maloney reminded him he was on 3 per cent (of purse money) and said he felt he was worth every penny. Lewis then explained the new arrangements he had in mind, with Ogun playing the primary managerial and promotional role, which meant a reduced workload for Frank. When Ogun dropped in a mention of Panos's idea that Frank should receive no more than a flat fee per fight, Maloney saw sense in compromise and agreed to have his share cut to 2 per cent. Adrian congratulated him on handling the situation well, but Maloney later said he felt like an invited guest or 'no more than a whore' because, like Panos, he was required to do very little work for his percentage. Incidentally, Lewis's purse for the Tua fight was $8 million, which meant Maloney's cut was $160,000.

When Lennox began training he took a keen interest in developments in the Sydney Olympics. He was excited about the progress of a confident and opinionated 28-year-old London super heavyweight called Audley Harrison. Lennox and Audley had very different public personas – the one cautious and sometimes diffident; the other garrulous, cocksure and combative – but they had a great deal in common: they were about the same size (Audley, at 6ft 5½in, is a fraction taller); both were London-born, with single mothers who were nurses of Jamaican origin; both were unmarried without any children; both were well-read intellectuals by the standards of the game; and both were prepared to gamble by delaying their professional start to pursue their goal of winning the Olympic gold medal.

Audley was the third of six brothers from west London. 'My mum and dad divorced when I was three,' he said, 'so I experienced the pain of family breakdown very early.' His main diversion was sport – particularly football – but it was not enough to keep him out of trouble. 'I grew up in quite a rough area and we all wanted to be bad boys. It's just what kids done. That's a phase I went through.' He was expelled from two schools, served eighteen months for robbing some members of a rival gang after a fight and was later fined for thumping a man who refused to put out his cigarette on the bus. He then decided to go straight by dedicating himself to boxing and education.

He set two goals: winning the Olympic super heavyweight gold medal and getting a university degree. After completing a couple of years at night school he spent four more at Brunel University and emerged with a BSc (Hons) degree. The boxing took longer. His arrogance saw him kicked out of London's leading amateur club, Repton, before he came back begging and was allowed to return. Then, after winning the British and Commonwealth championships he was offered £100,000 to turn professional but turned it down to pursue his dream of Olympic gold. But there were several setbacks, including an early loss in the World Amateur Championships, and he only qualified for Sydney at the last chance and then drew the Russian favourite in the opening round.

'Everybody thought, "Oh gosh, Audley's home time. He lost to that Russian the year before,"' he recalled. 'But I was glad because I knew I had the conviction and my resolve was strengthened.' He fell behind before blasting the Russian out with a southpaw left cross in the fourth. The punch won the fight but caused severe damage to his left hand. 'The tendon popped, the hood of the knuckle ruptured and the ligament tore, and it kept on swelling up,' he said Audley boxed one-handed to win his next two fights, by which stage Lennox was so caught up in his progress that he sent him a fax, encouraging him. 'That really helped me,' said Audley. 'My hand was killing me. I couldn't even make a proper knuckle and that fax from Lennox came through at the right time. It was perfect, and it just gave me the kick to get me into the zone. So really, a lot of credit to Lennox for that.' Audley, with his hair tied up in little elastic bands and his huge dimpled smile, won gold and became the British face of the Olympics. Soon after the Games he went to a delighted Lennox for advice on his professional future and was told to go it alone, without the middle men. 'To win the Olympic super heavyweight gold medal for Britain is quite an achievement,' Lewis said. 'I can see he's a very focused person who has taken his future in his own hands, and he's doing the right thing. It kind of reminds me of myself.'

The other backdrop to Lennox's preparations for Tua was one of the strangest presidential elections of the past century – and for a democrat, let alone a Democratic Party supporter like Lennox, one of the most disturbing. He watched with bemusement and dismay as the man winning the popularity contest by over half a million votes ended up the loser courtesy of a few hundred 'hanging chads' and a few thousand disenfranchised black people in Lewis's sometime home state of Florida. Lennox, an interested observer of American politics and certainly no fan of George W. Bush, drew on the memory that something analogous happened to him, albeit on a far less significant scale, in his first fight against Holyfield. The answer, it seemed, was to go all out for a knockout every time.

The Tua fight, however, was one that demanded caution. The squat Samoan was the heaviest puncher in the division, particularly with his left hook. 'I realise that David Tua is very powerful and has powerful hands,' he conceded. Or as Tua's manager, Kevin Barry elaborated, 'Dave can retain his power. He'll take you out whenever he hits you on the chin, whether it's the first round or the twelfth. There are a lot of guys who are big punchers for the first couple of rounds, but after that their power fades. That's not the case with Dave. It's a tremendous weapon because that power is always there, and power can change a fight like that. Lennox is going to get a chance to see that.'

Tua also owned one of the best chins in recent boxing history. He'd never wobbled despite getting hit flush by bangers like Ibeabuchi, Izon, Rahman and the top Russian Oleg Maskaev. As Tua liked to put it, while tapping his head and grinning, 'This coconut hasn't been dented yet.' Duva and Benton taught him the skills of bobbing, weaving and rolling his shoulders to slip punches, which also made him a difficult man to tag cleanly. The combination of his effective defence and his concrete chin guaranteed a long fight during which Lennox could not let his concentration slip for a second. On top of this, Lewis usually did best against taller heavyweights and Tua was eight inches shorter – more when you took his pronounced fighting crouch into account. He 'fought small', which meant that tall men had to punch down at the top of head. It was a point Lennox acknowledged. 'The fact that he's short may give me some problems,' he said.

Steward warned that one punch could decide it. 'He's a devastating puncher who has knocked out some of the best fighters of his generation,' he said, before adding, with a touch of self-interest, 'So I am one punch from being out of business.' It was a fight that worried him. 'I think Tua will force the situation and try to have a slugfest, although he's also good defensively and takes punches well, so it's one I'm excited about but I have a certain amount of nervousness also because Tua has a very good trainer in Ronnie Shields. I have a lot of respect for him.' Manny wanted plenty of aggression but seldom at close range where Tua could plant his killer hooks. He trained Lennox to punch down, to use his balance and footwork, to stay off the ropes where Tua was most dangerous, to keep his right glove up to protect his chin and to keep his sparring partners at arm's length.

It was one of his toughest training camps, and by the end of it, weighing a sleek and hard 249lb, all his people agreed he had reached new heights of brilliance. Despite the danger, they felt that if he maintained concentration there was a chance he could outclass Tua, and as the weeks passed their confidence grew. 'I see him do things in the gym on a daily basis that, if he did them in the ring, people would go, "Damn! Where did that come from?"' said Steward. 'Lennox is a different type of person, so sometimes the Americans judge him by our standards instead of by his. He's not inclined to be flashy or flamboyant and that translates to his boxing. I know how great he can be because when there's nobody around he'll make moves that are hard to believe, and now that he's getting confident you're starting to see them in the fights. He doesn't save it for the gym any more.'

Lennox had no difficulty convincing himself of his trainer's sunny perspective. He felt certain that at the age of 35 he was reaching his peak. He liked that term he'd come up with, 'pugilist specialist', and used it over and over, sensing he'd become a master boxer in a different league from the rest. 'I've stayed busy and I've fought so many guys I can't help but improve,' he said. 'I analyse fights a lot quicker now. I can spot what works and what won't work, and then I put it into practice. Before, it took me a while to figure that out, and maybe people interpreted that as me being conservative.' Despite Tua's reputation and the need to maintain his focus throughout the fight, he felt this was an occasion display his wares. 'I realise who I have in front of me, but I also realise that David Tua hasn't done anything to prepare for me. The only preparing he has done is in his training camp by getting a six foot six guy to spar with, but who is going to emulate me? Nobody. All of a sudden he steps into the ring with me, he'll say, "Whoa, what have I gotten myself into?" Tua has nothing for me. You can talk about all the fighters he's beaten but I'm in another league. This isn't the same old story for him. He's going to learn.'

Tua, however, was doing a lot more than going a few rounds with a giant. Leaving behind his girlfriend Robina and his toddler son Kayan for two months, he relocated to the Prince Ranch Resort in the foothills of Mount Charleston, half an hour outside Las Vegas, and worked significantly harder than ever before. He sparred 107 rounds – double his norm – with Shields tutoring him how to slip the jab, to step into firing range, to draw Lewis in and cut off the ring.

'It's no secret we have to get inside,' Shields said, using the old-fashioned trainer-speak of describing the fight as a joint venture. 'We're not going to win by David standing on the outside and jabbing Lennox. But there are plenty of ways for David to win and he knows all the scenarios. We've come up with a pretty good plan, but a plan doesn't mean a thing if you don't have a guy who can execute. Dave is a guy who can execute.'

When the sparring was over, he would do windsprints up and down one of the steeper hills of Mount Charleston. 'At the start of the camp I was doing it once and I could barely get up and my lungs were burning badly, but now I'm running up that hill four times, no problem,' he said. He looked quick and sharp, despite his designer, giant-busting bulk, and he felt he was in magnificent condition, although he later admitted to a sore rib caused by a hook to the body in sparring.

The odds in Las Vegas on a Lewis victory fell from 4–1 to 2–1 in the week before the fight, with huge bets placed on an upset. CNN and *Sports Illustrated* conducted a survey of US boxing fans and found 46 per cent were predicting a Tua knockout. Several top pundits also went this way. Bowe's former trainer Eddie Futch liked the way Tua worked against taller boxers. 'I think Tua will win,' he said. 'I think he will have the strength. He has the power in both hands. He boxes pretty well too. He is younger, stronger, punches just as hard, if not harder, with both hands and he is aggressive. He has what it takes.' Teddy Atlas agreed: 'I'm going with Tua. Lewis, even at his height, allows you to get close at times. Holyfield got close, and in both fights he stung Lewis. Tua can potentially do more than sting him. All Tua needs is that one left hook on the chin.'

The Mandalay Bay Events Center drew a capacity crowd of 12,085, with around a thousand extremely vocal New Zealanders and a handful of Samoans among them. When Tua, sporting an odd, electrified, King-like hairstyle that made his head look like a toilet brush, was heralded in by Polynesian drummers and shell blowers, the Americans roared along with him. Lennox's entrance (fireworks, maidens and knights) received a muted response. By fight time, Las Vegas had taken to Tua and was hoping for an upset.

It was soon clear Lewis wasn't going to try to bash him up like he did with Grant and Botha. This was essentially a jab-and-move job with Lennox moving in the opposite direction from normal – to his left, away from Tua's hook – while popping or prodding his jab into the face. Tua's strategy was to press forward, with slow advances suddenly transformed into explosive bursts when he would fling his whole body into massive, single punches that would bring chants of 'Tu-a! Tu-a! Tu-a!' The first of these, an over-committed launch of a violent left hook, came to nothing. It whooshed by and was easily avoided by Lennox, who countered with a quick right.

Round two offered more of the same, Tua bobbing and weaving and missing while Lennox landed quick jabs and sharp crosses, but it ended with Lewis being clipped on the chin with one of his big hooks, and even though he took it well, Steward was worried. 'When you get on the ropes, keep your hands up and keep moving to the left,' he said. Tua landed another left hook to the chin and an extremely hard right to the body in round three, but Lewis absorbed them without distress, throwing some eye-catching combinations and a stream of jabs. David caught him with two more stiff hooks early in the fourth, but Lennox countered with a sharp cross while gliding around the ring – a huge man moving with elegance and grace. Tua was missing more than landing and most that connected were blocked. 'A couple of times he tried some desperation left hooks,' said Lewis, 'and that's the only thing I was worried about, but I nullified his hook by keeping my right hand up.'

Until then the challenger was still in the fight, but the champion streaked ahead from the fifth. He started picking David off with harder punches, targeting the body as well as the head, while Tua couldn't time his counters to land. But the danger had not yet passed. David managed a heavy right and a left hook that rocked Lennox back on his heels, but Lennox replied with his own right and was soon off again, ending the round with a hard left to the body and another to the head.

Tua's left eye swelled after Lewis hit him with a right in round six; he then worked the body, followed by another right to the head. But just when it was becoming totally one-sided, Tua caught him with a right to the chin that knocked him back into the ropes. Once again he absorbed it well and came back with his first hard uppercut of the fight. 'There's no fucking tomorrow!' Shields screamed at David. 'You gotta come on now!'

Lennox's movement, his size and the pain of those long, quick punches were too much. By the end of the night he'd averaged 44 jabs per round (landing eighteen) – one every four seconds – and as the rounds passed the jabs became heavier. Late in round seven he fired a hard cross that snapped Tua's head back, followed by several hurtful combinations. 'You're not jabbing, you're not doing nothing!' Shields yelled. 'You gotta get the confidence to do something. You gotta get on top of the guy.'

But the 35-year-old Lewis, moving like the 25-year-old Ali, wasn't allowing him to do anything. When David came close he pushed him away like a cheeky child, then snapped his head back with another combination. Shields was beside himself. 'This is the champion!' You've gotta take the title and you're not working. The guy won't just sit down and say, "Here it is." You need a knockout now!' So Tua charged in for round nine and flung his hook at Lennox, who deftly stepped back, shifted to his left and came in with a short right cross, which he followed up with combinations of three or four. 'I was doing all the work in there,' he recalled. 'I thought he was trying to get me tired by getting me to use all my punches and then come in with some kind of offence in the later rounds, but all he did was plod, step around and throw his hook.'

Early in round ten Lewis staggered Tua for the first time in his career after landing an impeccably timed, extremely hard and fast left–right combination that forced an involuntary dip of the knees. But those 30-inch thighs were magnificent shock absorbers, and he recovered quickly. With the crowd chanting his name, he kept throwing hopeful hooks, but without the foot speed to cut off the ring, none came close. Once again, Shields pleaded, 'You gotta give me punches now,' but Tua simply had no clue how to get past the jab or to nullify the movement and the thud of hard punches proved so discouraging. Late in the eleventh a right cross–left hook combination had Tua retreating again. His left eye was closing, he seemed tired and thoroughly dispirited. Lewis still looked fresh and lively.

Sending his man into the final round, Shields had one more desperate attempt at engendering a response – if not through inspiration, then at least through guilt. 'You doing nothing to win the title. You got one round. You are the puncher. Now go out and punch!' Tua tried, with big, single punches that hit nothing but air or were expertly blocked. Midway through the round Lennox landed a hard, chopping right and Tua grinned defiantly in response. It was all he had to offer, but at least it was better than capitulation. 'David Tua has a great chin,' Lennox acknowledged. 'I'll give him credit for that. I hit him with some good right hands and he smiled at me, so I hit him again and he smiled again.' Over the final 45 seconds Lennox was back on his toes, putting on an exhibition of his skills for the crowd. Tua's final humiliation was a desperate and easily evaded charge that sent him careering head-first into the ropes. As he hurtled past, Lennox whacked him twice more in the body. When the bell rang his head was peering into the press benches, where he knew he could expect to find no comfort.

The CompuBox count showed Lewis landed 300 of 674 punches to Tua's 110 out of 413, indicating that for every three punches attempted by David, Lennox tried five, and for every one absorbed, Lennox landed three. It was hard to see that Tua had genuinely won anything more than the third round, but two of the judges gave him merit points for trying. Dave Moretti made it eleven rounds to one, which seemed right, while Chuck Giampa made it ten rounds to two and Jerry Roth nine rounds to three.

Lennox Lewis had achieved what he'd set out to do: retain his world title by completely nullifying the assets of an extremely dangerous opponent while showing off his own refined range of skills. It wasn't spectacular but for those who appreciated calculated, 'scientific' boxing, it was impressive stuff. Never before had such a big man been so light on his feet in a boxing ring, and despite Lewis's age he'd maintained it without any sign of exhaustion. There was a hint of disdain about his own assessment. 'When you declare war on me you've got to come with more than a left hook and a bad hairstyle,' he said. 'You bring your whole arsenal. I'm a pugilist specialist. I box inside and outside, I can move. I'm a boxer-puncher. You've got to be able to do all those things to be the best. What was wrong with David Tua was Lennox Lewis.' And because he'd boxed from the Ali template he offered an impromptu, ersatz Ali rhyme, although on this terrain his blows fell short: 'If Tyson wants to come test/I'll put him to rest./Remember, Lennox Lewis is the best.' Even Lennox seemed to cringe after this popped out of his mouth. He smiled, suggesting this wasn't to be taken seriously and quickly moved in a different direction, praising Tua's ability to take punches and his own pugilist specialist's ability to land them. 'You could say I'm like fine wine,' he concluded. 'I get better with age.'

And what of David Tua? While Kevin Barry muttered about the pain of a pre-fight rib injury, David said he had no excuses. All he could offer was a string of apologies to the peoples of Samoa and New Zealand and a vow to do better the next time he fought a giant. 'Lennox Lewis is a great champion,' he said. 'He came out and did what he had to do. Thank God I wasn't seriously injured. I give so much respect and credit to Lennox Lewis.'

CHAPTER TWENTY TWO
UPPER CLAPTON,
EAST LONDON, 2004

If you live in London it's a long way from WC1 to E5, particularly if you're thinking metaphorically. Certainly Panos Eliades' eastward journey gives the impression of a slide – from the plush Bloomsbury Square offices of the master liquidator and big league boxing promoter to the less salubrious surroundings of Theydon Road, Upper Clapton, where he's struggling to fight off the demand for the £3.5 million he owes Lennox Lewis after being found liable for civil fraud, racketeering and breach of fiduciary duty. Some would take such a tumble as cause for self-critical introspection. After all, the bare facts of his legal defeats suggest that, at best, his judgement was flawed. But with Panos, the question 'Where did I go wrong?' is seldom turned very far inwards. He prefers a different angle altogether: where did everyone else go wrong?

Over the last couple of years, ever since launching a legal suit against Lennox, Panos has had a terrible time of it in the American and British courts. His personal reputation, professional standing and financial well-being have been battered. First, in 2002 a New York jury found against him, and in favour of Lennox, on questions relating to his probity and trustworthiness to the tune of over $6 million plus interest, and he was also ordered to pay $600,000 to his American promotional partners Main Events. He then fought Lennox's attempt to get the judgement applied in Britain, but lost. Finally, in 2004, Panos was fined $73,000 by a US District Judge for contempt of court. But none of this shakes his conviction that he is right.

His starting point is a curious reading of the New York judgement. 'They found that Lennox owed me a million dollars and that I short-changed him by $56,000 and that I must pay an additional $300,000 penalty,' he begins. 'Because of this $56,000 irregularity, the court decided I had no right to earn 30 per cent for his future fights. On top of that American juries have the right to punish you and this jury found that because I was an accountant with financial expertise I should pay him damages to the tune of nearly ten million.' And he adds bitterly, 'That's the beauty of the American court system. When I started with Lennox he didn't have a dime to his name; when I left he had something like $63 million, and the jury punishes me for short-changing him by $56,000. And now they've decided to try to make me bankrupt by trying to enforce the judgement in the UK, although here in Britain the High Court knocked it down from ten million dollars to five million, so you can see it's already being reduced.'

It is worth pointing out that this version is not quite that of the courts. He was, in fact, held liable for $56,400 as damages for fraud (not for 'short-changing' or 'irregularities'), almost $400,000 (not $300,000) for violating the RICO anti-racketeering act, and $6.8 million for breach of fiduciary duty. These amounts were set against the $1 million owed by Lewis to Eliades for the Tua fight, leaving Panos liable for $6.27 million. The RICO proportion was subsequently trebled on appeal, taking the amount owed to over $7 million but reduced again to £3.5 million (just under $6 million; not $5 million) after Panos unsuccessfully contested the applicability of the American judgement in the British courts.

But to Panos these differences are neither here nor there, because he doesn't accept the view of the courts. By early 2005 his appeal to the House of Lords, and his US appeal to have the original trial declared a mistrial, will have been decided, and he talks of vindication. 'Lennox once said to me, "Panos, I would hate to go against you," and now he has,' he says in a tone chosen to suggest the wilful craziness of taking arms against such a deep sea of troubles. 'I'm too proud to accept the New York result and just walk away. It was disgraceful. Lennox should have paid me a million and then another million to say, "Thank you for all you've done, and I really appreciate it, but I've decided to go it alone," but instead they tried to take away my dignity in New York and made me look like a thief. Well, he's won the first eleven rounds but I win on a knockout in round twelve. These cases have cost Lennox millions and in the end could end up destroying him completely, because I believe in God. I'm a God-fearing person, and if there is justice then the truth will come out and the truth will set me free.'

Panos takes a scattergun approach to the question of why it came to all this, starting with the general and moving towards the specific. First, he blames the sport and those who populate it before honing in on Lennox's feckless friends and associates. 'When I was around we used to hire a limousine for the three hours that we needed it, but these hangers-on and good-for-nothings who I wouldn't tolerate, they would hire the limousine for twenty-four hours on standby and run up thousands of dollars in limousine fees. They would have sixteen people in a room in a top New York hotel, all ordering room service on Lennox's account; when I was around I would tell them to get out. These were people without two bob to their name.' His point is that the kind of person who filches on limousines and steak platters will take everything he can get his grubby hands on. 'These upstarts just earned money off Lennox without any investment. The fact of the matter is that I picked up Lennox when he didn't have a pot to piss in, and when I left he was at the top of the world. I was the only one who could negotiate with the likes of Don King. I'm expensive, but I'm good, and I made a major investment which none of them did. There's a saying, "when the plum is ripe, then you can eat it", and that's when the gang moved in.'

It isn't just that he doesn't care for Lennox's friends. He takes it further, because as he views it, these are not just any friends, they are 'black friends – a group of brothers, I think that's the word they use', whose whispering fed into Lennox's black-and-white view of the world. Perhaps a different way of looking at it is that the black-and-white view of the world is Panos's, because it has to be said that issues of race crop up rather a lot when he gets rolling. When talking about his meeting with Lennox and Dennis's other brother, for instance, he mentions he couldn't quite work out whether the man was older or younger than Lennox. 'because they all look pretty much the same to me – a bit like the Chinese'. And when talking about Eugene Maloney's resignation in 1994, he comments, 'Sometimes, when a black man is using a white man like a slave you create a huge amount of resentment. Black people can abuse white people because of slavery.'

His point is that this colour consciousness played a role. 'You see, Lennox is a very clever man and a very proud man but he's a proud black man who is prejudiced against the white man. Lennox will support the black against the white. He's very pro-black. When we went to a restaurant together he would count the number of black people working there and he wouldn't go back if there were too few blacks.' Panos concludes this leg of his case by claiming that the black friends took advantage of Lennox's 'pro-black' views. 'They started whispering that Panos is white and he's stealing from you and we can do the job at one-tenth the price, and their eventual proof was that I short-changed him out of $56,000 – out of $100 million. It's a mismatch of monsters.' He doesn't offer evidence that anything of the sort was whispered because, in his terms, it simply must be so. Why else?

His next thesis involves a stab at psychology. In essence, he claims that the peculiarities of Lennox's upbringing turned him into a self-centred bastard. 'You see, Lennox and I had a relationship like a father and son, but because he was never raised by his father he never learned how to treat a father figure, and that's one of the problems with him. You know, you can influence Lennox by giving him bullshit but he can also be manipulated by financial reward. He just discards people when he can afford to. That's why he got rid of his brother, Dennis.'

And finally, there's the corrupted-by-power explanation, as seen through the gothic novel or at least the Boris Karloff version. 'I began to see a different kind of human being from the one I first saw,' he says. 'He became a monster through the power I gave him. He became like Frankenstein's monster, and now he's trying to destroy his maker.'

The picture he paints of his own demise is certainly impressive in terms of depth of pathos. On the one hand there's the urchin 'without a dime to his name', 'without a pot to piss in', saved from the poorhouse by his worldly-wise but kindly maker/father who leads him along the path of righteousness to a pot of gold. And what does the urchin do? Why, of course, he kicks father in the balls, grabs the whole pot for himself and tries to take dad's house and the clothes off his back too. He does this because he's rotten inside, and because the money his father/maker earned for him turned him even more rotten, and because he was led astray by his even rottener group of grasping friends – rotten black friends, yes.

It's a version of Lewis, his career and Panos's role in it that few would recognise. By any other calculation Panos got quite a catch when he purchased the contract in 1991. By then the Olympic super heavyweight gold medallist was the European champion and an unbeaten top-twelve contender with considerable assets and an enormous earning potential. In the absence of Panos some other promoter would have taken up the reins, his career would probably have proceeded pretty much the same way, and he would still have ended up earning his £100 million. Here and there he might have done even better – like securing a get-out clause in his HBO contract that would have made negotiations with Tyson easier or not being forced to vacate his WBA title. Without Lennox Lewis, however, Panos Eliadis would never have entered boxing and would never have been able to take those 30 per cent bites at the boxer's million-dollar purses.

There is another explanation of why it all went wrong. The picture painted in the court during the New York trial, and unanimously accepted by the jury, was of a man who acted dishonestly and breached his fiduciary duty. In particular, there remains the question of the missing $56,400, which Panos does not dispute. The court called it plain and simple fraud; Panos prefers the softer word 'short-changed' but declines to offer an explanation of why he short-changed a boxer whose money he was supposed to protect. Instead he dismisses it as of no consequence. 'Losing $56,000 to Lennox Lewis is just like losing a farthing to you,' he says. 'If they still had farthings.'

Lennox was starting to relish his role as undisputed world heavyweight champion. He delighted in the sense of respect coming his way from both sides of the Atlantic and all over the world and for the first time in his career he felt a sense of contentment. 'I didn't enjoy it before because there were so many unbelievers out there,' he said, 'but now that they're believing and I've proved my point, I can relax and go live my life the way I want. I have the respect I wanted to get and now I can go out and have fun.' Despite HBO's reservations, his plan was to make an easy defence in South Africa against the American Hasim Rahman; then secure his final, career-defining fight against Mike Tyson. Part of this final furlong was to assume absolute control of his destiny – something he'd wanted for a couple of years. With his mandatory defence out of the way, he felt it was time to make a move. In future, those in his team playing a managerial role would be salaried employees – some with the usual bonuses and small percentage incentives but they would not be major shareholders or co-owners or partners, and they would have no ultimate authority.

This was fresh territory for a boxer, very different from the days when promoters decided exactly who would be the next opponent and how much each man would be earning without bothering to consult those on the giving and receiving ends; from the days when managers spoke for their boxers, using the pronoun 'we' as if their part in contractual negotiation could really stack up against the part of actually getting whacked. Ever since Muhammad Ali boxers have found it easier to find their individual voices, and a handful acquired sufficient financial pull to chop and change promoters, hire and fire and control their own destinies. For a boxer to promote himself, however, was a step further, although Lewis was not alone in this pioneering venture. Roy Jones and Oscar de la Hoya were also moving in this direction, while Naseem Hamed, Sheffield's declining world featherweight champion, decided to cash in on his status as the most marketable little man in boxing history by parting ways first with Warren and then with his manager-trainer Brendan Ingle. He ceded his management to his brothers, with

Barry Hearn retained as the hired help, paid a fee for the job of putting bums on seats but without a percentage of the profits.

Lennox examined these precedents and decided to take it further still, by becoming his own promoter, without outside help. But he has a gentler personality than the abrasively egocentric Prince Naseem, so he wanted to handle the change in a more dignified and less acrimonious way. He hoped to keep the backbiting out of the public arena, but this would depend on those who were dropped taking it philosophically. Dennis could be relied on to absorb the blow while keeping his toys in the cot, and Frank Maloney was being retained and restrained for the time being. Panos, however, was not one for a graceful bow.

Lewis held a press conference in London in February 2001. Maloney was chosen to read out a statement saying, 'Panos Eliades has no right to hold himself out as promoting any future Lennox Lewis bouts or representing Lennox Lewis in any capacity whatsoever in relation to any future bout.' Lennox hoped it would go no further and that the remaining details would be settled behind closed doors, but Panos was incandescent. He claimed to be protected by a long-term contract with both Lewis and HBO and felt this move was a betrayal and reflected a moral deterioration in the world champion. 'I feel like a father abandoned by his son,' he said. 'Lennox now has no time for those who helped make him. Lennox has changed. He is not the man you think he is. I gave him the crown and he has taken my head, but fame and money does funny things to people.' He built on this attack, based on the strange notion that he, Panos, had created Lewis, delivered the world title to him and that the champion therefore had an ethical duty to maintain the relationship. He also kept plugging the theme that handing the keys to a man like Adrian Ogun was a 'joke' and that it would end in tears. 'We created a huge monster, and look what happened,' he said. 'Lewis is ungrateful, and he suffers from selective memory loss. I think he is heading for disaster, if not in the ring then on a personal level.'

Maloney relished the chance to hit back. 'Panos is a very bitter and twisted man who is acting like a divorced wife on the poor end of a settlement,' he said with obvious glee because he enjoyed the spectacle of his old boss getting the sack while, once again, he survived. He then put the boot in by drawing attention to Panos's struggles. 'Since I left to join Frank Warren nothing has gone right for Panos. He's had three shows cancelled by Sky and has failed to deliver certain fights.' He even paid a minor compliment to Ogun in order to get in another kick in. 'At the end of the day, if Lennox Lewis is happy, that's all that counts. Adrian Ogun is prepared to listen, but Panos took all the decisions himself. He believes that when God handed out brains he was the only one in the room.'

Ogun and his boss eventually responded to Panos's attacks by accusing him of mismanagement. What followed was a bitter dispute over the issue of who owed whom. Ogun, Violet and others in the team convinced Lennox that it was possible he had not received all that was due to him. They felt that before any final payments were made his finances needed to be scrutinised and they pointed to the $200,000 from the Botha fight that had yet to be paid to Lewis. Ogun called for Eliades to be stripped of his promotional licence because of this shortfall.

Eliades had a different perspective on all this, insisting he was a greviously wronged man of honour. He acknowledged he did indeed owe $200,000 from the Botha fight but said he wanted to set this off against the $1 million owed to him for his minor role in the Tua fight. 'After the Tua fight I got two cheques,' he said, 'and we needed two signatures for each. My cheque was for one million dollars and Lennox's was for five million, so I signed both cheques and sent them to Adrian Ogun but then Adrian didn't sign my cheque. They said, "Pay us the $200,000 first," but I wasn't getting caught again, so I refused, and instead I sued Lennox for my million plus my fee for the remainder of my career as his promoter, because the HBO contract was a brilliant contract, and because I was on 30 per cent I would have received 30 million.'

This proved to be the most disastrous move of Panos' business career, and the decision to start in New York added to his woes. Lewis retained a top US trial attorney, Judd Burstein, whom Eliades now acknowledges is 'very good and very ruthless', and Burstein got to work on securing the best defence Lennox's money could buy. As happens in many major American civil trials, he initiated not only a legal search of the paper trail using a team of forensic accountants, but also a thorough investigation of Eliades's day-to-day dealings. Panos bitterly recalled: 'They went back eleven years for copies of all the documentation – sixty thousand pieces of paper – and they got a team of detectives to follow me around, and my wife and children, to find out who was screwing who.' Without Eliades's writ there would have been no Burstein, no private detectives, no investigation of his bookkeeping records and no counter-suit. As Burstein explained, the fraud came to light only because Eliades 'made the horrific mistake of actually suing Lennox Lewis'.

Much to Panos's irritation, Lennox attended each of the ten days of the New York trial and when the jury found in his favour he soberly stated: 'I am satisfied that justice has been done today.' Today he says he was astonished to discover Eliades was defrauding him and that he'd been reluctant to believe those, including his mother, who warned him on this score. 'At first, when people were telling me about it, I didn't really take it in,' he said. 'I heard the rumours but there were a lot of whispers and rumours about all sorts of things, and that doesn't make them true, and I just didn't believe he was ripping me off. So I was shocked at what came out.' Of the court case itself, he added, 'Listen, this is a big thing. It's not easy to sue someone without conclusive evidence and it's particularly hard to get a judgement against someone on racketeering allegations, yet he was proved to be a racketeer. Anyone who lies all the time like he does – he lies all the time – is a despicable person. He's just a thief. He ripped me off.'

Eliades insists his view will be vindicated. '$56,000 is insignificant if you look at all he's earned through me but he's trying to destroy me because he feels I stole ten million, which I didn't. If you examine the judgement you'll see that all but the $56,000 was in penalties, and if you consider I put well over a million pounds of my own money into Lennox Lewis College, why would I steal $56,000? You see, Lennox prefers to hear what he wants to hear, and it's very easy to believe what you want to believe.'

The Manhattan jury members were not the only ones to prefer the truth according to Lennox. When he left the New York court, a relieved Lewis said, 'I can now concentrate on my boxing career.' He thought it was over but, a bit like a more fortunate version of Kafka's K, his trial never seemed to end, taking hundreds of hours of his time, with the case knocked from one court to another, finally ending up at the Court of Appeal in London. Eliades's barristers argued that because of a conflict of law between the British and American legal systems the New York judgement could not be applied in the UK, which would mean that Lennox would be unable to make any claim on Panos's British assets. The issue of contention was the trebling of the anti-racketeering penalty, permitted under the American RICO Act, with no equivalent in British law. Eventually, in October 2003, the three law lords reached a simple solution – 'correcting' the trebling of the penalty by not applying it. As Lord Justice Potter ruled: 'The robust and sensible approach is not to treat the multiple damages element of the judgement as definitive or "infecting" its character as a whole.' Eliades was therefore ordered to pay up the rest, which amounted to £3.5 million when applied in sterling.

It seemed to Lennox that everything had finally been settled, but in March 2004 it was back in court in Manhattan. Two years earlier the US District Judge Harold Baer made a ruling to restrict Panos from making any financial transactions that could hide funds or make the money difficult to collect. Burstein appeared in court listing ten different ways he believed Eliades was defying this order, such as transferring ownership of his Mercedes-Benz to someone else and transferring his interest in some investments to avoid Lennox's discovering them. He asked Judge Baer to throw Panos in jail or to appoint a federal prosecutor to begin drawing up criminal charges. In the end, however, Baer found that Panos was in contempt of court only for exceeding the daily spending limits imposed by the order, and slapped him with a $73,000 fine, which he had to pay in 30 days. 'Another piece of bad news for Panos,' said a sardonic John Hornewer when he heard about the judgement. 'Although perhaps for Panos these days that would count as good news.'

It wasn't only Panos who suffered for his rash decision to challenge Lewis in court. Burstein was shocked to discover that Panos's lawyer, Milt Chwasky, was also Lennox's lawyer. Eliades had an endearing explanation for this double deal: 'You see, Lennox and I had a relationship like a father and son, and Milton was a lawyer I employed, and he's a lovely man, so, as a favour to Lennox, I used to ask Milt to give him advice. And let me tell you, he did a lot of good work for Lennox because Milton and I were the only people who could deal with Don King without giving King rights to his future fights, which is what we achieved with the Holyfield fight. But Burstein really is ruthless and he advised Lennox to sue Milton because, as my lawyer, he shouldn't have been giving Lennox legal advice, and therefore he must repay all the legal fees he received from Lennox. Milton is a seventy-five-year-old man with cancer, and it nearly destroyed him.'

Burstein viewed it from a different angle, arguing there was a fundamental conflict of interest that contributed to Lennox being defrauded. He pointed out that Chwasky was paid $1.6 million by Lewis in legal fees, while also representing Eliadis at the same time (and, in once case, the casino fight venue as well) but 'looked the other way when bad things started happening because he embraced every conflict imaginable. He's exactly what's wrong with boxing.' He advised Lewis to sue for damages. Chwasky responded with dismay, describing the accusations as 'a crock of shit' while his lawyer, Jethro Eisenstein, claimed Milt had given Lewis nothing but 'valuable and faithful service'.

The case rested heavily on Lewis's testimony in court. In essence he argued that Chwasky knew or should have known about Panos's manipulation of accounts. 'He should have kept me informed,' he told the jury of seven women and one man. 'He should have told me Panos was ripping me off.' When pressed by Eisenstein, he acknowledged the obvious point that he had made millions of dollars while working with Chwasky and that he couldn't be certain precisely what knowledge Milt retained about Panos's activities, but he kept pressing his contention that Chwasky never explained the conflict of interest in working for a boxer and his promoter at the same time. He also dismissed the rather odd suggestion that he should have made the lawyer more involved in the administration of his personal expenses. 'That part of the business was about paying the gardener, buying a car, buying fish,' Lennox said. 'Why do I need a lawyer to buy fish?' At one point Eisenstein became so exasperated at his inability to stump Lewis that he began screaming at him. 'Please stop yelling,' said Lennox softly. 'It confuses me when you shout.'

The jury found unanimously in Lennox's favour and awarded him $1.175 million in damages. Lennox gave a nod and a slight smile when he heard the result. 'I'm showing the rest of the world and other athletes, especially boxers, to fight for their rights,' he said.

But such fights can be more draining than those in the ring. Immediately after the judgement Chwasky, like Eliades, announced that 'the legal process is not over', and as these cases drag on the lawyers' bills mount while the spoils of legal victory remain frustratingly elusive. But at least Lennox Lewis knows that he has tens of millions to go before his own resources are drained.

As for Panos Eliades, well, he just about keeps afloat – at least until his remaining legal options are exhausted. 'I'm doing accountancy, liquidation, and I'm still involved with property,' he said. 'But I will have nothing to do with boxing any more. When you're dealing with boxing people you have to realise you're dealing with people who have no morals, and your word means nothing, It's a cesspit of the worst scum you can get.'

CHAPTER TWENTY THREE
JOHANNESBURG,
SOUTH AFRICA, 2001

It's the morning after Lennox Lewis's second professional defeat. Thirty hours earlier he was still the undisputed (or barely disputed) heavyweight champion of the world, but now he's back in the queue and already his conqueror is trying to wriggle out of the return clause. He's had a sad, slow day and night and even the close friends within his huge entourage are struggling to find the appropriate words of compassion. In fact, he seems to be doing more to console them than the other way around. He tells them over and over again that it was just a lucky punch, one of the occupational hazards of heavyweight boxing: you beat someone up for four and three-quarter rounds, batter them till they can almost take it no more, and then, boom! One 238lb whack on the jaw and you're gone. And no heavyweight in the world would have risen in time from that one, fast count or not.

The last time this happened he headed for the Jamaican hills to contemplate his future. This time he's heading for the game reserve, but there's an appointment to keep. He's cancelled a few outings in the past week, but this is one he wouldn't contemplate missing for anything. It's a moment he has dreamed about for over a decade.

Lennox first learned about Nelson Mandela when he was starting secondary school in Canada at a time when the man they call Madiba was still in his prison cell on Robben Island. In those days, neither Lewis nor Mandela would have been permitted to live in the leafy, high-walled suburb of Houghton where the fallen fighter is heading. If you had dark skin and hair that held a pencil then you were classified as Bantu, which meant you were required to carry your dompas (passbook) at all times if you hoped to work in or visit any part of white South Africa, which made up 70 per cent of the land. It's good to see this much, at least, has changed, although Lennox admits he's been a bit taken aback to discover how many things are still pretty much the same in this 'new' South Africa: mostly white people still at the top; mostly black people at the bottom. Anyway, ever since Madiba's 1990 release, Lennox has longed to meet him. They had a brief chat before the fight, but this is the real thing – the chance for a genuine conversation in his hero's home.

Hasim Rahman, the new heavyweight champion of the world, the successor to Johnson, Dempsey, Louis, Marciano, Ali, Tyson and Lewis, is also supposed to pay his respects. He'd been doing brilliantly over the previous few weeks, playing to the cameras and hugging the press. Only yesterday morning he told them he planned to return 'home' to defend his title – home, he explained, being 'Africa and South Africa'. But a few hours later he slipped off to another home, in Baltimore, missing his date with Madiba, because, after all, a rhetorical home is not the same as a real one. But for Lennox Lewis, responding to Nelson Mandela's invitation and finally meeting him was a major part of his decision to agree to this disastrous, cut-rate defence of his world title, so there is no consideration of moping the morning away in his hotel room and no chance of being late as usual.

The Mercedes arrives in the Houghton driveway at the appointed time and out steps the former world champion, this time without his post-fight shades, and with his locks tied up for the occasion, but otherwise looking relaxed in jeans and a blue South African T-shirt bearing a picture of the Johannesburg skyline. He's relieved Rahman won't be joining them. Without Hasim he'll get to spend time more or less alone – if you don't count the scores of journalists and photographers outside – with the man he most admires in the whole wide world. For today's chat it's just Lennox and Violet (dressed down in a white shirt and leggings), and there to greet them is Madiba in one of those loose, multi coloured shirts he always wears, with a conciliatory smile on his 82-year-old face.

Lennox has been briefed that Mandela follows boxing and even tried it in his youth, but, as he discovers, it went a bit further than that. Mandela was in prison for the Liston, Ali, Frazier, Foreman, Holmes and Tyson eras, but, one way or another, he kept himself informed. When you interview him and raise the subject of boxing, he seems delighted and speaks about it with a detailed knowledge, revealing an up-to-date interest.

In the early 1950s, when he was in his mid-thirties and Rocky Marciano was champion, he used to train up to four days a week, arriving home from his attorney's office, picking up his eldest son Thembi, and then driving to a community centre in Orlando, Soweto. Thembi would sometimes lead the sessions, picking out his dad for criticism. 'Mister Mandela, you are wasting our time this evening. If you cannot keep up, why not go home and sit with the old women,' he would say, and everyone would laugh, including his father. In those days Madiba was a beefy man, weighing about 30lb more than today, and he was classed as a heavyweight. Although he never took part in any official tournaments he sparred regularly with both amateurs and professionals, but acknowledges he was nothing special. As he put it in his autobiography, *A Long Walk to Freedom*, 'I had neither enough power to compensate for my lack of speed nor enough speed to make up for my lack of power.' But he liked what he called the 'egalitarian ethos' of the game, loved the physical exercise, and most of all appreciated the 'science' of boxing – the strategy and tactics of advance and retreat, defence and attack, and the need to pace yourself, which all seemed like a metaphor for the struggle to liberate his country.

It is in these areas he feels Lennox was lacking against Rahman, but he makes these points gently, placing less stress on the causes of failure than on the potential for overcoming it. When they go inside, Mandela puts his hand on Lennox's arm and tells him he was sorry to have missed the fight but he could not cancel an overseas trip and only returned a few hours after it was over, but he watched a recording on television as soon as he arrived home and, like everyone else, was shocked by the result. 'You know, Lennox, it is the nature of sport to have wins and losses but you will always be our champion and if you train properly for the rematch you will regain your titles,' he says, before revealing his grasp of heavyweight history. 'Joe

Louis was knocked out by Max Schmelling, but in the rematch knocked Schmelling out in the first round. Muhammad Ali won the heavyweight championship twice more after he had it taken from him the first time, and, Lennox, I think you will have a very, very good chance of coming back to beat this, uh, Hasim Rahman. That was a lucky shot he caught you with, but if I may be so bold to say, there is something you must look out for. When I saw the replay a few minutes after I arrived home, I saw that you weren't using your jab when you were knocked out.'

Lennox listens intently, nodding as the old man gives him encouragement and advice, and after a while they move off the subject of boxing and the former world champion finally has a chance to ask the former political prisoner a question he has been wanting to pose for several years. 'I have to ask you this,' he begins. 'Don't you feel hate because of what you went through under apartheid, and because of the fact that they put you in jail for so long? Didn't you feel hate for them when you came out of jail?' Mandela offers an understanding smile because he can appreciate why foreigners find this difficult to understand. He tells Lennox that he could hate the injustice of the system without hating individuals, and that he felt a sense of love for all South Africans after he was released.

When the photographers enter to take pictures of a beaming Mandela with his right arm around Lennox's shoulder and his left arm around Violet's, he turns to the former champion and reminds him, 'Don't worry, you'll always be our champion.' A few minutes later, with the press watching, he throws a playful right to the chin. 'I know that punch well now,' Lennox says to him, 'and I promise you Rahman will not catch me with it again.'

More than any other factor it was Mandela's appeal that persuaded Lewis to defend his world heavyweight title in South Africa in April 2001. When he first mooted the idea at the time of the Tua fight, there was strong opposition within his camp, particularly from Panos, who was not yet aware that he was about to be dropped. He preferred one of the alternative proposals, from Europe, Canada and America. There was also opposition from HBO, which had put up with Lennox's desire to hold the Botha fight in London and felt it was time to return to the real world – Las Vegas. But Lennox insisted, and his will prevailed. As he explained it while training in Vegas, 'Nelson Mandela was very involved in the idea. He is a great fan of boxing and he likes boxers, and I have the utmost respect for him. He has been through so much. I wanted to do something to show my admiration for Mr Mandela, and having this fight in South Africa is my way of honouring him.'

Aside from the Mandela factor he wanted to make a statement of identity with his African roots and provide inspiration and hope to African youth and to poor people. He'd seen the documentary *When We Were Kings* about Ali regaining his title by beating Foreman in what was then Zaire, and felt inspired to follow his example. But 27 years had passed since then and the world of satellite communication had changed. They needed a city that could easily cope with the organisational and technological demands of the twenty-first century. The only viable option was Johannesburg or somewhere nearby, and only one South African promoter had any hope of pulling it off. That was Rodney Berman, a friendly, usually easy-going but extremely astute white South African lawyer who was then in partnership with Cedric Kushner, the obese ex-Capetonian who was one of the major promoters who admitted bribing Bobby Lee for favours from the IBF.

Kushner had a contract with a hard-hitting American heavyweight contender called Hasim 'The Rock' Rahman, so he was chosen as the opponent, with Berman as co-promoter, Johannesburg the venue and 'Thunder in Africa' the billing. Lennox hoped for a big stadium where large numbers of black people could buy cut-rate tickets, but in the end he left the details to his aides who agreed to a casino venue in a place called Brakpan a few miles outside Johannesburg, which seated a mere 5,500 people. They were told this was the only viable option, partly because the fight would begin after five a.m. (so that the American HBO viewers could watch the fight at a civilised time), but the team was assured that Lennox would get plenty of opportunity to travel to the black townships and meet the people. Having concluded the agreement, Ogun sent Maloney out to Johannesburg to check it all out and he reported back that all was in order with the venue and accommodation, but warned that the altitude of over 6,000 feet could create acclimatisation problems and that it would be ideal to arrive there six weeks before the fight.

The difficulty was that Lennox had signed a contract to take part in Steven Soderbergh's remake of the Rat Pack classic *Ocean's Eleven*, starring George Clooney, Brad Pitt and Julia Roberts. His cameo was a familiar one: a world champion whose fight against his challenger (played by the Ukrainian Wladimir Klitschko) never happens. This meant a later arrival time in Johannesburg and a training camp in Las Vegas, where the film was set, rather than at high altitude in Big Bear. Maloney sent a memo to Lewis and Ogun, suggesting a compromise. 'We need to be in South Africa for no less than 21 days. We should arrive on Saturday, 31 March 2001, to start training on the Monday.' He listed some of the problems: 'Time difference, flying time, altitude (a big one).' Their altitude expert, Joe Dunbar, reiterated this advice. 'When Adrian made the agreement to fight in Johannesburg I don't think anybody realised it was at such altitude, but as soon as I heard I told Lennox, "You must be there six weeks before the fight," but he said he'd committed himself to doing *Ocean's Eleven* and would be sued for millions if he pulled out. So we had to work around that commitment, training in Las Vegas, which wasn't ideal, and arriving in Johannesburg two weeks after Rahman, which gave him a big advantage. It's a physiological fact that arriving late at high altitude will affect your performance. It was like running the hundred metres and giving the other guy a ten-metre start.'

The original film schedule meant he would be able to arrive on the date Maloney suggested but an eight-day postponement meant his departure date was delayed. The companion problem was that Manny Steward was contracted to work with Naseem Hamed for his world featherweight title defence against Mexico's Marco Antonio Barrera, two weeks before the Rahman fight. This meant that Steward would have to shuttle between the two camps and would not be able to give Lennox his consistent attention until the Hamed gig was over. Here, too, Lennox had no complaint. Manny would be able to do two jobs at once, and if there were gaps they could be filled by Harold. After all, Rahman was no Tyson. Lennox's work-plan reflected this low-level risk assessment.

Las Vegas proved a difficult place for full speed training. There was no sense of isolation, and this affected the unity in the camp. Lennox stayed with Scott in a double-storeyed wooden house overlooking a golf course, with Violet around the corner, still cooking his dinners, and the rest of the team members scattered in rented houses and hotels nearby. There was a lot of driving to be done – to the gym, to the hills, to restaurants – and it was hard to be on time when faced with Vegas gridlock. This created tension. Lennox and Scott were bickering, and so were others in the camp.

By the end the physical indicators suggested he was not as fit as he'd been for most of his previous fights. 'Everything he does in training camp is logged in incredible detail, right down to how many punches he throws at the bags,' said Dunbar, 'and the fact is, this was one of his lighter camps in terms of workload. But the reason wasn't so much that he took it too lightly, because his actual training was fairly good, but more down to circumstances. For a start, he had a short camp and then he had to break it for this movie and then the movie was delayed.' To make matters worse, once the shoot was done he decided to delay his departure by a couple more days, to give him the chance to cheer on his little friend Naseem Hamed, just as Hamed had done for him in the past.

Naseem, a first-generation Yemeni-Yorkshireman, was once a boxer of astonishing brilliance, with a combination of speed, reflexes and power never seen before in a British ring. He talked of winning world titles in six divisions and of leaving victims like Oscar de la Hoya in his wake. When he won his first version of the featherweight title at 21 he seemed untouchable, but instead of progressing he went into decline, despite effectively unifying the title and beating a string of champions. He reached America in 1997 where he became an instant celebrity, but by then he was past his best. His problem was hubris on a gargantuan scale: a belief that he'd been chosen by Allah to become a 'legend'. At 21 he gave up running; at 22 he stopped training between fights. He fought less often and refused to listen to his trainer, Brendan Ingle. He ate as he pleased, which meant training camps concentrated on weight reduction. He became impatient with working for openings, preferring to blast his way to victory. His ability to avoid punches, based entirely on reflexes, speed and anticipation, was dulled by neglect and he started taking hits he would once have avoided. He dumped Ingle, took on two new trainers – a yes-man called Oscar Suarez and to help him, Manny Steward – and required them to alternate between rounds.

For a while it worked and his record improved to 35 straight wins, but by the time he arrived in camp to train for the formidable former world champion Barerra he'd been out of the ring for seven months and was 25lb overweight. They struggled to bring him down to featherweight and Steward failed to convince him that he might need to box his way to victory. He spent time on the golf course and seemed more worried about his hairstyle than his opponent, believing one punch was all it would take. Naseem, who had started taking his Islamic upbringing more seriously, entered the ring to piped religious chants and went about the business of bashing up Barerra for God's glory and his own. But instead the Mexican brawler turned boxer, and Hamed failed to connect, losing his title on points. It was a bad day for British boxing and for Emmanuel Steward, whose reputation as a miracle man took a hit. And it was a good warning about the price of complacency.

Saddened by the demise of the Prince, Lennox left Las Vegas with the firm idea of vindicating British boxing by doing a job on Rahman. He arrived in Johannesburg eleven days before the fight, feeling exhausted after a long, sleepless flight, and was reluctant to do anything more than take the quickest route to his hotel. But when he walked through the concourse he was greeted by a crowd of cheering well-wishers and about 80 members of the local and foreign press, along with a group of Zulu dancers and a lioness cub, hired for the occasion by the South African promoters because, after all, this was Africa and the arriving champion was occasionally called Lennox 'The Lion' Lewis. 'Get that out of here,' growled one of his minders. 'It's dangerous for the champion.' The little lioness was returned to her cage while Lennox kept on walking, offering the crowd a wave and the tired remark, 'It's great to be here.' With that, he joined Violet in one of the cars and was whisked off for a long sleep in his hotel, while a couple of other members of his team lingered to explain that the champion was 'a little bit tired'. The local press felt snubbed and reflected it in their reports, beginning an eleven-day war.

Lennox took two days to recover from the time change and found the altitude problem worse than anticipated, although he was reluctant to admit it. 'We were immediately hit by it,' Dunbar recalled. 'When we arrived we found we could hardly walk up a flight of stairs, let alone start training. He usually trains hard the Monday before the fight and then winds down, but he didn't do that with Rahman because of the long flight and the impact of arriving at such high altitude, so he lost a little fitness.' His heavy-legged huffing and puffing on his morning runs and in sparring produced further sneers from antagonistic local journalists. Then his team found a problem with the gym in nearby Benoni, owned by one of the country's leading trainers, Harold Volbrecht, and they had to find an alternative, prompting further negative reports. 'I fitted everything out to their orders and paid for it myself,' Volbrecht complained. 'But they haven't bothered to come here to train and haven't had the decency to advise me of their changed plans.'

Lennox brought out a huge team of over 30, among them his Canadian mentor and trainer Arnie Boehm, and a large number of friends and family members, including his brother Dennis. Most got on with their tasks or enjoyed the ride but those entrusted with security irritated their hosts, who complained they were surly, uncooperative and took themselves too seriously. The local reporters also sneered when they noticed that wherever the team travelled or went for a run they were escorted by a pack of white ex-mercenaries who served as additional security, driving at high speed, never taking the same route twice because they were worried about carjackings and kidnap attempts – understandable in a country where 22,000 people a year are murdered but perhaps an over-reaction. These mercenaries generally did their best to look as heavy as possible, although there were times when their expertise in evasive driving techniques might have come in handy. For instance, Patrick Drayton, the running coach-cum-driver-bodyguard-cum-music man, was lucky to survive an accident on a Johannesburg freeway when the car in front of him blew a tyre and some of the rubber flew into the air and landed on the bonnet of his hired Mercedes – an everyday occurrence in South Africa where around 25,000 people die every year in road accidents.

Lennox began to suspect that Berman and Kushner were hatching a plot to make his life as difficult as possible in order to help their own man win the title. He felt his hotel was inferior to Rahman's and that the promoters had inspired the local media into their 'vilification campaign' and were trying to exhaust him with an over-packed schedule. Berman dismissed this as nonsense and said that while he had no problem working with Ogun, the rest of the team were distinguished by their arrogance – and the main scheduling problem was that the original three weeks was compressed into nine busy days, with a few extra events added in because of Lennox's desire to be an inspirational presence.

Shortly before the fight Lennox watched on television as a stadium collapsed at a football game between Soweto's two biggest sides, Orlando Pirates and Kaiser Chiefs, leaving 43 spectators dead and hundreds injured. He laid a wreath at the blessing and cleansing ceremony at the stadium and then stayed for hours afterwards, speaking with the victims' relatives. He also went with Frank and Violet to an Aids orphanage in Soweto, all three of them becoming tearful after viewing the dire conditions faced by these children in a country where it is estimated that one in ten people are HIV positive. He then took an impromptu walk among the street children of Soweto, passing tiny block shacks with the grannies looking out and the children joining them, feeling like the Pied Piper. He ended up missing his scheduled training session and spending seven hours in the township. 'With me coming over here as world champion and being a black man, I'm giving hope to a lot of youths,' he said. 'That's why it's important to go to Soweto, to go to the orphanages so the kids get a chance to see me.' Later he bought tickets for a group of eager but unemployed onlookers at one of his public workouts after complaining bitterly that there should be no charge and that he wasn't there to make money for himself or anyone else and that he wanted to be 'an inspiration to the black youth and the underprivileged'.

When Lennox planned this venture he saw himself playing the Muhammad Ali role, and certainly the response he received in Soweto, at the football stadium and during his open sparring sessions offered a glimpse of this kind of acclaim. But the media was placing him in the George Foreman role – the offish, over-protected, reluctant recluse – while his challenger, a Muslim like Ali, was being cast in the crowd-milking Ali role, despite doing comparatively little in terms of meeting 'the people'. Lewis blamed the white-dominated South African press and the white South African promoters for this distortion, but took it out on his opponent. 'I'm tired of the mind games these guys play,' he said. 'Rahman's trying to make it look to the people of South Africa that I don't care enough about them to be there while he's there training so hard. It simply isn't true.'

As the fight loomed, his sense of disappointment became more profound. Although all arrangements had been negotiated with Adrian Ogun and assessed by Maloney, Lewis had not absorbed all the details before he arrived and was unhappy with much of what he found. He hoped to be fighting in front of the masses with the event shown on terrestrial television (as it was in Britain: the BBC bought the rights) but instead discovered he was to perform in front of rich people in a circus tent decorated with fairy lights in a grotesque gambling complex called Carnival City, with the fight screened only on M-Net in South Africa (a subscription channel), and now poor people were being charged even to watch him spar. Berman and the Carnival City staff were taken aback, pointing out that this had all been cleared before he arrived, but for Lewis, it was not the African experience he anticipated. When he spoke to Mandela after arriving, he suggested that Berman had 'a forked tongue' and maintained this negative take. 'It is only six years or so since they came out of apartheid,' he observed. 'They've come a long way but still have a long way to go.'

Over the last few days he took to training after midnight – running at two a.m., followed by a gym session at 3.30 a.m. – to get his body ready for a fight scheduled to start after five a.m. South African time. This meant he had to sleep during the day, although he was finding it more difficult than usual to doze off. As a result he ended up cancelling another visit to Soweto and a public sparring session, and he turned down a studio interview with the national terrestrial broadcaster, the SABC, prompting further acrimony from the South African media. There were constant niggles around him and a sense of frustration in the camp. Even Manny Steward, despite his outward calm, was feeling uneasy and wanted this African adventure behind him. And Lennox was even starting to lose to Scott when they played chess – a rare turnaround. By 21 April he'd had enough. He was irritated with his South African promoters, the local media and his opponent. He simply wanted to get the fight over as quickly as possible so that he could finally have his meeting with Mandela and then head off on safari.

Meanwhile, Hasim was having a marvellous time, joking with the local press, always available for a pithy quote and opening most of his gym sessions to the public. Before arriving he put in seven weeks of intense training in the Catskills, living with his co-manager Stan Hoffman (the man who advised Lewis and Hornewer at the start of Lennox's career). He then flew to Johannesburg ahead of schedule, three and a half weeks before the fight, together with Hoffman, fellow manager Steve Nelson, his trainer Adrian Davis, his sparring partners, his mum Joyce and his wife Crystal but no huge entourage to get in the way, and promptly got down to work in an old-style gym in downtown Johannesburg, known as the 'house of pain' and owned by Nick Durandt, a beefy fellow with an absurd peroxided, shoulder-length mullet hairstyle, who had a reputation as one of the hardest-working and most capable trainers in South Africa.

Four years earlier a rival boxing camp went for Durandt after one of their boxers defected to his camp. Using ex-policemen to bug his phone, they taped a conversation between Durandt and his wife after she'd been carjacked. The doctored version included derogatory remarks about kaffirs ('niggers'), Indians and Jews and was sent to the SABC, which played it on television. As a result, most of Durandt's black boxers walked out while their promoter, Berman, announced he would cease working with Nick: 'I can't let this one pass. I can live with anti-Semitism – I've learned to expect it – but I can't live with employees or partners of mine talking of kaffirs. What was said was morally reprehensible and indefensible and I can't align myself with someone making racist remarks, whatever the circumstances.' But South Africans have learned to maintain short memories. Today, for instance, you will struggle to find many whites who admit to having supported apartheid, despite the fact that three-quarters of the white population voted for apartheid-backing parties. So Durandt's indiscretion was more or less forgotten, despite his refusal to apologise. He acquired a new stable of top black professionals, began to work with Berman again and was recommended to Rahman as a man who could make a difference. He was hired to assist with the training and to work in the corner.

Durandt drove his boxers hard, and the Rahman team fitted in with his altitude-busting methods. Hasim struggled, despite all his work in the Catskills, and was quickly out of breath, but started to adapt after a fortnight. 'Nick Durandt's gym was a sweatbox,' he said later. 'It was really tough.' In his final week he completed twelve four-minute rounds of sparring with only half a minute's rest between rounds, and still looked sharp at the end. 'Now he is fit,' Durandt declared. 'I seriously believe that unless Lewis wins early he is going to feel the altitude from the sixth round. That could be the turning point.'

Rahman was unusual for an American heavyweight in that he avoided addiction to alcohol or drugs on the way up, largely through growing up in a Muslim family. His problems, like Hamed's, were overeating and driving too fast, and as a youth in Baltimore, Maryland, there was also the lure of a life as a street enforcer because he was a big, strong lad who knew how to get his way. At the age of eighteen he was shot five times, and soon after that he was involved in a car accident in which his best friend, Michael, died. This left him with severe scarring around his right eye and cheek. 'I broke my wrist and they literally had to put my face back on,' he said. 'It was a tragic accident.' He believed he had survived for a reason and this made him think about his future. He decided he had a shot at winning a million dollars if he dedicated himself to boxing and after just ten amateur fights, turned professional at the age of 22, in 1994.

After three years he broke into the world rankings and some writers were comparing him with one of the great heavyweights of the past, Sonny Liston, because he was strong and big (6ft 2in and over 235lb) with sound skills, a heavy 82-inch jab and an extremely hard right cross. It was time for him to step up, and he accepted a crossroads fight against Tua. Hasim absorbed some heavy digs but kept well in front by using his jab to great effect. By the end of round nine he'd only lost one round. The only way Tua could win was by knockout, and he made sure of it by landing a monstrous hook on Rahman's jaw well after the bell, which should have led to disqualification or a recovery period of up to ten minutes. Instead, the still-groggy American was required to come out as scheduled for the tenth. Tua jumped on him, landed a few more hooks, and the fight was stopped. 'The Rock', as he was known, felt he had been the victim of a grave injustice.

His next failing, however, was entirely of his own making. He was offered a chance to break back into the rankings against the Russian contender Oleg Maskaev, but arrived unfit and began to tire. In round eight he was knocked out of the ring, bashed his head on a computer terminal on the way down, and was counted out. 'They robbed me against Tua but I didn't prepare properly for Maskaev because I knew Tua had beaten him easily and Tua was easy for me,' he said, and then drew an analogy between his attitude for the Maskaev fight and what he discerned might be Lewis's for this fight. 'It just goes to show what happens when you take people too lightly. If Lennox has underestimated me, he's in for a surprise because I'm a better fighter than Tua. I've got more tools and I know I can ask more questions of Lennox than Tua did.' Six months later, Rahman proved his point by getting himself into magnificent shape to face the extremely quick and hard-hitting South African southpaw Corrie Sanders in what turned out to be a war of attrition. He went down twice but kept on fighting back, dropping Sanders and then breaking his will, stopping him in round seven. He was back in the ratings, and after another quick win (taking his record to 34 wins, 28 on knockouts, and two defeats) Lennox picked him for the 22 April date.

He exuded confidence as he wound up his training. His magnificent physical condition and the late arrival of the heavier-than-expected champion boosted his optimism. 'Whatever he hits me with I'll be ready, and I'll hit him back with it, because there's no quit in me, believe that,' he said. 'When I get in that ring he's not Lennox Lewis, champion of the world, he's just Lennox Lewis, another man, and I don't believe I'm going to have a problem hitting him. He's never fought another person like me.' He pointed to a poster on the wall of Durandt's gym which read 'The harder you train, the luckier you get', and added, 'All I know is I'm ready and I'm prepared and I've never worked more for a fight in my life. I truly believe I'm going to be champion of the world.'

The way Lewis was speaking it was clear he was expecting a quick and one-sided knockout, but he also felt he was in shape for a longer fight. Taking his lead from Steward he dismissed the problems with altitude, feeling that after a week's intermittent work his body had adjusted. 'I've fought and trained at altitudes before, so this is nothing to me,' he said. He was clearly irritated with all the talk of his opponent's longer acclimatisation and exemplary fitness. 'Rahman says he's great, he's in superb condition – well, let's see what strange maladies he comes up with when I knock him out,' he said. 'People said I couldn't break Grant and Tua. And I made them look like amateurs. Do you realise most boxing writers picked Grant to beat me? I will break Rahman too, and since Tyson wants this so bad,' he added, holding up his fist, 'he can come and get it after Rahman.'

When they stepped on the scales on the evening of 20 April Rahman came in at 238 extremely muscular pounds. Lennox weighed 253½lb., 11½ more than when he beat Holyfield and the heaviest of his career. He didn't look fat, but there was no six pack and he lacked his usual muscular sheen. Steward insists his fitness not at issue. 'Lennox always stays in shape,' he said. 'He might go to parties and so on, but he doesn't let himself go like other heavyweights who have to lose over thirty pounds before you can really start training them for a fight. I've seen him between fights in Miami, where he does a lot of boating and diving, and he keeps up his jogging and plays a lot of golf and tennis. So he arrives in shape, and he certainly did his work for the Rahman as he always does and neither the altitude nor his weight was a problem. Not at all. The only reason he weighed what he did was because they held the weigh-in at eight p.m. instead of in the afternoon, so Lennox weighed-in after he had eaten.' Joe Dunbar offered a slightly different perspective: 'I'd say his training was fairly good for Rahman fight even though his total workload was lighter than for some of the others, but after we arrived he lost some of that fitness because of the circumstances there and this may have affected his weight, although I think too big a deal is made of it. The biggest factor was the altitude.'

The team left their Kaponong Hotel compound at 2.45 a.m., arrived at Carnival City half an hour later and got down to work in the hot, brightly lit changing room. Patrick put on the music – slow, soft reggae – and Lennox lay down on the massage table with his head covered in a beanie hat and resting on a pillow, his hands crossed over his chest, sunglasses keeping out the glare. He fell asleep within a few minutes, while Scott stood by him to ensure no one disturbed him. Lennox's Canadian friend Ron Hepburn cleared the room of outsiders and then stood beside Scott – two guards for the sleeping lion. Courtney collected the towels, Al Gavin, the cutman, prepared the ice buckets and cut solution, Manny prepared the bandages and hand tape, Harold organised the water bottles before leaving the room to inspect Rahman's hand wrapping while Frank pulled on his Union flag suit. Lennox woke sooner than normal, sat up and talked for a while, then began shadow boxing until the man from the Rahman camp arrived, after which he sat down again while Courtney laced his boots and Manny wrapped his hands. With the Casino woman telling them it was almost time to go, they strapped the red groin protector over his black underpants, pulled on his trunks and removed his sunglasses. Lennox shadow sparred with Egerton but stopped for an adjustment to his protector. Courtney greased down his body and took him through a stretching routine on a blanket on the floor. Harold taped the gloves and an official signed them, then Lewis pounded his fists together, shot out some jabs, hit the pad, and listened to a few words from Manny while the team started chanting. Courtney wiped the sweat off his body and they formed a circle, holding hands. Harold led, thanking God for bringing them to South Africa and asking him to protect Lennox and Hasim from pain or damage. With that, led along by a group of African dancers and serenaded by the sound of Marley singing 'Get up, stand up, stand up for your rights', they accompanied the man they adored to the ring.

Rahman, wearing his black dressing gown and bandana, looked intense as the mainly white and exclusively well-to-do crowd cheered him. Lennox, in contrast, looked casual, reflecting the view of the bookies, who made him a 15–1 favourite.

He came out purposefully, taking the initiative with several hard jabs, but Rahman managed to catch him with a decent jab and a half-decent right of his own and did not seem overawed. In round two Lewis stepped up his assault, jabbing hard. Hasim caught him with a sharp right, and a few seconds later a solid left–right combination, but Lennox came back to hurt him with a left uppercut–overhand right combination, and followed it with a chopping right to the ear and a right to the left eye, driving the American on to the back foot, but he was already breathing heavily through his mouth.

Lewis decided to abandon his jab and go for a quick result. He was particularly effective with hooks and uppercuts, and midway through the third round landed a heavy overhand right that caused Rahman's left eye to swell. But Hasim was punching with venom whenever Lennox came close, although landing mainly on the arms. With less than a minute to go Lewis caught him coming in with a sharp hook, but Rahman fought back hard, driving the champion away with a flurry of body punches, although he had to absorb a heavy left hook to the chest just before the bell. Both had their problems. Lennox was gasping for breath while Hasim had a swelling above and below his left eye.

Just as Lennox predicted, he was dominating, but it was turning into a scrappy fight, with Lewis's balance, work-rate, reflexes and rhythm affected by the altitude, and this contributed to a shift in momentum. He started hopefully enough in round four, slamming a power jab into Rahman's bruised eye and then whipping in yet another teeth-jarring uppercut. But Hasim fought back, landing several of his own jabs, attacking incessantly and hitting Lennox in the face with a big right cross a minute into the round. Because Lewis was tiring he preferred working at close quarters where Rahman was most effective, although he emerged from one exchange with a small cut. When the Belgian referee Daniel van de Wiele called 'Break!' after a clinch, requiring them to step back without punching, Hasim fouled Lennox. Van de Wiele raised a finger and declared, 'One, OK, box,' to suggest a first warning. Just before the bell Lewis landed a low blow but instead of complaining Hasim replied in kind. Steward instructed Lewis to make more use of the jab, to watch out for the right and to keep his hands up, but he also advised that Rahman was weakening. 'You start shooting the left hooks you're gonna knock him out of here.'

Early in round five Lennox walked Hasim down and pinned him in his own corner, and although the challenger escaped he was taking heavy punishment. Nearly two minutes into the round he caught Lennox with a powerful right to the jaw that seemed to shake him momentarily but for the next half minute normal service was resumed, the heavy-breathing champion smiling as he landed hurtful uppercuts and crosses without bothering to protect his chin. Hasim began touching his cut that was now bleeding more profusely, while Lennox, fighting with his hands low and that odd smile, was cavalier in his confidence. From ringside Rahman looked thoroughly discouraged and ready to give up – turning away from the punches with a look on his face suggesting serious distress, although he later denied he'd been on the verge of quitting. 'I kept pawing at my eye because there was blood dripping into it. I really couldn't see Lennox's punches and he was trying to finish me, but I knew the general area he was in.' Steward claimed that Rahman admitted to him after the fight that he had been ready to quit. In any event, his perturbed corner was frantic: 'Get off the ropes!' they screamed, and 'Throw some punches!'

The end was sudden and completely against play. Rahman poked out three tentative jabs and Lennox retreated to the ropes, where he planted his feet, apparently with the intention of catching him coming in. He was standing at a slight angle with his arms apart and his gloves low, and once again, smiling, feeling certain that his night's work was soon to end. Rahman moved in with his right cocked; Lennox caught a glimpse of this and started to bring up his gloves. But he was tired and his reactions were slower than normal. Trying to bounce off the ropes he crossed his legs, losing balance, and his left glove didn't make it up quite in time. Hasim took a step forward and put his full body weight behind the hardest and heaviest right cross he would ever throw in his career, and it landed flush with a cracking sound on the side of Lennox's still-unprotected jaw.

It was a rare thing of beauty, this punch – 'one of the greatest I've ever seen,' said Steward. Seldom do all the elements of a perfect right come together: a full-commitment, perfectly straight and extremely fast cross thrown from the bottom of the boot of the back foot, up the right leg, along the back, through the turning right shoulder, along the arm and into the fist, connecting at the most vulnerable point of the jaw with the elbow still bent, giving a further foot of neck-twisting extension. It was one of the finest in heavyweight history, and for the second and last time in his career Lewis went down. A few months later he described the blow that ended his reign: 'The punch was a great punch, but I never put my left hand in position to block it. My defence wasn't like it should have been. I wouldn't say I was cocky or arrogant – I think those are the wrong words – but I may have taken him a bit lightly and didn't realise he was able to throw a punch like that. I'm going to make sure my defence is up in a better position next time. There's no way I want to get caught by that punch again.' His fall was even more dramatic than in 1994, and his chances of rising in time were further diminished when his head banged hard against the canvas-covered ring floor, making a horrible thud that was audible from the other side of the ring.

Exhaustion also slows the process. As Dunbar put it, 'Your ability to recover from a punch diminishes if you're not perfectly fit.' He lifted his head off the canvas as Van de Wiele counted away the seconds with Rahman poised in the neutral corner. 'I was trying to get the referee to count eight, nine, ten, and I was ready to jump on him again,' Hasim said. When the referee reached four Lennox rolled over on his side and used his hands and knees to push himself up, but his left leg wobbled and his body drooped when he reached ten. Van de Wiele held him in his arms and removed his mouthpiece. Lewis' reign was over.

He later argued it was a quick count and that he beat it. 'I wasn't able to get off the canvas because the referee counted too fast. The ref was trying to count me out as fast as possible. When I was getting up he stopped the fight.' Steward, watching from his perch in the corner, reached the same conclusion. 'When Lennox went down the referee started counting like he was in a race. I know for a fact because

I was there. I've seen guys in heavyweight championship fights hurt much worse and come back to win. Holmes did it against Shavers and Snipes; Holyfield was hurt worse than that in the second Ruiz fight and they let it go on. The round was almost over. If the referee had given Lennox a normal count he would have been able to go on. This was the heavyweight champion of the world defending his title. You give the man a chance.'

Just like the count in the McCall fight, this one was only fractionally fast: just under ten seconds passed between the moment Lennox hit the canvas and the moment when Van de Wiele counted ten, with 28 seconds left in the round. Perhaps if he'd been given the kind of delayed count Douglas received before beating Tyson or the long count that helped Tunney survive his return against Dempsey or the extended post-count check-ups Golota and Briggs received in their failed world title challenges, he might have survived, but even then there would have been around twenty seconds left and Lewis did not look in great shape. This was certainly Rahman's view. 'The referee counted to ten,' he said. 'He could have counted to twenty and Lennox wouldn't have been able to go on. They refuse to deal with the truth.' In any event, Lennox could not rely on such favours, and he was legitimately counted out.

He immediately stood up and seemed to be firm-legged and fine, although Frank Maloney said he seemed confused. 'It was just like walking down a dark alley and, whoom!, you don't see a punch coming,' he said. 'In the ring, he didn't even know he had been stopped.' Lennox's first response was, 'I can't believe that, I can't believe that. I felt fine in there. I was going about my work, nice and comfortable. There's no way Hasim Rahman can beat me.' But he quickly absorbed the facts. 'He caught me with a good shot,' he said a minute later. 'But I felt fine afterwards. This is what happens in heavyweight boxing – you get hit with a good shot, you go down. If you don't beat the count, you're out. But I definitely want a rematch. I want to get in there as soon as possible.'

Violet climbed into the ring and gently stroked the side of her son's face. Manny and Harold removed his gloves while his Ghanaian friend and camp aide Prince Osei-Poku wiped the tears from his eyes with a clean white handkerchief. Arnie Boehm was also crying. In New York, in front of the computer on which she'd watched the fight, Lennox's girlfriend Aisha Mike was sobbing uncontrollably. 'As soon as I saw him go down and then his head bounce off the canvas I just felt my stomach sinking and I started to cry,' she said. 'And then I e-mailed him immediately because I couldn't get hold of him. It was the closest thing I'd seen to a loved one dying because I've never lost anyone. All four of my grandparents are still alive. But to me, seeing Lennox get knocked out like that felt as if I was seeing my brother die, and I felt an inner hysteria. I was very upset about it.'

In the other corner there was mania. Hasim laughed with his hands raised, saying, 'It was unbelievable, indescribable.' He then bent down to hug Joyce and Crystal. His American managers and trainers joined the scrum, with Nick Durandt bouncing and screaming on the outside, trying to get in, while below them at ringside Cedric Kushner and Rodney Berman were hugging each other. Berman's wildly excited, middle-aged press man Terry Pettifer was shouting, over and over again at the top of his voice, 'We control the heavyweight champion of the world!' and 'South Africa owns the world heavyweight title!' and 'I'm so glad, Rodney and Cedric have the world champion!' He was not to know that this 'ownership' was already in doubt, but for the moment his sense of vindication was absolute, and he turned to some of the British journalists and yelled, 'You thought Lennox Lewis was so great but he's one of the worst champions ever!'

As Lennox left the ring to the boos of this pro-Rahman crowd, George Foreman, the last world heavyweight champion to lose his title in Africa, expressed the verdict later shared by Nelson Mandela. 'Lennox didn't use his jab, which was a terrible fault, because he has a good jab. Like I did with Ali, Lewis just tried to take his man out with one punch and he paid the price. He was overconfident, and it showed. It is a reflection on him and his trainer. If you bring a guy to training camp you have to get him in shape, or you don't take him to the fight. Lennox had a right to be confident – he has been so dominant – but he also has to prepare properly. You don't take anything for granted against a 240lb guy. If you do, he creams you.'

Lennox went back to his changing room, where Maloney made a little speech about being positive, acting as a team and behaving with dignity. Lennox dutifully made it to the post-fight press conference, just as he'd done after the Oliver McCall catastrophe six and a half years earlier. He stressed there were no problems with fitness and no problems with altitude; it was just a lucky punch. When Rahman arrived a few minutes later, Lennox congratulated him, reminded him of the rematch clause and added, 'Hasim, you know it was a lucky punch.' Rahman smiled and shook his head while the former Lewis adviser Stan Hoffman countered, 'It wasn't an accident, it was a plan. There isn't a reporter in this room who hasn't heard me say Hasim would win by knockout.'

And with that, Rahman abandoned his African 'home' two days early, missed his meeting with Mandela and flew off home to Baltimore where he was greeted by the mayor and several thousand fans, by which stage he seemed to have forgotten about a return with Lewis. 'Let's bring Mike Tyson here to Baltimore – what do you think?' he asked the crowd, and they cheered their approval. But his was not to be a reign destined for happiness. As he was driving away from the rally, on his way to a television interview, another car jumped a red light and crashed into them. His three children were uninjured, but Hasim came away with a few cuts and his wife with cuts, bruises and a neck brace.

After leaving Carnival City, Lennox and his team were driven back to the Kaponong Hotel by the white ex-mercenary guards who once again chose a new route to foil the plans of any would-be kidnappers – this time taking an extra long time to get them back, just in case. Lennox showered, changed and was driven off again, as previously planned, to his post-fight party, where he played DJ while some danced and others cried and everyone drank lots of champagne. Later, Frank Maloney popped in to Lennox's crowded hotel apartment to say goodbye, but he soon left because he didn't like the smell of the smoke or the sense of being an outsider with this huge group of champagne-quaffing friends and hangers-on, many of whom he barely knew. Lennox and some of his team then went off for the week-long safari in the game reserve, easing off among the elephants, lions and hyenas, while Maloney flew home alone to face the British press.

Before the fight, Frank spoke off the record to several journalists, telling them of his misgivings about the preparations. Afterwards he went on the record, criticising Lennox's decision to go ahead with the *Ocean's Eleven* movie and to arrive so late in Johannesburg, as well as airing his irritation with the 'Johnny-cum-latelies' in camp. But his most trenchant criticism was reserved for Manny Steward. He accused the head trainer of getting it horribly wrong by telling Lennox not to worry about the altitude and of not giving Lennox his full attention by agreeing to work with Hamed. 'I think he made Lennox feel too complacent,' he said.

This provoked a furious response. Manny claimed Maloney was 'unravelling' under pressure and called on him to 'concentrate on being a manager.' And he added: 'He's the least qualified person I have ever dealt with to be making any criticism. He's supposed to be Lennox's manager but over the last three fights he hasn't been in any of the training camps to know what's been going on. This is a time when your team pulls together and you find out who your strong people are. Well, I guess he was asked to point some fingers and rather than accept blame he suggested I'm the cause of Lewis's loss. Normally I try to be a gentleman and just leave things alone, but I'm not going to do it. He shows up at the fights, wearing his lumberjack jackets around, more like a mascot, and doesn't even know half the time who Lennox Lewis is fighting. To me, for him to be out criticising is the most disgusting thing I've experienced in boxing. We're spending all these weeks and months getting up at three in the morning and Maloney is somewhere sleeping and waking up just in time to go to the bar with the British writers.'

Steward stuck to his line that Lennox had been fighting fit: 'He was in excellent condition and I don't think he could have done any better.' Contradicting Joe Dunbar he still insisted that altitude was not a problem. 'With people who travel internationally as much as we do, the altitude and climate doesn't hurt our bodies as much,' he said. 'Our bodies adjust extremely well.' Today he puts the blame on complacency of mind rather than of body. 'He was too relaxed in there, that was the problem. Rahman didn't seem to be up to the quality of the guys he'd beaten over the previous few years. There was the unbeaten Mavrovic and then the two fights with Holyfield, and then Grant who was unbeaten, and then Tua who'd beaten Rahman. Hasim just didn't seem to be up to that level and the result was that he wasn't focused enough in the ring. By the fourth round he'd dropped his level of intensity. His hands were down and he was very comfortable, which one round later would prove to be a huge mistake. He was just too relaxed.'

Lennox tacitly acknowledge that he could have been better prepared by saying that he would have trained harder and arrived in South Africa earlier had Tyson been his opponent. A day later he blamed Rodney Berman for engineering his downfall. 'That guy disgusts me,' he said. 'For him to do what he did to me after agreeing to come to fight to South Africa with so little money just proves how he is. They made all the tricks, dictating to me what to do. Eventually their tricks succeeded when Rahman knocked me out, but it will not last long because I will regain my titles.' A few months on, however, he decided to forgive and forget in true South African style. He bought Berman's Golden Gloves promotional company in order to expand his own Lion Promotions stable and retained Rodney and his son, Joel, to manage the show.

He still maintains it was a lucky punch, but unlike Steward he acknowledges he could have prepared better: 'I realised afterwards that I suffered as a result of the mistake of taking him too lightly. I didn't take him seriously enough and I was a bit unfocused. He got through with one great punch and we're in the heavyweight division where it can end with one punch. I didn't want to go through that again. So I definitely learned my lesson because I'm a competitor by heart and it's important for me to come out on top.'

His African experience was a disaster that would leave his 'legacy' permanently tarnished. But his memory of the trip does not pause too long on the frustrations of the build-up or that career-altering blow, but rather on that morning-after meeting with Mandela. It was the event that left him with the most interesting lessons, he says.

'One thing I remember vividly about that meeting was when he told me that when he came out from 27 years in jail he felt love and he spread love, and I thought that was a great thing to say – a great statement to make. That answer was definitely part of what made my meeting with him such a great experience for me. But there was another thing as well. You remember, we went around to his place just after I'd lost my world title, so what he said was particularly meaningful to me. He said, "Ah, that was just a lucky shot. Don't worry, you're going to come back and beat him." He said it in such a relaxed way that he made me feel very good. And that's what I was thinking of when I was training for the return fight. And then, when it actually happened, I thought this man, Nelson Mandela, must have some foresight. He knows what he's talking about, even when the subject is boxing. The fact that he said it made me feel like he'd seen the whole thing already.'

CHAPTER TWENTY FOUR
MANHATTAN, NEW YORK, 2004

Judd Burstein counts Lennox Lewis as a buddy he can chat with outside of work as well as a client. 'We speak regularly and get on very well,' he says. 'He sent me a Christmas present at Christmas, our working relationship is extremely cordial, there was definitely no falling out between us, and he really is still a friend.' The question arises because Lewis's 49-year-old American lawyer was also his business adviser before resigning from this role in January 2004 amid speculation of a difference of opinion, not so much with Lennox but with Adrian Ogun. Of his business relationship with Lewis, he says, 'I'll simply say I chose to remain his litigation counsel but didn't want to continue as his business adviser.' Of his relationship with Ogun, he says, 'My mother told me that if you can't say something good about something don't say anything, so I won't say anything about Adrian Ogun.'

So, while keeping clear of anything relating to contractual or investment advice, it's business as usual when it comes to suing and being sued, activities that have taken up a lot of Lewis' time over the last three years. With the appeals of Panos Eliades and Milton Chwasky still on the go, along with a couple of slow-brewing cases involving Don King, you can be sure that they'll be working together for a few years yet.

Their first meeting served only one purpose: to bring Judd to Lennox's attention, although that was not its prime aim. In other respects this opening contact was a dud. A Malaysian woman retained Judd's services in late 2000 to put together the Lewis–Tyson fight, claiming she had $60 million to share. Her plan was to offer Lennox $1 million for a 45-day option and use that as bait for Tyson. 'What happened after that,' says Burstein, 'is that I had discussions with Ogun about paying this option but in the end I felt obliged to withdraw because it became clear to me that my client was not above board.'

Burstein was used to below-board clients. He'd learned how to spot them, cultivate them and avoid them, although his early background gave no indication that these were among his talents. A *cum laude* graduate of Ivy League Brandeis, he went on to complete a master's degree in philosophy before teaching the subject for a couple of years. But when you talk to him you realise he's a man who likes a challenge, a gamble even, and the life of that kind of don didn't quite cut it. In a moment of boredom, he enrolled for law at New York University and soon discovered he had no passion for the academic dimensions of his new calling. Still, he sailed through and decided if he was to do anything with these new letters after his name it would have to be in the only dimension that excited him: crime. He was articled to a New York criminal attorney who specialised in representing the real-life equivalents of the Corleone family, and soon became a full partner.

He was raking it in, but his ethically firm Jewish upbringing meant this money came with niggling questions about the type of person he was defending – a problem brought home when the body of one of his mobster clients was found in the boot of a car. He felt it would be less troublesome to his conscience if he concentrated on criminal appeals because then he'd be dealing with legal principles rather than representing Tony Soprano directly. The risqué conclusion to his connection with the crime bosses came in 1990 when he had a romantic relationship with a state prosecutor. He received a warning that the New York Mafia boss John Gotti was 'displeased'. Burstein did not appreciate being threatened but was also afraid and decided he would no longer represent such clients (while the fling ran out of steam of its own accord). However, he'd acquired the label 'mob lawyer', which made it tricky when called upon to represent non-mob clients, so he decided the best option was to leave criminal law altogether.

The leap from there to the boxing world may seem like a half-step to outsiders but for Burstein it made a real change. He loved the sport and knew that boxers were more deserving than crime bosses. 'Most fighters are treated like indentured servants,' he said. 'Their exploitation makes me angry.' He started with failure, which was not his accustomed mode, representing Bowe and Newman against Holyfield. But soon he was on a roll, acting for the former world light middleweight champion Terry Norris, the former three-weight world champion Julio Cesar Chavez and the heavyweight Frans Botha in cases against Don King, and he earned a reputation as a relentlessly focused campaigner and a brilliantly feisty courtroom interrogator. Where other lawyers were battered back by King's resources, Burstein became his *bête noire*, beating him on a regular basis. With the Norris case, for example, King was forced to settle for $7 million. 'That was a very successful result,' says Burstein, who adds that he has a 'very unusual relationship with King', suing on behalf of clients, being sued by him and negotiating with him all at the same time. He came to regard keeping King in check as a moral calling. 'His modus operandi is to wait until the boxer's in the ring and then go into the locker room and pickpocket his wallet,' he said. 'It's not to take his wallet out and pay the fighters.'

By early 2001, when Ogun met Burstein to discuss the Lewis–Tyson fight, Adrian was well aware of the reputation of this tenacious, King-busting lawyer and he was impressed with the way Judd handled the negotiations and the integrity he showed when he discovered his Malaysian client wasn't on the level. Soon after, Eliades sued Lewis, who decided he needed a new American lawyer. 'He had some dissatisfaction with his existing lawyers,' says Judd, 'and my name came up because of the way I'd handled the Tyson fight negotiations and because of the success I'd had in those other cases involving boxers.' So Burstein, who has no partners but works from his Manhattan office with five associate lawyers and five administrative staffers, was hired for what at first looked like a tough assignment. He quickly turned it around by successfully counter-suing, drawing on his experience from his criminal law days to toss in anti-racketeering allegations. This was followed by his victory over Lewis's former US attorney Milt Chwasky.

Hiring Burstein is an expensive habit at up to $600 an hour, but without his courtroom skills it is unlikely that Lewis would have had the chance to regain his title. His most significant victory was also the first to come to court: Judd trounced King's lawyers and won an injunction forbidding Rahman to fight anyone before the Lewis rematch, and he continued to represent Lennox in a series of trials and appeals (most involving King) and, until 2004, also advised him on contractual negotiations and business decisions. It's a lucrative relationship but one he says he enjoys beyond its pecuniary advantages. He describes his most valued client as an intelligent, caring and cautious person who's had some bad times at the hands of some bad men. 'I feel he is a fundamentally decent person. Like everybody, he has been formed by his experiences. He's been taken advantage of, and there is no doubt that has left an impact on him, but he's one of those people I really enjoy spending time with and I regard him as a friend.'

When Rahman recovered from the cuts and scratches of his Baltimore car crash, he went on a pilgrimage to Mecca and returned more enthused than ever with the idea of making heap loads of money. His purse for the South African fight was $1.5 million (Lewis's was $7 million), but now it was time to cash in. The figures he had in his head – or those that were being put there by various suitors – went all the way to $100 million if he kept winning. 'Money, m-o-n-e-y,' a grinning Hasim said after returning home. 'It's about the money. We're not fools. This business is a money business. It's a chance for a guy like me to make sure my family is set for life. And that's a great motivator. If you have that carrot out in front of you, you don't get complacent.' And who gave him the chance to earn this money? Hasim had no illusions: 'I love Lennox! I love him because of all the money he made me. Lennox bought me a house. Lennox bought me a car. Lennox bought me a lot of nice jewellery. He bought me so many nice things, that's why I love him. Oh, thank you, Lennox. Thank you, thank you, thank you. I love you, man.'

Rahman, however, felt no obligations arising out of this love, neither to Lennox nor to anyone else except himself, his family and his God. Never had, never would. His contract for the South African fight included a clause obliging him to fight Lewis again within 150 days if he won, but he thought it was full of holes. His promoter, Cedric Kushner, had similar ideas and their position was strengthened by the fact that HBO decided before the fight to save money by turning down the chance to secure future options through signing this no-hoper to a multi-fight deal – why pay him extra when he's sure to lose? As Hasim put it, 'HBO had an arrogance about their fighter and now they have a hefty price to pay.' What it meant was that HBO's smaller rival, Showtime, which 'owned' Mike Tyson, could bid against HBO for Rahman's services on the understanding that Tyson's manager Shelly Finkel was pushing hard for the fight. 'I was barely out of the ring in South Africa when Shelly phoned me to ask when I was going back to New York, and he was disappointed it was not until the Tuesday after the fight,' said the gleeful Kushner.

The 5ft 8½in, 385lb Kushner felt he'd finally made it as a heavyweight promoter; he was the big man who controlled the world heavyweight title and could play the television giants against each other. He was enjoying himself, tickled by the knowledge that HBO's pre-fight penny pinching was now costing them a fortune. Showtime offered Rahman $19.5 million for the Tyson fight while HBO bid $14.15 million for the Lewis return, but they preferred the HBO deal because of its long-term possibilities and the certainty that a Tyson fight would earn him more in the future. Hasim went with his managers to the HBO offices in New York on Friday, 10 May 2001, said OK to their offer and was ready to sign. But HBO was used to the normal way in which these things are done, the way they dealt with Lennox and his managers: you reach an agreement, then you draw up the contract, then you meet again to sign. The contracts would be ready on Monday and Hasim would be $14.5 million richer.

The world heavyweight champion went back to his hotel and, as Lennox put it, 'he went ghetto crazy'. Don King saw in Hasim a way to control the heavyweight title again and also a way of cutting off Tyson's worrying $100 million lawsuit. If he could offer Mike a shot at the undisputed crown, he might just be persuaded to drop his suit. So, when no one was looking, he slipped under the net and came courting in one of the most cunning moves of his audacious career. What Don, the former numbers runner, understood and the suits at HBO didn't, was that former street enforcers like Hasim don't trust promises. What they trust are 'readies', cash in hand, dollar bills. So late on the Friday night Don arrived armed with a suitcase packed with 5,000 one-hundred-dollar bills – $500,000 in all. This was just a taster, a display of good faith between brothers from the same side of the tracks (unlike those white South Africans and Yankee college boys). Also from his suitcase he pulled out a contract that offered another $4.5 million for providing nothing more than his signature – a signing bonus. But wait, more: $5 million for a sleepwalking first defence in China (initially against a fat Dane called Brian Nielsen); $15 million for a 'showdown' with Holyfield in Nigeria; $20 million for a defence against Lewis; and finally, $30 million for a defence against Tyson. That's $75 million for just four fights – how about that? Hasim signed at 2.30 a.m. Later that day a hoarse King returned home with a triumphant smile. 'I've been a busy beaver,' he said. And when his voice had recovered he proceeded to 'big-up' Hasim in every way he knew, including the unique feat of praising his attributes as a God-fearing good guy in co-joined clichés: 'The proof of the pudding is in the eating, the family that prays together stays together.'

Kushner responded first with disbelief, then with fury. 'How does this young man feel he got to the heavyweight championship if it weren't for me?' the plummy-voiced, Long Island-based promoter asked. 'He wouldn't have if it wasn't for my efforts, if it wasn't for my relationships. Two fights earlier [*sic*] he was lying underneath the ring, not on the canvas. How does he think he got from there to here?' A few years earlier he'd had a similar problem with King and Rahman when Don tried to poach him, but on that occasion Cedric accused Don of tampering with their contract and sued successfully. He went to court again, but this time his rival had done his homework. A bit like HBO, Cedric had pinched the pennies by neglecting to pay Hasim a $75,000 signing bonus before the Lewis fight, which proved to be a breach of contract. Kushner emerged from court with the minor consolation prize of being allowed to collect a small portion of the promotional fee for the rematch. He treated himself by going off to hospital to have his stomach stapled, and halved in size. King emerged as the genuine big man, once again in total control.

Or so he assumed. As it turned out, the return fight clause signed by Rahman was a lot less porous than assumed. The court ruled that if Rahman failed to honour the contract he would be banned from fighting anyone else for eighteen months. King then threw in the towel, hoping that Hasim would prevail or that his own role as promoter of the return fight would reel Lewis in, and he played it both ways, keeping the champion sweet while trying to seduce the former champion. Lewis also played it both ways. Worried about what King might try to pull if he lost hope in the seduction stakes, he played a more friendly game than usual, laughing at King's jokes, accepting hospitality but leaving any agreements about future relations until after the fight. And when the fight was over it was thank you but no thank you. Once again he won the battle of wits.

Hasim's ghetto madness was not yet spent. HBO, learning from its mistakes, decided to secure its options by offering Rahman a multi-fight deal, which, his co-manager Steve Nelson said, could earn him $100 million. At King's prompting, however, the champion said no – why tie himself into a long-term contract when he'd be in a stronger position after the Lewis rematch, set for 17 November in Las Vegas? Getting locked in by HBO would make it more difficult to secure a fight against the Showtime-controlled Tyson. 'A TV contract is only an insurance policy for losing,' King said. 'I don't want to know what Rock gets if he loses, I want to know what Rock gets when he wins. Rock ain't no one-night stand. This is what you call rolling the dice, winner takes all.' It's what you call rolling the dice on someone else's future, but still, 'Rock', in his street-wisdom, turned HBO down. So while Lewis was guaranteed $11 million, Hasim accepted Don's $5 million purse deal plus a share of the pay-per-view profits once the sales target was met.

This might have netted a healthy balance if not for the 11 September terror attacks. The after-shock and period of national mourning, followed by the home-grown anthrax scare, limited King's ability to promote the fight and Hasim's to earn from it. At first boxing itself was off the agenda; even when it began to creep back it had to be handled in more muted tones than the usual King fare. Aside from sensibilities about too much frivolity, there was also the issue of Hasim's religion. Despite presidential assurances that the 'War on Terror' was not a war on Islam, Muslims were treated with suspicion. Although no one alluded to Rahman's faith directly, it made him harder to sell to boxing pay-per-view aficionadoes at $49.99 a pop. Eventually it began to turn, journalists finding an angle in the idea of a patriotic, apolitical American family man as an alternative Islamic role model who could speak for tolerance. 'Hate and ignorance are never a good thing,' Hasim said a month after the tragedy. 'That's not a solution to any problem. People should try to get knowledge of any situation before they just go and act. Ignorance is a reason for a lot of the turmoil we're having right now.' He added that problems like court cases over contractual disputes had become less important. 'What happened on September 11 should have helped us all put everything into its proper perspective. I feel I'm blessed with or without a contract. I feel everybody should thank God we're still here and save something for the people who didn't make it. If we have a good fight and give people a way to enjoy themselves, that's probably the best thing that can happen. So you could say that all this hard work I'm doing up here at seven thousand feet on this mountain is for the people.'

Rahman began his training at a camp in upstate New York for a couple of weeks before switching to the thin air of Big Bear for five weeks, and then rounding off in Las Vegas. The impression from his camps was of a man working with focused intensity who was thoroughly enjoying himself at the same time, displaying an attractive combination of quick-witted bonhomie and aggressive confidence. He felt he'd improved significantly and now had a better array of punches, particularly the left hook, which he'd spent many hours working on. He also claimed to have surpassed the level of fitness he'd reached in Johannesburg, although after the fight he admitted his relationship with his trainer, Adrian Davis, had become strained toward the end. 'We weren't really getting along for the last month of camp,' he said. 'There was a lot of tension and it was hard for me to be around him. I almost didn't let him work the corner. He was already paid so I felt like I had to keep him, but if he hadn't been paid he wouldn't have been at the fight.'

Lennox's training team united behind him for his longest-ever camp (almost twelve weeks), but he too was experiencing his share of unwanted distractions. By the time he entered his Pennsylvania retreat his relationship with his manager was ending. It had gradually weakened over the previous three years for several reasons. On Lennox's side was the fact that he was spending less time in Britain. He had a new group of friends and associates who had no relation to Maloney, and his decision to promote himself and take on Ogun as his business manager, Burstein as his lawyer and business adviser and his friend Kojo Amoafo as press agent meant Frank's role was becoming superfluous. On Maloney's side there was his flirtation with Don King and then his decision to defect to the arms of Lennox's sneerer-in-chief Frank Warren, his refusal to sign the confidentiality form and finally, and most decisively, his decision to go public with his criticisms of Lennox's preparations for the first Rahman fight and to call for Lewis's retirement.

Frank viewed his public criticism as no more than stating the obvious, but Lewis had a very different perspective. He saw Maloney's response as disloyalty and related it to the fact that his manager was working for Warren – a case of abandoning ship rather than working as part of a team to plug the holes. He was also angered by a story that someone from his team phoned Rahman trying to persuade him to fight Tyson first. Lennox said he later raised it with Rahman, who told him, 'Yo, your manager phoned me up trying to get a fight with me and Tyson.' Maloney was adamant that he had no part in this and no knowledge of it either, and took legal action against a Sunday newspaper that ran a story along these lines, winning what he called 'a substantial sum' as well as an apology.

Lennox held back from firing him. One reason was that Maloney represented his clearest connection to Britain. The rest of his team was a cosmopolitan mix reflecting his own mixed identity – Jamaicans, Canadians, Africans, Americans and Englishmen – but the only one with a public profile was Steward. Maloney represented a British counter-balance. To outsiders he was an English archetype; to insiders, an English type. The way he looked, spoke, drank, swore and laughed was unmistakably East End, London, England, Britain, depending on your angle, and this eased Lewis's acceptance in the country of his birth and established his identity as British when viewed from abroad. He might have smiled indulgently at the Union flag suit and little Englander politics, but he could see that his manager's image helped his own. More to the point, he could see that losing Frank might hurt his own image, particularly in Britain, where the easy-going, self-deprecating, lager-swigging Maloney was popular with sports journalists. The British press had had no particular feeling for the others he shed along the way but Frank was different. Firing him would come at a cost. So Lennox preferred to keep him on, even if it meant paying 2 per cent for a role that had become dispensable. But he also felt he could not afford Frank going his own way when the spirit moved him. Ogun presented Maloney with a new consultancy agreement containing a confidentiality provision. If he signed and then broke the provision, he could be fired; if he refused, it was becoming clear he would meet with a similar fate. Frank did not sign, and Lennox went off to train for Rahman.

By this stage Ogun had been appointed a director with a large agency with bases in the US and UK called the Sport Entertainment and Media Group (SEM), headed by former football agent, Jerome Anderson. SEM bought out Lennox's Lion Promotions, which in turn owned Berman's Golden Gloves, making it a significant player in world boxing for a short while. It also took over the management of Lennox's business affairs, with Anderson playing a central role. Early in November 2001, when Lennox was immersed in his final fortnight of training, Anderson spoke to Maloney, urging him to sign. He pointed out that Maloney's fee for the Rahman fight alone would be $225,000 and that he might double that for the Tyson fight. Frank refused, claiming it was a slave contract, and asked instead for a $750,000 settlement. Lewis decided he'd given Frank his final chance and time was up. Three days later, on 5 November, when Maloney was in California, he received a letter in Lewis's name (but signed on his behalf by Ogun) terminating his role as manager. It stated that the closeness of the Rahman bout (twelve days away) prevented Lewis from handling this in person and wished him success for the future. Lennox decided to keep his feelings to himself, honing in on the most easily explicable aspect of their differences – Frank's refusal to sign the consultancy contract and his new promotional allegiances. 'You do realise Frank Maloney is working for Frank Warren?' he asked. 'It is about conflicts of interest.' To which he later added, 'I felt Frank was no longer acting in my best interests.'

Maloney was incensed by the form of his dismissal and made comments he later regretted, in identical terms to Eliades's outburst nine months earlier: 'I'm certainly disappointed in the way Lennox has behaved. You come to expect it from people when you create a monster and that's obvious for all the world to see in the way he behaves and treats people. He is not the Lennox Lewis I first knew and worked with for quite a while. I haven't spoken to him in fifteen weeks and all there has been is a fax from his office.' Taking his cue, Panos leapt in: 'Frank, Dennis and myself created a huge monster, and look what happened. Forget the differences between Frank and myself, the three of us worked very well together, and Lennox became the best in the world despite a lot of obstacles. I think Lennox will realise one day he made a terrible mistake getting rid of Frank. He picked him up from nowhere, and Frank is responsible for where Lennox is today. The decision was disgraceful. Lewis is ungrateful.'

Over the next fortnight Maloney elaborated on their differences, claiming the real cause of his dismissal was his insistence on telling the truth and his principled refusal to sign a gagging order. The story continued to run in the British sports pages, and the general tone of the reporting was far more sympathetic to the fired manager than to the beleaguered boxer who was in the final stages of training for one of the biggest fights of his life. Maloney had reached the point of desiring Lennox's demise and went public with his prediction that he would once again get knocked out, although he changed his mind on his way to the Sky studio and phoned Joe Dunbar, sending Lennox his best wishes. He now admits that his early prediction was a case of emotion clouding logic.

The rumblings continued for several months. Lennox took out a court injunction effectively barring Maloney from discussing his private life, which annoyed Frank, who insisted he had no intention of spilling any fresh details in this area. Lennox doubts this and refers to his dealings with Maloney's autobiography, *No Baloney*. 'When Frank decided to write his book I decided I didn't want anything private about me in it and I had to hire lawyers to make sure of this, and in the end, the reason there wasn't anything too heavy about me was because I had to see it before it was published, and we went through it very carefully and cut a few things out – things he shouldn't have said – and I had to pay my lawyers to make sure. I've got the bills to prove it.' Maloney, however, says it was his own initiative to send Lewis the book before publication. 'When I wrote the book I told them I'd let them read it and that they could take anything out they objected to, and they did slightly change three things, but nothing major. Only three small things were removed and they had nothing to do with his private life. They were things I thought showed Lennox in a more human light, but when he wanted them removed, I agreed. I honestly didn't write anything about his private life. I would never betray his trust, because that's not my nature, and you can't do that if you want to survive in this business. I really wasn't about to spill any secrets. What I always said when people asked me is that I have no interest in what he does in his private life – I'm only interested in what he does in the ring.'

Today, Maloney says he no longer feels angry about their falling out and looks back on their years together with more satisfaction than regret. Like several others who parted with Lennox, he remains particularly fond of Violet, praising her as a wonderful woman and pointing out, for example, that after his dismissal she made a point of coming round to his house to see his new baby daughter. He also retains a high opinion of Lennox as a boxer and accepts he displayed admirable qualities as a human being, stressing his kindness and his love of children, including his own, although he still feels that his dismissal was badly handled. 'I must admit I was a bit annoyed and, really, a bit fucking angry over that issue, because I feel I was ill-treated, but if I look back now that's the only thing I still feel bad about – that Lennox didn't have the decency to pick up the telephone and tell me himself after all we've been through together. To get a fax sent to me signed by Adrian Ogun was an absolute fucking insult because I never in my whole career done nothing wrong to Lennox Lewis. If anything, I made Lennox – not the fighter, but Lennox Lewis the person in Britain. I made him English with the English people, and since I left he lost that touch with the English people, because I don't think he handled his career very well in his last couple of years – badly, in fact, because the people around him didn't know what they were doing. But other than that gripe about the fax I don't have any problem with Lennox. We're both stubborn people, and I admit that at the time of our parting I felt bitter and there was a temptation to start saying bad things about him, but I soon realised that would be stupid. I don't think I've ever really badmouthed him, and whatever I know about his personal life will stay with me. I would never get into that discussion.'

Lennox does not dispute his manager played a positive role for most of his career and makes it clear their parting should not be compared to the Eliades fall-out and that Frank would have continued as manager if not for his public response to the Rahman defeat. 'Eliades was despicable but I've never had a bad thing to say about Frank Maloney in the sense of strong words in the press even though he's had bad things to say about me. As far as I'm concerned, me and Frank are still cool and I don't have a problem with him. The problem he's dealing with is a sour grapes thing, which I find disappointing. Yeah, I would say my main feeling is that he's just a big disappointment. I feel I did a lot for him. In a way, I made him the major figure he became because without me where would he be? And there were also personal things, like going to his wedding, but when I look back I'd have to say he's disappointed me a lot. For a start, I have a different point of view from him on his decision to go to Frank Warren, and I never understood his response to my demand that he sign the confidentiality agreement.

'When I lost to Rahman, I saw him going the other way and felt he was doing that because he was basically looking out for his own future. After that the team had a meeting and I said, "Nobody talk to the press right until we decide what way we're gonna go and what we're gonna do in the future." But he was the first person talking to the press and TV, and I'm wondering, "What's this all about? He's hardly spoken to me, so why is he speaking for me?" And it was all over the news – him saying Lennox should quit, and this and that – and I really didn't think that was for him to say. I should be the one talking on my behalf about that kind of thing, not him. And then I realised that he was talking lots of bad things about me in the press, saying negative things about me to journalists and I didn't appreciate that. So there was definitely a breach of trust and then since we parted company he's been putting me down, slagging me off, then saying I'd lose to Tyson. It was just sour grapes. But despite all that I never said a bad word about him because, you know, I believe you don't shit in your own patch.'

Lennox seemed unusually tense in the build-up to the return fight while Rahman came across as relaxed and full of bubbly confidence. Hasim was invariably quicker off the mark in their verbal exchanges, his insults more pointed and his repartees wittier. 'Trash talking is something I did all my life,' he said. 'It just so happens he can't respond to it.' He could not resist taking this trash talking into the touchy territory for a boxer of his manhood and sexuality. Hasim was by no means the first or last fighter to venture into this territory as a pre-fight tactic. It has a long history. In 1963, for example, the Cuban Benny Kid Paret called his American opponent Emile Griffiths the Spanish equivalent of a 'faggot' and was beaten up so badly that he died in the ring. In 2001 the Mexican world featherweight champion Erik Morales made a gay allusion to his countryman Marco Antonio Barrera, who then whacked him in the face at their press conference and beat him in the ring. In 2004 the Nicaraguan welterweight champion Antonio Mayorga used similar terms to describe the American Cory Spinks and ended up a surprise loser of their unification bout.

For the normally slow-to-rile Lennox Lewis, this was a sensitive issue because he never seemed quite able to shake it off. In 1999, he declared in the *Sun* that he was not gay, hoping it would end the rumours. Instead the *Sun* launched its trawling expedition, and from then on tabloid innuendo was stepped up, along with the chatter on gay websites and in boxing gyms. In January 2001, Peter Tatchell, the British human rights campaigner, famous first for 'outing' prominent gays and later for confronting human rights abusers, wrote to Lennox warning him that some tabloids were 'digging for dirt' about his sexuality and urging him to maintain his dignity by not making a fuss. 'Be evasive if you must, but please do not go down the road of denial,' he instructed. 'It will only demean your integrity.'

But ignoring the issue or offering evasive replies would be impossible for someone from his background and position. Professional sport is not exactly lovey territory, and in boxing the issue is even trickier, not just because of its hard-man, working-class base but because of its intimate, one-on-one nature. Sections of the gay world may want to discern an erotic element here, but this perception invites incredulity from those directly involved. The suggestion that any boxer might swing the other way invariably produces a frantic response. The relatively recent phenomenon of professional athletes coming out or being outed has largely been confined to white middle-class sports, and usually only after the stars have safely retired. One exception was the footballer Justin Fashanu, whose pressured decision to come out made his playing life even more difficult than it had been when he was in the closet, and in the end may have contributed to his suicide. The only prominent public example in boxing history was Britain's world light heavyweight champion Freddie Mills, although his bisexual dalliances were exposed only long after his death. Still, they have remained a subject for speculation for 30 years.

Tatchell issued a long and strange public statement on this issue before the Rahman return, in which he discussed the difficulties faced by gay British sports stars who 'worry constantly about being found out' and therefore 'lead lonely miserable lives' going to 'absurd lengths to project a straight image, even to the extent of having phoney girlfriends'. In an odd twist, he detoured into a 'what if fantasy' applied directly to Lewis, picturing him coming out on television, facing down the 'notorious homophobia of the boxing profession' and becoming a gay role model, before finally concluding, 'Sadly, it is only a fantasy.' For a gay or bisexual boxer to follow this fantasy would take courage verging on bravado; for a 'straight' boxer simply to turn his cheek in the face of such rumours on grounds of principle would seem absurd. Perhaps the perfect example of a balanced response is Oscar de la Hoya's. He faced similar rumours at about the same time, and eventually a Latino magazine popped the question: are you gay? 'No, not at all,' he began, but Oscar knew how to deflect the impact of this bald denial. 'And I don't mean that in a bad way. I respect the whole world. I am not gay, but I do have a lot of gay fans and I am grateful to all of them for the support they have always given me in my career.'

Lewis is not as smooth as Oscar and faced the questions more persistently. Once he denied it to the *Sun*, he found himself having to respond to other papers. For instance, when asked this question shortly before his first fight with Rahman, he replied. 'How can they call me gay? I am a hundred and twenty per cent a man's man. At first it upset me because it was disrespect. How can they call me gay? People say, "I don't see him out with lots of women, he looks too good, so he must be gay," but I have realised if you are famous they always say you are gay, so let them. I'm no longer bothered.' Soon after, however, his response suggested he was bothered. 'It's such a disrespectful thing to accuse me of being like that. So, no, I'm not gay. I can't believe people are still coming with that.' And again: 'Nobody ever says it to my face. I was upset about being called gay. Was there a fly-on-the-wall camera in my bedroom? How could anyone know what I do in my own home? I am definitely, definitely not gay and never have been. I love women.' Once more: 'I don't have anything against homosexuals but I'm a woman's man and I'm sick of the rumours.'

Rahman taunted Lewis on this terrain, believing it would give him an edge. It started with a radio interview when he snidely said it was a 'gay move' for Lewis to take him to court. For Lennox, it was bad enough that Hasim dishonoured their contract and that he had to take him to court to force him to fight, but to call that 'gay' was too much. When they appeared face to face in the ESPN studio on 30 August for a chat show, the host, Gary Miller, decided to toss a flame at these sensitivities and see what happened. He asked, 'During your radio gigs here did he question your sexuality?', Lewis replied that Rahman had done just that and emphasised that he wasn't gay. He then glared at Hasim. 'Why are you calling me gay?'

Rahman smiled, and when Miller asked what he'd said, he replied, 'I said what he did was gay, that he wanted to take it to the courts to get a rematch. I don't know why he was offended.' Lennox was becoming exasperated. 'I'm a hundred per cent a woman's man, so don't even play that,' he snapped and then added a comment that won't go down as one of his smartest: 'If you are worried about that, bring your sister, bring anyone!'

It was Hasim's turn to get testy. 'Whoa, whoa, whoa, whoa,' he said in descending register. 'I'm gonna say this right now. If you don't want me saying anything about your mother, your father or anybody else in your family do not say anything about my family.'

'Listen!' Lennox cut in but Rahman was having none of it. 'Do not say anything about my family,' he repeated.

'Be careful what you say,' said Lennox.

'Do not say anything about my family,' Rahman repeated.

'Be careful what you say to me,' Lewis said in a quiet voice, glaring at him.

Rahman raised his voice. 'Man, you ain't nobody. I'll say what I want to you!'

'Go ahead, man.'

'I'll say what I want.'

'Go ahead.'

They had reached an impasse that required escalation or backing down. Hasim cranked it up by leaping to his feet: 'I'll just say it. What do you want me to say?' Lennox joined Rahman on his feet, staring down at him from three inches away, but could not think of anything clever, so replied, 'Anything.' By this point the confrontation had reached a level of verbal absurdity, but there was no intervention from Miller, who was obviously enjoying the spectacle, or at least its implications for ratings.

'Like what?' Rahman asked.

Lennox, unable to find something suitably pithy, repeated, 'Anything you want.'

'Like what?'

The verbal crescendo had reached its limits. Lennox looked Hasim up and down while considering his options and eventually grabbed his arm. Rahman responded in kind, and they scuffled for a few seconds. Miller stood up and said, 'Fellas, fellas, fellas, OK, we do not want this.' It seemed to calm them but then Rahman pushed again and they continued to wrestle until Lennox's path was blocked by a low glass table that tripped him up and he tumbled backwards, breaking it. When security men started pulling Rahman he was still holding the lapels of Lewis's jacket. Lennox was also holding Hasim while kicking upwards, trying to get a foot or knee into Rahman's face. Finally, with Hasim held from behind, Lennox went for him but was grabbed by security men before he could close in. The clips shown on television did not show the cause of the fall nor Lewis's attempt to continue the fight, and gave the impression that Hasim had not only had the better of the verbal exchange but also the wrestling match, a view the partisan Steward vociferously disputed. The odds on a Lewis victory, which started at 4–1, began to fall.

The next day, at another press conference, they were given the chance to explain themselves. Lewis, who said Rahman started it by leaping to his feet, claimed to have kicked Hasim twice in the face when they were on the floor. 'I would have thrown some punches,' he added. Hasim seemed calmer, saying Miller provoked the confrontation but Lewis needed to realise that while 'trash talking and all that is part of the promotion, as far as touching, that is out of order'. He gave the impression that he was wallowing in the dispute and took the opportunity to goad Lennox some more. 'The man is denying,' he said. 'Why do you keep losing it? This man is bitter. He is upset. He is in denial. He certainly can't beat me. He can't control himself.'

When they returned to Las Vegas in November they continued where they had left off, Lennox sullen and ill at ease in verbal exchanges, Hasim confident, relaxed and comfortable with the quick repartee required for trash talking. During one press conference a reporter mentioned that Lewis had called Holyfield a hypocrite for fathering children with different women while preaching Christian values. Rahman asked suggestively, 'Well, how many babies does Lennox have?' The reporters burst out laughing and one asked if he was calling Lewis gay. 'How many children does Lennox have?' Hasim repeated, before adding. 'Emmanuel is trying to make his baby nice and comfortable.' Eventually Lennox responded: 'You have to understand I'm not soft to sit here and let somebody insult me. If you're that kind of person, well then, you're that kind of person. But I'm not.' And then he added, 'I have to store my emotions up and save them for the fight. I'll do my damage in the ring.'

Hasim seemed thoroughly pleased with himself, convinced he'd upset Lewis and undermined his self-confidence. 'I'm in his head, big. You know what I'm saying? I can punch hard and Lennox knows that now. But the thing is, even though he's aware of it this time, there's nothing he can do to stop it. I humiliated this man. I knocked him out and the same thing is coming this time, only faster.' By fight time the odds had fallen to 2–1.

Both men looked in magnificent nick – Rahman weighed in at 236lb (two lighter than last time), Lewis at 246½lb (seven lighter) – but once again he seemed significantly tenser, a perception confirmed by his blood pressure (150 over 88) and pulse rate (80, compared to his pre-fight resting rate of 43). Rahman's blood pressure was 120 over 80 and his pulse rate 65, and he looked relaxed. When the neurologist Dr Margaret Goodman took them through their final pre-fight medical Hasim jauntily told her he'd probably eat pizza as his pre-fight meal; Lennox said he'd eat fried eggs and sweet plantains for breakfast and that his last meal, pasta, would be at four p.m. After examining Lewis she informed him that it appeared his nose had been broken since the Tua fight and that the cartilage on the right side had collapsed, restricting the inflow of air through his right nostril. He told her he had no trouble breathing and no colds or flu.

The contrast between his tension and Rahman's joyful cockiness continued until about eight p.m. on fight night, but in the final hour the world champion's bravado dissipated. He tried to get into the Lewis changing room in an attempt to upset him, but Lennox shook his head and smiled inside as Rahman became agitated. He lost focus, and then – suddenly, too soon – the moment to get ready arrived and he began to doubt.

When American folk-rock singer Jewell was done with a particularly poignant post-9/11 rendition of the 'Star Spangled Banner', a full-bearded Lennox Lewis entered to the sound of James Brown's 'The Big Payback' with his head covered in a white hood and his eyes still and focused on the middle distance, concentrating intently on the job to do. When his gown was removed, his body looked sleeker and harder than last time. Hasim followed a few minutes later, also wearing a hood, with a bandanna beneath it, all in stars and stripes to make it clear to his country-men that here was a Muslim who was also a four-square patriot. For the first time in the entire build-up he looked worried, and it was noticeable that his magnifi-cently honed body was dry.

Lennox landed the first punch, a right hook to the body after Hasim blocked his opening jab, but this was not to be a repeat of the tactics of the first fight. As Mandela and Foreman advised, Lewis was basing his offence behind the jab, and not the tentative probe he sometimes used but a snappy straight left, sometimes doubled up. Rahman, too, had been instructed to work behind an offensive jab and managed to get a few in, one of them jolting back the head and bringing a smile of appreciation to Adrian Davis's face. But most missed while Lennox's were finding their mark. By the end of the round a glancing jab opened a nick in the corner of Hasim's left eye. 'He got my eye good in the first round,' he said, 'and I could feel the blood dripping.' It was a Lewis round but Davis wasn't perturbed. 'Jab to the face, then throw the right hand to the stomach,' he advised. 'You're hurting him already with the jab. Now put the right hand behind it.'

Rahman attacked behind his own long jab, but Lewis's 36-year-old reflexes seemed sound enough. He was slipping punches and countering with perfect tim-ing. A minute into round two he landed his first left hook – a punch that turned Rahman's head – and a few seconds later another left hook and a short, brutal right hook to the ribs and then a textbook three-punch combination. It was noticeable that Lennox's balance and footwork, so leaden in South Africa, were back to their best, his movements fluid and timing sharp. He was dancing more than usual, mak-ing full use of the ring and keeping the American on the end of his punches, and when Rahman managed to find his way inside Lewis would use his superior strength to hold him. 'I thought he would attack more, but he'd prepared well and he kept his distance good,' Rahman said. 'It wasn't only his jab. It was his distance and footwork, and he stopped me landing my own jab.' At the bell Rahman threw a hard left–right combination, but Lennox bent his knees, dipped at the waist and managed to duck under both punches before skipping off to his corner, where Manny told him he could take away Rahman's jab without dancing and that he was moving too much.

He began the third by jabbing with impressive accuracy. He also took a few in the first half minute, but kept to Manny's instruction to cut down the movement and work offensively. For a few seconds this advice seemed questionable. Rahman, who had practised the hook incessantly in training, came in with a thumping left jab and followed it a few seconds later with a punch that started like a jab but then hooked slightly at the end of its trajectory and landed squarely on the side of the jaw. Hasim later said he felt sure he saw Lennox's legs dip and this made him feel he would soon get another chance and could finish the job. Lennox said he never felt the punch –

'In fact I can't remember getting hit in that whole fight.' In any event, there was no time for Hasim to admire his work because Lewis, still circling to his right but no longer on his toes, came back with a left hook–right cross combination and followed this up with an even heavier hook and a crunching cross. Hasim staggered back, looking disorganised, but had the presence of mind to stave off the follow-up by pushing out his arms – another move practised in training. He recovered his poise and came back with a decent hook of his own. Lewis ended the round by planting several hard jabs into his face, widening the cut around his left eye.

Lennox had won all three rounds, but Manny wanted even more aggression. Before the fight he advised that Hasim was not one of the game's sharpest counter-punchers – effective when taking the lead but less so when trying to take advantage of an effective offence, which meant that Lennox could start boxing off the front foot without too much danger. It was a possibility that worried Adrian Davis. This was a completely different Lewis from the South African version, and nothing they'd practised seemed to be working. He'd negated Hasim's jab and now he was starting to land the right cross. Davis's advice carried a note of defensive despera-tion. 'Every time he comes in with the right, put your arms out,' he instructed, 'and try that right hand. Try it!'

Coming out aggressively for round four, Lennox landed a lead right cross and soon after that hurt Rahman with a big overhand right. He had achieved a state of total domination and felt ready to draw the champion in with a feint to finish him. Several times he'd tried a move of throwing a decoy left hook to get Rahman to move his head before swatting him with the right cross. Midway through the round he tried it again with a crucial variation: the expected cross became a right hook. The left hook glanced off Rahman's chin as he pulled back, leaving the left side of his jaw exposed. Lennox immediately followed up with an extremely fast, wide-arc right hook that carried his full, swivelling weight and was thrown with maximum leverage. It was a monstrous punch, magnificently executed, and it landed with per-fect timing and accuracy on the side of Rahman's jaw, opening a two-inch gash above his mouth. He was out cold well before he crashed spectacularly on to his back. He made a semi-comatose attempt to pick himself up and managed to push his knees and pull his hands off the canvas before collapsing again, landing face-first on the floor. He was counted out at the one-minute-45-second mark.

While still on the canvas he asked, 'What happened?' Dr Margaret Goodman replied, 'You got knocked out.' Rahman slowly absorbed that point and said, 'I did-n't see the punch.' It took another 45 seconds before he could make it to his feet. He then looked up at the giant screen above the ring as they played the knockout over and over again, to the woos of the crowd, and said to himself, 'Wow! He's the real champion.'

Lennox explained that final, beautiful, blow: 'I noticed every time I tried to reach him with the left hook he put his arms up because he was watching out for the straight right, so I turned it around and made it into a round-house right hook. It was a planned punch, not a lucky one. A lucky punch is one like Rahman hit me with in South Africa – a punch you throw just one time and connect. But the punch

I knocked him out with was one I meant to throw. I tried variations four times in the fight before I hit him flush by hooking it.' A humbled Rahman acknowledged the brilliance behind his own demise. 'I just didn't see that punch coming. He blinded me with the left hook and that's how he got in with that right hook. He has an enormous amount of weight and put it all behind that punch. I've gotta give him credit. It was a good shot and I wasn't able to recover. He had a good game plan, he took away my jab and fought a very smart, intelligent fight.'

With his arm around the shoulder of his ten-year-old son, also wearing a Stars and Stripes bandanna and a resigned smile on his face, Hasim promised his day would come again. He preferred to avoid the fact that he'd made several astonishingly stupid mistakes – not least in turning down a long-term deal with HBO. As it turned out he would make less money in three years with King than he would have made in one fight had he stayed with Kushner. From then on he would have to take whatever morsels King chose to hand him, but he struggled to digest the retreads thrown his way. Like so many Lewis victims – Mason, Ruddock, Jackson, Butler, Golota, Briggs, Holyfield, Tua – Rahman was never the same after losing to Lewis. It was not just the physical effects of such a one-sided thrashing but also the psychological impact of being so thoroughly outclassed on a night he felt he was at the absolute peak of his powers. It drained him of confidence and inspiration, so that while he could still talk a good fight, he could no longer fight.

Lennox was in no mood for magnanimity. He ran around the ring beating his chest, all his pent-up anger coming out in a display of vindication. He was shouting, 'Hasim the Has-been! I told you he's a freshman in the game.' He pointed to the title belts and yelled, 'They were on loan.' This triumphalism continued until he had to bend down to allow his mother to kiss him, after which they began dancing and whooping together, with huge smiles on their faces, and the mood shifted into one of ecstatic celebration. Midway through a quick interview with HBO's Larry Merchant, he remembered what Nelson Mandela had told him seven months earlier and shouted into the microphone, 'Madiba! The people of South Africa!' And then, less congruously, after a pause, 'Winnie!' And finally, 'The blacks!' A bit later, feeling light and full of fun, he began to 'big up!' the cities and countries of his past and present.

Today, he remembers this as the favourite occasion of his entire boxing life: the most satisfying fight and most perfect knockout of his career. All the frustration of the long preamble went into a performance he believes was the closest to perfection he came. Only with Bowe had his emotional state ever come as close to basic, visceral hatred.

'Hasim Rahman? Who knows of him now?' he asked, his voice still full of loathing. 'I changed his name. It became Has-been. Now he's living a fairytale where he says he can't get breaks. The worst thing for him was that he had to fight me again. I wanted to knock him out quicker than he knocked me out so I could get one up on him because he showed me so much disrespect, and that helped me because I stored it up inside me and this is what he paid for. A lot of people were saying I was too old, I would wreck my future, but I knew what I wanted and I went out and did it. I wanted to show him: "This is what I mean when I say you caught me with a lucky punch," so I went out and beat him every minute of every round. The reason it was so rewarding was that he gave me so much mouth. He even tried to come to my dressing room before the fight, but I was just laughing at him inside. That man loved his fifteen minutes of fame so much, he loved the camera so much. After I knocked him out he wanted to come and be interviewed with me but my people just ran a defence and blocked him out. He must have expected me to speak to him but I never said a word to him. I just knocked him out and left. He had his moment, he took full advantage, and that's it. His six months was up.

'For me it was more personal than any other fight I had before. I wanted to take it to him because of the way he insulted me and disrespected me. If you're coming into a game like boxing you should know it's already hard enough without having to take disrespect. I'm the one who gave Rahman the chance to fight for the title. I gave him the chance to win my belts, and that was his only hope of winning them and he was able to go through with it. But then I had to take him to court to get him back into the ring. He was forced to fight me again. After he insulted me all the way I was saying to myself, "Right, the rematch is coming, your fifteen minutes of fame is over, you're going to be toast." This is one guy I'm giving no respect to whatsoever because he gave me no respect. So it was very satisfying for me. I took that return so seriously, and the way it ended up gave me and all my friends a great Christmas that year. I was so happy and they were so happy, and there were smiles on our faces for at least three weeks.'

CHAPTER TWENTY FIVE
PHOENIX, ARIZONA, 2001

When you're tiptoeing through a human minefield, images get distorted. Hair-trigger aggression, unpredictable menace, overwhelming physical presence – these are a few of Mike Tyson's favourite things, so anything approaching norma-lity is bound to be anti-climactic once fear subsides. Perhaps it's the rising heat of the Madison Gym. Maybe it's tiredness. But it has to be said: today's opening glimpse is both deflating and a relief. For a start, there's his size – always a surprise when you see him in the flesh, but particularly today. He's an official 5ft 11in but looks smaller, perhaps because he's dressed in a black T-shirt and black tracksuit pants that make him look more compact, and also because he's nine inches shorter than the bodyguard minding the door, and a lot less intimidating. 'I don't have nothing to do with you and I can't tell you my name,' the minder says as he lets the English visitors pass. 'I'd have to kill you if I told you my name.'

Mike grows as you get closer. With that snub-nosed bullet head sinking into twenty inches of neck and a body that looks solid at 240lb, you soon appreciate his bulk. Yet, still this version is less imposing than normal. He's slumping in a round-shouldered crouch, moving at a somnambulist's crawl, prompting whispered comparisons with the contemporary Muhammad Ali. Mike offers a quiet word to this or that gym rat, a couple of autographs to the patient fans sweating on the peripheries, but despite the pleasantries his face is sad, his posture tired. There's no sign of inspiration, and you wonder whether this has to do with mood-modifying prescription drugs or something more profound.

In mitigation, he's had an exasperating time preparing to fight the Great Dane Brian Nielsen – a former Olympic super heavyweight bronze medallist with an impressive-sounding professional record of 62 wins (43 knockouts) and one defeat but without the ability to worry even the dopiest version of Tyson. And today's ver-sion certainly looks dopey, but then so does everyone else in his twelve-man entourage (trainers, handwrappers, jesters, music players, sparring partners, gym owners, hangers-on) – a dozen wilting cabbages longing for the fridge. The rising puddles of perspiration are a tribute to his insistence on training without the bene-fit of air conditioning, but there's also heat of a different kind, which may just be why he's here.

He started in Big Bear, California, but there was a sudden change of plans that relocated him to this 115-degree gym in downtown Phoenix. Mike's people say he rearranged his plans to 'get some eyedrops' – a quirky excuse for a desert drive. Mike himself says he relocated because 'I just like being here. It's real hot and I do the heat to lose a few pounds.' But there was also a little corner-shop incident in Big

Bear, when Mike walked out with $25 worth of the sweets. Problem is, he didn't pay, leaving that job to his aides, although this time Mike returned and grovelled, explaining it was all a mistake, and the matter was sorted. This was followed by an incident of familiar vintage, a rape allegation – this time not from a teenage beauty contestant but a 50-year-old granny (although the police later dropped the charges). You can't help feeling that he might have concluded it was easier to be out of the state, and at times like this he tends towards the unpredictable.

To be on the safe side, his crew is eager to please. Some wear Team Tyson tattoos on their forearms – signs of obeisance that may long survive the object of their sycophancy. They swear they're friends but you wonder, especially today when he isn't cooperating. Not snubbing them, but offering a pittance in return. They look starved of affection and turn to those with notebooks and cameras for approval. 'Hey, remember me?' says Crocodile, Tyson's self-styled 'Master Motivator' ('don't call me his cheerleader – promise'). Crocodile, also known as Steve Fitch, is dressed, as ever, in his military fatigues and shades. When on duty he does throat-cutting gestures for Mike's opponents. This together with yelps of abuse and praise-singing chants pass as his stock-in-trade, but today, with Mike so glum, he couldn't be cuddlier. 'Saw you in Scotland. Great time. Good people, you British' – although once he gets chatting he can't restrain himself from making the usual insinuations about the sexuality of Britain's best heavyweight.

Next to approach is Rickie Rodriguez, the plump, white-bearded, gold-chained gym owner who is delighted about Tyson's fortuitous change of plans. 'Mike's been coming here since the second Holyfield fight,' he says. 'You know that little deli around the corner? Well, I own that, and Mike really likes the candy so I keep him supplied. His favourite is caramel apple popsicles. Loves those. I'm like his brother now. He's been beautiful to me.' He's joined by a young, white super middleweight called Danny Batchelder, who nods his cropped head enthusiastically. 'I've known Mike for seventeen years, since I was a little kid, and I've been training with him for five,' he begins, then pauses to pull off his top, revealing his seven tattoos. He looks nervously in Mike's direction and nods. 'He always lets me join him. He's watched my fights and I'm always with him. Mike has always been a great guy to me. We're close.'

And finally, to complete the cosy picture, another regular, Anthony Macdonald, who doubles as Danny's manager. 'Yep, Mike's got the best people around him that money can buy,' he says, scanning the gym with his eyes and settling on Tommy Brooks, Mike's head trainer. 'He's even got his own personal chef so that his fight diet is perfect, and let me tell you, Mike's truly awesome at the moment. He's the hardest puncher I've ever seen in my life. Like last Friday, he knocked all three of his sparring partners out, and when he pounds that big bag there you can hear it a mile off. He's real sharp.'

Right now, however, you can't quite picture Mike bashing a punchbag let alone another man. He passes the praise-singing group without a greeting, gives a nod in the direction of a plastic chair, slumps down and with a little prompting begins to talk about a recent trip to Mexico where he took some street urchins for breakfast, because something similar happened to him in the distant days when he was a street urchin in Brooklyn.

Just as he's shorter than he appears on television, he also has a smaller voice and the incongruity between the slab-like body and the little squeak from his mouth comes as a surprise. It really is a little boy's voice, offering the last clue to his childhood nickname, Fairy Boy. Even if you've heard it often before, that high-pitched lisp remains a curiosity in one so strong. There's an odd tradition of heavyweight champions with high voices (all those low blows?) going back to the wife-beating, racist bully Jack Dempsey, 80 years ago. But with Tyson there's also a childlike quality, and today it's being served up in a mild monotone that makes you feel more sad than afraid – a common emotion when watching and listening to him, along with the residual wariness of an unpredictable explosion. The way he sits and uses his hands compounds this sense of pity. His eyes are impassive but his hands are busy, now clasped tightly together, then wiping away trickles of sweat, or covering his face, or being used as a prop to rest his huge, tired head.

He settles into a mode of polite apathy – short, noncommittal answers – and goes through the motions. It's only when the subject of Sonny Liston pops up that Mike responds with interest. Sonny, currently enjoying a spell of posthumous revival (no longer just a monster but a victim too) was a rapist, thug, jailbird and man of violence who was also a heavyweight champion of the world, and there are many who see in Mike a case of history repeating itself. He has often speculated about Sonny's demise: he died of a heroin overdose while still boxing, although many suspect he was really murdered by the Mob, and there are still those who believe he took a dive in the second Ali fight.

Mike skirts the human dimensions of the Liston comparison and sticks to business. 'I don't really see any particular similarities between the two of us, just that we're two good punchers,' he begins. 'We have two different fighting styles.' But then, what the hell, he decides to offer something more. 'Sonny was just a person who was at the wrong time of life, and society was different then from what it is now. They perceived black fighters and black individuals differently to what they do now, and he got a rough deal. But back then it didn't matter. Only people like us appreciate that – the big issue.'

For Tyson, a man who frequently makes reference to the way he's been abused as an individual and as a black person, particularly in childhood, this stress on today's world being a better one is unusual. A gentler Tyson, less driven by past demons? 'I don't know if I'm mellowing out any, but God, it's just as stressful,' he says, but a moment later he adds, 'I just thank God I'm alive, and thank God I'm successful.' He went through a spell of reading the classics behind bars, even though he says jail made him a worse person: 'Changed my whole outlook on life; really screwed me up; my attitude became ugly and really nasty. It made pretty much an animal out of me.' But now, three years after release, his hinterland is more restricted. The pigeon fancier is now a keeper of white tigers, but as he puts it, 'I don't have much time for hobbies, like I used to. I miss it, but that's the life I chose.' Boxing is still good, he insists, because he doesn't have much else. 'I'm glad I became a fighter. It's quite a life. Life has ups and life has downs. Sometimes you're up, sometimes you're down, but one of the best things I decided to do was take up fighting.'

He talks of his early fighting days when he blazed a trail of speed and ferocity while living a wild life out of the ring, until these two competing universes began to clash and it all burnt out of control, first in the ring, then in a hotel bedroom. 'I don't remember much of anything – it was just all a blur,' he says. 'I didn't basically work on getting and staying in the best shape possible then.' He suffered greatly, so now he's pared his life down to the essentials – buying stuff for his children, women and friends, expanding his fleet of expensive cars, smoking the odd spliff, visiting strip clubs and wherever follows, and being a Muslim. But mainly it's boxing. He says he's learned what it takes. 'Once I'm in good shape, in good condition, I can handle my whole surroundings pretty good.'

Tyson likes discussing his first mentor, Cus D'Amato, the man who taught him how to fight, prompting speculation about what Cus would have advised were he still alive. He ponders for a couple of seconds and smiles lugubriously. 'He'd say, "Be confident and relaxed. Basically it's all about relaxation and believing in yourself." Relaxation just comes naturally when you get into the ring.' He sees his profession as an antidote to depression and chaos. Yet the subtext is one of reticence, resentment and distaste. The ring is still a refuge but hardly a place of joy. 'I just start to hate the fight people,' he says, and you begin to see why the entourage is so edgy. 'They're just not my kind of people. Not the people I want to hang around and associate with.'

He was once a dedicated student of boxing history, desperate to cement his place within it, but he's no longer driven by this quest (as he puts it, 'I don't try to overwhelm myself with a bunch of political things'). Still, when asked if he has it within him to regain what he lost, he says softly, 'Yes,' then pauses before repeating more emphatically, 'Yes!' He does not place too much weight on Lewis's flop in Johannesburg and respects him as a fighter – but not too much. 'He wasn't training and he came in and he took this guy lightly' – a predicament Tyson knows only too well – 'but Lewis has an interesting style. I think of him as a straight-up, English-type fighter and I'm definitely prepared for him.'

It sounds convincing, but if you look into his sad eyes it's hard to avoid the impression that he's going through the motions for negative reasons: because he has massive debts and doesn't know anything else and has no alternative strategy for keeping his demons under control. He finds it hard to think as far as his next fight, let alone the post-boxing void, insisting he can't 'choreograph' his life. 'I don't know what I'll do,' he answers when pressed. 'I don't dwell on that too much. I haven't given it thought.' He drifts off for a few seconds, allowing himself the luxury of a daydream. 'Maybe I'll just go away somewhere. I'm really considering going away for a while, getting away from America. But I don't know what I want to do. I just need to take everything I've done concerning my life, look at it in retrospect, and see what I'm going to do after that.'

But enough of that. He pushes away the plastic chair, rises and turns to face the ring. A few minutes later his assistant trainer Stacey McKinley wraps his hands while his DJ spins a big beat rap number and the rest of the gang returns to hovermode. Only Tommy Brooks, a wise man with a firm demeanour, stays aloof. He climbs into the ring to prepare Mike for his sparring session. There are three sparring partners: lanky Maurice Harris (the fringe contender who regularly works with Lennox), stocky Lawrence Clay-Bey (a former US Olympic heavyweight who has won thirteen out of fourteen professional fights) and long Leroy Seals, a professional sparring partner. Clay-Bey was knocked cold yesterday so it's Seals's turn to take the heat. He follows Mike through the ropes, absorbing the pre-session instructions from Brooks – things like 'keep your distance', 'jab and move'. Tommy then turns to his English visitors, explains, 'He has to do that 'cause no one in the world can stand and trade with Mike,' and then glances and nods at the door minder. This is the cue to order the Englishmen out of the hothouse and into the sun.

An hour and a half later the door opens and Mike emerges, sprightlier after the violent exertions that seem to give purpose to his life. He signs a few more autographs then makes his way to a man they call 'his Islamic brother'. 'We'll talk later,' the suited one says, and the smiling, satiated Mike is driven away. The crew is emerging too, and with the object of their genuflection out of sight they are sighing with relief. It's been one of his better days. They crowd around again to favour the English visitors with their versions of the last hours and weeks – the speed! the power! the glory! the love! the man!

The loudest, as always, is Crocodile, who slips into his ululating mode. 'Mike's thirty-five years *young*. He's a young thirty-five. He's ferocious now. I tell ya, mystique is a powerful force, and Mike has it. He's real pumped up and he's shakin' everything up.' He raises a sweaty arm and points backwards. 'You know that heavy bag with them big chains? Know how much it weighs? Five hundred pounds. Well, Mike's pounding it and he lands a left hook and a right cross – boom-boom! And I ain't lying, that bag gets torn clean off its hinges and goes crashing down for the full count, and he's gonna do the same to your Lennox. It's gonna be guerrilla warfare. It's to be or not to be time, and Mike will be champion again. He's kicking ass again.'

For affirmation he looks towards Seals, who comes in on cue. 'I tell ya, his jab is harder than most guys' rights. I'm, like, five inches taller than him but he bobs and weaves and is able to get under my jab and he's knocked me down a few times, and then they bring on another sparring partner because they don't want us to get too badly hurt. I never met nobody with power like that. I mean, his body punching is devastating – it goes right through you. He goes for one side one day, the other the next, and today he went for both sides.' To illustrate his point, he touches his sides and grimaces, sucking the air in through his back teeth. 'I'm going back to the hotel room now. My body feels real sore.'

Stacey McKinley has been with Mike ever since he emerged from prison, and he's a man who keeps his place partly through his preparedness to fall into the Crocodile mode of insulting the opposition while praising his own man to the hilt. Brian Nielsen is not really worth insulting, so he settles on Lewis, calling him a coward while claiming that Tyson is in the best shape of his life. 'I've been with Mike longer than anyone else in his camp and we have a real good working relation – real good – and I can tell you he trains extremely hard for each fight these days so he's in tip-top shape. You ask about his weight, but look at him. Does he carry any excess? I don't think so. When he was younger he weighed around 217lb but we've taken him past 225lb, which means he's definitely got more weight behind those punches, yet he's still just as quick.'

And finally, Tommy Brooks – not one for group huddles but still glad to offer his opinion: 'I would say Mike has definitely matured. He's as fast as most middleweights and he really is hitting harder than ever. We tell the sparring part-ners to stay at long range and then get Mike to slip the jab and counter on the inside, and he's been knocking all of them out – every day someone goes down. That's how it will be when he fights Lewis.' He chuckles for a while. 'You guys must get your cokes and nachos before that first bell 'cause it'll be over quick. Mike'll get inside and knock Lennox out inside three rounds.'

Mike Tyson's previous fight – his first since bowling over of Lou Savarese and refer-ee John Coyle in Glasgow four months before – was intended as the most serious of his latest comebacks. For one round Andrej Golota looked competitive, but then Tyson head butted him, opening a cut, and dropped him with a short right, after which the big Pole decided he'd had enough and refused to come out for round three, claiming his jaw was broken. But what looked like an impressive stoppage was compromised when Mike tested positive for THC, the active ingredient in cannabis. THC slows the reflexes and pacifies the emotions making it the opposite of a per-formance-enhancing drug, but, presumably for 'just-say-no' reasons, it falls into the same category as growth hormones and anabolic steroids, which meant the result was changed to 'no contest'.

The engagement with Nielsen was intended as his last before taking on the Lewis–Rahman winner. When Mike arrived in Copenhagen on 1 October 2001 he looked in shape, but over the final thirteen days he lost ground, heading for the strip clubs rather than the gym. He came in at a career-heaviest of 239lb, still hard but bulkier than normal. Nielsen, at a less 'cut' 259½lb, arrived, as always, to the jaunty *Monty Python's Life of Brian* crucifixion-scene song 'Always look on the bright side of life' and found himself battered, fouled and then dropped heavily in the third round. After further punishment that left him with severely cut over both eyes, a broken nose, bruised ribs and painful testicles, the Dane felt he'd done enough and declined to come out for round seven. It was a solid performance and Mike's longest piece of work since losing his title to Holyfield.

Five weeks later Lennox regained the title from Rahman, and the negotiations were finalised. The biggest stumbling block had been the fact that the fighters were contracted to rival cable television networks – Tyson to Showtime and Lewis to HBO – but in the end they made the unprecedented agreement that all the spoils would be shared equally: a minimum of $35 million in purse money split between the two boxers and the pay-per-view revenues between the television companies.

The tricker problem was how to get Mike to Las Vegas on 6 April 2002 before he assaulted someone else or self-destructed in some other way. The idea was to minimise all risk factors. When Tyson decided he needed another warm-up and chose the ageing but still hard-hitting and hard-chinned Ray Mercer, the Lewis camp took legal steps to stop him on the grounds that it was a breach of contract. From the precedent of his previous eight fights there were just too many things that could go wrong. It wasn't worth the risk.

Desperate for his payday, Mike tried to be helpful in making it all possible. His only wobble came when spending New Year in Cuba (a holiday that so angered right-wing Cuban-American groups that they tried to get him prosecuted). Tyson arrived in the lobby of his hotel wearing jeans and no shirt and sporting a new tattoo of Che Guevara on his ample belly; he was confronted by a posse of journalists and photographers who had the temerity to question him and take pictures. This was not one of his happy days so he tossed out a few choice insults, raised his fists, tapped a photographer on the head, threw some glasses and Christmas decorations in their direction and stormed out.

Still, no one expected trouble at a pre-fight press conference in New York three weeks later. What followed fell either into the category of misunderstanding loaded on misunderstanding (the Tyson camp's version) or insanity (everyone else's). As Lewis stepped on to the small stage platform, Mike started to march towards him, looking threatening. He later said he was doing no more than going ahead with a pre-arranged eyeballing and that he had no intention of causing any real trouble. 'My motivation for approaching Lennox was to stage a face-off, which I was told both camps had agreed to,' he explained. No one else could recall agreeing to anything of the sort.

As he moved in, a Lewis bodyguard blocked his path and touched him. In the Tyson version, this was a big mistake because no one touches Mike and gets away with it. Tyson threw a hook and the bodyguard fell – a bit like Bruce Seldon, because the punch missed. Tyson kept walking, his body bristling with intent, his hands moving into punching position. Seeing this, Lewis raised his own guard, and as Tyson moved within range, seemingly about to strike, Lennox got in first with an overhand right that caught Mike on the top of his head, opening a cut and raising a bump. Tyson went down, and once there he began to feel he was the victim of a mugging. 'I was here to promote the fight, not to be intimidated,' he later explained. 'I will never be intimidated by anyone. It was Lennox's bodyguard who panicked and shoved me. Lennox then threw a right.' All their assorted minders, team members and hangers-on entered the fray, and Lewis joined Tyson on the floor. Mike went down on him and munched on his left thigh, breaking the skin and leaving toothmarks. As Lewis later explained: 'He bit me on the thigh. That was pretty close to my willy. When he's talking about eating my kids, that's what he's talking about.' Meanwhile, Gary Shaw (of Main Events) was punched several times, while WBC president Jose Sulaiman, who was not above throwing punches of his own in times of exasperation, was knocked unconscious when he hit his head on a table.

When it all calmed down Tyson was feeling heavily put-upon. He moved to the front of the stage, thrust his arms into the air in a triumphant gesture (another triumphant bite, presumably) and grabbed his crotch in a gesture aimed at the press. When a journalist shouted 'Put him in a straitjacket!' Tyson gesticulated with his right pointer finger while still gripping his groin with the left. 'I'll put your mother in a straitjacket, you punk ass white boy,' he began. 'I'll fuck you in the ass till you love me, faggot. You're a little white pussy scared of a real man. You wouldn't last two minutes in my world, bitch.' With that he left, refusing any more questions, and went for a stroll around the block to cool off. By the time he returned he was smiling, signing autographs and getting kissed by women.

Peter Tatchell was beside himself, interpreting Tyson's invective against the reporter as an anti-Lennox slur. He began by writing a long letter (public, of course) to the general secretary of the British Boxing Board of Control, Simon Block, urging him to 'liaise with the international boxing authorities to take action against the boxers, managers and promoters who have subjected Lewis to a stream of anti-gay insults over the last nine months'. As to the guilty promoters and managers he gave no clues, but he specifically cited Rahman's 'vulgar bigotry' and Tyson's 'stream of violent homophobic threats' and said it was 'appalling that the BBBC and other boxing governing bodies have not taken disciplinary action against Rahman and Tyson over their disgraceful homophobic rants'.

This would have garnered little attention had it not been for Tatchell's decision to confront Tyson directly – a move as courageous as his most famous piece of direct action, when he tried to citizen's arrest Robert Mugabe. He went to Memphis before the fight and called for a meeting with Tyson to discuss his 'homophobic campaign against Lewis'. When this was ignored he led a protest outside Mike's gym, with gay activists holding banners saying things like 'Mike Tyson! Stop your homophobia!' and 'Knock out Tyson sexism and homophobia'. Team Tyson arrived in a van, Mike saw the protesters and stepped out. Tatchell took his life into his hands, marched up, looked him in the eye, shook his hand and challenged him on his 'faggot' statement. Tyson, in one of his charming moods, beamed with delight and replied, 'I've got nothing against gay people. I am not homophobic,' and then illustrated the point by hugging the local leader of a gay lobby group who a few seconds earlier had been shouting 'Stop homophobia!' at him. They then posed together and smiled for the cameras, after which Mike signed autographs while explaining that his use of the word 'faggot' wasn't of the offensive variety.

Naturally, this drew attention to Lennox, who once again had to field a string of 'Well, are you?' questions. 'I'm not gay,' he repeated once again. 'The way Tyson talks he certainly sounds more that way than I do. It's such a disrespectful thing to accuse me of being like that. It's a star thing, and people also wonder about me being close to my mother or whatever. They're gonna say things like that, but it's totally off-base.' And when pushed once more for his take on Tyson's 'I'll fuck you up the ass' comment, he replied, 'I think he's gay when he says things like that. They are stupid comments.'

All this excitement inspired some of the tabloids into new fishing expeditions, including fresh attempts to get Lennox's former girlfriend Aisha Mike to disclose something juicy. 'I got a lot of e-mails because of my address being on my website, and gossip columnists and others would try to get hold of me that way, but I always turned them down,' she said. 'In the end I gave an interview to one British paper. They said to me, "We'll do a story on you as a musician if you tell us about Lennox." Well, I wasn't interested in being promoted as a musician on the basis of my past relationship with Lennox because I wanted to be seen as an artist in my own right, so I said no to that side of the story, but he was about to fight Tyson and I thought this is really not the time to be assaulting his character with this kind of story, and I felt he never really gets a fair assessment from the press, so I agreed to comment.'

The story in the biggest-selling British Sunday tabloid the *News of the World* (sister to the *Sun*) was picked up by the *Chicago Sun-Times* where it was run under the headline GAY IT AIN'T SO, LENNOX. Aisha, described as Lennox's 'lover' despite the fact that they'd broken up a year earlier, was quoted as saying, 'He is not gay. I want to set the record straight. He's a beautiful person – and let me tell you, he's secure in his manhood. If calling him gay is a psychological thing by his opponents, they're fighting a losing battle.' The paper dropped in the observation that 'some folks have wondered about Lewis's companions because he rarely was seen in public with a woman' and questioned Aisha further. 'There are things he has to keep private,' she replied. She felt irritated when she read the story, mainly because they 'twisted' her words to give the impression she and Lennox were still together and were contemplating marriage 'when I made it very clear to them this wasn't the case and that I hadn't spoken to him in ages'.

One spinoff of the incessant questioning was to push Lennox into a more reticent, distanced approach to any discussion of his personal life. Over the previous three years he'd gradually started to open up, something he found difficult. As his mother put it, 'I don't think he's shy. I think he's just … there's a lot of movie stars who don't like a lot of attention and I think he's one of those people, but I don't think he's shy at all. He just likes to be in the background.' The decision to move his private life closer to the foreground was a conscious one he came to regard as a necessary obligation of fame. 'I find the media blow things way out of proportion, but I'm trying to be more accessible to them,' he said. 'I know that I do have to open the book, but not that much, not like Mike Tyson. I know people out there want to know who Lennox Lewis is, how Lennox Lewis ticks, so I have to learn that, yeah, there's a lot of people who want to know me and so I have to open myself up a bit. I'm definitely accessible and getting more so.'

He began to mention girlfriends and to be seen with them in public. He talked about his feelings. He joked about being in touch with his feminine side, about deodorants and body lotions and launching his own underwear range. At times his efforts were a little gauche, but you could see he was trying. For instance, he talked playfully about standing in front of the mirror and admiring his physique. 'And I thank the Lord,' he said. 'I thank the Lord for what he has given me.' And when this seemed to be taken too seriously, he added, 'I looked at myself and thought, "Sheesh!" Now I'm not perfect any more. But you know what I am saying? Two little scars or ten million dollars? Heh heh. Who cares?' In another interview he admitted his face was his least favourite part of his body.

His team were delighted with this change, feeling it was helping to break down the barrier between Lennox and his public. They had found it exasperating trying to explain the gap between the reserved public persona and the relaxed, garrulous friend who was constantly playing practical jokes and imitating other people's accents. 'He was always guarded and he chose certain shows he wanted to go on,' said Harold Knight. 'But now he's like gung-ho. He wants to go on all the shows because not only the boxing public has accepted him worldwide, the people world-wide have accepted him. He's got the floodgates open, welcoming them in, and the real Lennox Lewis is still to be seen.'

But the persistent prying at the time of the Rahman and Tyson fights closed those floodgates. 'You have to realise he's had some very bad experiences with journalists,' said Steward, 'experiences where they've twisted his words completely out of context or just put words into his mouth, or just made things up that he never said, or turned things he said against him. He's been in the limelight ever since he went to the Los Angeles Olympics twenty years ago and has never really been out of the public eye since, but I think some of these bad experiences made him wary of journalists, so he became reserved in interviews. I can understand it, but I think it's the one thing in his career that hurt him.'

Lennox's more immediate pain, however, came from the diminishing likelihood of a Tyson showdown, which he'd long viewed as the defining fight of his career. The short-term impact of the press conference fracas was that the April date in Las Vegas was cancelled, and for a while it looked like it might never be revived. Lennox began to suspect that Tyson's behaviour was his way of backing out without losing face. As he put it, 'When he bit me I said to myself, "He's definitely trying to get out of the fight," so I kept the bite quiet at first. I went up to my room, got it checked out, got my tetanus shot and had pictures taken of it. I didn't want to help him get out of the fight.' When negotiations resumed, he decided to set a number of conditions aimed at preventing any further fight-stopping outrages, including compensation for the bite, financial forfeits for any foul play in the ring and no physical contact between the fighters until the first bell rang. Memphis volunteered to host the event in the 21,000-seater Pyramid Arena for a site fee of $12.5 million (with ringside seats sold at $2,400) and a new date of 8 June was set.

Lewis's attitude had hardened. 'Since that bite he's been obsessed with knocking Tyson out,' Steward said. Until then he had heeded the attitude of his mother, who went out of her way to show kindness to Tyson, always making a point of talking to Mike and generally feeling sorry for him because he'd had such an unloved background. Following a few steps behind, Lennox talked of Mike as a basket case and stressed the reason he wanted the fight had to do with vindication rather than antipathy. As he put it before the bite, 'I'm going to say to the Americans who have not shown me much respect over the years, "Hey, I'm really the very best." Tyson was a good champion once, no doubt. He matured very early and I matured late, but when they talk about him now they're really talking about the past. I'm operating in the present. I've answered a lot of questions about myself, fighting people like Morrison, Golota, Mercer and Holyfield. There were all kinds of questions about me – my chin, my stamina, my heart, whether I could take it when the going gets tough. Throughout my career I've answered all those questions. Mike Tyson is the last question. This is about the history of boxing in my time.'

But the brawl changed his mood, shifting his focus. He joked about the bite but still felt the need to punish Tyson's behaviour to restore the image of his sport. 'Up until that, Mike was just another guy I was going to fight,' he said. 'But now I feel like beating him would be a victory for decency in boxing. Tyson talks about being a victim, but anyone could say that. I never grew up in a nice place, a nice world, but look how I turned out. Tyson can choose how he turns out. He's got to stop using his background as an excuse. It's such a silly excuse because when you look at it, it doesn't mean anything, especially to me. I'm tired of Tyson's talk, of the attention he gets for simply being someone who can't take control of his life. I'll be glad to see him coming into the ring because that's where it gets hard, where whatever you say doesn't mean a thing and you have to be honest and just fight. For a long time there has been a need to put an end to the Mike Tyson story. It has become increasingly bad for boxing. People look at the sport; they see Tyson and they wonder how could this man who doesn't respect women, doesn't really respect anything, become some kind of icon? The sooner the Mike Tyson story is over, the better.'

In his idiosyncratic way, Tyson wasn't far off reaching a similar conclusion. During a break from training in his Hawaiian retreat in Wailea on the island of Maui, he spoke of the contradistinction between his iconic public status and his unacceptability to corporate America. 'Mike Tyson is a bad nigger but he's very popular,' he began. 'He's a big nigger and he's a bad nigger and we can use him. You don't like that word, do you? I'm just a dark shadowy figure from the bowels of iniquity. I wish I could be Mike who gets an endorsement deal, but you can't make a lie and truth go together. I would love to be Tiger Woods. I would love to be Michael Jordan.' It was beginning to sound like reflective logic, but with Mike it never stops there. Self-pity invariably follows: 'I love my babies, don't crucify me for what I am. You guys have written so much bad stuff about me, I can't remember the last time I fucked a decent woman. I have to go with strippers and whores and bitches because you put that image on me.' Later the husband of long-suffering paediatrician Dr Monica Turner told a female journalist that he didn't do interviews with women unless he was having sex with them; then he told a group of male journalists that he wished he could stomp on the testicles of their children 'so you could feel my pain'.

Yet despite this sad and vile tone, he seemed highly motivated in training, working far harder than for any fight in recent years. He lived in a beachside villa for three months, working away at his hotel's health club and sparring in a ring set up for his purposes. As was his custom, he took on a new head trainer, this time Ronnie Shields, who knew Lennox well from the Tua fight, along with familiars like McKinley and Crocodile, with additional help from the Jamaican three-weight world champion Mike McCallum and the notorious Panama Lewis. They worked on resistance exercises and heavy weights to build muscle, figuring he needed to match Lennox's strength and that the extra weight would mean additional power, increasing the chance of a quick knockout.

'Fighting is fun,' he said after working over his sparring partners seven weeks before the fight. 'Why shouldn't fighting be fun? Lennox thinks I'm afraid of him but I'm going to show him differently. I can't wait.' He looked like he meant it, although with Tyson you could never be sure. After all, this was a man who also said, 'I'm a great manipulator. You have to understand, in order to be the greatest fighter in the world, you have to be the greatest liar in the world.' His objective was 'to be professional and to kill him', adding that he meant to 'take Lennox's title, his soul and smear his pompous brains all over the ring'. He elaborated: 'I wish he was dead. I wish I could kill him now.' When asked about the leg-biting, he said that Lewis 'should have died that night'.

Reaching Memphis two weeks before the fight and training at a casino gym in Tunica, Mississippi, about 35 miles south, he maintained this tone, and his team regulars took their cue, laying on the insults. 'Lewis is a coward,' McKinley repeated. 'He's a good fighter but he doesn't have a big heart. You know he has a lot of bitch in him. He's a bitch.'

None of this had much impact on Lewis, who worked for nearly eight weeks in Pennsylvania. Insults from opponents and their trainers seemed to rile him for past fights but he just laughed at the comments of Tyson and his people. 'Mike Tyson has always been saying things,' he said with a shrug. 'He's always carrying on. Through life there's evolution, and he's shown that he hasn't graduated. After a while we need to self-teach, and he's obviously not teaching himself. He sounds like a cartoon character when he says those things. To me, it's coming from an ignorant person.'

Steward reinforced Lewis's perception that despite Tyson's swagger he really was afraid of him. This was not simply a case of the trainer 'bigging up' his boxer. After all, Manny had been saying more or less the same thing ever since Lennox knocked out Mike Weaver over a decade earlier and was adamant that Lennox would do a job on Mike when the fight was first seriously mooted over six years before. 'I've watched Tyson,' he said. 'He's always had this thing about Lennox where Lennox intimidates him a lot. Mike has admitted that. In fact, he's continually making comments about Lennox intimidating him and picking on him. That's a role that Mike isn't used to. That, plus the fact that Mike doesn't want to fight Lennox, has him in a terrible state of mind. You can see that in the man's face when he speaks. And Lennox has no fear of Tyson. He almost laughs at Tyson. He's going to knock Tyson out. I don't think the fight will go four rounds. It will be a total mismatch after the first forty-five seconds or so.'

Lewis, too, was convinced he could have beaten any previous version of Tyson – that his best was better than Mike's. 'Sometimes I would watch Tyson in those days and agree that, yeah, that was a good knockout,' he recalled, 'and other times I'm like, "He's fighting nobodies." You see, TV has a way of making you seem greater than you are, but if you turn off the sound and watch it yourself you realise it's not that great. It would have been the same fight as now because when we sparred as teenagers it was the same thing. That's why Tyson is afraid of me. He remembers the sparring.'

Although Lennox was a slight favourite with the bookies, there was a strong line among the supposed experts that Tyson's speed and power would prove too much for him, including the usual suspects, Bowe, Holmes, Holyfield and, more surprising, Foreman. Some of these predictions seemed motivated by desire as much as by analysis. Frank Maloney once again followed the lead of his employer Frank Warren, despite having got it so wrong in the Rahman return. 'I believe Mike Tyson will stop Lennox Lewis and win,' he predicted. 'I feel Tyson will win within the first five rounds, although if Lennox gets past five rounds he might have a chance. I'm convinced Tyson will win because of what I know of the two fighters and the body language and behaviour of the two fighters.'

This perception was strengthened in the final weeks because Mike seemed so quick and aggressive, and after 160 rounds of sparring his footwork, timing and powers of anticipation were sharp. He was using his jab, moving his head, throwing fast combinations – things he hadn't done for years. Some were surprised when he weighed $234^{1}/_{2}$lb – four and a half less than against Nielsen (and $14^{1}/_{2}$ less than Lewis) but ten more than usual – although as his trainers emphasised, this was solid muscle, not fat.

Over the final fortnight Lewis kept quipping 'Can I fight tomorrow?' and Manny had to hold him back to avoid peaking too soon. On the morning of the fight he told his team, 'I've never felt so energised for a fight in a decade.' In his changing room he listened to the hard reggae of the homophobic Jamaican Capleton, and for the shaven-headed Tyson he came out, as usual, to Marley's 'We're gonna chase those crazy baldheads out of town'.

The immediate prelude was one of the strangest in heavyweight history, and this continued until the first bell. Both camps were permitted a maximum of six people to accompany their man into the ring. When they got there, the ring was divided in half by a line of twelve men in yellow shirts and black trousers whose job it was to keep them separated, but in the end none of this was necessary. Tyson swaggered in, wearing, as always, his black shorts and boots and white singlet. He paced around the ring for a few minutes until Lennox emerged from his changing room, his feet dancing but his eyes still and hard. Tyson then removed his singlet to reveal a body that looked significantly more cut than in his last fight. He was clearly in great shape.

The opening joust came not from the boxers but the ring announcers. Part of the deal between HBO and Showtime was that each introduced their own man. In a fitting prelude to what was to follow, this was no contest. Alongside HBO's tall, handsome, perpetually tanned grey eminence Michael Buffer, Showtime's Jimmy Lennon Jr had the look of a pet rodent, with his ginger-blonde hair, pinkish complexion and pale, long-lidded eyes, but it was their voices and their calling card slogans that really told. Lennon's nasal whine completed its preamble with the tired climax, 'It's Showtime!' Buffer, in his booming baritone, his phrases laden with purple hyperbole, completed his preamble for what he called 'another chapter in the history book of boxing legend' by introducing his company's man as 'the linear, legitimate, universally recognised, undisputed heavyweight champion of the world, Lennnn–oxxxx Lewis!' And though his 'Let's get ready to rumble!' climax was well into its second decade, it seemed to do the job for the 21,000 capacity crowd. The tension and sense of anticipation surpassed that of any previous Lewis fight, largely because no one knew what to expect from Tyson.

Tyson's strategy was immediately apparent: all out for a quick knockout. His idea was to get it over quickly by overwhelming Lennox with power and aggression. He later admitted he'd entered the ring believing this was all it would take – some time in the opening round he'd connect and the fight would be over. He rushed forward from his bob and weave crouch, intent on exploding bombs. But there was more than just force and momentum. He was moving his head to avoid counters – something he'd neglected for a few years. He shot out two fast jabs that were slipped; then landed a hard jab and a right; Lennox held and leant on Mike. The pattern was repeated five times, then Lewis began to land his own jab and caught Tyson with a right uppercut on the inside, shaking him momentarily, followed with a left hook and another right, forcing Mike to cover up on the ropes. Lennox was trying to meet his challenger punch-for-punch and was starting to get the better of the exchanges when Mike caught him with a heavy hook to the jaw, and although it had no effect on Lewis's equilibrium, Tyson shaded the round.

Lewis later acknowledged he'd been edgy and over-keen to please. 'I made a mistake because there was so much emphasis on what would happen. Everyone was saying Tyson's going to kill me, will I be able to handle it? Will I be able to deal with Tyson's rush? And on the other side they were saying Lennox is a chicken with no heart and they wanted me to get into a real fight. Tyson had the public behind him saying he was the best, so I was trying to show him I'm the best, mentally and physically. I went out to show him, "I don't care who you are, you ain't ruling this first round, you're not going to knock me out. You're coming with force, I'm coming back with force." Ordinarily I wouldn't do that because of the kind of boxer I am, but it was an ego thing. That first round was a bit rough for me because I never settled down, so Manny told me to settle.'

When Tyson returned to his corner he complained to Ronnie Shields about Lennox's holding, and Shields made a loud complaint to the referee, Eddie Cotton, before telling Mike, 'Just one body shot is all you need, OK? Start using your jab and come over the top and then use the uppercut. You won the round.' Meanwhile, Manny Steward was issuing his emphatic instructions to Lennox: 'Just settle down! If you could see how bad you're looking you'd be surprised. Just take your time.'

Cotton gave Lennox a fierce warning for holding; he cautioned him again a later, giving him a ten-second ticking off. But Lewis was settling into a relaxed rhythm and starting to control the action at his own pace, pumping out hard jabs and bringing in his right cross, sometimes in combination, working the body with hooks and using the uppercut up close. It was soon clear how much stronger he was. He landed a heavy right uppercut and then shoved Tyson away contemptuously, and ended the round with another uppercut and a sharp jab. It was a clear Lewis round that delighted Steward. 'He's slowing down real bad now,' he said. 'Work your jab. Your jab is pumping. You're on your way, baby.' Shields was agitated: 'You can't let this man throw that many jabs without coming back at him! You gotta get close and make this an ugly fight – now! I want you right in front of him. You have to be on his chest. And move your head!'

Tyson made a better start in the third, connecting with a couple of jabs, a hard left hook and a snappy left uppercut while moving his head more to slip his opponent's punches. He also got away with a head butt and hitting Lennox on the break – offences Cotton ignored. But Lewis was in charge, sitting down on his jabs, thrusting them out with added power from a low guard. He was fighting at long range, pulling back from Tyson's punches or slipping them and then countering. Late in the round a Lewis jab opened a cut above Tyson's right eye. Mike replied by using his head again, but it was becoming clear that his tactical options were limited. Shortly before the bell Lennox hit him with a hard right cross, and then a quick left-right after the bell. 'Shoot that damn uppercut some!' Steward shouted. 'The man is tired.' Tyson slumped down, looking dispirited. 'You're letting this guy have his way on the outside – don't let him!' Shields yelled. 'When you get inside you gotta let it go with both hands.'

Tyson struggled to find a way in, and when he came close he was worried about the uppercuts. He'd never fought a man with anything close to Lewis's size or strength and the attacking strategy he'd planned during those 160 rounds of sparring just didn't seem to be working. He was also surprised by Lennox's ability to take his punches. Early in the fourth he got in with another butt and then a stiff left hook to the chin, but Lewis barely blinked and came back with two heavy crosses. Everything Tyson tried was countered, and this made him wary of charging or throwing combinations. Instead he started to lunge with hooks in the hope he'd get lucky, but Lewis had no trouble evading these and made Mike pay with that thumping jab and the big right, and once with a huge left hook to the body. With a couple of thousand Brits shouting 'Lew-WIS! Lew-WIS! Lew-WIS!' the world champion threw two fast jabs, a clubbing overhand right and then a left uppercut that knocked Tyson's head back. He was dazed, and Lewis moved to finish him with two more jabs and then a perfectly timed right hook to the chin. Tyson started to fall, his body sliding down Lewis's. To get him off, Lennox leaned on him and threw a right to the body. But it was clear he was on his way down anyway and it was a legitimate knockdown. Any doubts were dispelled by the fact that it took ten seconds for Mike to regain his feet.

Usually it takes several warnings before a point is deducted for a minor infringement (like a push). This was Lewis's first warning for pushing, yet Cotton deducted a point and issued another long lecture. By this stage Lewis felt sure he was fighting two men, the depleted Tyson and the combative Cotton. 'I had to be very careful as it was so apparent the referee was against me from the start,' he said. 'Why? I'm not a dirty fighter. I've hardly ever been cautioned, and here's this ref making me out to be a dirty fighter and I'm fighting against the dirtiest of fighters. This was an oxymoron. It didn't make sense. Manny told me to take him out in the fourth but I wanted to use my jab and soften him up because he was still determined and tough and he can take a helluva punch. I was thinking this could be Tyson at his best, so I was taking no chances after the first round, just waiting for my time. The pressure was on me throughout the fight even though it might have looked easy, because if Tyson had hit me one good shot and wobbled me for a second, that ref would have stopped the fight.' Manny had a similar perception and was worried Cotton was looking for an excuse to throw Lewis out. He took out his frustration on his boxer. 'Turn and bang him to the body and get this motherfucker out of here, man!' he screamed, giving Lennox a slap. 'Step it up! The man is ready! And don't fuck and get caught with some crazy shit! Step it up and take it to him!'

Tyson's face had cuts around both eyes and there was a severe swelling above his right eye. Shields had little to offer. 'Get your hands up – your right hand is down – and use your jab,' he tried. 'Just give me three minutes, OK?' Tyson did his best, charging and swinging with a huge hook that missed by a foot and taking a stiff jab in reply. He tried a hook on the inside but Lennox blocked it, moved away and landed several more jabs to the eyes and then some heavy body blows and neck-snapping uppercuts. Again Tyson tried to come in, and Lewis caught him with a short right that made him grab. It was Cotton's turn again. He gave Tyson a rest while giving Lennox a drawn-out lecture for holding, even though Tyson initiated the clinch. He broke off midway through to cast a quick glance at Mike, then continued with his lecture, which lasted seventeen seconds. Lennox resumed his assault with long, hard jabs that rocked Tyson's head back. By the end of the round Lennox, at 36 years and nine months, was dancing around the ring in complete control.

Steward was still worried about Cotton. 'Finish him off!' he screamed. 'Take him out! Left–left–right! Let it go! Left–right, it's all over. That's it, man.' Shields was reduced to pleading. 'Give me all you got for one round and get your hands moving. You gotta move your hands.' His boxer hadn't quite given up and charged again, but Lennox caught him with the jab, and as Tyson tried to hold, pushed him off. He was manhandling Tyson, shoving him away every time he grabbed. A few seconds later he fired a one-two combination, the right landing around Tyson's temple, and then dug in a hook to the body. Tyson held for survival and Cotton let him get away with it, as he did again later in the round. Lewis was landing with every mesmerising jab and the uppercuts and crosses were huge punches that would have dropped most heavyweights. But Mike had reached the point of stoicism. He decided to soak up whatever came his way in the hope of luck, and if there was no luck, he'd go out with honour. 'I'm telling you, some of those punches I caught him with on the right side, he took like a man,' said Lewis. 'I was shocked he was able to take them because I felt them right through my hand.'

His trainer was worried about the combination of Lennox losing concentration and the referee taking advantage. 'Keep throwing those big uppercuts,' he urged.

'There's no way this man should be in here so long, and the longer he's here the more dangerous it gets. Take him out! Keep working the jab, but you gotta add to it. The man ain't that dangerous.' Tyson's corner was losing self-control. Everyone was shouting and Shields couldn't shut them up, despite yelling at them, 'One at a fucking time, OK?' Eventually he managed to get in his words of desperate advice. 'Come back with your right hand, understand? Let your hands go. Listen, Mike: be first, understand me? Be first.'

But it was Lewis who got in first with a heavy cross, followed by a three-punch combination and then a series of hard jabs and rights, and again Tyson looked wounded. At this point Cotton stepped in, taking his time by warning Lennox he was pushing with the elbow. When the action resumed, Lewis landed five jabs in a row and Tyson responded with two low blows that Cotton ignored. Late in the round, with Tyson in retreat, Lewis caught him with a massive right hook to the temple that knocked his head sideways, and followed up with a left hook. Mike's right eye was closing, the left was cut and he was soaking up severe abuse. When he slumped down on his stool he mumbled, 'I'm done,' and when they applied pressure to his cuts he let out a little whine of pain. But Shields and Cotton were being vicariously brave and instead of pulling out a badly beaten man they allowed him to continue, hoping for a miracle. McKinley tried to persuade him that he'd taken the best the tiring Lewis had to offer. 'You have to throw punches, champ,' Shields cut in. 'You have two hands. Just let your hands go. I want those hands to move, and slip the jab.' Tyson shook his head, 'I can't, that's all. I can't.'

When the bell tolled for round eight Tyson dutifully rose as if to disprove all the taunts that he'd gutted out of the Holyfield return by taking a bite – and prove that he could take a brave beating. So he gave it one last go, charging out to face the heavy guns, but Lennox covered up and then started firing again. First came a stream of power jabs; then a massive left uppercut under the chin and a right cross. Tyson's knees buckled and he went into a crouch before straightening up again immediately. It was not a knockdown, but Cotton could see Mike needed one and gave him a prolonged standing eight count, even though there was no provision for this in the rules. By the time he'd allowed the action to resume seventeen and a half seconds had elapsed.

Lewis closed in to finish, landing huge, unanswered hooks and uppercuts, but Tyson had one trick left. As Lennox moved in to hit him with another uppercut, he swung a right hook, but even though Lewis was a year older, his reflexes were sharper and he ducked under it. Tyson bent his knees and put all his remaining strength into his best punch of the night, a right uppercut that landed flush under the chin when least expected. Lennox stepped back but showed no sign of serious distress. His head was obviously clear because his next move came out of the Rahman 2 form book – a distracting jab and then a momentous right hook to the chin. Tyson's legs gave way and he collapsed on to his conqueror; Lennox gave him a little farewell shove downwards. 'I was noticing he was ducking to his left and my right, so I just wanted to catch him while he was doing that, and I caught him on the chin and he went down.'

Mike landed on his back with blood dripping from both of his eyes and from his nose. Lennox patted his chest. Cotton hesitated, turning towards Lewis as if contemplating whether to disqualify him for some imaginary infringement, before picking up the count. Tyson raised his head off the canvas and tried to get up but fell down again from the effort and was counted out. Cotton cradled him in his arms, and it was 30 seconds before Mike's legs had the strength to hold him. Manny Steward, babbling on about a perfect performance, went up and patted his man on the tummy while Violet kissed him on the lips. Lennox then went over to hug his victim.

Even by Tyson's standards, his post-fight demeanour was bizarre, going beyond the humble acceptance of defeat and into the territory of the bitch-whipped bully rolling over for the new big man of the prison yard. While Lewis was being interviewed, Mike looked up at him adoringly and in his little boy's voice began, 'I've known Lennox for fifteen years [sic] and we've always been friends.' Lennox was too magnanimous to disagree, but later commented, 'Tyson said we are friends. We're not, but there is a sort of respect aspect to our relationship.' Mike then thanked Lennox for giving him the chance but felt the need to bend his knee further. 'He was just splendid,' he said. 'A masterful boxer. I take my hat off to him, and if he'd just give me one more chance I'd really appreciate it.' (When he'd thought about it some more, he had a different idea: 'I might just fade into oblivion. I'm just fortunate Lewis didn't kill me in there. I don't know if I can ever beat him if he fights like that. I might just go to New York and feed my pigeons on the roof.')

He couldn't restrain himself, gently stroking a swelling under the left eye of the big man – three long, soft strokes. 'I've known this man since he was sixteen or fifteen years old [sic],' he said. 'I have respect. Everything I said was to promote the fight. If he thinks I don't respect and love him, he's crazy. He knows I love him. And his mother. He knows I have respect. He knows I respect him. He's just a prolific fighter. He knows I love and respect him too much to do anything respectful to him. He knows that, and if he thinks I disrespect him he's crazy.' He leant over to a bemused Violet and kissed her on the cheek.

The world heavyweight champion left the arena with the unambiguous praise of the Americans ringing in his satisfied ears, and to the sound of commentators scratching around for fresh superlatives. None made a bigger effort than a penitent George Foreman. 'Lennox is beyond doubt the greatest heavyweight of all time,' he said. 'He is not second any more; he is there at the top of the tree. It reminded me of a young George Foreman and an elusive Muhammad Ali – everything you want in a fighter.' Lennox always left it to others to rate him on the all-time list but knew what this victory meant to his present standing. 'This was my defining fight,' he said. 'People had to see me against Mike Tyson before they believed I was the best fighter on the planet. It's been a long road and I've finally completed what I wanted to do. I'm just glad I was able to come through.'

Yet with Lennox there is always an element of ambiguity. Once the euphoria diminished, he began to feel that a little more definition was required, that the road was not yet completed. 'The thing about the Tyson fight,' he said, 'is that I only hit him with two combinations, which were the right hand, the jab and the upper-cut, and I've got an arsenal that I can unleash at any given moment. The world still hasn't seen the best of me.'

CHAPTER TWENTY SIX
MANHATTAN, NEW YORK, 2003

Mr White is asleep in bed when the phone rings. He groans and reaches over, but the receiver is on the other side, so his girlfriend fumbles for it and answers in a sleepy voice. She hands it to her man, who listens to a wide-awake, unAmerican voice babbling away about a forthcoming interview.

'Uh, what time is it?' the sleepy man asks.

'Eight a.m. here and one p.m. there, yeah. Um, as I was saying—'

'No, it's actually about three o'clock in the morning here.'

'What? Three o'clock? What ? Oh, shit! Shit! So sorry. I'll speak to you later.'

'Yeah, OK. Make it quite a bit later. Bye.'

Lennox, identified at the Tropical International Hotel as 'Mr White', and his girlfriend Violet Chang roll over and go back to sleep, but they're able to smile about this craziness over breakfast a few hours later. When their penitent caller rings again, grovelling, early the next afternoon – 'I've never done this before. I added five hours instead of subtracting. I'm an idiot, sorry, sorry, sorry' – the world heavyweight champion bursts out laughing and says, 'No problem, no problem, these things happen. And to think I just assumed it was another one of those crank calls.' Sitting on a couch in the penthouse suite with its big bay window overlooking Central Park on a warm spring Saturday afternoon, after a night with the love of his life and a long, late breakfast, Lennox is in a happily forgiving mood – not easy to upset.

He's reaching the end of a nine-month holiday and will soon be heading back to the Poconos to go back to what he does best – not a prospect he particularly relishes on languid afternoons and it's not a destination that either of the Violets – Chang or Blake (as Lennox's remarried mother is by now known) – are exactly pushing him towards, but he's decided it must be done. The plan goes like this: First, a comeback against an unthreatening Canadian called Kirk Johnson, just to get his eye in; then a mandatory defence against the huge German-based Ukrainian Vitali Klitschko; and then perhaps an easy-money return against Tyson, if he's up for it (which is looking unlikely). 'I would say there's at least two fights in me and then I retire,' he muses. Two in total, or two after Johnson? He laughs again; today, everything's a laugh. 'Anyway you want to put it.'

But why prolong the agony? Surely after Tyson there's nothing left to prove? 'You know, it definitely crossed my mind to retire,' he admits. 'But I realised, well, let me see what's going on. I did some television commentating and I watched those other heavyweight title belts go back and forth and that made me think, and then everywhere I went people would say to me, "Yo! Why you retire, man? You can still beat those guys." And then Manny said, "You should come back and beat the rest of these guys. You've still got a number of years left in you. You can deal with the longevity question because you don't get hit much in fights and you don't really get hit much in training, and you still have a lot of spark left in your spark plug." So I've been getting a lot of encouragement to fight on, and also I just feel that the world still hasn't seen the best of me.'

Put like this, the fighting-on decision sounds so painless, especially since Johnson is three inches shorter, lighter despite being fat, and although he has decent skills, speed and power, he's lacking in heart, chin, killer instinct. Lennox, promoter of the event, does his best to talk him up – 'an explosive fighter who throws power shots from all angles' – but essentially this is a tune-up for the more imposing Klitschko, although Lennox doesn't find him very intimidating either. 'In a way Vitali boxes a bit like me and he wants to get out of my shadow, but, really, I don't believe anybody my size can beat me,' he says. 'I still see Vitali as another Michael Grant, and I like fighting big guys like that because something gets in me that I want to go and beat them up, so if they want to put that big lamb to the slaughter, no problem. You know, I've always said these Klitschkos have a lot of hype about them but they haven't been through the wars I have, but all of a sudden they feel they can step in there against the kings. They need to go to school first which is why I've been saying I could have one for breakfast and the other for lunch.'

He's been saying that quite a lot lately, this breakfast–lunch thing, ever since he appeared with Vitali's younger brother Wladimir in the movie *Ocean's Eleven* before the first Rahman fight. Breakfast, then lunch, and he was expecting Tyson for supper, but then Mike lost interest. 'We signed for two fights, so the return was always on the grill and he said he wanted it,' says Lennox, 'but now all of a sudden he's said he doesn't want to fight me any more, and the reason is that he doesn't want to get beat up again. I understand that, and I'm not going to force a man to fight unless he wants to fight. I saw the return with Tyson as an opportunity to make some money, but now it looks like I might not get the opportunity because I blew it out of the water by beating him too badly the first time.'

Manny is talking up the idea of 'closure' against the best boxer, pound for pound, in the world, the world light heavyweight champion, Roy Jones Jr, but Lennox knows Roy well enough and doesn't believe he'll be prepared to step up that far. He suspects there will be much time-consuming talk but no movement. 'I admire and respect Jones enormously but everyone knows who'd win,' he says, 'so there's no point, and I don't believe he will risk it because he realises he could get seriously hurt and no one needs the money that bad.'

So basically he's on his final furlong, and then he'll get into promoting more seriously, and he'll take on a range of other business ventures, criss-crossing the world. Over the last nine months he has commuted regularly between New York and Miami, Montego Bay and Kingston, Kitchener and London and Accra in Ghana. He wants to settle down, start a family, but he'd also like to spend even more time seeing the world.

'If someone asks me where I live, I say my prime home is planet earth,' he says. 'I've had the opportunity of going all around the world, but I realise that a lot of people, especially here in America, have never even left their town, so they don't know what it's like anywhere else. I mean, if you look at this war situation America is in, with Iraq, people here may see pictures of the country but, of course, they've never been there so all they get are the images that television shows them, but because of the opportunities I've had to travel I've learned to love all parts of the world, and also not to just rely on television to understand them. I also want to read about them.'

He refers to a book at his bedside on Iraqi history. 'I love history books because they teach me things I never knew, and how the present came about. If things are hard today in some part of the world, look back in history and you'll find out why. Like now, I'm reading a lot about Iraq and I've discovered how the British controlled that country for a while and then gave all the power back to Saddam, and then the Americans helped keep Saddam in power to challenge the Iranians, and that helped create the situation we see today. So, when I look at this war, I have strong views on it. They say you can't get no peace without war, but I feel very badly for all the innocent people made to suffer through this war. I really feel for the Iraqi people.'

He seems relieved to have a break from talking about boxing, to get on to some of his other pet subjects: the different forms of racism he's seen in America, Britain and Germany; Nelson Mandela's tolerance and insight; the need for tougher laws protecting children and the environment; the importance of maternal love in character development; the philosophical influence of Rastafarianism; the impact of reggae and hip-hop in his life – areas he's been able to explore more during his long sabbatical. But in a week he'll be off to camp and back to work and he has to get his mind firmly set on fighting again.

The team slotted in quickly once he made his decision. 'I made a phone call and everybody was ready to go,' he says. 'They know their jobs already, so it's very organised – a great team. I'll have people there counting my punches each round so we know exactly what level we want to get to. We know how to prepare for fights and I get in shape really fast – that's a big advantage for me. I'm a multi-athlete, so between fights I'm playing basketball and tennis and keeping up some kind of conditioning, and definitely my strength, so if it's anything like most other fights I'll have to take days off by the end of my training camp. Like before the Tyson fight I took a week off because Manny and Courtney didn't want me to over-prepare. There's always a perfect level you have to reach.'

But the gap between the hotel couch and that ideal level seems wider than usual. His long, dreadlocked hair is thinning at the forehead and greying all over; his beard is also flecked with white (or 'platinum' as he prefers). His waist is thicker than a few years ago and his face chubbier. By mid-June he'll be two months short of his thirty-eighth birthday after over a year without a fight. He admits to taking this changing reality into account.

'The only thing is the injuries you go through in training at my age. They may take longer to recover from, and that was one of the reasons I needed a long lay-off, because I had some nagging injuries that needed time to heal. Injuries are part of the package with this sport and the older you get the higher the risk because the endorphins don't kick in as quickly. I probably get more aches and pains than when I was younger, and boy, the training gets harder and harder. But Courtney has a programme to ensure I don't get injured and I'm certainly not taking this fight lightly because I realise I've suffered from those mistakes before and I've learned my lesson. It's important for me to come out on top.'

Soon after the Tyson fight Lennox headed off to Jamaica for what he called 'girl-friend time', moving between his home in Montego Bay, his family home in Port Antonio and the capital, Kingston, where Violet Chang lives and where he was wanted as a presidential guest at the country's fortieth anniversary independence celebrations. He was becoming a homeboy for many Jamaicans, spending at least a month a year there, sometimes more. He'd also been taking on more of a Jamaican identity, stressing his parental roots, growing his locks, switching to patois when with friends from the island, talking about reggae, ragga and ska and showing public pride in the country's achievements. 'I'm amazed that many people just cannot understand the importance of being an independent nation,' he said. 'It's a big deal, and I really enjoy being part of it.'

Another dimension of Jamaica's appeal was it left him relatively free from the intrusive press interest, and he made it clear that he was not prepared to conduct long interviews with the non-Jamaican journalists while on holiday. Aside from an occasional social obligation and the odd chat with local reporters, he could go his own way, which meant plenty of time on the beach or anywhere else in the sun. 'Jamaica is not a huge island, and when I'm there I'm all over it, seeking out the sun, because when I train in cold climates I miss the heat,' he said. 'I grew up in Britain and Canada, but I really love the warmth of the sun, day after day, and that's one of the reasons I spend more time there, the heat, although Jamaicans are cool.'

He found another reason to spend time there in 2001 when he started dating Violet Chang, a master's student who doubled as a beauty contestant (she was runner-up at the Miss Jamaica Universe Pageant) and is 12 years younger than him. He began travelling more regularly to Kingston, where she was studying, and she would join him in Miami or on his travels. For a while the press confused her with Aisha Mike (despite several inches' difference in height), but eventually they got it right and began to push the couple on their intentions. 'Everybody expects us to marry, but it's important to spend time knowing each other,' Lennox said when he was with her in Jamaica shortly after the Tyson fight. 'I've never been married and have no children. The woman I settle down with will be the mother of all my children, and I plan to have lots. I see myself taking my children out, doing whatever my kids want me to do with them. You see, I'm doing everything backwards, my career and then family.'

Early in 2003 he proposed to Violet and soon afterwards they quietly announced their engagement, while leaving marriage plans until some time after his retirement.

He began to speak more openly about their relationship. 'Well, it's important that every great man needs a great woman,' he said, bursting into laughter before changing tone. 'To have a long relationship it's important that we must be in sync, and Violet's like that with me. I would say we have a great chemistry together. She gives me no stress and she really helps me in all my endeavours and I help her, and we've become very close friends. We learn things about each other every day.'

After his spell in Jamaica Lennox took his girlfriend, his mum, his trainer and 36 other friends and family members to Ghana for ten days to celebrate his thirty-seventh birthday, attend the engagement ceremony of his aide Prince Osei-Poku, meet with the country's president and investigate setting up the Lennox Lewis Garments Factory in Accra as a job creation venture. He was pursued by Don King who was going through a stage of playing homage, calling Lewis 'The Emperor' while manoeuvring to claim another piece of the heavyweight title. King suggested that a return with Tyson would not be credible and that his best option was to retire immediately. When this failed to impress, he had another idea: why not relinquish just the IBF version of the title for $1 million, with a Range Rover thrown in as a further sweetener? To the surprise of many boxing traditionalists, Lennox agreed. As he viewed it, this was money for nothing.

The IBF's mandatory contender was a tricky little southpaw called Chris Byrd, who was signed up by King. The 6ft 1in Byrd was an Olympic silver medal winner at middleweight who turned professional at light heavyweight, but after a couple of wins he decided the money lay with the big boys and beefed up to 210lb. He remained quick and skilful but lacked the power and strength to move giants. His first bout against a genuine contender saw him battered to defeat in five rounds by the crazy Nigerian Ike Ibeabuchi. A year later he took on the even bigger Vitali Klitschko and was knocked around for eight rounds but Klitschko severely damaged his shoulder in round nine and decided his career would be endangered if he continued. Six months later Byrd fought Vitali's brother, Wladimir, and was dropped twice while losing eleven of the twelve rounds. But with King behind him he regrouped and found himself back in contention.

Steward advised Lewis it was a no-gain fight. 'You thrive on a challenge but Byrd presents no kind of challenge. Byrd's boring. He's not a boxer who goes all out to win and he's never done well against big heavyweights. Ibeabuchi stopped him, and Ike was smaller than you. Wladimir dropped him and dominated him. Vitali was beating him easily until his shoulder went. It wouldn't be competitive. You'd just knock him around for three or four rounds and then stop him, but no one would be interested and no one would get excited about the result because that's what everyone would expect.'

Lewis had long since decided he would only take fights that excited him. 'I looked carefully at Chris and realised he's not an explosive fighter, nobody likes to see him box and he offers no competitive challenge to me.' He felt this fight could turn out to be an Akinwande-type stinker, with the smaller man running and spoiling until he was finally broken down. If Byrd could genuinely beat one of the Klitschkos, he might change his mind, but for the moment this latest King man did not deserve his slot as top contender. So, instead of being stripped by the IBF, he took King's money. Byrd won the vacant belt by outpointing the ancient Holyfield. This meant Lewis was down to one established title, the WBC version he'd started with, but this hardly mattered because everyone else recognised him as world champion. The Tyson victory secured this without dispute.

One of those who watched that career-defining fight from ringside was Lennox's amateur coach from Kitchener, Arnie Boehm, who proudly described the Tyson knockout as 'my crowning achievement'. Lennox had regularly offered Arnie financial assistance, helped to equip his gym and invited him to his training camps and to all his fights. Arnie would usually make it, and you'd see him standing alongside his former pupils, smiling like a proud father whose lad had won or doing his best to console him on the two occasions he lost. But the Tyson fight turned out to be his last: four months later he died of a heart attack while training young boxers at the gym. He was 69 years old.

Lennox returned to Kitchener to attend Arnie's funeral, later describing it as one of the saddest occasions of his life. 'You know, Arnie was still training young kids to be responsible men right up until his death, travelling all over Canada and often using his own money, just like he did with me when I was growing up. He did so much for me during those years – not just teaching me how to box and planting the seeds that made me become world champion, but also teaching me about life and helping me through difficult times, taking me camping, teaching me how to drive and talking to me about girls. He was more of a father figure to me than any other person in my life, and he was also a trusted friend, and even though I know that everybody's time comes up, I wished that he'd lived on. So it was a very, very sad occasion for me when I learned that he'd died.'

As 2002 ended Lennox had not yet made his decision about whether to plough on with boxing. He flew to London to receive his CBE from Prince Charles (he'd already had the MBE), arriving at Buckingham Palace in his top hat and morning suit, this time with another prince, Osei-Poku, in tow as well as Adrian and his mum. Prince Charles politely asked him about the Tyson fight; Lennox, who said he had 'good chemistry' with Charles, gave him a summary and promised to send him a tape, 'so he could see what this big man did'. He also talked about whether he would retire, admitting he was still undecided partly because he was still unsure of Tyson's intentions. Before their fight they agreed to a return, and though Lewis didn't feel much enthusiasm for a re-run, he recognised he was contractually tied. 'But if they don't pay thirty million dollars I'll retire,' he said after leaving Buckingham Palace. 'This is the perfect opportunity to retire and it's the pending question. Retirement is definitely floating around as an option for me.'

Tyson's people realised he could not go straight into a Lewis return – Mike wasn't ready and the public wouldn't accept it. So he signed for a warm-up against a decent fighter, Clifford Etienne, employed another top trainer, Freddie Roach, and worked himself into shape. But a week before the fight he went walkabout and acquired a new, Polynesian-style facial tattoo around his left eye after claiming variously that he had flu or backache, Eventually, he was coaxed back to work. 'They offered me more money and that makes you better real quick,' he explained. 'If I didn't get it, I'd have been sick again.' Suitably enriched, he flattened Etienne in one round, after which he gabbled on about having broken his back and other such nonsense. Maintaining this form, he claimed he underestimated Lewis last time, could still knock him out and wanted the rematch. 'I want to fight Lewis again to beat his ass. I might have kissed him after the fight but I'll still want to crush his head when we're in the ring again.'

The two teams, along with their cable companies, met to begin plotting Lewis–Tyson 2. They decided to steer Mike through three more fights to rebuild his reputation. Mike's attorney and his manager Shelly Finkel agreed to a contract for Mike to begin with a ten-rounder against Russia's Oleg Maskaev on 21 June while Lewis would defend against Johnson on the same bill. But then King stepped in, devising a scheme to persuade Mike not to sign. King's motive was transparent: Tyson was suing him for $100 million for allegedly stealing his money and King feared that if he lost it would bankrupt him; he hoped by offering Mike a few short-term millions, along with some more cars and favours, he could get him to drop his suit and, as an added bonus, perhaps even sign him up again.

Tyson pulled out of the 21 June bill and there seemed a real possibility that Mike would sign with King – until Judd Burstein, acting for Lewis, stepped in, slapping Don with a lawsuit for up to $385 million for illegally interfering in a contract. The suit claimed that King cost Lewis $10 million by keeping Tyson off the June bill and $25 million by stopping him from signing a deal for an eventual rematch, with the rest of the money claimed as damages. 'Don King should be hanging his head in shame,' Judd said.

Tyson was named as a co-defendant (and sued for $20 million) because it was alleged he had breached his original agreement for a second Lewis fight. This created the curious situation of the world heavyweight champion suing one of his contenders for not fighting him, but Burstein insisted this rather unusual arrangement was the right way to go. 'This is not about whether Tyson should have fought Lewis,' he explained. 'This is about whether Tyson, who entered into a contract, should be held to the financial consequences of deciding not to honour it. Nobody forced Tyson to seek a rematch. Four days after the first fight he sent a letter demanding a rematch. Decisions were made on the basis of that. All too often people in boxing don't care about whether they have contractual obligations.'

The case against King was more serious. Burstein claimed Don threatened the life of Tyson's friend and adviser, the Los Angeles agent Jeff Wald, and conspired with a female friend of Tyson's, Jackie Rowe, to keep Mike sequestered in New York's Peninsula Hotel in April, preventing him from signing the Lewis contract. He said King paid for the expensive suites and bribed Rowe to keep Tyson away from Finkel and his attorneys, and to keep on telling Mike he should not agree to the 21 June fight because he would be treated as a 'second-class citizen'. He also alleged that King gave Tyson large amounts of cash and bought him several cars (worth $303,000), putting them in other people's names because Tyson still owed the Internal Revenue Service millions of dollars in back taxes.

The immediate effect was to prevent King getting his way with Tyson (who then decided to pursue his suit for a while longer). Don was apoplectic, furiously denying the allegations against him, and he tried, and failed, to get the case thrown out of court. He hit back with two counter-suits, the first (for $60 million), claiming that Lewis, 'by wrongful means, induced Tyson not to enter into the settlement [with King] … and the promotional agreement with Don King Promotions'. Burstein dismissed the suit as 'frivolous'.

Stranger still was King's suit for defamation. In his rage he called Burstein 'a shyster lawyer'. Judd responded by calling King an 'anti-Semite'. King then sued both Burstein and Lennox for libel, claiming 'shyster' had no Jewish connotation and that he was 'highly offended', having given money to Jewish charities. Judd hit back by citing several other examples of King's alleged anti-Semitism – imitating Hitler at a press conference, calling Shelly Finkel 'Finkelstein', refusing to allow his lawyer to apologise for demanding action from Judd on Yom Kippur. The oddest angle was that King chose to launch it in Britain. 'When I asked Don why he was suing me in London, he said, "Judd, I need some leverage." It's a remarkable thing that he's suing there, when he's an American and I'm an American and the interview was with an American boxing website maybe read by about two people in Britain, but I have a very unusual relationship with King.'

Burstein believed he was watching the final unravelling of King's empire. He called Don 'way past his prime', adding ' his world is collapsing around him and he is looking everywhere but the mirror for an explanation of that collapse.'

Aside from the court cases, Lewis had problems with the 21 June bill he was promoting. He sold it to HBO on the basis it was a Lewis and Tyson doubleheader; now he had to sell it alone against an undemanding opponent, which meant it could no longer be a pay-per-view event. The original idea was to go straight into a mandatory defence against Klitschko, but Vitali's German management were tough negotiating partners and they ran out of time, so decided instead that Vitali would fight on the undercard while Lewis would find a filler opponent, and they would then fight each other later in the year. Lewis chose Johnson, whose only loss in 36 fights was on a disqualification. Kirk was Canadian, and the plan was to stage it in Canada as his way of giving something back to the country that introduced them to boxing. But the financing didn't work out so the bill was moved to Los Angeles, where Johnson was an unknown quantity.

Steward was disappointed when the Klitschko fight was put off. 'Frankly, I'm more worried about Johnson,' he said. 'He has speed, skill, knockout power and that long amateur pedigree, and I think he could present difficulties because of his movement, but I don't think Klitschko will create difficulties. He's slower and more of a lumbering type of guy. He doesn't have the equipment to trouble Lennox, who would get much more publicity from beating him.' Lennox wasn't entirely convinced but did his best to talk up the low-profile Canadian, even after Johnson turned up at a press conference looking fat and bloated, and even after the WBC refused to recognise the event as a title fight.

Lennox headed to Pennsylvania to train for his first fight in nearly thirteen months, asking his 'team' to leave their families once more for the good of the cause and their pockets. Aside from the main players on the technical side of his training – his mum, whom he described as 'leader of the team', Steward, Knight, Shand, Dunbar, masseur Leigh McGinniss, Egerton Marcus and five other sparring partners – all his mates were there too: Prince Osei-Poku – 'he helps a bit on the training, he's a close friend and adviser and plays an important conciliatory role, sorting out any disputes in camp'; Kojo Amoafo – 'he's become camp coordinator, he helps with the press work and looks after my website'; his Canadian friend Ron Hepburn and his English friend Patrick Drayton – 'they're both multitalented, doing the driving, cooking, running and playing the role in security'; and his closest friend, the Jamaican Scott DeMercado – 'he does so much more than just the cycling – all sorts of things, like playing chess with me, going running and so much more.'

Over the past three years Shand, Marcus, Drayton and Hepburn had become fathers, some for the first time, DeMercado and Osei-Poku had married, and Violet's bubbly young granddaughter Marissa had come to live with her. Lennox paid for the team members to meet up outside camp to celebrate these events, which strengthened Manny's impressions of his boxer. 'He's very close to all of them,' he said. 'He pays them well and treats them well, and with each new wedding or baby he flies them out first class, and he's just so wonderful with their children. I've watched him over the years and even sparring partners and hotel staff he treats with a great deal of courtesy and respect, so he sets a very good example for all of them. And now that he's in a long-term relationship of his own, I think he's very contented. He really is a man I have developed a great deal of respect for. We have a very good relationship – as friends as well as boxer and trainer. We're close.'

Once they arrived they would all get out of bed at the same time and, with the exception of Leigh and Violet, join Lennox on his morning runs; then they'd have breakfast before getting down to their individual tasks. By the end of his first week in camp Steward declared, 'He's already sharp, in shape and very focused. Actually, I think the long break has been good for him, and it's been good for me too. His fights against Rahman and Tyson were emotional fights, so he needed a good break, and I can see from the way he's working that it's been good for him.' However, not everyone in camp shared his perception about his condition. Joe Dunbar, for one, noticed that after so long out of the ring he was not in the shape he'd been in when he'd arrived for earlier fights. 'I always preferred it when he was fighting more often,' he said. 'I know he says he's active between fights, playing a bit of basketball and sometimes running, and it's true he wasn't totally unfit when starting camp, but, let's just say I suspect he exaggerates how much he does.'

Steward, a businessman as much as a boxing man, looked forward to three more big-earning Lewis fights. Two years earlier, when testifying in the case against Rahman, he'd suggested that Lennox might already be in decline but he seemed to have changed his mind. If there were signs of deterioration, he wasn't admitting to them. 'Even though he's nearly thirty-eight he's boxing better than ever,' he claimed. 'He hasn't taken punishment in fights or training, so it's not like Ali who, after thirty-two, was getting hurt in almost every fight, and really Lennox enjoys his training camps. And also, you have to realise he's the best tactician in heavyweight history, so he makes people fight his fight, at his pace and rhythm, which is a huge advantage when you're getting older. There's no skill erosion there at all. I honestly think he could easily go on until he's forty if he wanted to. The only danger is complacency, but I can't see that happening again. I can't see him beaten again. I think he'll beat Johnson, then Vitali Klitschko, then Roy Jones, then retire.'

They worked on tactics required for a shorter man known for skittish attacks and evasive movement and Manny chose sparring partners who fitted this mould. After over a hundred rounds of sparring Steward felt he was ready and declared, 'Kirk Johnson won't make it out of the fourth round.' But it wasn't Johnson he was fighting.

Lewis was winding down and preparing to relocate to Los Angeles when he received news that his Canadian opponent had pulled out with an injured pectoral muscle. There were only two options: cancel and lose a fortune or fight Klitschko, who'd been training long and hard for his undercard fight against the unbeaten American Cedric Boswell. 'HBO told me it was Klitschko or nobody, and if I didn't fight then I would have to wait until November,' he recalled. 'Both Manny and Adrian were saying, go for it. I looked at the whole spectrum – the business as well as the boxing aspects – and decided I might as well fight him now. I'd been sparring with short, skilful guys but I thought I'd be able to adjust to Klitschko's style as the fight went on.' He phoned his trainer at midnight, twelve days before the fight: 'Manny, let's go through with this fight against Vitali,' he said. 'I'll take my chances.' The next day he announced a decision widely regarded as surprising: to take on his mandatory contender.

He believed he was in for an easy fight. 'Vitali is all about retreat and doesn't like to mix it up, but I'm going to come out quickly,' he said. 'I'm not going to waste time and plod around with him. I love fighting big guys because I don't have to punch down. I'm going to show him what he's been asking for. I still think I'd have had to work harder to beat Johnson, who's more of a mover and gives more angles.'

As for Klitschko, he had no hesitation, knowing that he could not have trained harder. 'When they told me, I had no emotion,' he said. 'I knew I was prepared.' Over the next three days Ogun drew up the contracts and both men signed. They had just eleven days to prepare for each other.

Vitali had been studying Lewis since his amateur days and had been preparing for him ever since watching him perform with his brother Wladimir on the set of *Ocean's Eleven*. 'It wasn't a real fight, but the movements were real and I was always watching from the corner,' he said. 'I saw then some mistakes – ways to keep him off, openings I can take advantage of.' On that occasion he was watching mainly for his little brother, the designated dauphin of the division.

The brothers had always been tight, the 6ft 7½in Vitali, the taller, harder, uglier one, generally minding the 6ft 6in Wladimir, who was five years younger. They came as a package: similar look and size, both chess players, and both Magic Circle members with Kiev University PhDs to their names (Wladimir's curiously acquired by the age of 20), spoke four languages and worked in each other's corners. Their extraordinary closeness came through their being constantly on the move as a military family, first in the old Soviet Union and then in newly independent Ukraine, and having to rely on each other for support. Their father was an air force colonel shifted from one air base to another within the old Soviet bloc. Vitali took up boxing at the age of fourteen when his father was based in Czechoslovakia, and his brother soon followed. But while Wladmir stuck to the conventional form, Vitali mixed his boxing with his obsession for a variety of martial arts. He won the European professional heavyweight title in kick boxing and the world military gold medal in amateur boxing. They were picked to represent the Ukraine at the 1996 Atlanta Olympics, Vitali at super heavyweight and Wladimir at heavyweight, but the older brother (who boasted an amateur record of 195 wins, 80 on knockouts, and fifteen losses) was struck off the team after testing positive for steroids (he claimed he'd received them from a doctor who was treating a calf injury sustained in a kick boxing tournament). Wladimir replaced him at super heavyweight and returned with the Olympic gold medal.

Immediately after the Olympics, their mother Nadia received offers from professional promoters, plied the brothers with vodka to see how they would react. She turned down Don King, among others, and told her sons to go with Germany's top promoter, Klaus-Peter Kohl. They turned professional on the same German bill in November 1996, and it was the heavy-handed younger brother, with his smoother style and gold medal, who gained most attention. But six weeks after Vitali won the European title, Wladimir suffered a shock defeat, getting stopped in the eleventh round against an American journeyman called Ross Puritty (whom Vitali later stopped). He'd been knocked down early in his professional career and there were doubts about his chin and stamina. A few months later Vitali widened the gap by knocking out Britain's Herbie Hide to win the WBO title. For the moment he was the brother to watch.

Then came his routine defence against Byrd, which he was winning easily until he quit in his corner. Larry Merchant, the HBO broadcaster, told his viewers that this act of surrender was clear proof 'the Klitschkos have no balls'. The gutless epithet stuck, despite subsequent medical evidence that Vitali had torn rotator cuff ligaments. 'The injury to my shoulder was very, very bad,' he protested. 'I did not want to stop fighting but I knew if I continued the injury could have become so much worse and I may not have been able to fight again for the rest of my life. The shoulder could have been irreparably damaged. The doctor who performed the surgery said the pain I went through was enough to make me go blind – to see black and nothing else. It was terrible.' Wladimir outclassed Byrd six months later and then picked off several other contenders to complete another reputation reversal and establish himself as the primary threat to Lewis's crown. Vitali spent a year recuperating before moving to Los Angeles and working his way back via the European title towards a final WBC eliminator that he won by stopping yet another King man.

HBO's attitude was that Lennox would see off Vitali as a warm-up for a 'super fight' against the more talented, marketable and long-lasting Wladimir, but the brothers had a different approach: joint control – Vitali beating Lewis for the WBC and linear titles and Wladimir winning the other versions. 'Our ambition is to win every heavyweight championship belt and to hold it in the family,' Vitali said. 'But we promised our mother that we will never ever fight against each other. It would hurt her to see us fight each other. No money or championship title would be worth that. It would break her heart. We never have fought or even sparred. It's the closest a brother relationship can be.'

Vitali was dutifully playing the supporting role when Wladimir went through a routine defence of his WBO title against one of Lewis's promotional protégés, the 37-year-old South African Corrie Sanders – a risky choice, because the 6ft 4in Afrikaner southpaw was quick and dangerous. His record showed two defeats in 41 bouts, including one against Rahman three years earlier, but there were few heavyweights to match his speed or natural ability. He had the balance and reflexes of a born ball player – he'd once played centre for the reserve team of one of South Africa's top provincial rugby squads, Northern Transvaal, he ran 100 metres in eleven seconds, and he became a scratch golfer who won pro-am tournaments – but for most of his career he was lacking in motivation. For Klitschko, however, he took on a sports psychologist to build up his confidence and trained like never before, viewing it as the last big break of his under-achieving career.

Lennox phoned Corrie on the eve of the fight to offer advice. 'I did that partly because he's promoted by Lion Promotions,' he said, 'but also because he's a very nice guy who always treated me with respect.' Sanders later said this call made a significant difference to his confidence. 'I really appreciated what Lennox did for me then. He went out of his way to call me, telling me not to hold back and to get in quickly. He said that if he was fighting Wladimir he would pressure him from the start, and he suggested I do the same thing – really go at him from the first bell, because he wouldn't be able to handle that, and I took his advice very seriously because I have a lot of respect for him.'

Sanders did as Lewis proposed, dropping Wladimir twice in the first round with his perfectly timed left crosses, and twice more in the second to end his reign as crown prince. The protective instincts of the older brother kicked in and the distraught Vitali tried to start a fight with Sanders in the ring. Corrie returned to his dressing room and received another call from a delighted Lewis, congratulating him on a perfect job. When Lennox put down the phone he commented, 'I knew Corrie could win. These Klitschkos have a lot of hype about them but they haven't been through what we've been through.'

There was, however, a contrary view: that it was dangerous to talk of 'them'. They had different styles, strengths and weaknesses, and those who fought them both or observed them closely tended to dispute the conventional wisdom that Wladimir was superior. Vitali, taller, leaner and stronger than his broad-backed brother, tended to pick opponents off from a distance with long, accurate punches. While his legs-wide-apart style was awkwardly jerky and not aesthetically pleasing, he had an effective defence and quick hands. He would tuck his chin over his shoulder, flick out his left, and once he found his range he would hook off the jab or step in with powerful chopping crosses. His power brought him 31 knockouts in 32 wins; perhaps even more important, he seemed to take a good shot, never getting rocked, dropped or stopped.

When you watched them together this impression of Vitali's dominance was reinforced: the more aggressive older brother was in command. Chris Byrd's father and trainer Joe, who watched from the corner when his son fought both brothers, had no doubts. 'Vitali's the better of the brothers,' he said. 'He's so strong, and I think he is the better scientific boxer. He was really beating Chris until he came undone with that shoulder problem and he's been under-rated ever since.' He said Vitali had the style to beat Lewis. 'He keeps his left hand taped to the side of his face so Lennox is going to have trouble landing that right, and I also think Vitali will be able to smother it,' he said. 'Any day now Lennox is going to come to the end of the road. My opinion? I just don't see Lennox beating this guy. Vitali Klitschko is going to knock Lennox Lewis out.'

Vitali had several advantages, aside from being over two inches taller and six years younger. His last fight – an 11th-round win – came five months after the Lewis-Tyson fight and he retained his high level of fitness. He then spent ten weeks in a training camp with the idea of making a big impression in America. He was in far better shape than Lennox at the start and still fitter when he signed to fight him. Over those final days he was able to devote himself to the task of taking on a boxer whose style he'd studied carefully over the years. Throughout his camp he worked closely with his 6ft 6in brother (though never in full-contact sparring) and two other 6ft 5in sparring partners; Lennox, in contrast, worked exclusively with smaller men and failed to find any Vitali-sized sparring partners over those final days. As Vitali put it, 'Lennox has had less than two weeks of preparation for me, which is not enough, but I have been waiting for this fight for almost three years and I really am prepared.' Lewis also had to do far more work to sell the fight – attending endless press events, television interviews and appearances at baseball games all over California – which meant he lost his edge and gained a few extra pounds.

Klitschko looked hard at 248lb, Lewis, softer at 256½lb – his heaviest ever. His people made light of his weight, insisting he was in fine condition and illustrating this by claiming he'd broken his previous record for one of his runs and sparred more rounds than for Tyson. 'He wasn't fat,' said Steward. 'Obviously, taking a year off between fights is not ideal and what happened was his muscle became solid and lost some of its flexibility. It would have been bad for him to have taken off more weight.' This time Dunbar agreed: 'We were all quite happy with his fitness by the time he arrived in Los Angeles. Weight is obviously important but not quite as important as some journalists seem to think. In a way I'd have been more concerned if he came in too light because as you get older you have greater muscle mass, so putting on weight is natural, and Lennox does a lot of strength training in the gym. I actually thought his fitness was quite good by the end of camp.' Lewis, however, had doubts. 'I could have been in better shape. If I'd been in Tyson shape or

Rahman-rematch shape it would have been better, and if I fought him again I'd definitely come in lighter.' Shortly after the fight John Davenport phoned him about promoting one of his boxers – their first contact since parting over a decade earlier. Before settling into a friendly chat the forthright ex-Marine told Lennox he'd looked 'terrible', and, he said, Lewis replied, 'Yeah, coach, but just between you and me, I wasn't in shape.'

Still, he had reason to be satisfied with his promotional graft. Almost 16,000 people packed the Staples Centre in Los Angeles, with 4.6 million homes tuning into HBO's broadcast – the highest rating for an HBO heavyweight fight in six years. In Germany, where the fight was shown at four a.m., nearly five million households watched it live, a further 2.3 million watched the re-run later that morning, while three million watched a live interview with Vitali later that day. And Lennox, inadvertently, gave them a treat – not the short, sharp treat he'd intended but a longer, give-and-take thriller that changed public perceptions about him. He revealed a big heart, a solid chin and a mean streak never seen before, along with a range of vulnerabilities resulting from age, inactivity and hubris.

It was clear when Klitschko walked to the ring, blowing kisses to the sound of 'Hotel California', that he was not about to suffer a nervous crisis like Golota. But as he later acknowledged, the decision to go to war was not his. The world champion had one thing in mind: to test this display of cool. He wanted to bash Klitschko up, take away his heart and legs, and drag him into territory he'd never seen before. 'I wanted to dog him,' he said after the fight. 'I wanted to be in a dogfight. I'm tougher than him and I just wanted to go after him and slug it out. I got away from the boxing aspect but I felt this would work for me, given the time I had to prepare, although part of my problem was that I went in there just wanting to knock him out. I said, "Let's leave the boxing out of the way, we're two big boys," so we threw boxing out of the window and I loved it. We were going to go heart to heart, but I knew I had a bigger heart.'

His tactics may have been ideal against the more fragile and conventional Wladimir, but with Vitali's stand-off style they were dangerous. Lewis bulled forward and after a few exploratory jabs and a missed hook they collided and began to wrestle – the first of several clinches. Unlike previous opponents, Vitali was able to match Lewis's physical strength, although at first the champion felt he had it all under control. 'In the clinches he was looking at me and winking, thinking he was covered when he wasn't,' said Steward. 'And I was thinking to myself, "Oh my God." Then he thought if he just controlled the centre of the ring he couldn't be hit. He just wasn't used to fighting a guy that tall.' Lennox, who enjoyed a six-inch reach advantage, kept missing with his jab while Vitali's was landing. From the jab Klitschko stepped in from his legs-wide stance and landed the right cross. He did this three times, and the last of them, a chopping punch that made Lewis take a backwards step, was enough for the judges to give him the round.

Lewis started round two with a hard jab and a right, but the Ukrainian was unmoved and came back with his own right, landing flush. Lennox's reaction speed was slower than usual: he was being hit by punches he normally would have avoided. Vitali followed up with a hard jab and stepped in with a short, hard, perfectly timed right cross that landed flush on the chin – the kind of punch that had stopped 31 victims. 'I had the feeling when I landed that punch I could have ended the fight at that point,' he said. Lewis looked shaken but was clear-headed enough to duck and lean away from the next couple of punches and then hold. When they broke, he absorbed another jab and then a heavy left hook, and Vitali continued his bombardment, landing several more hard rights. Lewis, who was already breathing heavily with an open mouth, soaked them up, revealing a chin more solid than many believed. 'I took some shots but they didn't really hurt me that much,' he recalled. 'With all that weight coming from behind a punch, Vitali's obviously got some good power, but nothing wobbled me.'

Again, all the judges agreed it was Vitali's round. 'He's definitely an awkward guy to fight,' Lennox acknowledged. 'He has an unusual European style and it took me a while to figure it out. He impressed me. He threw some good punches, punches I wasn't used to seeing, especially coming from that height, and he definitely won the first two rounds.' Manny admitted they'd underestimated him: 'Vitali fought a much more determined fight than I expected. The height differential gave Lennox a problem because we did not have time to prepare for that, and I could see it was making Lennox struggle to get into his rhythm, so it was a very frustrating fight. I was worried after the first two rounds. I told Lennox, "You are not going to look good tonight but the main thing is still drive in your jab." I decided he was just going to have to start pushing forward some more. I got him to run at Klitschko at the opening bell each time a round began. I wanted Lennox to lunge at him, throw looping shots because even when he missed Klitschko never counter-punched. He doesn't punch back if you're the aggressor.'

Lewis landed several huge jabs, including one that visibly hurt the Ukrainian, and then threw a long right. Klitschko pulled back and the punch caught the side of his left eyebrow, ripping it open. It was a terrible cut – more like a hole – and the blood began to pour. Lewis now had a target, and he rammed his jab into the eye, once using the heel of his glove to exacerbate the damage. His movement was slow, his balance poor and he was tired, but he was hurting Vitali with his meaty single power jabs. He was also starting to win the exchanges and land his right. Vitali was fighting back hard to the roar of his adoptive crowd but the damage was severe enough for the ringside physician, Dr Paul Wallace, a plastic surgeon, to call time-out to examine the gaping wound. It seemed like a clear Lewis round, although one of the three judges went the other way.

Vitali continued to throw and land more, particularly his jab, but Lewis's blows were more damaging. He kept going for that eye, mainly with the jab and the cross. Much of the work was at close quarters, and at one point in the fourth they fell to the floor together, Lewis taking the opportunity to paw the cut, which prompted an angry Vitali to try to knee him. Lennox leapt up first, then bent down to help his rival up, receiving several jabs in the face for his troubles. It was a Klitschko round, but the gash was clearly worsening, even though his cutman, Joe Souza, succeeded in temporarily stemming the flow by sticking adrenalin swabs inside the chasm, and at one point he stuck his whole thumb in. It looked like he was about to climb in, head-first.

Round five was brutal. Lewis worked up close where he could conserve energy by leaning on Klitschko while ripping in massive uppercuts. One of these shook Vitali and he held. Lennox responded by whacking him to the body twelve times in a row, but the effort seemed to exhaust him and for a moment he sagged on the ropes. Klitschko came back, landing several jabs and some good rights but Lewis took them well. 'It was a tough fight,' said Steward, 'Even though Lennox was a little clumsy-looking because he was really having problems with the height, he wasn't really hurt. I talked to him between rounds and he was fully aware of everything.' Dunbar thought the way Lewis soaked up punishment proved his fitness. 'Lennox took a lot of punches, more than in his previous three fights combined, and he took them particularly well. If he was as unfit as some claimed he would have gone down from some of those punches, and there's an argument that the extra weight might have helped him to take them better.' The judges were divided again, one giving it to Lewis on the basis of his heavier blows and the others to Klitschko.

The Ukrainian's facial damage was dire. One of Lennox's uppercuts cut the inside of his lip, a clubbing right caused severe bruising and swelling around his left eye, and two jabs opened a pair of cuts on the left cheekbone, but far more serious was a new cut on the left eyelid. Klitschko's German trainer, Fritz Sdunek, told him that time was running out and he desperately needed a knockout. He had to go all out for a win.

Vitali started well, landing accurate jabs and rights while doing his best to protect his eye. He was looking the fresher of the two but he was up against a champion who knew how to ride rough patches and was always dangerous. As Klitschko moved in, Lennox put all his weight into his biggest uppercut of the night. It collided with Vitali's chin, rocking his head far back on his shoulders and deepening the cuts in his mouth. His legs shook and it drained him of strength and energy. Suddenly there were two exhausted men in the ring. Klitschko clung on, waiting for his head to clear, and tried the jab again. But this time Lennox was able to walk through to land more big jabs of his own, then another jarring uppercut. As Klitschko came to clinch, Lewis hit him with a short, hard right to the jaw, and again he seemed hurt. 'He said I wasn't in shape, but I wasn't the one that was holding,' said Lennox. 'He was holding for dear life, all the time, every time, and I was trying to push him off. He was the one getting tired.' Klitschko clinched again, and Lennox allowed himself to be walked across the ring while he caught his breath.

Vitali sagged on to his stool, utterly exhausted, his chest heaving. He'd lost the sixth on all three cards and looked like he had very little left. Lennox, his eyes and lip puffy and sporting a small cut on the nose, took a slow walk to his corner before plonking himself down, but despite his tiredness he felt he was on top and that Klitschko's blows had lost their sting. 'I was getting to him, and I'd made him punch his load,' he said.

Dr Wallace made his second visit to the Klitschko corner. The damage appeared extraordinary. The hole in his left brow was horrific and he now had three cuts below the swollen eye zone, a bleeding nose and a bloody mouth. But the cut that interested Wallace was the one on his eyelid. It had widened, opening up horizontal and vertical flaps. One more punch would rip it down to the eyeball, leaving the optic nerves vulnerable to serious damage. Later, when the doctor tried to insert a needle for the anaesthetic, he couldn't find an appropriate spot because wherever he tried the skin just shredded away. Sixty-three stitches were required to close Klitschko's cuts.

Wallace informed the referee, Lou Moret, that he was in no condition to continue. As he later explained, 'When I went into the ring a second time I asked him to look at me. When he did, his upper lid covered his field of vision. He had to raise his head to see me. In that condition there was no way he would be able to defend himself or see a punch coming. I had no option but to stop the fight.' Vitali shouted 'No! No! No!' and vehemently disputed this view. 'I see everything,' he protested, later adding, 'I understand the doctor is worried about my health but I think I'm wronged by the doctor's decision.'

Lennox watched, feeling relieved, but as his breath returned, what prevailed was a sense of disappointment at being denied the chance to complete his night's work. He reasoned that in past fights he'd come through tired patches to prevail and that he was about to do so again. 'I'm a slow starter,' he said, 'but as a fight goes on I get stronger, and I was getting my second wind.' In fact, no boxer gets stronger as a fight progresses, not unless he takes a stimulant mid-fight. What can happen, is that his opponent weakens more quickly, and Lewis felt this was happening: that he would have won, even without the cuts.

'I brought Vitali into the deep water, and if the doctor hadn't stopped it he would have drowned,' he said. 'In my opinion the referee saved his face, but it would have been a matter of time before I would have knocked him out – definitely some time in the next two rounds – so I'm actually sorry that he stopped the fight because I wanted to knock him out for real and then they would have nothing to complain about.' Steward shared this belief. 'When Lennox hit him with those two tremendous uppercuts in round six I knew the fight was over. He was badly hurt. It wasn't going to be a great polished victory, but Lennox would have knocked him out without any doubt in the next couple of rounds – probably the seventh. I knew he'd been in this place before – in his fights with Mercer and Bruno – so I knew when it counted he'd always found a way to win when things were tough. Being behind on the score cards was unimportant because there was no way Klitschko was going to last. The important question is, what direction was the fighting going when it was stopped? Definitely in Lennox's direction. He'd have put Klitschko to bed. I'm proud of what he did that night and told him so.'

The crowd decided collectively that Lewis benefited from a dubious medical decision and booed when it was announced while cheering Vitali as he raised his hands. Lennox initially dismissed this as 'an underdog thing' and said he wasn't taking it personally. 'This is just a crowd mentality,' he said. 'A lot of people were disappointed that the good fight they were seeing got stopped. They wanted to see a knockout.' But he later admitted it had hurt him. 'Yeah, the booing bothered me, because we'd both fought as hard as we could. We'd fought and fought, giving it everything we had.'

Perhaps for this reason, he showed irritation in his post-fight interview with HBO's Larry Merchant, snapping out impatient answers, refusing to give Klitschko much credit and declining to hand back Merchant's microphone until he'd had his say. But what bothered him even more was his opponent's reaction. Vitali crossed the ring, knocked Lennox with his glove in his exasperation and demanded a rematch. Lewis turned to him and, according to the beaten boxer, said, 'Vitali, don't worry. I will give you a rematch.'

When Vitali learned he'd been ahead on all three cards by margins of 58 to 56 (four rounds to two) he decided he deserved to be champion. 'Right now I feel like I'm the people's champion,' he said an hour after the fight. 'I have some feeling Lennox Lewis lose energy and lose his condition, and you've seen my record. I can punch hard in all twelve rounds and I think I have very big chance in this fight.' He later admitted he'd never been hit so hard, that Lennox was by far the strongest man he'd ever fought, and that he'd taken too many punches, but at the time he was reluctant to admit to weakness. 'Lennox is a great fighter, but I don't give him chance to use his great weapon, the right hand. I controlled the fight, but it was not so easy to fight Lewis – he's good – but he doesn't punch very hard. I punch him with every jab. I saw his punches come. He makes great fight, but I know I would have won.' He soon took this a step further. 'Lennox is world champion, and on June twenty-one I beat him. Many people doubt that he's world champion, that he beat me in our last fight. I don't feel like the loser. I beat him on points.'

He also claimed that his cuts were opened by head butts – a view later disproved by footage that clearly proved a right cross started the Ukrainian's troubles and there was no careless use of the head. This attitude exasperated Lewis. 'Take that out of your vocabulary,' he snapped, 'it's crazy. I've never head butted anyone in my life.' He responded to Klitschko's rematch demand. 'If he wants a rematch there is no problem with that – if the money is right. I will have much more time to prepare. My performance can only get better. He caught me at my worst and I still beat him. Show me the money and I am happy to give him a rematch because I'll bust up the other side of his face too.'

This was a more belligerent version of Lewis than his public knew. He brawled aggressively, took big hits in order to land his own and after the fight was a hard man, talking about the pain he wanted to inflict. The general verdict was that he'd lost a lot in terms of speed, balance, timing and fitness but had gained in terms of his reputation for guts, chin and attitude. More vulnerable, certainly, but also more exciting.

But once again he found himself eclipsed. The new American darling was the man he had just beaten, Vitali Klitschko. The false perception – that this adopted Californian had been cruelly deprived of the title by the bad luck of an over-officious doctor – stuck. The bailing out against Chris Byrd was forgotten, and as he tramped the circuit of Jay Leno, Jimmy Kimmel and morning television, his relationship with the American sporting public gelled. If the United States could no longer produce a dominant heavyweight then they would settle for this huge multi-lingual resident of Los Angeles, with his big heart, big punch and hard chin.

CHAPTER TWENTY SEVEN
MANHATTAN, NEW YORK, 2004

Everything is bigger now – the body, the face, and particularly the smile. Today Lennox exudes contentment. He seems delighted with his lot, hugely relieved that he's finally made his decision to retire, although he knows, as do those around him, that in his line of work finality can be more elusive than it appears. But for the moment, anyway, he's done with the physical side of boxing and he's doing his best to convince himself and everyone else that he'll never return to it. He's about to leave for London to help promote a title fight (a minor one) of his friend Audley Harrison. Then he's off to Los Angeles to play a role in the promotion of his protégé Corrie Sanders, who will be fighting for his old title against his old opponent Vitali Klitschko, who will be coached by his old trainer, Manny Steward – funny how things turn out. So he's still in there, still involved, still interested, but as yet just about resisting the temptation to take up arms again.

'You ask about being tempted by boredom to get back into the ring. No, I don't see it,' he says, with another smile that for a moment makes you wonder. 'I've been trying to get out of the ring for a long time, and now I've finally done it. I couldn't get out without fighting Tyson, because when I was growing up in boxing his name was synonymous with being a real man and I felt if I didn't fight him people would still be saying he's the man. Well, I fought him, and the public saw that he wasn't the man, and by the way, I honestly think that's why he didn't want to fight me in the early days. If we'd fought back in 1996 I would have done what Buster Douglas did, because Douglas and I basically boxed him the same way. But once I'd beaten Tyson, what more was there to prove?'

The way he portrays it is that ever since vanquishing Tyson he's been staying afloat as champion for the benefit of other people, which is certainly part of the truth but not the whole truth. 'They wanted me to fight Klitschko, so when the Johnson fight was cancelled I went ahead with it, and I know the fight wasn't pretty but I was on my way to knocking him out. At first he claimed I butted him, but then they found that was untrue and the cut was caused by a punch, so they said, well, he only lost on cuts, but of course the point they missed was that I was the one who cut him with my fists. So the call went out that I should go back to camp and do it all over again, and I can tell you, if I had done that the result would have been the same. I would have stopped him again. I could easily have done that.'

Well, then, why not? With Klitschko's newfound celebrity status, the return would have been huge – big enough to confirm the Lewis 'legacy'. Why endure the boos of the crowds? Lennox sighs, aware that everything he does in life comes with a layer of uncertainty. 'Sure, I could have gone ahead with the return, and I know I'd

have beaten him again, and in a way carrying on would have been the easiest decision because I'm sure I could have kept on winning at that level for a while longer. I
could easily have done that if I had the hunger but I didn't have the hunger to go
through all that again. I didn't have the hunger to beat the same guy a second time,
and to box at that level you need the passion and desire. I realised I just didn't have
it any more, and that without it I really shouldn't be boxing. And then I started
thinking, I know what happens to boxers when they get old, and really, all I'm doing
is feeding other people's wishes. I considered all the options, as I always do, and in
the end I felt retirement was the best way to go.'

This time he provides a more ambiguous grin. 'It's you guys who want me to carry
on, but you don't take the punches and I do. Don't get me wrong, I understand why
you want to see me fight a guy like Klitschko again because it was a great fight, but
the reason it was great was that I got hit far more than in the past. Think about that.'
He shrugs, aware that the kind of fights that are good for the public are not the kind
that are good for boxers. 'I'm into the sweet science of hitting without getting hit,
and I suppose that is why some people don't find me an exciting fighter because they
don't appreciate the defensive side, and maybe what I do is not always attractive to
fans who just want to see blood, but my idea was always to show people that there is
more to my sport than blood, and now my idea is to show them that there is more to
me than boxing.'

What other things, then? He talks a bit about Harrison and Sanders, but that hardly takes him far from base, so he moves on to the subject of the US presidential
election. He's just heard that Don King has come out in support of George W. Bush.
He laughs at this and admits to a sneaking admiration for Colin Powell and Condi
Rice, black people who've made it to the top of the American political tree, but that's
not where his political identity lies. 'I've never met Bush but I have met John Kerry and
I hope he wins,' he says. 'Actually, I went to a private lecture he gave at a house in
Miami, and afterwards he came over and thanked me for coming. We talked for a while
and he said I was doing a great job in representing my sport, and I was really impressed
with his policies and what he had to say, so I was very pleased to hear it when he
announced his candidature in the presidential election, and I'll be supporting him.'

Audley Harrison, Corrie Sanders and John Kerry – a mixture of big winners and
brave losers, it would seem. And as for Lennox himself, well, for the moment he's
content to watch and wait while taking on fresh charitable causes, seeing to his new,
more hands-on role as a director of the Sport, Entertainment & Media Group
(SEM) and playing his part as a boxing promoter and television commentator.
There are a few older causes too, like those court cases against Don King, and
between all that lots more beach time, some more fiancée and family time, and
maybe soon marriage and children time. He thinks it's full enough to satisfy him for
the time being. He hopes so. But if heavyweight history offers any precedents then
the urge to return will take a while longer to settle.

The end to Lennox Lewis' boxing career – or at least this phase of it – was a
bit like the start fifteen years earlier: a period of indecision, a testing of options,
a long spell of keeping everyone waiting and finally the big announcement in

London. Just as he'd done when choosing a new trainer after his first defeat in 1994, he listened to conflicting advice and pondered over it. He then turned to history to help himself to analyse his predicament, picking out the retirement trends over the past 110 years and finding two historical poles to avoid: those who retired too soon for their own obsessive desires or for their pockets and came back to failure, and those who left it too late, prolonging the agony. Thinly interspersed between these cautionary examples were the few who left at the right time, never to return. He regularly cited the example of Marvelous Marvin Hagler, the world middleweight champion who retired after his disputed loss to Sugar Ray Leonard and never mounted a comeback, and he also began talking about the happy two heavyweights who bowed out as winners and stayed out. 'Gene Tunney and Rocky Marciano retired as champions and stayed retired, and I promise you, I will be the third,' he said.

Tunney is the champion who first comes to mind when trying to find historical resonance. He too was a handsome working-class lad who read books, tried out new ideas and fraternised with authors and politicians (quoting Shakespeare and sitting at the knee of George Bernard Shaw, and he later had a son who was elected as a Democrat senator for California). Like Lennox, he preferred hitting without getting hit (although Gene was a light-fisted light heavy rather than a heavy-hitting super heavy). He too suffered an unexpected defeat when he was supposedly reaching his peak, a horrific mauling by the great middleweight Harry Greb, but came back to beat a declining Greb and then to outbox the wildly popular and over-rated Jack Dempsey to win the heavyweight title, but, like Lewis after Tyson, he had to endure the taunt that he was lucky to miss the peak version. He retired at 31 after two defences, using the opportunity to announce his engagement to steel heiress Polly Lauder. 'I have fought my way to the goal of my ambition,' he said. 'I became a professional fighter because I realised it afforded me the quickest way to earn a fortune and now that I have it I shall retire.' He said he considered fighting on, 'but it looks like it might be two or three years before a dangerous opponent is developed. That is too long to stand and wait.' Instead he married Polly and made another fortune; about as successful a post-boxing life as you get – at least if you excise his final decade when his schizophrenic daughter murdered her English husband and ended up in a psychiatric hospital, and the distraught Gene descended into alcoholism, dying in despair at 81.

In one sense, Rocky Marciano's career was even more successful: 49 fights, 49 wins and 43 knockouts, although he did lose an amateur bout after turning professional and got away with at least one dubious decision. The heavy-handed Italian-American seemed crude and clumsy, bled when you breathed on him, and at 5ft 10½in and 185lb looked too small to make a big impression. But the combination of his tenacity, power, strength, chin and superb conditioning, plus the good fortune of peaking when the division was at its weakest, together with some creative side-stepping of the best big men, saw him through three years as champion and six title defences. He retired at 32, planned a comeback five years later, but decided against it and settled for a staged 'computer fight' against Muhammad Ali.

Still, Rocky's last years weren't quite as anodyne as the press image of his time. An obsessive miser, he took to hiding money under mattresses and doing his own heavy-weather debt collecting. At the age of 46 he saved a few pennies by taking a cheap flight in a single-engine aircraft and died in a crash. These are the positive models for Lennox to follow. The rest are less salutary.

The first world heavyweight champion to mount a comeback was big, crude Jim Jeffries, who bowed out in 1904 after just twenty bouts. Then the brilliant Jack Johnson became the first black man to win the title, and the likes of John L. Sullivan and Jim Corbett – the last bare-knuckle and the first gloved champion – shuddered with disgust. The author Jack London appealed to Jim as 'the chosen representative of the white race' and called on him 'to wipe the golden smile off that Nigger's face'. Dim Jim, who once remarked that 'all coons look alike to me', needed the money, answered the call and was beaten to a pulp.

Jack Dempsey ruled for seven years during the 1920s through a combination of his savagery in the ring, his refusal to fight black men ('I will draw the colour line and pay no attention to Negro challengers') and his undemanding workload (five low-risk defences in seven years). After two defeats at the hands of Tunney he retired, but returned four years later, aged 36, for an eight-month spell packed with 59 exhibition bouts. His plan to take it to the next level was scotched when he was soundly outboxed by a better class journeyman called Kingfish Levinsky. Jack tried again at 45 and then retired to become a wrestling referee, Coast Guard commander and restaurant owner.

The comebacks of his successors were even less encouraging. The second black heavyweight champion, Joe Louis, retired at 34 after reigning for over eleven years, with 25 defences, but tax troubles forced him back, and Ezzard Charles, who gave away 34lb, bashed him up for fifteen painful rounds. Joe pressed on until his thirty-eighth year, when Marciano stopped him, after which his life spiralled into the despair of chronic debt, heroin addiction, delusional paranoia and commitment to a psychiatric hospital. He ended his days at the age of 66, as a wheelchair-ridden Las Vegas greeter.

Muhammad Ali was never the same after October 1975, when he arrived unfit for his third, brutal fight against Joe Frazier in Manila. After that he remained champion partly through the courtesy of judges who awarded bonus points for fame, before losing to seven-fight novice Leon Spinks. He finally retired after beating Spinks (who forgot to train), but the whispers in his own head and the tugging at his coattails could not be denied. 'Thirty-six is getting to the age you know it's time to leave,' he admitted, 'but something tells you you've got to take one more gamble.' He took a horrible hiding from Larry Holmes but tried once more, losing again. Finally, nearing 40, he learned to say no, after which punch-exacerbated Parkinson's robbed him of his once remarkable powers of movement and speech, even if his powers of perception remained sound. And it was even sadder for Frazier, without his realising it. After a second, one-sided beating by George Foreman he retired, but couldn't help himself and looked pathetic when scraping a comeback draw with a no-hoper, after which he returned to his default state of seething hatred for Ali, mocking Muhammad's condition with slurred words and muddled thoughts.

In Foreman's case, it took ten years, but even though his return was a triumph that prompted an even more lucrative career selling grilling machines, he had to endure some beatings along the way. He drifted back into retirement after his third comeback loss, aged 49, but six years later discovered he wasn't quite satisfied and announced he would fight on. His example was followed by Holmes, who'd enjoyed a memorable reign of twenty wins in over seven years as champion but retired a bitter 36-year-old after losing a poor decision. Greed prompted his first return, which saw him flattened by Tyson, and envy his second, in his forties. He wanted what Foreman had, and like George, lost three times, but unlike George none of his wins gained him a title. At 54, rich but unsatisfied, Holmes is still chasing Foreman, berating Lewis and trumpeting his heroic past.

When it comes to those who just couldn't retire, history is even less encouraging. Lewis's British-born predecessor, Bob Fitzsimmons, fought on with diminishing returns until the age of 50, dying a poor man three years later. Jack Johnson once beat up an aged Fitz, but he too couldn't say no, boxing until the age of 54 and making another losing return at 60. He spent his later years displaying his resentment of his black successor, Joe Louis, while at the same time pleading to be allowed to help him. Joe gave way to the brilliant Ezzard Charles, who began his gradual decline as a 26-year-old light heavyweight after killing an opponent but went on to win the heavyweight title and defend it eight times. By 30 he was losing to men he'd previously outclassed, but pressed on for eight more years, ending with a series of defeats and dying, broken and crippled, from Lou Gehrig's disease at 53. Floyd Patterson, the youngest man to win the title until Tyson and the first to regain it, plugged on until Ali stopped him for a second time when he was nearly 38. Two decades later the effect of all those punches contributed to the early onset of Alzheimer's disease. His worst batterings came at the hands of Sonny Liston, who was frozen out of contention after his second, dubious loss to Ali and fought on aimlessly, dying of a heroin overdose shortly after his last fight when he was probably 43 years old.

These, then, are the sad precedents from the division's history, lending credence to the idea that careers in boxing, as in politics, almost always end in failure. And the picture was even direr when Lennox considered the plight of his contemporaries.

None more so than Frank Bruno, who announced his intention to return at 41 despite warnings that his eyesight was at risk if he boxed again. He decided Audley Harrison was, 'ready to be picked like an orange' and appeared in the ring before a Harrison fight but despite the obligatory ovation, this time he looked a forlorn, insecure figure. A week later he checked himself into The Priory, a rest-home-cum-dry-out clinic used by celebrities on the skids, after acknowledging he was suffering from depression, but quickly checked out again, only to return and leave again. After his third spell he complained, 'I've had a lot of mugs and creeps in my house but I've had a lot of good people and I stick with the good people I know. It's jealousy and power and money. They're trying to turn me into the English Mike Tyson. I'm not. I'm the English Frank Bruno I always was. I'm a prisoner in my own home. Just let me chill.'

But 'chilling' wasn't his accustomed mode. He was consumed by loneliness, isolation and confusion. He sometimes slept in a tent in the garden, or in the boxing ring used for his WBC title win, which he bought. He told friends he was really Frankie Dettori, the champion jockey, and accused his tailor, who was fitting him for a pantomime costume, of trying to put him into a straitjacket. He drove to Liverpool and began wandering the streets, knocking on the doors of strangers; he drove to Land's End, 'crazily weaving in and out of the traffic lanes', as he admitted. He started giving away hundreds of thousands of pounds. In conversation he struggled to hold his end, sometimes not making sense. Eventually, at the prompting of his oldest daughter and his ex-wife, Laura, two doctors signed the order sectioning him under the Mental Health Act and he was committed to a psychiatric hospital for observation. He was later diagnosed as a manic-depressive with an obsessive disorder. Soon after, he attempted to force his way out and ten policemen had to restrain him, after which he was given injections to calm him down. He explained, 'It was a man thing. People run ten miles when they hear you're mentally ill, but it's not as bad as people think.' The *Sun,* however, had a different perspective, surpassing itself with the headline BONKERS BRUNO LOCKED UP.

Lennox, who'd long since forgotten their feud, was one of the first to offer support. 'It must be a terrible time for Frank,' he said. 'All boxers think about the future but they're only as good as their last fight. Once you lose, what will you do? What will you do when you stop? We should all do better. We should look into these situations and look after the interests of boxers when they retire. You can see by Frank's behaviour – sleeping in his boxing ring – how much he misses boxing, so he should get involved with a young boxer and help him achieve his dreams. People love Frank and he should love himself because of the effect he has on people when he meets them. He helps them in a very positive way. It's a sad situation, and I can only wish him the best and hope he gets things sorted out.'

One week Frank was talking about picking the Audley orange, the next he was detained in a psychiatric hospital, but it was not as sudden as it seemed. The finality of his timid defeat against Tyson and what it revealed about his body and mind chipped away at his self-confidence. At 34, when his doctors said no more, he had to find a new purpose in life. 'When I came out of boxing it was like a bereavement,' he said. 'For twenty years I had got out of bed at six every morning to train, even on Christmas Day. Now I get out of bed at six and have nothing to do. Retirement is like taking your heart out and putting it in a drawer. I miss everything about boxing.' Unlike so many boxers, he continued to earn reasonably well and to stay in shape. He built on his early success as a pantomime star, did the rounds as a DJ, put in appearances as a boxing pundit and the odd stint as a celebrity guest on talk and game shows, and campaigned for the Conservative Party. But it never satisfied him. Like so many ex-boxers, or former revolutionaries or soldiers after a war, he found nothing could compare with the bright colours of his heroic past. He spent £100,000 on a christening party for his son, inviting 1,500 people; he blew £350,000 in two years on clothes, and the same again on cars. 'I just couldn't stop,' he said.

In 1997, Laura secured a court injunction restraining Frank from 'molesting, harassing and assaulting her'; the *Sun*'s front-page take was WILD-EYED FRANK MADE ME QUAKE IN TERROR. It quoted her on her husband's 'frightening, unnerving and aggressive behaviour', although her account made no allegations of actual physical violence. She left him, returned briefly, then left again, divorcing him in 2001 and taking their three children with her, along with a phased £5 million settlement. His last remaining friend was his trainer, 'Uncle' George Francis, the man who taught him the basics of professional boxing, cradled his head when he was knocked out, listened to his problems and offered him advice and solace. But in April 2002 Francis committed suicide, hanging himself in his garage. 'It was weird,' said Frank. 'I knew he suffered from depression but I didn't know it was so bad.' Frank was alone, and the foundations of his psyche wobbled to the point where former boxers and friends began advising him to seek professional help.

He was released from hospital after 28 days, coming out to read the first of several long interviews by his ex-wife in the *Sun*, billed as 'The Laura Bruno Story'. She described his 'awful decline into mental illness' and chronicled how he'd turned into 'an empty shell who forgot to eat' and how he'd turned to drugs and bombarded her with calls begging her to look after him.

The British boxing community was more sensitive, rallying behind Frank, with several former champions speaking about the hell they had gone through in the search for meaning in their lives after hanging up their gloves. 'I wish I could have looked at myself in the mirror,' Bruno said. 'It's embarrassing, really. I needed to slow down. I was talking hibbery-jibbery for a long time. They battered me from pillar to post in hospital, but I needed it. When three policemen and two ambulance men came to my house to take me away I thought they were joking. I couldn't believe what was happening, but after a week I realised I needed to be there. I took it as a joke, but was burning out. It weren't funny. But some good has come out of this. One in four families has someone with mental problems. I'm far from perfect and there are lots of people who need help.'

Riddick Bowe also needed help, but instead plotted a comeback. His troubles went back to the ghetto – Rock Newman said they came from growing up in a 'pretty dysfunctional family' – but he was not helped by taking too many punches. Some boxers have the constitution to take thousands for decades without any sign of mental decline; others start talking funny before they're out of their twenties, and none more so than Bowe. As Newman belatedly recognised, 'Bowe was not a guy who had a lot of self-motivation, and once he got money he wasn't motivated any more', which meant he got fat and slow and took more hits than necessary. The beatings he absorbed from Holyfield and Golota and the thousands of punches taken in sparring had him slurring before the age of 30.

He'd never been the sweetheart of early press notices, but brain damage, combined with boredom and declining self-esteem, released the monsters. 'Once I retired everything fell apart,' he said. 'My personal life, everything, just went crazy.' He began beating his wife, Judy, although he insisted it wasn't one-sided. 'There were times when she hit me as well. If you hit me, I'm gonna get mine back, and I'm not waiting. I'm gonna hit you right back.' Even a woman? 'I don't care who it is,' he replied, stressing she was six feet tall, although, like so many wife beaters, he admitted to periodic remorse. 'I would feel bad. She'd feel bad. We'd apologise to one another and say we wouldn't do that no more, but as time progressed we just kinda forgot and it would happen again.' One minute contrite, the next self-justifying. 'Me and Judy were like two peas in a pod, but I found out when I was in training camp she was having affairs. I was so naive, but when you are in love you never understand. Riddick Junior had blood tests and it turned out he's not my child. How do you think I felt when I learnt that? After seventeen years with my name he turns out to be not my child. When I found out everything went haywire. Judy should have shot me. It would have been easier.' He knocked Judy unconscious in April 1997. 'I remember my youngest boy telling the other kids that Daddy killed Mommy,' she recalled. 'They had stopped noticing and stopped crying. They had gotten used to too much.' She fled from the family estate in Maryland with their five children and headed for the hills of North Carolina.

Without Judy and his children, Riddick was distraught. 'I just wanted my family back,' he said. 'I felt I couldn't live without them.' In February 1998 he armed himself with a long knife, duct tape, handcuffs and pepper spray, and with his brother as driver, pulled into Judy's new home at six a.m. and ordered: 'Judy, get up!' She did as she was told, and climbed into the car, still wearing her pyjamas. He then spotted three of their children at the bus stop and ordered them in too. Riddick sat in the back with his knife out, threatening to kill Judy. Just to make his point, he gave her a little cut on one of her breasts. She eventually persuaded him she needed the toilet and they pulled over – appropriately, at a McDonald's, where she called the police on a cellphone. They drove on, but the car was pulled over a few miles later. Riddick was arrested and charged with kidnapping. He protested it was no more than a 'crime of passion', because 'how can you kidnap your own family?' Later he added, 'I wouldn't say I regret it. I regret being there.'

In his trial, Bowe's attorney Johnny Cochran (of O.J. Simpson fame) made a successful plea for a non-custodial sentence, arguing that Bowe had diminished responsibility because of his boxing-induced brain damage, but the prosecutors appealed successfully, and in 2003 'Big Daddy' began an eighteen-month jail sentence in the Federal Correctional Institute in Cumberland, Maryland, for the relatively low-level crime of 'interstate domestic violence'. By then he had another wife, Terri, who also had Bowe troubles. She laid charges of second-degree assault after he allegedly hit her, her two children and a family friend, but he was acquitted when Terri and three other witnesses failed to arrive in court. Judy also remarried, after which Riddick lost contact with his children (except for their pictures, tattooed on his back). They did not visit him in jail. Nor did Rock Newman – much to the disgust of Lennox, who believes a manager should stand by his man, especially if he portrays himself as a father figure – and much to Riddick's disappointment too. 'He's a shyster,' Bowe complained. 'He hasn't even sent me a care package. I would have died for Rock. He don't know that. He keeps saying how he feels sorry for me. How come all the time I've been in here he's never contacted me?'

While going about his day job of cleaning prison staircases, prisoner number 13603 decided salvation lay in boxing. 'In order for me not to come back to jail, I've got to fight – unless you want me to steal for the rest of my life,' he said. 'I was born to fight, and I don't know how to do anything else. The biggest mistake I ever made was listening to Rock and letting him talk me into retiring. I have only two regrets in my life: marrying Judy and hiring Rock.' He accused Newman of stealing his earnings; then apologised profusely when Rock produced the accounts, proving all was on the level. He also had second thoughts about his lawyers' plea about brain damage. 'These cats said, "He's a fighter and we can make up this frontal lobe thing,"' he recalled, waving around test results from his own doctor stating that he was mentally fit to fight. 'They said I couldn't make rational decisions, but the truth is I made a mistake. I'm sorry, and that's how it goes. All I can say is it will never happen again. There's nothing I can do to change the past. I realise what I did was wrong, I'm paying my debt to society, and I'm hoping and praying that when I get out of here the American public will give me a second opportunity to show I'm sorry for what I did. I just want a second opportunity to be a fighter.'

Riddick's speech seems clearer than after his second Golota fight, perhaps because it has been shown that some brain regeneration is possible as long as the cause is not repeated, but when you compare the way he talks now with recordings of his speech from twelve years ago it is evident there is still some residual brain damage. He slurs slightly, particularly when speaking for a while but like so many former fighters refuses to recognise the symptoms. Sitting in his khaki prison uniform, wearing wire-rimmed glasses and a corn-row haircut, and looking 50lb slimmer than the 320lb slob of a year earlier, he declared, 'I'm still sharp. If there was something wrong I wouldn't put my life on the line, but in the end I will be declared medically fine. I have a report from the government doctors that I don't have a brain injury. They knew it was a ploy to get me off.'

He began to plan his comeback and started to get fit again. By 8.30 a.m. he would complete his cleaning work, run three miles around the prison yard and do some push-ups and sit-ups and other floor exercises. At first he talked of a tune-up programme of fifteen easy fights against men who weren't 'Bengal tigers'; later he pared that down to three. 'Just being fair to me they should let me have two or three fights to see if I can still do it.' His ultimate goal was to fight the man he'd avoided for so long, Lennox Lewis. 'I hope he can hold on until I get out of here,' he said. 'The game needs some excitement, and I'm the man for the job. All I need is a couple of warm-ups then I will be three-time heavyweight champ, and I just hope Lennox doesn't retire. I want to put everything on the line: the gold medal, the championship belt. The best man wins.' He was released in May 2004 and began working toward his first comeback fight.

But as Manny Steward put it, 'There's one guy he should never think about fighting and that's Lennox. It's in bad taste that there are people encouraging him to fight at all because quite aside from his mental problems seven years, retirement will make it very difficult for him, but if he does come back with a few wins Lennox will want to fight him because he doesn't care about Bowe's problems. He has a really hard attitude towards him and I think he would come back if he thought there was a chance of it happening. Riddick would run the risk of being seriously hurt because Lennox would show him no mercy.'

Evander Holyfield presents a more wholesome image, but in a way his situation is also disturbing. There were several moments when he could have retired, but none more so than after his two beatings at the hands of Lennox Lewis. He persuaded himself he would rise again to glory but there is no redemption for little old heavies who fluff their consonants. The evidence of deterioration between his throwback losing performance in the Lewis return and his sluggish winning performance over John Ruiz nine months later was unmistakable, but still he pressed on. With Holyfield there was always room for doubt because of his phoenix-like past, and this inconsistency continued, even if the overall trajectory was downhill. In some rounds and fights he did better than others and when things went wrong there were always excuses. Just over three years after his defeat against Lewis he suffered a wide points defeat against the shorter, lighter Chris Byrd, and it was clear the game was up. Instead, he blamed a rotator cuff injury and promised, once again, to regain the undisputed title. He then took on the 35-year-old cruiserweight champion (and former middleweight and super middleweight champion) James Toney. For one round he looked like the Evander of old, for another two he remained competitive, and then ran out of energy, speed and ideas, and received a severe beating. Finally, in round nine, Evander was dropped and his trainer, Don Turner, threw in the towel. His response? To fire Turner. 'The fight was not over,' he protested. 'I was not badly hurt and I could have continued fighting.'

Evander decided there were all sorts of things he could do to improve at 41 – he could iron out those 'lingering bad habits', for one – and offered his routine public reassurance: 'I understand the risks better than anyone. I have undergone probably the most extensive medical testing of any boxer in history. The tests do not indicate that I have suffered any damage or face any increased risk by fighting again.' And so on, before reminding us he 'prayed a lot about this decision' and concluding, as ever, 'I still want to leave boxing as the undisputed heavyweight champion of the world. I believe that a setback is nothing but an opportunity for a comeback.' And he ended his declaration, 'I am not fearful and I ask you not to be, but instead to have faith as I do. God bless you all.'

Five years after losing to Lewis he is still deluding himself that glory days are around the corner while struggling to get his combinations flowing, whether in punches or words. For Lennox, this is the kind of behaviour to avoid. 'What more is there for me to prove?' he asked. 'That I can be Holyfield and not know how to quit; prove that I can stay stuck in boxing until I'm speaking so that no one understands what I'm saying?'

And finally to Tyson, who speaks clearly but acts as oddly as ever, mixing lucidity with madness. After pulling out of the June 2003 Lewis bill he lost interest in fighting and turned inwards. 'I got some serious, serious demons I'm fighting,' he said. 'I hate my life now. Maybe in the next life I'll have a better life. That's why I'm just looking forward to going to the other world.' Despite earning $300 million he filed for bankruptcy, claiming debts of $27 million (and spends $220,000 a year on just clothes). His only real hope of returning to solvency – aside from his lawsuit against Don King – was to fight again. But as he admitted, 'I'm old, I'm tired, I'm out of shape. I don't know. It's probably too difficult to get into shape now. I'm exhausted.'

Still, he was capable of punching when provoked, as he revealed when a thuggish pair approached him aggressively for his autograph. He told them where to get off and walked away, but they became belligerent, suggesting they might just shoot him, so he turned around and flattened them both. He pleaded guilty to disorderly conduct and a sympathetic judge sentenced him to a hundred hours of cushy community service – spent teaching children how to box at a New York gym. Soon he began to talk of regaining the world title but it was too late to tempt Lennox, who felt he'd been burnt once too often. Living in a small flat and complaining that he had to take out his own garbage, he was desperate for money, and so, in 2004, he finally settled with King, accepting a $14million out of court settlement rather than wait a while longer for the chance to win $100million. But he still owed his creditors $40million and so began to work his way towards another shot at the world title. Finally, on 30 July 2004, after 17 months out of the ring, Mike made his return and was knocked out in four rounds by Britain's Danny Williams.

With Roy Jones returning to light heavyweight (and then losing) and Chris Byrd surviving only by the grace of some myopic judges, only the scar-faced Vitali was standing. Lennox prevaricated. 'It's one more fight or nothing, and right now it's looking more like nothing, but my mind changes from day to day,' he admitted four weeks after their fight. A month later: 'One day I wake up and want to bash up Klitschko and the next I wake up and think I should retire. If we do fight my performance can only get better. He caught me at my worst and I still beat him, but my mind changes every day. I ask myself, "Why am I still fighting?" It's not for the money and I've achieved all my goals. Maybe it's because I enjoy it. But retirement is getting close.'

He began to phone friends and trainers, gauging opinions. Violet Blake says she tried to persuade him to retire; Manny Steward, to fight on. 'I told him to be very careful before making a decision because that decision should be the final one you make,' he said. 'And I begged him to take the rematch with Vitali because he is such a great talent. I was hoping he wouldn't retire.' He phoned Harold, who advised, 'Fight Klitschko again and knock him out so there are no questions to ask. That's what I would do if I was you: beat him in what people will say is the right way.' Teodorescu played it more cautiously, telling Lennox he had nothing to prove before adding, 'But if you want to take away the bad taste of the Klitschko fight, you should take ten weeks out of the rest of your life and fight him again: knock him out, take the money and then retire happy.'

Vitali's cuts healed quicker than expected and HBO set aside 6 December 2003 for the rematch, but Lennox declared he would not fight again in 2003. HBO then put on Klitschko against Lennox's original opponent, Kirk Johnson, in Madison

Square Garden, and once again the huge Ukrainian proved his marketability as well as his talent by stopping the overweight Johnson in two emphatic rounds. Earlier that day Lennox and the team were in Kitchener to attend Courtney Shand's wedding. By this stage he knew where most of them stood, although some, like Joe Dunbar, were playing it by ear. 'My feeling was that it's much better to give up one fight too early than one fight too late,' Joe said. 'If he'd asked me directly, I would have said retire, but at Courtney's wedding we spoke about it more in a roundabout way, so I didn't answer directly. In the past he often asked me, "Joe, should I stop boxing?" The first time was after the Tua fight and I said I'd tell him when it was time if he asked again. I would have told him it was time after the Klitschko fight, even though I was very confident he would have beaten Klitschko if he'd gone ahead with the return, but I could see he hadn't yet decided because it was the biggest decision of his career.'

Steward noticed that Lennox appeared slimmer and harder than when he'd seen him in New York a month before. He approached his man with a grin and said, 'You look like you're in shape and you've been working out.' Lennox replied, yeah, sure, a bit of running, a bit of gym work. Violet Blake then approached Steward and asked what he thought. Manny, mindful of Violet's view, did his best to present a neutral front. 'It's Lennox's decision to make,' he said. Lennox overheard this and playfully asked Steward, 'So Manny, what do *you* think I'll do?' Steward replied, 'I think you're gonna fight again.' Lennox smiled knowingly. For the first time in six months Steward emerged feeling optimistic that Lennox would settle for at least one more fight. 'My gut feeling,' he said at the time, 'is that he's going to come back, although he came short of saying it then.'

The next morning Lennox went for a long run, then turned up for brunch at Kitchener's Charcoal Steakhouse and worked his way through ten thick waffles and a side order of crêpes along with his coffee – the rigours of training set against the perks of retirement. He thought some more about the big question and once again decided to leave it a bit longer, but eventually the WBC forced his hand. The future of the WBC and its boss Jose Sulaiman was already in doubt after it lost a $31million lawsuit against the German light heavyweight Graciano Rocchiagiani, who was unjustly stripped of the WBC world title to accomodate the more lucrative whims of Roy Jones – a case of getting away with many big crimes only to be bust, like Al Capone, for a relatively small one. They were eventually forced into bankruptcy, but at the time they were desperate to avoid any additional legal troubles. And so, worried about another lawsuit from the Klitschko camp – the Ukrainian had previously taken legal action to press his claim as mandatory contender – they gave Lennox an ultimatum: sign for the fight by 15 March 2004 or get stripped of the title. As the weeks passed, Steward grew concerned and went public with his campaign. 'I would love him to finish his career by knocking out Klitschko,' he said. 'Lennox is too strong and too powerful a man for Klitschko to hold off. It won't take Lennox more than four rounds to finish him off this time.'

Finally, under pressure from the ultimatum and not wanting the ignominy of being stripped, Lennox made up his mind. In February he returned to London where it had all begun, booked a room at the Grosvenor House Hotel, put on his best black suit and, with Violet Blake in prime place, Violet Chang beside him and his team behind him, declared, 'I am announcing the end of an important chapter of my life and the beginning of a new one. June twenty-one 2003 was my last fight as a professional boxer.' He thanked all those still working for him (with special thanks for Manny, Courtney and Harold), as well as two who'd been dropped, Dennis and former coach Adrian, but there were no words for Maloney, Hornewer and Davenport or any of the others who'd parted acrimoniously. He began to dip into heavyweight history: the precedent set by Tunney and Marciano in retiring without returning; his belief that he was 'the best heavyweight of my time, a distinction which links me with great boxers like Jack Johnson, Jack Dempsey, Joe Louis, Muhammad Ali and Larry Holmes'. He even had words of thanks for 'boxers like Ray Mercer, Evander Holyfield and Mike Tyson, who brought out the best in me in the defining fights of my career'. Following Tunney's example, he then displayed Violet Chang's engagement ring and kissed his mother, praising her for teaching him about loyalty and love and for 'the sacrifices she made to help me' and saying, 'Thanks, Mum, I love you.' A beaming Violet Blake expressed her delight that he'd reached this decision. 'I think it's great,' she said. 'I think it's the right time. He accomplished all he wanted to do and he did everything he set out to do. Every moment in Lennox's life are my favourite moments. He's always been so special to me. Every day of his life is special.'

At the age of 38 years and five months, which made him the third oldest world heavyweight champion of all time, Lennox Lewis retired by noting that 'I'm still a young man. Many exciting experiences await me. Let the new era begin.' He returned to New York, and then back to London in his new role as a director of SEM to promote a bill featuring the fighter he felt best represented this new era, Audley Harrison.

By the time Audley returned from the 2000 Olympics he had a PR company working for him and had written his own autobiography. He was courted by several promoters, particularly Frank Warren, but decided not to make any move before approaching Lennox for advice, after which he turned Warren down and decided there was more to be gained from his fights being televised on the BBC mass market than on the specialised satellite market of Sky. 'After the Olympics I took a lot of advice from Lennox,' he said, 'and this was one reason why I decided to promote myself. I saw that Lennox had his own company and I realised boxing is a cash cow and that boxers go into the ring and take the risk but they don't get the benefits. I decided I'm Britain's first gold medal winner in thirty-two years and I want to run my own company. That's why I went to university, so I did my deal directly with the BBC, without any middle men.'

As with Lewis, there was a long delay before his professional debut, and he then decided to head his own bills. Injury, stamina problems and feeble opponents prompted more sneering than cheering, particularly from Warren. 'He was so bitter about not signing me because he was the one most actively seeking me of all the promoters,' said Audley. 'He really came after me, so his attacks just amuse me.'

Lewis, however, went out of his way to defend his friend. 'He kind of reminds me of myself,' he said. 'He's an Olympic gold medallist, which is quite an achievement, and he's now in a situation where people are insulting him, and where he's getting a lot of pressure from the press, but he's keeping that focus. He's taken his future in his own hands and he's doing the right thing.'

Trained by Thell Torrance, the man Lennox came close to taking on as his own trainer, Harrison kept on winning, and eventually began campaigning in the United States, where he continued to seek the advice of the older heavyweight. 'Lennox and I have a great relationship and I've got a lot of time for him because he's always backing me,' said the self-trumpeting Olympic champion. 'Like one time he got me a seat at the Oscar de la Hoya–Shane Mosley fight and the two of us were sitting together and through the whole fight he was telling me technical stuff, like "I wouldn't be putting my feet there" or "I would be feinting like this", and he'd show me. It's been a real benefit. He's the nearest thing to me as my idol. He's won everything there is to possibly win, and he's someone whose done what I'd like to be doing in two or three years time.'

Lennox returned to London to stage a Harrison bill, afterwards praising him as already possessing better in-fighting technique than he ever mastered. Audley, he felt, represented the hopeful future – a bright, good-looking, independently minded Englishman with the size and skill to beat the Americans and Europeans. 'Although they might criticise him now, in the end they will praise him,' he declared. 'This is the way it will happen.'

Meanwhile, Manny Steward made a move that surprised Lennox: he cut a deal to assist with the training of the Klitschko brothers, which meant he would be backing Vitali against the Lewis-promoted South African Corrie Sanders when they met for the vacant WBC title in Los Angeles in April 2004. He promptly announced that if Lennox came out of retirement he would be in the opposite corner. 'I'm a professional, and when I'm with a fighter, I'm with a fighter one hundred per cent,' he declared, and went on to praise the Klitschko brothers at Lennox's expense, explaining that he would have worked with them earlier if it hadn't been for a promise to Violet Blake that he would remain with her son to the end. 'But now I'm with Vitali, and that means I'm only with Vitali,' he said. 'I hope Lennox stays retired and enjoys his retirement and everything he's worked for and never returns, because if he did return I'd be working with Vitali to defeat Lennox.'

Lennox went to Los Angeles for the Klitschko–Sanders fight and once again found himself booed when introduced, the crowd refusing to forgive him for not giving Vitali a return. He then watched his man do to Vitali what he'd done to Wladimir – whack him on the chin with his fast left cross. But Sanders was to discover that the fault line in the brother's fragile jaw was not a universal Klitschko trait. Vitali took the punches, wore Sanders down and pounded him to defeat in the eighth round. Sanders later noted that Vitali not only took a better punch than his brother, he was also harder to tag, but Lennox was not particularly impressed. He went to Klitschko's dressing room to congratulate him and emerged smiling. 'The temptation is already there,' he admitted when asked the inevitable comeback question. 'If I'd trained for the right fight last time I would have taken him out easily, and I would still do so if we did it again.'

He might have been playing with his audience and with himself, but the boos and the certainty that even at 39 he could turn it all around by taking out this big white giant left him with a niggling itch to scratch, and the beginnings of an internal debate: the push of the boos of the boxing crowd versus the pull of the cheers of the home crowd, and always the competing questions. Is my legacy secure? Will it be endangered by one more fight? And so, as with all boxers, especially the great ones, the temptation of Icarus was there for the taking – to fly that little bit higher, just once more, just once. Yet by any reasonable standards he'd already reached as close to the sun as he could possibly go.

Rating fighters of different eras is hard enough in the lighter divisions where you have to balance advances in terms of technique, fitness, diet and strength against the larger competitive pools of some past eras, but with heavyweights it is absurd. Most of the greats of the distant past were cruiserweights or light heavyweights by today's standards – too light and weak for a man of Lewis's size, strength and power. Picture Marciano giving away seven inches in height, sixteen in reach and 60lb. to a man with Lennox's speed and skill. Even Liston, Ali and Holmes at their best were lighter and weaker than Holyfield, who was Lennox's smallest serious opponent. So the game doesn't work. Just as Haile Gebrselassie would have left Emil Zatopek standing, so the Louis of 1938 would have been too small and fragile for the Lewis of 1998.

The only plausible way to compare heavyweights of different eras is in terms of what they achieved in their time. Considered purely in fighting terms, Lewis is among the best. For eleven years he was at or near the top of his division. He fought in eighteen 'world' title fights (eleven for the linear title, nine for the undisputed title) and lost just two out of 44, avenging both, and most of his opposition were genuine top contenders or fellow champions. He was a more consistent performer than the best of his contemporaries – Tyson, Holyfield and Bowe – and, overall, beat a better list of opponents. Holyfield pulled off magnificent triumphs over Bowe and Tyson but his heavyweight record is spotty and he never managed a sustained winning spell. Tyson overcame several good men but no giants near their best and lost four times. Bowe's finest hour came with his first win over Holyfield, but he was also beaten by Evander and twice beaten up by Golota.

In Lennox's peak years, 1997 to 2002, his assets were among the most formidable in heavyweight history. He did not always use his jab effectively, but when he did it was up there with the best: here quick like Ali's, there heavy like Liston's, and often a bit of both, like Holmes's. Under Steward's tuition he developed an impressive arsenal of power punches, especially the right cross and uppercut but also the left and right hook, taking him to a 73 per cent stoppage record. He was a fine counter-puncher, usually showed good balance and footwork, and his defence, particularly blocking and parrying, was hard to penetrate. He was probably the strongest heavyweight champion of all time, and one of the biggest, and he was usually in peak shape, contributing to his longevity. He was also adept at controlling the pace and range of a fight, was able to adjust his strategy as a fight progressed, and he was equally comfortable boxing aggressively or off the back foot.

Lennox's chin often gets first mention when negatives are listed. Those two stoppage defeats count against him because while McCall and Rahman were big hitters neither belonged among the elite. Both bouts followed a lapse in concentration or dedication and were ended by a huge punches, connecting perfectly: McCall's on the front of the chin when Lennox's momentum was propelling him forward, and Rahman's the perfect right cross, landing on the side of the jaw. Yet those were the only counts in his fourteen-year professional career, and he took flush hits from several other noted bangers without going down. Compare that to some of the genuinely 'chinny' champions: Louis was down ten times and out twice; Patterson, twenty times and stopped five; Moorer, eleven times, out three. Even champions known for resilience tumbled more often. Frazier, for example, was dropped eleven times in 37 fights and stopped three times. The reality is that while Lewis's chin was not of the McCall tungsten standard, he took a good punch.

His heart was also questioned because of his caution, but there was never any basis for this criticism. He used the best strategy he could find to win and preferred not to take chances, but could also suck it up and brawl his way to victory, taking punches to land them, as he showed in particular against Mercer and Klitschko. He usually preferred to control a fight at long range, but despite a reluctance to work on the inside, even the best in-fighters struggled to make an impression on him because when they came close he would either drill them with uppercuts or use his strength to tie them up and lean on them. Stamina was a more serious fault line because he sometimes went through periods of exhaustion when his mouth would hang open and his arms and legs would look leaden. Invariably, however, he would pull himself through and finish strongly.

So, not a perfect fighting machine, but the best of his generation. As Manny Steward put it, 'You have to conclude that Lennox is the dominant heavyweight of the decade. There were spells when others rose or fell but he was there throughout. Tyson gave up the WBC title rather than fight him; Bowe did the same because he was scared of Lewis after the beating he received in the Olympics; but Lennox avoided no one and eventually beat everyone, including the two men who beat him. He will go down as one of the all-time greats, and after a few years of retirement people will start to appreciate him more.'

But heavyweight champions are not just boxers: they represent their sport, and very occasionally stand for something more. Jack Johnson, who reigned from 1908 to 1915, had no great cause beyond his own self-gratification, but as the first black heavyweight champion and a brilliant boxer who took pleasure in making fun of his white opponents, flaunting his white wives and taunting the white establishment he became a symbol of black pride and, conversely, an excuse for white prejudice. In contrast, Joe Louis, who ruled in the more benign 1930s and 1940s, obeyed orders to be seen as the anti-Johnson: the good 'race man', never to be seen with a white woman, always living and fighting clean, forever maintaining a deadpan expression and letting his fists do the talking. And they spoke loudly enough. When he lost to the Nazi-backed German Max Schmelling racist America was delighted. Jack Dempsey, for instance, declared it 'the finest thing to happen to boxing in a long time'. But when he signed to fight Schmelling again two years later President Roosevelt told him, 'Joe, we need muscles like yours to beat Germany.' This time Joe overwhelmed Max in two minutes and, as Jesse Jackson put it, he freed black Americans 'from the midst of inferiority'. He went on to donate two of his purses to the war effort, to serve in the US army and to be seen as an American hero. 'He's a credit to his race,' idiotic mayors would say at civic receptions. 'He's a credit to his race – the human race,' the patronising sportswriter Jimmy Cannon responded.

To Muhammad Ali, the old Brown Bomber was an Uncle Tom. Ali unsettled the white boxing, political and military establishments in the 1960s with his innovative defiance, sometimes with a big smile on his handsome face but also with a sneer. At first it was just the boasting, the hands-down dancing style and the snappy dogger-el, but soon he abandoned his 'slave name' and in place of integration argued for separation; in place of Jesus a strange version of Muhammad. In contrast to Louis he refused to fight for Uncle Sam, even though that meant being stripped of his title and the risk of jail. Black America, black Britain, Africa, Asia, the Islamic world, all adored him, and he inspired thousands of wannabes in just about every sport. When he re-emerged in the 1970s white America also came to embrace him and he became as an icon who transcended his sport and all sport.

From Ali downhill to Tyson, the last iconic world heavyweight champion – volatile, angry, wild and always compulsive. He spoke for the ghetto, but not in any considered way; he was more symbolic of its dangers, violence and unpredictabi-lity – the rapist, the thug, the metaphorical killer. In the ring he'd explode, and then talk of driving nose bones into his opponents' brains. He might also bite them, try to break their arms or keep on punching after it was over. Outside the ring there were no restraints. The boxing world loved Tyson but despised him too, because they could see he was damaging their image. They wanted Tiger Woods; instead their man was a maniac whose antics drew attention to those of all the rest, in a divi-sion whose top ranks were littered with drug abusers, wife batterers, drunkards, gluttons and thugs. Each new batch seemed worse than ever, yet in some ways all that changed was the way it was reported.

Go back to the 1920s and you find a public image of tomcat transformed into pussycat outside the ring, in the form of Jack Dempsey, but this illusion had little bearing on reality. Skip the multiplicity of fouls he committed, side step the fact that he was openly racist and settle on the everyday Jack. His first wife was a prostitute, and for a while he was her pimp. It has been claimed that he supplemented his early purses as 'a professional rapist of virgins' who would be sent to brothels to perform this service. He regularly beat up his women and his friends, and his protector was Al Capone. Leap forward 40 years and you get to Sonny Liston. As well as his scores of assault charges, his years as a brutal mob enforcer and his spells in prison for crimes of violence, during his short spell as world champion he was an alcoholic and committed at least one rape – facts not reported at the time. Even the gods had their blind spots. Ali? You won't see it in the Will Smith movie, but he once slapped around his first wife, as well as his father. Louis? A serial philanderer who would have put Ali and Holyfield to shame. He treated his wives abysmally and may have beaten one of them. He later fell to heroin.

Lennox's personal example seems exemplary in comparison. Like just about every boxer of his generation he drew inspiration from Ali, but in one sense his behaviour was more redolent of an earlier generation: he expected his private life to escape scrutiny as long as he behaved with dignity but this was not a bargain that interested the media, so it became a defining battleground. He never sought to become an enigma, but through the tussle between tabloid desire for scandal and Lewis's desire for privacy, he ended up that way. But he persisted, and, largely, won. The rumours lingered but the press failed to find anything resembling a smoking gun. As for the rest, there were no drunken brawls, swollen-faced women, positive drugs tests or late-night arrests. The worst they could find hardly qualified: a studio wrestling match, a post-fight hangover and some disputes with past employees and promoters. Not much meat there when you've got the very public–private lives of Tyson, Bowe, Holyfield and Bruno to chew on.

His emphasis on dignity had little in common with the version thrust on Louis when he turned professional seventy years ago. It was bound up both with his personal credo and with his notion of black pride. On the one hand he observed the decline of Tyson's image and his loss of self-respect until he became a 'prod him and see how he snarls' parody of his once fearsome past; on the other he saw Bruno, compliant and smiling – the white man's hero. He wanted to avoid both these extremes. He would hold his head high, watch his tongue, think before he acted and speak out when he saw the need. In the recent past most of his attention has been focused on his long walk to vindication in the ring and he was too introspective to become a campaigning force in the wider world, but he was also no back-turning, lips-closed Tiger Woods. When asked for his opinions on social issues Lennox seldom held back. He had strong views on racial discrimination, black solidarity, the environment, poverty, education, the war in Iraq, gun control and the American presidential election, to name but a few, and he never hid them.

When you put it all together, he emerges not only as one of the great heavyweight boxing champions but as a man with a substantial hinterland outside his line of work. On 15 June 2004, that hinterland grew by 8lbs 2oz, when his fiancée, Violet, gave birth to a son, Landon. At the time of writing he's having to fight against the undertow of temptation – that pull to go back to the thing that has defined the last two decades of his life, just one more time, for $30 million, to end on the right note. But the more interesting challenge will be to see if he can defy the history of his sport and build something of substance beyond a reputation for fighting well. It's a challenge he accepts, hypothetically at least. 'I tried to show people that boxing has to do with more than just brutality and blood,' he says. 'And now I want to show them that as much as I love this sport, there really is more to me than just being a boxer. You see, now I have to think of my whole life.'

SELECT BIBLIOGRAPHY

Howard Bingham and Max Wallace, *Muhammad Ali's Greatest Fight: Cassius Clay vs. The United States of America* (Robson Books, 2001)

Bert Blewett, *The A-Z of World Boxing* (Robson Books, 1996)

Gavin Evans, *Prince of the Ring: The Naseem Hamed Story* (Robson Books, 1996); *Wicked!* (Robson Books, 1999); *Dancing Shoes is Dead: A tale of fighting men in South Africa* (Doubleday 2002, Black Swan, 2003)

Fight Fax Inc., *The Boxing Record Book 2004* (Fight Fax Inc., 2004)

Blaise Hart and Melissa Mathison, *Lennox* (Little, Brown, 2002)

Thomas Hauser, *Muhammad Ali: His Life and Times* (Robson Books, 1991) and *A Year at the fights* (University of Arkansas Press, 2003)

Bill Hughes & Patrick King (eds) *Come Out Writing: A Boxing Anthology* (Queen Anne Press, 1991)

James Lawton, *Mission Impossible: How Lennox Lewis Unified the World Heavyweight Title* (Mainstream, 2000)

Lennox Lewis (with Joe Steeples), *Lennox Lewis: The Autobiography of the WBC Heavyweight Champion of the World* (Faber and Faber, 1993, and with Ken Gorman, 1997)

Frank Maloney, *No Baloney* (Mainstream, 2003)

Hugh McIlvanney, *McIlvanney on Boxing* (Mainstream, 1996)

Donald McRae, *Dark Trade: Lost in Boxing* (Mainstream, 1996) and *In the Black & White: The Untold Story of Joe Louis and Jesse Owens* (Simon & Schuster, 2002)

Joyce Carol Oates and Daniel Halpern (eds), *Reading the Fights: The Best Writing about the Most Controversial of Sports* (Simon and Schuster, 1990)

Ferdie Pacheco, M.D., *The 12 Greatest Rounds of Boxing: The Untold Stories* (Robson Books, 2001)

The Ring, *The 2004 Boxing Almanac* (London Publishing Company, 2004)

Mickey Vann (with Richard Coomber), *Give Me a Ring* (Mainstream, 2003)

INDEX

Page numbers in **bold** denote significant references to headings.

INDEX

INDEX